MW00440699

THE AMERICAN
DEMOCRAT AND OTHER
POLITICAL WRITINGS

CONSERVATIVE LEADERSHIP SERIES

EAGLE PUBLISHING, INC.

EAGLE BOOK CLUBS, INC.

CONSERVATIVE BOOK CLUB

REGNERY PUBLISHING, INC.

The Conservative Leadership Series is a joint project of Regnery Publishing, Inc. and Eagle Book Clubs, Inc., divisions of Eagle Publishing, Inc., to make the classics of conservative thought available in hardcover collectors' editions.

The American Democrat and Other Political Writings

James Fenimore Cooper

Edited with an Introduction by Bradley J. Birzer and John Willson

REGNERY PUBLISHING, INC.

WASHINGTON, D.C.

Notions of the Americans: Picked Up By a Travelling Bachelor was originally published in two volumes in London in 1828 by Henry Colburn.

A Letter to His Countrymen was originally published in New York in 1834 by John Wiley.

The American Democrat, Or Hints on the Social and Civic Relations of the United States of America was originally published in Cooperstown, New York in 1838 by H. E. Phinney.

Library of Congress Cataloging-in-Publication Data

Cooper, James Fenimore, 1789-1851
    The American democrat and other political writings / by James Fenimore Cooper ;
    Edited with an introduction by Bradley J. Birzer and John Willson.
        p.   cm.
    ISBN 0-89526-242-8 (alk. paper)
        1. United States—Politics and government—19th century. 2. Political science. I.
    Birzer, Bradley J., 1967- II. Willson, John, 1940- III. Title.

    JK216.C69 2000
    973.5—cd21   00-062543

Published in the United States by
Regnery Publishing, Inc.
An Eagle Publishing Company
One Massachusetts Avenue, NW
Washington, DC 20001

Distributed to the trade by
National Book Network
4720-A Boston Way
Lanham, MD 20706

Printed on acid-free paper.
Manufactured in the United States of America

10 9 8 7 6 5 4 3 2 1

Books are available in quantity for promotional or premium use. Write to Director of Special Sales, Regnery Publishing, Inc., One Massachusetts Avenue, NW, Washington, DC 20001, for information on discounts and terms or call (202) 216-0600.

CONTENTS

A line rendering of James Fenimore Cooper done around the time of his death (1851). Courtesy of the Burlington County Historical Society, Burlington, New Jersey, birthplace of the author.

INTRODUCTION

"Places for the worship of God abound with that frequency which characterizes a moral and reflecting people, and with that variety of exterior and canonical government which flows from unfettered liberty of conscience," James Fenimore Cooper wrote in the first Leatherstocking Tale, *The Pioneers.* "The whole district," he continued, "is hourly exhibiting how much can be done, in even a rugged country, and with a severe climate, under the dominion of mild laws, and where every man feels a direct interest in the prosperity of the commonwealth of which he knows himself to form a part."[1]

Reflecting many thinkers before him, Cooper argued in all of his works that America had a biblical duty to be the "Light Upon the Hill." Anything less would prove reprehensible to God and to America's ancestors, who had shed much blood for the creation of the new nation. Indeed, reliance on European art, manners, or political forms would only destroy the United States and deny our covenant with God. It would end the American promise to the world.

Whether writing fiction or social criticism, Cooper consistently stressed the significance of American politics and culture for the world. He believed that both republicanism and the frontier made America unique, vigorous, and consequential. Though fiction, the above passage from *The Pioneers* reveals Cooper's passionate commitment to the American regime. The freedom of the wilderness, in the process of being subdued, and the republican form of government precipitated faith, liberty, and natural progress. Blessed from above, a prosperous America spread quickly.

---

[1] James Fenimore Cooper, *The Pioneers* (1823; New York: Signet, 1980), 13–14.

Cooper spent his adult life advocating a purely American form of art, chastising those who adopted or maintained European conventions. His three explicit works of social criticism—*Notions of the Americans* (1828); *A Letter to His Countrymen* (1834); and *The American Democrat* (1838)—advocated a similar cultural and political nationalism. In *Notions*, he is naively optimistic, simplistic, and giddy about America's prospects. In *A Letter*, he is overly strident and bitter, though very nuanced in his argumentation. In the final work of social criticism, *The American Democrat*, Cooper lays out clearly his ideas on a variety of subjects, ranging from equality to slavery to the press. More restrained, Cooper's *American Democrat* tempers the euphoria of *Notions* and the seething resentment of *A Letter*.

Cooper's project met with mixed results. Numerous Americans of his day despised Cooper, believing him pretentious and, because he refused to swim in the rising tide of plebiscitary democracy, possibly traitorously un-American. Still, they devoured his romance novels (ironically enough, a European convention), as did countless Europeans.

1789–1821: Learning Self-Discipline

Cooper received his convictions regarding republicanism, nationalism, and the frontier from his relatively idyllic childhood. Born in 1789 to a well-to-do Quaker family in New Jersey, young James soon moved to upstate New York where his father, William, had already founded the prosperous community of Cooper's Town.[2] The twelfth of thirteen children, James ran wild through the town and the surrounding woods. As Hannah, a sister, wrote of him and his brothers, they "show plainly that they have been bred in the Woods."[3]

Cooper's "wild" streak continued to irrupt during Cooper's childhood. As a young man, Cooper attended Yale College from 1803 to 1805, but the school dismissed him for disciplinary reasons. He had performed a series of

---

[2] For an excellent exploration of early Cooperstown and its founder, see Alan Taylor's Pulitzer prize–winning *William Cooper's Town: Power and Persuasion on the Frontier of the Early American Republic* (New York: Knopf, 1995).

[3] Quoted in Robert Emmet Long, *James Fenimore Cooper* (New York: Continuum, 1990), 14. This introduction benefits significantly from Long's excellent opening chapter on Cooper.

harmless pranks that had infuriated the wrong people. Afterwards, Cooper's family wanted him to go to Princeton, but that school had banned any Cooper after one of James's brothers had burned down a building on campus. Prior to his failed college career, however, Cooper had received a strong classic liberal arts education. His teachers remembered him as a good student, a voracious reader, and an excellent storyteller.

With few options and a drive for adventure, Cooper became a common sailor, hoping to prepare for a naval career. In 1806, Cooper joined a merchant vessel, the *Stirling*. Once aboard, he certainly experienced the adventure he had sought. He survived violent storms, outran pirates, and even faced impressment into the British navy. The action suited Cooper, and on 1 January 1808, President Thomas Jefferson signed the documents placing Cooper in the Navy as a midshipman. He served the Navy well and hoped to make it his lifelong career. He aspired to the rank of admiral.

Two events derailed Cooper's plans. First, he inherited a considerable amount of wealth and property in 1809 when an angry politician violently and mortally struck Judge William Cooper from behind in Albany after a disagreement. The wealth and land allowed James to set up as a gentleman. Second, he met and fell in love with wealthy Susan De Lancey of a prominent New York family. Not wanting her husband absent for long stretches of time, she convinced James to retire from the Navy. Though he complied, his love for the ocean remained unabated. During his writing career, he wrote fondly of the sea and the United States Navy in his fiction and nonfiction alike. Many historians still consider his *The History of the Navy of the United States of America* (1839), *The Cruise of the Somers* (1844), and *Lives of Distinguished American Naval Officers* (1846) masterful works of scholarship.[4] The famous philosopher and historian George Bancroft praised Cooper's historical works during his lifetime.[5]

In 1810s, Cooper settled into the life of leisure. He farmed, landscaped, developed local voluntary associations based on agriculture and the Bible, actively participated in the local Episcopal Church, and served as a colonel in the New York state militia.

---

[4] George H. Callcott, *History in the United States, 1800–1860: Its Practice and Purpose* (Baltimore, Md.: Johns Hopkins University Press, 1970), 70.

[5] Long, *James Fenimore Cooper*, 26.

During the same decade, Cooper's four brothers, all of whom shared the father's estate with James, spent their money unwisely, driving the family's collective finances into deep debt. By 1819 all four had died, joining their mother, who had died in 1818.

These tragedies left a huge burden of debt for James. He sold the family estate and attempted a number of (mostly failed) speculative ventures to raise money to pay off creditors. One of the ventures, the one his wife considered the strangest, was fiction writing. Upon throwing down a trashy English novel, Cooper complained of its poor quality. His wife challenged him to write something better, and, much to her surprise, James accepted her offer and did. Though his first novel, *Precaution* (1820), received only moderate success, Cooper's second novel, *The Spy* (1821), achieved instant fame in Europe.

1822–1827: Republicanism and the American Frontier

With his third novel, *The Pioneers*, Cooper secured his place as the first true American novelist. Cooper introduced his greatest literary creation, the character of Natty Bumppo. He followed *The Pioneers* with four more novels involving Natty, collectively known as the Leatherstocking Tales: *The Last of the Mohicans* (1826); *The Prairie* (1827); *The Pathfinder* (1840); and *The Deerslayer* (1841).

Natty Bumppo, though of European descent, personifies the American frontier. Natty's parents had died when he was a very young child, and a family of Christianized (Moravian) Delaware Indians had raised him. According to Cooper, Natty, therefore, embodies the best of both worlds. Though shunning Christianity as a doctrine, Natty excels at virtue, spending most of his life helping those in need. An excellent hunter and warrior, Natty prefers the company of Indians, white woodsmen, and frontier soldiers to "civilized" and class-conscious persons of the town or city. For Cooper, Natty Bumppo represents the true American: virtuous, innovative, and free.

Cooper impressively anticipated Frederick Jackson Turner's famous historical arguments as presented in his "Significance of the Frontier in American History" (1893). Turner's frontier thesis stated that the frontier had made the American. The American characteristics of individualism, innovation, and equality had manifested themselves at the point where "savagry" had met "civilization." "American social development has been continually beginning over again on the frontier," Turner said. The American was neither European nor Indian. Instead, he was something altogether different, a synthesis: more than either individually.

"This perennial rebirth, this fluidity of American life, this expansion westward with its new opportunities, its continuous touch with the simplicity of primitive society," Turner stated unequivocally, "furnish the forces dominating American character." In a famous passage that could be taken as a perfect descrition of Natty Bumpo, Turner wrote, "The frontier is the line of most rapid and effective Americanization. The wilderness masters the colonist. It finds him a European in dress, industries, tools, modes of travel, and thought. It takes him from the railroad car and puts him in the birch canoe. It strips off the garments of civilization and arrays him in the hunting shirt and the moccasin. It puts him in the log cabin of the Cherokee and Iroquois and runs an Indian palisade around him. Before long he has gone to planting Indian corn and plowing with a sharp stick, he shouts the war cry and takes the scalp in orthodox Indian fashion."[6]

Though essentially correct in his description of the frontier, Turner offers a simple two-dimensional theory. There exists in Turner's argument little or no room for those of non-European descent, and the argument especially ignores the frontier's effects on American Indians. Implicit in Turner is the view that indigenous people had served as a mere catalyst in making Europeans Americans. Once the transformation is complete, the Indians are no longer needed; they simply disappear from Turner's story.

But Cooper presented a far more nuanced and realistic view of the frontier than Turner's better known theory. Surprisingly similar to Turner's wording regarding the effects of the frontier on those of European descent, Cooper wrote of Natty Bumppo as he stands next to his closest friend, Chingachgook, a Delaware Indian: "the habits of the 'Leatherstocking' were so nearly assimilated to those of the savages, the conjunction of their interests excited no surprise. They resided in the same cabin, ate of the same food, and were chiefly occupied in the same pursuits."[7]

---

[6] Frederick Jackson Turner, "The Significance of the Frontier in American History" in *Rereading Frederick Jackson Turner: "The Significance of the Frontier in American History" and Other Essays*, ed. John Mack Faragher (New York: Holt, 1994), 32–33.

[7] Cooper, *The Pioneers*, 80.

But far from being merely a catalyst to make Natty a true American, Chingachgook plays a vital role in the five Leatherstocking Tales. Indeed, Chingachgook is Natty's equal in almost every respect, and in terms of his Christianity, he seems to be the better of the two. While Natty holds great respect for Christian arguments, he thinks very little of Christians them-selves. He believes that as a philosophy it puts too much emphasis on mercy, ignoring justice.[8] Chingachgook agrees with Natty in this aspect but also treats the Christian God and His ministers with great respect. The minis-ters, in turn, think highly of Chingachgook. They see him traveling on the right path.[9]

For Cooper, the Indians were also good republicans. Their republican beliefs gave them freedom and, therefore, allowed them to discover virtue, though they usually took their republicanism to extremes by nearly abol-ishing all government.[10]

Despite Cooper's language in the above quoted passages, one should not conclude that Chingachgook represents Rousseau's Noble Savage, as many scholars have argued. Though elements of the Noble Savage exist within Cooper's works, Cooper nuanced his characterizations of the Indians. Like all humans, Cooper's Indians appear to be moral, immoral, and, often, some-where in between. Turner should have read his Cooper more carefully.

In addition, Cooper's version of the frontier, unlike that of Turner's, transcends race and sex. This issue is extremely important for Cooper, not only in his fiction, but in all of his written works. The American is not a white man with Indian characteristics. Instead, the frontier can make anyone—regardless of background or sex—a true American, noble, liberty-loving, and virtuous. Ultimately, then, one cannot base "Americanness" on racial or ethnic background or terms. Instead, Americanness is individual and cultural; it is based on virtue and merit.

The character Cora Munro in the *Last of the Mohicans* exemplified Cooper's frontier. From the first, beautiful Cora is skilled, intelligent, and virtuous. She is also of dark complexion. Her sister, Alice, equally beautiful, is timid and, consequently, lacks the virtue of Cora. While Alice may want

---

[8] James Fenimore Cooper, *The Last of the Mohicans* (1826; New York: Bantam, 1989), 290.

[9] Cooper, *The Pioneers*, chapter 12.

[10] Cooper, *The Pioneers*, 80.

to do the right thing, her diffidence holds her back. Cooper points out that Alice is blond and fair skinned.

The reader must wait until the middle of the novel to discover why Cooper repeatedly distinguishes the two female characters by their complexions. Cora is actually part African; as a young Scottish officer in the British army her father had had an intimate relationship in the West Indies. Once Cooper reveals Cora's background, several pointed conversations occur between the main characters regarding the issue. Accusations of prejudice fly.[11] Through his characters, Cooper chastises those who hold racial prejudice. "The dogs and crows of their tribes [white men]" Tamenund, a Delaware Sachem, says, "would bark and caw before they would take a woman to their wigwams whose blood was not of the color of snow." The sagacious Indian suggests that God may send a plague against those who put race above virtue.[12]

While modern readers do not find this shocking, American readers in the 1820s would have been aghast to find the heroine of the story to possess any amount of African blood. Cooper wanted to make a significant point. Being American transcends the narrow biological categories and confines of race or sex. Instead, the frontier provided the freedom for each person to discover and use his moral gifts, to submit to his God-given teleology. In the end, Cora proves the most moral and virtuous of all characters in *The Last of the Mohicans*, even more so than Leatherstocking or Chingachgook. She does everything well, and she does it without hesitation—even if it involves the ultimate sacrifice, her own life, for her friends and loved ones.

Cooper's Leatherstocking novels proved astoundingly successful, especially in Europe. Publishers throughout Europe—Britain, France (18 different ones), the German states (30 different ones)—competed to print Cooper's works. Cooper saw little, if no, money from these publishers. Editions of the Leatherstocking tales also appeared in Russian, Egyptian, Turkish, Persian, Spanish, Italian, and Portuguese. Within a decade of the publication of *The Pioneers*, children throughout Europe and the Middle East played "Indian," inspired by Natty and Chingachgook.[13] The Leatherstocking Tales even

---

[11] Cooper, *Last of the Mohicans*, 164–65.

[12] Cooper, *Last of the Mohicans*, 324.

[13] Paul Johnson, *A History of the American People* (New York: HarperCollins, 1997), 404–5.

served as a recruiting agent for European immigrants, who saw America's wilderness as a site of opportunity and adventure.[14]

Cooper's ideas also significantly influenced American artists and scholars regarding the Indians and the frontier. Cooper's portrait of the Indians, for example, inspired later artists such as George Catlin to visit and paint the scenes of everyday Indian life. Catlin's extant paintings remain as some of the best ethnographical evidence regarding the indigenous people of the Great Plains.[15]

1828: *Notions of the Americans*

By the late 1820s, Cooper, a thoroughgoing American patriot, had come to resent the highly popular British travelogues purporting to describe America. Cooper believed British arrogance ineluctably obscured the truth about the United States in the minds of His Britannic's Majesty's subjects. Cooper also indicted laziness in British travel writers as a source of the distorted picture of the new nation in their works. Preferring speculation and reliance on rumor to research and investigation, many a British author affected expertise. In addition, Europeans had never experienced anything like republican America; republicanism seemed little better than anarchy to the minds of most Europeans. Cooper noted that the British intentionally distorted America's success, fearing to face the failures of their own non-republics. The upshot was that the British public, as well as the rest of Europe, were horribly misled regarding the meaning and significance of American character and nation.

To correct the problems of the travelogues, Cooper decided to write one. The superficially fictional story of *Notions* follows the wanderings of an open-minded, quasi pro-republican European aristocrat, a member of a club of travelers who network with one another via letters. Cooper inserted himself into the story as the American traveling companion, John

---

[14] Paul Johnson, *The Birth of the Modern* (New York: HarperCollins, 1991), 224.

[15] See, for example, George Catlin, *Letters and Notes on the North American Indian* (New York: Gramercy, 1975); William H. Goetzmann and William N. Goetzmann, *The West of the Imagination* (New York: W.W. Norton, 1986), 16–17; and Paul Reddin, *Wild West Shows* (Urbana: University of Illinois Press, 1999), 1–52.

Cadwallader of Cadwallader, New York (James Fenimore Cooper of Cooper's Town, New York!).

Cooper's description of an American girl could easily be his take on America itself. The American girl exhibits a "gentle, natural, and nymph-like deportment, no less than . . . spirited and intelligent." The moment, however, that the European protagonist approaches her, her demeanor changes dramatically. In a story that anticipates Henry James's *Daisy Miller*, the American girl's "joyous, natural, and enticing [ ] merriment," the aristocrat laments, "was instantly changed into the cold and regulated smiles of artificial breeding" (vol. 1, letter 3). The young girl's grandfather also becomes instantly vigilant, casting a wary eye toward the aristocrat. With his fake title, an artificial construct, the aristocrat had disrupted the natural flow of American society, culture, and history. The girl, like America, feels the need to put on airs to interact with the affected Europeans. Cooper believed that such unnatural reaction is the American's first response to the affected.

Cooper defends republicanism from its detractors in Europe, even advocating universal suffrage and attacking property qualifications. Far from being artificial and contrived as were European institutions and titles, Americans based their government on the laws of nature. Composed of several individual and nearly autonomous republics (as Cooper referred to the states), the country inspired pride and patriotism. Being an American was the equivalent of being a lover of truth (vol. 1, letter 16).

In this sense, then, the American founders were not revolutionaries. They did not advocate a change in society through the "adoption of sudden and violent means." Rather, the Americans of that day understood the British system to be based on a lie, a violation of the natural order. The American founders, according to Cooper, reestablished the natural law and right reason (vol. 2, letters 15 and 16).

In one of the truly inspired moments of the book, Cooper has several fictional European aristocrats debate the merits of the various forms of polities. It is a scene reminiscent of both Herodotus' debate among the conquering Persians in *The Histories* and Plato's argument in *The Republic* regarding democracy's inevitable devolution into tyranny. In the *Notions*, though, the Europeans have not yet conquered America, and Cooper stressed that the European idea of monarchy will never prevail. As long as

American institutions remain rooted in the laws of nature, they cannot fail; liberty will prevail (vol. 1, letter 16).

According to Cooper, the American character serves as probably the greatest bulwark against tyranny, providing one of the most important reasons that republicanism will survive in the United States. Americans, argued Cooper, are rooted in truth, ignoring, for the most part, class standing. Americans judge one another through merit and common sense. This has, according to Cooper, been tested many times in battle. Americans fight bravely, he contended, because they fight for truth. Europeans, in contrast, fight for artifice and consequently lack virtue and the spirit of manhood (vol.1, letters 5, 10, 13).

Cooper concluded rather optimistically that America is the most civilized nation in the world. "In this particular [common-sense sympathy for another American, adherence to the truth]," Cooper wrote, "America is, beyond a doubt, the most civilized nation in the world, inasmuch as the aggregate of her humanity, intelligence and comfort, compared with her numbers, has nothing like an equal" (vol. 1, letter 5). Ultimately, because America—in its character and institutions—is based on truth, it will prevail in a world built on a shaky foundation of lies. Like the "City upon a hill," it will serve as a light to the world. "It is not difficult to see, that the day is at hand when this republic will be felt in the great general political questions of christendom," Cooper wrote. "It may be then fortunate for humanity, that the mighty power she will shortly wield, is not to be exercised to satisfy the ambition of individuals, but that they who will have to bear the burthen of the contests will also have a direct influence on their existence." The impetus for this spreading of American republican influence will not come from military action. Instead, it will derive from two sources: leadership through example and through commerce (vol. 1, letter 13, vol. 2, letter 21).[16]

In attempting to rectify the misinformation of the British travelogues, Cooper, unfortunately, overcompensated. According to Cooper, America is

---

[16] Interestingly, Cooper supported the Mexican War, 1846–1848. Unlike most of his northern counterparts, he viewed it as a republican war, a war against tyranny and, most likely, against the Roman Catholic papacy. See James Franklin Beard, ed., *The Letters and Journals of James Fenimore Cooper* (Cambridge, Mass.: Belknap Press, 1960), 139–40.

nearly perfect, an assertion that weakens the importance and substance of his arguments.

1828–1851: Nationalistic Struggles

With his success as a novelist secure, and overconfident in his vision of America, Cooper and his wife moved their four daughters and one son to Europe in 1828. Several reasons prompted Cooper and his family to move. First, he wanted to see Europe as someone other than a tourist; after all, he had criticized European travelers for merely touring. Second, he wanted his family to experience Europe; there was no gainsaying, even by the American Cooper, the cultural benefits of a Grand Tour for the family. Third, and perhaps most important, he want to secure copyright of his novels in several European countries. He was losing considerable money to publishers who had pirated his works.

Cooper met all of his objectives, and his move to Europe solidified his reputation as the first true American novelist. Throughout Europe, he met with important persons and received a great deal of critical acclaim. The French especially loved Cooper, comparing him favorably to Sir Walter Scott. Cooper took copious notes during his travels, and he even involved himself in revolutionary republican activities, which would get him into considerable trouble with the upper crust of Europe. *A Letter to His Countrymen* is, at least in part, a self-assessment of his revolutionary activities.

When Cooper returned to the United States in 1833, America greatly disappointed him. It seemed to Cooper that it had changed dramatically since his departure in 1828. The number of immigrants—which he had unwittingly helped precipitate through the popularity of his novels—the drive for material gain, and the demands for radical equality surprised him. Even worse, the Whig opposition to him and his republican activities in Europe stunned him. Distraught, Cooper penned *A Letter to His Countrymen*. In it, he attacked the Whigs, editors subservient to European literary standards, and the European nobility. He also defended President Andrew Jackson against the Congress, which Cooper saw as America's conniving aristocracy. Most shocking, though, to his readership was the regret he now expressed in having written such romances as *The Pioneers* and *The Last of the Mohicans* that had borrowed heavily from their European counterparts.

Cooper lamented his contribution to "non-American" art forms and promised never to write another romance.

1834: *A Letter to His Countrymen*

Unlike the gushing and naive *Notions*, Cooper's *Letter* seethes with bitterness and cynicism. Though written in 1834, only six-years after its relatively immature forerunner, it remains a sophisticated and nuanced argument for cultural nationalism and republicanism. The essay deals, in a complicated manner, with issues of free speech, the roles of the American presidency and Congress, and the expectations and duties of a man of letters. It represents the best of an open society, with Cooper as a critic and reformer from within playing the Jeremiah.

Letter is a true essay, unlike Cooper's other two nonfiction works of social criticism, which are collections of essays. Cooper addressed it, appropriately enough, "To the Public." After all, he believed, his God-given duty was to support republicanism and its manifestation in North America. The strength of American republicanism originated with its people—their character and institutions. If the people fall in their moral righteousness, America will fail to correct its errors. Republican society can exist only as long as its citizens remain vigilant and virtuous.

While living in Europe with his family, he served as an honorary, unpaid consul in France and had become involved in revolutionary activities in both France and Poland. The European aristocracy, disgruntled with Cooper and suspicious of him, launched a series of attacks against him and his writings in the European press. Much to Cooper's chagrin, many American editors simply reprinted the aristocratic attacks on Cooper without comment. In the vein of Cato the Elder, Cooper found it necessary to defend himself. Cooper thought the best way—that is, the republican or manly way—was to defend his actions directly to the American republic, the audience worthy of his attention.

A strong supporter of President Andrew Jackson, though not a Jacksonian in the classic sense, Cooper blamed the Whig press for being ignorant, incompetent, and obsequious to its European counterpart. Whig actions, he argued, would ultimately lead to the downfall of America. America, after all, depended on its natural character, honest and tied to the truth, for its survival. If it looked to Europe for its opinions on anything, it would become corrupt, and republicanism would go the way of Rome. "It can be shown that [accepting the opinions of non-Americans] is destructive of those sentiments of self-respect, and of that manliness and independence of thought," Cooper argued, "that are necessary to render a free people great, or a nation respectable."

Acquiescence to foreign opinion would destroy America in a number of ways, most of them in a subtle, undetectable manner. Americans, as already noted, lose self-respect and their habit of self-reliance when they begin to depend on the opinions of Europeans. This dependency affects first the leaders and, soon after, the people. "The habit of listening to another people, and of imbibing their prejudices and peculiar ways of thinking, does not limit its injury to the representation of the country," Cooper argued. "The constituency itself becomes tainted by the communion, and ceases to judge of its own interests on its own principles." The result of listening or attempting to listen to the opinions of others resulted in the War of 1812, a war that ravaged America when one party aligned itself with France and the other with England.

While other countries certainly want the United States dependent upon them, America must maintain its independent course. It must, Cooper stressed, recognize the bounty that God has given it. "One of the most melancholy consequences of this habit of deferring to other nations, and to other systems, is the fact that it causes us to undervalue the high blessings we so peculiarly enjoy; to render us ungrateful towards God," Cooper argued, "and to make us unjust to our fellow men, by throwing obstacles in their progress towards liberty." Additionally, no other country completely understands the American experiment. Other countries have contrived, unnatural polities. It is impossible for them to understand the organic, natural, and truthful beliefs undergirding American republicanism. They possess neither the reference point nor the ability. Because of false information being propagated by the European aristocracy, the average European believes that America is in a constant state of chaos and revolution. They hear so many bad things about republicanism that they simply cannot comprehend that it might actually work.

The question then became for Cooper, what can America do to protect itself from foreign corruption, to regain the path to righteousness?

Certainly, from Cooper's point of view, republicanism is the only virtuous and manly political philosophy. America must maintain its spirit. It can only do that by recognizing a number of vital realities. First, it must strictly adhere to the United States Constitution, itself a brilliant republican document. Deviation would mean a move toward special interest control as well as a breaking of the proverbial dike. Once one person or group changes the Constitution for his or its benefit, it sets a dangerous precedent that others will follow. The Constitution has a built-in safety guard, the tenth amendment, which states that "all powers not delegated to the United States, nor prohibited to the states, 'are reserved to the states respectively, or to the people,'" Cooper wrote. "Common prudence would seem to say, that construction, under a compact like our own, should be jealously limited to clear inferences from the powers that are granted in terms," he continued. By limiting the role of government, persons can freely associate with one another in the market or community. Voluntary associations represent the only true, non-exploitative engine of progress. Here is an heir of the high Federalist tradition arguing in favor of a compact theory of government.

Second, Americans must recognize the corrupting nature of power. As human nature is flawed due to the fall of Adam, that nature is easily tempted. Because of this, Americans must keep government limited so as to not put too much power in the hands of any one individual. As Cooper wisely noted, one also should avoid becoming involved with party politics, as parties enslave men's souls as well as serve as mechanisms to appropriate wealth from the unprotected. True republicans should remain dedicated to ideas, never to parties.

Third, parties are not the only groups attempting to exploit others in society. For Cooper, history demonstrates that society itself is based on those who oppress and those who are oppressed. "Monarchy versus democracy" is simply a ruse, Cooper assured his readers. The real struggle is between the elite and the non-elite. "I had had abundant occasion to observe that the great political contest of the age was not, as is usually pretended, between the two antagonist principles of monarchy and democracy, but in reality between those who, under the shallow pretence of limiting power to the elite of society, were contending for exclusive advantages at the expense of the mass of their fellow-creatures," argued Cooper.

"The monarchical principle, except as it is fraudulently maintained as a cover to the designs of the aristocrats, its greatest enemies, is virtually extinct in christendom."

The debate over elites and non-elites manifested itself in the United States in the power struggle between Congress and the President. In this contest, Cooper clearly backed the President—Andrew Jackson at the time—as he had to perform his duties openly. Consequently, power tempted him less than it did Congressmen who could individually hide behind their collective institution. In Cooper's view, Congressmen behave deviously and only to their own benefit. Jackson, Cooper believed, represented all of the people of the United States.[17]

Finally, Cooper addressed his role, the role of the "man of letters" in a republic. As a true republican and nationalist, Cooper argued that his purpose was to promote American forms of art. Europeans and Americans, unfortunately for him, began to refer to him as the "American Sir Walter Scott." Cooper could not honestly deny this. He wrote romances such as the Leatherstocking Tales in the vein of Scott. With no small amount of irony, the first real American hero, Natty Bumppo, existed within a foreign framework. Cooper's medium, if not his message, was indeed European. For this, Cooper apologized to the American people. He renounced his past and promised to write no more romances.

Undoubtedly, Cooper believed he could abide by this promise in 1834. How could he, a "man of letters," criticize his fellow American republicans for obsequiousness to European forms of art and thought when he himself profited from it? In his bitterness and cynicism, Cooper went too far. At least temporarily. Only a year later, Cooper published another romance. He could not escape his nature as an author of fiction, even if it meant employing what he considered a foreign medium.

Cooper's own contradictions of word and action revealed the tensions within him. By nature, he was a republican and a loyal son of the new country, but he was not a dogmatist, a creator of systems, ideologies, or, as he called them, "innovations." What, then, was it the American should reject and what was it he should inherit and preserve? In 1834, all foreign things

---

[17] It is worth noting, however, that Cooper strongly disagreed with Jackson's Indian removal policy.

were corrupt and corrupting, but the process was a slow one and far from irreversible at the point he was writing.

Cooper wrestled with these questions again and again in his fiction and non-fiction, especially in *The American Democrat*. He did, though, reach a part of the necessary conclusion in the *Letter*. "The democracy of this country is in every sense strong enough to protect itself," Cooper wrote. "Here, the democrat is the conservative, and, thank God, he has something worth preserving."

1838: *The American Democrat*

Cooper continued to fight the Whigs, especially in his fiction, which began to include evil or incompetent Whig editors as characters. In return, naturally, the Whigs attacked Cooper at every opportunity. One particularly nasty controversy revolved around a small segment of Cooper's land that townspeople had been using as a public park. When Cooper forbade them from using it, the public was outraged. Not knowing that Cooper owned it, they assumed it was public property and that Cooper was merely playing king over it. Though they knew better, Whig editors exacerbated the controversy, intentionally failing to mention that Cooper did indeed own the land. Cooper successfully sued the editors but only after much inconvenience to himself and damage to his reputation.

Believing that Whig editors had too much power, encouraging the majority to override the rights—property or otherwise—of the minority, Cooper responded by writing *The American Democrat*. This third and final non-fiction work of social criticism reveals a maturity in Cooper's political thinking. Far less giddy than *Notions*, Cooper offered a realistic yet critical assessment of America and its political institutions. And while not as sophisticated in argument as in *A Letter*, *The American Democrat* covered a much greater number of topics in a more straightforward and clearer manner. It balances the best of both previous works without falling into the faults of either. As one of Cooper's twentieth-century intellectual heirs, Russell Kirk, writes, *The American Democrat* is "a book full of perspicuity and courage, cogent and dignified."[18]

---

[18] Russell Kirk, *The Conservative Mind: From Burke to Eliot* 7th Revised ed. (Chicago: Regnery, 1986), 200.

Cooper published his most profound commentary on American political culture on the edge of a decade that would produce more systematic challenges to democratic order than any in the nation's history, except maybe the 1960s. The book invites comparison to Alexis de Tocqueville's *Democracy in America*, the first volume of which had appeared in 1835. The authors also may be profitably compared. Both Cooper and Tocqueville were aristocrats in their own ways; both had lived on each side of the Atlantic; both were fascinated by the explosion of interest around the Western world in democracy and equality. And both were well aware of how susceptible democracies were to disorder in times of rapid change.

Tocqueville observed American institutions with the eye of an anthropologist. He believed that in America lay the future—"The gradual development of the principle of equality is a Providential fact"—and therefore a successful dissection of its democratic system was both a scientific and a prophetic exercise. He also understood that equality as a condition was both a cause and effect of democracy, but that democracy required something more permanent at its foundation than an abstraction. Left to itself, equality was a volatile and unruly beast. And since "the very essence of democratic government consists in the absolute sovereignty of the majority," the beast could well produce its own despotism, what in his famous phrase Tocqueville called "the tyranny of the majority."

There is in Cooper's *American Democrat* a pervasive tone of concern over this very problem. "The disposition of all power is to abuses," he says, "nor does it at all mend the matter that its possessors are a majority. Unrestrained political authority, though it be confined to the masses, cannot be trusted without positive limitations, men in bodies being but an aggregation of the passions, weaknesses and interests of men as individuals." He recognized as clearly as Tocqueville the central problem of democracy.

Tocqueville concluded that what made American democracy work was religion and morality (or *mores*) and the characteristic local institutions they produced—what Robert Nisbet would later call the "intermediate institutions" between the unrestrained individual and unrestrained government (families, churches, schools, local government, voluntary associations, etc.). Cooper also sees that point—the longest chapter in *The American Democrat* is "On the Private Duties of Station"—but is interested less in institutions than in moral lessons.

The American Democrat is, finally, a moral primer on what gives democracy a decent chance to work. Cooper is a patriot and a believer in democracy; he is also a moralist trying to convince his fellow Americans that chaos is around the corner if they fail to conform to the created order of things. "The writer believes himself to be as good a democrat as there is in America," he writes, but then adds that "he is not a believer in the scheme of raising men very far above their natural propensities." Furthermore, the "terms liberty, equality, right and justice, used in a political sense, are merely terms of convention, and of comparative excellence, there being no such thing, in practice, as either of these qualities being carried out purely, according to the abstract notions of theories."

It is Cooper's rejection of ideological abstractions that gives The American Democrat enduring value. Today's readers would certainly find some of his positions quaint. For example, in discussing reasonable limitations on equality he says about women, "females are, almost generally, excluded from the possession of political rights. There can be no doubt that society is greatly the gainer, by thus excluding one half its members, and the half that is best adapted to give a tone to its domestic happiness, from the strife of parties, and the fierce struggles of political controversies." Particular positions aside, Cooper's insight that democracy demands restraint, discipline, and a sound understanding of the created order is timeless.

THE LAST YEARS: 1838–1851

In his works of fiction, Cooper continued to attack Whigs, the press, and democracy run amok. The most significant controversy for Cooper in the late 1830s and early 1840s was the New York Anti-Rent War. Radicals in New York demanded reform of the large estates. In essence, they advocated squatting on already-owned land. Though the battle raged for several years, fought valiantly by Cooper on the side of the landed, the radicals won. The New York landed elite simply ceased to exist, and the leveling passions of American democracy, as both Cooper and Alexis de Tocqueville sagaciously noted, continued their juggernaut plow through the American regime.

Unrepentant to the end, Cooper, either avoiding or ignoring political controversies, spent the majority of the 1840s writing fiction prolifically. He died a day short of his sixty-second birthday on 14 September 1851.

NOTE ON THE TEXT

All the pieces in this collection of James Fenimore Cooper's most important political writings were set from original sources, and as many elements of nineteenth-century typography as possible have been preserved. The editors believe that the experience of reading texts from another age is warped if these elements are eliminated. However, the editors have rendered Cooper's inconsistent use of double and single quotation marks consistent with current American practice, and obvious errors in the original texts have been corrected. One other note: the reader should know that *Notions of the Americans* was originally published in two volumes, with both volumes commencing with a Letter I. Instead of numbering the letters consecutively for this volume, the editors have instead chosen to number the letters as they appeared in their respective volumes. The selective yet thorough nature of this collection is thereby emphasized.

PART I

Notions of the Americans:

Picked up By a Travelling Bachelor

PREFACE.

The writer of these Letters is not without some of the yearnings of pater-
nity in committing the offspring of his brain to the world. His chief concern is that the book may pass as near as possible for what it was intended
in the design, however the execution may fall short of the plan.

A close and detailed statistical work on the United States of America,
could not keep its place as an authority for five years. What is true this year
would the next become liable to so many explanations, that the curious
would soon cease to consult its pages. The principles of the government, and
the state of society, are certainly more permanent; but the latter varies rapidly
in the different stages of a life that is so progressive. Nothing more has, therefore, been attempted here, than to give a hasty and general sketch of most
things of interest, and to communicate what is told in as unpretending and
familiar a way as the subjects themselves would conveniently allow.

The facts of these volumes are believed to be, in general, correct. The
Author does not claim to be exempt from error; but as he has given some
thought and a great deal of time to the subjects of which he has treated, he
hopes that refutation will not easily attack him in the shape of evidence. His
reasoning—if rapid, discursive, and ill-arranged arguments can aspire to so
high a name—must, of course, depend on its own value. A great number
will certainly condemn it, for it as certainly opposes the opinions of a vast
number of very honest people in Europe. Still, as he has no one object but
the good of all his fellow-creatures in view, he hopes no unworthy motive
will be ascribed to his publication.

A great number of readers will be indisposed to believe that the United
States of America are of the importance which the writer does not disguise

he has attempted to shew that they are of to the rest of the world. On this subject there will, probably, remain a diversity of opinion, that time only can decide. As it is probable that in this unfortunate dispute there will be many against him, the Author will endeavour to content himself with the consideration that time is working much faster than common on the points that are most involved in the matter. He is quite satisfied with the umpire.

There is a much graver offence against the rights of readers than any contained in the opinions of this work. A vast deal has been printed that should not have been, and much has been omitted that might have been properly said. But circumstances allowed of no choice between great and acknowledged imperfectious, or total silence. Something of the extent of this demerit, therefore, must depend on the fact of whether enough has been told to justify the publication at all. The writer has not treated the public with so little ceremony as to usher a work into their notice without, at least, believing that a fair proportion of this apology is contained in its pages. If he deceives himself, it will be his misfortune; and if he does not deceive his readers, he will rejoice.

The circumstances to which allusion has just been made, involve haste in printing no less than haste in selection. There are errors of style, and some faults of grammar, that are perhaps the result of combined neglect on the part of the author, the copyists, and the printers. The word "assured" is, for instance, used for "insured," and adverbs have, in several cases, been converted into adjectives. In one or two instances, negatives have been introduced where it was not intended to use them. But they who detect most of these blunders will know how to make allowances for their existence; and to those who do not, it will be a matter of but little interest. The author has far less ambition to be thought a fine writer, than to be thought an accurate observer and a faithful narrator of what he has witnessed.

It will be seen that much use has been made of the opinions and information of a native American. Without some such counsellor, the facts of this book could never have been collected. There is, perhaps, no Christian country on earth in which a foreigner is so liable to fall into errors as in the United States of America. The institutions, the state of society, and even the impulses of the people, are in some measure new and peculiar. The European, under such circumstances, has a great deal to *unlearn* before he can begin to learn correctly.

America has commonly been viewed in the exceptions rather than in the rules. This is a common fault with all travellers, since it at once gratifies their spleen and indulges their laziness. It is a bad compliment to human nature, but not the less true, to say that no young traveller enters a foreign country without early commencing the task of invidious comparison. This is natural enough, certainly, for we instantly miss the things to which we have been accustomed, and which may owe half their value to use; and it requires time and habit to create new attachments. This trait of character is by no means confined to Europe. The writer can assure his contemporaries, that few men travel among foreign nations with a more laudable disdain than the native of the States of which these volumes treat. He has his joke and his sneer, and not unfrequently his reason, as well as the veriest *petit maître* of the Tuileries, or any exquisite of a London club-house. Ere long he will begin to make books, too; and as he has an unaccommodating manner of separating the owner from the soil, it is not improbable that he may find a process by which he will give all due interest to the recollections of former ages, while he pays a passing tribute to this.

The writer has not the smallest doubt that many orthodox unbelievers will listen to what he has said of America in this work, with incredulous ears. He invites all such stout adherents to their own preconceived opinions, to submit to a certain examination of facts that are perfectly within their reach. He would propose that they inquire into the state of America as it existed fifty years ago, and that they then compare it with its present condition. After they have struck a balance between the two results, they can safely be left to their own ruminations as to the probability of a people, as barbarous, as ignorant, and as disorganized, as they have been accustomed to consider the Americans, being very likely to work such miracles. When they have honestly come to a conclusion, it is possible they may be disposed to give some credit to the contents of the following pages.

It is not pretended that the actual names of the individuals to whom these letters are addressed are given in the text. It is hoped that eight or ten single gentlemen can meet once in three years in a club, and that they can pass the intermediate time in journeying about the world, occasionally publishing a few ideas on what they have seen, without being reduced to the necessity of doing so much violence to their modesty as to call each other unequivocally by their proper appellations. Had they been disposed to lives of free comment and criticism, it is more than probable that they would have all been married men these——years.

One more word on the subject-matter of these pages, and the writer will then commit them to the judgment of his readers without further comment. In producing a work on the United States, the truth was to be dealt with fearlessly, or the task had better have been let alone. In such a country, existing facts are, however, of consequence only as they are likely to affect the future. It is of little moment to know that so many houses are in a town, or so many straw beds in such a house, when premises are at hand to demonstrate clearly, that in a year or two the roofs of the city will be doubled, and the inmates of the dwelling will repose on down. The highest compliment that is, or that can be, paid to the people of the United States, is paid by writers, who are evidently guilty of their politeness under any other state of feeling than that of complacency. The Englishman, for instance (he is quoted, because the most industrious in the pursuit), lands in America, and he immediately commences the work of comparison between the republics and his own country. He is careful enough to avoid all those topics which might produce an unfavourable result (and they are sufficiently numerous), but he instantly seizes on some unfortunate tavern, or highway, or church, or theatre, or something else of the kind, which he puts in glaring contrast with, not the worst, nor the middling, but the best similar object in his own country. Really there must be something extraordinary in a people, who, having had so much to do, and so very short a time to do it in, have already become the subjects, not only of envy, but of a seemingly formidable rivalry, to one of the oldest and wealthiest nations of Europe! It strikes the writer, that, while these gentlemen are so industriously struggling to prove the existence of some petty object of spleen, they prove a great moral truth in favour of America. What should we think of the boy whose intellect, and labours, and intelligence, were drawn into bold and invidious comparison with those of aged and experienced men!

The writer has said very little on the subject of the ordinary vices of mankind; for he has hoped that no one will read his book, who has yet to learn that they exist everywhere. If any one supposes that he wishes to paint the people of America as existing in a state superior to human passion, free from all uncharitableness and guile, he takes the liberty to assure him he will fall into an egregious blunder. He has not yet met with such an elysium in his travels.

If the bile of any one shall be stirred by the anticipations in which the writer has indulged in favour of the United States of America, he will be sorry; but as he cannot see how the truth is to be affected, or the fortunes of a great people materially varied, by the dissatisfaction of this or that individual, he has thought it safest for his own reputation to say what he thinks, without taking the pains to ascertain to how many it may be agreeable, or to how many disagreeable. He has avoided personalities, and that, as a traveller, is all he feels bound to do, and hopes he shall always do; for he is not of that impertinent class of persons, who think the world cannot be sufficiently enlightened without invading the sacred precincts of private life.

Vol. I, Letter 3

Cooper introduces the European reader to the American young woman. Like the nation as a whole, she is wholesome and honest, radiating innocence, but she is also wary, at least at a certain level, of the predatory and rapacious nature of European men and, thus, European governments.

TO THE BARON VON KEMPERFELT,
&c. &c.
New York, ——

I threw aside my pen abruptly, dear Baron, in order to catch a first view of America. There is something so imposing in the sound of the word—*continent,* that I believe it had served to lead me into a delusion, at which a little reflection has induced me to be the first to smile. My ideas of this remote and little known moiety of the world, have ever been so vague and general, that I confess the folly of having expected to see the land make its appearance *en masse,* and with a dignity worthy of its imposing name. The mind has been so long accustomed to divide the rest of the globe into parts, and to think of them in their several divisions of countries and provinces, that one expects to see no more of each, at a *coup d'œil,* than what the sight can embrace.★ Now,

---

★ The Americans say, it is a common and absurd blunder of the European to blend all his images of America in one confused whole. Thus one talks of the climate of America! of the soil of America! and even of the people and manners of America! (meaning always the continent too, and not the United States.) No doubt there are thousands who know better; but still there is a good deal of truth in the charge. The writer was fre-

ridiculous as it may seem, I had, unaccountably, imbibed the impression that America was to appear, at the first glance, larger to the senses than the little island I had left behind me. You are at perfect liberty to make yourself just as merry as you please at this acknowledgment; but, if the truth could be fairly sifted, I have no doubt it would be found that most European adventurers, who seek these western regions, have formed expectations of its physical or moral attributes, quite as extravagant as was my own unfortunate image of its presence. I have taken the disappointment as a salutary admonition, that a traveller has no right to draw these visionary scenes, and then quarrel with the people he has come to visit, because he finds that he has seen fit to throw into a strong light, those parts which nature has every where been pleased to keep in shadow; or to colour highest the moral properties, which the same wise dame has sagaciously kept down, in order that those qualities, which it has been her greatest delight to lavish on man, may for ever stand the boldest and most prominent in her own universal picture.

Instead of beholding, on reaching the deck, some immense mountain, clad in a verdant dress of luxurious and unknown vegetation, lifting its tall head out of the sea, and imperiously frowning on the sister element, my first view was of that same monotonous waste with which my eyes had been sated to weariness, during the last three weeks. The eager question of "Where is America?" was answered by Cadwallader, who silently pointed to a little, blue, cloud-like mound, that rose above the western horizon in three or four undulating swells, and then fell away to the north and to the south, losing itself in the water. I believe I should have expressed my disappointment aloud, but for the presence, and, more particularly, for the air of my companion. His eye was riveted on the spot with all the fondness of a child who is greeting the countenance of a well-beloved parent. It appeared to me

---

quently amused, during his voyage, by hearing the passengers (mostly Americans) relate the ridiculous mistakes that have been made by Europeans, otherwise well informed, when conversing on the subject of the trans-atlantic continent. Countries which lie on different sides of the equator, are strangely brought in contact, and people, between whom there is little affinity of manners, religion, government, language, or, indeed, of any thing else, are strangely blended in one and the same image. It would seem to be an every day occurrence, for Americans to have inquiries made concerning individuals, estates, or events which exist, or have had an existence, at some two or three thousand miles from their own places of residence, just as if the Dane should be expected to answer interrogatories concerning the condition of a farm situate on the Po!

that it penetrated far beyond those little hills of blue, and that it was gifted with power to roam over the broad vallies, vast lakes, and thousand rivers of his native land. I fancied that his philanthropic spirit was deeply enjoying those scenes of domestic happiness, of quiet, of abundance, and of peace, which he has so often assured me exist, beyond a parallel, within her borders. Perhaps a secret consciousness of my own absurdity, came in season, also, to prevent so unfortunate an exposure of my high-wrought expectations.

The season of the year, a soft, balmy, southerly breeze, and the air from the land, however, were all present to restore good humour. The little hillocks soon swelled into modest mountains; and then a range of low, sandy, and certainly not inviting, coast, was gradually rising along the western margin of the view. The sea was dotted with a hundred sails, all of which were either receding from, or approaching, a low point that was as yet scarcely visible, and which extended a few miles to the northward of the high land already mentioned. Beyond, in that direction, nothing more was as yet apparent, than the tame view of the sea. Three or four small schooners were lying off and on, under jib and mainsail, gliding about, like so many marine birds soaring over their native waters. From time to time, they threw pilots on board of, or received them from, the different ships that were quitting or entering the haven within the Cape. On the whole, the scene was lively, cheering, and, compared to the past, filled with the most animating expectations.

It was not long before a beautiful little sloop, of a formation and rig quite different from any I had ever before seen, came skimming the waves directly in our track. Her motion was swift and graceful, and likely to bring us soon within speaking distance. It was a fishing smack, out of which the captain was disposed to obtain some of the delicious bass that are said to abound on certain banks that lie along this coast. We were disappointed of our treat, for the fisherman answered the signal by intimating that he had sold the last of his stock, but the manœuvres of the two vessels brought us near enough to hail. "Is there any news?" roared the captain, through his trumpet, while we were gliding past each other. The answer came against the breeze, and was nearly indistinct. The words "Cadmus in," were, however, affirmed by more than one eager listener, to form part of the reply. Every body now pressed about our commander, to inquire who or what was this Cadmus, and what he or she might be in? But the captain was not able to gratify our curiosity.

Cadmus was the name of a ship in the French trade, it seemed, and formed one in a line of packets between Havre and New York, just as our own vessel did between the latter port and Liverpool. "It is not surprising that she should be in," continued our honest commander, "for she sailed on the 13th, whereas, we only got clear of the land, as you well know, gentlemen, on the 18th of the same month; a passage of one and twenty days, at this season of the year, cannot be called a bad one." As it was quite evident the ideas of the worthy seaman were in a channel very different from our own, we were fain to wait for some more satisfactory means of arriving at the truth. Another opportunity was not long wanting. A large coasting schooner passed within two hundred feet of us. A tar was standing on her quarter-deck, both hands thrust into the bosom of his sea-jacket, eyeing our ship with a certain understanding air that need not be explained to one who claims himself to be so promising a child of Neptune. This individual proved to be the master of the coaster, and to him our captain again roared "Any news?" "Ay, ay; all alive up in the bay," was the answer. The vessels were sweeping by each other with tantalizing rapidity, and without paying the customary deference to nautical etiquette, some six or seven of the passengers united in bawling out, as with one voice, "What news, what news?" The envious winds again bore away the answer, of which no more reached our ears than the same perplexing words of "Cadmus is in."

In the absence of all certainty, I ventured to ask Cadwallader, whether an important election had not just passed, in which some favourite namesake of the founder of Thebes had proved successful. This surmise, however, was not treated with any particular deference, and then we were left to devise our own manner of explaining the little we had heard by the aid of sheer invention.

In the mean time the ship was pressing steadily towards her haven. The high land which, in contra-distinction to the low, sandy beach, that extends for hundreds of leagues along the coast of this country, has obtained the name of "Neversink," ceased to rise, and objects had become distinct on its brown acclivity. A light-house on the Cape was soon plainly visible, and a large buoy was seen, heaving and setting with the unquiet waters, to mark the proper entrance to a wide bay, that stretched, farther than the eye could reach, to the westward. Just without this rolling beacon, lay a low, graceful, rakish, little schooner, in waiting to give us a pilot. The wind was getting

light, and there was no necessity to arrest the progress of the ship to receive
this welcome harbinger of the comforts of the land. It may be unnecessary
to add, that we all pressed around him, in a body, to attain the solution of
our recent doubts, and to hear the tidings of another hemisphere.

I was struck with the singular air of exultation with which this sturdy
marine guide delivered himself of the intelligence with which he was evidently teeming. To the usual question, he gave a quick answer, and in nearly
the same language as the seaman of the fishing-smack. "Cadmus in," again
rung in our ears, without leaving us any wiser than before we had heard the
inexplicable words. "She has been long enough from Havre, to be out
again," retorted our captain, with a dryness that savoured a little of discontent. "If you think so much of the arrival of the Cadmus in thirty days, from
France, what will you say to that of my ship, in twenty-one, from Liverpool?" "Your owners may be glad to see you, but then, you've not got the
old man aboard." "We have them here of all ages: and, what is far better, some
of both sexes!" returned one of the passengers, throwing a glance at the
interested features of a beautiful young creature, who was eagerly listening
to catch the syllables that should first impart intelligence from her native
country. "Ay, ay; but you have no La Fayette in the ship." "La Fayette!"
echoed, certainly every American within hearing. "Is La Fayette arrived?"
demanded Cadwallader, with the quickness of lightning, and with an ani-
mation far greater than I had ever given him credit for possessing. "That is
he, safe and well. He has been on the island with the vice-president since
yesterday. This morning he is to go up to town, where he will find himself
a welcome guest. The bay above is alive," our guide concluded, jerking his
thumb over one shoulder, and looking as if he were master of a secret of
some importance. Here, then, was a simple and brief explanation of the
event on which we had been exercising our faculties for the last two hours.
For myself, I confess, I was disappointed, expecting little short of some revolution in the politics of the state. But the effect on most of my companions was as remarkable as it was sudden. Cadwallader did not speak again
for many minutes. He walked apart; and I saw, by his elevated head and
proud step, that the man was full of lofty and patriotic recollections. The
eyes of the fair girl just mentioned, were glistening, and her pretty lip was
actually quivering with emotion. A similar interest in the event was
manifested, in a greater or less degree, by every individual in the ship, who

claimed the land we were approaching as the country of his birth. The captain lost every shade of discontent on the instant, and even the native portion of the crew, suspended their labour to listen to what was said, with a general air of gratification and pride.

I will acknowledge, Baron, that I was touched myself, at the common feeling thus betrayed by so many differently constituted individuals; and, at so simple an occurrence. There was none of that noisy acclamation with which the English seamen are apt to welcome any grateful intelligence, nor a single exaggerated exclamation, like those which characterize the manners of most of the continental nations of Europe, in their manifestations of pleasure.

It was not long ere Cadwallader had taken the pilot apart, and was earnestly engaged in extracting all the information he deemed necessary, on a subject he found so interesting. I was soon made acquainted with the result. It seems, that after an absence of forty years, La Fayette had returned to visit the land in which he had laid the foundation of his fame. That he had reached a country where hearts and arms would alike be open to receive him, was sufficiently manifest in the manner of all around me; and I could not but felicitate myself, in being so fortunate as to have arrived at a moment likely to elicit some of the stronger emotions of a people, who are often accused of insensibility to all lively impressions, and most of whose thoughts, like their time, are said to be occupied in heedful considerations of the future. Here was, at least, an occasion to awaken recollections of the past, and to elicit something like a popular display of those generous qualities which constitute, what may not improperly be called, the chivalry of nations. It would be curious, also, to observe, how far political management was mingled, in a perfect democracy, with any demonstrations of pleasure it might be thought expedient to exhibit, or in what degree the true popular sentiment sympathized with feelings that, in one section of the earth, are, as you well know, not unfrequently played off by the engines of governmental power.

I was not sorry, therefore, to listen to the plans of my companion. A boat, in the employment of the journals of the city, was by this time alongside the ship, and having obtained the little news we had to impart, it was about to return into the haven, in order to anticipate the arrival of the vessel, which was likely to be delayed for many hours by a flat calm and an adverse tide. In this boat it was proposed that we should take passage, as far, at least, as the place where La Fayette had made his temporary abode. The earnestness with which Cadwallader pressed this plan, was not likely to meet with any objections from me. Tired of the ship, and eager to place my foot on the soil of the western world, the proposal was no sooner made than it was accepted. The boat was instantly engaged for our exclusive benefit, and the necessary preparations made for our departure.

And now a little incident occurred, which, as it manifests a marked difference in the manners, and perhaps in the characters of those who inhabit this republic, and the possessors of our own Europe, I shall take the liberty to introduce.

I have already mentioned a fair creature as being among our passengers. She is of that age when, in our eyes, the sex is most alluring, because we know it to be the most innocent. I do not think her years can much exceed seventeen. Happily, your Belgic temperament is too mercurial to require a tincture of romance to give interest to a simple picture, in which delicacy, feminine beauty, and the most commendable ingenuousness, were admirably mingled. Neither am I, albeit, past the time of day-dreams, and wakeful nights, so utterly insensible to the attractions of such a being, as to have passed three weeks in her society, without experiencing some portion of that manly interest in her welfare, which, I fear, it has been my evil fortune to have felt for too many of the syrens in general, to permit a sufficient concentration of the sentiment, in favour of any one in particular. I had certainly not forgotten, during the passage, to manifest a proper spirit of homage to the loveliness of the sex, in the person of this young American; nor do I think that my manner failed to express a prudent and saving degree of the admiration that was excited by her gentle, natural, and nymph-like deportment, no less than by her spirited and intelligent discourse. In short—but you were not born in Rotterdam, nor reared upon the Zuy der Zee, to need a madrigal on such a topic. The whole affair passed on the ocean, and, as a nautical man, you will not fail to comprehend it. Notwithstanding I had made every effort to appear, what you know I really am, sufficiently amiable, during the voyage, and, notwithstanding Cadwallader had not given himself any particular trouble on the subject at all, it was not to be denied that there was a marked distinction in the reception of our respective civilities, and that, always in his favour. I confess that, for a long time, I was disposed (in the entire absence of all better reasons) to ascribe this preference to an illiberal national prejudice. Still, it was only by comparison that I had the smallest rational grounds of complaint. But a peculiarly odious quality attaches itself to comparisons of this nature. There is a good deal of the Cæsar in my composition, as respects the sex; unless I could be first with the Houries, I believe I should be willing to abandon Paradise itself, in order to seek pre-eminence in some humbler sphere. I fear this ambitious temperament has been our bane, and has condemned us to the heartless and unsocial life we lead! Our fair fellow passenger was under the care of an aged and invalid grandfather, who had been passing a few years in Italy, in pursuit of health. Now, it is not easy to imagine a more cuttingly polite communication, than that which this vigilant old guardian permitted between me and his youthful charge. If I approached, her joyous, natural, and enticing (I will not, because a little piqued, deny the truth, Baron,) merriment was instantly changed into the cold and regulated smiles of artificial breeding. Nature seemed banished at my footstep: and yet it was the artlessness and irresistible attractions of those fas-cinations, which so peculiarly denote the influence of the mighty dame, that were constantly tempting me to obtrude my withering presence on her enjoyments. With Cadwallader, every thing was reversed. In his society, she laughed without ceasing; chatted, disputed, was natural and happy. To all this intercourse, the lynx-eyed grandfather paid not the smallest attention. He merely seemed pleased that his child had found an agreeable, and an instruc-tive companion; while, on the contrary, there existed so much of attractive-ness in our respective systems, that it was impossible for me to approach the person of the daughter, without producing a corresponding proximity on the part of the parent.

Something nettled by a circumstance that, to one who is sensible he is not as interesting as formerly, really began to grow a little personal, I took occasion to joke Cadwallader on his superior happiness, and to felicitate myself on the probability, that I might yet enjoy the honour of officiating, in my character of a confirmed celibite, at his nuptials. He heard me without surprise, and answered me without emotion. "I thought the cir-cumstance could not long escape one so quick sighted," he said. "You think I am better received than yourself? The fact is indisputable; and, as the motive exists in customs that distinguish us, in a greater or less degree, from every other people, I will endeavour to account for it. In no other country, is the same freedom of intercourse between the unmarried of the two sexes, permitted, as in America. In no other christian country, is there more restraint imposed on the communications between the married: in this particular, we reverse the usages of all other civilized nations. The why, and the wherefore, shall be pointed out to you, in proper time; but the present case requires its own explanation. Surprising, and possibly suspicious, as may seem to you the easy intercourse I hold with my young countrywoman, there is nothing in it beyond what you will see every day in our society. The father permits it, because *I am his countryman,* and he is watchful of you, because you are *not!* Men of my time of life, are not considered particularly dangerous to the affections of young ladies of seventeen, for unequal matches are of exceedingly rare occurrence among us. And, if I were what I have been," he added, smiling, "I do not know that the case would be materially altered. In every thing but years, the grandfather of the fair Isabel, knows that I am the equal of his charge. It would be quite in the ordinary course of things, that a marriage should grow out of this communication. Ninety-nine, in one hundred, of our family connexions, are formed very much in this manner. Taste and inclination, rather guided, than controlled, by the prudence of older heads, form most of our matches; and just as much freedom as comports with that prudence, and a vast deal more than you probably deem safe, is allowed between the young of the two sexes. We, who ought to, and who do know best, think otherwise. Women are, literally, our better halves. Their frailty is to be ascribed to the seductions of man. In a community like ours, where almost every man has some healthful and absorbing occupation, there is neither leisure, nor inclination, to devote much time to unworthy pursuits. I need not tell you that vice must be familiar, before it ceases to be odious. In Europe, a successful intrigue often gives *éclat,* even to an otherwise contemptible individual; in America, he must be a peculiarly fortunate man, who can withstand its odium. But the abuse of youth and innocence with us, is comparatively rare indeed. In consequence, suspicion slumbers; *voila tout.*"

"But why this difference, then, between you and me?" I demanded. "Why does this Cerberus sleep only while you are nigh? I confess I looked for higher courtesy in a man who has travelled."

"It is precisely because *he has travelled,*" my friend interrupted, a little dryly. "But you can console yourself with the expectation, that those of his countrymen, who have never quitted home, will be less vigilant, because less practised in foreign manners."

This introduction brings me to my incident. It was no sooner known that we were about to quit the ship, than a dozen longing faces gathered about us. Our example was followed by others, and one or two more boats from the land were engaged to transport the passengers into the bay, in order that they might witness the reception of La Fayette. I had observed a cloud of disappointment on the fair brow of the little Isabel, from the moment our intentions were known. The circumstance was mentioned to Cadwallader, who was not slow to detect its reason. After a little thought, he approached the grandfather, and made an offer of as many seats, in our own boat, as might be necessary for the accommodation of his party. It seems the health of the old man would not permit the risk. The offer was, therefore, politely declined. The cloud thickened on the brow of Isabel; but it vanished entirely when her aged grandfather proposed that she should accompany us, attended by a maid, and *under the especial protection* of my companion. In all this arrangement, singular as it appeared to my eastern vision, there was the utmost simplicity and confidence. It was evident, by the tremulous and hesitating assent of the young lady, that even the customs of the country were slightly invaded; but, then, the occasion was deemed sufficiently extraordinary to justify the innovation. "So much for the privileges of two score and five," whispered Cadwallader, after he had handed his charge into the boat. For myself, I admit I rejoiced in an omen that was so flattering to those personal pretensions which, in my own case, are getting to be a little weakened by time. Before closing this relation, of what I consider a distinctive custom, it is proper to add, that had not the parties been of the very highest class of society, even far less hesitation would have been manifested; and that the little reluctance exhibited by Isabel, was rather a tribute paid to that retiring delicacy which is thought to be so proper to her sex, than to the most remote suspicion of any positive impropriety. Had she been a young married woman, there would, probably, have been the same little struggle with timidity, and the same triumph of the curiosity of the sex. But the interest which our fair companion took in the approaching ceremony, deserves a better name. It was plain, by her sparkling eyes and flushed features, that a more worthy sentiment was at the bottom of her impulses—it was almost patriotism.

Behold us then in the boat; Cadwallader, the gentle Isabel, and our three attendants, and impelled by the vigorous arms of four lusty watermen. We were still upon the open sea, and our distance from the city not less than seven leagues. The weather, however, was propitious, and our little bark, no less than its crew, was admirably adapted to inspire confidence. The former was long and narrow, but buoyant, and of beautiful construction, being both light and strong. The latter, it appears, are of a class of watermen, that are renowned in this country, under the name of Whitehallers. I have every reason to believe their reputation is fairly earned; for they urged the boat onward with great speed, and with the most extraordinary ease to themselves. I remarked, that their stroke was rather short, and somewhat quick, and that it was made entirely with the arm, the body remaining as nearly upright as possible when the limbs are exerted. At first, I thought these men were less civil than comported with their condition. They touched their hats to us, it is true, on entering the boat, but it was rather too much in the manner of a salutation of equality; at least, there was no very visible manifestation of a sense of inferiority. Closer observation, however, furnished no additional grounds of complaint. Their whole deportment was civil, nor, though far from humble, could it be termed in any degree obtrusive; still it was not precisely European. There seemed no sin of commission, but something of omission, that was offensive to the established superiority of a man of a certain number of quarterings. Perhaps I was more alive to this jealous feeling, from knowing that I was in a republican country, and from the fact, that I had so recently quitted one where the lower classes bow more, and the higher less, than among any other christian people. The strokesman of the boat took some interest in seeing us all properly bestowed. With the utmost coolness he appropriated the best place to Isabel, and then with the same *sang froid* intimated that her attendant should occupy the next. Neither was he ignorant that the object of his care was a domestic, for he called her "the young woman," while he distinguished her mistress as "the young lady." I was a little surprised to see that Cadwallader quietly conceded the place to this Abigail; for, during the passage, the distinctions of master and servant always had been sufficiently observed between all our passengers. I even ventured to speak to him on the subject, in German, of which he has a tolerable knowledge. "Notwithstanding all that the old world has said of itself on this subject," he coolly answered, "you are now in the true Paradise of women. They receive, perhaps, less idolatry, but more manly care here, than in any country I have visited." Truly, Baron, I begin to deem the omens propitious!

After passing at a short distance from the low sandy point already named, we were fairly within the estuary. This bay is of considerable extent, and is bounded on the north and on the south by land of some elevation. It receives a river or two, from the west, and is partially protected from the ocean, on the east, by a low beach, which terminates in the point named, and by an island on the opposite side of the entrance. The mouth is a few miles in width, possessing several shallow channels, but only one of a depth sufficient to admit vessels of a heavy draught. The latter are obliged to pass within musket shot of the point, Cape, or *Hook,* as it is here called. Thence to the city, a distance of some six leagues, the navigation is so intricate as to render a pilot indispensable.

The ruins of an imperfect and insignificant military work were visible on the cape; but I was told the government is seriously occupied in erecting more formidable fortifications, some of which were shortly visible. A shoal was pointed out, on which it is contemplated to construct an immense castle, at a vast expense, and which, with the other forts built and building, will make the place impregnable against all marine attacks. I have been thus diffuse in my details, dear Baron, because I believe every traveller has a prescriptive right to prove that he enters all strange lands with his eyes open; and, because it is quite out of my power to say at what moment your royal master, the good King William, may see fit to send you at the head of a fleet to regain those possessions, of which his ancestors, of the olden time, were ruthlessly robbed by the cupidity of the piratical English!

I presume, that renowned navigator, the indefatigable Hudson, laboured under some such delusion as myself, when his adventurous bark first steered within the capes of this estuary. My eyes were constantly bent towards the west, in expectation of seeing the spires of a town, rearing themselves from the water, which still bounded the view in that direction. The boat, however, held its course towards the north, though nothing was visible there, but an unbroken outline of undulating hills. It seems we were only in an outer harbour, on a magnificent scale, which takes its name (Raritan Bay) from that of the principal river it receives from the west. A passage through the northern range of hills, became visible as we approached them, and then glimpses of the cheerful and smiling scene within, were first caught. This passage, though near a mile in width, is a strait, compared with the bays within and without, and it is not improperly termed "the Narrows."

Directly in the mouth of this passage, and a little on its eastern side, arises a large, massive fortress, in stone, washed by the water on all its sides, and mounting some sixty or seventy pieces of heavy ordnance. The heights on the adjoining shores, are also crowned with works, though of a less imposing aspect. The latter are the remains of the temporary defences of the late war, while the former, constitutes part of the great plan of permanent defence. Labourers are, however, unceasingly employed on the new forts.

The shores, on both hands, were now dotted with marine villas and farm-houses, and the view was alive with all the pleasing objects of civilized life. On our left, a little distance above the passage, a group of houses came into view, and some fifty sail were seen anchored in the offing. "That, then, is New York!" I said, with a feeling a little allied to disappointment. My companion was silent, for his thoughts kept him dumb, if not deaf. "Gentlemen are apt to think they get into the heart of America at the first step," very coolly returned our strokesman; "we are eight good miles from Whitehall slip, and that village is the quarantine ground." This was said without any visible disrespect, but with an air of self-possession that proved our Whitehaller thought it a subject on which long experience had given him a perfect right to bestow an opinion. As I felt in no haste to take the second step into a country where the first had proved so unreasonably long, I was fain to await the development of things, with patience. My companions did not manifest any disposition to converse. Even the petite Isabel, though her strong native attachments had been sufficiently apparent, by her previous discourse, was no longer heard. Like our male companion, a sentiment of deep interest in the ensuing scene, kept her silent. At length the exclamation of "there they come!" burst from the lips of Cadwallader; and there they did come, of a certainty, in all the majesty of a fine aquatic procession, and that too on a scale of magnificence that was admirably suited to the surrounding waters, and as an American would also probably say, "to the occasion." In order that you may form a better idea of the particular scene, it is necessary that I should attempt a description of some of its parts.

The harbour of New York is formed by a junction of the Hudson with an arm of the sea. The latter connects the waters of Raritan Bay with those of a large sound, which commences a few leagues further eastward, and which separates, for more than a hundred miles, the state of Connecticut from the long narrow island of Nassau. The Americans call this district Long

Island, in common parlance; but I love to continue those names which perpetuate the recollection of your former dominion. Some six or seven rivers unite here to pour their waters into a vast basin, of perhaps sixty or seventy miles in circuit. This basin is subdivided into two unequal parts by a second island, which is known by the name of Staten, another memento of your ancient power. The Narrows is the connecting passage. The inner bay cannot be less than twenty miles in circumference. It contains three or four small islands, and possesses water enough for all the purposes of navigation, with good anchorage in almost every part. The land around it is low, with the exception of the hills near its entrance, and certain rocky precipices of a very striking elevation that on one side line the Hudson, for some miles, commencing a short distance from its mouth.

On the present occasion every thing combined to lend to a scenery, that is sufficiently pleasing of itself, its best and fullest effect. The heavens were without a cloud; the expanse beneath, supporting such an arch as would do not discredit to the climate of sunny Italy herself. The bay, stretched as far as eye could reach, like a mirror, unruffled and shining. The heat was rather genial than excessive, and, in fine, as our imaginative young companion poetically expressed it, "the very airs were loyal, nor had the climate forgotten to be true to the feelings of the hour!"

It is necessary to have seen something of the ordinarily subdued and quiet manner of these people, in order to enter fully into a just appreciation of the common feeling, which certainly influenced all who were with me in the boat. You probably know that we in Europe are apt to charge the Americans with being cold of temperament, and little sensible of lively impressions of any sort. I have learnt enough to know, that in return, they charge us, in gross, with living in a constant state of exaggeration, and with affecting sentiments we do not feel. I fear the truth will be found as much with them as against them. It is always hazardous to judge of the heart by what the mouth utters: nor is he any more likely to arrive at the truth, who believes that every time an European shows his teeth in a smile, he will do you no harm, than he is right who thinks the dog that growls will as infallibly bite. I believe, after all, it must be conceded, that sophistication is not the most favourable science possible for the cultivation of the passions. No man is, in common, more imperturbable than the American savage; and who is there more terrible in his anger, or more firm in his attachments!

Let this be as it may, these republicans certainly exhibit their ordinary emotions in no very dramatic manner. I had never before seen Cadwallader so much excited, and yet his countenance manifested thought, rather than joy. Determined to probe him a little closer, I ventured to inquire into the nature of those ties which united La Fayette, a foreigner, and a native of a country that possesses so little in manners and opinions in common with his own, to a people so very differently constituted from those among whom he was born and educated.

"It is then fortunate for mankind," returned Cadwallader, "that there exist, in nature, principles which can remove these obstacles of our own creation. Though habit and education do place wide and frequently lamentable barriers between the sympathies of nations, he who has had the address to break through them, without a sacrifice of any natural duty, possesses a merit, which, as it places him above the level of his fellow-creatures, should, and will protect him from their prejudices. It is no small part of the glory of La Fayette, that while he has taken such a hold of our affections as no man probably ever before possessed in those of a foreign nation, he has never, for an instant, forgotten that he was a Frenchman. In order, however, to appreciate the strength and the reasons of this attachment, as well as the glory it should reflect on its subject, it is necessary to remember the causes which first brought our present guest among us.

"If any man may claim a character for manful and undeviating adherence to what he has deemed the right, under circumstances of nearly irresistible temptation to go wrong, it is La Fayette. His love of liberal principles was even conceived under the most unfavourable circumstances. The blandishments of a sensual, but alluring court, the prejudices of a highly privileged caste, with youth, wealth, and constitution, were not auspicious to the discovery of truth. None but a man who was impelled by high and generous intentions, could have thrown away a load which weighs so many gifted minds to the earth. He has the high merit of being the first French nobleman who was willing to devote his life and fortune to the benefit of the inferior classes. Some vapid and self-sufficient commentators have chosen to term this impulse an inordinate and vain ambition. If their appellation be just, it has been an ambition which has ever proved itself singularly regardful of others, and as singularly regardless of self. In the same spirit of detraction have these declaimers attempted to assail the virtue they could not imitate, and to depreciate services, whose very object their contracted minds have not the power to comprehend. I shall not speak of events connected with the revolution in his own country, for they form no other part of our admiration of La Fayette, than as they serve to show us how true and how fearless he has ever been in adhering to what we, in common, believe to be the right. Had he been fitted to control that revolution, as it existed in its worst and most revolting aspects, he would have failed in some of those qualities which are necessary to our esteem.

"In the remembrance of the connection between La Fayette and his own country, the American finds the purest gratification. It is not enough to say that other men have devoted themselves to the cause of human nature, since we seek, in vain, for one who has done it with so little prospect of future gain, or at so great hazard of present loss. His detractors pretend that he was led into our quarrel by that longing for notoriety, which is so common to youth. It is worthy of remark, that this longing should have been as peculiarly his own by its commencement as by its duration. It is exhibited in the man of seventy, under precisely the same forms that it was first seen in the youth of nineteen. In this particular, at least, it partakes of the immutable quality of truth.

"Separate from all those common principles, which, in themselves, would unite us to any man, there are ties of a peculiarly endearing nature between us and La Fayette. His devotion to our cause was not only first in point of time, but it has ever been first in all its moral features. He came to bestow, and not to receive. While others, who brought little beside their names, were seeking rank and emoluments, he sought the field of battle. His first commission had scarcely received the stamp of official forms, before it had received the still more honourable seal of his own blood. A boy in years, a native of a country towards which we had a hereditary dislike, he caused his prudence to be respected among the most prudent and wary people of the earth. He taught us to forget our prejudices: we not only loved him, but we began to love his nation for his sake. Throughout the half century of our intercourse, a period more fraught with eventful changes than any that has preceded it, nothing has occurred to diminish, or to disturb, this affection. As his devotion to our cause never wavered, not even in the darkest days of our adversity, so has our attachment continued steady to the everlasting obligations of gratitude. Whatever occurred in the revolutions of the old world, the eye of America was turned on La Fayette. She watched his movements with all the solicitude of a tender parent; triumphed in his successes; sympathised in his reverses; mourned in his sufferings, but always exulted in his constancy. The knowledge of passing events is extended in our country, to a degree that is elsewhere unknown. We heard of the downfall of thrones; of changes in dynasties; of victories, defeats, rapine, and war, until curiosity itself was sated with repetitions of the same ruthless events. Secure in our position, and firm in our principles, the political tornadoes, that overturned the most ancient establishments of the old world, sounded in our ears, with no greater effect than the sighings of our own autumnal gales. But no event, coupled with the interests of our friend, was suffered to escape our notice. The statesman, the yeoman, or the school-boy; the matron among her offspring; the housewife amid her avocations; and the beauty in the blaze of her triumph, forgot alike the passions or interests of the moment, forgot their apathy in the distresses of a portion of the world that they believed was wanting in some of its duty to itself, to suffer at all, and drew near to listen at the name of La Fayette. I remember the deep, reverential, I might almost say awful, attention, with which a school of some sixty children, on a remote frontier, listened to the tale of his sufferings in the castle of Olmutz, as it was recounted to us by the instructor, who had been a soldier in his youth, and fought the battles of his country, under the orders of the 'young and gallant Frenchman.' We plotted among ourselves, the means of his deliverance; wondered that the nation was not in arms to redress his wrongs, and were animated by a sort of reflection of his own youthful and generous chivalry. Washington was then with us, and, as he was said to be exerting the influence of his powerful name, which, even at that early day, was beginning to obtain the high ascendancy of acknowledged virtue, we consoled ourselves with the reflection, that he, at least, could never fail. Few Americans, at this hour, enjoy a happier celebrity than Huger, who, in conjunction with a brave German, risked life and liberty to effect the release of our benefactor.

"Though subsequent events have tranquillized this interest in the fortunes of La Fayette, we must become recreant to our principles, before it can become extinct. It is now forty years since he was last among us; but scarcely an American can enter France without paying the homage of a visit to La Grange. Our admiration of his disinterestedness, of his sacrifices, and of his consistency, is just as strong as ever; and, I confess, I anticipate that the country will receive him in such a manner as shall prove this attachment to the world. But, you are not to expect, in our people, manifestations of joy similar to those you have witnessed in Europe. We are neither clamorous nor exaggerated, in the exhibitions of our feelings. The prevailing character of the nation is that of moderation. Still am I persuaded that, in the case of La Fayette, some of our self-restraint will give way before the force of affection. We consider ourselves as the guardians of his fame. They who live a century hence, may live to know how high a superstructure of renown can be reared, when it is based on the broad foundations of the gratitude of a people like our own. The decision of common sense to-day, will become the decision of posterity."

Cadwallader spoke with an earnestness that, at least, attested the sincerity of his own feelings. I may have given to his language the stiffness of a written essay, but I am certain of having preserved all the ideas, and even most of the words. The humid eyes of the fair Isabel responded to all he uttered, and even our Whitehallers bent to their oars, and listened with charmed ears.—Adieu.

VOL. I, LETTER 5

Cooper offers a complex discussion of New England, its character, economy, and geography. The Yankee, Cooper concludes, helps make America the most civilized and humane of all nations.

TO SIR EDWARD WALLER, BART.
&c. &c.
New York ———

*In consequence of this temporary separation from Cadwallader, I was left for a few days, the master of my own movements. I determined to employ them in a rapid excursion through a part of the eastern states of this great confederation, in order to obtain a *coup d'œil* of a portion of the interior. It would have been the most obvious, and perhaps the most pleasing route, to have followed the coast as far as Boston; but this would have brought me in the train of La Fayette, where the natural aspect of society was disturbed by the universal joy and excitement produced by his reception. I chose, therefore, a direction farther from the water, through the centre of Connecticut, entering Massachusetts by its southern border, and traversing that state to Vermont. After looking a little at the latter, and New Hampshire, I returned through the heart of Massachusetts to Rhode Island, re-entering and quitting Connecticut at new points, and regaining this city through the adjacent county of Westchester. The whole excursion has exceeded a thousand miles,

---

* The commencement of this, and of many of the succeeding letters, are omitted, since they contain matter already known to the reader.

though the distance from New York has at no time been equal to three hundred. By naming some of the principal towns through which I passed, you will be able to trace the route on a map, and may better understand the little I have to communicate. I entered Connecticut near Danbury, and left it at Suffield, having passed a night in Hartford, one of its two capital towns. The river was followed in crossing Massachusetts, and my journey in Vermont terminated at Windsor. I then crossed the Connecticut (river) into New Hampshire, to Concord, and turning south, re-entered Massachusetts, proceeding to Worcester. The journey from this point back to New York, was a little circuitous, embracing Providence and Newport, (in Rhode Island), and New London, New Haven and Fairfield, in Connecticut.

As experience had long since shown me that the people on all great, and much frequented, roads, acquire a species of conventional and artificial character, I determined, if possible, to penetrate at once into that part of the country within my reach, which might be supposed to be the least sophisticated, and which, of course, would afford the truest specimen of the national character. Cadwallader has examined my track, and he tells me I have visited the very portion of New England, which is the best adapted to such an object. I saw no great town during my absence, and if I travelled much of the time amid secluded and peaceful husbandmen, I occasionally touched at points where all was alive with the bustle and activity of commerce and manufactures.

A review of the impressions left by this short excursion has convinced me of the difficulty of conveying to an European, by the pen, any accurate, general impression, of even the external appearance of this country. What is so true of one part, is so false of the others, and descriptions of sensible things which were exact a short time since, become so very soon erroneous through changes, that one should hesitate to assume the responsibility of making them. Still, such as they are, mine are at your service. In order, however, to estimate their value, some little preliminary explanation may be necessary.

The six eastern states of this union comprise what is called New England. Their inhabitants are known here by the familiar appellation of "Yankees." This word is most commonly supposed to be a corruption of "Yengeese," the manner in which the native tribes, first known to the colonists, pronounced "English." Some, however, deny this derivation, at the same time that they confess their inability to produce a plausible substitute.

It is a little singular that the origin of a soubriquet, which is in such general use, and which cannot be of any very long existence, should already be a matter of doubt. It is said to have been used by the English as a term of contempt, when the American was a colonist, and it is also said, that the latter often adopts it as an indirect and playful means of retaliation. It is necessary to remember one material distinction in its use, which is infallibly made by every American. At home, the native of even New York, though of English origin, will tell you he is not a Yankee. The term here, is supposed to be perfectly provincial in its application; being, as I have said, confined to the inhabitants, or rather the natives of New England. But, out of the United States, even the Georgian does not hesitate to call himself a "Yankee." The Americans are particularly fond of distinguishing any thing connected with their general enterprise, skill, or reputation, by this term. Thus, the southern planter, who is probably more averse than any other to admit a community of those personal qualities, which are thought to mark the differences in provincial or rather state character, will talk of what a "Yankee merchant," a "Yankee negociator," or a "Yankee soldier," can and has done; meaning always the people of the United States. I have heard a naval officer of rank, who was born south of the Potomac, and whose vessel has just been constructed in this port, speak of the latter with a sort of suppressed pride, as a "Yankee man-of-war." Now, I had overheard the same individual allude to another in a manner that appeared reproachful, and in which he used the word "Yankee," with peculiar emphasis. Thus it is apparent, that the term has two significations among the Americans themselves, one of which may be called its national, and the other its local meaning. The New-Englandman evidently exults in the appellation at all times. Those of the other states with whom I have come in contact, are manifestly quite as well pleased to lay no claim to the title, though all use it freely, in its foreign, or national sense. I think it would result from these facts, that the people of New England are thought, by the rest of their countrymen, to possess some minor points of character, in which the latter do not care to participate, and of which the New Englandman is unconscious, or in which, perhaps, he deems himself fortunate, while, on the other hand, they possess certain other and more important qualities, which are admitted to be creditable to the whole nation. Cadwallader, who is a native of New York, smiled when I proposed this theory, but desired me to have a little patience until I had been able to judge for myself. After all, there is little or no feeling excited on the subject. The inhabitants of states, living a thousand miles asunder, speak of each other with more kindness, in common, than the inhabitants of adjoining counties in England, or provinces in France. Indeed, the candour and manliness with which the northern man generally admits the acknowledged superiority of his southern countryman, on certain points, and *vice versa,* is matter of surprise to me, who, as you know, have witnessed so much illiberality on similar subjects, among the natives of half the countries of Europe.

New England embraces an area of between sixty and seventy thousand square miles. Thus, you see, it is larger in extent than England and Wales united. It has about seven hundred miles of sea coast, and contains a population of something less than 1,800,000. This would give about twenty-seven to the square mile. But in order to arrive at an accurate idea of the populousness of the inhabited parts of the country, it is necessary to exclude from the calculation, that part of it which is not peopled. We should then reject a very large portion of Maine, and a good deal of land in the northern parts of Vermont and New Hampshire, including, perhaps, twenty thousand square miles. This estimate would leave forty inhabitants to the square mile. But we will confine ourselves to Massachusetts, Connecticut, and Rhode Island; neither of which, for America, has an unusual quantity of vacant land. Their surface embraces about 14,000 square miles. The population is not quite a million. This will give an average of a little less than seventy to the square mile. Here, then, we have what may be considered the maximum of the density of American population on any very extended surface. There is a fair proportion of town and country, and a more equal distribution of the labour of society, between commerce, manufactures, and agriculture, than perhaps in any other section of the Union. You are not, however, to suppose that this amount of population is confined to these three states. A great deal of New York, Ohio, and Pennsylvania, and certain districts in many other states, have attained, or even exceed, this ratio. Thus the highest comparative rate of population in this country, estimating it in districts of any considerable extent, is a little less than that of the whole kingdom of Denmark, and very materially exceeding that of Spain.

Still you will scarcely be able to obtain a just idea of the outward appearance of New England from a knowledge of these facts. You must have often observed, in travelling through the most populous countries of Europe, how few of their people are seen. France, for instance, only shows the millions with which she is teeming, in her cities and villages. Nor are you struck with the populousness of even the latter, unless you happen to enter them on fêtes, or have an opportunity of examining them in the evening, after the labourers have returned from the fields. This is, more, or less, true with every other country in Europe. Even in England, one does not see much of the population out of the towns, unless at fairs, or merry-makings. Now I do not remember to have ever travelled so far through any country which appeared more populous than the parts of New England described.* This peculiarity may be ascribed to several causes.

The whole country is subdivided into small freeholds, which are commonly tilled by their owners. The average size of these estates is probably less than a hundred acres. Each, as a general rule, has its house and out-houses. These buildings are usually very near the public roads, and consequently in plain view of the traveller. The field labour is also commonly done at no great distance from the highway. In addition to these reasons, the Americans are thought to perform more journeys, and, consequently, to be more before the eye of their visiters than common. Cadwallader accounts for the latter circumstance in various ways. The greatness of the intermediate distances is the chief of his reasons. But the mental activity of the people, together with the absence of want, are thought to have a proportionate effect. I hear wonders of the throngs that are seen, at certain seasons, on the avenues which lead from the interior to any of the great markets. My companion assures me he once counted eight hundred waggons in the distance of forty miles, most of which were conveying wheat to the city of Albany. On the same road there were sixty taverns in a distance of as many miles; a sufficient proof in itself of the amount of travelling.

Now, all this does not at all comport with our vague European notions of America. We are apt to imagine it a thinly populated, wooded, and fertile, though little cultivated region. Thinly populated it assuredly is, when the whole number of its square miles is compared to the whole amount of its population. But from what I have seen and heard, I feel persuaded, that an American, who understood his ground, might conduct a stranger, who

---

* Part of the North of Italy may, perhaps, be excepted.

knew nothing of the true numbers of the country, over a territory which shall greatly exceed France in extent, and leave the impression on the mind of his guest, that it was more populous than the latter kingdom. In hazarding this opinion, however, I except the effect of the great towns, and of the villages on fête days and at evenings. In continental Europe the traveller often feels a sense of loneliness, though surrounded by millions of human beings. He sees no houses out of the villages; he meets few on the highways; even the field labourers are half the time removed from sight, and when he enters a wood, it is usually a tenantless forest. In the parts of America I have as yet visited, the very reverse is the case. Unless in particular instances, houses occurred at very short intervals; the highways were not thronged as described by Cadwallader, it is true, but I saw more travellers than is usual in the season of harvest; and I scarcely recollect the moment when my eye could not discover groups of field labourers. Of wood there was certainly plenty; but of forests, with the exception of now and then a mountain, scarcely any. At the latter fact, no less than at the air of populousness which distinguishes this portion of the country, I have been greatly surprised. I passed several comparatively barren tracts which were suffered to sustain what wood they might, and I saw ridges of uneven, broken land, that probably still lay in their native shades; but the character of the whole district was that of a succession of fields, sprinkled with houses, and embellished with little groves, that were reserved for the domestic supply of their respective owners. Indeed, in some quarters, there actually appeared less wood than was necessary, when it is remembered the inhabitants use little other fuel, and how expensive the transportation of an article so heavy soon becomes.

I should not describe New England as a particularly fertile region. A large proportion of its surface, at least of the part I saw, was rugged and difficult of tillage, though but little of it was positively sterile. It is rather a grazing, than a grain country. For the former, it is well adapted; the land apparently producing rich and sweet grasses in almost every quarter. There were, however, large districts of deep alluvial soil, where any plant that will thrive in this climate might be successfully grown. I scarcely remember so beautiful a country, or a more fertile looking one, than some of that I passed along the borders of the Connecticut. The river bottoms were loaded with their products, and the adjacent swells were every where crowned with evidences of the abundance they had lavished on their possessors, in the shape of well-stored barns and spacious and comfortable dwellings. In this excursion I first saw extensive and luxuriant fields of that favourite American plant—the maize. It is deemed an infallible test of the quality of the soil, no less than of the climate, throughout most of the Union. Where maize will not grow, the husbandman is reluctant to dwell. It furnishes a healthful nourishment for man and beast, nor is there any useful animal that will not thrive upon its food. I do not think I passed a solitary farm that had not more or less maize in cultivation. It is universally called "corn" *par excellence.* As it is indigenous to the country, sometimes the word Indian is prefixed. But when an American says "corn," he invariably means "maize." It is a splendid plant as it grows in this country, surpassing in appearance any other that appertains to husbandry. It is said to be still finer and more luxuriant to the south, but to me, there was great pleasure, as I saw it here, in gazing at its broad, gracefully curving, dark green blades, as they waved in the wind. It was in the tassel, and its ordinary height could not be much less than eight feet. Many fields must have exceeded this growth.

New England may justly glory in its villages! Notwithstanding the number of detached houses that are every where seen, villages are far from unfrequent, and often contain a population of some two or three thousand. In space, freshness, an air of neatness and of comfort, they far exceed any thing I have ever seen, even in the mother country. With now and then an exception of some one among them that possesses a more crowded, commercial, or manufacturing population, than common, they all partake of the same character. I have passed, in one day, six or seven of these beautiful, tranquil and enviable looking hamlets, for not one of which have I been able to recollect an equal in the course of all my European travelling. They tell me, here, that villages, or small towns, abound in the newer portions of the northern and western states, that even eclipse those of New England, since they unite, to all the neatness and space of the latter, the improvements of a still more modern origin.

In order to bring to your mind's eye a sketch of New England scenery, you are to draw upon your imagination for the following objects. Fancy yourself on some elevation that will command the view of a horizon that embraces a dozen miles. The country within this boundary must be undulating, rising in bold swells, or occasionally exhibiting a broken, if not a ragged surface. But these inequalities must be counterbalanced by broad and rich swales of land, that frequently spread out into lovely little vallies. If there be a continued range of precipitous heights in view, let it be clad in the verdure of the forest. If not, wood must be scattered in profusion over the landscape, in leafy shadows that cover surfaces of twenty and thirty acres. Buildings, many white, relieved by Venetian blinds in green, some of the dun colour of time, and others of a dusky red, must be seen standing amid orchards, and marking, by their positions, the courses of the number- less highways. Here and there, a spire, or often two, may be seen pointing towards the skies from the centre of a cluster of roofs. Perhaps a line of blue mountains is to be traced in the distance, or the course of a river to be fol- lowed by a long succession of fertile meadows. The whole country is to be subdivided by low stone walls, or wooden fences, made in various fashions, the quality of each improving, or deteriorating, as you approach, or recede from the dwelling of the owner of the soil. Cattle are to be seen grazing in the fields, or ruminating beneath the branches of single trees, that are left for shade in every pasture, and flocks are to be seen clipping the closer herbage of the hill sides. In the midst of this picture must man be placed, quiet, orderly, and industrious. By limiting this rural picture to greater, or less extensive, scenes of similar quiet and abundance, or occasionally swelling it out, until a succession of villages, a wider range of hills, and some broad valley, through which a third rate American river winds its way to the ocean, are included, your imagination can embrace almost every variety of landscape I beheld in the course of my journey.

Concerning the character of the people, you cannot expect me to write very profoundly on so short an acquaintance. In order, however, that you may know how to estimate the value of the opinions I shall venture to give, it is necessary that you should learn the circumstances under which they have been formed. Before parting from Cadwallader, I requested he would give me some brief written directions, not only of the route I was to pur- sue, but of the manner in which I was to regulate my intercourse with the people. I extract the substance of his reply, omitting the line of route he advised, which is already known to you.

"As respects intercourse with the inhabitants, your path is perfectly plain. You speak the language with what we call the intonation of an Eng- lishman. In America, while there are provincial, or state peculiarities, in tone, and even in the pronunciation and use of certain words, there is no patois. An American may distinguish between the Georgian and the New Englandman, but you cannot. In this particular our ears are very accurate, and while we can, and do pass for natives every day in England, it is next to impossible for an Englishman to escape detection in America. Five out of six of the whole English nation, let them be educated ever so much, retain something of the peculiarity of their native county. The exceptions are much fewer than they suppose themselves, and are chiefly in the very highest circles. But there is also a slang of society in England, which forms no part of the true language. Most of those who escape the patois, adopt something of the slang of the day. There is also a fashion of intonation in the mother country which it is often thought vulgar to omit. All these differences, with many others, which it may be curious to notice hereafter, mark the Englishman at once. I think, therefore, you will be mistaken for a native of some of the less accurate counties of England. It will, in consequence, be necessary for you to be more on your guard against offence than if you were thought a German, or a Frenchman. The reasons for this caution are perfectly obvious. It is not because the American is more disposed to seek grounds of complaint against his English visiter, but because he has been more accustomed to find them.

"All *young* travellers are, as a matter of course, grumblers; but an Englishman is proverbially *the* grumbler. It is generally enough for him, that he meets an usage different from that to which he has been accustomed, to condemn it. It is positively true, that an intelligent and highly talented individual of that country, once complained to me, that in the month of January the days were so much *shorter* in New York than in London!★ His native propensity had blinded him to the material fact, that the former city was in 41°, while the latter lay 10° higher. Now, the Englishman may grumble any where else with more impunity than in America. In France, in Germany, or in Italy, he is not often understood, and half the time, a Frenchman, in particular, is disposed to think his country is receiving compliments, instead of anathemas. But with an American, there can of course be no such mistake. He not only understands the sneer, but he knows whence it comes. Though

---

★ This mistake is not, in truth, as absurd as it first seems. The twilight, in high latitudes, serves to eke out the day, so as greatly to subtract from the amount of total darkness. Had the gentleman in question chosen any other part of England than London, he might have found some pretext for his opinion.

far from obtrusive on such occasions, it is not rare for the offended party to retort, whenever the case will admit of his interference. The consequence has been, that, as a class, the English travellers now behave themselves better in America than in any other country. But a character has been gained, and it will require a good deal of time to eradicate it. The servant of the respectable Mr. Hodgson tells his master that the people of the inns 'are surprised to find Englishmen behave so well.' But after all, with a great deal that is not only absurd, but offensive, there is something that may be excused in the discontent of an Englishman, when travelling in a foreign country. The wealth of an immense empire has centered at home, in a comparatively diminutive kingdom, and he who can command a tolerable proportion of that wealth may purchase a degree of comfort that is certainly not to be obtained out of it. But comfort is not the only consequence of those broad distinctions between the very rich, and the very poor. It is saying nothing new, to say that the lower orders of the English, more particularly those who are brought in immediate contact with the rich, exceed all other Christians in abject servility to their superiors. It may be new, but in reflecting on the causes, you will perceive it is not surprising, that on the contrary, the common American should be more natural, and less reserved in his communications with men above him in the scale of society, than the peasant of Europe. While the English traveller, therefore, is more exacting, the American labourer is less disposed to be submissive than usual. But every attention within the bounds of reason will be shewn you, though it is not thought in reason, in New England especially, that one man should assume a tone of confirmed superiority over the rest of mankind, merely because he wears a better coat, or has more money in his purse. Notwithstanding this stubborn temper of independence, no man better understands the obligations between him who pays, and him who receives, than the native of New England. The inn-keeper of Old England, and the inn-keeper of New England, form the very extremes of their class. The one is obsequious to the rich, the other unmoved, and often apparently cold. The first seems to calculate, at a glance, the amount of profit you are likely to leave behind you; while his opposite appears only to calculate in what manner he can most contribute to your comfort, without materially impairing his own. It is a mistake, however, that the latter is filled with a sense of his own imaginary importance. It troubles him as little as the subject does any other possessor of a certain established rank, since there is no one to dispute it. He is often a magistrate, the chief of a battalion of militia, or even a member of a state legislature. He is almost always a man of character; for it is difficult for any other to obtain a license to exercise the calling. If he has the pride of conscious superiority, he is not wanting in its principles. He has often even more: he has frequently a peculiar pride in his profession. I have known a publican, who filled a high and responsible situation in the government of the first state of this confederation, officiously convey my baggage to a place of security, because he thought it was his duty to protect my property when under his roof. An English inn-keeper would not have impaired his domestic importance by such an act. He would have called upon John, the head-waiter, and John would have probably have bid Thomas Ostler, or Boots, to come to his assistance. In both cases, the work would be done, I grant you; but under very different feelings. I profess to no more knowledge of the boasted English inn-keeper, than what any one may gain, who has travelled among them, in every manner, from a seat on the top of a stage coach, to one in a post-chaise and four. But, with the publican of New England, I have a long and intimate acquaintance, and I fearlessly affirm, that he has been the subject of much and groundless calumny.

"If servility, an air of *empressement,* and a mercenary interest in your comforts, form essentials to your happiness and self-complacency, England, with a full pocket, against the world. But, if you can be content to receive consistent civility, great kindness, and a tempered respect, in which he who serves you consults his own character no less than yours, and all at a cheap rate, you will travel not only in New England, but throughout most of the United States, with perfect satisfaction. God protect the wretch, whom poverty and disease shall attack in an English inn! Depend on it, their eulogies have been written by men who were unaccustomed to want. It is even a calamity to be obliged to have a saving regard to the contents of your purse, under the observation of their mercenary legions! There seems an intuitive ability in all that belongs to them, to graduate your wealth, your importance, and the extent of their own servility. Now, on the other hand, a certain reasoning distinction usually controls the manner in which the American inn-keeper receives his guests. He pays greater attention to the gentleman than to the tin-pedlar, because he knows it is necessary to the habits of the former, and because he thinks it is no more than a just return for the greater price he pays. But he is civil, and even kind, to both alike. He sometimes makes blunders, it is true, for he meets with characters that are new to him, or is required to decide on distinctions of which he has no idea. A hale, well-looking, active, and intelligent American, will scarcely ever submit his personal comforts, or the hourly control of his movements, to the caprices of another, by becoming a domestic servant. Neither would the European, if he could do any thing better. It is not astonishing, therefore, that a publican, in a retired quarter of the country, should sometimes be willing to think that the European servants he sees, are entitled to eat with their masters, or that he calls both 'gentlemen.' A striking and national trait in the American, is a constant and grave regard to the feelings of others. It is even more peculiar to New England, than to any other section of our country. It is the best and surest fruit of high civiliza-tion. Not that civilization which chisels marble and gilds *salons,* but that which marks the progress of reason, and which, under certain circum-stances, makes men polished, and, under all, renders them humane. In this particular, America is, beyond a doubt, the most civilized nation in the world, inasmuch as the aggregate of her humanity, intelligence and com-fort, compared with her numbers, has nothing like an equal.

"From these facts, you may easily glean a knowledge of the personal treatment you are likely to receive in your approaching excursion. There will be an absence of many of those forms to which you have been accus-tomed, but their place will be supplied by a disinterested kindness, that it may require time to understand, but which, once properly understood, can never be supplied by any meretricious substitute. I never knew an Ameri-can of healthful feelings, who did not find more disgust than satisfaction, in the obsequiousness of the English domestics. For myself, I will avow that the servility, which I can readily understand may become so necessary by indulgence, gave me a pain that you will, perhaps, find it difficult to com-prehend. I do not say it may not be necessary in Europe, particularly in England, but I do say, thank God, it is not necessary here.

"It will be prudent, at all times, to treat those who serve you with great attention to their feelings. An instance may serve as an example. A few years since, I was in a boat, on one of our interior waters, accompanied by a fine, gentlemanlike, manly, aristocratic young Englishman. One of the boatmen incommoded us with his feet. 'Go forward, Sir,' said my English companion, in a tone that would have answered better on the Thames, than on the Cayuga. The boatman looked a little surprised, and a good deal determined. There was an evident struggle, between his pride and his desire, not to give offense to a stranger. 'We have scarcely room here for our feet,' I observed; 'if you will go forward, we shall be more comfortable.' 'Oh! with all my heart, Sir,' returned the man, who complied without any further hesitation. The same individual, if left to his own suggestions, or not assailed in his pride, would probably have plunged into the lake for our pleasure, and that, too, without stopping to consider whether he was to get sixpence for his ducking. With this single caution, you may go from Maine to Georgia with perfect safety, and, most of the distance, with sufficient comfort; often with more even than in England, and, generally, at a price which, compared with what you receive, is infinitely below the cheapest rate of travelling in any part of Europe. It is a ludicrous mistake, that you must treat every American as your companion in society, but it is very necessary that he should be treated as your equal in the eye of God."

I must leave you, for the moment, with this morceau from the pen of Cadwallader, who writes as he speaks, like a man who thinks better of his countrymen than we have been accustomed to believe they deserve. I must postpone, to my next, the commentaries that my own trifling experience has suggested on his theory.—Adieu.

This letter is a continuation of Cooper's analysis of New England. It focuses on the character of the Yankee and the importance of ideas in northeastern culture. Yankees, Cooper argues, are well known throughout America for their "enterprise, frugality, order, and intelligence."

TO SIR EDWARD WALLER, BART.
&c. &c.
New York, ——

The six North Eastern States of this great union compose what is called New England.★ The appellation is one of convention, and is unknown to the laws. It is a name given by a King of England, who appeared willing to conciliate that portion of his subjects, who had deserted their homes in quest of liberty of conscience, by a high-sounding title. It will be remembered that colonies of the Dutch and Swedes, at that time, separated the northern possessions of the English from those they held in Virginia. It is most probably owing to the latter circumstance that the inhabitants of the New England provinces so long retained their distinctive character, which was scarcely less at variance with that of the slave-holding planters of the south, than with that of their more immediate neighbours, the Dutch. The pacific colonists of Penn brought with them but little to soften the lines of distinction, and after New York became subject to the Crown of Britain, it was a *mélange* of Dutch quietude and English aristocracy. It was

---

★Maine, Massachusetts, New Hampshire, Vermont, Rhode Island, and Connecticut.

not until the Revolution had broken down the barriers of provincial prejudices, and cleared the way for the unrestrained exercise of the true national enterprise, that these territorial obstacles were entirely removed, and a thorough amalgamation of the people commenced. A few observations on the effect of this amalgamation, and the influence it has had on the character of the nation, may not be thrown away here. The little I shall say is written under the inspection of Cadwallader, confirmed, if not improved, by my own observation.

The people of New England are, even to this hour, distinguished among their own active and quick-witted countrymen, for their enterprise, frugality, order, and intelligence. The three latter qualities, taken in conjunction, I believe they have a right to claim to a degree that is elsewhere unequalled. The Scot and the Swiss, the Dane and the Swede, the German, the Belgian, or even the Frenchman, may be often as frugal, but there is always something of compulsion in European frugality. The inhabitant of New England seems thrifty on principle; since he neglects no duty, forgets no decency, nor overlooks any of the higher obligations in order to save his money. He is eminently economical and provident in the midst of abundance. A sentiment of deep morality seems to influence his savings, which he hoards, in order that the superfluity of his wealth may be serviceable, as wealth should be, in securing his own private respectability, and in advancing the interests of the whole. No doubt, in a great community, where economy is rigidly practised as a virtue, some mistake its object, and pervert a quality, which is so eminently adapted to advance the general good, to the purposes of individual rapacity. But it is impossible to journey through New England and witness its air of abundance, its decency, the absence of want, the elevation of character, which is imparted to the meanest of its people, without respecting the sources whence they flow. A prudent and discreet economy is, in itself, an evidence of a reflecting and instructed being, as order is the necessary attendant of abundance and thought. You may form some estimate of the degree of intelligence which is diffused throughout the community in New England, by the facts contained in a report I lately read concerning the progress of general instruction in Massachusetts. That State contains nearly 600,000 souls, all of whom (of proper age), with the exception of about 400, could read and write. It is probable that the latter number was composed chiefly of foreigners, blacks from other States, and those

who laboured under natural disabilities. But reading, writing, and arithmetic, are far from being the limits of the ordinary instruction of the lower
American schools. A vast deal of useful and creditable knowledge, moral
and useful, is also obtained in learning to read. I have known Cadwallader
to say repeatedly, that in referring to familiar history and geography, he
invariably passes by all his later acquisitions in the academies and university,
to draw upon the stores he obtained during his infancy in one of the common schools of the country. Perhaps, in this particular, he differs but little
from most educated men everywhere; but it is an important fact to remember that the children of his father's tradesmen, and indeed of every other
man in the place, enjoyed precisely the same means of obtaining this species
of information, as the son of the affluent landlord. He also pointed out
another important fact, as distinguishing the quality of the knowledge
acquired in the schools of America from that which is obtained in a similar manner, in most, if not all, of Europe. There is no lethargy of ideas in
this country. What is known to one (under the usual limits of learning) soon
becomes the property of all. This is strictly true, as respects all the minor
acquisitions of the school. It is also true as respects every sudden and important political event, in any quarter of the world. The former species of information is obtained through new and improved editions of their
geographies, histories, and grammars, and the latter through the powerful
agency of the public press. A new division of the German empire, for
instance, would be change enough to circulate a new geography through
all the schools of America. Improved systems of arithmetic are as numerous
as the leaves on the trees, nor is there any scarcity of annals to record the
events of the day. My companion pointed out the difference, between his
own country and France for instance, in this particular. He has three or four
young female relatives at school in the latter country. Curiosity had induced
him to bring away several of the class-books that had been put into their
hands, in conformity to the system which governs these matters there. In
the history of France itself, the Revolution is scarcely mentioned! The reign
of Napoleon is passed over in silence, and the events of 1814 and 1815 consigned to an oblivion, which does not conceal the siege of Troy. One can
understand the motives of this doubtful policy; but Cadwallader pointed
out defects in the geographies, which can only be accounted for on the
grounds of utter indifference. One example shall suffice for numberless

similar instances of gross and culpable neglect, since it could not be ignorance, in a country where the science of geography is certainly as well
understood as in any other part of the earth. With an excusable sensitiveness, he shewed me, in a recent edition of an authorized geography, the
account of his own confederation. It is said to be composed of *eighteen*
states, though *twenty-one* are actually named, and *twenty-four,* in truth,
existed! Even the palpable contradiction seems to have escaped the proof-
readers of the work. Now this book, excessively meagre in itself, is put into
the hands of the future mothers of France. Their own kingdom is certainly
dealt with a little more liberally; but, though it is perhaps the highest effort
of human knowledge, to know one's self, in order to a right understanding
of our own character, it is absolutely necessary to have a pretty intimate
acquaintance with those of other people. I speak understandingly, when I
tell you, that the geographies and modern histories which are read by the
commonest American children, are vastly more minute and accurate than
those read in most of the fashionable pensions of Paris.

The effects of this diffusion of common instruction is pre-eminently
apparent throughout New England, in the self-respect, decency, order, and
individuality of its inhabitants. I say individuality, because, by giving ideas to
a man, you impart the principles of a new existence, which supply additional motives of concern to his respectability and well-being. You are not
to suppose that men become selfish by arriving nearer to a right understanding of their own natures and true interests, since all experience proves
that we become humane and charitable precisely as we become conscious
of our own defects, and obtain a knowledge of the means necessary to
repair them. A remarkable example of this truth is to be found in New England itself. Beyond a doubt, no where is to be found a population so well
instructed, in elementary knowledge, as the people of these six states. It is
equally true, that I have no where witnessed such an universality of that
self-respect which preserves men from moral degradation. I very well know
that in Europe, while we lend a faint attention to these statements concerning American order and prosperity, we are fond of seeking causes
which shall refer their origin to circumstances peculiar to her geographical
situation, and which soothe our self-love, by enabling us to predict their
downfall, when the existence of European pressure shall reduce the American to the level of our own necessities. I confess, I entered the country with

very similar impressions myself; but nearer observation has disturbed a theory which is generally adopted, because it is both consolatory and simple. We are apt to say that the ability of the Americans to maintain order at so little cost of money and personal freedom, is derived from the thinness of population and the absence of want: but the American will tell you it proceeds from the high civilization of his country, which gives to every member of the community a certain interest in its quiet and character. I confess, I was a little startled to hear a people who scarcely possess a work of art that attains to mediocrity,—among whom most of the sciences are comparatively in their infancy,—who rarely push learning beyond its practical and most useful points, and who deal far less in the graces than in the more simple forms of manners, speak of their pre-eminent civilization with so evident a complacency. But there is a simple dignity in moral truths, that dims the lustre of all the meretricious gloss which art and elegance can confer on life. I fear that it is very possible to live in a gilded palace—to feast the eyes on the *beau ideal* of form and proportions,—to be an adept in the polished deceptions of conventional intercourse,—to smile when others smile, and weep when others weep,—to patronize and to court,—to cringe and to domineer, in short, to reach the *ne plus ultra* of eastern refinement, and still to have a strong flavour of barbarity about one after all. There can be no true humanity, which is the essence of all civilization, until man comes to treat and consider man as his fellow. That society can never exist, or, at least, that it could never advance, under a too fastidiously strict interpretation of this duty, needs no proof, since all incentive to exertion would be deadened in a condition where each member of the community had an equal right to participate in the general abundance. The great desideratum of the social compact would then seem to be, to produce such a state of things as shall call the most individual enterprise into action, while it should secure a proper consideration for the interests of the whole;—to avail of the talents of the gifted few, while the long train of humbler beings shall have scope and leisure also for the privileges of their mortality: in short, to profit by the suggestions of policy, without forgetting the eternal obligations of humanity. If a union of the utmost scope to individual enterprise with the most sacred regard to the rights and feelings of the less fortunate of our species, be any evidence of an approximation to this desired condition of society, I think the inhabitant of New England has a better right to claim an elevated state of being than any other people I have ever visited. The activity of personal efforts is every where visible on the face of the land, in their comforts, abundance, improvements, and progressive wealth, while the effect of a humanity that approaches almost to refinement, was felt at every house I entered. Let me not be misunderstood: I can readily conceive that an European gentleman, who had not been, like myself, put on his guard, would have found numberless grounds of complaint, because he was not treated as belonging to a superior class of beings by those with whom he was compelled to hold communication. Servility forms no part of the civilization of New England, though civility be its essence. I can say with truth, that after traversing the country for near a thousand miles, in no instance did I hear or witness a rude act: not the slightest imposition was practised, or attempted, on my purse; all my inquiries were heard with patience, and answered with extraordinary intelligence: not a farthing was asked for divers extra services that were performed in my behalf; but, on the contrary, money offered in the way of *douceurs* was repeatedly declined, and that too with perfect modesty, as if it were unusual to receive rewards for trifles. My comforts and tastes, too, were uniformly consulted; and, although I often travelled in a portion of the country that was but little frequented, at every inn I met with neatness, abundance, and a manner in which a desire to oblige me was blended with a singular respect for themselves. Nor was this rare combination of advantages at all the effect of that simplicity which is the attendant of a half-civilized condition; on the contrary, I found an intelligence that surprised me at every turn, and which, in itself, gave the true character to the humanity of which I was the subject. I repeatedly found copies of your standard English authors, in retired dwellings where one would not expect to meet any production of a cast higher than an almanack, or a horn-book; nor were they read with that acquiescent criticism which gives a fashion to taste, and which makes a joke of Molière better than a joke of any other man. Young women (with whom my situation, no less than my tastes, oftenest brought me into literary discussions) frequently surprised me with the extent of their acquaintance with, and the soundness of their opinions concerning the merits and morality of Pope and Addison, of Young and Tillotson, and even of Milton and Shakspeare. This may sound to you ridiculous, and certainly, if taken without a saving clause for the other acquirements of my female critics, it is liable to some exception; but I repeat I have often known professed blues acquit themselves with less credit than did several of my passing acquaintances at the tea-tables of different New England inns. I can, however, readily conceive that a traveller might pass weeks in this very portion of the country, and remain profoundly ignorant of all these things. In order to acquire information one must possess the disposition to learn. I sought out these traits of national character, and I flatter myself that by the aid of good dispositions, and a certain something that distinguishes all of our fraternity in the presence of the softer sex, a commendable progress, in reference to the time and opportunity, was always made in their kind estimation. The great roads, as I have said, and as you well know, are rarely favourable in any country to an accurate acquaintance with the character of its inhabitants. One may arrive at a general knowledge of the standard of honesty, disinterestedness, and civilization of a people, it is true, by mingling with them in much frequented places, for these qualities are always comparative; but he who would form an opinion of the whole by such specimens, must do it under the correction of great allowances. I believe the New Englandman, however, has less reason than common to deprecate a general decision of this nature. A good deal of my journey was unavoidably on a great route, and though I found some inconveniences, and rather more difficulty in penetrating their domestic reserve there, than in the retired vallies of the interior, still the great distinctive features of the population were every where decidedly the same.

It is worthy of remark that nearly all of the English travellers who have written of America, pass lightly over this important section of the Union. Neither do they seem to dwell with much complacency on those adjoining states, where the habits and characteristics of New England prevail to a great extent, through the emigrants or their immediate descendants. I am taught to believe that, including the inhabitants of the six original states, not less than four millions of the American people are descended from the settlers of Plymouth, and their successors. This number is about four-tenths of the white population. If one recalls the peculiar energy and activity which distinguish these people, he may be able to form some idea of their probable influence on the character of the whole country. The distinctive habits of the Dutch, which lingered among the possessors of the adjoining province of New York even until the commencement of the present century, have nearly disappeared before the tide of eastern emigration; and there is said to be scarcely a state in the whole confederation which has not imbibed more or less of the impetus of its inexhaustable activity.

Suspicion might easily ascribe an unworthy motive to a silence that is so very uniform on the part of interested observers. Volumes have been written concerning the half-tenanted districts of the west, while the manners and condition of the original states, where the true effects of the American system can alone be traced, are usually disposed of in a few hurried pages. It is true there are some few of the authors in my collection, who have been more impartial in their notices, but most of them appear to have sought so eagerly for subjects of derision, as to have overlooked the more dignified materials of observation. Even the respectable Mr. Hodgson, who seems at all times ready to do justice to the Americans, has contented himself with giving some thirty or forty pages to the state of New York, and disposes of all New England (if the extraneous matter be deducted), Pennsylvania, New Jersey, and Ohio, in about the same space that he has devoted to a passage through the wild regions on the Gulf of Mexico. Though the states just mentioned make but a comparatively indifferent figure on the map, they contain nearly, if not quite, half of the entire population of the country. If to this be added the fact, that in extent they cover a surface about equal to that of the kingdom of France, one may be permitted to express some surprise that they are usually treated with so little deference. An American would be very much inclined to ascribe this uniform neglect to an illiberality which found no pleasure in any description but caricature, though I think few of them would judge so harshly of the author whose name I have just mentioned. As Cadwallader expressed it, even the mistakes of such a man are entitled to be treated with respect. A much more charitable, and in the instance of Mr. Hodgson, I am fully persuaded a more just explanation would be to ascribe this apparent partiality to the woods, rather to a love of novelty, than to any bare thirst of detraction. There is little to appease the longings of curiosity, even in the most striking characteristics of common sense: nor does a picture of the best endowed and most rational state of being, present half the attractions to our imaginations, as one in which scenes of civilization are a little coloured by the fresher and more vivid tints of a border life.

Still he who would seek the great moving principles which give no small part of its peculiar tone to the American character, must study the people of New England deeply. It is there that he will find the germ of that tree of intelligence which has shot forth so luxuriantly, and is already shading the land with its branches, bringing forth most excellent fruits. It is there that religion, and order, and frugality, and even liberty, have taken deepest root: and no liberal American, however he may cherish some of the peculiarities of his own particular state, will deny them the meed of these high and honourable distinctions. It may be premature in one who has kept aloof from their large towns, to pronounce on the polish of a people whom he has only seen in the retirement and simplicity of the provinces. Their more southern neighbours say they are wanting in some of the nicer tact of polite intercourse, and that however they may shine in the more homely and domestic virtues, they are somewhat deficient in those of manner. I think nothing, taken with a certain limitation, to be more probable.

I saw every where the strongest evidences of a greater equality of condition than I remember ever before to have witnessed. Where this equality exists, it has an obvious tendency to bring the extremes of the community together. What the peasant gains, the gentleman must in some measure lose. The colours get intermingled, where the shades in society are so much softened. Great leisure, nay, every idleness, is perhaps necessary to exclusive attention to manner. How few, dear Waller, excel in it, even in your own aristocratic island, where it is found that a man needs no small servitude in the more graceful schools of the continent, to figure to advantage in a saloon. Perhaps there is something in the common habits of the parent and the child that is not favourable to a cultivation of the graces. Institutions which serve to give man pride in himself, sometimes lessen his respect for others: and yet I see nothing in a republican government that is at all incompatible with the highest possible refinement. It is difficult to conceive that a state of things which has a tendency to elevate the less fortunate classes of our species, should necessarily debase those whose lots have been cast in the highest. The peculiar exterior of the New Englandman may be ascribed with more justice to the restrained and little enticing manners of his puritan ancestors. Climate, habits of thrift, and unexampled equality of rights and fortune, may have aided to perpetuate a rigid aspect. But after all, this defect in manner must, as I have already said, be taken under great limitation. Considered in reference to every class below those in which, from

their pursuits and education, more refinement and tact might certainly be
expected, it does not exist. On the contrary, as they are more universally
intelligent than their counterparts in the most favoured European countries, so do they exhibit, in their deportment, a happier union of self-respect
with consideration for others. The deficiency is oftener manifested in certain probing inquiries into the individual concerns of other people, and in
a neglect of forms entirely conventional, but which by their generality have
become established rules of breeding, than by any coarse or brutal trans-
gressions of natural politeness. The former liberty may indeed easily degenerate into every thing that is both repulsive and disagreeable; but there is
that in the manner of a New Englandman, when he most startles you by
his familiarity, which proves he means no harm. The common, vulgar
account of such questions, as "How far are you travelling, *stranger?* and
where do you come from? and what may your name be?" if ever true, is now
a gross caricature. The New Englandman is too kind in all his habits to call
any man stranger.* His usual address is "friend," or sometimes he compliments a stranger of a gentlemanly appearance, with the title of "squire." I
sought the least reserved intercourse that was possible with them, and in no
instance was I the subject of the smallest intentional rudeness.† I say intentional, for the country physician, or lawyer, or divine (and I mingled with
them all), was ignorant that he trespassed on the rules of rigid breeding,
when he made allusions, however guarded, to my individual movements or
situation. Indeed I am inclined to suspect that the Americans, in all parts of
the Union, are less reserved on personal subjects than we of Europe, and
precisely for the reason that in general they have less to conceal. I cannot
attribute a coarser motive than innocent curiosity, to the familiar habits of
a people who in every other particular are so singularly tender of each
other's feelings. The usage is not denied even by themselves; and a professor of one of their universities accounted for it in the following manner.
The people of New England were, and are still, intimately allied in feeling
no less than in blood. Their enterprise early separated them from each other

---

* Cadwallader told me that this appellation is, indeed, used in the new states to the south-
west, where it is more apposite, and subsequent observation has confirmed the fact.

† It is singular that every English traveler the writer has read, in the midst of all his exaggerations, either directly or indirectly admits this fact.

by wide tracts of country; and before the introduction of journals and public mails, the inhabitants must have been dependent on travelers for most of their passing intelligence. It is not difficult to conceive that, in a country where thought is so active, inquiry was not suffered to slumber. You may probably remember to have seen, when we were last at Pompeii, the little place where the townsmen were said to collect in order to glean intelligence from upper Italy. A similar state of things must, in a greater or less degree, have existed in all civilized countries before the art of printing was known; and, in this particular, the only difference between New and Old England probably was, that as the people of the former had more ideas to appease, they were compelled to use greater exertions to attain their object. But apart from this, I will confess startling familiarity, there was a delicacy of demeanour that is surprising in a population so remote from the polish of the large towns. I have often seen the wishes of the meanest individual consulted before any trifling change was made that might be supposed to affect the comfort of all. In this species of courtesy, I think them a people unequalled. Scarcely any one, however elevated his rank, would presume to make a change in any of the dispositions of a public coach, (for I left my waggon for a time,) in a window of a hotel, or indeed in any thing in which others might have an equal concern, without a suitable deference to their wishes. And yet I have seen the glance of one woman's eye, and she of humble condition too, instantly change the unanimous decision of a dozen men. By the hand of the fair Isabel, Waller, there is something noble and touching, in the universal and yet simple and unpretending homage with which these people treat the weaker sex. I am sure a woman here has only to respect herself in order to meet with universal deference. I now understand what Cadwallader meant when he said that America was the real Paradise of woman. The attention and manliness which he exhibited for the Abigail of the little Isabel, is common to the meanest man, at least in New England. I traversed the country in harvest time, and scarcely recollect to have seen six females in the fields, and even they appeared there only on the emergency of some passing shower. When one considers the price which labour bears, this solitary fact is in itself pregnant with meaning. A little boy whom I conveyed with his father in my waggon a dozen miles, (for I neglected no opportunity to mix with the people,) laughed aloud as he pointed with his finger and cried, "There is a woman at work among the men!" Had he seen her riding a war horse *"en militaire,"* he could scarcely have been more amused. After all, what nobler or more convincing proof of high civilization can be given than this habitual respect of the strong for the weak. The condition of women in this country is solely owing to the elevation of its moral feeling. As she is never misplaced in society, her influence is only felt in the channels of ordinary and domestic life. I have heard young and silly Europeans, whose vanity has probably been wounded in finding themselves objects of secondary interest, affect to ridicule the absorbed attention which the youthful American matron bestows on her family; and some have gone so far in my presence, as to assert that a lady of this country was no more than an upper servant in the house of her husband. They pay us of the eastern hemisphere but an indifferent compliment, when they assume that this beautiful devotion to the first, the highest, and most lovely office of the sex, is peculiar to the women of station in America only. I have ever repelled the insinuation as becomes a man; but, alas! what is the testimony of one who can point to no fireside, or household of his own, but the dreaming reverie of a heated brain. Imaginary or not, I think one might repose his affections on hundreds of the fair, artless creatures he meets with here, with an entire confidence that the world has not the first place in her thoughts. To me, woman appears to fill in America the very station for which she was designed by nature. In the lowest conditions of life she is treated with the tenderness and respect that is due to beings whom we believe to be the repositories of the better principles of our nature. Retired within the sacred precincts of her own abode, she is preserved from the destroying taint of excessive intercourse with the world. She makes no bargains beyond those which supply her own little personal wants, and her heart is not early corrupted by the baneful and unfeminine vice of selfishness; she is often the friend and adviser of her husband, but never his chapman. She must be sought in the haunts of her domestic privacy, and not amid the wranglings, deceptions, and heart-burnings of keen and sordid traffic. So true and general is this fact, that I have remarked a vast proportion of that class who frequent the markets, or vend trifles in the streets of this city, occupations that are not unsuited to the feebleness of the sex, are either foreigners, or females descended from certain insulated colonies of the Dutch, which still retain many of the habits of their ancestors amidst the improvements that are throwing them among the forgotten usages of another century. The effect of this natural and inestimable division of employment, is in itself enough to produce an impression on the characters of a whole people. It leaves the heart and principles of woman untainted by the dire temptations of strife with her fellows. The husband can retire from his own sordid struggles with the world to seek consolation and correction from one who is placed beyond their influence. The first impressions of the child are drawn from the purest sources known to our nature; and the son, even long after he has been compelled to enter on the thorny track of the father, preserves the memorial of the pure and unalloyed lessons that he has received from the lips, and, what is far better, from the example of the mother. Though every picture of life in which these bright colours are made, the strongest must be deadened by deep and painful shadows, I do firmly believe that the undeniable truth I have just written may be applied with as much, if not with more justice, to the condition and influence of the sex in New England as in any portion of the globe. I saw every where the utmost possible care to preserve the females from undue or unwomanly employments. If there was a burthen, it was in the arms or on the shoulders of the man. Even labours that seem properly to belong to the household, were often performed by the latter; and I never heard the voice of the wife calling on the husband for assistance, that it was not answered by a ready, many, and cheerful compliance. The neatness of the cottage, the farm-house, and the inn; the clean, tidy, healthful, and vigorous look of the children, united to attest the usefulness of this system. What renders all this more striking and more touching, is the circumstance that not only is labour in so great demand, but, contrary to the fact in all the rest of christendom, the women materially exceed the men in numbers. This seeming departure from what is almost an established law of nature, is owing to the emigration westward. By the census of 1820, it appears, that in the six states of New England there were rather more than thirteen females to every twelve males over the age of sixteen. It is vain to say that absence of selfishness, and all the kinder, of man, are no more than the concomitants of abundance and simplicity, which in themselves are the fruits of a spare population and of provincial retirement. If this be so strictly true, why do not the same qualities prevail in the more favoured regions of this very continent? why do not order, and industry, and enterprise, and all the active and healthful virtues abound in South as in North America? why is not the fertile province of Upper Canada, for instance, as much distinguished for its advancement in all the useful arts of life as the states of the neighbouring republic? and why, under so many physical disadvantages, are the comparatively sterile and rocky states of New England remarkable for these very qualities amid their own flourishing and healthful sisters? It cannot be the religious principles they derived from their ancestors, since the Pennsylvanian and the New Jerseyman, and even the peaceful and honest Hollander of New York, can claim just as virtuous a descent. It cannot be any exclusive succession to the principles and habits of their English ancestors, since, with exceptions too slight to affect the great body of the nation, this has been an inheritance common to all. It cannot be that time has matured their institutions, and given play and energy to their mental advantages, since Brazil, and Chili, and Mexico, and many other nations of this continent, date a century older, and Virginia and New York, Canada and Louisiana, are of coëval existence. In short, it cannot even be their elastic and inciting liberty, for that too is a principle which has never been suffered to slumber in any of the vast and varied regions of this great confederation. We must seek the solution in a cause which is the parent of all that is excellent and great in communities, no less than in individuals. I mean intelligence. That pitiful and narrow theory which, thank God, is now getting into disuse in Europe, and which taught the doctrine that instruction became dangerous to those who could not push learning to its limits, was never in fashion here. The limits of learning! As if any one could yet pronounce on the boundaries which the Almighty has been pleased to set between the efforts of our reason and his own omniscience. It is true that the wisest men are always the most truly modest; for, having outstripped their competitors in the attainment of human knowledge, they alone can know how much there is necessarily beyond their reach, and how impossible it is for mortals to attain it. But who could ever yet say he had taxed his faculties to the utmost. The world has been amusing itself with assumed axioms on this subject, when it might have been better employed in investigating the truth in its more useful and practical forms. The self-sufficiency of pretenders has been tortured into an evidence of the danger of empiricism in knowledge. As well might the pedantry and foibles of the student himself be perverted to an argument against learning, as to say that thought must be kept in subjection because it sometimes leads to error. The fruits of knowledge are not to be weighed by the credit they reflect on this or that searcher after truth, but by the influence they produce on the mass of society. The man who, from defect of powers, or from any other adverse circumstance, cannot assist in the advancement of intelligence, may, notwithstanding, become the wholesome recipient of truth; and the community which encourages a dissemination of the sacred quality, enjoys an incalculable advantage over all others, inasmuch as each of its members starts so much nearer to the goal for which every people must strive, (and that too through its individual members,) in order to secure a distinguished place in the great competition of nations. It is a remarkable fact, that the retired, distant, and little regarded states of which I am writing, had matured and were reaping the rare fruits of a system of extended general instruction, for quite a century, when a distinguished advocate for reform (Mr. Brougham), in the Parliament of your own country, that country which was then, and is still giving lessons to Europe in liberty and government, charmed the ears of the liberal by visions of a similar plan for yourselves, which then existed, as it now exists, only in the wishes of the truly wise and benevolent. And yet one hears of the great moral debt that the people of New owe to the people of Old England! The common ancestors may have left a goodly inheritance to their children; but on this subject, at least, it appears to me that the emigrant to the western hemisphere has made of his talent ten talents, while his kinsman, who remained at home, has done little more than imitate the example of him who met with any thing but unqualified approbation.

In reviewing my letter, I see that I have written warmly, and with a portion of that interest which the two subjects that have been its themes rarely fail to inspire. As I know you enter fully into all my feelings, both for the fair and for general instruction, (for however lame and defective may have been the policy of your nation, compared with that of your kinsmen here, there still exists in England, as in Denmark, and a few other nations, a high and noble spirit of emulation,) I shall not repress a single sentence of that which has escaped my pen. But the subject must be left, until further opportunity shall be given to look into the society of New England in its large towns.

During the whole of my recent excursion, though I purposely avoided encountering La Fayette, his visit has been a constant and inexhaustible topic of conversation. His journey along the coast has been like the passage of a brilliant meteor. In every village he has been received with modest, but heartfelt rejoicings, while his entrances into the cities have been literally triumphant. That there have been some exhibitions of joy which a fastidious taste might reject, cannot be denied; but you will remember that the people of this country are left to express their own sentiments in their own fashion. The surprise should be, not that the addresses and receptions of which you will doubtless see some account in Europe, are characterised by so little, but that they are distinguished by so much soundness of discrimination, truth of principle, and propriety of manner.—Adieu.

Cooper discusses the importance of birth and social distinctions to American society. While Americans, it seems, prefer merit and earned respect, a lingering fascination continues for those born into "good" and historically important families. Religion and common sense, however, serve to push Americans toward respecting merit rather than birth. Because they like to think of themselves in terms of merit, Americans consider merchants to be the best element in society.

TO THE COMTE JULES DE BéTHIZY.
&c. &c.
New York, ———

It may be premature to pretend to speak with any certainty concerning the true state of ordinary American society. My opinions have already undergone two or three revolutions on the subject, for it is so easy, where no acknowledged distinctions prevail, for a stranger to glide imperceptibly from one circle to another, that the impressions they leave are very apt to be confounded. I have never yet conversed with any declaimer on the bad tone of republican manners (and they are not wanting), who has not been ready enough to confess this, or that, individual an eminent exception. Now, it never appears to enter into the heads of these Chesterfieldian critics, that the very individuals in question are so many members of a great class, that very well know how to marshal themselves in their ordinary intercourse with each other, although, to a stranger, they may seem no more than insulated exceptions, floating, as it were by accident, on the bosom of a motley, and frequently far from inviting state of society. I think, however, that it is not difficult to see, at a glance, that even the best bred people here maintain their intercourse among each other, under far fewer artificial forms than are to be found in almost any other country. Simplicity of deportment is usually the concomitant of good sense every where; but, in America, it is particularly in good taste. It would be a gratuitous weakness in a people who have boldly denounced the dominion of courts, to descend to imitate the cumberous forms which are perhaps necessary to their existence, and which so insensibly get disseminated, in mawkish imitations, among those who live in their purlieus. Direct in their thoughts, above the necessity of any systematic counterfeiting, and in almost every instance, secure of the ordinary means of existence, it is quite in nature that the American, in his daily communications, should consult the truth more, and conventional deception less, than those who are fettered and restrained by the thousand pressures of a highly artificial state of being. The boasted refinement of the most polished court in Europe is, after all, no more than expertness in a practice, which the Persian, with his semi-barbarous education, understands better than the veriest courtier of them all. That rare and lofty courtesy, in which the party knows how to respect himself, by sacrificing no principle while be reconciles his companion to the stern character of his morals by grace of mien and charity to his weaknesses, is, I think, quite as common here as we are wont to find it in Europe. In respect to those purely conventional forms, that receive value only from their use, and which are so highly prized by weak minds, because so completely within their reach, and which even become familiar to strong ones from an indisposition to dispute their sway, are in no great favour here. Perhaps the circumstance that people of education, fortune, connections, and, of course, of similar turn of mind, are so much separated by the peculiarity of the state governments, into the coteries of twenty capital towns instead of those of one, is the chief reason that they are neglected; for all experience proves that fashion is a folly which merely needs soil to take deep root. Indeed I am not sure that this species of exotic will not, at some future day, luxuriate in America to a greater degree, than it even thrives in the fertile regions of the east. It is certain, that in England, the country most resembling this, fashionable society is more tramelled by fictitious forms, both of speech and deportment, than in any other European nation. Every where else, after certain sacrifices are made to deception and the self-love of second persons, the actor is left to play his part at the instigations of nature; but in England there is a fashion for drinking a glass of wine, for pronouncing, and *mis*-pronouncing a word, for even perverting its meaning, for being polite, and what is still more strange, sometimes for being rude and vulgar. Any one who has lived twenty years may recal a multitude of changes that have occurred in the most cherished usages of what is called good-breeding. Now, there must be a reason for all this whimsical absurdity. Is it not owing to the peculiarly vacillating nature of her aristocracy? In a country where wealth is constantly bringing new claimants for consideration into the arena of fashion, (for it is, after all, no more than a struggle for notoriety that may be more bloodless, but is not less bitter than that of the gladiators,) those who are in its possession contrive all possible means of distinction between themselves and those who are about to dispute their ascendancy. Beyond a doubt what is called high English society, is more repulsive, arti-ficial and cumbered, and, in short, more absurd and frequently less graceful than that of any other European nation. Still the English are a rational, sound, highly reasoning, manly and enlightened people. It is difficult to account for the inconsistency, but by believing that the struggle for supremacy gives birth to every species of high-bred folly, among which is to be numbered no small portion of customs that would be more honoured in the breach than in the observance.

If like causes are always to produce like effects, the day may come when the same reasons shall induce the American fashionables of two generations to lead the fashionables of one, a similar wild goose chase in quest of the *ne plus ultra* of elegance. As the fact now stands, the accessions to the *coteries* are so very numerous, and are commonly made with strides so rapid, that it is as yet, fortunately, more likely to give distinction to be rationally polite, than genteely vulgar.

Of one truth, however, I am firmly persuaded, that nineteen out of twenty of the strangers who visit this country, can give no correct analysis of the manners which prevail in the different circles that divide this, like all other great communities. The pursuits and the inclinations of the men bring them much oftener together than those of the women. It is therefore among the females that the nicer and more delicate shades of distinction are to be sought. The very prevalent notion of Europe, that society must, of necessity, exist, in a pure democracy, on terms of promiscuous association, is too manifestly absurd to need any contradiction with one who knows life as well as yourself.

It would require the magical power which that renowned philanthropist, Mr. Owen, ascribes to his system, to destroy the influence of education, talents, money, or even of birth. They all, in fact, exist in America, just as they do with us, only modified, and in some degree curtailed.

You may perhaps be startled to hear of distinction conferred by birth among a people whose laws deny it a single privilege or immunity. Even thousands of Americans themselves, who have scarcely descended into their own system farther than is absolutely requisite to acquire its general maxims, will stoutly maintain that it has no reality. I remember to have heard one of these generalizers characterise the folly of a young acquaintance by saying, with peculiar bitterness of tone, "he presumes on his being the son of ———." Now, if some portion of the consideration of the father were not transmissible to the descendant, the latter clearly could in no degree presume on his birth. It is fortunate here, as elsewhere, to be the child of a worthy, or even of an affluent parent. The goods of the latter descend, by process of law, to the offspring, and, by aid of public opinion, the son receives some portion of the renown that has been earned by the merit of the father. It is useless to dwell on those secret and deep rooted feelings by which man, in all ages, and under every circumstance, has been willing to permit this hereditary reflection of character, in order to prove that human nature must have sway in the republics of North America, as in the monarchies of the east. A thousand examples might be quoted to show that the influence of this sentiment of birth, (just so far as it is a *sentiment* and not a *prejudice,*) is not only felt by the people, but is openly acknowledged by the government of the country in its practices. Unless I am grossly misinformed, the relative of one who had served the state, for instance, would, *cæteris paribus,* prevail in an application for the public favour, over a competitor who could urge no such additional claim; and the reason of the decision would be deemed satisfactory by the nation. No one would be hardy enough to deny, that, had Washington left a child, he would have passed through society, or even before the public, on a perfect equality with men similarly endowed, though not similarly born. Just as this hereditary advantage would be true in the case of a son of Washington, it is true, with a lessened effect, in those of other men. It would be a weak and a vain, because an impracticable and an unwise attempt, in any people, to reject so sweet an incentive to virtue on the part of the parent, or so noble a motive of emulation on that of the child. It is enough for the most democratic opinions, that the feeling should be kept within the limits of reason. The community, in a government trammelled by so few factitious forms, always holds in its own power a sufficient check on the abuse of the privilege; and here, in fact, is to be found the true point of distinction, not only between the governments of this and other countries, but between the conditions of their ordinary society also. In America, while the claims of individuals are admitted, it is easy to satisfy, to weaken, or to lose them. It is not enough simply to be the son of a great man; in order to render it of essential advantage, some portion of his merit must become hereditary, or the claim had better be suppressed. Even an honourable name may become matter of reproach, since, when the public esteem is once forfeited, the recollection of the ancestor only serves to heighten the demerit of his delinquent child. There is no privileged rank under which he can stalk abroad and flout at the morals, or offend the honesty of men better than himself, and the councils of the nation are for ever hermetically sealed against his entrance.

In society, the punishment of this unworthiness, though necessarily less imposing, is scarcely less direct and salutary. Nothing is easier than for a member of any circle to forfeit the privileges of caste. It is a fact highly creditable to the morals of this people, unless close observation and the opinions of Cadwallader greatly mislead me, that a circle confessedly inferior will not receive an outcast from one above it. The great qualifications for all are, in moral essentials, the same. It is not pretended that all men, or even all women, in the United States, are exemplary in their habits, or that they live in a state of entire innocence, compared with that of their fellow mortals elsewhere; but there is not a doubt that the tone of manners here requires the utmost seemliness of deportment; that suspicion even may become dangerous to a man, and is almost always fatal to a woman; and that as access to the circles is effected with less difficulty than with us, so is the path of egress much more readily to be found.

There is a very summary way of accounting for these things, by saying that all this is no more than the result of a simple state of society, and that in the absence of luxury, and especially in a country where the population is scattered, the result is precisely that which was to be expected. Why then is not the tone of manners as high in South as in North America, or why are the moralists in the cities quite as fastidious, or even more so, than those on the most remote borders? The truth is, that neither the polity nor the manners of the Americans bear that recent origin we are wont to give them. Both have substantially endured the test of two centuries; and though they are becoming meliorated and more accommodating by time, it is idle to say that they are merely the experiments of the hour. Nor is it very safe to ascribe any quality, good or bad, to the Americans on account of their being removed from the temptations of luxury. That they have abstained from excessive indulgence, is more the effect of taste or principle, than of necessity. I have never yet visited any country where luxuries were so completely within the reach of the majority. It is true that their manners are not exposed to the temptations of courts; but it is equally true that they have deliberately rejected the use of such a form of government as renders them necessary.

Before leaving this subject I must explain a little, or what I have already written may possibly lead you into error. The influence of birth, though undoubted, is not to be understood as existing here in any thing like the extent, or even under the same forms, as in Europe.★ The very nation, which, in tenderness to the father, might be disposed to accord a certain deference to the child who had received his early impressions under such a man as Washington, would be very apt to turn a cold and displeased eye on the follies or vices of a more distant descendant. You may be prepared to answer, "all this reads well, but we will wait the effects of time on a system that pretends to elevate itself above the established prejudices of the rest of the world." But in what is reason weaker than prejudice, after its conclusions have been confirmed by practice? I repeat, these people are not experimenting, but living in conformity to usages, and under institutions that

---

★ We have the authority of a great contemporary (the biographer of Napoleon) for believing that the science of heraldry reverses the inferences of reason, by shedding more lustre on the remote descendant than on the founder of an illustrious name. This is, at the best, but an equivocal acknowledgment, and it is undeniably far too sublimated for the straight going common sense of the Americans. The writer is inclined to believe that the very opposite ground is maintained by the proficients in American heraldry, or, in other words, that the great man himself is thought to be the greatest man of his family, and that the reflection of his talents, probity, courage, or for whatever quality he may have been most remarkable, is thought to shed most lustre on those of his offspring who have lived nearest to its influence.

have already been subject to the trials of two hundred years. So far as I can learn, instead of imperceptibly falling into the train of European ideas, they have rather been silently receding; and if there has been the least approximation between the opinions of the two hemispheres on these subjects, the change has been wrought among ourselves. While travelling in the interior of New England, an honest looking farmer endeavoured to read the blazonry that, by the negligence of a servant, had been suffered to remain on the plate of one of my travelling cases. I endeavoured to solve the difficulties of the good man by explaining the use and meaning of the arms. No sooner did the American find that I was disposed to humour his curiosity, than he asked several home questions, that, it must be confessed, were not without their embarrassment. It was necessary finally to tell him that these were distinctions that had been conferred by different sovereigns on the ancestors of the owner of the case. "If there is no harm in't, may I ask for what?" "For their courage in battle, and devotion to their princes." The worthy republican regarded the plate for some time intently; and then bluntly inquired "if this was all the reward they had received?" As it was useless to contend against the prejudices of an ignorant man, a retreat was effected as soon as convenient.★ Notwithstanding these instances of ignorance, the mass of the people are surprisingly familiar with the divisions of a society that is so different from their own. While alluding to armorial bearings, it may be well to add, that I saw a great number, emblazoned in different materials, suspended from the walls of the dwellings, especially in New England. They are frequently seen on carriages, and perhaps oftener still on watch seals. My travelling companion was asked to explain why these evidences of an aristocratical feeling were seen among a people so thoroughly democratic. The substance of his answer shall be given: "Though the Americans do not always venerate their ancestors, for

---

★ The simplicity which one finds on these subjects in America, is often not without amusement. The general use of books, and the multitude of journals in the United States, certainly prevent the inhabitants of the country from being as ignorant of the usages of Europe, as the people of Europe, even of the better classes, are commonly of them; still there are thousands who form droll opinions on the subject of our distinctive habits. A German prince of the family of Saxe Weimar, was travelling in the United States during the visit of the writer. He made himself acceptable every where, by his simplicity and good sense. A little crowd had collected round an inn where he had stopped, and a new comer inquired of one of his acquaintance, "why he stared at the big man in the piazza?" "Oh, for nothing at all, only they say he is a Duke!" "A Duke! I wonder what he does for a living?"

precisely the same reasons as are acknowledged in Europe, they are nevertheless descended from the same sort of progenitors. Those who emigrated to this hemisphere, brought with them most of the opinions of the old world. Such of them as bore coats of arms did not forget the distinction, and those that you see are the relics of times long since past. They have not been disposed of, for no other reason that I can discover, than because it is difficult to find a use for them. Most of the trinkets are heir-looms; though many individuals find a personal convenience in the use of seals which are appropriate to themselves. There are others who openly adopt arms for the sake of this convenience, sometimes rejecting those which have long been used by their families, simply because they are not sufficiently exclusive; and there are certainly some who are willing to creep under the mantle of gentility at so cheap a rate. Foreigners, when they see these exhibitions, and find self-established heralds in the shape of seal cutters, &c. in the country, sometimes believe that wealth is gradually producing a change in the manners of the people to the prejudice of democracy. But they fall into an egregious error. The fact is, that even this innocent, though perhaps absurd vanity, is getting rapidly into disuse, together with most of the other distinctive usages of orders in society, that are not purely connected with character and deportment. No one, for instance, thinks now of exhibiting the arms on any portion of the dwelling, in hatchments, or on tomb-stones, though all were practised openly within thirty years. Liveries are scarcely so frequent now as formerly, while coaches, coachmen, and footmen are multiplied fifty-fold. In short, the whole country, not only in its government, but in all its habits, is daily getting to be more purely democratic, instead of making the smallest approaches to the opposite extreme. I state this merely as a fact that any well-informed American will corroborate, leaving you to your own reasoning and inferences."

It is a peculiar feature of American democracy, and it is one which marks its ancient date and its entire security, that it is unaccompanied by any jealousy of aristocracy beyond that which distinguishes the usual rancour of personal envy. One may sometimes hear remarks that denote the sourness of an unsuccessful rivalry, but the feeling can no where be traced in the conduct of the nation. The little states of Connecticut and Rhode Island contain, beyond a doubt, the two most purely democratic communities in the civilized world. In both, the public will is obeyed with the submission that a despot would exact; and, in the latter, it is consulted to a minuteness of detail that would be inconvenient, if not impracticable, in a community of more extended interests. Now, mark one effect of this excessive democracy which you may not be prepared to expect. No less than three governors of Connecticut have been named to me, who, in due progress of time, and at suitable ages, have been selected to sit in the chair which their fathers had filled with credit. Many inferior offices also exist, which, were it not for the annual decision of the people, might be thought to have become hereditary in certain families.★ Here is proof that the sovereign people can be as stable in their will, as the will of any other sovereign. Of the five presidents who have filled the chair, since the adoption of the present constitution in 1789, but one has left a son. That son is now a candidate for the same high office; and though the circumstance, amid a thousand other absurdities, is sometimes urged against his election, it is plain there is not a man in the whole nation who deems it of the least importance.†

As might be expected, the general society of New York bears a strong impression of its commercial character. In consequence of the rapid growth of the city, the number of families that may be properly classed among those which have long been distinguished in its history for their wealth and importance, bears a much smaller proportion to its entire population than that of most other places. A great many of the principal personages were swept away by the Revolution. Under these constant and progressive changes, as might be expected, the influence of their manners is, I think, less perceptible than, for instance, in Philadelphia. Still, a much larger class of what in Europe forms the *élite* of society exists here, than strangers commonly suppose. My letters first threw me, as a matter of course, among the mercantile men; and I found that mixture of manners, information, and character, that distinguish the class every where. It was my lot frequently to occupy a seat at a banquet between some fine, spirited, intelligent individual, whose mind and manners had been improved by travel and education, and, perhaps, another votary of Plutus, (one hardly dare say of Mercury, in this stage of the world,) whose ideas were never above the level of a sordid calculation, and all of whose calculations were as egotistical as his discourse. It strikes me that both a higher and a lower order

---

★ The writer was assured that the office of Secretary of State, in Rhode Island, had been in one family for near seventy years.

† Mr. John Quincy Adams: he was chosen the following winter, and is now president.

of men mingle in commerce here, than is seen elsewhere, if, perhaps, the better sort of English merchants be excepted. Their intimate relations on "Change" bring them all, more or less, together in the saloons; nor can the associations well be avoided, until the place shall attain a size, which must leave every one the perfect master of his own manner of living. That hour is fast approaching for New York, and with it, I think, must come a corresponding change in the marshalling of its coteries.

When Cadwallader returned from the country, I fell into a very different circle. His connections were strictly of New York, and they were altogether among the principal and longest established families. Here I met with many men of great leisure and large fortunes, who had imparted to their children what they had received from their fathers; and it would not have been easy, after making some slight allowances for a trifling tinge of Dutch customs, to have distinguished between their society and that portion of the English who live in great abundance, without falling into the current of what is called high or fashionable life. Although many, not only of the best informed, but of the best bred of the Americans, are merchants, the tone of manners in this circle was decidedly more even and graceful than in that which strictly belongs to the former. But it is not difficult to see that society in New York, in consequence of its extraordinary increase, is rather in a state of effervescence than settled, and, where that is the case, I presume you will not be surprised to know, that the lees sometimes get nearer to the surface than is desirable. Nothing is easier than for a well-behaved man, who is tolerably recommended, to get admission into the houses of the larger proportion of those who seek notoriety by courting a general intercourse; but I am inclined to think that the doors of those who are secure of their stations are guarded with the customary watchfulness. Still you will always remember, that suspicion is less alert than in Europe; for where temptations to abuse confidence are so rare, one is not much disposed to clog the enjoyments of life by admitting so sullen a guest. The effect of this general confidence is a less restrained and more natural communication.

There is a common accusation against the Americans, men and women, of being cold in their manners. Some carry their distaste of the alleged defect so far, as to impute it to a want of feeling. I have even listened to speculations so ingenious, as to refer it to a peculiarity in the climate—a reasoning that was thought to be supported by the well-known imperturbability of the Aborigines. Whether the theory be true or false, the argument that is brought to maintain it is of most unfortunate application. The tornado itself is not more furious than the anger of the Indian, nor is it easy to imagine a conformation of the human mind that embraces a wider range of emotions, from the fiercest to the most gentle, than what the original owners of this country possess. Civilization might multiply the changes of their humour, but it would scarcely exhibit it in more decided forms. I confess, however, that even in Cadwallader I thought, during the first weeks of our intercourse, something of this restraint of manner was perceptible. In his countrymen, and more particularly his countrywomen, the defect seemed no less apparent. In New England, notwithstanding their extraordinary kindness in deeds, there was often an apparent coldness of demeanour that certainly lessened, though it could not destroy its effect.★

This national trait can neither be likened to, nor accounted for, by any of those causes which are supposed to produce the approximating qualities in some of the people of our hemisphere. It is not the effect of climate, since it exists equally in 45° and 30°. It is not the phlegm of the German, for no one

---

★ An instance of this suppressed manner occurred while the author was at New York in the summer of 1825. An English frigate (the Hussar) entered the port, and anchored a short distance below the town. Her captain was the owner of a London-built wherry, which he kept for his private sport, as his countrymen on shore are known to keep racers. It seems that some conversation concerning the model of this boat, and of those of New York, and perhaps, too, respecting the comparative skill of four London watermen whom he was said to retain as a sort of grooms, and the renowned Whitehallers, induced him to insert a challenge in the journals, wherein he threw down the glove, for a trial of speed, to all the mariners or sportsmen of the city. The Whitehallers took up the gage, and a day was publicly named for the trial. It was quite evident that the citizens, who are keenly alive to any thing that affects their reputation on the water, let it be ever so trifling, took great interest in the result. Thousands of spectators assembled on the battery; and, to keep alive the excitement, there were not five Englishmen or English women in the city who did not appear to back the enterprise of their countrymen. The distance run (about two miles) was from the frigate to a boat anchored in the Hudson, and thence to another which lay at a short distance from the Castle Garden, already described. On board of the latter, the judges (who, it is presumed, were of both nations,) had adopted those delicate symbols of victory which had so recently been pitted against each other in far less friendly encounters, i.e. the national flags. The writer and his friend, who, notwithstanding his philosophy, felt great interest in the result, took their stand on the belvidere of the castle, which commanded a fine view of the whole bay. On their right hand stood a young American naval officer, and on their left a pretty and

can be more vivacious, frank, cordial, and communicative than the American, when you have effected the easy task of breaking through the barrier of his reserve. It cannot be the insulated pride of the Spaniard, brooding under his cloak on the miserable condition of to-day, or dreaming of the glories of the past; nor is it the repulsive hauteur of the Englishman, for no one is more disposed to admit of the perfect equality of his fellow creatures than the native of this country. By some it has been supposed to be the fruits of the metaphysical, religious dogmas and stern discipline that were long taught and practised in so many of the original colonies. That the religion of the Puritans and of the Friends left their impressions, is, I think, beyond a doubt; for the very peculiarity of manner to which we have reference, is to be found, in different sections of the Union, modified by the absence or prevalence of their self-mortifying doctrines. Still, one finds degrees of this same exterior among the Episcopalians of New York, the Catholics of Mary-

---

highly excited young Englishwoman. The frigate fired a gun, and the two boats were seen dashing ahead at the signal. One soon took the lead, and maintained it to the end of the race, beating by near a quarter of a mile, though the oarsmen came in pulling only with one hand each. For some time the distance prevented a clear view of which was likely to be the victor. A report spread on the left that it was the boat of the frigate. The eyes of the fair Englishwoman danced with pleasure, and she murmured her satisfaction so audibly as to reach the ears of all near her. The writer turned to see the effect on his right-hand neighbour. He was smiling at the feeling of the lady, but soon gravely turned his eyes in the direction of the boats. He was asked which was ahead. He answered, "The Whitehallers!" and directed the attention to a simple fact to confirm his opinion. The victors were pulling with so swift and equal a stroke, as to render their oars (at that distance) imperceptible, whereas there were moments when the blades of those in the beaten boat could be distinctly seen. This young lieutenant described as a "man-of-war stroke," which, be said, "could never beat a dead Whitehall-pull, let the rowers come from where they would." The fact proved that he was right. The English flag was lowered amid three manful cheers from the goal-boat, which was no other than the launch of the Hussar. With the exception of a few boys, the Americans, though secretly much elated, made no answer, and it was difficult to trace the least change in the countenances of the spectators. On quitting the battery, the writer and his friend met a French gentleman of their acquaintance descending the Broadway to witness the race. He held up both hands, and shook his head, by the way of condolence. His error was explained. "Victors!" he exclaimed, looking around him in ludicrous surprise, "I could have sworn by the gravity of every face I see, that the Englishmen had beaten you half the distance!" It is no more than fair to add, that something was said of an accident to the Hussar's boat, of which the writer pretends to know nothing, but of which he is sure the grave crowd by which he was surrounded was quite as ignorant as himself.

land, the merchants of the east, the great landed proprietors of the middle states, and the planters of the south. It is rather tempered than destroyed by the division of states, of religion, or of habits. It is said even to begin to exhibit itself among the French of Louisiana, who are already to be distinguished from their kinsmen in Europe by greater gravity of eye and mien. It is even so contagious, that no foreigner can long dwell within its influence without contracting more or less of its exterior. It does not arise from unavoidable care, since no people have less reason to brood over the calamities of life. There is no Cassius-like discontent to lead the minds of men into plots and treasons; for, from the time I entered the country to the present moment, amidst the utmost latitude of political discussion, I have not heard even a whisper against the great leading principles of the government.★

In despair of ever arriving at the solution of doubts which so completely baffled all conjecture and experience, I threw myself on the greater observation of Cadwallader for the explanation of a habit which, the more I reflected, only assumed more of the character of an enigma. His answer was sufficiently sententious, though, when pressed upon the subject, he was not unwilling to support it by reasons that certainly are rather plausible, if not just. To the question—"To what do you ascribe the characteristic grave demeanour of your countrymen?" the reply was, "To the simplicity of common sense!" This was startling, and at first, perhaps, a little offensive; but you shall have his reasons in his own words.

"You admit yourself that the peculiarity which you mention is solely confined to manner. The host, the friend, the man of business, or the lady in her drawing-room, who receives you with less *empressement* than you have been accustomed to meet elsewhere, omits no duty or material act of kindness. While each seems to enter less into the interests of your existence, not one of them is selfishly engaged in the exclusive pursuits of his own.

"While the Americans have lived in the centre of the moral world, their distance from Europe, and their scattered population, have kept them, as respects association, in comparative retirement. They have had great leisure for reflection. Even England, which has so long and so richly supplied us with food for the mind, labours under a mental disadvantage which is not

★ The author will add, nor to the hour of his departure. The United States of America are, perhaps, the only country in Christendom where political disaffection does not in a greater or less degree prevail.

known here. Her artificial and aged institutions require the prop of concerted opinions, which, if it be not fatal to change, have at least acquired an influence that it is thought dangerous to disturb. In America, no such restraint has ever been laid on the human mind, unless it might be through the ordinary operation of passing prejudices. But those prejudices have always been limited in their duration, and have never possessed the important prerogative of exclusive reverence. Men combated them at will, and generally with impunity. Even the peculiar maxims of the monarchy came to us, across the Atlantic, weakened by distance and obnoxious to criticism. They were assailed, shaken, and destroyed.

"Thought is the inevitable fruit of a state of being where the individual is thus permitted to enjoy the best effects of the highest civilization, with as little as possible of its disadvantages. I should have said thought itself was the reason of that gravity you observe, did I not believe it is more true to ascribe it to the nearest approximate quality in which that thought is exhibited. When there is much leisure, and all the other means to reflect on life, apart from those temptations which hurry us into its vortex, the mind is not slow to strip it of its gloss, and to arrive at truths that lie so near the surface. The result has been, in America, to establish common sense as the sovereign guide of the public will. In the possession of this quality, the nation is unrivalled. It tempers its religion, its morals, its politics, and finally, as in the case in question, its manners. The first is equally without bigotry or licentiousness; the second are generally consistent and sound; the third are purely democratic without the slightest approach to disorder; and the last are, as you see them, less attractive to you, perhaps, because unusual; but more in consonance with common sense than your own, inasmuch as they fail of an exaggeration which our reason would condemn. Many nations excel us in the arts, but none in the truths of human existence. The former constitute the poetry of life, and they are desirable so far as they temper society; but when they possess it to the exclusion of still nobler objects, their dominion is dangerous, and may easily become fatal. Like all other pursuits in which the imagination predominates, they have a tendency to diminish the directness with which reason regards every thing that appertains to our nature.

"Although there is nothing incompatible between perfect political freedom and high rational refinement, there is certainly a greater addiction to factitious complaisance in a despotism than in a republic. The artificial deference which, in the former, is exacted by him who rules, descends through all the gradations of society, until its tone becomes imparted to an entire nation. I think it will be found, by referring to Europe, that manners, though certainly modified by national temperament and other causes, have become artificial in proportion as the sovereign power has exercised its influence. Though France, under the old regime, was not in theory more monarchical than many of the adjoining countries, the monarch, in fact, filled a greater space in the public mind. It would be difficult to find any other nation in which sacrifices so heavy, indeed, it may be said, so fatal, were daily and hourly made to appearances, as under the reign of Louis XIV. They were only the more dangerous, inasmuch as the great advancement of the nation made the most gifted men auxiliary to the propagation of deception. The part which Racine with his piety, Boileau with wit, and even Fontaine with his boasted simplicity, did not disdain to play, humbler men might well desire to imitate. The consequences of this factitious tone in manners prevail to the present day in France, which, notwithstanding her vast improvements, has yet a great deal to concede to the immutable and sacred empire of truth, before either religion, government, or morals, shall reach that degree of perfection which each and all may hope to attain. However agreeable habitual deference to forms may become, the pleasure is bought too dearly, when a just knowledge of ourselves, deceptive views of life, or even of sacred liberty itself, may be the price. I should cite America as furnishing the very reverse of this proposition. Here, without pretending to any infallibility of judgment, all matters are mooted with the most fearless indifference of the consequences. In the tossings and agitations of the public opinion, the fine and precious grains of truth gradually get winnowed from the chaff of empiricism and interestedness, and, to pursue the figure, literally become the mental aliment of the nation. After the mind is thoroughly imbued with healthful moral truths, it admits the blandishments and exaggerations of conventional politeness with great distrust, and not unfrequently with distaste. When the principle is pushed into extremes, men become Trappists, and Puritans, and Quakers. Now, in this respect, every American, taken of course with the necessary allowances, is, more or less, a Puritan. He will not tell you he is enchanted to see you, when, in truth, he is perfectly indifferent to the matter; his thoughts are too direct for so gross a deception. Although he may not literally mean what he says, he means something much nearer to it than one meets with in what is called good society any where else.

"The native of New England has certainly more of this peculiar exterior than the native of any other part of our country. This difference is unquestionably a result of the manners of the Puritans. But you are right in believing that it is, more or less, to be seen in the air of most Americans; perhaps of all, with the exception of those who have lived from infancy in what is called the most polished, which of itself implies the most artificial circles.

"A great deal of this exterior is also hereditary. The Englishman is the man of the coldest aspect in Europe, when you compare his ordinary temperament with his deportment. Has not the Englishman a sounder view of life than any other man in your hemisphere? If not, he has been singularly fortunate in preceding all his competitors in the enjoyment of its most material advantages.

"France has been proverbial for grace of manner. But the manners of France are undergoing a sensible change, under the influence of the new order of things. Her gentlemen are becoming grave as they become thoughtful. Any one may observe, in passing through French society, the difference between the two schools. I confess that my taste is for the modern. I have been so much accustomed to the simplicity of American manners, as to find something that is congenial in the well-bred English, that is wanting in the well-bred French deportment, and precisely for the reason that it is still a little more natural. So far as this distinction goes, I honestly believe the Englishman has the advantage. But, with honourable exceptions, it will not do to push English complaisance too far. Perhaps, if we attempt a comparison, I shall be better understood.

"The Englishman and the American have, in a great degree, a common manner. I do not now speak of the gentlemen of the two countries, for much intercourse is rapidly assimilating the class every where, but of the deportment of the two entire nations. *You* will find both cold. There is certainly no great difference in the men, though more may be observed in the women. The English say that our women are much too cold, and we say that theirs are artificial without always being graceful. Of course, I speak of the mass, and not of exceptions, in either case. Our women are, as you see, eminently feminine, in air, conversation, and feeling, and they are also eminently natural. You may find them cold, for, to be honest, they find you a little artificial; but, with their countrymen, they are frank, sincere, unreserved and natural, while I challenge the world to produce finer instances of genuine, shrinking delicacy, or of greater feminine propriety.

"The French gentleman has certainly one advantage over his island neighbour. He is uniformly polite; his conventional habits having apparently gotten the better of all his native humours. You are sure, so far as manner is concerned, of finding him to-morrow as you left him today. There may be some question on this point with the Englishman, but none with the American. Common-sense is quite as equal as good breeding. The American gentleman is less graceful than the Frenchman, and may be even less conventional in his air than the Englishman, but he is commonly gravely considerate of the feelings. Were he disposed to abuse his situation, his countrymen would not tolerate his airs. I have already told you that humanity is a distinctive feature of American intercourse. The men of secondary manners may be more subdued in air than those of Europe, but it is altogether confined to appearance. No man is kinder in all his feelings or habits.★

"But this digression is leading me from what you call the peculiar coldness of the American manner. The word is not well chosen, since coldness implies a want of feeling, and want of feeling cannot exist where every concession is made to humanity, except in words and looks. Mr. Hodgson says, he does not think the habit of which he complains is to be seen in the better classes of the men, though he appears, unwillingly enough too, to admit that the females are not quite so free from the charge. Mr. Hodgson, it will be remembered, was a bachelor, and he ought to have known that this is a class of men far less in demand in America than in England. Without appearing to make the smallest allowance for the momentary warmth that is always excited by countrymen meeting in a foreign land, he puts the seeming cordiality of the wives of certain English soldiers whom he met at

---

★ The writer landed in England, on his return to Europe. Curiosity led him to the gallery of the House of Commons. The member on the floor was a stranger to him. A well dressed man stood at his elbow, and he ventured to ask him if he knew who was speaking. "No," was the answer, and it was given with an elevation and a peculiar sententiousness of voice which cannot be committed to paper. The writer was induced to repeat the experiment, simply as an experiment, four times, and always with the same success, except that in the last instance be obtained the name, but in a note pitched in the same key. He is bold to say, that the coldest looking man in America would have answered in a tone of more *"civilization."*

Niagara, in strong contrast with the cold demeanour of the wives of the thousands of Americans whom he had just left. This gentleman does not pretend that there was actually more of feeling in the one case than in the other; he seems perfectly willing to ascribe the difference to its true cause, viz., a simple difference in manner. Just to this extent I admit the justice of his remark, and I have endeavoured to give you some reasons for its existence. One would not gather from the book of Mr. Hodgson, rational and candid as it is, that the author had ever seen many countries besides his own; if he has, he must be aware that the air and manner of a French *paysanne* would still be more likely to flatter his self-complacency than the cordiality of the soldiers' wives. It would not be difficult for you and me to quote still stronger instances of the extent to which this manner is carried among different people, and people, too, who have no very extraordinary reputation either for morals or civilization.

"I think it will be found, too, on reflection, that the subdued manner (the word is more just than cold) of the Americans, is more owing to the simple and common sense habit they have of viewing things, than even to rusticity, or indeed to any other cause. It cannot be the former, since it is to be traced among those who have passed their lives in the most polished intercourse in the cities no less than in the country, and amid elegance as well as rural simplicity. While we have very few certainly who devote their leisure to the exclusive cultivation of the mere refinements of life, there is perhaps a smaller degree of rustic awkwardness in the country than can be found among an equal number of the inhabitants of any other nation. The very quality which keeps down the superfluous courtesy of the upper, has an agency in elevating the manners of the lower classes, who, considering their situations, are at all times surprisingly self-possessed and at their ease. A far more just objection to the social usages of the Americans, might be discovered in the rough and hardy manner in which they support their opinions, than in this absence of assumed cordiality. The latter, though it may become necessary by indulgence, can, after all, only impose upon a novice, whereas the former may easily become offensive, without in the slightest degree advancing what they urge. But it is so difficult, and even so dangerous, to say how far courtesy shall infringe on truth, that one can tolerate a little inconvenience to favour the latter; and depend on it, though the practice is often excessively unpleasant in the individual (and much oftener here than in Europe), it is a sound, healthful, national failing, that purchases great good at a small price."

I shall make no comments on the opinions of my friend. There is, however, one thing that may be said on the subject which will go to prove the justice of his theory. There is, at least, nothing conventional in this coldness of manner of his countrymen. Men do not admit it as a part of their gentility; but it has altogether the air of being either the effect of their national temperament, or, as Cadwallader would prove, of habits that proceed from a reflection so general and uniform, as to have perfectly acquired the simplicity and force of nature. I think also that he has not laid sufficient stress on the effect of republican institutions and the want of a court; but one cannot expect so thorough a democrat to speak with much reverence of the latter. He has explained that, by the prevalence of "common sense," he does not mean that every man in America is wise enough to discriminate between the substance and the shadow of things, but that so many are as to have given a tone to the general department of the whole: a case that may very well exist in a reading and instructed nation.

Vol. I, Letter 13

Cooper claims American soldiers are, in general, physically larger, braver, and more moral than their European counterparts. Because the Atlantic protects America, it will not have to prepare for the foreseeable future for offensive wars. Nevertheless, America will one day make itself "felt in the great general political questions" of Christendom.

TO THE COMTE JULES DE BéTHIZY.

&c. &c.

New York, ⸺

Neither the geographical situation of the United States, nor the habits of their citizens, are very favourable to the formation of a military character. Though the republic has actually been engaged in six wars, since the year 1776, only two have been of a nature to require the services of land troops in the field. The two struggles with England were close, and always, for the number engaged in the combats, obstinate and bloody, but the episode of a war with France in 1799, the two with Algiers, and that with Tripoli, only gave occasion for the courage and skill of the marine.

By studying the character of the people, and by looking closely into their history, it will be found that they contain the elements to form the best of troops. In point of *physique* they are certainly not surpassed. So far as the eye can judge, I should say that men of great stature and strength are about as common in America as elsewhere; while small men are more rare. I am much inclined to think that the aggregate of mere animal force would be found to be somewhat above the level of Europe in its best parts. This is not at all surprising, when one remembers the excellence and abundance of nutriment which is within the reach of the very poorest. Though little men are, without doubt, seen here, they are by no means as frequent as in England, in the southern provinces of France, in Italy, Austria, and indeed almost every where else.*

As might be expected, the military qualities which the Americans have hitherto exhibited, are more resembling those which distinguish the individual character of the soldier, than those higher attainments which mark an advanced knowledge of the art of war. As courage in its best aspect is a moral attribute, a nation of freemen must always be comparatively brave. In that collective energy which is the fruit of discipline, the Americans, except in a few instances, have been sadly deficient; but in that personal spirit, for which discipline is merely a substitute, they have as often been remarkable. They are certainly the only people who have been known to resist, with repeated success, in their character of armed citizens, the efforts of the disciplined troops of modern times. The militia and national guards of Europe should not be compared to the militia of America, for the former have always been commanded and drilled by experienced soldiers; while the latter, though regularly officered, have been led to the field by men in all respects as ignorant as themselves. And yet, when placed in situations to rely on their personal efforts, and on their manual dexterity in the use of arms, they have often been found respectable, and sometimes stubborn and unconquerable enemies.

The investigation of this subject has led me, perhaps, into a singular comparison. At the great battle of Waterloo, the actual English force in the field is said to have been 36,000 men. These troops undauntedly bore the assault of perhaps rather more than an equal number. This assault was supported by a tremendous train of artillery, and directed by the talents of the greatest captain of the age. It endured, including the cannonading of the artillery, for at least five hours. The official account of the British loss is 9,999 men, killed and wounded. At the affair of Bunker's-hill, the Americans might have had between 2,000 and 2,500 yeomen actually engaged. Though these men were marshalled in companies, their captains knew

---

* The writer afterwards found what he is almost tempted to call a race of big men in the south-western states.

little more of military service than the men themselves. There was positively no commander in the usual sense of the word. The aptitude of these people soon enables them to assume the form of an army; but it is plain that nothing except practice can impart the habits necessary to create good troops. At Bunker's-hill they enjoyed, in their preliminary proceedings, the advantage of a certain degree of order and method, that elevated them something, it is true, above an armed mob; but it is probable that they could not have made, with any tolerable accuracy, a single complicated movement at their greatest leisure, much less in the confusion of a combat. Just so far, then, as the ability to place themselves behind their imperfect defences with a certain military front was an advantage, they might be deemed soldiers; but in all other respects they were literally the ordinary inhabitants of the country, with very indifferent firearms in their bands. A great deal has been said of the defences and of the position of Bunker's-hill. It is not possible to conceive a redoubt better situated for an assault than the little mound of earth in question. It could be approached within a short distance with perfect impunity, and might easily be turned. It *was* approached in this manner, and it *was* turned. As to the rail fences on the level land beneath, where much of the combat was fought, and where the British were twice repulsed with terrible loss, the defences were rather ideal than positive. Now, against this force, and thus posted, the English general directed 3,000 of his best troops. His attack was supported by field artillery, by the fire of a heavy battery on an adjacent height, and by that of several vessels of war. The Americans were incapable of making any movements to profit by the trifling advantages their position did afford, and they had no artillery. They merely remained stationary to await the assault, relying solely on that quality of moral firmness, and on that aptitude which it is the object of this statement to elucidate by a comparison of the results of this combat with the results of Waterloo. The English made three different attacks. Their average continuance under the fire of the Americans was less than fifteen minutes. Their loss was certainly 1,056 men, and possibly more, for it is not probable that their general would be fond, under the peculiar circumstances, of proclaiming its full extent. Here, then, assuming our data to be true, (and that they are substantially so I fully believe,) we have a greater comparative loss produced by 2,500 husbandmen, armed solely with muskets, in forty-five minutes, than was produced by all the reiterated and bloody attacks at Waterloo. After making the necessary deductions for the difference in effect between great and small numbers, it will be found that there is something peculiar in the destruction occasioned by the peaceful citizens of this country. I should not have drawn this comparison, if it were not to demonstrate what I believe to be one of the inevitable consequences of the general dissemination of thought in a people. The same directness of application is observable in the manner that the American handles his arms, as in handling his plough. The battles of this country, both by sea and land, when there has been sufficient inducement to make their undisciplined bodies fight at all, have always been distinguished for their destruction. Many of their officers have been so conscious of the fatal effects of their own fire as to have implored their men (militia) to give but two or three discharges, and they would answer for the victory with their heads. No doubt they often failed in their entreaties, for the history of their wars are full of frank and manly acknowledgments of cases in which the militia yielded to the force of nature; but it is also full of instances in which their eloquence or influence had more effect, and these have always proved fatally destructive to their enemies. The battle of New Orleans will furnish a subject for a similar comparison.

There is another point of view, in which it is consolatory to study the short military history of this country. The states of New England, in which information has been so generally diffused, have always been the most dangerous to assail. A powerful force (for the times and the duty) was, in the war of 1775, early driven disgracefully from their soil by the people of New England. It is true, rapid, predatory excursions were afterwards made in the country, but always under the protection of a superior naval force, and with the most jealous watchfulness of detention. The only time that an army of any magnitude was trusted to manœuvre near their borders for a campaign, it was assailed, surrounded, and captured. Such are the fruits of intelligence, disseminated among a people, that, while it adds to all their sources of enjoyment, it gives a double security to their possession.

It would be vain to deny the excellence of the American troops when properly equipped and disciplined. If the English soldiers are admitted to be as good as common, the Americans are equal to the best. I have examined with deep interest the annals of both their wars, and I can find but a solitary instance in which (other things being equal) their *disciplined* troops have been defeated in open combat. Their generals have often been out-manœuvred and deservedly disgraced; but their disciplined soldiers, when fairly engaged, have, except in the case named (Hobkirk's-hill), invariably done well. The instances in which drilled soldiers have been left to their own efforts, are certainly rare, compared to those in which they have been blended with nominal regulars and militia; but they are sufficiently numer-ous to show the qualities of the troops. I refer you to the affairs of Cow-pens, Eutaw, and to the whole war of the south, under Greene, which was almost all the service that was exclusively done with drilled men in the rev-olution, and to the battles on the Niagara, during the late war. There are also many instances in which the regular troops (drilled men) did excellent service, in battles where they were defeated in consequence of being too few to turn the fate of the day.

It is another evidence of the effects of general intelligence that, disciplined or not, the Americans are always formidable when entrenched. They have been surprised (not as often, perhaps, as they have surprised), taken by siege, though rarely, and frequently disgraced by the want of ability in their chiefs, but seldom carried by open assault. Indeed, I can find but one instance of the latter (if Bunker's-hill be excepted, where they retreated for want of ammu-nition, after repelling the British as long as they had it), in a case of any impor-tance, and in that the assault partook of the nature of a surprise (Fort Montgomery). There are fifty instances, on the contrary, in which they have given their foes a rough reception, both against attacks by land and by sea. Bunker's-hill was certainly a victory, while the means of resistance lasted. To these may be added, the affairs of New Orleans, Fort Mifflin, Fort Moultries, Sandusky, Red Bank, Tiger River, Fort Erie, and numberless others.

With this brief review of their military character, which does not stand as high as it deserves, merely because there has been a sad dearth of efficient leaders, capable of conducting operations on a concerted and extensive scale, I think you will agree with me that the Americans are not in much danger of being the victims of a conquest. They turn the idea themselves into high ridicule. Some of them go so far as to assert, that Europe, united, could not subdue a people so remote, so free, and protected by so many nat-ural advantages. It is very certain, that whatever Europe might do now, she could not overturn this republic, if it shall remain united, fifty years hence.

The Americans seem quite determined that a future war shall not find them so entirely without preparation as the last. In the great concerns of the day, few of us, in Europe, had time or inclination to lend our attention to the details of that war; and with the exception of the actors, and perhaps a few of the leading events, little is known of it, even by the English who were parties to the struggle. As I intend to close this chapter with a brief account of the present military system of the United States, it may be well to revert to the means they employed in their two former contests.

The insurrection of 1775, was commenced under every military disadvantage. It is a well known fact that Washington kept the British army beleaguered in Boston, with an undisciplined force not always numerically superior, and which was for a long period so destitute of ammunition, that it could not have maintained a sharp conflict of half an hour. Yet the high resolution of this people supported them in the field, not as an enthusiastic and momentarily excited mob, but as grave and thoughtful men, intently bent on their object, and who knew how to assume such an aspect of order and method, in the midst of all their wants, as should and did impose on their skilful and brave enemies. Some minute calculations may be useful in furnishing a correct opinion of that contest, and, of course, in enabling us to judge of the effects which intelligence (the distinctive property of the American community) has on the military character of a nation.

In the year 1790, there were in the United States 814,000 white males over the age of sixteen (fractions are excluded). It is known that the population of the country has doubled in about twenty-three years. This calculation should give 407,000 of the same description of males, in the year 1767; or about 600,000 in the year 1779, which was the epoch when the final issue of the revolution might be said to have been decided by the capture of Burgoyne. If we deduct for age, physical disabilities, religious scruples, (as among the Quakers,) and disaffection to the cause, 100,000, a number probably greatly within the truth, we shall have half a million of men capable of bearing arms, to resist the power of Britain. I am sensible that this enumeration rather exceeds than falls short of the truth. England employed, at one time, not less than fifty thousand soldiers to reduce the revolted colonies, and she was in possession of all the strong holds of the country, at the commencement of the contest. The half million, badly armed, without supplies, discipline, money, or scarcely any other requisite but resolution, were scattered over a wide surface, a fact which, though, *with* their intelligence, and determination, it was favourable to their success, *without* it would have assured their defeat in detail. The formidable army of their enemies was sustained by the presence of powerful fleets; was led by experienced generals, and always fought bravely, and with perfect good will. Yet what was it able to perform? From New England, the only portion of the whole country where a tolerable dense population existed, a great force was early expelled in disgrace. A few cities on the sea coast were held by strong garrisons, which rarely ventured out with success. The only great expedition attempted in the north, was signally defeated. In the middle districts, marches of one or two hundred miles were made, it is true, and several battles were fought, commonly to the advantage of discipline and numbers; but in the only instance where an extended chain of communication was attempted, it was destroyed by the vigour of Washington. In the south, a scattered population, and the presence of slaves, allowed a temporary, but a treacherous success. Reverses soon followed; the conquered territory was regained, and triumph ensued. This is a summary of the outline of that war. If to the soldiers, be added the seamen of the fleet, a species of force nearly, or quite, as useful in such a war as the troops, there could scarcely be less than 80,000 men employed in endeavouring to reduce the malcontents. When the magnitude of the stake, and the power of Britain be considered, this number will scarcely appear sufficient. Here, then, admitting these estimates to be just, you have a regular, combined and disciplined force of 80,000 men, aided by large bodies of the disaffected to the American cause, contending against an unprovided, scattered, population of half a million of males, who had to resist to till their land, and to discharge all the customary obligations of society. The aid of the French was certainly of great use to shorten the conflict; but the men who had gone through the dark period of 1776, '77, and '78, and who had cleared the southern and eastern states, by their own exertions, were not likely to sub-mit to a power they had so often baffled.

In the war of 1812, the country was much better provided, though still miserably defective in military preparation, and in scientific knowledge. The whole population was about 8,000,000, and, though joined as one man on the subject of independence, and the maintenance of territory, nearly equally divided on the question of the policy of the war. A capital blunder was committed at the very commencement of the struggle. Instead of plac-ing young and talented men at the head of the armies, officers of the revolution were sought for to fill those situations. The Greenes, the Waynes, the Lincolns, Knoxes, &c. of that war had followed, or preceded, their great chief to the tomb, and few or none were left, of sufficient distinction, to yield a pledge for their future usefulness. The very fact that a man had served in a revolution without *éclat,* should have been *prima facie* evidence of his incapacity. Still, ancient officers, who had commanded regiments, or battalions, in the war of 1770, were thought preferable to those who had acquired their information in studying the more modern tactics. The result proved as might be expected. Not a single officer of the old school (one excepted) did any thing to justify his appointment, while several of them inflicted heavy disgraces on the arms of the country. The exception was general Jackson, who was far too young to have arrived at eminence in the revolution, and who gained his renown by departing from the Fabian policy of that struggle, instead of pursuing it.

The last war commenced in the middle of 1812, and terminated at the commencement of 1815. With the usual exceptions of personal enterprise and courage, the two first campaigns were disgraceful, expensive, and unmilitary. But time was already beginning to correct the blunders of a fatal prejudice, or rather fatal partiality. Men of character and talents forced themselves into notice; and although there existed, in the conceptions of the manner in which the war was to be conducted, a most lamentable impotency in the cabinet, the campaign of 1814 was brilliant in achievement. With the solitary exception of a rapid expedition to Washington, through a barren and nearly uninhabited country, the English were not successful in a single attempt of any importance. Four bloody affairs were fought on the Niagara, to the advantage of the Americans; formidable invasions on the north and on the south were successfully, and, in one instance, brilliantly repelled; and, in fine, the troops of the confederation, better drilled, and better led, began to exhibit some of the finest qualities of first rate soldiers. There is no doubt that England nobly maintained her colonies, which, of necessity, became the disputed point in such a war; but it is just as true, that so soon as, encouraged by finding herself unexpectedly released from her great European struggle, she attempted conquest in her turn, that she was quite as signally foiled.

Another quarter of a century may be necessary to raise the United States to the importance of a first rate power, in the European sense. At the end of that time, their population will be about 25,000,000, which, though not compact, according to our ideas, will be sufficiently available for all military purpose, by means of the extraordinary facilities of intercommunication that already exist, and are hourly increasing in the country. I think, before that period arrives, the republic will be felt as a military (or, more properly, a naval) power, in the affairs of Christendom. What she will become before the end of the century must depend more on herself, than on any thing the rest of the world can do to forward, or to retard, the result.

The present military condition of the United States, though far from imposing, is altogether more respectable than it has ever before been. One who is accustomed to see kings manœuvre large bodies of household troops as their ordinary play things, might smile to be told that the whole army of this great republic contains but 6,000 men. The Bourbons seldom lie down, dear Count, without as strong a force to watch their slumbers. But he who estimates the power of this people to injure, or to resist, by the number of its regular troops, makes a miserable blunder. The habit of discipline and the knowledge of military details are kept alive by the practice of this small force. They are chiefly employed on the western frontier, or they garrison, by companies, the posts on the sea board. They answer all the objects of preserving order on the one, and of guarding the public property in the other. But the vast improvement of the country is in the progress, and in the gradual diffusion of professional knowledge. All the subordinate ranks in this little army are filled by young men, who have received rigid military educations, tempered by a morality, and a deference to the institutions of the land, that are elsewhere little cultivated, and which tend to elevate the profession, by rendering a soldier strictly the support, and not the master of the community.

It is not probable that the jealousy of the Americans will ever admit of the employment of a very large regular force in time of peace. They prefer trusting to the care of armed citizens. Though the militia never can be, compared with its numbers, as formidable as disciplined troops, it is certainly sufficient to maintain order, and to resist invasion. With respect to the two latter objects, you may possibly believe that America is peculiarly favoured by her geographical situation. It is scarcely fair for governments to refuse to give a population the necessary degree of intelligence, and then to say it will be dangerous to entrust them with arms. We know that a child may do mischief with a weapon, but we also know that Nature has decreed that the time shall come when they may be made highly useful to him. For my part, I firmly believe, that if Europe would put the school-book into one hand, the other might be safely trusted with the musket. It is commonly the interest of the vast majority in every nation to preserve order; and they will certainly do it best, if the means are freely furnished. When the interests of the majority are in favour of a change, there is something very like true wisdom and justice in permitting it. Fancy, for a moment, twelve or fifteen millions, resembling the population of New England, in possession of a sufficient territory in the heart of Europe, every man with a musket, a reasonable supply of military munitions in readiness, and a moderate, disciplined force to furnish the nucleus of a regular army. What nation could hope to invade them with success? It is very true that the king of Prussia, now, is probably more dangerous to his neighbours than he would be at the head of such a nation; but a good deal of the truth of all these questions lies in the fact, whether a nation is any the better for being externally so very formidable. Three or four communities, intelligent, content with their condition, and entrusted with arms, like the Americans, properly dispersed over the surface of Europe, would be sufficient to insure the tranquillity of one quarter of the globe of themselves. It is odd enough, that the world should have been contending so long about the balance of power, without hitting on the cheapest mode of affecting it. Ink costs far less than gunpowder; and no reasonable man can doubt that, if properly expended, it would go farther, in one generation, to establish the natural and useful boundaries of nations, than rivers of blood. It is not a century since the fate of the British empire was decided by less than twenty thousand soldiers. It became Protestant, when it might have been Catholic. Here was a balance of power, so far as England and her dependencies were concerned, settled by a handful of men. It would require Europe united to do the same thing over again, and all because new generations have acquired more liberal ideas of their natural rights. And yet England is far, in this particular, very far, from what she might be. Even this country has still a great deal to do in advancing the mighty work of education.

We have an obstinate habit of insisting that, though America is prospering with all her freedom and economy, that her system would be fatal to any European nation. I once ventured to assert this position to my travelling friend, who met my opinion by bluntly asking—"How do you know it? In what age, or in what country did you ever try the experiment? I grant that certain desperate political adventures have been attempted, in which a few good men have joined a great many bad ones, in overturning governments, and that the mockery of liberty has been assumed by the latter, until it suited their convenience to throw aside the mask, and then tyranny has succeeded to the temporary deception, as a perfect matter of course. But so far as the experience of Europe goes, and considering the question altogether in a military point of view, I think it will be found that the freest nations have, *cœteris paribus,* always been found the most difficult to conquer. I might quote Scotland, Holland, and Switzerland, in favour of this theory. You will say, perhaps, that the first and the last were more indebted for their independence to their peculiar condition and poverty than to any actual political institutions, more particularly the former. Granted. And yet you find that it is only necessary to make a man feel a direct interest in preserving his actual condition to make him resolute in defending it. One would think there was far less to fight for in the hills of Scotland, than in the plains of Italy; and yet Italy has been overrun a hundred times by invaders, and Scotland never. But you think the hills and the fastnesses composed the strength of Scotland and Wales. No doubt they added; but will any man accuse the Netherlands, particularly Holland, of being a mountainous country? Do you think Napoleon would have ventured to march his vast army into a country so remote from France as Russia, had the latter been peopled with 20,000,000 of Americans, and had even the climate been as temperate as that of Paris. What were the facts in similar invasions, though certainly on a greatly lessened scale? Ten or twelve thousand yeomen, intermingled with a few regular troops, who were animated by the same spirit, intercepted and destroyed Burgoyne, at the head of ten thousand regulars, who were quite as good troops as any in the imperial guard. Prevost, at the head of an admirable force of many thousand men, who had been fighting the best battles of Europe, was checked by a handful of countrymen, and would have shared the fate of Burgoyne near the same spot, had he not been timely admonished to make a disgraceful retreat, by the fortune of his predecessor. Jackson, with some five or six thousand Tenesseans, Kentuckians, and Louisianians, did not even permit his enemy to involve himself in the difficulties of a distant retreat. The situation of a wealthy city required that the spirit of these freemen should be shown in its front; and well did they make it known. A similar fate would have attended the excursion to Washington, had time been given for arrangement, and the collection of a force sufficient for the object. But the experience of even the most despotic governments goes to show how much more formidable they become, when each man is made to believe it is his interest to resist aggression."

But the Americans appear sensible, that while the irresistible force of every nation exists in giving all of its citizens the deepest possible interest in its welfare, they do not neglect such rational means of rendering their numbers as effective as may be, without rendering the system of defence unnecessarily burthensome. There can be no doubt, that in this respect at least the republic is greatly favoured by its geographical position. Removed from all the ordinary dangers of external aggression, the country is able to advance in its career of improvement, with the freedom of a child, whose limbs are permitted to grow, and whose chest expands, unshackled by the vicious effects of swaddlings, or any other artificial correctives.

Compared with its state in 1812, the present military condition of the United States presents the following points of difference. Instead of possessing a few indifferently educated graduates of an infant military school, it has now hundreds, who have long enjoyed the advantages of far higher instruction. The corps of engineers, in particular, is rapidly improving, and is already exceedingly respectable. A system of order and exactitude has been introduced into the police and commissariat of the army, which will serve to render any future force doubly effective, and which may be readily extended to meet the exigencies of the largest armies. Formidable fortresses have been erected, or are in progress of erection, which will give security to most of the coast, and protection to the commerce of the country. By the aid of canals and great roads, armies on the frontiers can now be supplied at one-sixth of the former cost, and in half the time. Arms, artillery, and all the munitions of war, woollen and cotton clothing, in short, the whole materiel of an army, could now be furnished in the country at a reasonable cost; whereas, as late as 1812, the Americans were so entirely dependent on their enemy for a supply, that regiments were absolutely unable to march for want of so simple an article as blankets. The population has advanced from 8 to 12,000,000, and the revenue in even a greater proportion. The debt is in about the same ratio to the inhabitants as before the

war; but as the expenditures are not increased in the proportion of the revenue, it is in the course of rapid extinguishment. A very few years more of
peace will effect this desirable object.*

It is a mistaken idea that the Americans are a people so much engaged
in commerce as to be indifferent to the nicer points of national honour and
military renown. It is far more true to describe them as a people who have
hitherto been removed from the temptation of aggression, and in whom
the native principles of justice have, in consequence, never been weakened.
One hears a great deal in France, among the upper classes, of the French
honour, and in England of British character, &c. &c.; but neither of these
nations has ever manifested one half the jealous watchfulness of their rights
as these simple republicans. They dared the war of their independence in
the maintenance of a perfectly abstract principle, for no one pretends that
the taxation of England was oppressive in fact, and at this hour it becomes
very necessary for the graver heads of the nation to temper the public mind
at the smallest rumour of any assault on their dignity or national character.
The politicians are moderate, because they see that aggression bears an
aspect with them different from that which it assumes towards other people. An aggression by England, for instance, on America, is much like an
insult offered by a man to a boy. The latter may bear it, because he can say
to himself, the other will not dare to repeat it next year. Thus the American politician reasons, or rather has reasoned, that time is all-important to
them. Nations do not often go to war for indemnity, but to maintain established rights by showing spirit and force, or for conquest. Conquest the
Americans do not need, and there is no fear of injuries growing into precedent against a people who are rich, out of debt, free, intelligent, intrinsically
brave, however prudent they may be, and who in fifty years will number
50,000,000! I think, however, that the spirit of the people rather runs ahead
of their actual force, than otherwise. Perhaps their revolution was twenty
years too soon; and now, though lovers of peace, and frequently religiously
indisposed to war, it is quite easy to see that they chafe, to a man, at the idea
of any invasion on what they deem their natural rights.

It may serve to give you an idea of the different attitude which this

---

* The average amount of customs for ten years before the war, a little exceeded
12,000,000 of dollars a year; it may now be stated at about 20,000,000.

country takes in 1825, from what it maintained in 1812, by stating two facts. It is well known that thousands of their citizens were impressed, with impunity, into the British navy before the latter period. There was a false rumour the other day, that a similar act had occurred on the coast of Africa. I heard but one opinion on the subject. "We must have explanation and justice without delay." Cadwallader says, that he can hardly imagine a case in which two or three impressments (unless subject to clear explanations) would not now produce a war. The rumour, that England was to become mistress of Cuba, has also been circulated during my visit. I have sought opportunities to demand the consequences. The answer has been, at least five times in six, "war."

It is not difficult to see, that the day is at hand when this republic will be felt in the great general political questions of Christendom. It may then be fortunate for humanity, that the mighty power she will shortly wield, is not to be exercised to satisfy the ambition of individuals, but that they who will have to bear the burthen of the contests, will also have a direct influence on their existence. Neither the institutions, nor the necessities of America, are ominous of a thirst for conquest; but, with her widely-spread commerce, it will be impossible to avoid frequent and keen collisions with other nations. I think, for a long time to come, that her armies will be chiefly confined to the defensive, but another and a very different question presents itself when we turn our attention towards her fleets.

Vol. I, Letter 15

Cooper considers the merits of American political institutions. The most democratic of all American institutions is the New England town meeting. Competition there occurs among men of good will and good humor; rarely do candidates resort to mud slinging. Cooper also argues for universal suffrage and the end to property qualifications. In addition, Cooper maintains that power corrupts, and Americans, Cooper insists, must recognize that the American War for Independence was in reality a reformation, not a revolution. Revolution, especially its violence and suddeness, is alien to the American character.

TO SIR EDWARD WALLER, BART.
&c. &c.
New York, ——

The day after we had quitted Cooperstown, we saw a collection of people assembled in front of an inn, which was the principal edifice in a hamlet of perhaps a dozen houses. Cadwallader told me this was the first day of the state election, and that this spot was one of the polls, a name which answers in some degree to the English term, "hustings." Fortunately, the stage changed horses at the inn, and I had an opportunity of examining the incipient step in that process which literally dictates all the national policy of this great republic.

Although each state controls its own forms, not only in the elections, but in every thing else, a description of the usages of one poll will be sufficiently near the truth to give a correct general idea of them all. I now speak literally only of the state of New York, though, generally, of the whole

Union. The elections occur once a year.* They last three days. In the large towns, they are stationary, there being no inconvenience in such an arrangement where the population is dense, and the distances short. But in the country they are held on each successive day at a different place, in order to accommodate the voters. The state is divided into counties which cover, on an average, 900 square miles each. Some are, however, larger, and some smaller. These counties are again subdivided into townships, covering, perhaps, eighty or ninety square miles. There is, also, great inequality in the size of these minor districts. These are the two great divisions of territory for all the ordinary purposes of government and police. The counties have courts of their own, and a certain sort of legislative body, which regulates many of their financial affairs. In order that the whole subject, however, may be rendered as clear as possible, we will begin at the base, and ascend to the super-structure of their government.

The most democratic assemblage known to the laws, in which legal and binding resolutions can be enacted, are the town meetings. Any number of the people may assemble when and where they please, to remonstrate, to petition, or even to plot, if they see fit; but their acts can only be recommendatory. The town meetings are held annually, and every citizen who has attained his majority can vote. A moderator (no bad name for a perfectly popular assembly) is chosen by acclamation to preside. The meeting is commonly held in some school-house, but very often in the open air. In some places, though rarely, there are town-houses. At these meetings, all the town officers are chosen. They consist of a supervisor; three assessors, who apportion all the taxes on the individuals, whether imposed by town, county, state, or United States; collectors, who collect all the taxes, except those laid by the United States government, which, in time of peace, are just nothing at all; a town-clerk, who keeps certain registers; constable, poor-officers, overseers of highways, path-masters, and a few others. The names of most of these officers indicate their duties. The overseers of the highway are the men who lay out the ordinary roads of the town, and who say how much

---

* There is one state where they occur twice—the little state of Rhode Island, which is still governed by the form of its ancient charter, as granted by Charles II. in 1663. As this is practically the most democratic state in the Union, it affords pretty good evidence that the experiment of a democratic government is not so new in America as some pretend.

tax each individual shall contribute in work or in money; and the path-masters inspect the labour. Men of property and education frequently seek the latter employment. The voting in this popular assembly may be by bal-lot, but it is generally done by acclamation. There is a penalty if an individ-ual refuse to serve, though they are sometimes excused by the citizens, if a good reason can be rendered. The courts have also a discretionary power in imposing and in laying fines. I was present during the course of this excur-sion at one of these town-meetings. There might have been two hundred citizens assembled before the door of a large school-house. Much good humour was blended with a sufficient dispatch of business. The Americans mingle with a perfect consciousness of their influence on the government, an admirable respect for the laws and institutions of their country. I heard jokes, and one or two open nominations of men of property and character, to fill the humble offices of constable and pound-keeper; but the most per-fect good sense and practical usefulness appeared to distinguish all their decisions. There was a contest for the office of supervisor, and it was decided by a close vote. The two candidates were present, and on seemingly very good terms. They were respectable looking yeomen, and he who lost told his rival that he thought the people had shewn their judgment. There was no noise, no drinking, nor any excitement beyond that which one would feel in seeing an ordinary foot-race. One farmer observed, that the crows had got the taste of his corn, and unless something was done, there could be little hope for the year's crop. He therefore would propose that a reward of six cents should be paid for every dozen that should be killed, within their town, for the next six months. The resolution was opposed by a hatter, who insisted that he could take care of his hats, and that the farm-ers ought to take care of their corn. This logic was unsuccessful; the price was reduced a trifle, and the resolution was passed. It was then just as much a law as that which hangs a man for murder. The sum voted to meet the expense was to be apportioned with the other taxes, among the citizens by the assessors, collected by the collector, received and paid by another offi-cer, &c. &c. After this important act of legislation, the meeting adjourned.

The next body in the scale of the government is the board of supervi-sors. It is composed of the supervisors of each town in a county, who have a very similar legislative authority over the more familiar interests of the county, as is possessed by their constituents in the towns themselves. They impose taxes for all objects connected with the expenses of the county. Their authority is, however, a good deal circumscribed; enactments by the state legislature being often necessary to enforce their recommendations. When the question involves an expense heavier than common, and its effects are entirely local, the questions is often referred to a final decision of the people in their town meetings. This board audits the accounts, and I believe it appoints a treasurer for the county. So far you see the process of government is exceedingly simple. The whole legislative duty is discharged in three or four days, and yet the decisions have great influence on the comfort and property of the people. The duties of the officers named, continue for one year, but the same incumbents are frequently continued for a whole life, especially the collectors, treasurers, constables, and clerks.

Each town is also subdivided into school districts, and road districts. There are overseers of the schools, who regulate all that belongs to the familiar duties of the common schools of the country, to which any body may go.

Each township is also a petty electoral district of itself, for all the ordinary purposes of the state and the United States' elections, which are held at the same time and place. The three stations taken for the convenience of the elections, as already mentioned, are selected by the inspectors of the poll, who are five or six of the town officers, named by law, and of course chosen annually by the people in their original capacity. Each county chooses its own representatives to the lower branch of the state legislature, the number being according to the amount of the population. The state is again divided into what are called senatorial districts, composed of several contiguous counties, each of which chooses a certain number of representatives, who sit in the upper body of the state legislature. Each state has a right to send to the lower House of Congress a number of representatives, in proportion to its entire population. These representatives must be chosen by the people, but the states themselves may regulate the form. Some choose them by a general ticket; that is to say, each citizen votes for the whole number; and some choose them by districts, in which case each citizen votes for the member, or members, who represent his particular district. The latter is the course adopted by New York, and in most of the other large states, in which it is difficult for the characters of so many individuals to be intimately known to every body.

Now, complicated as this system may seem in words, it is perfectly simple in practice. It is astonishing how clearly it is understood by those who exercise it, and how difficult it is to make a foreigner get a correct idea of its details. All the elections, except those which are made at the town meetings, where other duties necessarily assemble the citizens, are held at the same time, and at the same place. Thus an American in one of the more populous states, can exercise all his constitutional rights at an expense commonly of a ride of four or five miles at the outside, and of three hours of time.

The election on the present occasion embraced senators, (always for the state,) representatives in the assembly,★ governor, lieutenant-governor, &c. The inspectors were assembled in a quiet room of the inn, with the ballot boxes placed before them, on a table. The voters entered at their leisure, and delivered their different ballots to the officers, who, holding them up as lottery numbers are usually exhibited, called the name of the voter aloud, and then deposited the ballot in its proper box. "I challenge that vote," cried an individual, as the name of one man was thus proclaimed. It appeared there were doubts of its legality. An inquiry was instituted, an oath proffered explanations were made, and the challenge was withdrawn. The vote was then received. Any one who votes may challenge. Nothing could be more quiet and orderly than this meeting. A few handbills were posted around the house, proclaiming the names, and extolling the qualities of the different candidates, and I heard one or two men disputing the wisdom of certain public measures, rather in irony than in heat. The election was not, however, esteemed a warm one, and perhaps quite one third of the people did not attend the polls at all. Mr. Clinton, the governor, under whose administration the canal policy, as it is called, has been fostered, had declined a re-election, at the expiration of the official term preceding the one now in existence. His place had been filled by another. In the mean time his political adversaries profiting by a momentary possession of a legislative majority, had ventured to assail him in a manner the people were not disposed to relish. He was removed from a seat at the "canal board," a measure which was undoubtedly intended to separate him, as far as possible, from a policy that was already conferring incalculable advantage on the state. The instant Cadwallader was told of this ill-

---

★ The more popular branch of the State Legislature, as it is sometimes called, though both are popular alike. The difference is principally in the term of service, and in some little exercise of power.

advised and illiberal measure, he exclaimed, that the political adversaries of this gentleman had reseated him in the chair of the government. When asked for an explanation, my friend answered, that the people, though they sometimes visited political blunders with great severity, rarely tolerated persecution. The event has justified his predictions. Although a popular candidate was selected to oppose him, Mr. Clinton has triumphed in this election by an immense majority, and, in a few days, he will become governor of the state for another term of two years.★

After quitting the poll, we familiarly discussed the merits and demerits of this system of popular elections. In order to extract the opinions of my friend, several of the more obvious and ordinary objections were started, with a freedom that induced him to speak with some seriousness.

"You see a thousand dangers in universal suffrage," he said, "merely because you have been taught to think so, without ever having seen the experiment tried. The Austrian would be very apt to say, under the influence of mere speculation too, that it would be fatal to government to have any representation at all; and a vizier of the Grand Turk might find the mild exercise of the laws, which is certainly practised in Austria Proper, altogether fatal to good order. Now we know, not from the practice of fifty years only, but from the practice of two centuries, that it is very possible to have both order and prosperity under a form of government which admits of the utmost extension of the suffrage. It is a never failing argument on these subjects, that American order is owing to the morality of a simple condition of life, and that our prosperity is incidental to our particular geographical situation. There are many good men, and, in other respects, wise men, even among ourselves, who retain so much of the political theory which pervades the literature of our language, as to believe the same thing. For myself, I cannot see the truth of either of these positions. Our prosperity is owing to our intelligence, and our intelligence to our institutions. Every discreet man in America is deeply impressed with the importance of diffusing instruction among our people, just as many very well-meaning persons in your hemisphere honestly enough entertain a singular horror of the danger of school-books. Thus it is our natural means of safety to do the

---

★ No voter can put in two ballots, since all are compelled to place them in the hands of an inspector. In case two ballots are found rolled together, both are rejected. Thus fraud is impossible.

very thing which must, of necessity, have the greatest possible influence on the happiness, civilization, and power of a nation.

"There can be no doubt that, under a bald theory, a representation would be all the better if the most ignorant, profligate, and vagabond part of the community were excluded from the right of voting. It is just as true, that if all the rogues and corrupt politicians, even including those who read Latin, and have well-lined pockets, could be refused the right of voting, honest men would fare all the better. But as it is very well known that the latter are not, nor cannot well be excluded from the right of suffrage any where, except in a despotism, we have come to the conclusion, that it is scarcely worth while to do so much violence to natural justice, without sufficient reason, as to disfranchise a man merely because he is poor. Though a trifling *qualification* of property may sometimes be useful, in particular conditions of society, there can be no greater fallacy than its *representation*. The most vehement declaimers in favour of the justice of the representation of property, overlook two or three very important points of the argument. A man may be a voluntary associate in a joint stock company, and justly have a right to a participation in its management, in proportion to his pecuniary interest; but life is not a chartered institution. Men are born with all their wants and passions, their means of enjoyment, and their sources of misery, without any agency of their own, and frequently to their great discomfort. Now, though government is, beyond a doubt, a sort of compact, it would seem that those who prescribe its conditions are under a natural obligation to consult the rights of the whole. If men, when a little better than common, were any thing like perfect, we might hope to see power lodged with safety in the hands of a reasonable portion of the enlightened, without any danger of its abuse. But the experience of the world goes to prove, that there is a tendency to monopoly, wherever power is reposed in the hands of a minority. Nothing is more likely to be true, than that twenty wise men will unite in opinion in opposition to a hundred fools; but nothing is more certain than that, if placed in situations to control all the interests of their less-gifted neighbours, the chance is, that fifteen or sixteen of them would pervert their philosophy to selfishness. This was at least our political creed, and we therefore admitted a vast majority of the community to a right of voting. Since the hour of the revolution, the habits, opinions, laws, and I may say principles of the Americans, are getting daily to be more democratic. We are perfectly aware, that while the votes of a few thousand scattered individuals can make no great or lasting impression on the prosperity or policy of the country, their disaffection at being excluded might give a great deal of trouble. I do not mean to say that the suffrage may not, in most countries, be extended too far. I only wish to show you that it is not here.

"The theory of representation of property says, that the man who has little shall not dispose of the money of him who has more.* Now, what say experience and common sense? It is the man who has *much* that is prodigal of the public purse. A sum that is trifling in his account, may constitute the substance of one who is poorer. Beyond all doubt, the government of the world, which is most reckless of the public money, is that in which power is the exclusive property of the very rich; and, beyond all doubt, the government of the world which, compared with its means, is infinitely the most sparing of its resources, is that in which they who enact the laws are compelled to consult the wishes of those who have the least to bestow. It is idle to say that an enlarged and liberal policy governs the measures of the one, and that the other is renowned for a narrowness which has lessened its influence and circumscribed its prosperity. I know not, nor care not, what men, who are dazzled with the glitter of things, may choose to say, but I am thoroughly convinced, from observation, that if the advice of those who were influenced by what is called a liberal policy, had been followed in our country, we should have been a poorer and, consequently, a less important and less happy people than at present. The relations between political liberality, and what is called political prodigality, are wonderfully intimate.

"We find that our government is cheaper, and even stronger, for being popular. There is no doubt that the jealousy of those who have little, often induces a false economy, and that money might frequently be saved by bidding higher for talent. We lay no claims to perfection, but we do say, that more good is attained in this manner than in any other which is practised elsewhere. We look at the aggregate of advantage, and neither our calculations nor our hopes have, as yet, been greatly deceived.

"As to the forms of our elections, you see that they are beyond example

---

* When the numbers of those who have nothing, get to be so great as to make their voices of importance, it is time to think of some serious change.

simple and orderly. After an experience of near forty years, I can say that I have never seen a blow struck, nor any other violent proceeding, at a poll. These things certainly do happen, but, in comparison with the opportunities, at remarkably long intervals. So far from the frequency of elections tending to disturb society, they produce an exactly different effect. A contest which is so soon to be repeated loses half its interest by familiarity. Vast numbers of electors are content to be lookers-on, rarely approaching a poll, except to vote on some question of peculiar concern. The struggle is generally whether A or B shall enjoy the temporary honour or the trifling emolument in dispute, the community seldom being much the better or the worse for the choice. People talk of the fluctuations which are necessarily the consequences of a popular government. They do not understand what they say. Every other enlightened nation of the earth is at this moment divided between great opposing principles, whereas here, if we except the trifling collisions of pecuniary interests, every body is of the same mind, except as to the ordinarily immaterial question of a choice between men. We have settled all the formidable points of policy, by conceding every thing that any reasonable man can ask. The only danger which exists to the duration of our confederacy (and that is not a question of a form of government, but one of mere policy), proceeds from the little that is aristocratical in our Union. The concentrated power of a state may become, like the overgrown power of an individual, dangerous to our harmony, though we think, and with very good reason, that, on the whole, even this peculiarity adds to the durability of the Union.

It is unnecessary to say, that so far as mere convenience goes, this method of election can be practised by a hundred millions of people, as easily as by twelve. As to corruption, comparatively speaking, it cannot exist. No man can buy a state, a county, or even a town. In a hotly contested election it is certainly sometimes practicable to influence votes enough to turn the scale; but, unless the question involve the peculiar interests of the less fortunate class of society, it is clear both parties can bribe alike, and then the evil corrects itself. If the question be one likely to unite the interests and the prejudices of the humbler classes, nine times in ten it is both more humane and wiser that they should prevail. That sort of splendid and treacherous policy which gives a fallacious lustre to a nation by oppressing those who have the most need of support, is manifestly as unwise as it is unjust. It violates the very principles of the compact, since governments are not formed to achieve, but to protect. After a sufficient force has been obtained to effect the first great objects of the association, the governed, and not the governors, are the true agents in every act of national prosperity. Look at America. What people, or what monarch, if you will, has done half so much as we have done, (compared to our means,) in the last half century, and precisely for the reason that the government is obliged to content itself with protection, or, at the most, with that assistance which, in the nature of things, strictly requires a concentrated action.

"It is of far less importance, according to our notions, what the executive of a nation is called, than that all classes should have a direct influence on its policy. We have no king, it is true, for the word carries with it, to our ears, an idea of expenditure; but we have a head, who, for the time being, has a very reasonable portion of power. We are not jealous of him, for we have taken good care he shall do no harm.

"Though we are glad to find that principles which we have practised, and under which we have prospered so long, are coming more in fashion in Europe, I think you must do us the justice to say, that we are not a nation much addicted to the desire of proselyting. For ourselves we have no fears, and as for other people, if they make some faint imitations of our system, and then felicitate themselves on their progress, we are well content they should have all the merit of inventors. That is a miserable rivalry which would make a monopoly of happiness. I think, as a people, we rather admire you most when we see you advancing with moderation to your object, than when we hear of the adoption of sudden and violent means. We have ever been reformers rather than revolutionists. Our own struggle for independence was not in its aspect a revolution. We contrived to give it all the dignity of a war from the first blow. Although our generals and soldiers might not have been so well trained as those they fought against, they were far more humane, considerate, and, in the end, successful than their adversaries. Our own progress has been gradual. It is not long since a trifling restriction existed on the suffrage of this very state. Experience proved that it excluded quite as many discreet men as its removal would admit of vagabonds. Now it is the distinguishing feature of our policy that we consider man a reasonable being, and that we rather court, than avoid, the struggle between ignorance and intelligence. We find that this policy rarely fails to assure the victory of the latter, while it keeps down its baneful monopolies. We extended the suffrage to include every body, and while complaint is removed, we find no difference in the representation. As yet, it is rather an improvement. Should it become an evil, however, we shall find easy and moderate means to change it, since we are certain that a majority will be sufficiently sagacious to know their own interests. You have only to convince us that it is the best government, and we will become an absolute monarchy to-morrow. It is wonderful how prone we are to adopt that which expectation induces us to think will be expedient, and to reject that which experience teaches us is bad. It must be confessed that, so far, all our experiments have been in favour of democracy. I very well know that you in Europe prophesy that our career will end in monarchy. To be candid, your prophecies excite but little feeling here, since we have taken up the opinion you don't very well understand the subject. But should it prove true, *à la bonne heure;* when we find that form of government best, depend on it, we shall not hesitate to adopt it. You are at perfect liberty, if you will, to establish a journal in favour of despotism under the windows of the capitol. I will not promise you much patronage at first, neither do I think you will be troubled with much serious opposition. At all events there is nothing in the law to molest the speculation. Now look behind you at the 'poll' we have just left; reflect on this fact, and then draw your conclusion, of our own opinion, of the stability of our institutions. We may deceive ourselves, but you of Europe must exhibit a far more accurate knowledge of the state of our country, before we shall rely on your crude prognostics rather than on our own experience."

I could scarcely assure myself that Cadwallader was not laughing at me during a good deal of the time he was speaking, but after all, it must be confessed there is some common sense in what he said. There were three or four other passengers in the stage, men of decent and sober exterior, among whom I detected certain interchanges of queer glances, though none of them appeared to think the subject of any very engrossing interest. Provoked at their unreasonable indifference to a theme so delightful as liberty, I asked one of them "If he did not apprehend there would be an end to the republic, should General Jackson become the next President?" "I rather think not," was his deliberate, and somewhat laconic answer. "Why not? He is a soldier, and a man of ambition." My unmoved yeoman did not care to dispute either of these qualities, but he still persevered in thinking there was not much danger, since "he did not know any one in his neighbourhood who was much disposed to help a man in such an undertaking."

It is provoking to find a whole nation dwelling in this species of alarming security, for no other reason than that their vulgar and every-day practices teach them to rely on themselves, instead of trusting to the rational inferences of philanthropic theorists, who have so long been racking their ingenuity to demonstrate that a condition of society which has delusively endured for nearly two hundred years, has been in existence all that time in direct opposition to the legitimate deductions of the science of government.

Vol. I, Letter 16

Cooper creates a debate about the best polity among several European aristocrats. Though concerned with the long-term affects of slavery, Cooper concludes that America is the country most rooted in truth and patriotism. "There is less falsehood uttered in the United States (if you exclude the slaves) than in any other Christian country."

TO SIR EDWARD WALLER, BART.
&c. &c.
Philadelphia, ——

Since my last letter, I have visited New Jersey, the eastern parts of Pennsylvania, and Delaware. With the exception of Maine, Illinois, and Indiana, (quite new states,) I have now seen something of all those communities, which, in common parlance, are called the "free states," in contradistinction to those which still encourage the existence of domestic slavery. As respects this material point of policy, the confederation is nearly equally divided in the number of states, thirteen having virtually gotten rid of slavery, and eleven still adhering to the system. The difference between the white population, however, is vastly more in favour of the "free states." We shall not be far out of the way in stating the whole of the white population of the United States at a little more than ten millions. Of this number near, if not quite, seven millions are contained in the thirteen northern, middle, and north western states.

This portion of the Union is governed by the same policy, and its inhabitants seek their prosperity in the same sources of wealth and in the same spirit of improvement. More than half of them are either natives of New England, or are descended from those who were born in that district of the country. Together, the states I have named cover a surface of little less than 300,000 square miles. If the territory of Michigan be included, (which is not yet sufficiently populous to be a state,) the amount will be swelled to near 330,000. The former will give rather more than twenty-three to the square mile, as the rate of the whole population on the whole surface. But in making the estimate, what I have already said of the vast regions that are not peopled at all, must be kept in view. Perhaps one-third of the territory should be excluded from the calculation altogether. This would leave something more than thirty to the square mile, for the average. But even this estimate is necessarily delusive, as it is known that in the old states there are sixty and seventy souls to the square mile, and in some parts of them many more.

In the course of reflection on this subject, I have been led to inquire when these republics are to reach that ratio of population which, of necessity, is to compel them to adapt their institutions to the usages of European policy. The result is not quite so conclusive as one might at first be disposed to believe. I find that despotism flourishes with little or no opposition in Russia, a country of about twenty-five to the square mile; in Turkey, one of about fifty;* in Spain, one of, say sixty; in Denmark, one of about eighty, &c., &c.; and that liberty is beginning to thrive, or has long thriven, in England, one of more than two hundred; in the Netherlands, one of an equal rate; and, in short, in France, in several of the most populous states of Germany, some of which mount as high as six and nine hundred to the square mile, more particularly the *free* towns!

Here is pretty clear evidence, by that unanswerable argument—fact, that the populousness of a country is not necessarily to control the freedom or despotism of its institutions. But the United States have carried the freedom of their institutions too far, since they go much farther than we have ever found it wise or safe to go in Europe. England herself has stopped short of such excessive freedom. The latter position is certainly much nearer to the truth than the other, and yet if we should assemble even the travelled brethren of our own club, and put the question to

---

* Both in Europe.

them—"How far do you think that liberty and equality of political rights can be carried in a government without danger to its foundations?"—it would be seen that the replies would smack a little of the early impressions of the different worthies who compose the fraternity. Let us fancy ourselves for a moment in solemn conclave on this knotty point, and we will endeavour to anticipate the different answers. We will begin with the Prince André Kutmynoseandeyesoff.

"I am of opinion," says our accomplished, intelligent, and loyal prince, "that without a vast standing army, a nation can neither secure its frontiers, nor on occasion bring them properly within a ring fence. In what manner is a serf to be made to respect his lord, unless he see that the latter can enforce his rights by having recourse to the bayonet, or in what manner is even rank among ourselves to be regulated, without a common centre whence it must flow? It would be utterly impossible to keep an empire composed of subjects born in the arctic circle and subjects born on the Caspian, men speaking different languages, and worshipping Jesus and Mahomet, together, without such a concentration of power as shall place each in salutary fear of the ruler. It is quite clear that a nation without a vast standing army—"

"I beg pardon for the interruption, mon Prince," cries Professor Jansen: "I agree with you *in toto,* except as to the army. Certainly no spectacle is more beautiful than that of a kind and benevolent monarch, dwelling in the midst of his people like a father in the bosom of a vast family, and at once the source of order and the fountain of honour. Still I can see no great use in an overgrown army, which infallibly leads to a waste of money and a misspending of time. Soldiers are unquestionably necessary to prevent invasion or aggression, and to be in readiness to look down any sudden attempts at revolution; but they are dangerous and extravagant play-things. When a sovereign begins to stir his battalions as he does his chess-men, one can never calculate what move he means to make next; and as to rank, what can be more venerable or more noble than the class of Counts, for instance— ["Hear, hear," from Sir Edward Waller]—a set of nobles who hold so happy and so respected an intermediate station between the prince and his people. That is clearly the happiest government in the whole world, where the labour of ruling is devolved on one man: but I shall always protest against the wisdom of a large standing army."

"*Quant à moi,*" observes the colonel, making an apologetic bow, "I cannot agree with either the one or the other. An army before all things, but
no despot; and, least of all, a despot who does nothing but stay at home and
vegetate on his throne. If I must have an absolute monarch, King Stork any
day to King Log. In my youth, I will confess, certain visions of glory floated
before my eyes, and conquest appeared the best good of life; but time and
hard service have weakened these impressions, and I can now plainly perceive all the advantages of *La Charte*. In a constitutional monarchy one can
enjoy the advantages of a despotism without any of its disadvantages. You
have an army to vindicate the national honour, as ready, as brave, and as efficient, as though the power of its head were unlimited; and yet you have not
the constant danger of *lettres de cachet,* bastilles, and monks. By a judicious
division of estates, those odious monopolies, which have so fatal a tendency
to aristocracy—"

"If you stop there, dear Jules," interrupts a certain Sir Edward Waller, "we
shall be in the majority, and the question is our own. Nothing can be more
dangerous than a despotism, every one must allow" (though two worthy
members had just held the contrary doctrine). "But you are touching on
the very thing now, that must unavoidably prove fatal to your monarchy, *la
charte,* and all, since it is clear, that a monarch needs the support of an aristocracy, and an aristocracy is nothing without money.—An enlightened,
unpaid, disinterested gentry, who possess all the property.—"

"Money!" echoes the colonel, in heat; "it is that money which is the
curse of you English. You have it all, and yet you see you are hourly in ter-
ror of bankruptcy. Thank God, if the revolution has done nothing else, it has
cut up root and branch all our odious seignories, with their feudal follies,
and man now begins to think himself the owner of the soil, and not a plant."

"Nay, my dear Béthizy, keep your temper; you are not now storming the
bridge of Lodi. Reflect one moment; what will become of France when
her whole territory shall be subdivided in freeholds not bigger than a
pocket-handkerchief?"

"And your island! what will the poor devils of paupers do when Lord
——— shall own the whole island?"

"I think," observes the abbate, perceiving that the argument is likely to
wax hot, "that it is a question that will admit of much to be said on both
sides, whether a people will leave more lasting and brilliant recollections, if

their career has been run under a republican or a monarchical form of government. In Italy we find arguments to maintain both positions; though at present we are somewhat divided between a hierarchy and such minute geographical divisions as shall ensure a close inspection into the interests of all who have any right at all to be consulted in these matters. I can neither agree with the prince, nor with the professor, nor with the count, nor yet with Sir Edward, though I think all of us must be of opinion that a popular government is a thing quite impracticable."

"Oh! all, all, all, all."

"It is quite certain that your Lazzaroni would scarcely know what to do with political power if they had it," continues the abbate.

"Nor a serf," says the prince.

"I can see no use in giving it even to a count," mutters the Dane.

"Nor to a Manchester reformer," puts in Sir Edward.

"It is quite certain the *canaille* do not know how to use it," adds Jules Béthizy, with a melancholy sigh; and so the question is disposed of.

Now, if my friend Cadwallader were a member of the club (and I hope to live long enough to see the day when he shall become one), he might give a very different opinion from them all. Let us imagine, for an instant, what would be the nature of his argument. He would probably say, that, "my countrymen have taken care there shall be neither Lazzaroni, nor serf, (he might gag a little at the thought of the blacks,)* nor counts, nor Manchester reformers, and any opinions which may be formed on premises of this nature are, in consequence, utterly inapplicable to us. I dare say the abbate will very willingly admit, that if there were nothing but cardinals in Italy, a popular government would do very well; and perhaps Sir Edward will allow if the English population were all baronets of seven-thousand a year, the elective franchise might be extended even in his kingdom without any very imminent danger. It is wonderful how very difficult it is to make men comprehend that a thing can be done by any one else which they have long been used to consider as exceeding their own ability to perform. This feeling of selfishness, or of vanity, whichever you please,

---

* It is manifestly unsafe to found any arguments concerning the political institutions of this country on the existence of slavery, since the slaves have no more to do with government than inanimate objects.

insinuates itself into all our actions, and finally warps our opinions, and obscures our judgments.

"I do not believe it is in the power of man to make a Turk comprehend the nature of English liberty; simply because, when he looks around him, and sees the state of society in which he himself vegetates, he can neither understand the energy of character which requires such latitude for its exertion, nor the state of things which can possibly render it safe. It appears to me, that it is very nearly as difficult to make an Englishman comprehend that it is very possible for a people to prosper under a degree of liberty still greater than that he enjoys. His self-love, his prejudices, and his habits are all opposed to the admission. Experience and fact go for nothing. He is determined there shall be some drawback to all the seeming prosperity of a state of things which exceeds his own notions of the sources whence prosperity ought to flow; and though he may not be sufficiently conversant with the details to lay his finger on the sore spot, he is quite confident there must be one. He swears it is festering, and that by-and-bye we shall hear something of it worth knowing. I remember once to have conversed with a renowned English statesman on this very subject. He was sufficiently complimentary on the institutions of my country, and on the character of my countrymen, but we were neither of us the dupes of such simple courtesy. I believe he did me the justice to see that I understood him, for he very soon took occasion to remark that he should like the government of the United States better if it were a 'Frank Republic.' Perceiving that I looked surprised, and possibly understanding the expression of my countenance to say how much I wondered that a man of his experience should expect great *frankness* in any government, he went on to explain; 'I mean,' he continued, 'that I should like your government better, if there were no pageant of a head, and if Congress would act for itself directly, without the intervention of a President.'

"This conversation occurred shortly after the senate of the United States had rejected a treaty with Great Britain, which the President had made (through the public minister), and which the King of Great Britain had previously ratified. '*Hinc illæ lachrymæ.*' I confined my answer to a simple observation, that the actual power of the President was very little, but that we should unnecessarily impede the execution of the laws, and embarrass our intercourse with foreign nations, by abolishing the office, which added greatly to the convenience of the country, without in the slightest degree invading or endangering the liberties of the people.

"Now, what was the amount of the argument which this gifted man agitated in his own mind, on a subject so important to the policy of a great nation. He could understand that a right might exist somewhere to annual the bargain of a minister, for in his proper person he had just before refused to ratify a treaty made by one of his own agents,* but he could not understand that this power should, or could, with propriety, be lodged in hands where he was not accustomed to see it. Napoleon would have told him that he himself submitted to a thousand vain and restrictive regulations which only tended to embarrass his operations and to lessen his influence abroad.

"Again, it is quite common for the American to gather in discourse with Englishmen, either by inuendos, or direct assertions, that there is little or no religion in his country! Nine times in ten the former is content to laugh in his sleeve at what he terms the egregious ignorance of his relative, or perhaps he makes a circle of friends merry by enumerating this instance, among fifty others, of the jaundiced views that the folks on the homestead take of the condition of those who have wandered beyond the paternal estate. But should he be tempted to probe the feeling (I will not call it reason) which induces so many warm-hearted, and kindly intentioned individuals in the mother country, to entertain a notion so unjust, not to say so uncharitable, of their fellow Christians, under another *régime,* he will find that it is in truth bottomed on no other foundation than the circumstance that we have no established church. And yet it is a known fact that the peculiar faith of England is, in America, on the comparative increase, and that in England itself, it is on a comparative decrease, one half of the whole population being, at this moment, if I am rightly informed, dissenters from the very church they think so necessary to religion, morals and order. In America, we think the change in the latter country is owing to the establishment itself, and the change in our own, to the fact that men are always willing to acknowledge the merits of any thing which is not too violently obtruded on their notice. We may be wrong, and so may they; but if the fact were only half as well authenticated as is the one that we are competent to maintain our present political institutions, I should consider it a question not worth the trouble of discussion."

---

* With Mexico.

That Cadwallader would use some such manner of reply I know, for the anecdote of his conversation with the English statesman (now unhappily no more) I have actually heard him mention. I confess the justice of many of his remarks, for I am perfectly conscious of having been the subject of a great many of these vague and general conjectures on American policy; but a closer observation of the actual state of the country is gradually forcing me to different conclusions. The more candid European will admit that a vast number of our usages and institutions owe their existence, at the present hour, to prejudice. Now, is it not possible that prejudice may have quite as active an agency in keeping down aristocracy, as in keeping it up? It is perfectly absurd to say that it is an ordering of nature; for nature, so far from decreeing that the inequality of her gifts is to be perpetuated in a direct male line, and in conformity to the rights of primogeniture, is commonly content with visiting a single family with her smiles, at long intervals, and with a very unequal bounty. So far as nature is concerned, then, she is diametrically opposed to the perpetuation of power or consideration in the regular descent. Neither talents, nor physical force, nor courage, nor beauty, are often continued long in any one race. But men do get, and do keep too, the control of things in their own families, in most of the countries of the earth. This is a practical argument, which it will be found difficult to controvert. It is precisely for this reason that I begin to think the people of the United States will not soon part with the power of which they are at present in such absolute possession. But knowledge you will say is power, and knowledge is confined to the few. I am inclined to think, after all, that the degree of knowledge which is necessary to make a man obstinate in the defence of rights which he has been educated to believe inherent, is far from being very profound. It is well known that despots have often failed in attempts on the personal privileges of their subjects. Paul could send a prince to Siberia, but he could not make a Boyer shave. Now, the rights of suffrage, of perfect political equality, of freedom in religion, and of all other political privileges, are the beards of these people. It will be excessively hazardous to attempt to shorten them by a hair. The ornaments of the chin are not more effectually a gift of nature, than are the political privileges of the American his birth-right. Great as is the power of the English aristocracy, there are limits to its exercise, as you very well know, and any man can predict a revolution should they attempt to exceed them. I fancy the only difference between the mother and child in this particular is, that the latter, so far as political rights go, has rather a richer inheritance than the former. Time has clearly little to do with the matter beyond the date of our individual existence, since a human life is quite long enough to get thoroughly obstinate opinions on any subject, even though prejudice should be their basis.

From this familiar and obvious manner of reasoning (and I think it will be found to contain a fair proportion of the truth) it would seem to result that there is quite as little likelihood the American will lose any of his extreme liberty, as that the Dutchman, the Frenchman, or the Englishman, will lose any great portion of that which he now enjoys. The question is then narrowed to the use the former will make of his power.

The past speaks for itself, and in language sufficiently plain for any man to comprehend, who is not obstinately bent on refusing credit to institutions to which he is unaccustomed. The future is necessarily, in some degree, matter of conjecture; but, in order to anticipate it with an approach to accuracy, we will continue our investigation of facts.

You are already master of my opinions on the general character of the inhabitants of New England. If I add the results of the observations made in the recent tour, you will possess the remarks I have made on more than half of the whole population of the country, and this too without excluding the slaves from the calculation.

The great national characteristics throughout this whole people are, with few and limited exceptions, every where essentially the same. But shades of difference do assuredly exist, which may serve rather to modify the several states of society, than to effect any material change. I think the principal distinctions emanate from slavery, and from the greater or less support that is given to the common schools. The Americans themselves rightly esteem knowledge as the palladium of their liberty, no less than the mighty agent of their comparative importance; and wherever a sound and wholesome policy prevails, the utmost attention is paid to the means of its diffusion. You should constantly remember, however, that each state has the entire control of all these subjects in its own hands. Consequently, although the mighty truth is universally admitted, very different means have been resorted to, in order to promote its advancement.

The policy of New York and Ohio differs but little from that of New England in this particular. Unhappily that of Pennsylvania is less enlightened. In the former state, during the current year (1814), when the population is rather under 1,600,000, there are 7,642 common schools; 402,940 scholars have been taught in these schools for an average of nine months. These are in addition to all the *private* schools, which are numerous, especially in the towns; and which include all who push education beyond reading, writing, arithmetic, and a little grammar and geography.*

From these numbers, which are taken from official reports, you gain two important facts; the extent of the common education, and the number of the children compared to that of the adults. During the same year (1824) there were 11,553 marriages, 61,383 births, and 22,544 deaths, or nearly three births to one death. It must be remembered that this state contains more populous towns than any other, and that the deaths in the city of New York alone, from the wandering character of so great a portion of its population, must necessarily exceed the regular proportion of nature.

While on this subject, it may be well to advert to a few other facts, of which I propose to make some use, when further observation shall entitle me to comment on the present condition and future fortunes of the slaves. In 1790, the whole population of the state of New York was 340,120. Of this number 25,975 were blacks, chiefly slaves. In 1800 there were 586,050 persons, of whom 30,988 were blacks, chiefly slaves. In 1810, 959,049 persons, and 40,350 blacks, of whom, perhaps, nearly half were free. In 1820 the population was 1,372,812, of whom only 39,367 were blacks; viz., 10,088 slaves, and 29,279 free people of colour. In 1825 the population was 1,616,458, of whom 39,999 were blacks, all free, or, what was the same thing, all to be free on the 4th of July, 1827; and by far the most of them were free at the time the census was actually taken.

It will be well to recollect that the state of New York, so far from being a place avoided by the blacks, is rather one they seek. The scarcity of domestics, and the large proportion of families who keep servants, induce thousands of free people of colour to resort there for employment. A great many are also hired as labourers on board of vessels. Still they do not increase amid the vast increase of the whites. A trifling migration to Hayti may have affected the returns a little, but there is no doubt that the migration into the state exceeds that from it. One must remember how few marriages take

---

* In 1825, there were 7,773 common schools, and 425,530 scholars, exclusive of those who attended 656 schools, from which no returns were made in time to be included.

place among these people; their moral condition, their vagrant habits, their exposure, their dirt, and all the accumulated misfortunes of their race.*

I think it is quite fair to infer, from these statements, that freedom is not favourable to the continuation of the blacks, while society exists under the influence of its present prejudices. The general returns of the number of the free blacks in the whole of the United States, certainly show that they are on the increase; but this fact is to be ascribed to the constant manumissions, and not to any natural cause. In Massachusetts there have been no slaves since the declaration of independence. It has, of course, been a favourite residence of the blacks, some of whom have risen to respectable situations in life. Among them, there have been traders, ship-masters, and even ship owners; and yet they have scarcely increased in number, during the last thirty years. In 1790 there were 5,463 blacks in that state; and in 1820 there were 6,740. During the same time the whole population has advanced from 378,787 to 523,287.† A vast emigration to the New States has kept down the population of Massachusetts. Thus, you see, that while the whites have increased in thirty years more than thirty-eight per cent., the blacks have not reached the rate of twenty-four per cent., and this, too, under as favourable circumstances, as they are probably fated to enjoy, for a long time to come, in these republics. But Massachusetts was alone for many years in the protection and favour she extended to this unfortunate race. The rate of their increase was vastly greater, before the manumission laws went into force in the adjoining states, than now. Thus, between 1790 and 1800, they increased one hundred and eighty per cent., a rate much greater than that of the whites during the same period (a consequence of the influx of the former, and of the emigration of the latter). Between 1800 and 1810 their increase was forty-four per cent., and between 1810 and 1820 only five per cent. There being only three more blacks in 1820 than in 1810, while the whites, notwithstanding emigration, had augmented 51,116.

Now it is quite certain that, in a country subject to so many changes as

---

* At the census of 1825, there were in the state of New York 1,513,421 neat cattle; 349,628 horses; 3,496,539 sheep; 1,467,573 hogs; 2,269 grist mills, chiefly by water; 5,195 saw mills, almost all by water; 1,222 fulling mills; 1,584 carding mills; 76 cotton, and 189 woollen manufactories of cloth for sale. There were 645 deaf and dumb, 1,421 idiots, and 819 lunatics. It should, however, be remembered, that unfortunate subjects of these maladies are frequently sent from other states to the benevolent institutions of this.

† Census of 1820.

this, and where man is so very active, all statistical calculations are liable to the influences of minute and familiar causes, which are very likely to escape the detection of a stranger. When Cadwallader first directed my attention to the foregoing reports, I was about to jump to the instant conclusion that the free blacks did not propagate their species at all, and that, as the gross increase of their numbers in the country was owing to manumissions, nothing remained but to give them all their freedom, in order to render the race extinct. But my companion, like most of his countrymen, is a calculator too wary and too ingenious to fall into so gross an error.

There is no doubt that the free blacks, like the Aborigines, gradually disappear before the superior moral and physical influence of the whites, but the rate of their decrease is not to be calculated by that in the state of Massachusetts, nor even by that of the native possessors of the soil. A black man, unlike an Indian, can be easily civilized; and perhaps there are no peasants in the world who require a greater indulgence of their personal comforts than the people of colour in the northern and middle states of this Union. In this respect they are like the menials of most other nations, having acquired from their masters a reflected taste for luxury. But it is well known that cold is not congenial to the physical temperament of a black.* The free

---

* All experience proves, that ages and generations must elapse before the descendants of the African can acquire habits of endurance which shall enable him effectually to resist frost, if, indeed, it can ever be done. Indeed, while the negro is often powerful of frame, and generally supple and active, it may be questioned whether he can endure extreme fatigue of any sort, as well as a white man; at least as well as the hardy and vigorous whites of this country. A thousand instances might be adduced to prove this position, but two must suffice. A few years since, an American whaler was struck by a whale in the Pacific Ocean, and the vessel instantly bilged. The crew was compelled to traverse half of that vast ocean in their boats, subject to the utmost privation, and sustaining the most horrible sufferings. But few survived to reach the land. The blacks, of whom there were a fair proportion, died, being the first to sink under their abstinence and labour.—A few years since, a small vessel ran into a bay on Long Island, during a severe snow storm, at a time that Cadwallader was near the spot. She was soon surrounded by a thin ice, and as her crew had no fire, nor boat, they were reduced to the utmost distress. A signal was made to that effect. A young gentleman proceeded to the rescue of the unfortunate mariners, seconded by two servants, one of whom was white, and the other black. The latter was a farm labourer of great strength and activity. The ice was to be broken near a mile, in the face of a cutting wind, and while the thermometer (Fahrenheit) stood several degrees below Zero. The crew were rescued, but the black was near dying, and had to be landed before half the toil was completed, and a white man was taken in his place.

blacks are found hovering as near as possible to the slave states, because the climate of the south is what they crave. Thus, in Pennsylvania they increase, while in New York they decrease. Some portion of this effect is no doubt produced by the more extensive commerce of the latter (which works up a great number of blacks as sailors), and by the peculiar policy of the Quakers, as well as of the descendants of the Germans, in the former state, both of whom display singular care of their black dependants. But, on the whole, I think it must be assumed as a fact for our future reasoning, that the free blacks rather decrease than otherwise (always excepting the effects of manumission); and it is well known, that the whole white population grows rather faster than the whole black.

Before closing these remarks I will add, that the whites, with the exception of certain districts in the southern states, attain a greater degree of longevity than the blacks, and that it is known that the slaves have more children than the free people of colour.

It is not improbable that there are some immaterial errors in the reports, from which the number of children in the common schools of New York have been taken, since the state bestows its bounty in proportion to the wants of the district; but, on the other hand, it must be remembered, that the amounts are gathered by public and qualified officers, and that each school district is obliged to tax itself for just as much money as it receives, in order to raise the sum necessary to defray the current expenses of common education, so that, on the whole, it is probable there is no great exaggeration; nor is a traveller, who has witnessed the immense number of white-headed and chubby little urchins he sees all over the country, at all disposed to suspect it.

We of Europe, when we listen to the wonders of these regions, in the way of increase and prosperity, are a little addicted to suspect the native narrators of the prodigies of a love of the marvellous. I once ventured to ask Cadwallader his opinion on this delicate point. His answer was sufficiently to the point, and you shall have it, without the smallest qualification:—

"That the Europeans," he said, "will not believe facts, which have a daily existence before our eyes, proves nothing but their ignorance. In my own opinion, and this is but a matter of opinion, there is less falsehood uttered in the United States (if you exclude the slaves) than in any other Christian country, though Heaven knows there is quite enough. In saying falsehood,

I mean untruths, whether intentional or not. A certain degree of gross credulity is absolutely necessary, that one very numerous class of vulgar falsehoods should flourish anywhere. Our European kinsmen, who are quite as enlightened as any other people of your hemisphere, are far from being exempt from the foible of excessive credulity. The tales one hears on the top of a stage-coach would scarcely do in an American vehicle; for the shrewd, practical, quick-witted, and restless people of this country, would be ashamed to believe, and consequently ashamed to tell, half the extraordinary feats of such or such a subject of notoriety, merely because they have been accustomed to think understandingly of what a man can do in almost every situation in which he is ordinarily placed. Nowhere is a lie so soon and so thoroughly sifted as here. Even the institutions of the country are favourable to the discovery of truth, as no man is *ex-officio* considered immaculate. Love of country, a stronger passion in America than even in England, or rather a more general one, has never protected an officer in a false colouring of a victory or a defeat, when the truth was within the reach of the multitude. The attempts are comparatively rare, for the hazard is notorious. During the war of the revolution, the public documents of the nation, which were issued in something like the form of bulletins, were found to be so true, that the signature of the Secretary of Congress was universally deemed conclusive as to all interesting facts.

"In no one instance were the people ever intentionally deceived, and it is rare indeed that they were ever deceived at all. History, in 1824, gives in substance the same accounts of our battles, fortunes, and reverses, as did Charles Thompson in 1776. Indeed, it would be just as impracticable for the government to mislead, for any length of time, as it would for an individual to make people think a man could work a miracle, or get into a quart bottle. Thus we are spared a prodigious amount of falsehood, which prevails elsewhere, merely because no one will believe it; or, at least, there will not be enough of the credulous to permit an improbable lie to flourish. Then the servile deception, which is a necessary attendant of great inequality of condition, cannot be, and is not, as frequent here as in Europe. A mechanic will be very apt to tell any man his mind who offends him, whether he be a governor or merely a brother in the trade.

"Moral influence is also quite as strong in the United States as in the most moral countries of the east. Indeed I know but one cause why deception should be more active here than in Europe, while I can see and do know a multitude why it should not. The frequency of elections certainly gives rise to a greater frequency of those amiable misrepresentations that are so peculiar to all political struggles. But, in point of effect, these election lies, as they are called, defeat themselves; they indeed do even more; they often defeat the truth, as most people are predisposed to incredulity. And yet, four-fifths of our elections pass away like this you have just witnessed, without exciting sufficient interest to raise a lie about them at all.

"Facts, undeniable, manifest, and, to an American, familiar facts, do certainly often assume to the unpractised ears of an European, an air of startling exaggeration. There appears in mankind a disposition always to believe too much, or to believe too little. The exact and true medium is hit by very few, who, by uniting a sufficiency of experience to a necessary amount of native penetration, are enabled to estimate testimony with accuracy. I have repeatedly felt, while in Europe, the embarrassment of encountering those who were disposed to believe miracles on the subject of my country, and those who were not disposed to believe that things, under any circumstances, could vary materially from the state in which they existed, before their own eyes. Even educated men cease to resemble each other in this respect, for all the books in the world cannot qualify a man to estimate the power of his species, half so well as personal observation. Our very obstinacy in incredulity on practical things, goes to prove the general sense of mankind concerning the value of experience, by showing how apt we are to refuse credit to acts which exceed any thing we have ourselves witnessed. Perhaps, in a country where so much is actually done, there is some disposition, on the part of vulgar minds, to exceed possibility in their anticipations, and even in their narrations, but this would prove the quality rather than the amount of our misrepresentation. On the whole, I incline to the opinion, that there are more untruths told in denying the unparalleled advances of this country, than in affirming it."

VOL. II, LETTER 2

In this analysis of Congress, Cooper claims that most representatives are yeoman or mechanics, not gentlemen. Americans understand that class matters little in their selecting representatives. Instead, the communities advocate morality and intelligence as criteria.

TO THE ABBATE GIROMACHI.
&c. &c.
Washington, ——

My attention, after our arrival at this place, was early called to the great body, which was about to assemble. We had taken a little suite of rooms in a lodging house, or rather tavern, which soon began to fill with members of congress from all quarters of the country. Perhaps of the whole legislative corps of the country, there is not a single individual who is the proprietor of a dwelling at the seat of government. Those who are of sufficient estate to maintain two houses, have their town residences in the capitals of their own particular states, though a very large majority of the members are far from being men of large fortunes at all.[*] There are a few individuals who appear at the capital with their wives and families, but by far the greater part of those who have them, leave them at home. The common practice is, for a certain number of the members who are acquainted with

---

[*] Does not this fact go to confirm the opinion of Cadwallader, that frugality in the public expenditure of a country, is by no means a necessary consequence of power resting in the hands of the comparatively poor?

each other, to make what is called a "mess," at some chosen boarding-house. Here they reside together, during the session, like the members of one large family. Even ladies are often included in these arrangements. Others again choose to live entirely secluded: and, in some few instances, families keep their regular winter establishments, in such narrow accommodations as the place affords. The fact that a member is so completely dependant on the public will, for his election, is enough in itself to prevent any one but a man of very large estate from incurring the expense of building on so uncertain a tenure.

A member of the congress of the United States is, in fact, what the office professes to be, a representative of the people. It is not pretended that he should be, as a matter of course, a gentleman, in the ordinary acceptation of the term. On the contrary, he is very commonly a plain, though always a respectable yeoman, and not unfrequently a mechanic. I remember to have passed a night, in one of the northern states, in a very good, cleanly, cheap and comfortable inn, whose master was a member of the lower house. In the southern states, where the white men of smaller fortunes are by no means of so elevated a character as their brethren of the north, a choice from the middling classes rarely happens; but from the more northern, eastern, and north-western states, such selections are by no means uncommon.

When Cadwallader first directed my attention to this fact, I confess a little surprise entered into my view of the composition of the American legislature. Perhaps the circumstance of so material a difference between the congress and the British parliament was at the bottom of my wonder; for we in Europe are perhaps a little too apt to try all experiments in liberty by those which England has so long practised with such comparative success. I alluded, a little freely, to the circumstance of their having so far departed from the practice of the mother country, with a view of extracting an opinion on the subject from my companion. The plan was successful.

"If departure from the policy of our ancestors is to create your wonder, the feeling should be neither new nor trifling. What we do now, in this particular, we have practised, not only without inconvenience, but with signal success, for near seven generations. The representation under the crown differed but little from that of the present day. It is, in truth, a representation; and the surprise should be, not that the people choose so many men of a situation in life closely resembling that of the majority, but rather that they choose so few. There is a practical good sense in the mass of the community, here, that tells them a certain degree of intelligence and of respectability of character is needed in a representative of the nation. No one will deny that they sometimes deceive themselves, but, on the whole, they are sufficiently critical. For native talent, practical intelligence, moral character, and political honesty, the congress of the United States need not dread a comparison with the legislature of any other country. I do not mean to say that they are perfect, but I am quite certain, from tolerably close observation, that they do as much good and as little harm as any other similar body in the world.

"He who enters the halls of congress, expecting to find the same conventional finish of personal deportment, or the same degree of education, as he will find in the British parliament, or in the French chambers, enters it under a gross misconception of the nature of its organization. But he who enters either of the two foreign legislative bodies I have named, expecting to meet with the same useful and practical knowledge of life, in those details on which a legislator is called every hour to act, the same degree of native capacity, or even the same aptitude of applying the great principles of government to their direct and desirable uses, will fall into an error quite as gross. We have men, and very many men, in our legislature, that may be safely placed at the side of the most eminent politicians of Europe; and perhaps no people in the world could more easily fill every chair on the floors of the two houses with representatives who, by their intelligence, practical knowledge, independence, and honesty, would do high credit to a nation, than ourselves. But there are many reasons why we do not. The first, and the most important of all, is, that we have happily got the country into that onward movement, that there is little or no occasion for legislative impulses. As a rule, besides the ordinary grants of money, and the usual watchfulness over the proceedings of the executive, the less they do the better. We find it useful to place the check of plain men, with moderated views of life, on the speculations of educated theorists. Besides, every class of society has its interests, and it is proper that they should have their representation. It is certainly true, that many members of congress sometimes believe it necessary to yield to the mistaken prejudices of a majority of their constituents; but it may be well questioned, whether as much evil to the community results from this pliancy, as from that which obeys the beck of a minister. In America we have some of the former and none of the latter; in Europe you have a great deal of the latter, and none of the former. Now, in the United States, if the mistake of the people entails inconvenience on themselves, they are sure to get rid of it; but I am yet to learn in what manner you dispose of a blunder, or of an intentional innovation, of a minister. You must always remember that we claim no perfection; it is not a quality of earth. All we wish to maintain is, that our system is the best known, and perhaps the best practicable; but if you will shew us a better, we will adopt it. Nothing can be more absurd than to accuse almost the only nation on the earth that is constantly endeavouring to amend its institutions, of a besotted opinion of its own immaculate wisdom. I know you will say, that changes are frequently dangerous, and that they too often lead to evil. Now, I am not at all disposed to deny that you are partially right as respects yourselves; but we know that we can improve, or even afford to deteriorate a little, without much danger; and therein we think we have no small advantage over all the rest of the world. If you doubt the fact, compare our actual situation, the past, and what we have done and are doing, with what other governments have done and are about, and let the result speak for itself.

"You will see on the floors of congress men belonging to every condition of society known to our community, with the exception of that which necessarily infers great ignorance and vulgarity. All the members are respectable, and very many of them are gentlemen. There are some who are scholars, and not a few have been improved by travel and by observation of other countries. A remote frontier district, however, must send such men as it possesses, or trust its peculiar interests to those who have but little concern in its welfare. The senate is, in some respects, rather more select than the lower house, because their constituents have a state instead of a district to choose from, and because that body is expected to temper the proceedings of legislation with a peculiar degree of moderation and dignity.

"In the British parliament there is some show of this universality of representation. Certain corporations send men of their own stamp; but in England every thing has a tendency to aristocracy, while, in this country, every thing which pertains to the government must seek its support in the democracy. The 'worthy alderman,' who may have commenced life behind a counter, endeavours to forget his apron when he takes his seat on the opposition benches. Instead of returning to his shop when the session is ended, he becomes a deserter to aristocracy, the moment he has received the seal of office from the people. How far he may contribute to the boasted refinement of the higher classes, I cannot pretend to say; but it is certain that he does not, like his American prototype, assist to give respectability and elevation to that of which he was originally a member. It is this elevation of character among the middling, and even among the more inferior classes of our community, which chiefly distinguishes us from all other nations. Europe must shew a population as much accustomed to political power, as moderate in its exercise, as practised in all that controls the general interests of life, and as shrewd in their estimate of character, as this of ours, before she should pretend to infer the results of democratic institutions by any facts drawn from her own experience. We do not deny the universality of human impulses, we only insist that governments have not the habit of giving them fair play. The two houses of congress are, and ever have been, living proofs that the majority of men are not disposed to abuse power when it is once fairly entrusted to them. There is not a doubt that the comparatively poor and ignorant might fill all our legislative chairs with men of their own class, and yet they rather take pride in seeing the representation respectable for information. Some part of this seeming generosity is, no doubt, owing to the superior influence of intelligence; but you must allow there is a prospect of quiet and durability under a system in which the majority find no reason to complain, and in which the minority must see the folly of usurpation. But as the two houses are by this time organized, we will go to the capitol, and hear the message. When on the spot, I will endeavour to direct your attention to such individuals as may serve to elucidate what you have just heard."

We proceeded to the capitol in a coach. Alighting at the foot of the hill, we mounted it to a door on the western facade, and entered the edifice through its *substratum*. Passing among a multitude of eating-rooms, &c. &c., we ascended, by a noble flight of massive steps, to the true basement, or to that story which runs through the whole building. Directly under the dome is a gloomy vaulted hall, that I have heard called the "caucus;" more, I believe, from its fancied fitness for the political meetings that are thus termed, than from the fact that it has ever actually been appropriated to such an use. It has the air, however, of being admirably adapted to the purposes of a secret conclave, though, in truth, it is a common thoroughfare of the building. Immediately above the "caucus" is the principal hall. It is circular, large, high, and covered with a fine dome. There is not much richness in the ornaments of this hall, though it is sufficiently wrought to prevent the appearance of nakedness. It contains, among other things, four bas-reliefs in stone, which are intended to illustrate as many of the most striking incidents in the original settlement of the country.* I have no disposition to criticise their execution. Historical pictures are to be placed in the pannels beneath.

From the great hall we passed into that of the house of representatives. My friend was formerly a member, and by an usage he is permitted to enter the body of the chamber, or rather to occupy a seat that is only separated from those of the actual members by a slight division. Under his auspices, and by the aid of a little interest, I was permitted to be his companion.

The hall of the house of representatives, without being particularly rich, or highly wrought, is one of the most beautiful apartments I have ever entered. The form is semicircular. It is lighted from above, and from windows on its straight side. Between these windows and the body of the hall, is a sort of lobby or gallery, which is separated from the other parts by a colonnade. Here the members and privileged persons promenade, converse, stand, listen, or repose, without, in fact, quitting the room. It is sufficiently withdrawn to prevent the appearance of disorder, and yet near enough to render the debates audible.

---

* The writer is himself but a traveller, and he should, therefore, speak reverently of the craft. But he will seize this occasion to express his surprise at the very different view which he has taken of visible objects from those of some others of the class, who, like himself, have been pleased to put their observations before the world. In the "Personal Narrative of Lieutenant the Honourable Frederic de Roos," p. 15, is the following sentence, while speaking of the apartment just named: "The walls are destitute of ornament, if we except some pieces of sculpture, representing various wars and treaties with the Indians. The artist might have selected subjects more creditable to his country." Now, if the writer has not been greatly deceived, these four bas-reliefs are on the following subjects: the landing of the pilgrims on the Rock of Plymouth; the Treaty of William Penn with the natives for the possession of their soil; the beautiful and touching story of Pocahontas saving the life of Captain Smith, and a personal rencontre of Colonel Boon, the patriarch of Kentucky, with the savages. These are four distinct historical events, which are connected with the settlement of the four principal parts of the Union. More illustrious incidents might have been chosen, beyond a doubt: but there is certainly nothing discreditable to the American character in those they have selected for this purpose.

In the centre of the diameter which cuts the circle is the speaker's chair. It is, in fact, a little sofa, sufficiently large to hold, on occasion, the president of the United States, the president of the senate, and the speaker. Immediately in front, and four or five feet lower, is a chair for the presiding member, when the house acts as a committee. On a line with the speaker the clerks have their places. In front of the chair there is a vacant semicircular space of perhaps five-and-twenty feet in diameter. Then the seats of the members commence. They are arranged in semicircular rows, preserving the form of the exterior walls, and are separated by a great number of little openings, to admit of a passage between them. Each member has an arm-chair and a low desk, in mahogany. In the first row, they sit in pairs, or there is a vacant space between every two, and each successive row increases its number by one member. Thus, in the last row, some six or seven are placed side by side, as on a bench (though actually on chairs), while those in front are in pairs. The practice is for those who arrive first to choose their seats, and the choice is invariably respected.

There is no such thing known as a political division of seats. Members of the same politics certainly often choose to be placed near to each other, and sometimes the entire representation of a particular state is to be seen as near together as possible. But there is no rule in the matter.

The seats of the members are separated from the semicircular passage in which Cadwallader and myself were placed, by no other division than a low railing. Sofas lined the whole of the exterior wall: and as the floor rises a little from the centre, or the area in front of the speaker, we had the best possible opportunity for seeing and hearing. A spacious and commodious gallery, of the same form as the hall, completed the outline of the apartment. It was raised several feet above the level of the chamber, and is intended for the use of spectators.

The house was organized when we entered, and was engaged in some business of form. Nearly all the seats were occupied; and, as the message was expected, the gallery was crowded with ladies and well-dressed men. The privileged places around the floor of the hall were nearly all filled. The speaker was uncovered, but most of the members wore their hats. No one appeared in costume, nor is there any official dress prescribed to the members of congress for any ceremony whatever.

After what Cadwallader had told me of the true character of the representation of his country, I confess I was rather surprised with the appearance of the individuals who composed this assembly. It was to be expected that they should all be well attired, but, on the whole, with some very few exceptions, they had quite as much the air of the world about them as those who compose the chambers of the two first nations of Europe. No one is allowed to sit in the lower house who has not attained the age of five-and-twenty; but, in point of fact, there is not, probably, a single member of congress who has seen less than thirty years. The greater number seemed to be men between the ages of thirty-five and fifty-five. There were but very few who could be termed old. All, or very nearly all, were natives of the country.

I was struck with the simple but imposing aspect of this assembly. Though so totally destitute of any personal decorations, the beauty of the hall, with its magnificent row of massive columns,* the great neatness of the faut'uil and desks, the beautifully carpeted floors, and the long range of sofas, serve to relieve a scene that might otherwise have been too naked. It appeared as if the members had said, thus much may you do for the benefit of comfort, for the encouragement of the arts, and, perhaps, as a testimonial of the respect due to the sacred uses of the place, but man must be left in the fullest force of his simplicity. None of the attendants even wore any badges of their offices. There were neither swords, chains, collars, stars, bayonets, nor maces, seen about the place, though a quiet, and order, and decency reigned in the hall that bespoke the despotic dominion of that mighty, though invisible, monarch—the Law.

A discussion on some question of order was getting to be a little general, and one member was addressing the chair [they speak from their places, as in the British Parliament] with some earnestness, when the principal door was thrown open, and an officer proclaimed aloud, "A message from the president." The members all rose in their places, the speaker included, when a young gentleman entered, and passed through the body of the house to the chair. He was attired in a neat morning dress, and having placed his document in the hand of the speaker, he bowed and

---

* The roof of the hall of the house of representatives is supported by a noble semicircle of columns of pudding stone. They are highly polished, and have a pleasing no less than a striking effect.

withdrew. It was then decided that the communication should be read.★
There was much interest to hear this document, which always contains a
great outline of the state of the republic. It was a clear, succinct narrative of
what had been done in the course of the past year, of the condition of the

---

★ The instance of a propensity in Europeans to misconstrue the political and moral condition of the United States are numberless. One may be quoted here with propriety. Since
the return of the writer to Europe, he has, on more than one occasion, heard the fact that
the president of the United States sends a message to congress, commented on in a significant manner, as if the circumstance were portentous of some great political change!
"Parliament would scarcely brook a *message,*" said an Englishman, with emphasis, when the
subject was alluded to. The writer saw nothing, at the time, in the thing itself, but the most
perfect simplicity; but, determined to sift the matter to the bottom, he mentioned the subject in a letter to his American friend, and extracts a part of his reply: "I am not at all surprised," said Cadwallader, "that thousands in Europe should easily pervert every possible
circumstance into an evidence of a state of things which they rather desire than seriously
expect. There has not been a single change, however, in all our usages, which goes less to
prove the justness of their anticipations, than the fact you have mentioned. When the government, as it now exists, was first organized, Washington met the two houses and made
his annual communication in a speech. The practice had prevailed in the colonial legislatures. We have never been in a hurry to make unnecessary innovations. Reform marches
with a dignified pace—it is revolution that is violent. The states continued the practice of
the colonies. It was quite natural that the first presidents should conform to existing usages
for a time. We have never been great sticklers for shadows, though no principle is ever listened to that is likely to entail a disadvantage. In the course of a few years, men began to
ask themselves, why does the president make a *speech* at the opening of a session? He sends
messages at all other times, and why not on this occasion? The substance of what he has
to communicate, can be told by a message quite as well as by a speech. The amount of it
all then is, that the parade of a speech is a mere matter of state and show, and although
some little ceremony is, perhaps, necessary, we ought to have as little as possible, since common sense, which is our palladium, is always a sufferer in ceremonies. You will understand
me; a state of society may exist, in which it is good sense to adopt ceremony, but such is
not the case in the year 1827, in the United States of America. Every sage physician adapts
his remedy to the disease. Mr. Jefferson dispensed with speeches, because they did no good,
and might do harm by drawing us nearer to the usages of Europe, when it is so often our
business to recede from them. For my own part, I think it rather better as it is, though it
cannot be a matter of much moment. It is, however, odd enough, that the very usage
which has been adopted for its simplicity and republicanism, should be tortured into a
proof of a directly contrary tendency. It may be a sufficient answer to the remark of your
English friend, 'that the British parliament would be apt to grumble at receiving a message from the king,' to say that should congress not receive one from the president at a
pretty early day in the session, they would be very apt to appoint a committee to inquire
why he had forgotten to lay the state of the nation before them. I am no quarreller about
terms, and I leave you to decide where the substance of things is to be found."

finances, of the several negociations, and concluded with a statement of what the people had a right to anticipate for the future.

When the message was ended, Cadwallader introduced me to several of the members to whom he was personally known. Most of them were men of good manners, and of education, though one or two were certainly individuals who had paid far more attention to the substance of things than to forms. The former were of course of that class of society which, in Europe, would be termed the gentry, and the others were probably farmers, if not mechanics. There was an air of great self-possession and decorum in the latter, nor could the slightest visible difference be traced between the respect which they received, and that which their more polished confederates bestowed on each other. A simple, quiet courtesy is certainly the tone of manners in congress. While we stood together in the lobby, a grave-looking, middle-aged man, of a slightly rustic air, approached, and addressed my companion. His manner was manly and independent, but at the same time decent, and I think it was to be distinguished by a shade of respect. They shook hands, and conversed a little concerning some questions of local politics. Promises were made of exchanging visits. "This is my friend, the ———," said Cadwallader; "a gentleman who is travelling in our country." The stranger saluted me, offering his hand with the utmost simplicity. "If this gentleman comes into our part of the country, I hope to see him," he said, and soon after took his leave. When he was gone, I learned that this individual was a member of congress from the county in which the paternal estates of my friend lie; that he was a farmer of moderate means and good character, whom his fellow citizens had sent to represent them. His constituents might very possibly have made a better choice, and yet this man was not useless, since he served as a check on the schemes of those who would be legislating for effect. A gentleman-like man of sixty came next, and he and my friend met as equals in all respects, except that the latter paid a slight deference to the years of his acquaintance. I was introduced. We touched our hats, and exchanged a few words. The next day, I received this gentleman's card, and as soon as his visit was returned, an invitation to dine in his private lodgings followed. This was Mr. ———, a man of immense hereditary landed estate. His alliances, fortune, and habits, (though tempered by the institutions of his country,) are, to all intents and purposes, the same as those of a gentleman or nobleman in Europe. His character is excellent, and, in consequence, he is now, and may be to the day of his death, the representative of his native district. Here you have the two extremes of the representation of this country—a yeoman, and a great proprietor whose income would put him on a level with most of the great men of our hemisphere. They represent no particular interests, for all interests unite to send them here. They happen to please their constituents, and the fact that the one is a yeoman, and the other a species of lord of the manor, produces no effect whatever. These men meet in congress on terms of perfect equality. It often happens that a yeoman, possessed of a vigorous native mind, has vast influence.

While quitting the capitol, two more members of congress spoke to Cadwallader. They walked with us the whole length of the avenue. One of them was a man of a fashionable air, and of exceedingly good manners. He spoke French, and we conversed together for some time in that tongue. I found him agreeable and intelligent, and was glad to perceive he was disposed to renew the interview. But the other individual puzzled me not a little. In dress and externals he differed but little from his more agreeable companion. His air, however, was not that of a man of the world, and his language was sufficiently provincial to be remarked. I should not have taken him for one of a station in life to be found in such company, did I not know his official rank, and were I not prepared for the great admixture of ordinary American society. But if I was a little perplexed by the provincialisms of this individual, I was not less surprised at his shrewdness and intelligence. He used his words with great discrimination, and with perfect grammatical accuracy; and he spoke not only with good sense, but frequently with power, and always with prodigious clearness. When we parted, I again expressed surprise at the manifest difference in manners that existed between the two members.

"You will begin to know us in time," returned Cadwallader. "Those men are both lawyers. He whose air and language are so unexceptionable, is a member of a family long known in this country for its importance. You see he has not lost, nor will he be likely to let his posterity lose, the manners of the world. He is far from being rich, nor is he remarkable for talent, though rather clever. You find he has a seat in congress. The other is the child of an affluent tradesman, who has given his son an education for the bar, but who could not give him what he had not himself,—a polished exterior. But he is gleaning, and, before he dies, he will be in the way of imparting a better air to his descendants. In this manner is the whole of our community slowly rising in the scale of mere manners. As to talent, this provincial lawyer, for he is provincial in practice as well as by birth, has, as you must have observed, enough of it. He is a good man in congress, whatever he may be in the saloons. He has got the intelligence, and no small part of the feelings of a gentleman; he may never get the air, for he began too late for that, and, like most men, he probably affects to despise an unattainable advantage. But as it is in nature to wish for distinction, rely on it, he is secretly determined to amend. Perhaps one of these parties loses a little by the intimate association which is a necessary consequence of their common situation; but the gradual approximation is, on the whole, produced by the improvement of the other. In the great essentials of soundness of feeling, morals, and common sense, they are quite on an equality."

Vol. II, Letter 4

A continuation of the discussion on the relationship between citizens and their representatives. The focus is on titles within the government and between officials and citizens. Common culture as well as the Constitution have prevented a significant social and political distinction between the ruled and the rulers. The handshake and use of informal titles best exemplify the ideas of republican manhood and the equality of men within politics.

TO THE COUNT JULES DE BéTHIZY.
&c. &c.
Washington, ——

To you, who so stoutly maintain that the regulations of etiquette are necessary to order, it may be surprising to learn with how little of preparation the functionaries of this government get through the ceremonials of their offices. Just so far as etiquette is of use in facilitating intercourse, is it rational; but these people very rightly believe, that their institutions enable them to move on with far less than is practised in Europe. We will seize a moment to discuss the matter in some of its general bearings.

In point of style there is none whatever practised in addressing any one officer of the government. The naked appellation of the office is used in conversation sometimes, and commonly, though not always, in notes and letters. The tone can be taken best from the incumbents themselves. An invitation to dine at the "White House," always runs, "The president requests the pleasure," &c. A secretary commonly says, "Mr. ——— requests, &c." Now, the best style, and that which is expected, is to reply in the same form. Thus a note should be addressed "To Mr. ———," to "the president," "To Mr. Adams, (the secretary of state,)" or "to Mr. Southard (the secretary of the navy)." The use of honourable to either, or indeed to any one else, is not deemed *bon ton*. It is done, however, quite frequently by those who are ignorant of the tone of the place. The use of the terms "excellency" and "honourable," came in with the colonial practices. I have more than once had occasion to say that these people have never been violent in their innovations. The changes in things not deemed material, have always been gradual, and the work of time. Washington, at the head of the army, was called "his excellency," as a matter of course, and he carried the title with him to the chair of state. The colonial governors had the same title, and one of the states (Massachusetts) continued it in its constitution. But, though often observed, even now, it is a practice gradually falling into disuse. It is not seriously pretended there is any thing anti-republican in giving a title to a public officer; indeed many contend it should be done, as a way of imparting more consideration to the rank; but, as near as I can learn, the taste of the nation is silently receding from the custom. Cadwallader tells me that, twenty years ago, it would have been thought rather a breach of politeness to address a letter to a member of congress, without prefixing "honourable" to the name, though the better practice now is to omit it. When I asked him if he saw any reason for the change, he answered, none, but the fact that the thing grew contemptible from its frequency.

"Twenty years ago," he continued, "an officer of the militia, above the rank of captain, was sure of bearing his title; but now, among men of a certain class, it is getting into disuse, unless one has reached the rank perhaps of general. There is no general rule, however, as the people of the country are fond of calling a man by the title of an office which they may have had an agency in conferring. I think there is a quiet waggery in the nation, that takes pleasure in giving quaint names. Thus, dwarfs are often called 'major'*—heaven knows

---

* The writer has just seen an American play-bill, in which Major Stevens, a dwarf, is advertised to enact the part of Tom Thumb. There is also a strange effect, in the way of names, produced by reading. The writer met several men, who were called *Don* Sebastian, *Don* Alonzo, &c. &c. In one instance, he knew a person who was called Lord George Gordon. The latter proceeded from waggery, but the mothers of the former had] found names in books that captivated their fancy. Women of a similar rank of life in Europe, would know but little of titles beyond the limits of their own parishes.

why! but I have met three who all bore this title. I have a gardener, who is universally stiled judge, and an old black family servant is never known by any other name than that of governor. Nicknames are rather too much in use with us. The liberty is not often taken, of course, with men of the better orders. They are much disposed to dispense with all sorts of titles. We call a gentleman an esquire, by courtesy, according to a practice imported from England; though some one-sided masters of ceremonies deny that any but magistrates, counsellors, &c. have a right to the title; just as if even they could find better authority for their claims than any body else. The truth is, the courts continue a few of the colonial forms, which may be well enough, and their officers sometimes think that use has grown into a law. In New England the custom goes so far as to call a deacon of a church by his title; and I have even seen 'serjeant' placed before the name of a respectable yeoman. The practice, as it confines the appellation to the office, is rather republican than otherwise; but, as I have just said, it is getting into disuse, because it is no longer a distinction."

In conversation, the actual president, I find, is called Colonel Monroe. I am told his predecessors were addressed as Mr. Madison, Mr. Jefferson, Mr. Adams, and General Washington.* The secretaries and the members of congress are addressed as other gentlemen. In the two houses, the etiquette is to speak of another member as "the gentleman from Virginia," "the gentleman from Connecticut, who spoke last," and, sometimes, as "the honourable gentleman," &c. The president is commonly alluded to, in debate, as "the executive." Other indirect means of indicating the members meant, are sometimes adopted; but, as in the British parliament, names are always avoided.

No civil officer of the government has a costume, except the judges of the supreme court. The latter wear, in court, plain black silk gowns. They commenced with wigs and scarlet robes, but soon discarded them as inconvenient. The president might, on occasion, appear attired either as a general or an admiral; and, in some instances, Washington did as the former; but it is the usage for the president to dress like any other gentleman, consulting his own taste and appearance. The same is true of the vice-president, of the speaker of the house of representatives, and of all other officers and members. You know there is no order of knighthood in the country. At the

---

* The present president (1828) is called Mr. Adams. The writer never heard the term "excellency" used, in speaking to him or to his predecessor.

close of the war of the revolution, the officers of the army formed themselves into a society called the Society of Cincinnati. They adopted a little enamelled badge, which bears some resemblance to a simple European cross. Even this immaterial distinction gave offence, and some of the state societies were abolished many years ago. The plan was to perpetuate the feeling which had united them as a corps, through their descendants, it being intended that the eldest male heir should succeed to the father. You may trace, in this little circumstance, the lingering of ancient prejudices. Still, had not Washington been at the head of this society, and had not the services of its members been so undeniable, and so pitifully rewarded, this trifling consolation to their pride would not have been endured even at that time. The society is daily getting of less importance, though possibly of more interest, and there is no doubt but it will disappear entirely, with the individuals who were personal actors in the scenes which called it into existence. It is probable there will be no more members of the Cincinnati a dozen years hence.

The constitution has shown a marked jealousy of the introduction of any distinctions that are not solely attached to office, which, as you know, are fluctuating, and entirely dependant on popular favour. Thus, no American can receive a title, or a decoration, from a foreign court, without losing his citizenship; nor can any officer of the government receive even a trifling present from another power. There are a good many people here whose fathers bore titles. In all cases, where use had not become too strong, they were dropped. In short, I think the tone in all such matters in America, is to follow the natural course of things. It is not natural for a community, like this, to cherish hereditary titles, and yet it would be doing violence to usage by attempting to change the appellation of an individual, who had been known by a title for perhaps half a century. The Dutch in New York had a sort of lords of the manor, who were known by the title of patroons (paterons). Cadwallader tells me that, in his youth, he knew several of these patroons. But they have all disappeared, except one. The exception is a gentleman resident at Albany, who is perhaps the greatest landed proprietor in the United States. Every body, who is familiar with the habits of that part of the country, calls this gentleman "the patroon." His father, and several of his ancestors, bore the same appellation. There is not the slightest jealousy or feeling on the subject. He is a member of congress; and though persons from other parts of the Union address him by his real name, my friend always calls him "patroon." The immense estate of this gentleman was entailed, and he came into possession about the time of the revolution. But there are no more entails in any of the states; and although the possessions of the patroon will undoubtedly go to his children, it is more than probable that the appellation will cease with his own life.

The etiquette of the American government is as simple as possible. Some attention to forms is found convenient, and as so many foreign ministers reside here, perhaps it is necessary. The practice of all American society, in respect to precedency, is very much like your own, always excepting the great officers of the two governments. Age, talent, and character, exercise a great and a natural influence, and there, I think, the matter is permitted to rest. A governor of a state, or even a senator of the United States, would be expected to lead the mistress of the house to the table, perhaps, just as a stranger, or a man of particular personal claims, would be permitted to do the same thing. But the deference paid to official rank would be very apt to end there. A mere member of the lower house may receive certain distinctions in public ceremonies, but scarcely in society. It would be intolerable for a son of the president to presume on his birth in any situation. He might, and certainly would be more caressed, on account of the circumstance; but he must always content himself with precisely the degree of attention that is offered. The son of any other gentleman is, in every respect, his equal in society, and the son of any other man his equal before the world. You will understand me to speak now with direct reference to practice, for in theory there is no difference at all.★

★ The writer, since his return to Europe, has had an opportunity of ascertaining how far the question of precedency is sometimes pushed in England. At an entertainment given not long since in London, there were present, besides many Englishmen of rank, a Russian and a Roman Prince. The high-bred English peers could not hesitate to give the *pas* to the strangers; but these gentlemen were delicate in respect of each other. The question was one far too awful for the mistress of the house to attempt to decide. After the whole party had stood in reverential silence for a sufficiently awkward minute, the ladies moved to the banquet in a body, followed by the gentlemen in the same solitary order. Within a fortnight of that memorable *coup d'étiquette,* the writer was present at a similar entertainment at Paris. Here there were also men of distinction from different countries, without any graduated scale to determine their co-relative rank. There was, however, one gentleman whose claims, though a countryman of the hostess, might in all fairness, be considered to be pre-eminent, since, to personal rank, he united the highest talents, and the utmost private merit. The lady of the house, in order to anticipate any doubts, took his arm, and then, with exquisite grace and tact, she saw each of the other claimants accommodated with a proper companion, and every one advanced towards the *salle à manger* in less than a minute.

The present secretary of state* undertook, in great simplicity, to give his opinions lately on some questions of etiquette connected with the subject of official intercourse. There was probably a great deal of good sense in what he published, and no doubt the practices he recommended were not without convenience. But it is generally thought he committed an error in writing about them at all. Now, it is just in this fact that I think the common sense of the Americans is to be traced. Whatever is convenient, in the way of ceremony, they are very apt to adopt; but they are not disposed to make trifles matters of serious discussion. The secretary was a good deal quizzed for his essay, though I dare say most people practised the very thing they laughed at.

At Washington official rank is certainly more attended to than elsewhere. I cannot give you an insight into the whole table of precedency, but some of its secrets have been practically divulged in my presence. The day after our arrival, Cadwallader and myself left cards at the President's House; at the houses of the heads of departments; at those of the foreign ministers; and at the lodgings of a dozen senators. We met sundry members of congress, but my friend did not appear to think it necessary to treat them as personages entitled to particular deference. Their claims form a disputed point, I find; but Cadwallader knows his own foothold in society too well to trouble himself with a disputed point. We called on a few, as "good fellows," but on none officially.

Our cards were all returned, except by the president. During the session this functionary never visits, though he receives twice a-week. Between the sessions, when the society of Washington is reduced to a very few families, I understand he consults his own pleasure. In the course of the week we received notes to attend the "evenings" of those who opened their houses; and invitations to dine with the secretaries soon followed. The dinner of the president came last; but as it contains the essence of all the etiquette of this simple court, I shall select it for a short description.

Cadwallader was personally known to Mr. Monroe (the president), and we took an opportunity to repeat our call between the time of leaving our cards and the day of the dinner. The principal entrance of the "White House" communicates with a spacious vestibule, or rather a hall. From this

---

* The actual president.

we passed into an apartment, where those who visit the president, in the mornings, are to wait their turns for the interview. Our names had been given in at the door, and after two or three, who preceded us, had been admitted, we were desired to follow the domestic. Our reception was in a cabinet, and the visit of course quite short. Colonel Monroe received us politely, but with an American gravity, which perhaps was not misplaced in such an officer. He offered his hand to me, though an entire stranger, and asked the common-place questions concerning my visit to the country. We took our leave in less than ten minutes.

I found the president a man of a gentlemanlike, but of a grave and simple deportment. He expressed his hope of seeing us soon again, in a way to make me suspect we had rather been invited to his dinner, as a matter of course, than by any express commands. Let that be as it might, we went on the appointed day, with as much confidence as if the banquet were expressly spread in our behalf.

On this occasion we were honoured with the presence of Mrs. Monroe, and of two or three of her female relatives. Crossing the hall, we were admitted to a drawing room, in which most of the company was already assembled. The hour was six. By far the greater part of the guests were men, and perhaps two-thirds were members of congress. It is unnecessary to describe a company that was composed of a very fair representation of congress, which, as you already know, is composed of a very fair representation of the whole country, the very lowest classes always excepted. There was great gravity of mien in most of the company, and neither any very marked exhibition, nor any positively striking want, of grace of manner. The conversation was common-place, and a little sombre, though two or three men of the world got around the ladies, where the battle of words was maintained with sufficient spirit. I do not know that it differed materially from a reunion any where else. To me the entertainment had rather a cold than a formal air. When dinner was announced, the oldest senator present (there were two, and seniority of service is meant) took Mrs. Monroe and led her to the table.* The rest of the party followed without much order. The president took a lady, as usual, and preceded the rest of the guests.

The drawing room was an apartment of a good size, and of just

---

* The wife of the president is always styled the same as any other lady.

proportions. It might have been about as large as a better sort of Paris *salon,* in a private hotel. It was furnished in a mixed style, partly English, and partly French, a custom that prevails a good deal in all the fashions of this country. It was neat, sufficiently rich, without being at all magnificent, and, on the whole, was very much like a similar apartment in the house of a man of rank and fortune in Europe. The dining room was in a better taste than is common here, being quite simple, and but little furnished. The table was large and rather handsome. The service was in china, as is uniformly the case, plate being exceedingly rare, if at all used. There was, however, a rich plateau, and a great abundance of the smaller articles of table plate. The cloth, napkins, &c. &c., were fine and beautiful.

The dinner was served in the French style, a little Americanized. The dishes were handed round, though some of the guests, appearing to prefer their own customs, very coolly helped themselves, to what they found at hand. Of attendants there were a good many. They were neatly dressed, out of livery, and sufficient. To conclude, the whole entertainment might have passed for a better sort of European dinner party, at which the guests were too numerous for general, or very agreeable discourse, and some of them too *new* to be entirely at their ease. Mrs. Monroe arose at the end of the dessert, and withdrew, attended by two or three of the most gallant of the company. Being a stranger, Jules, I forgot the credit of the club, and remained to see it out. No sooner was his wife's back turned, than the president of the United States reseated himself, inviting his guests to imitate the action, with a wave of the hand, that seemed to say, "Now have we a matrimonial fourth of July." Has it never struck you, Comte de Béthizy, that these domestic subjects feel a species of momentary triumph, as they figure at the head of their tables without any rival in authority near? Your Englishman, and his cis-atlantic kinsman, are the only real slaves in their own households. Most other husbands consider matrimony, more or less, a convenience; but these downright moralists talk of its obligations and duties. Obligations! There is our triumph. It is when they feel the man within them waxing bold, as they imbibe courage with their wine, that the wife prudently retires, rather than remain to dispute a sway that she knows is about to weaken itself, by libations to victory. I never feel so thoroughly independent as when I see one of your immoderately hen-pecked heroes, bristling up and chuckling with glee as he looks around on the domestic throne which has just been momentarily abandoned by her who is seated there all the rest of the twenty-four hours. No one need seek deeper into the history of customs, than the date of this triumph, to find the origin of drunkenness after dinner.

I cannot say that Colonel Monroe abused his opportunity. After allowing all his guests sufficient time to renew, in a few glasses, the recollections of similar enjoyments of their own, he arose himself, giving the hint to his company, that it was time to join the ladies. In the drawing-room coffee was served, and every body left the house before nine.

On the succeeding Wednesday, Mrs. Monroe opened her doors to all the world. No invitation was necessary, it being the usage for the wife of the president to receive once a-fortnight during the session, without distinction of persons. I waited for this evening with more curiosity than any that I remember ever to have sighed for. I could not imagine what would be the result. To my fancy, a more hazardous experiment could not be attempted. "How dare she risk the chance of insult—of degradation? or how can she tolerate the vulgarity and coarseness to which she must be exposed?" was the question I put to Cadwallader. *"Nous verrons,"* was the phlegmatic answer.

We reached the White House at nine. The court (or rather the grounds,) was filled with carriages, and the company was arriving in great numbers. On this occasion two or three additional drawing-rooms were opened, though the frugality of congress has prevented them from finishing the principal reception-room of the building.* I will acknowledge the same sort of surprise that I felt at the Castle Garden fête, at finding the assemblage so respectable, in air, dress, and deportment. Determined to know exactly in what view to consider this ceremony, I gave my companion no peace until every thing was explained.

The "evening" at the White House, or the drawing-room, as it is sometimes pleasantly called, is in fact a collection of all classes of people who choose to go to the trouble and expense of appearing in dresses suited to an ordinary evening party. I am not sure that even dress is much regarded; for I certainly saw a good many men there in boots. The females were all neatly and properly attired, though few were ornamented with jewelry. Of

---

* The people furnish the entire house. It is the practice to make a moderate appropriation for that purpose, at the accession of each new president.

course the poorer and labouring classes of the community would find lit-tle or no pleasure in such a scene. They consequently stay away. The infa-mous, if known, would not be admitted; for it is a peculiar consequence of the high tone of morals in this country, that grave and notorious offenders rarely presume to violate the public feeling by invading society. Perhaps if Washington were a large town, the "evenings" could not exist; but as it is, no inconvenience is experienced.

Squeezing through the crowd, we achieved a passage to a part of the room where Mrs. Monroe was standing, surrounded by a bevy of female friends. After making our bows here, we sought the president. The latter had posted himself at the top of the room, where he remained most of the evening, shaking hands with all who approached.★ Near him stood all the secretaries, and a great number of the most distinguished men of the nation. Cadwallader pointed out the different judges, and several members of both houses of congress, whose reputations were quite familiar to me. Individu-als of importance from all parts of the Union were also here, and were employed in the manner usual to such scenes. Thus far the "evening" would have been like any other excessively crowded assembly; but while my eyes were roving over the different faces, they accidentally fell on one they knew. It was the master of an inn, in one of the larger towns. My friend and myself had passed a fortnight in his house. I pointed him out to Cadwal-lader, and I am afraid there was something like an European sneer in my manner as I did so.

"Yes, I have just shaken hands with him," returned my friend, coolly. "He keeps an excellent tavern, you must allow; and, what is more, had not that circumstance been the means of your making his acquaintance, you might have mistaken him for one of the magnates of the land. I understand your look, Count de ——, better than you understand the subject at which

---

★ It is a mistaken opinion, however, that shaking hands is a custom not to be dispensed with in America. Most people practise it certainly, for it is thought to be a frank, manly, and, if you will, a republican usage. But, in a certain class, it is not considered a mark of breeding to be too free with the hand, in casual introductions. Two gentlemen meeting would be apt to touch their hats (unless intimates) just as in Europe, though either of them would offer his hand to any one who he thought expected it. When an European, therefore, offers to shake hands with an American of breeding, unless on familiar terms, he mistakes the manners of the country. The natural feeling of gentlemanly reserve is the guide there, as it is with us.

you are smiling. Fancy, for a moment, that this assembly were confined to a hundred or two, like those eminent men you see collected in that corner, and to these beautiful and remarkably delicate women you see standing near us; in what, except name, would it be inferior to the best collections of your side of the ocean? You need not apologize, for we understand one another perfectly. I know Europe rather better than you know America, for the simple reason, that one part of Europe is so much like another, that it is by no means an abstruse study, so far as mere manners are concerned; whereas, in America, there exists a state of things that is entirely new. We will make the comparison, not in the way you are at this moment employed in doing, but in the way common sense dictates.

"It is very true that you meet here a great variety of people of very many conditions of life. This person you see on my left is a shopkeeper from New York: no—not the one in black, but the genteel-looking man in blue—I dare say you took him for an *attaché* of one of the legations. And this lovely creature, who demeans herself with so much elegance and propriety, is the daughter of a mechanic of Baltimore. In this manner we might dissect half the company, perhaps; some being of better, and some of worse, exteriors. But what does it all prove? Not that the president of the United States is obliged to throw open his doors to the rabble, as you might be tempted to call it, for he is under no sort of obligation to open his doors to any body. But he chooses to see the world, and he must do one of two things. He must make invidious and difficult selections, which, in a public man, would excite just remarks in a government like ours, or he must run the hazard of remaining three or four hours in a room filled with a promiscuous assembly. He has wisely chosen the latter.

"What is the consequence? Your ears are not offended by improper discourse. Your individuality is not wounded by impertinence, nor even your taste annoyed by any very striking coarseness of manner. Now it appears to me, that every American should exult in this very exhibition. Not for the vulgar reason that it is a proof of the equality of our rights, for it is a mistake to think that society is a necessary dependant of government. In this respect the 'evenings' are some such deception as that ceremony one hears of in Europe, in which sovereigns wash the feet of beggars. But he should exult that the house of his first magistrate can be thrown open to the world, and an assembly so well behaved, so decent, so reasonable, so free alike from sheepishness and presumption, in short so completely creditable, in every point of view, is collected by the liberty. Open the doors of one of your palaces in this manner, and let us see what would be the character of the company.

"There is a good sense in our community, which removes all dangers of unpleasant consequences from too much familiarity. It imposes the necessity on him who would be thought a gentleman, of being circumspect and reasonable, but it leaves him sufficiently the master of all his movements and associations. The seeming scarcity of high bred men in this country, compared with the number one sees in Europe, is much less owing to our form of government, than the fact that they are so widely scattered. Quite half, too, of what is called fastidious breeding, is purely conventional, and, to make conventions, men must meet.

"I have known a cartman leave his horse in the street, and go into a reception room to shake hands with the president. He offended the good sense of all present, because it was not thought decent that a labourer should come in a dirty dress on such an occasion; but while he made a trifling mistake in this particular, he proved how well he understood the difference between government and society. He knew the levee was a sort of homage paid to political equality in the person of the first magistrate, but he would not have presumed to enter the house of the same person as a private individual without being invited, or without a reasonable excuse in the way of business.

"There are, no doubt, individuals who mistake the character of these assemblies, but the great majority do not. They are simply a periodical acknowledgment that there is no legal barrier to the advancement of any one to the first association in the Union. You perceive there are no masters of ceremonies, no ushers, no announcing, nor indeed any let or hindrance to the ingress of all who please to come; and yet how few, in comparison to the whole number who might enter, do actually appear. If there is any man, in Washington, so dull as to suppose equality means a right to thrust himself into any company he pleases, it is probable he satisfies his vanity by boasting that he can go to the White House once a fortnight as well as a governor or any body else. You will confess his pride is appeased at a cheap rate. Any prince can collect a well dressed and well behaved crowd by calling his nobles around him; but I fancy the president of the United States is the only head of a nation who need feel no apprehension of throwing open his doors

to every body. Until you can show an assembly composed of similar materials, which shall equal this, not only in decency, but in ease and in general
manners, you ought in reason to be content to confess your inferiority."

You will perceive the utter impossibility of having an opinion of your
own, dear Jules, when a man is obstinately bent on considering things
always in reference to common sense, instead of consulting the reverend
usages which have been established by the world, whether founded on
prejudice or not. So far as mere appearance goes, I must confess, however,
my friend was not very wrong, since the company at the White House, on
this occasion, was certainly as well behaved, all things considered, as could
be wished.

VOL. II, LETTER 6

Cooper discusses the importance of printers, colleges, and writers to the creation of a distinct American culture. While America is doing well regarding the former two, good writers have yet to appear on the cultural scene. If they do, printers and publishers, knowing they can make more money by selling European novels, rarely give the natives a chance. Additionally, the newness of America and the integrity of most Americans combine to reduce in American social life the frequency of highly dramatic events, which are necessary for the genre.

TO THE ABBATE GIROMACHI,
&c. &c.
FLORENCE.
Washington, ——

You ask me to write freely on the subject of the literature and the arts of the United States. The subjects are so meagre as to render it a task that would require no small portion of the talents necessary to figure in either, in order to render them of interest. Still, as the request has come in so urgent a form, I shall endeavour to oblige you.

The Americans have been placed, as respects moral and intellectual advancement, different from all other infant nations. They have never been without the wants of civilization, nor have they ever been entirely without the means of a supply. Thus pictures, and books, and statuary, and every thing else which appertains to elegant life, have always been known to them in an abundance, and of a quality exactly proportioned to their cost. Books, being the cheapest, and the nation having great leisure and prodigious zest for information, are not only the most common, as you will readily suppose, but they are probably more common than among any other people. I scarcely remember ever to have entered an American dwelling, however humble, without finding fewer or more books. As they form the most essential division of the subject, not only on account of their greater frequency, but on account of their far greater importance, I shall give them the first notice in this letter.

Unlike the progress of the two professions in the countries of our hemisphere, in America the printer came into existence before the author. Reprints of English works gave the first employment to the press. Then came almanacks, psalm-books, religious tracts, sermons, journals, political essays, and even rude attempts at poetry. All these preceded the revolution. The first journal was established in Boston at the commencement of the last century. There are several original polemical works of great originality and power that belong to the same period. I do not know that more learning and talents existed at that early day in the states of New England than in Virginia, Maryland and the Carolinas, but there was certainly a stronger desire to exhibit them.

The colleges or universities, as they were somewhat prematurely called, date very far back in the brief history of the country. There is no stronger evidence of the intellectual character, or of the judicious ambition of these people, than what this simple fact furnishes. Harvard College, now the university of Cambridge—(it better deserves the title at this day)—was founded in 1638; within less than *twenty years* after the landing of the first settlers in New England! Yale (in Connecticut) was founded in 1701. Columbia (in the city of New York) was founded in 1754. Nassau Hall (in New Jersey) in 1738; and William and Mary (in Virginia) as far back as 1691. These are the oldest literary institutions in the United States, and all but the last are in flourishing conditions to the present hour. The first has given degrees to about five thousand graduates, and rarely has less than three hundred and fifty or four hundred students. Yale is about as well attended. The others contain from a hundred and fifty to two hundred under-graduates. But these are not a moiety of the present colleges, or universities, (as they all aspire to be called,) existing in the country. There is no state, except a few of the newest, without at least one, and several have two or three.

Less attention is paid to classical learning here than in Europe; and, as the term of residence rarely exceeds four years, profound scholars are by no means common. This country possesses neither the population nor the endowments to maintain a large class of learned idlers, in order that one man in a hundred may contribute a mite to the growing stock of general knowledge. There is a luxury in this expenditure of animal force, to which the Americans have not yet attained. The good is far too problematical and remote, and the expense of man too certain, to be prematurely sought. I have heard, I will confess, an American legislator quote Horace and Cicero; but it is far from being the humour of the country. I thought the taste of the orator questionable. A learned quotation is rarely of any use in an argument, since few men are fools enough not to see that the application of any maxim to politics is liable to a thousand practical objections, and, nine times in ten, they are evidences of the want of a direct, natural, and vigorous train of thought. They are the affectations, but rarely the ebullitions of true talent. When a man feels strongly, or thinks strongly, or speaks strongly, he is just as apt to do it in his native tongue as he is to laugh when he is tickled, or to weep when in sorrow. The Americans are strong speakers and acute thinkers, but no great quoters of the morals and axioms of a heathen age, because they happen to be recorded in Latin.

The higher branches of learning are certainly on the advance in this country. The gentlemen of the middle and southern states, before the revolution, were very generally educated in Europe, and they were consequently, in this particular, like our own people. Those who came into life during the struggle, and shortly after, fared worse. Even the next generation had little to boast of in the way of instruction. I find that boys entered the colleges so late as the commencement of the present century, who had read a part of the Greek Testament, and a few books of Cicero and Virgil, with perhaps a little of Horace. But great changes have been made, and are still making, in the degree of previous qualification.

Still, it would be premature to say that there is any one of the American universities where classical knowledge, or even science is profoundly attained, even at the present day. Some of the professors push their studies, for a life, certainly; and you well know, after all, that little short of a life, and a long one too, will make any man a good general scholar. In 1820, near eight thousand graduates of the twelve oldest colleges of this country (according to their catalogues) were then living. Of this number, 1,406 were clergymen. As some of the catalogues consulted were several years old, this number was, of necessity, greatly within the truth. Between the years 1800 and 1810, it is found that of 2,792 graduates, four hundred and fifty-three became clergymen. Here is pretty good evidence that religion is not neglected in America, and that its ministers are not, as a matter of course, absolutely ignorant.

But the effects of the literary institutions of the United States are somewhat peculiar. Few men devote their lives to scholarship. The knowledge that is actually acquired, is perhaps quite sufficient for the more practical and useful pursuits. Thousands of young men, who have read the more familiar classics, who have gone through enough of mathematics to obtain a sense of their own tastes, and of the value of precision, who have cultivated *belles lettres* to a reasonable extent, and who have been moderately instructed in the arts of composition, and in the rules of taste, are given forth to the country to mingle in its active employments. I am inclined to believe that a class of American graduates carries away with it quite as much general and diversified knowledge, as a class from one of our own universities. The excellence in particular branches is commonly wanting; but the deficiency is more than supplied by variety of information. The youth who has passed four years within the walls of a college, goes into the office of a lawyer for a few more. The profession of the law is not subdivided in America. The same man is counsellor, attorney, and conveyancer. Here the student gets a general insight into the principles, and a familiarity with the practice of the law, rather than an acquaintance with the study as a science. With this instruction he enters the world as a practitioner. Instead of existing in a state of dreaming retrospection, lost in a maze of theories, he is at once turned loose into the jostlings of the world. If perchance he encounters an antagonist a little more erudite than himself, he seizes the natural truth for his sheet anchor, and leaves precedent and quaint follies to him who has made them his study and delight. No doubt he often blunders, and is frequently, of necessity, defeated. But in the course of this irreverent treatment, usages and opinions, which are bottomed in no better foundation than antiquity, and which are as inapplicable to the present state of the world, as the present state of the world is, or ought to be, unfavourable to all feudal absurdities, come to receive their death warrants. In the mean time, by dint of sheer experience, and by the collision of intellects, the practitioner gets a stock of learning, that is acquired in the best possible school; and, what is of far more importance, the laws themselves get a dress which brings them within the fashions of the day. This same man becomes a legislator perhaps, and, if particularly clever, he is made to take an active part in the framing of laws that are not to harmonize with the other parts of an elaborate theory, but which are intended to make men comfortable and happy. Now, taken with more or less qualification, this is the history of thousands in this country, and it is also an important part of the history of the country itself.

In considering the course of instruction in the United States, you are always to commence at the foundation. The common schools, which so generally exist, have certainly elevated the population above that of any other country, and are still elevating it higher, as they improve and increase in numbers. Law is getting every day to be more of a science, but it is a science that is forming rules better adapted to the spirit of the age. Medicine is improving, and in the cities it is, perhaps now, in point of practice, quite on a level with that of Europe. Indeed, the well-educated American physician very commonly enjoys an advantage that is little known in Europe. After obtaining a degree in his own country, he passes a few years in London, Edinburgh, Paris, and frequently in Germany, and returns with his gleanings from their several schools. This is not the case with one individual, but with many, annually. Indeed, there is so much of a fashion in it, and the custom is attended by so many positive advantages, that its neglect would be a serious obstacle to any very eminent success. Good operators are by no means scarce, and as surgery and medicine are united in the same person, there is great judgment in their practice. Human life is something more valuable in America than in Europe, and I think a critical attention to patients more common here than with us, especially when the sufferer belongs to an inferior condition in life. The profession is highly respectable; and in all parts of the country the better sort of its practitioners mingle, on terms of perfect equality, with the highest classes of society. There are several physicians in congress, and a great many in the different state legislatures.

Of the ministry it is unnecessary to speak. The clergy are of all denominations, and they are educated, or not, precisely as they belong to sects which consider the gift of human knowledge of any importance. You have already seen how large a proportion of the graduates of some of the colleges enter the desk.

As respects authorship, there is not much to be said. Compared to the books that are printed and read, those of native origin are few indeed. The principal reason of this poverty of original writers, is owing to the circumstance that men are not yet driven to their wits for bread. The United States are the first nation that possessed institutions, and, of course, distinctive opinions of its own, that was ever dependant on a foreign people for its literature. Speaking the same language as the English, and long in the habit of importing their books from the mother country, the revolution effected no immediate change in the nature of their studies, or mental amusements. The works were reprinted, it is true, for the purposes of economy, but they still continued English. Had the latter nation used this powerful engine with tolerable address, I think they would have secured such an ally in this country as would have rendered their own decline not only more secure, but as illustrious as had been their rise. There are many theories entertained as to the effect produced in this country by the falsehoods and jealous calumnies which have been undeniably uttered in the mother country, by means of the press, concerning her republican descendant. It is my own opinion that, like all other ridiculous absurdities, they have defeated themselves, and that they are now more laughed at and derided, even here, than resented. By all that I can learn, twenty years ago, the Americans were, perhaps, far too much disposed to receive the opinions and to adopt the prejudices of their relatives; whereas, I think it is very apparent that they are now beginning to receive them with singular distrust. It is not worth our while to enter further into this subject, except as it has had, or is likely to have, an influence on the national literature.★

It is quite obvious, that, so far as taste and forms alone are concerned, the literature of England and that of America must be fashioned after the same models. The authors, previously to the revolution, are common

---

★ The writer might give, in proof of this opinion, one fact. He is led to believe that, so lately as within ten years, several English periodical works were re-printed, and much read in the United States, and that now they patronize their own, while the former are far less sought, though the demand, by means of the increased population, should have been nearly doubled. Some of the works are no longer even re-printed.

property, and it is quite idle to say that the American has not just as good a right to claim Milton, and Shakspeare, and all the old masters of the language, for his countrymen, as an Englishman. The Americans having continued to cultivate, and to cultivate extensively, an acquaintance with the writers of the mother country, since the separation, it is evident they must have kept pace with the trifling changes of the day. The only peculiarity that can, or ought to be expected in their literature, is that which is connected with the promulgation of their distinctive political opinions. They have not been remiss in this duty, as any one may see, who chooses to examine their books. But we will devote a few minutes to a more minute account of the actual condition of American literature.

The first, and the most important, though certainly the most familiar branch of this subject, is connected with the public journals. It is not easy to say how many newspapers are printed in the United States. The estimated number varies from six hundred to a thousand. In the State of New York there are more than fifty counties. Now, it is rare that a county, in a state as old as that of New York (especially in the more northern parts of the country), does not possess one paper at least. The cities have many. The smaller towns sometimes have three or four, and very many of the counties four or five. There cannot be many less than one hundred and fifty journals in the state of New York alone. Pennsylvania is said to possess eighty. But we will suppose that these two states publish two hundred journals. They contain about 3,000,000 of inhabitants. As the former is an enlightened state, and the latter rather below the scale of the general intelligence of the nation, it may not be a very bad average of the whole population. This rate would give eight hundred journals for the United States, which is probably something within the truth. I confess, however, this manner of equalizing estimates in America, is very uncertain in general, since a great deal, in such a question, must depend on the progress of society in each particular section of the country.

As might be expected, there is nearly every degree of merit to be found in these journals. No one of them has the benefit of that collected talent which is so often enlisted in the support of the more important journals of Europe. There is not often more than one editor to the best; but he is usually some man who has seen, in his own person, enough of men and things to enable him to speak with tolerable discretion on passing events. The usefulness of the American journals, however, does not consist in their giving the tone to the public mind, in politics and morals, but in imparting facts. It is certain that, could the journals agree, they might, by their united efforts, give a powerful inclination to the common will. But, in point of fact, they do not agree on any one subject or set of subjects, except, perhaps, on those which directly affect their own interests. They, consequently, counteract, instead of aiding each other, on all points of disputed policy; and it is in the bold and sturdy discussions that follow, that men arrive at the truth. The occasional union in their own favour, is a thing too easily seen through to do either good or harm. So far, then, from the journals succeeding in leading the public opinion astray, they are invariably obliged to submit to it. They serve to keep it alive, by furnishing the means for its expression, but they rarely do more. Of course, the influence of each particular press is in proportion to the constancy and the ability with which it is found to support what is thought to be sound principles; but those principles must be in accordance with the private opinions of men, or most of their labour is lost.

The public press in America is rather more decent than that of England, and less decorous than that of France. The tone of the nation, and the respect for private feelings, which are, perhaps, in some measure, the consequence of a less artificial state of society, produce the former; and the liberty, which is a necessary attendant of fearless discussion, is, I think, the cause of the latter. The affairs of an individual are rarely touched upon in the journals of this country; never, unless it is thought they have a direct connection with the public interests, or from a wish to do him good. Still there is a habit, getting into use in America, no less than in France, that is borrowed from the English, which proves that the more unworthy feelings of our nature are common to men under all systems, and only need opportunity to find encouragement. I allude to the practice of repeating the proceedings of the courts of justice, in order to cater to a vicious appetite for amusement in the public.

It is pretended that, as a court of justice is open to the world, there can be no harm in giving the utmost publicity to its proceedings. It is strange the courts should act so rigidly on the principle, that it is better a dozen guilty men should go free, than that one innocent man should suffer, and yet permit the gross injustice that is daily done by means of this practice.

One would think, that if a court of justice is so open to the world, that it should be the business of the people of the world to enter it, in order that they might be certain that the information they crave should be without colouring or exaggeration. It is idle to say that the reports are accurate, and that he who reads is enabled to do justice to the accused, by comparing the facts that are laid before him. A reporter may give the expression of the tongue; but can he convey that of the eye, of the countenance, or of the form?—without regarding all of which no man is perfectly master of the degree of credibility that is due to any witness of whose character he is necessarily ignorant. But every man has an infallible means of assuring himself of the value of these reports. Who has ever read a dozen of them without meeting with one (or perhaps more), in which the decision of the court and jury is to him a matter of surprise? It is true he assumes, that those who were present knew best, and as he has no great interest in the matter, he is commonly satisfied. But how is it with the unfortunate man who is wrongfully brought out of his retirement to repel an unjust attack against his person, his property, or his character? If he be a man of virtue, he is a man of sensibility; and not only he, but, what is far worse, those tender beings, whose existence is wrapped up in his own, are to be wounded daily and hourly, for weeks at a time, in order that a depraved appetite should be glutted. It is enough for justice that her proceedings should be so public as to prevent the danger of corruption; but we pervert a blessing to a curse, in making that which was intended for our protection, the means of so much individual misery. It is an unavoidable evil of the law that it necessarily works some wrong, in order to do much good; but it is cruel that even the acquittal of a man should be unnecessarily circulated, in a manner to make all men remember that he had been accused. We have proof of the consequences of this practice in England. Men daily shrink from resistance to base frauds, rather than expose themselves to the observatious and comments of those who enliven their breakfasts by sporting with these exhibitions of their fellow creatures. There are, undoubtedly, cases of that magnitude which require some sacrifice of private feelings, in order that the community should reap the advantage; but the regular books are sufficient for authorities—the decisions of the courts are sufficient for justice—and the utmost possible oblivion should prove as nearly sufficient as may be to serve the ends of a prudent and a righteous humanity.

Nothing can be more free than the press of this country, on all subjects connected with politics. Treason cannot be written, unless by communicating with an open enemy. There is no other protection to a public man than that which is given by an independent jury, which punishes, of course, in proportion to the dignity and importance of the injured party. But the utmost lenity is always used in construing the right of the press to canvass the public acts of public men. Mere common place charges defeat themselves, and get into discredit so soon as to be lost, while graver accusations are met by grave replies. There is no doubt that the complacency of individuals is sometimes disturbed by these liberties; but they serve to keep the officers of the government to their work, while they rarely do any lasting, or even temporary injury. Serious and criminal accusations against a public man, if groundless, are, by the law of reason, a crime against the community, and, as such, they are punished. The general principle observed in these matters is very simple. If A. accuse B. of an act that is an offence against law, he may be called on for his proof, and if he fail he must take the consequences. But an editor of a paper, or any one else, who should bring a criminal charge, no matter how grave, against the president, and who could prove it, is just as certain of doing it with impunity, as if he held the whole power in his own hands. He would be protected by the invincible shield of public opinion, which is not only in consonance with the law, but which, in this country, makes law.

Actions for injuries done by the press, considering the number of journals, are astonishingly rare in America. When one remembers the usual difficulty of obtaining legal proof, which is a constant temptation, even to the guilty, to appeal to the courts; and, on the other hand, the great freedom of the press, which is a constant temptation to abuse the trust, this fact, in itself, furnishes irresistible evidence of the general tone of decency which predominates in this nation. The truth is, that public opinion, among its other laws, has imperiously prescribed that, amidst the utmost latitude of discussion, certain limits shall not be passed; and public opinion, which is so completely the offspring of a free press, must be obeyed in this, as well as in other matters.

Leaving the journals, we come to those publications which make their appearance periodically. Of these there are a good many, some few of which are well supported. There are several scientific works, that are printed monthly, or quarterly, of respectable merit, and four or five reviews. Magazines of a more general character are not much encouraged. England, which is teeming with educated men, who are glad to make their bread by writing for these works, still affords too strong a competition for the success of any American attempts, in this species of literature. Though few, perhaps no English magazine is actually republished in America, a vast number are imported and read in the towns, where the support for any similar original production must first be found.

The literature of the United States has, indeed, too powerful obstacles to conquer before (to use a mercantile expression) it can ever enter the markets of its own country on terms of perfect equality with that of England. Solitary and individual works of genius may, indeed, be occasionally brought to light, under the impulses of the high feeling which has conceived them; but, I fear, a good, wholesome, profitable, and continued pecuniary support is the applause that talent most craves. The fact, that an American publisher can get an English work without money, must, for a few years longer (unless legislative protection shall be extended to their own authors), have a tendency to repress a national literature. No man will pay a writer for an epic, a tragedy, a sonnet, a history, or a romance, when he can get a work of equal merit for nothing. I have conversed with those who are conversant on the subject, and, I confess, I have been astonished at the information they imparted.

A capital American publisher has assured me that there are not a dozen writers in this country, whose works he should feel confidence in publishing at all, while he reprints hundreds of English books without the least hesitation. This preference is by no means so much owing to any difference in merit, as to the fact that, when the price of the original author is to be added to the uniform hazard which accompanies all literary speculations, the risk becomes too great. The general taste of the reading world in this country is better than that of England.* The fact is both proved and explained by the circumstance that thousands of works that are printed and read in the mother country, are not printed and read here. The publisher on

---

* The writer does not mean that the best taste of America is better than that of England; perhaps it is not quite so good; but, as a whole, the American reading world requires better books than the whole of the English reading world.

this side of the Atlantic has the advantage of seeing the reviews of every book he wishes to print, and, what is of far more importance, he knows, with the exception of books that he is sure of selling, by means of a name, the decision of the English critics before he makes his choice. Nine times in ten, popularity, which is all he looks for, is a sufficient test of general merit. Thus, while you find every English work of character, or notoriety, on the shelves of an American book-store, you may ask in vain for most of the trash that is so greedily devoured in the circulating libraries of the mother country, and which would be just as eagerly devoured here, had not a better taste been created by a compelled abstinence. That taste must now be overcome before such works could be sold at all.

When I say that books are not rejected here, from any want of talent in the writers, perhaps I ought to explain. I wish to express something a little different. Talent is sure of too many avenues to wealth and honours, in America, to seek, unnecessarily, an unknown and hazardous path. It is better paid in the ordinary pursuits of life, than it would be likely to be paid by an adventure in which an extraordinary and skilful, because practised, foreign competition is certain. Perhaps high talent does not often make the trial with the American bookseller; but it is precisely for the reason I have named.

The second obstacle against which American literature has to contend is in the poverty of materials. There is scarcely an ore which contributes to the wealth of the author, that is found, here, in veins as rich as in Europe. There are no annals for the historian; no follies (beyond the most vulgar and common place) for the satirist; no manners for the dramatist; no obscure fictions for the writer of romance; no gross and hardy offences against decorum for the moralist; nor any of the rich artificial auxiliaries of poetry. The weakest hand can extract a spark from the flint, but it would baffle the strength of a giant to attempt kindling a flame with a pudding stone. I very well know there are theorists who assume that the society and institutions of this country are, or ought to be, particularly favourable to novelties and variety. But the experience of one month, in these states, is sufficient to show any observant man the falsity of their position. The effect of a promiscuous assemblage any where, is to create a standard of deportment; and great liberty permits every one to aim at its attainment. I have never seen a nation so much alike in my life, as the people of the United States, and what is more, they are not only like each other, but they are remarkably like that which common sense tells them they ought to resemble. No doubt, traits of character that are a little peculiar, without, however, being either very poetical, or very rich, are to be found in remote districts; but they are rare, and not always happy exceptions. In short, it is not possible to conceive a state of society in which more of the attributes of plain good sense, or fewer of the artificial absurdities of life, are to be found, than here. There is no costume for the peasant, (there is scarcely a peasant at all,) no wig for the judge, no baton for the general, no diadem for the chief magistrate. The darkest ages of their history are illuminated by the light of truth; the utmost efforts of their chivalry are limited by the laws of God; and even the deeds of their sages and heroes are to be sung in a language that would differ but little from a version of the ten commandments. However useful and respectable all this may be in actual life, it indicates but one direction to the man of genius.

It is very true there are a few young poets now living in this country, who have known how to extract sweets from even these wholesome, but scentless native plants. They have, however, been compelled to seek their inspiration in the universal laws of nature, and they have succeeded, precisely in proportion as they have been most general in their application. Among these gifted young men, there is one (Halleck) who is remarkable for an exquisite vein of ironical wit, mingled with a fine, poetical, and, frequently, a lofty expression. This gentleman commenced his career as a satirist in one of the journals of New York. Heaven knows, his materials were none of the richest; and yet the melody of his verse, the quaintness and force of his comparisons, and the exceeding humour of his strong points, brought him instantly into notice. He then attempted a general satire, by giving the history of the early days of a *belle*. He was again successful, though every body, at least every body of any talent, felt that he wrote in leading-strings. But he happened, shortly after the appearance of the little volume just named (Fanny), to visit England. Here his spirit was properly excited, and, probably on a rainy day, he was induced to try his hand at a *jeu d'esprit,* in the mother country. The result was one of the finest semi-heroic ironical descriptions to be found in the English language.* This simple fact, in itself, proves the truth of a great deal of what I have just been

---

* This little *morceau* of pleasant irony is called Alnwick Castle.

writing, since it shews the effect a superiority of material can produce on the efforts of a man of true genius.

Notwithstanding the difficulties of the subject, talent has even done more than in the instance of Mr. Halleck. I could mention several other young poets of this country of rare merit. By mentioning Bryant, Percival, and Sprague, I shall direct your attention to the names of those whose works would be most likely to give you pleasure. Unfortunately they are not yet known in Italian, but I think even you would not turn in distaste from the task of translation which the best of their effusions will invite.

The next, though certainly an inferior branch of imaginative writing, is fictitious composition. From the facts just named, you cannot expect that the novelists, or romance writers of the United States, should be very successful. The same reason will be likely, for a long time to come, to repress the ardour of dramatic genius. Still, tales and plays are no novelties in the literature of this country. Of the former, there are many as old as soon after the revolution; and a vast number have been published within the last five years. One of their authors of romance, who curbed his talents by as few allusions as possible to actual society, is distinguished for power and comprehensiveness of thought. I remember to have read one of his books (Wieland) when a boy, and I take it to be a never-failing evidence of genius, that, amid a thousand similar pictures which have succeeded, the images it has left still stand distinct and prominent in my recollection. This author (Mr. Brockden Brown) enjoys a high reputation among his countrymen, whose opinions are sufficiently impartial, since he flattered no particular prejudice of the nation in any of his works.

The reputation of Irving is well known to you. He is an author distinguished for a quality (humour) that has been denied his countrymen; and his merit is the more rare, that it has been shewn in a state of society so cold and so restrained. Besides these writers, there are many others of a similar character, who enjoy a greater or less degree of favour in their own country. The works of two or three have even been translated (into French) in Europe, and a great many are reprinted in England. Though every writer of fiction in America has to contend against the difficulties I have named, there is a certain interest in the novelty of the subject, which is not without its charm. I think, however, it will be found that they have all been successful, or the reverse, just as they have drawn warily, or freely, on the distinctive habits of their own country. I now speak of their success purely as writers of romance. It certainly would be possible for an American to give a description of the manners of his own country, in a book that he might choose to call a romance, which should be read, because the world is curious on the subject, but which would certainly never be read for that nearly indefinable poetical interest which attaches itself to a description of manners less bald and uniform. All the attempts to blend history with romance in America, have been comparative failures, (and perhaps fortunately,) since the subjects are too familiar to be treated with the freedom that the imagination absolutely requires. Some of the descriptions of the progress of society on the borders, have had a rather better success, since there is a positive, though no very poetical, novelty in the subject; but, on the whole, the books which have been best received, are those in which the authors have trusted most to their own conceptions of character, and to qualities that are common to the rest of the world and to human nature. This fact, if its truth be admitted, will serve to prove that the American writer must seek his renown in the exhibition of qualities that are general, while he is confessedly compelled to limit his observations to a state of society that has a wonderful tendency not only to repress passion, but to equalize humours.

The Americans have always been prolific writers on polemics and politics. Their sermons and fourth of July orations are numberless. Their historians, without being very classical or very profound, are remarkable for truth and good sense. There is not, perhaps, in the language a closer reasoner in metaphysics than Edwards; and their theological writers find great favour among the sectarians of their respective schools.

The stage of the United States is decidedly English. Both plays and players, with few exceptions, are imported. Theatres are numerous, and they are to be found in places where a traveller would little expect to meet them. Of course they are of all sizes and of every degree of decoration and architectural beauty known in Europe, below the very highest. The facade of the principal theatre in Philadelphia is a chaste specimen in marble, of the Ionic, if my memory is correct. In New York, there are two theatres about as large as the Théatre Français (in the interior), and not much inferior in embellishments. Besides these, there is a very pretty little theatre, where lighter pieces are performed, and another with a vast stage for melo-dramas.

There are also one or two other places of dramatic representation in this city, in which horses and men contend for the bays.

The Americans pay well for dramatic talent. Cooke, the greatest English tragedian of our age, died on this side of the Atlantic; and there are few players of eminence in the mother country who are not tempted, at some time or other, to cross the ocean. Shakspeare, is of course, the great author of America, as he is of England, and I think he is quite as well relished here as there. In point of taste, if all the rest of the world be any thing against England, that of America is the best, since it unquestionably approaches nearest to that of the continent of Europe. Nearly one half of the theatrical taste of the English is condemned by their own judgments, since the stage is not much supported by those who have had an opportunity of seeing any other. You will be apt to ask me how it happens, then, that the American taste is better? Because the people, being less exaggerated in their habits, are less disposed to tolerate caricatures, and because the theatres are not yet sufficiently numerous (though that hour is near) to admit of a representation that shall not be subject to the control of a certain degree of intelligence. I have heard an English player complain that he never saw such a dull audience as the one before which he had just been exhibiting; and I heard the same audience complain that they never listened to such dull jokes. Now, there was talent enough in both parties; but the one had formed his taste in a coarse school, and the others had formed theirs under the dominion of common sense. Independently of this peculiarity, there is a vast deal of acquired, travelled taste in this country. English tragedy, and high English comedy, both of which, you know, are excellent, never fail here, if well played; that is, they never fail under the usual limits of all amusement. One will cloy of sweets. But the fact of the taste and judgment of these people, in theatrical exhibitions, is proved by the number of their good theatres, compared to their population.

Of dramatic writers there are none, or next to none. The remarks I have made in respect to novels apply with double force to this species of composition. A witty and successful American comedy could only proceed from extraordinary talent. There would be less difficulty, certainly, with a tragedy; but still, there is rather too much foreign competition, and too much domestic employment in other pursuits, to invite genius to so doubtful an enterprise. The very baldness of ordinary American life is in deadly hostility to scenic representation. The character must be supported solely by its intrinsic power. The judge, the footman, the clown, the lawyer, the belle, or the beau, can receive no great assistance from dress. Melo-dramas, except the scene should be laid in the woods, are out of the question. It would be necessary to seek the great clock, which is to strike the portentous twelve blows, in the nearest church; a vaulted passage would degenerate into a cellar; and, as for ghosts, the country was discovered, since their visitations have ceased. The smallest departure from the incidents of ordinary life would do violence to every man's experience; and, as already mentioned, the passions which belong to human nature must be delineated, in America, subject to the influence of that despot—common sense.

Notwithstanding the overwhelming influence of British publications, and all the difficulties I have named, original books are getting to be numerous in the United States. The impulses of talent and intelligence are bearing down a thousand obstacles. I think the new works will increase rapidly, and that they are destined to produce a powerful influence on the world. We will pursue this subject another time.—Adieu.

A continuation of the relationship of art to the American character. Cooper focuses on architecture (a failure in America) and landscape painting, specifically on the success of the Hudson River School. One reason America lags behind in art and literature derives from the fact that no real leisure class exists in a republic.

TO THE ABBATE GIROMACHI
&c. &c.
FLORENCE.
Washington, ——

You will be satisfied with these reasons for the abrupt conclusion of my last. I shall now tax your patience for a short continuation of the subject.

Although there are so many reasons why an imaginative literature should not be speedily created in this country, there is none, but that general activity of employment which is not favourable to study, why science and all the useful arts should not be cultivated here, perhaps, more than any where else. Great attention is already paid to the latter. Though there is scarce such a thing as a capital picture in this whole country, I have seen more beautiful, graceful, and convenient ploughs in positive use here, than are probably to be found in the whole of Europe united. In this single fact may be traced the history of the character of the people, and the germ of their future greatness. Their axe is admirable for form, for neatness, and precision of weight, and it is wielded with a skill that is next to incredible. Reapers are nearly unknown, but I have seen single individuals enter a field of grain in the morning, and clear acres of its golden burthen, by means of the *cradle*,★ with a rapidity that has amazed me. The vast multitude of their inventions, as they are exhibited in the patent office in this city, ought to furnish food for grave reflection to every stranger. Several large rooms are filled with the models, many of which give evidence of the most acute ingenuity. When one recollects the average proportion of adults to which the population must have been confined during the last thirty-five years,† the number of their inventions is marvellous. A great many of these models contain no new principle, nor any new application of an old principle; but, as in such cases, money has been paid by those who deposit them there without an object, it is fair to presume that they were inventions so far as the claimants were concerned. There are so few means by which men, in remote districts of this country, can profit by the ideas of other people in these matters, that it is probable there is not a dozen machines lodged in the office, of which the parties concerned did not honestly believe themselves the inventors. You may estimate the activity of thought, which distinguishes the mass of this nation from all other people, by this fact. It is in itself a prodigious triumph to a young people to have given form and useful existence to the greatest improvement of our age; but the steam-boats are not the only gift of this nature, by many, that Europe has already received from the western hemisphere.

The general accumulation of science in this country is exceedingly great, though it is quite likely that few men have yet attained to a very eminent degree of knowledge in any one particular branch. Still it is probable, that the amount of science in the United States, at this day, compared to what it was even fifteen years ago, and without reference to the increase of the population, is as five to one, or even in a still much greater proportion. Like all other learning, it is greatly on the advance.

In architecture the Americans have certainly no great reason to exult. They appear to have inherited the peculiarity of their ancestors, in all matters of mere taste. Their houses are mostly built of wood in the country and in the villages, and of bricks in the towns. There are, however, exceptions, in all cases, which reverse the rule. There are many farm-houses,

---

★ The writer does not know whether this implement is an American invention or not.
† The whole period that the Patent Office has been in existence.

seats, churches, court-houses, &c. in the country and smaller towns, which are of stone. Marble and granite are getting a good deal into use, too, in the more northern cities. The principal motive which controls their taste is economy. It is commonly cheapest to build of wood in the country, but where stone is at hand, and of a good quality, it begins to be preferred, in what may be called the second and third stages of the settlements. As the materials are cheap, the buildings are in common much larger than would be occupied by men of the same wealth in Europe. A house of forty or of forty-five feet front, and of thirty or thirty-five feet in depth, of two stories, with cellars, and garret, and with offices attached, is a usual dwelling for the owner of one or of two hundred acres of land, in a part of the country that has been under cultivation thirty or forty years. Such a man may be worth from five to ten thousand dollars. He has his growing orchard; fifty sheep; some eight or ten cows; a stock of young cattle; three or four horses; one or two yoke of oxen; hogs, poultry, and all the other provisions of a small farm. He grows his own maize; fattens his own pork; makes his own cider; kills his own beef; raises his own wheat, rye, and flax; and, in short, lives as much as possible on the articles of his own production. There are thousands and tens of thousands of these sturdy, independent yeomen in the eastern, middle and north-western states.

The villas and country-seats are commonly pretty, without ever attaining much elegance or size. A better sort of American country-house will cover perhaps sixty or seventy feet of ground in length, and from fifty to sixty in depth. There are some of twice this size; but I should say the first was a fair average. There are a great many a size smaller. The expense of building is, of course, in proportion to the general cost of every article in the particular place where the house is erected. I am told the best buildings in New York cost from thirty to forty thousand dollars. A few are even much more expensive. But the town houses, occupied by a majority of their gentlemen (those who own their own dwellings), cost probably something under twenty thousand.★ These are

---

★ The writer afterwards saw a row of buildings in New York of the following cost and dimensions; twenty-five feet front, (in marble) fifty-five feet deep, and of three stories, besides the basement. The lots, were two-hundred feet in depth. The buildings were about as well finished as a third-rate London town house. The cost of the whole was ten thousand dollars, and the rent six hundred dollars a-year. These houses were in the dearest city of America, but not in the dearest part of the town.

the habitations of the rich, exclusively. They are every where exceedingly neat, prettily furnished, frequently with great elegance, and are always comfortable.

As some general idea of the state of the useful arts must have been obtained, in the course of my previous letters to the fraternity, I shall now pass to those which are intended exclusively to embellish life.

The United States, considered with reference to their means and opportunities, have been exceedingly prolific in painters. It is rather remarkable, that, in a country where active and less hazardous employments are so open to talent, men should take an inclination to a pursuit that is rarely profitable, and in which mediocrity is as annoying as success is triumphant. I cannot say that the majority of these gentlemen acknowledge that the fine arts are greatly encouraged in America, nor has it yet been my happy lot to enter a country in which artists and authors were very generally of opinion that the pen and the pencil received the rewards and honours which no one will deny they merit. A very great majority of the American artists are portrait painters. Some of them are highly esteemed by their own countrymen, and certainly there are a few of a good deal of merit. They are generally more distinguished for spirit and character than for finish or grace; but it is quite evident that, as a class, they are rapidly improving. Drawing is the point in which they chiefly fail; and this, too, is probably an inherited defect, since most of them are disciples of the English school.

There are some highly respectable professional landscape painters. One of them (a Mr. Cole) possesses the rare faculty of giving to his pictures the impression of nature, to a degree so extraordinary, that he promises to become eminent. You know my eye is only for nature. I have heard both high eulogiums and sneering critiques on the powers of this young man, as an artist, some declaring that he has reached a point far beyond that attained by any of his competitors, and others denying that he knows how to make a sky look blue, *secundum artem*. To me his scenery is like the scenery from which he drew; and as he has taste and skill enough to reject what is disagreeable, and to arrange the attractive parts of his pictures, I only hope he will continue to study the great master from whom he has drawn his first inspirations. America has produced several historical painters. West, though a native of this country, and, perhaps with a pardonable vanity, claimed as such by these people, was, to all intents and purposes, an English artist. There are one or two of his pupils who practise their skill here, and a few others have aspired to the highest branch of their art. One of them (Mr. Alston) is said to be employed on a great and elaborate picture (the hand-writing on the wall); and as his taste and merit are universally admitted, a good deal is expected from his pencil. It may serve to give you a better idea of the taste for pictures in this country, or rather of the desire which exists to encourage talent, if I mention the price he is to receive for this work. A company of gentlemen are said to have bought the picture, in advance, by agreeing to pay ten thousand dollars: I believe it is their intention to remunerate themselves by exhibiting it, and then to deposit the work in some public place. Cabinet pieces, by this artist, are readily sold for prices of between three hundred and a thousand dollars, and the pencil of Cole is employed as much as he pleases. There are many other artists that paint portraits and landscapes, who seldom want orders. The government of the United States has paid Trumbull thirty-two thousand dollars for the four historical paintings that are destined to fill as many compartments in the rotunda, or the great hall of the capitol.

It is plain that the system of elementary education pursued by this country, must bring an extraordinary quantity of talent, within the influence of those causes which lead to renown. If we suppose one hundred men in America to possess the same amount of native talent as one hundred men in any other part of the world, more of it will, of necessity, be excited to action, since more individuals are placed in situations to feel and to improve their infant powers. Although a certain degree of excellence in the higher branches of learning and of art, may yet be necessary to create a standard, and even for the establishments of higher schools or real universities, still the truth of this position is proved by the fact, that there already exists, among this people, a far more advanced state of improvement in all that relates to the familiar interests of life than among any other. It is true that a division of labour, and vast competition may create a degree of minute perfection in many articles of European manufacture that is not known in the same articles manufactured here; but I think it will be commonly found in all such cases, that these wary people have counted the profit and the cost with sufficient accuracy. As circumstances vary, they instantly improve, and once induced to persevere they soon fearlessly challenge competition.

The purely intellectual day of America is yet in its dawn. But its sun will not arise from darkness, like those of nations with whose experience we are familiar; nor is the approach of its meridian to be calculated by the known progress of any other people. The learned professions are now full to overflowing, not so much with learning as with incumbents, certainly, but so much so, as to begin to give a new direction to education and talents. Writers are already getting to be numerous, for literature is beginning to be profitable. Those authors who are successful receive prices for their labours, which exceed those paid to the authors of any country, England alone excepted; and which exceed even the prices paid to the most distinguished authors of the mother country, if the difference in the relative value of money in the two countries, and in the luxury of the press, be computed. The same work which is sold in England for six dollars, is sold in the United States for two. The profit to the publisher is obtained out of a common rate of per centage. Now, as thirty three and a third per cent. on six thousand dollars, is two thousand,* and on two thousand dollars, only six hundred and sixty-six, it is quite evident, that if both parties sell one thousand copies of a work, the English publisher pockets three times the most profit. And yet, with one or two exceptions, and notwithstanding the great difference in the population of the two countries, the English bookseller rarely sells more, if he does as many, copies of a book, than the American. It is the extraordinary demand which enables the American publisher to pay so well, and which, provided there was no English competition, would enable him to pay still better, or rather still more generally, than he does at present.

The literature of the United States is a subject of the highest interest to the civilized world; for when it does begin to be felt, it will be felt with a force, a directness, and a common sense in its application, that has never yet been known. If there were no other points of difference between this country and other nations, those of its political and religious freedom, alone, would give a colour of the highest importance to the writings of a people so thoroughly imbued with their distinctive principles, and so keenly alive to their advantages. The example of America has been silently operating on Europe for half a century, but its doctrines and its experience, exhibited with

---

* This calculation supposes one-third of the price to go to the trade in discount, one-third to the expenses, and the other third to constitute the joint profit of the author and publisher.

the understanding of those familiar with both, have never yet been pressed on our attention. I think the time for the experiment is getting near.

A curious inquiry might be raised as to the probable fate of the English language among so many people having equal claims to its possession. I put this question to my friend, who has kindly permitted me to give you the substance of his reply. You will at once understand that this is a subject which requires a greater knowledge of the matter in dispute, than what I, as a foreigner, can claim.—

"In order to decide which nation speaks the English language best, it becomes necessary to refer to some standard. If it be assumed that the higher classes in London are always to set the fashion in pronunciation, and the best living writers in England are to fix the meaning of words, the point is clearly decided in their favour, since one cannot see on what principle they are to be put in the wrong. That the better company of London must set the fashion for the pronunciation of words in England, and indeed for the whole English empire, is quite plain; for, as this very company, comprises all those whose manners, birth, fortune, and political distinction, make them the objects of admiration, it becomes necessary to imitate their affectations, whether of speech or air, in order to create the impression that one belongs to their society. It is absurd to think that either parliament, or the stage, or the universities, or the church, can produce any very serious effect on the slighter forms of utterance adopted by this powerful caste. The player may hint at the laws of prosody for ever, unless his rule happens to suit the public ear, it becomes no more than the pronunciation of the stage. The fellow, when he gets beyond his cloisters, is glad to conceal the habits of retirement in the language of the world; and as for the member of parliament, if he happen to be of the caste, he speaks like the rest of them; and if not, he is no better than a vulgar fellow who is very glad to conceal his provincialisms by having as little said about them as possible. In short, the bishop might just as well expect to induce the exquisite to wear a copy of his wig, or the representative of Othello, to set the fashion of smooty faces, as either of them to think of giving the tone to pronunciation, or even to the meaning of words. A secret and lasting influence is no doubt produced by education; but fashion is far more imperious than even the laws of the schools. It is, I think, a capital mistake, to believe that either of the professions named, produce any great impression on the spoken language of

England. They receive more from fashion than they give to it; and they each have their particular phrases, but they rarely go no farther than their own limits. This is more or less the case in all other European nations. The rule is more absolute, however, in England than in France, for instance, because the former has no academy, and because men of letters have far less circulation, and, of course, far less influence in society there, than in the neighbouring kingdom. The tendency of every thing in England is to aristocracy. I can conceive that the King of England might very well set a fashion in the pronunciation of a word, because being the greatest aristocrat of the nation, the smaller ones might be ambitious of showing that they kept enough of his company to catch his imperfections of speech; but, as for the King of France, he sits too much on a pinnacle for men to presume to imitate his blunders. A powerful, wealthy, hereditary, but subsidizing aristocracy, rules all things in England; but, while wit gives up to the king and *la charte,* the control of politics in France, it asserts its own prerogative over every other interest of the empire, religion, perhaps, a little excepted.

"There exists a very different state of things in America. If we had a great capital, like London, where men of leisure, and fortune, and education periodically assembled to amuse themselves, I think we should establish a fashionable aristocracy, too, which should give the mode to the forms of speech as well as to that of dress and deportment. Perhaps the influence of talent and wit would be as much felt in such a town as in Paris; for it is the great peculiarity of our institutions to give more influence to talents than to any one other thing. But we have no such capital, nor are we likely, for a long time to come, to have one of sufficient magnitude to produce any great effect on the language. In those states where many men of leisure and education are to be found, there are large towns, in which they pass their winters, and where, of course, they observe all those forms which are more or less peculiar to themselves. The habits of polite life, and even the pronunciation of Boston, of New York, of Baltimore, and of Philadelphia, vary in many things, and a practised ear may tell a native of either of these places, from a native of any one of the others, by some little peculiarity of speech. There is yet no predominating influence to induce the fashionables of these towns to wish to imitate the fashionables of any other. If any place is to possess this influence, it will certainly be New York; but I think, on an examination of the subject, that it can be made to appear that an entirely different standard for the language must be established in the United States, from that which governs so absolutely in England.

"If the people of this country were like the people of any other country on earth, we should be speaking at this moment a great variety of nearly unintelligible patois; but, in point of fact, the people of the United States, with the exception of a few of German and French descent, speak, as a body, an incomparably better English than the people of the mother country. There is not, probably, a man (of English descent) born in this country, who would not be perfectly intelligible to all whom he should meet in the streets of London, though a vast number of those he met in the streets of London would be nearly unintelligible to him. In fine, we speak our language, as a nation, better than any other people speak their language.* When one reflects on the immense surface of country that we occupy, the general accuracy, in pronunciation and in the use of words, is quite astonishing. This resemblance in speech can only be ascribed to the great diffusion of intelligence, and to the inexhaustible activity of the population, which, in a manner, destroys space.

"It is another peculiarity of our institutions, that the language of the country, instead of becoming more divided into provincial dialects, is becoming, not only more assimilated to itself as a whole, but more assimilated to a standard which sound general principles, and the best authorities among our old writers, would justify. The distinctions in speech between New England and New York, or Pennsylvania, or any other state, were far greater twenty years ago than they are now. Emigration alone would produce a large portion of this change; but emigration would often introduce provincialisms without correcting them, did it not also, by bringing acute men together, sharpen wits, provoke comparisons, challenge investigations, and, finally, fix a standard.

"It has been a matter of hot dispute, for the last twenty years, in which of our large towns the best English is spoken. The result of this discussion has been to convince most people who know any thing of the matter, that a perfectly pure English is spoken no where, and to establish the superiority, on one point, in favour of Boston, on another in favour of New York,

---

* Of course the writer calls Italy one nation, and all Germany one nation, so far as language is concerned.

and so on to the end of the chapter. The effect of all this controversy is, to make men think seriously on the subject, and thinking seriously is the first step in amendment. We do amend, and each year introduces a better and purer English into our country. We are obliged, as you may suppose, to have recourse to some standard to settle these contentions. What shall this standard be? It is not society, for that itself is divided on the disputed points; it cannot be the church, for there is none that will be acknowledged by all parties; it cannot be the stage, for that is composed of foreigners, and possesses little influence on morals, politics, or any thing else; nor the universities, for they are provincial, and parties to the dispute; nor congress, for that does not represent the fashion and education of the nation; nor the court, for there is none but the president, and he is often a hot partizan; nor the fashions of speech in England, for we often find as much fault with them as we do with our own. Thus, you see, we are reduced to the necessity of consulting reason, and authority, and analogy, and all the known laws of language, in order to arrive at our object. This we are daily doing, and I think the consequence will be, that, in another generation or two, far more *reasonable* English will be used in this country than exists here now. How far this melioration or purification of our language will affect the mother country, is another question.

"It is, perhaps, twenty years too soon to expect that England will very complacently submit to receive opinions or fashions very directly from America." [What she will do twenty years later, is a question that little concerns us, dear Abbate, since I have not, and you ought not to have, any very direct interests in the fortunes of posterity.] "But the time has already arrived, when America is beginning to receive with great distrust fashions and opinions from England. Until within the last fifteen years, the influence of the mother country, in all things connected with mere usages, was predominant to an incredible extent; but every day is making a greater change.

"On a thousand subjects we have been rudely provoked into comparisons, an experiment that the most faultless generally find to be attended with hazard. We are a bold though a quiet people, and names and fashions go for but little when set in opposition to the unaccommodating and downright good sense of this nation. It may be enough for an Englishman that an innovation on language is supported by the pretty lips of such or such a belle of quality and high degree; but the American sees too many pretty lips at home to be very submissive to any foreign dictation of this sort. I think it plain, therefore, that the language must be reduced to known general rules, and rules, too, that shall be respected as such rules should be, or else we shall have a dialect distinct from that of the mother country. I have not, however, the slightest apprehensions of any thing of the kind arriving, since any one who understands the use of figures can estimate the probable influence of the two nations half a century hence. I think it will be just as much the desire of England then to be in our fashion, as it was our desire twenty years ago to be in hers, and for precisely the same reason. The influence of fifty millions of people, living under one government, backed by enormous wealth, extended intelligence, a powerful literature, and unrivalled freedom, cannot be very problematical, in the eyes of any man who is capable of regarding the subject free from prejudice or passion. I very well know there is a fashion of predicting the separation of our states, and a consequent disorganization of society, which would certainly weaken that influence. These predictions were made fifty years ago with rather more confidence than they are made now, and those who know most in the matter, treat them with very little deference. But, admitting that they should be realized, in what particular will the result materially affect the question before us? A division of this republic into two or three republics is the utmost that can be expected. There would still exist those intimate relations between the parts of our present empire which find their support in a conformity of principles, and our intercourse and literature would necessarily be essentially the same. I cannot see that the impression on the language would in any degree be weakened, except that, by dividing our power, we might retard a little the period when the weight of that power should obtain its natural and necessary preponderance. You may be assured, that, in thinking on this subject, I have not forgotten that history supplies sufficient evidence that small communities may exercise a vast influence over larger; but I do not know where to find a precedent for a large community, possessing equal activity and intelligence, submitting to be controlled, either morally or politically, by one physically much weaker. Our own history already furnishes a striking example of the very reverse; and as we are bent on perpetuating all the means of our present independence, it is fair to presume that we shall gain a moral ascendancy in the world, in proportion as we gain physical force. If a pretty duchess can now set a fashion in speech, what will not a combination of two hundred millions of persons do, (the number is not at all exaggerated if we carry the time forward a century and a half,) more especially if all of them shall happen to possess a reasonable knowledge of the use of letters.

"You may have a curiosity to know something of the present state of the language in America. I have already said that there is no patois throughout the whole of this country. There is broken English among the Germans, French, and other foreigners, but nothing that is very widely distinct from the language of London. Still there are words of perfectly provincial use, most of which were brought from certain parts of the mother country, and which have been preserved here, and a few which have been introduced from wantonness or necessity. There is much more difference in intonation and in the pronunciation of particular words than in the use of terms unknown to England. The best English is spoken by the natives of the middle states, who are purely the descendants of English parents, without being the descendants of emigrants from New England. The educated men of all the southern Atlantic states, especially the members of those families which have long been accustomed to the better society of their towns, also speak an English but little to be distinguished from that of the best circles of the mother country. Still there are shades of difference between these very persons that a nice and practised ear can detect, and which, as they denote the parts of the Union to which they belong, must be called provincialisms. These little irregularities of language solely arise from the want of a capital.

"Throughout all New England, and among most of the descendants of the people of New England, the English language is spoken with more or less of an intonation derived, I believe, from the western counties of England, and with a pronunciation that is often peculiar to themselves. They form so large a proportion of the entire population of the country, that some of their provincialisms are getting to form a part of our ordinary language. The peculiarity of the New England dialect (the term is almost too strong) is most discernible in the manner in which they dwell on the last word of a sentence, or the last syllable of a word. It is not properly drawling, for they speak very quick in common, much quicker than the English; so quick, indeed, as to render syllables frequently indistinct: but, in consequence of the peculiar pause they make on the last word, I question if they utter a sentence in less time than those who dwell more equally on its separate parts.* Among men of the world and of education this peculiarity is, of course, often lost; but education is so common, and the state of society so simple in New England, as to produce less apparent distinction in speech and manners than it is usual to find elsewhere.

"Another marked peculiarity of New England is in the pronunciation of a great many words. The fact that a vast improvement has occurred in this respect within the last thirty years, however, goes to prove the truth of what I have just told you, no less than of the increasing intelligence of the nation.

"When I was a boy, I was sent from a middle state, for my education, to Connecticut. I took with me, of course, the language of my father's house. In the first year I was laughed out of a great many correct sounds, and into a great many vulgar and disagreeable substitutes. At my return home to pass a vacation, I almost threw a sister into fits by calling one of her female friends a 'virtoous *an*-gel,' pronouncing the first syllable of the last word like the article. It was in vain that I supported my new reading by the authorities of *the university*. The whole six weeks were passed in hot discussions between my sister and myself, amidst the laughter and merriment of a facetious father, who had the habit of trotting me through my Connecticut prosody by inducing me to recite Pope's Temple of Fame, to the infinite delight of two or three waggish elder brothers, who had got their English longs and shorts in a more southern school. It was at a time of life when shaving was a delight instead of a torment. I remember they were always sure of drawing me out by introducing the subject of my beard, which I pedantically called *berd;* or, for which, if pushed a little harder than common, I gave them a choice between *berd* and *baird.* Even to this hour, it is rare to find a native of New England who does not possess some of these marked provincialisms of speech. By a singular corruption, the word *stone* is often pronounced *stun,* while *none* is pronounced *noane,* or nearly like *known.* The latter is almost a shibboleth, as is *nothing,* pronounced according to the natural power of the letters, instead of *nuthing.* I think, however, a great deal of the peculiarity of New England pronunciation is to be ascribed to the intelligence of its inhabitants. This may appear a paradox; but it can easily be explained. They

---

* The phrase of "I wonder if he did," is very common in New England. It is usually uttered "I wonder if he de-e-e-e-ed," with a falling of the voice at the last word, to nearly an octave below the rest of the sentence. Sometimes there is more than one resting point in a sentence of any length.

all read and write; but the New Englandman, at home, is a man of exceedingly domestic habits. He has a theoretical knowledge of the language, without its practice. Those who migrate lose many of their peculiarities in the mixed multitudes they encounter; but *into* New England the current of emigration, with the exception of that which originally came from the mother country, has never set. It is vain to tell a man who has his book before him, that *cham* spells *chame*, as in *chamber;* or *an, ane*, as in *angel;* or *dan, dane*, as in *danger.* He replies by asking what sound is produced by *an, dan*, and *cham.* I believe it would be found, on pursuing the inquiry, that a great number of their peculiar sounds are introduced through their spelling-books, and yet there are some, certainly, that cannot be thus explained. It is not too much to say that nine people in ten, in New England, pronounce *does, dooze*, when the mere power of the letters would make it nearer *doze.* There is one more singular corruption, which I shall mention before I go farther south, and which often comes from the mouths of men, even in Boston, who, in other respects, would not be much criticised for their language: the verb *to show* was formerly, and is even now, spelt *shew*, and *shewed* in its participle; I have heard men of education and manners, in Boston, say, "he *shew* me that," for, he *showed* me that.

"With these exceptions, which are sufficiently numerous, and the hard sound they almost always give the letter *u*, the people of New England speak the language more like the people of Old England than any other parts of our country. They speak with a closer mouth, both physically and morally, than those who live further south and west. There is also a little of a nasal sound among some of them, but it is far from being as general as the other peculiarities I have named.

"The middle states certainly speak a softer English than their brethren of the east. I should say that when you get as far south as Maryland, the softest, and perhaps as pure an English is spoken as is any where heard. No rule on such a subject, however, is without many exceptions in the United States. The emigration alone would, as yet, prevent perfect uniformity. The voices of the American females are particularly soft and silvery; and I think the language, a harsh one at the best, is made softer by our women, especially of the middle and southern states, than you often hear it in Europe.

"New York, Philadelphia, and Baltimore, have each their peculiar phrases. Some of the women have a habit of dwelling a little too long on the final syllables, but I think it is rare among the higher classes of society. I don't know that it exists at all as far south as Baltimore. As you go further south, it is true, you get a slower utterance, and other slight varieties of provincialism. In Georgia you find a positive drawl, among what are called the 'crackers.' More or less of this drawl, and of all the peculiar sounds, are found in the south-western and western states; but they are all too new to have any fixed habits of speech of their own.

"The usual vulgar phrases which are put into the mouths of Americans, are commonly caricatured, though always founded in truth. 'I guess,' is a phrase of New England. It is used a great deal, though not as often, as 'you know,' by a cockney. It proceeds, I think, from the cautious and subdued habit of speaking which is characteristic of these people. The gentlemen rarely use it, though I confess I have heard it, interlarding the conversation of pretty lips that derived none of their beauty from the Puritans. You see, therefore, that it has been partially introduced by the emigrants into the middle states. Criticism is here so active, just now, that it is rapidly getting into disuse. The New Yorker frequently says, 'I suspect,' and the Virginian, 'I reckon.' But the two last are often used in the best society in the mother country.★

"The difference in pronunciation and in the use of words, between the really good society of this country and that of England, is not very great. In America we can always tell an Englishman by what we are pleased to call his provincialisms (and quite half the time the term is correct), I was struck at the close resemblance between the language of the higher classes in the mother country, and the higher classes of my own, especially if the latter belong to the middle states. There are certainly points of difference, but they as often proceed from affectation in individuals, as from the general habits of the two countries. Cockneyisms are quite as frequent in the language of an English gentleman, as provincialisms in the mouth of an American gentleman of the middle states. I now use the word gentleman in its strict meaning. I have heard many people of high rank in England, for instance, pronounce 'yours' as if it were spelt 'yers.' If affectations are to become laws, because they are conceived in the smoke of London, then they are right;

★ The negroes have a habit of saying, "you sabber dat," for, you know that; can this be one of their African terms, or is it a corruption of "saber," or "savoir," that has found its way to the continent from the neighbouring islands?

but, if old usage, the rules of the language, and the voices of even educated men are to prevail, then are they wrong. This is but one among a hundred similar affectations that are detected every day by an attentive and critical ear. But mere rank, after all, is not always a criterion of correct pronunciation in an Englishman or in an Englishwoman. I have met with people of rank who have spoken in very perceptible provincial dialects. Parliament is very far from being faultless in its English, putting the Irish, Scotch, and aldermen out of the question. I have heard a minister of state speak of the 'o-casion,' with a heavy emphasis; and just before we sailed, I remember to have burst into involuntary laughter at hearing a distinguished orator denounce a man for having been the 'recipient of a bribe of ten guineas.' The language of parliament is undeniably far more correct than that of congress; but when it is recollected that the one body is a representation of the aristocracy of a condensed community, and the other a representation of the various classes of a widely spread people, the rational odds is immensely in our favour. I am not sure that one, who took pleasure in finding fault, might not detect quite as many corruptions of the English language in the good society of the mother country, as in the good society of our own. The latter, strictly considered, bears a less proportion to our numbers, however, than the same class bears to the population of England. The amount of the whole subject I take to be simply this: allowing for all the difference in numbers, there is vastly more bad English, and a thousand times more bad grammar spoken in England than in America; and there is much more good English (also allowing for the difference in numbers) spoken there than here. Among the higher and better educated classes, there are purists in both countries, who may write and talk to the end of time; innovations have been made, are made, and will be made in both countries; but as two nations now sit in judgment on them, I think when words once get fairly into use, their triumph affords a sufficient evidence of merit to entitle them to patronage."

VOL. II, LETTER 9

A thorough and exhaustive examination of America's court systems. Cooper espe-
cially appreciates the use of common and natural law in America. "I am a great ven-
erator of those laws which are enacted by custom, since I entertain the opinion that
the stamp of usage is worth a dozen legislative seals."

TO THE PROFESSOR CHRISTIAN JANSEN,
&c. &c.
Washington, ——

—IT was a week before I recovered from the shock of such an alarm. But
on more mature thought, (especially when I came coolly to reflect on some
recent dangers through which I had myself passed in triumph, as well as on
the numberless instances in which I had felt symptoms of the same disorder,) I began to consider your case as far from hopeless. We become more
liable to these attacks as we advance in life, and I warn you of being constantly on your guard against them. I also beg leave to recommend exercise
and change of scene as the most effectual cure. I am fully persuaded that
had not fortune made us all travellers, we should long since have ceased to
be the independent beings we are. Waller spoke, in his last letter, of a Venetian beauty, in language that seemed ominous; but I know too well that deep
inward eccentricity of the man, which he so prettily calls *mauvaise honte,* to
dread any thing serious from the affair. I think his eminently impartial manner of viewing things, will for ever save him from the sin of matrimony.
Besides, the girl is only descended from two doges of the fifteenth century,
and four or five old admirals of the thirteenth and fourteenth, a genealogy

that surely cannot pretend to compete with the descent of a Somersetshire baronet, whose great grandfather was an alderman of Lincoln, and whose great grandmother was the youngest daughter of a British officer. If you doubt the truth of the last circumstance, I refer you to the half-pay list of lieutenants of dragoons, in the reign of George the Second.

You have made a much more formidable request than you appear to think, when you desire that I will give you a detailed account of the system of jurisprudence, of the laws, and of the different courts of this country. The subject, properly and ably considered, would require a year of time, and infinitely more legal science than I can lay claim to possess. Still, as I may tell you some things of which you are as yet a stranger, I shall not shrink from the task of communicating the little I do know, under the stale plea of incompetency.

About a week after our arrival in this place, Cadwallader and myself had descended from the hall of the house of representatives to the caucus, and we were about to leave the capitol, when my friend made a sudden inclination to the left, motioning for me to follow. He passed into the basement of the northern wing of the edifice. I had seen but a few minutes before, by the naked flag staff, that the senate had adjourned,* and, was about to say as much, when I observed, that in place of ascending the stairs which led to their chamber, he proceeded deeper into the lower apartments of the wing. Opening a simple door, we entered a spacious, but low and far from brilliant apartment. It was lighted only from one of its sides. Directly in front of the windows, and a little elevated above the rest of the floor, sat seven grave looking men, most of whom had passed the meridian of life. They were clad in simple black silk robes, not unlike those worn by the students of universities, and most of them were busily occupied in taking notes. Immediately in their front some ten or twelve respectable men were seated, who had nothing in attire to distinguish them from the ordinary gentlemen of the country. There were two or three others who had the air of being inferior *employés* of some grave and important body; though, with the exception of the black silk robes, I saw no other badges of office. On the right, and on the left, there were benches in rows, and perhaps thirty or forty more

---

* A flag is kept flying over the wings in which the two houses meet, when they are in session, and they are struck as either body adjourns. These are signals that enable people at a distance to learn whether the senate, or lower house, are still together or not.

gentlemen were seated on them, listening to what was said. Among these auditors there might have been a dozen genteel looking women. This assemblage was composed of the judges, the advocates, the officers, and the suitors of the supreme court of the United States. All present who did not come within one or the other of the above mentioned denominations, were, like ourselves, merely curious witnesses of the proceedings.

We staid an hour listening to the argument of a distinguished advocate. He was a member of congress from one of the eastern states, and by the simplicity of his language, and the acuteness and force of his thoughts, he was clearly a man who would have done credit to any tribunal in the world. The manner of the speaker was rather cold, but it was dignified, and he paid the highest compliment to his auditors by addressing all he said to their reasons. The judges listened with grave attention, and indeed the whole scene wore the air of a calm and a highly reasonable investigation.

My attention was given more to the severe simplicity which marked the aspect and proceedings of this powerful tribunal, than to the particular subject before it. I found high authority again reposing with confidence on the most naked ceremonials, and I again found it surrounded by an air of deep reverence, which proves how little the vulgar auxiliaries of our eastern inventions are necessary to insure it respect and obedience. On no other occasion was I ever so completely sensible of the feebleness of an artificial, or of the majesty of a true, because a natural dignity, as on this. I have heard the wigs, and robes, and badges of office of half the tribunals of Europe laughed at, even by those who become familiar with their absurdities; but I do not know on what the most satirical wit could seize, in a body like this, to turn into ridicule. It is no small proof of the superiority that is obtained by the habit of considering things in their direct and natural aspects, that wigs, and other similar incumbrances, which are heaped upon the human form, with us, in order to heighten respect, in this country are avoided, in order to protect those, who should be venerated, from undeserved ridicule.

Considered in reference to its functions, and to the importance of the trusts which it discharges, the supreme court of the United States is the most august tribunal of the world. It may not yet be called upon to decide on causes which involve as great an amount of property, perhaps, as some of the courts of England; but, as the wealth and power of this country shall increase with its growth, the matters it decides will become still greater; and it now produces a mighty influence on the interests of the whole Union. You will better understand the subject, if we take a rapid view of the judicial system of the confederation, as it is connected with those of the several states.

You already know that the theory of the American government assumes that all power is the natural and necessary right of the people. The accidental circumstances of colonization had thrown the settlers into a certain number of body politics, before the era of their revolution. Until that event arrived, each province was entirely distinct and independent of all the others, except as they had common relations through their allegiance to the crown of England, and through those commercial and general interests which united them as the subjects of the same empire.

For the purpose of achieving their independence, the different provinces entered into a compact which partook of the nature of an intimate and indissoluble alliance. The articles of the confederation were a sort of treaty, that was not, however, limited to definite, but which embraced general objects, and which was to know no limits to its duration, but such as necessity must put to all things. Still it was little more than an intimate alliance between thirteen separate and independent governments. Money was to be raised for avowed and general purposes; but it was done in the way of subsidies rather than of taxation. Each state collected its own resources in its own manner, and it had fulfilled most of its obligations to the confederation when it had paid its quota, and when it permitted the few public agents appointed by the congress to discharge the particular trusts that were delegated to the Union.

Notwithstanding this imperfect and clumsy organization of their general government, the inhabitants of the United States were, even at that early day, essentially the same people. They had the same views of policy, the same general spirit, substantially the same origin,* and a community of interests that constantly invited a more intimate association. The country was scarcely relieved from the pressure and struggle of the war of the revolution, before its wisest citizens began to consider the means of effecting so desirable an object. Peace was concluded in 1783; and, in 1787, a

---

* A gross error exists in Europe, on the subject of the mixed character of this people. The whole population of Louisiana, for instance, but a little exceeded 75,000 souls (blacks included), in 1810. It was ceded to the Union in 1804.

convention was called to frame a constitution for the United States. The very word *constitution* implies the control of all those interests which distinguish an identified community. If we speak with technical accuracy, the convention of 1787 was assembled for the purpose of improving an existing compact, rather than for the purpose of creating one entirely new. But it will simplify our theory, and answer all the desirable purposes of the present object, if we assume that the states entered into the bargain perfectly unincumbered by any pre-existing engagements.

Under this view of the case, each state possessed all the rights of a distinct sovereignty, when it sent its delegates to the convention. There was no power which of necessity belongs to any other government of the world, that each of these states could not of itself exercise, subject always to the restrictions of its own institutions and laws. But then, each state possessed the power of altering its own institutions as it saw fit; it had its own laws, its own tribunals, and it preserved its policy in all things, except that, in point of fact, by the ancient confederation, it was bound not to enter into wars, and certain other engagements, with foreign nations, without the rest of the states being parties to the transaction.

The constitution of 1787 wrought a vital change in this system. The Americans now became one people in their institutions, as well as in their origin and in their feelings. It is important to remember that the two latter induced the former circumstance, and not the former the latter.

You can readily imagine that the principal point to be decided in a body which had professedly assembled with such intentions, was that of the continuation or annihilation of the state governments. There were not a few in favour of the first policy, though the influence of those who supported the authority of the states happily prevailed. I say happily, since, I think, it can be made plain that the existence of the Union at the present hour, no less than its future continuance, is entirely dependent on the existence of the governments of the several states.

In consequence of the policy that prevailed, a species of mixed and complicated government was established, which was before unknown to the world, but which promises to prove that territory may be extended *ad libitum* without materially impairing the strength of a country by its extent. It strikes me, that as the confederation of the United States is the most natural government known, that it is consequently the only empire on whose stability the fullest confidence can be placed. It is a superstructure regularly reared on a solid foundation, and not a tower from which a number of heavy and ill-balanced dependants are suspended. As to the prognostics of its dissolution, they are founded on theories that are getting to be a little obsolete; and the best argument that is urged to prove their truth, after all, is merely the fact that the confederation of the United States has not existed more than the full term of fifty years during the last half century. Perhaps it may console these impatient reasoners to know, that, while the records of the country are certainly limited to the brief period named, so far as improvement, wealth, power, and a general advancement are concerned, it has every appearance of having been in existence two or three centuries.

In order to effect the material objects of the new confederation, it became necessary that the states should part freely with their power. The principle was adopted that every thing which was necessary to the general welfare should be yielded to the general government, while the states should, of course, retain all the rest of their authority. But, with a view to give the utmost efficiency to the new system, an executive, courts, and subordinate functionaries were created, who were to act on the people sometimes through, but oftener without, the intermediate agency of the state authorities. As our present business is with the courts, we will confine ourselves to that branch of the subject.

Although the several states preserve the outlines of the judicial institutions which they inherited from their ancestors, there are not, probably, two in the whole confederation whose forms of jurisprudence are precisely the same. There is necessarily a difference in the policy of a large state and the policy of a small one; in that of a large, *new* state and that of a large *old* one; in that of a state without and in that of a state with slaves; in a commercial and in a purely agricultural state; and, in short, in a society which exists under the direct influence of certain interests, and in a society which exists under the influence of certain others. You may trace in this power of accommodating their minute policy to their own particular condition, and, what is probably quite as important, to their own pleasure, one of the great reasons for the durability of the Union.

Had I the necessary knowledge to impart it, you would not possess the patience to read a detailed account of the shades of difference which exist in the jurisprudence of twenty-four separate communities. I shall therefore take the outline of that of New York, the most populous of the states, and point out its connection with that of the Union. It will be sufficiently exact to give you an idea of the whole.

The foundation of the laws of New York, is the common law of England. Some of the provisions of this law, and a few of its principles, have been destroyed by the constitution of the state, which, of course, has substituted the maxims of a republic for those of a monarchy. Statute law has changed, and is daily changing certain other decrees of the common law, which are found to be inapplicable to the peculiar state of this society. I know no better evidence of the boldness and usefulness of reform, as it exists in this country, than is to be found in the early changes they made in the common law. It is now near half a century since they destroyed the right of entail, the trial by battle, the detestable and unnatural law of the half-blood, and a variety of other similar usages that are just beginning to become obnoxious to European censure. The Americans themselves say that New York has still a great deal to do, and daily complaints are heard against impediments to justice, which are to be traced to the usages of a comparatively dark age.★

The lowest tribunal known to the laws, is what is called a justices' court, or the suits before a justice of the peace. In each county there is also a regular court for the trial of criminal causes, and for the common pleas of that county. The presiding officers of these courts are termed judges; they are commonly five in number, and are sometimes aided by what are called assistant justices. In the older counties these judges are usually men of education, and always men of character. They are frequently lawyers, who continue to practise in the higher courts, and they are often men of landed estate, yeomen of good characters and influence, and sometimes merchants. Their criminal duties are not unlike those of the quarter sessions in

---

★ There are people who may find it curious to know, that the advancement of public opinion, and the consequent security of liberty, is making bold inroads on those practices which are known to have given birth to political rights. In the state of Louisiana, and, the writer believes, in one or two others, the use of a jury is dispensed with, in all civil cases, in which it is not demanded by one of the parties. It is said that more than five-sixths of the civil actions are tried by the court. Still the *right* of a trial by jury is guaranteed by the constitution of the United States.

England. Executions in civil actions issued out of this court, take effect on all property found within the limits of the county, and judgments are liens on real estate, according to priority of date, without reference to the courts where any other similar claims may be recorded.

The state is next subdivided into judicial circuits. For each of these circuits there is one judge. This officer presides at the circuit courts, assisted by the judges of the county; and as the judgments obtained under verdicts in this court are perfected before the supreme court of the state, they have a lien on all property belonging to the party concerned within the bounds of the state. Both of these courts take cognizance of crimes.

The supreme court (of the State of New York) is composed of three judges. They constitute a court of law, to which appeals are made from the inferior tribunals. The judges do not regularly preside at any of the circuits, though it is within the scope of their powers to do so if they please.* They settle all causes, and the reports of their proceedings form the ordinary books of precedents.

There is a chancellor who hears and decides in all cases where equity is claimed, and who exercises the usual authority in granting injunctions against the consummation of proceedings at law. In many of the states the equitable power is lodged in the same courts as the legal, the judges hearing causes on what is termed the equity side. The chancellor of the state is purely a law officer, exercising no other functions, and holding his commission by the same tenures as the judges. In one or two of the states, however, the governor acts as chancellor.

The senate of the state, (of New York,) assisted by the chancellor and judges of the supreme court form a tribunal for appeals, and for the correction of errors in the last resort. Their decision is final, unless the defendant should happen to be a foreigner or a citizen of another state, in which

---

* There has been a recent change in the courts of New York. A few years since there were five judges of the supreme court, and they tried all causes at Nisi Prius, holding the circuits in person. It was found that the business accumulated, and, in order to repair the evil, the circuit judges were appointed; those of the supreme court were reduced in number, and the common duties of the latter were limited to the terms. The better opinion in the state is, that this departure from a practice which has been sanctioned by so many centuries is not successful. A return to the former system is already contemplated, with an increase of the judges, that shall make their whole number equal to the labour they have to undergo.

case the cause can be carried into the courts of the United States* under certain circumstances. This court is not known to many of the states.

The jurisdiction of the courts of a state, embraces most of the ordinary interests of life. Nearly all offences against persons and things, whether considered in reference to the protection of the individual, or in reference to the dignity and security of society, can be tried before some one of the tribunals mentioned. In many cases the tribunals have concurrent power, those of the United States always being supreme, when they have a right to interfere at all.

The lowest tribunal established by the United States is that of the district courts. The rule is to make each state a district for the trial of causes under the laws of the Union, though some of the larger states are divided into two. Each of these courts has its particular judge, its recording, and its executive officers. The latter are called marshals; they exercise all the ordinary duties of an English sheriff.† Original causes are tried before the district judge. If A. should fail in the conditions of an ordinary contract made with B., the latter would bring his suit in the county in which the former resided, or in the supreme court of the state, as he might please; but if the contract had direct reference to matter which is exclusively controlled by the laws of the United States, he would probably bring his action in the circuit court of the state in which the defendant lived. In matters that arise from seizures under the customs, or that affect any other of the direct interests of the United States, the *District Court* is always competent to proceed. If process issues on execution from the courts of the state, it is to the sheriff; but from the United States' courts it is directed to the marshal. The same distinction is observed for the execution of sentences under the respective criminal laws of the two authorities. Thus, it would be possible, as in the cases of an ordinary murder and of piracy, for two convicts to issue from the same gaol, and to go to the same gallows, though the one should be hanged under the orders of a sheriff, and the other under the orders of a marshal. Though there are no points of collision, in matters of mere dignity, the

---

* The plaintiff, being an alien, or a citizen of another state, can do the same thing in the first stages of the suit. But it is impossible to be minute in a work like this; the writer merely aims at giving a general idea of the system of the jurisprudence of the United States.

† Each county has a sheriff under the laws of the state.

marshal is a man of more importance than a sheriff, inasmuch as his baili-wick embraces a whole state instead of a county; and he executes the supreme law of the land, though, in fact, his functions are often limited to a course of concurrent, or rather to a division of familiar powers.★

Each state also forms a district for the circuit courts of the United States. At the circuit, a judge of the supreme court of the United States presides, assisted by the judge of the district. They hear original cases, and such appeals as, by law, can be brought from the tribunals of the state. It fre-quently happens that actions affecting parties residing in different states are brought in the courts of a particular state, because the property in dispute lies there, and the defendant then carries his appeal to one of the circuit courts of the United States. You will see that, of necessity, the laws of the several states must be known to the judges of these circuits, as a great deal of their power goes no further than to take care that these laws shall not infringe on the rights which are guaranteed by the confederation.

The judges of the supreme court of the United States sit once a year, to hear appeals and questions of law. They have all the equity powers which are necessarily incident to justice, there being no chancellor of the United States. Their decisions are final, no appeal lying to any other body of the land. This dignified and powerful tribunal not only decides on the interests of individuals, but on the interests of states. Communities that are, even now, larger than the smallest kingdoms of Europe, can come before them, in their corporate capacity as suitors and defendants.

The affairs of this immensely important tribunal have ever been con-ducted with surprising dignity and moderation. The judges are amenable to public opinion, the severest punishment and the tightest check in a free community, and their corruption can be punished by impeachment. An instance of the latter occurred during high party times, and while the doc-trines of Europe were more in fashion than they are at present, but the accused was not found guilty.

★ The United States have, as yet, no gaols. There is such perfect understanding between the two authorities, that the states lend their gaols, and court-rooms, &c. to the officers of the United States, though it is probable that, ere long, provision will be made for both. A convict, sentenced to hard labour by a court of the United States, is sent to the Penitentiary of the state where he is convicted, the former defraying any excess of expense over the fruits of his earnings.

The duties of the supreme court are often of a highly delicate nature, but the judges have contrived to create a great degree of reverence for, and of confidence in, their decisions. As the population of the country increases, the number of the judges will be increased to meet its wants.*

You know that steam was first successfully applied to boats in America. The celebrated Fulton obtained a law (in the State of New York) creating a monopoly of its use in his favour for a term of years. At first, the experiment was deemed so hazardous, that he enjoyed this exclusive right without molestation. But, when the immense profits of the speculation became apparent, men began to question the legality of the monopoly. Boats were built, without the consent of the assignees of Fulton. The chancellor of the State of New York, regarding the act of his own legislature, granted an injunction, prohibiting their use. The parties then joined issue, and the case was carried through the courts of the state, until it reached the Court of Errors, where it was decided in favour of the law of the state. New parties appealed to the circuit court of the United States, as citizens of another state, and as citizens claiming the protection of the laws of the confederacy. It was contended that the law of New York was unconstitutional, inasmuch as the states had conceded the right to protect inventions, &c. &c. to the general government, and that no state had a right to grant a monopoly on waters, that might interfere with the commerce of the whole country. So the supreme court decided, and, since that decision, there has been an end of the monopoly. Many of the states have enacted laws, of different natures, that have always been treated with great reflection and candour, but which have been as effectually destroyed by this court.

In respect of mere dignity, the judges of the supreme court of the United States stand foremost over all others. A judge of the district court is, as a rule, perhaps, about equal to a judge of the supreme court of a state, though these parallels are entirely arbitrary. In point of variety of power, the judges of the states have much the most; but, in point of importance, those of the United States are the greatest, since appeals can be made to, but not from, them.

You can easily imagine that numberless questions of jurisdiction between the courts of the confederation and those of the states still remain

---

* It has recently been raised to nine.

to be decided. Although the laws of the United States, when constitutional, are called supreme, yet there are points where the two authorities must of necessity meet. To take a strong case, the life of the citizen is, in most instances, to be protected by the laws of the state; but it is possible to conceive a case in which some of the rights that are fairly enough incidental to the discharge of the powers ceded to the United States, might impair the force of a state law for the protection of the life of its citizen. In such a case reason must decide the limits of the two authorities, as it has had to decide the limits of concurrent authorities elsewhere. It would be folly to say always that the United States law being paramount, should prevail. In fact, in such questions, it is not supreme, even in theory; for the states, having reserved to themselves all the power they have not expressly yielded to the United States, have clearly the same claim to the rights incidental to the powers reserved, as the United States possess to the rights incidental to the powers which have been conceded. The courts of the states (which are bound to know and respect the authority of the United States) might have a natural leaning to extend these incidental powers, and it is in fixing their limits that the supreme court of the United States, which is placed above all petty and local interests, exhibits most of its usefulness and majesty.

A species of natural law is growing up under this system, that promises to be eminently useful, inasmuch as it is adapted to actual necessity I am a great venerator of those laws which are enacted by custom, since I entertain the opinion that the stamp of usage is worth a dozen legislative seals, especially in a community where men, being as free as possible, have every opportunity of consulting the useful.

The states have conceded all power to congress to regulate commerce. Now congress has jurisdiction over more than twenty degrees of latitude. It has not, however, yet seen fit to establish quarantine regulations for the numerous ports within its jurisdiction, though it is scarcely possible to imagine any measure which more intimately affects commerce than these laws. But the states do continue to pass quarantine laws, under their natural right to protect the lives of their citizens. Should any state, under this plea, attempt to pass such laws, however, as would operate unjustly towards another state, the court of the United States might then pronounce a decision affecting the question. There is as yet a divided opinion, in theory, on the subject of this right, while the practice is just what it ought to be; that is to say, those who are most familiar with the subject provide for its wants, and should any abuses arise, there is a power in the country competent to put them down.

As its institutions get matured by time, the power of the confederation is every day receiving strength. A vast deal of constitutional law, however, remains to be decided; but as new cases arise, the ability to make discreet decisions, grows with experience. Laws are enacted to meet the regulations necessary to the common good, and as the legislators are themselves citizens of the states to be governed, and one body of them (the senate) are the legal protectors of their corporate rights, there is little fear that the general government will ever reach that point of authority that shall make it weak by setting it up in opposition to a force that it would vainly strive to subdue. It may appear paradoxical, but the secret of the actual durability of this confederation consists in its apparent weakness. So long as the influence of the several states shall be of sufficient importance to satisfy their jealousy, I think it will endure; and so long as the present representative system shall prevail, there is every motive to believe the states will possess, with a reasonable portion of the power, a share in all the honour, and the profit, and the security of being members of an Union that must shortly stand foremost among the nations of the earth.

The true balance of power, which elsewhere is found to exist in the hands of individuals, exists here in the hands of legislative bodies, who are the direct representatives of those whose interests are controlled by the government.

VOL. II, LETTER 10

Cooper presents a history of the electoral college and the various presidents. Elections, Cooper notes somewhat ominously, are gradually precipitating sectional conflicts between the North and South. Cooper also reveals great personal admiration for Andrew Jackson.

TO SIR EDWARD WALLER, BART.
&c. &c.
Washington, ——

A great event has just been decided in this city. The ceremony of the election of a president of the United States, for the four years which shall commence on the fourth day of March next, took place yesterday. The circumstances which led to the peculiar forms of this choice, the characters of the candidates, and the probable result that it will have on the policy of the country, may not be without interest to one who studies mankind as generally as yourself.

The first president, you know, was Washington. He was succeeded by the vice-president, the elder Adams.* At the end of four years, a hot contest occurred between Mr. Adams and Mr. Jefferson, the president and

---

* An absurd story is told by a recent traveller, or a pretended traveller, in the United States, concerning the wish of Mr. Adams, when vice-president, to have the title of "Highness, and Protector of our Liberties," given to the president of the United States. It is said he introduced a resolution to that effect in the senate. Now, it happens, independently of the gross folly of the title, that the vice-president, who is merely a presiding officer, has no right to introduce any law or resolution, into the *senate* at all.

vice-president of the day, for the chair. In order to give you a proper understanding of the case, it will be necessary to explain the law for the election to this high office.

You know that the sovereignty of the states is represented by the senate. Thus, Rhode Island, with 70,000 inhabitants, has two members in the senate, as well as New York with 1,700,000. But the members of the lower house, which is the connecting link between the states, are apportioned according to the population. The state of Rhode Island has, therefore, two representatives, and the state of New York thirty-seven. In all ordinary cases of legislation, each individual, whether a senator or a representative, gives one vote. While New York has, consequently, eighteen times more influence in the lower house than Rhode Island, in the upper house they are equal. It is in this division of power that another system of the checks and balances of this government are to be traced.

For the election of the president, bodies are especially convened that are at other times unknown to the constitution. They are called electoral colleges, of which there are as many as there are states. These colleges are composed of citizens chosen in each state, in such a manner as its own laws may prescribe. They are sometimes elected by the legislatures, sometimes in districts by the people, and sometimes again by the people in what is called a general ticket; that is to say, every citizen votes for the whole of the electors that his state is entitled to choose. The number is determined by the population of the state. The number of representatives is added to the two senators, and the amount forms the body of the electors. Thus New York, having thirty-seven representatives and two senators, chooses thirty-nine electors; while Rhode Island, having but two of each class, is limited to four electors.

Within a certain number of days after their own election, the electors of each state meet at some indicated place, and form the several colleges. The time is fixed at so short a period as to prevent, as much as possible, the danger of corruption. There is undoubtedly a preconcert between parties, and an understanding in the way of pledges; but there cannot well be any direct bribery on the part of powerful individuals. Each elector gives one vote for president, and another for vice-president. As the constitution formerly stood, the citizen who received the greatest number of votes, provided they made more than half of the whole number, was chosen for the former office, and the citizen who received the next greatest number, under the same provision, was chosen for the latter office. The constitution has, however, been changed, so as to make it necessary that each vote should express for which officer it is given. These votes are counted in the presence of the college, and of any body else who may choose to attend, and the result is properly authenticated and sent to the department of state; the president of the senate opens and compares the returns in the presence of both houses of congress, after which the result is officially announced to the country. But as the votes of each state are known the day they are actually given, the public press uniformly anticipates the public documents by several weeks. If there should be no election, the final choice is referred to congress.

In 1801, the contest between Mr. Adams and Mr. Jefferson had a singular termination. Mr. Pinckney, of South Carolina, was the candidate for the vice-presidency, supported by the friends of the former; and Mr. Burr, of New York, the candidate supported by the friends of the latter. Adams was the head of what was called the federal party, and Jefferson the head of the democrats.★ The election of 1801 was the first triumph of the democrats.

★ A singular mistake is prevalent in Europe, concerning the origin and objects of the two great political parties, which, for twenty years, nearly equally divided the people of the United States. It is often asserted, and sometimes believed, that the federalists, were the secret friends of a monarchy, and that the democrats were, what their name would imply, the only friends of the people. The gross absurdity of this belief is completely exposed, by the fact, that a great majority of the people of New England, and of New York were, for a long time, federalists, and it is difficult to conceive that the mass of communities, so completely republican in practice, should entertain a *secret* wish to overthrow institutions which they had been the first to form, and which were so completely confirmed by long habit. Washington was, undoubtedly a federalist, as, indeed, were a very large proportion of the ancient officers and patriots of the revolution. But this party was more lukewarm in the cause of the French revolution, than the other, and its members were the advocates of a rather stronger government than the democrats. It is also true that, as some of its leaders acknowledged more of the maxims of the ancient monarchy than their opponents, all those who had a bias in favour of the mother country joined their ranks, and served to keep alive an impression which their enemies, of course, industriously circulated, that the party leaned to aristocracy. It was easy to raise this cry, both for the reasons named, and because a large proportion of the men of wealth in the middle and eastern states, were enrolled in its ranks. But there can be no greater absurdity than to suppose that any party has existed in America, since the revolution, with an intention of destroying, or, indeed, with the intention of seriously modifying, the present form of government. When the constitution was formed, and before all its principles were settled by practice, it was to be expected that men should differ on the subject of the *degree* of change that was prudent;

Mr. Adams and Mr. Pinckney were both handsomely defeated; but, by an oversight of the electors, Jefferson and Burr received the same number of votes in the colleges. This left the question of the presidency to be still decided, as the constitution then prescribed that the choice should be in favour of the candidate who had the greatest number of votes, provided always that he had a majority of the whole number.

---

but, as early as the year 1800, the federalists and the democrats were, essentially, nothing more than two great parties, struggling for place, and who adopted different politics about as much for the purpose of opposition as for any other reason. This got to be eminently the case a few years later, when the federal party grew desperate in the minority, and lost sight of character altogether in the conduct it pursued on the subject of the war with England. Some of the eastern politicians during that war, believing the moment favourable to a final effort, concerted a plan, by which the whole of the eastern, and some of the middle states were to unite in an attack on the policy of the general government, the result of which was to be the expulsion of the administration. This plan gave rise to the famous Hartford Convention. The opponents of the Hartford Convention accused its founders of a design to divide the Union. It is difficult to say what crude projects may have floated in the heated brains of individuals of that body, but this is a country in which individuals do less than elsewhere, especially in matters of great moment. The New England states themselves would never have encouraged a scheme so destructive to their own interests; but, had they entertained the wish, it would have been a mad policy without the connivance of New York, a state that was then, and has been since, daily draining them of their population, and which already numbers nearly, if not quite, as many souls as all New England united. It is well known that the great body of the federalists of New York refused to join the convention, even with a view to remonstrate, at the time when the country was engaged single-handed against England. The best evidence of what would have been the fate of an attempt to separate the Union, is to be found in the fact that the people of New England themselves treat with great coldness, the principal members of the Hartford Convention, although most men acquit them of entertaining so mad a scheme. But the federal party was destroyed by the policy it pursued in the war. The Hartford Convention was its dying effort, and its last moments were as impotent as those of any other worn out nature. The older members of the party sometimes act together, now, from habit and intimacy, but the generation that is just appearing on the stage, already read of the party struggles in which their fathers were engaged as matters of history. There is no such party known in the United States, as a party unfriendly to their institutions, though, doubtless, there are still a few men living who retain some of their ancient attachments for the sort of government under which they were born. It is worthy of remark, that the children of these men are almost always decided democrats, and in many instances, the complete success of the confederative system has overcome the prejudices of old and bigoted tories. It must be remembered, also, that though a majority of the people of Massachusetts and Connecticut, &c. were willing to try the experiment of the Hartford Convention, there were powerful minorities in every state concerned, without counting the influence of all the rest of the Union.

The choice of a president, by the provisions of the constitution, now devolved on congress. In the event of a referred election, the senators have no voices, the representatives of each state in the lower house giving but one vote; so that the final decision is made by the states, and not by the people. In 1810, there were sixteen states in the confederation. By a singular coincidence, two of these states had a tie in themselves; so that they defeated their own votes; and of the remainder, eight gave their votes for Mr. Jefferson and six for Mr. Burr. You should be told that the same law which referred this question to congress requires that the successful candidate should have a majority of *all* the states. Mr. Jefferson, therefore, required nine votes for success, which was the number necessary to make a majority of sixteen.

The members of congress voted thirty-five times on this interesting question, and always with the same result. At length, a member or two belonging to the states which had lost their votes by a tie, changed their minds, and gave their voices for Jefferson. This decided the matter, and placed that distinguished statesman in the chair for the next four years. At the expiration of the regular period of service, he was re-elected; but, imitating the example of Washington, he retired at the end of his second term.

Until now the vice-president had been the successor of the president: but although Mr. Burr, having the next greatest number of votes, was necessarily vice-president for the first of Mr. Jefferson's terms of office, he was superseded at the second election. The constitution had been altered so as to stand as at present, making it necessary to indicate the situation it is intended the candidate shall fill. A veteran of the revolution, but a man past the expectation of further preferment, had been selected to supply the place of Mr. Burr. The friends of the administration now turned their eyes on the secretary of state, as a successor to the president of the day. This gentleman (Mr. Madison) was elected, and a sort of change in the descent of power was effected. After a service of two terms, Mr. Madison also retired, and the secretary of the time being (Mr. Monroe) became the successful candidate. The second term of this gentleman's service is now near its close, and he retires too, as a matter of course. You are not to suppose that the constitution prescribes any other limits to the presidency of an individual, but that of a new election every four years but the example of Washington, and, perhaps, the period of life to which all the presidents have attained, after filling the chair for two terms, have induced them, in succession, to decline elections for a third.

On the present occasion, an entirely new state of politics presents itself. The old party distinctions of federalists and democrats are broken down, and the country is no longer divided into two great political factions. Mr. Adams, the secretary of state (and a son of the second president), is considered by a great number of people as the natural and the best successor to Colonel Monroe. When I say natural, you must confine the meaning of the word to a natural expediency, and not to any natural right. His claims consist of a long experience in the politics of the country, great familiarity with foreign diplomacy, and the intimate connection that he has so long had with the particular measures of the existing administration. He is a man of extensive acquirements, great honesty, and unquestionable patriotism. He is also a northern, or, as it would be expressed here, an eastern man (coming from New England); and hitherto Virginia has given four out of the five presidents. But the circumstance of birth-place has far less influence than you would suppose in a government like this. It is worthy of remark, that while Europeans are constantly predicting sectional divisions in this country, that the people of the country themselves appear to think very little about them. Mr. Adams has both a warm support and a warm opposition in the northern states, it being evident that men follow the bent of their humours or judgments, without thinking much on the question of north and south. It is an important circumstance, which always should be remembered in considering this subject, that though the south has, in consequence of its physical inferiority and peculiar situation, a jealous watchfulness of the north, that the north regards the south with no such feelings. It is clear that the sentiment must be active enough in both to induce men to overlook their interests, before it can produce any important changes.

Mr. Crawford, the secretary of the treasury, was another candidate for the presidency; Mr. Calhoun, the secretary of war, was a third; Mr. Clay, the speaker of the house of representatives, a fourth; and General Jackson, a senator of Tenesse, was a fifth.

The two first of these gentlemen sit in the cabinet with Mr. Adams, and present the singular spectacle of men united in administering the affairs of the nation, openly and honourably opposed to each other in a matter of the greatest personal interest.

Mr. Crawford was for a long time thought to be the strongest candidate. He is said to have been a man admirably qualified to fill the high station to which he aspired; but a paralytic attack had greatly weakened his claims, before the meeting of the colleges. His friends, too, had committed a vulgar blunder, which is more likely to be fatal here than in any country I know. They commenced their electioneering campaign by bold assertions of their strength, and the most confident predictions of success. I have heard a hundred men of independence and of influence say that disgust, at having themselves disposed of in this cavalier manner, disinclined them to a cause that they might otherwise have been induced to support. It is the opinion of Cadwallader that Mr. Crawford would not have succeeded had his health not so unhappily suffered. He was but little known to the northern states, and men of character and talents always choose to have at least the air of judging for themselves. He succeeded, however, in receiving enough votes to include his name among the three highest candidates, and consequently he came before congress on the final question.

Mr. Calhoun, who is still a young man, and who probably aimed as much as any thing at getting his name prominently before the nation, to be ready for a future struggle, prudently withdrew from the contest. As he is universally admitted to be a man of high talents, he was put up, in opposition to the celebrated Albert Gallatin, for the vice-presidency; and as that gentleman declined the election, Mr. Calhoun was chosen by the colleges nearly unanimously.

Mr. Clay had many warm friends, and was supported by his own state (Kentucky) with great zeal; but he failed in getting his name included on the list of the three highest. He is a self-created man, of unquestionable genius, and of a manner and eloquence that will always render him formidable to his opponents, and of immense value to his political friends. His direct interest in this election, however, ceased, of necessity, with the returns of the colleges.

General Jackson is a gentleman who has long been employed in offices of high trust in his own state, but who only came prominently before the nation during the late war. He is a lawyer by education, and has filled the civil stations of a judge, a member of congress, and, lastly, of a senator. In early life he served as a soldier, during the struggle for independence; but he was much too young to be distinguished. As a military man his merit is unquestionable. He led two or three difficult expeditions against the Indians of the south with great decision and effect, and with an uniformity of success that has been rare indeed against the savages of this continent. In consequence of the skill and energy he displayed on these occasions as a general of militia, he received a commission in the regular army, soon after the declaration of war against

Great Britain. Fortunately, he was chosen to defend New Orleans against the formidable attack of that country. He was lying a short distance above the town, with a small body of men,* when it was unexpectedly announced that the enemy had landed at a point, whence a forced march of two or three hours would put them in possession of the place. Mustering as many of his motley troops as he could spare from other points of defence, (something less than sixteen hundred men,) he led them to the attack against a regular and much superior force, whom he attacked with a spirit and effect which left an impression that he was far stronger than the truth would have shewn. By this bold measure he gained time to throw up entrenchments and to receive reinforcements. Before his works were completed, or one half of the necessary troops had arrived, the British risked the celebrated attack of the 8th of January. They were repulsed with horrible slaughter to themselves, and with an impunity to the defendants that was next to a miracle. The works were entered at an incomplete point; but all who presented themselves were either slain or captured. The great modesty of the account of his success given by General Jackson is as worthy of commendation as was his indomitable resolution. Contrary to the usage of the times, he gave his opinion that the loss of the enemy was several hundreds less than what they acknowledged it to be themselves, and, indeed, nearly a thousand less than what further observation gave him reason to believe it actually was. If the decision of this extraordinary man was so brilliantly manifested in the moment of need, his subsequent prudence is worthy of the highest commendation. Although he had not hesitated an instant to attack nearly twice his force on the open plain, when nothing short of desperate courage could save the town, he did not allow success to lure him from a position which experience had shewn he could maintain. He suffered his beaten, but still greatly superior enemy to retire unmolested; and it is probable that, had they asked for succour, he would cheerfully have yielded them assistance to embark.†

---

* Less than three thousand men. As late as the 29th December, General Jackson, in an official letter, states his whole force at 3000 effectives. In the report of the battle of the 8th January, he says, that though a detachment of Kentucky militia had arrived, they added but very little to his force, as most of them were unarmed.

† The force with which General Jackson defended New Orleans, according to the official returns, was less than 6000 men, imperfectly armed and organized: and all of whom, with

General Jackson obtained immense popularity in the country by this brilliant success. His political honesty is unquestionable, and his patriotism without a blot. Still his want of experience in matters of state, and even his military

---

the exception of a few marines and sailors, and two battalions of new levies for the army, in all about one thousand men, were the citizens of the country. It is believed that, sailors and marines included, General Packenham landed nearly ten thousand men. It would be a curious study, to those who have any desire to sift the truth, to examine the documents of England and America in relation to the events of their two wars. The writer must say he has met many Americans who are familiar with the documents of England, but he never yet met one Englishman who was familiar with those of America. Nations lose nothing by looking a little closely into their own affairs, as well as into those of other people. One circumstance first drew the writer into a closer investigation of these subjects, than he might otherwise have been induced to undertake. He will relate it.

It is well known that, in 1814, a bloody battle was fought near the great cataract of Niagara. The American general says, that a brigade of his army met a portion of the British army, and engaged it. That he arrived with reinforcements, the enemy reinforcing at the same time; that he was much annoyed by certain pieces of artillery, stationed on an eminence that formed the key of the English position; that he carried this hill at the point of the bayonet, and captured the artillery; that the enemy made three desperate attempts to regain the position and their guns, in all of which they were defeated, and that they finally relinquished the attempt. He gives his enemy a small superiority of force, and he conveys an implied censure against the officer third in command (he and his second in command having been obliged to retire, from their wounds), for not securing the fruits of this victory on the morning succeeding the day of the battle. So much for the American. On the other hand, the English general gives a sufficiently similar account of the commencement of the battle. He also admits the charge up the hill, that "our artillerymen were bayonetted by the enemy in the act of loading;" that "our troops having for a moment been pushed back, some of our guns remained for a few minutes in the enemy's hands;" that they were, however, soon recovered; and that, instead of his making attacks for the recovery of the lost position, the Americans were the assailants; and that they were uniformly defeated in their attempts. He estimates the force of the Americans at nearly double what their official reports state it to have been. Both parties nearly double the (presumed) loss of their enemy; and the American, though something nearer to the admission of the Englishman than the Englishman was to the admission of the American, estimated the force of his enemy considerably over the official account.

The writer was struck with these official discrepancies. The documents were uttered to the world under the same forms, in the same language, and by people acknowledging the same moral influences. He was induced to exclaim. Where is the truth of history! The writer knows nothing more of the merits of this question than is contained in the documents he has examined, and which any one may also examine, who has a curiosity equal to his own. The circumstance should, however, teach moderation to partizans, as it abundantly proves that the data on which they found their opinions cannot always be of the most unexceptionable nature.

habits, were strongly urged against him. The former may be a solid objection, but, it is more than absurd, it is wicked to urge the military character of a citizen, who meritoriously leaves his retirement in the hour of danger to carry those qualities with which nature has endowed him, into the most perilous, and commonly the least requited service of his country, as an argument against his filling any station whatever. A thousand falsehoods have been circulated at the expense of General Jackson, and even some admitted inequality of temper has been grossly exaggerated. Notwithstanding the industry and affected contempt of the adversaries of this gentleman, he received more of the electoral votes than the highest of the three candidates in the returned list.

The day of the final decision by congress was one of great interest here. All the candidates were on the spot, in the discharge of their official duties, and large bodies of their friends had assembled to witness, and if possible, to influence the result. Cadwallader obtained a convenient position where we both witnessed the whole manner of the election.

Although three names were returned to congress for the choice, it was universally understood that the selection would be made between Messrs. Adams and Jackson. It would have been indecent in the representatives to prefer Mr. Crawford over two men, both of whom had received nearly double the number of the popular votes that had been given in his favour, though by the constitution they certainly had a right to elect which of the three they pleased. It was thought that the representatives of those states in which the electors had given their votes for this gentleman, would make a single demonstration in his favour, and then give their voices for one or the other of the two candidates, who, it was well known, must eventually succeed.

The gallery of the hall of congress was crowded nearly to suffocation. The senators were present as a sort of legal witnesses of the election, and many men of high political consideration were in the lobbies and behind the desks. In short, every one was there who could gain admission by art or influence. The arrangements for this important proceeding were exceedingly unpretending, though remarkably imposing by their simplicity, and that air of grave composure which usually reigns over all the legislative proceedings of this country.

The members of the different states were now seated together, since they composed so many separate colleges which, on this momentous question, were to pronounce the voices of their particular communities. Here, sat the numerous and grave-looking representation of the powerful state of

New York, and by their side was a solitary individual, who, in his own person, held all the authority that was to be exercised on that important day, by the younger community of Indiana. This gentleman, and one or two others, were men of peculiar importance in an event like this, since accident had placed them individually on a level with large bodies of enlightened and discreet men. Still it is not probable that they dared to depart from the known wishes of the people they represented, so direct and certain is the punishment which usually attends popular displeasure in this country.

At the appointed hour, the states began to collect the voices among themselves. The members voted by ballot, having established for that purpose, a set of simple forms by which the votes were collected and reported to tellers appointed to receive them by the house. Fraud was impossible, since each college knew the precise number of its votes, and each individual deposited his ballot with his own hand. The duty was soon performed by the smaller states, and a moment of breathless suspense succeeded while the representatives of New York were collecting their votes. The friends of Mr. Adams had counted on twelve states with great confidence, but the number and the peculiar policy of the members from New York had rendered their vote more doubtful. The result was, however, soon known on the floor of the house, as was quite apparent by the look of suppressed triumph that was playing about the eyes of certain partizans, and the air of forced composure that was assumed by their adversaries.

The result was communicated to the speaker, (who had himself been a candidate before the electoral colleges,) and then it was officially announced "that *thirteen* states had given their votes for John Quincy Adams, for President of the United States during the four years, commencing on the fourth of March next, and that the said John Quincy Adams was duly elected."*

While the sweet, clear, voice of Mr. Clay was announcing this important news, I never witnessed a more intense silence in any assembly. The stillness continued a moment after his words had ceased, and then followed the low hum of whispers, and immediately after, a half involuntary and feeble clapping of hands was heard in the galleries. This little burst of exultation on the part of some indiscreet spectators, gave me an opportunity of witnessing

---

* Thirteen states being a majority of the twenty-four which now compose the Union, were necessary to a choice.

the manner in which the American legislators maintain order and assert their dignity. "Serjeant at arms, clear the galleries!" commanded the speaker, in a voice, that of itself hushed the slightest sound of approbation. The officers of the house instantly performed their duty, and in a few moments those spacious and commodious seats which were so lately teeming with conscious human countenances, presented nothing to the eye but its magnificent colonnade and long rows of empty benches.

The house soon adjourned, and every body quitted the capitol, some filled with joy they could ill suppress, and others evidently struggling to conceal the defeat of expectations which had probably been more fed by hope than reason. The important question was, however, irretrievably decided by a first vote, notwithstanding hundreds had anticipated that a struggle similar to that of 1801 was about to occur again.

The election had been conducted with great heat, especially in the public prints, and so much seeming violence of denunciation had been used during the discussions, that I confess I was induced to look about me, as we quitted the edifice, in quest of the legions that were to tame so many unquiet spirits, and to teach them submission to an authority that exercised its functions in forms so simple as those I had just witnessed. I had heard so much of revolution, and of the disorders of popular governments, that it did not appear possible a question which, an hour before, had filled the minds and voices of men with so much bitterness, could peaceably subside in quiet, and in submission to a force that was invisible.

During the preceding week, more than one foreign functionary had whispered in my ear something that implied a sneer on the folly of periodically throwing society so near the verge of dissolution by enlisting the passions of the community in a question that embraced so many important interests as these frequent elections, and one of them had intimated an expectation that, in the event of his failure, there would be a rising in favour of a military hero, who was not accustomed to defeat. I remembered the reply of my quiet yeoman in the stage-coach, and did not certainly carry my expectations quite so far; but still it was inconceivable that passions which had been so strongly excited, should subside without at least some of the usual indications of a disappointed resentment.

While descending Capitol-hill, we met a warm partizan of the unsuccessful candidate, who was known to us both. "Well, ——," said Cadwallader,

"what do you intend to do now? Your man has, beyond all hope, lost the day."
"We shall change the face of things four years hence," was the answer. The
reply was given in the tone of one who seemed conscious that he and his
friends had been mistaken in their force, but who, at the same time, felt that
legal means of obtaining a triumph were always before him. I must acknowledge when I found that one of the most violent partizans I had ever met, was
for deferring his schemes of revenge to a day so distant as four years, and that
he even then contemplated to effect his object by means of the ballot box, I
began to despair of seeing a revolution in America during my visit. It is true
that the defeated party have begun already to raise a clamour against corruptions and bargains, but it is very evident that they are doing it as mariners
place an extra anchor to windward, to be in readiness for the tempest which
is known to come on periodically.*

The result of this election, and the sudden calm that succeeded to so
much apparent warmth, have again led me to reflect on the vague and imperfect impressions which we get in Europe, of the actual political condition of
America. During the war of 1812, one saw monthly accounts, in the journals
of England, that this, or that, state of the confederation was on the verge of a
separation from the Union, and that distress had driven men to madness and
all sorts of political desperation. If these accounts were published in good
faith, they imply an inconceivable ignorance of the actual state of the
country; for, unless the opinions of intelligent men of all parties grossly
deceive me, there never has been one hour since the adoption of the present
constitution, when probably one thousand *natives* of the whole United States
have seriously contemplated any such event as likely to be near. If the paragraphs to which I allude, were published with a view to deceive the people

---

* The writer had an excellent opportunity of witnessing the effect of the American
Institutions, shortly after the event above described, while on a visit to the city of
Philadelphia. A foreigner, who conducted a paper in that city, was so profoundly ignorant of the people among whom he lived, as to invite a meeting of the citizens of Pennsylvania, in order to provide the means of marching to Washington to put down Mr.
Adams, who, it was affirmed, had been elected by means of corruption. Curiosity drew
thousands of spectators to the appointed spot, in order to see what would be done at
such a meeting. No officers appeared to oppose it, and yet the affair ended in the utter
disdain of the whole community. The miserable intruder on the peaceful habits and
common sense of the Americans was too much despised to be punished for his impudence, though he could not escape contempt and ridicule.

of Europe, it has induced the inevitable consequences of a wilful ignorance, *viz.* disappointment. I am perfectly satisfied that a vast majority of the citizens of this country have more confidence in their own institutions than in those of any other nation, nor can I find, on a reasonably close examination of the subject, that they are so very wrong. One thing is certain, that other nations have made much nearer approaches to their opinions during the last half century, than they have made to the opinions of other nations.★

I have conversed freely on this matter with my friend Cadwallader. I cannot say that he discusses the subject with particular gravity; but one of his remarks struck me as possessing singular force. "How is it," he said, "that you, or any stranger who enters our country, can and does freely discuss the danger of a dissolution of our confederacy, or the probability that we shall one day become a monarchy, and that, too, without giving offence or finding any difficulty in meeting with disputants; or how is it that an American never goes into an European country, Switzerland, perhaps, excepted, without finding men, let their breeding be what it may, who very unequivocally let him know that they consider his government as a chimerical project, and the constitution of his empire exceedingly frail; while, on the other hand, if the American attempt a comparison between his own government and that of his assailant, he is generally silenced by cold looks and an averted eye? It is odd that all this sensitiveness, more especially as the parties exhibiting it rarely fail of being bold enough on the subject of American democracy, should abide in the midst of such conscious security. We all of us know that most Europeans so far identify themselves with their soil as to believe they have a moral superiority over the American that is exactly in

---

★ What are all the changes that have occurred in so many kingdoms on the continent of Europe, but approaches to the American system? It is certainly the fashion, and for obvious reasons, to look to England as the model for the new constitutions, but what is England herself about? The American would say, that the recent repeal or alteration of the Test Act, the state of the Catholic question, the disfranchisement of rotten boroughs, the improvement of the common law, and, in short, the whole plan of rational reform which now pervades England, rests on principles, that rather than abandon, his ancestor preferred to emigrate. When a man states this undeniable truth, with a view to exult in the superior penetration of his own people, he should be reminded how very far the most faultless are from perfection in any thing; but when an European insolently and ignorantly assumes that the United States are existing in a state of political insecurity, every day and every hour, the citizen of the latter country has a natural right to throw these stubborn facts into the teeth of such supercilious commentators.

proportion to the antiquity of their governments; but *we* also know a fact that commonly escapes their acuteness. The practices of Europe form part of our experience; while Europe knows nothing of our practices. Answer me one thing. Why does America trouble herself so little about the governments of Europe, while all Europe is demonstrating on paper that our republics cannot endure? I think, when you find the motive of this marked difference, you will not be far from the secret consciousness which the two parties have in the strength and durability of their respective systems."

The evening of the day of the election was one of those on which Mrs. Monroe opens the doors of the White-house to the motley assemblage I have already described. Great anxiety was felt by every one to be present, because it was known that the principal personages, who had been so recently exerting themselves in the question which was just decided, were in the habit of paying their respects, on these occasions, to the wife of the first magistrate. We went at ten.

Perhaps the company on this evening was a little more numerous than on the preceding drawing-room. It was composed of the same sort of visitors, and it was characterized by the same decency of exterior and of deportment. We found the President and Mrs. Monroe in their usual places; the former encircled by a knot of politicians, and the latter attended by a circle of women, of rather brilliant appearance. Most of the secretaries were near, conversing cheerfully, like men who had just got rid of an irksome and onerous toil; and I thought, by the placid air of the venerable chief justice, that he was well content that the harassing question was decided. The assistant justices of the supreme court were also present, near the person of the president; and a group had collected in the same room; in the midst of which I discovered the smiling features and playful eye of La Fayette. The speaker was known to have favoured the election of Mr. Adams, and I thought I could trace secret satisfaction at the result in a countenance that his height elevated above those of most of his companions. There was no coarse exultation on the part of the victors, nor any unmanly dejection on that of the defeated. Several of the latter spoke to us; and, in reply to the laughing condolences of my friend, they made but one remark—"We shall see what the next four years will do."

"How do you do, General Jackson?" said Cadwallader, as we passed out of one drawing-room into another. The unsuccessful candidate returned the greeting with his usual mild and graceful mien. I watched his manly and marked features narrowly, during the courteous dialogue that followed; but, with all my suspicions, it was impossible to trace the slightest symptoms of a lurking disappointment. He left us laughing and conversing cheerfully with some ladies, who induced him to join their party. A minute before, he had been seen congratulating his successful rival with great dignity, and with perfect good nature.

We now entered the last apartment of the suite, with the hope of finding a cooler atmosphere. A group of men, among whom perhaps a dozen women were intermingled, had collected about some object of common interest. Drawing near, I caught a glimpse of the cold air which, in contrast to an uncommonly fine and piercing eye, forms so remarkable an expression in the countenance of Mr. Adams. He was certainly in good spirits; though, had we not known his recent victory, it is probable that his manner would not have been at all remarked. He soon extricated himself from the crowd, and spoke to two or three of us who stood together. "Why have you not been to see us lately?" he inquired of a member of congress, from Virginia: "Mrs. Adams complains that you were not at her last evening." "I have been there so often this winter, that I began to think it necessary to be absent for the sake of form." "Is that the etiquette?" "We must ask that question of you;" returned the Virginian, laughing, in allusion to the secretary's well-known strictures on the subject; "*you* are our authority in all matters of etiquette." "Well then," returned the president elect, with great good humour, and with the tact of a courtier; "I pronounce it to be always etiquette for Mr. —— to visit Mrs. Adams."*

---

* Mr. Adams and General Jackson are again candidates for the presidency. As the contest is as yet confined to these two, and it is so shortly to be decided (in December of 1828), it is probable that one of them will be chosen. What the writer now states, he says understandingly. A good deal is certainly said concerning the inexperience of General Jackson, and some press the circumstance of his chief merit being military, as a reason against him. There is not a man in the Union, however, who seriously apprehends any danger from his election. It is false that he is not supported by wary and prudent men. The writer can name a hundred gentlemen in the middle states, of education, of fortune, and of religion, too, who are his warm friends. The question is altogether one of men, there being scarcely a measure of policy that is likely to be much affected by the result. A great deal of the popularity of General Jackson is owing to an injudicious and presuming opposition, which has foolishly ascribed a danger to his success, that is as false, as his friends are determined to manifest it is ridiculous. But men may well hesitate about rejecting so tried a patriot, and so experienced a statesman as Mr. Adams.

A discussion of government's spending and income. Cooper details the expenses of the branches of federal government as well as the army, navy, and a sampling of states.

TO THE PROFESSOR JANSEN,
&c. &c.
Philadelphia, ——

Congress necessarily rose on the night of the 4th of March. You must have learned from my previous letters, that a congress lasts but two years, commencing on the 4th of March of one year, and terminating on the 3rd of March of the year but one following. Of course it would be necessary to convene the new members, in order to proceed in legislation after the prescribed period. This can be, and has been, done, in times of need, but the usual practice is to let the bodies separate, at the end of what is called the "short session." The terms of short and long session are easily explained. The constitution requires that congress should assemble on the first Monday in December of each year, unless it has adjourned to a different period, or is expressly convened by a call from the president. On the first year of the service of the members, it is plain they may sit as long as they please; but on the second, their term of service expires on the 3d of March. As one third of the senators, and perhaps about the same number of the representatives, usually retire every two years, it would be necessary to summon those who supply their places, should the public service require an immediate continuation of the legislative duties. The senate sometimes sits a day or two after the lower house has adjourned, in order to attend to what is called executive business (the approval of nominations to office). The practice is, I believe, uniform, at the end of a presidential term, in order to give the new incumbent an opportunity to name his cabinet. In all such cases the new senators are summoned in time to attend. Of course no legislative business can then be done.

Late on the evening of the 3d of March, congress rose; but, in point of fact, the change of executive power was not made until the president elect took the oath of office. This ceremony took place about noon of the following day. In 1801, when Mr. Adams, the elder, went out of office, he made sundry nominations which were confirmed by the old senators on the evening of the 3d of March. Mr. Jefferson, his successor, refused to ratify these appointments. He took the ground that, as president, he had the power to appoint to office, the senate only possessing, in effect, a veto. Now, the new functionaries had not received their commissions, and no one could, constitutionally, sign them but the actual president; this, the actual president refused to do, and of course there were no appointments, since it is by no means incumbent on the president to appoint an officer, even after the senate has approved of his name, the power of the latter going no farther than their negative. It could be of no moment, except in the appointment of a judge, whether the president appointed these officers or not, since, in all other cases, he possesses the power of removal, the commissions invariably running—"this commission to continue in force during the pleasure of the president of the United States for the time being."

The president absolutely appoints certain inferior officers of the government, such as midshipmen, masters, gunners, &c. &c., in the navy, and all the cadets that enter the army; but, in point of fact, a great deal of republican equality is observed in the distribution of even these small favours. The plan is to give to each state officers in proportion to its representatives; still the absolute selection is with the president. All the postmasters in the country, who are, in truth, only deputies of the post-master-general, receive their commissions from the latter officer. Of course the president, who can at any time remove the post-master-general, has a controlling voice in all the superior appointments of that department. The secretaries also appoint their own clerks, and there is a considerable patronage in the hands of the secretary of the treasury, who names several hundred officers, in the different custom-houses, that receive salaries of between five hundred and a thousand dollars each. The constitution indicates certain officers who *shall* be nominated to the senate. It then goes on to say, that all others must be similarly appointed, unless congress, by law, shall see fit to trust the power in the president, or in the heads of departments. As yet, congress has seen fit to do both; but should the trusts be abused, it always possesses the power to repeal its own enactments.

A great deal is said in Europe concerning the economy of this government. It is the subject of much ridicule and of high praise on our side of the Atlantic. In order to form a just opinion on the subject, it is necessary to ascertain some of the leading facts.

You will always remember, that as there exists a double form of government, there are double sets of officers to be paid. This circumstance, however, does not add in any great degree to the expense, since no duty is performed twice. The president of the United States receives a salary of twenty-five thousand dollars a year. This sum can neither be increased nor diminished during his term of service. He is also supplied with a furnished house. On this salary the president can live like a gentleman who receives a good deal of company, and it is thought he may even lay by a reasonable excess yearly. Perhaps, considering the nature of the government, the income is about what it should be. The heads of departments receive six thousand dollars each, and no house. Their salaries are too low, since they scarcely afford the means of creditable subsistence to men in their public situations. It is probable, however, that the country will, ere long, erect buildings for the residence of these officers, and increase their pay a little. There is no plausible reason why it should be so much inferior to that of the president. The chief justice of the United States receives five thousand dollars a year, and each of the assistant justices four thousand five hundred. The judges of the district courts are paid from eight hundred to three thousand dollars a year, according to the amount of their services. The vice-president gets five thousand dollars a year. The members of congress receive eight dollars a day, each, while at Washington, and eight dollars for every twenty miles of their route in going and returning. Ministers plenipotentiary receive nine thousand dollars a year salary, the same sum for an outfit, and one-fourth of it to defray the expences of their return home. This pay is much too small, certainly; and it is as unwise in its generality, as in its amount. It is unjust to pay a man who is compelled to live in London, for instance, the same sum as a man who is compelled to live in Madrid. It is unwise to neglect to use, in a rational degree, an influence that other people acknowledge, whatever may be its inherent merit, or whatever may be the opinion of the people of the United States themselves on the subject. Their motive in sending ministers abroad, is interest: and we, who know the effect of a little appearance in our hemisphere, know that he is a gainer who consults the prejudices of those with whom he is required to dwell. But independently of this truth, which must, however, be taken with a proper degree of qualification, in many places, the agents of this government cannot subsist with a proper degree of comfort on their salaries. No man can maintain the establishment of a private gentleman and educate four or five children well, on two thousand pounds a year, in London. Consuls receive no pay (as such). The collectors of the customs are paid in proportion to their duties, limiting the receipts to less than five thousand dollars a year. A similar plan is observed with post-masters, and sundry other officers; the maximum of pay varying according to the importance of the office. Although the higher functionaries of this government are not often paid as well as they should be, the lower officers are very generally well rewarded. Salaries of two or three thousand dollars, for situations of no great dignity, are not uncommon, and there are many subordinates who receive from eight to twelve hundred. In short, the object, though it sometimes fails, is to make all classes of men comfortable, without furnishing the means of a useless splendour to any. The errors that have undoubtedly been made, are the unavoidable results of a popular government, in which official men are sometimes reluctant to incur a responsibility that leads to no very important results. I think that time will correct them, and should it not, the evil is one of far less magnitude than that which is entailed by a lavish expenditure of the public money.

The whole of the civil, diplomatic, and miscellaneous expences of this government, for the year 1826, were 2,600,177 dollars. This is, however, exclusive of the cost of the state governments, and the cost of collecting the revenue. The latter is about 750,000 dollars. The military expenditure was 6,243,236 dollars. But the greater part of this sum was for the erection of fortifications, for ordnance, arming the militia, Indian department, and pensions of soldiers of the revolution, &c. The actual cost of the army, pay, subsistence and clothing included, was about 2,000,000 of dollars. That so extensive a country can protect itself at so cheap a rate, is in some measure owing to its remote situation, but chiefly to its institutions, which trusts its defence to the citizens. A vast deal is clearly gained by thus limiting resistance to its foreign enemies. I do not think that the pressure of a crowded population can produce any material difference, since the present system of America must ever make it the interest of a great majority to preserve order. A soldier in the army receives five dollars a month pay, with his clothes and victuals. The officers are paid according to rank.★ The other expences of the army are of a temporary nature, and furnish no clue to future estimates.

The navy of the United States, for the same year (1826) cost 4,218,902 dollars. But this sum is also liable to a great deal of explanation. The United States, to be in readiness to meet any emergency, maintain a corps of about 950 officers. Their present policy is to foster this corps, and consequently no one member of it is put on half pay, except at his own desire. The pay and subsistence of the officers, and the pay of the men, actually afloat (rather more than 5,000 in all), somewhat exceeds a million of dollars. In this number, too, about one-tenth are quarter-deck officers. Much of the money is for the expenses of navy yards, and the ordinary. About 300,000 dollars are for the provisions of the men. The rest is for the increase of the navy, arrearages, and for the support of the marine corps, of whom nearly 1000 are employed. The latter are, of course, in addition to the sea officers and seamen. It would be troublesome to separate the several parts of these expenditures in such a manner as to give a clear and simple statement of each and all of them; but as the American government publishes the most minute documents on these subjects, it is in the power of any one to do it who has sufficient interest in the subject to pursue so elaborate an inquiry. I shall content myself with the main results, coupled

---

★ A soldier enlists for five years. He receives the following articles of clothing during that period, viz. five uniform coats; three cotton jackets with sleeves; three woollen ditto ditto; ten pairs of grey woollen overalls; ten pairs of drilling ditto; three fatigue frocks: five trowsers; ten pairs of laced boots; ten ditto shoes; ten flannel shirts; ten cotton ditto; ten pairs of stockings; ten ditto socks; two leathern stocks: one great coat; three blankets; five pairs of wings; four pompons; two cockades and eagles; four bands and tassels; one leathern cap cover, plate, scales and ball; one forage cap, and ten pairs of flannel drawers.

with such facts of a general nature, as I think may reward you for the pain of decyphering my letters.*

All the appointments of a captain of the navy, in command of a shore station, are worth something less than four thousand dollars a year, exclusive of a house. When in command of a vessel, his pay is considerably less. There is a difference made in the case of a vessel of a very small size, though the commander of a 44 receives as much as the commander of a 74. But the pay of both the army and navy should not be considered as permanently established, especially of the latter service, which is just beginning to receive, in all its branches, that grave attention that its vital importance to the security and dignity of the nation demands.

You will perceive that, as a rule, the inferior agents of the American

---

* In the January number (LXXIII.) of the Quarterly Review, there is an article on the United States of America. The reviewer speaks boldly of the American navy, for he professes to treat of a work written by an English naval officer, who, in his turn, had also written a little decidedly on the same subject. In a note attached to the end of this volume, the writer has endeavoured to show in what points his information differs from that of both reviewer and reviewed, in respect to this important branch of the American policy. His present object is, however, confined to expenditure. In page 279 of the said Review, is the following sentence, "With this small number of men" (4,268), "the establishments of the dockyards on a very limited scale, and the civil branches of the service, a mere trifle, the sum expended for the naval department in 1826, was 4,222,952 dollars, or close upon one million sterling." In the printed report of the secretary of the treasury, now before the writer, Letter F. page 39, is a minute statement of the expenditure of the naval establishment for the year 1826. The gross amount is 4,218,902 dollars, 45 cents. From this report the following items are extracted: "Repairs of vessels, 485,970; ship houses, 44,296; gradual increase of the navy 793,704: ten sloops of war, 506,163; prohibition of slave trade, 22,220; pay and subsistence of marine corps (which is not included in the before mentioned number of men), 219,686;" and no less a sum than 294,380 for improvements and additions to navy yards, besides a number of small miscellaneous items, that make together about 110,000 more. The figures are all meant to represent dollars, and together they make 2,576,419, or something more than one-half the sum that the reviewer has taken for premises by which he wishes to show that the Americans maintain a small force at an enormous expense. Not one of the items here enumerated, properly belongs to the expense of the small number of men, the civil branches of the service, or the establishments of the dock-yards, unless additions and improvements to the latter can be thus considered. Independently of all this, the balance not only supports the service afloat, &c. &c. but it keeps *all* the officers of the navy (with perhaps a dozen voluntary exceptions) on *full pay*. The writer here leaves the matter between the secretary of the treasury of the United States, and the contributor to the Quarterly Review.—See Note A. end of the volume.

government are better paid than the same description of individuals in the employment of almost any other nation, while the higher officers receive less.*

The positive annual expenses of the American government are not far from 13,000,000 dollars. Of this sum rather more than three millions and a half are for the interest of the national debt. But the odd half million is met by the dividends of bank stock, for the purchase of which several millions of the debt were created. The actual outgoings, therefore, for the current service of the country, all improvements and constructions included, are within 10,000,000 dollars. Every thing is so much on the advance in the United States, that it is difficult to arrive at an exact understanding of what is meant by current expenditure. Thus, of 2,600,177 dollars, which formed the amount of the civil, miscellaneous and diplomatic head of the account (for the year 1826), near 1,200,000 dollars were miscellaneous enough, as the charges included 188,000 dollars for light-houses, near 300,000 for canal stock, and more than 200,000 for old claims arising out of the war of 1812. The real civil list of that year, exclusive of diplomacy, was 1,256,745 dollars, and the cost of all the diplomacy of the country was 180,103 dollars. This trifling sum supported the whole expense and contingencies, in short, the entire cost of more than twenty different missions in Europe, Africa, and America. It is worthy of remark, that the diplomacy of this country is managed about as well as that of most nations; and I am of opinion, that, when its power shall become sufficiently great to be dreaded, it will be found to be still more successful.

The clear revenue of the United States, from the customs alone, is now (1828) about 20,000,000 of dollars. As this source of receipts produces in itself a great excess over all the outgoings, there are no direct impositions laid by the general government. The debt is in the course of rapid extinguishment, and as the interest is annually diminished, the ability of the country to increase its expenditure is of course increased. Notwithstanding

---

* The expenditure for the year 1828, is estimated as follows; the result rarely differing materially from these calculations. Civil, diplomatic, and miscellaneous, 1,828,385 dollars; military service, including fortifications, ordnance, Indian department, provisions, arming of militia, &c. 4,332,091 dollars; naval service, including the gradual increase of the navy, 3,788,349 dollars, making a total for the regular expences of the government, including sums previously voted for erecting forts and building ships, of 9,947,125 dollars. The interest of the debt is not contained in this amount.

this prosperous state of the public purse, the most rigid economy is observed, a circumstance that it is idle to say is produced by any other cause than the direct agency of the people on the administration.

Thus far we have not touched on the salaries of the state governments at all. They are graduated, however, on the same scale of expense, the richest and largest of these communities rarely paying as much to the public servants as the general government. There is undoubtedly, in some few instances, as in the legislatures and judiciaries, a double set of officers to support but, when one remembers the great extent of the country, it will be seen that, under any other form of government, it would be impossible to avoid this expense. No single set of judges could travel over this great surface in times sufficiently short to administer justice equally and promptly, nor could one great and central legislative body enact all the local laws that are absolutely necessary to a country so new and so vast.

The only reply that the enemies of America (and they are all the enemies of liberty) can urge, when her example is pointed to in support of the doctrine of economy, is founded on the fact of the double form of its government, and the additional expense that is consequently incurred. I know of but two ways in which we can arrive sufficiently near the truth to ascertain whether this additional cost raises the expenses of the American to the level of those of the European or not. The one (and is it not infallible?) is to compare the amount of contributions paid by the parties; and the other is to attempt to reach the cost of governing some particular portion of the confederacy, and then to make the necessary comparisons between it and some equal community in our hemisphere. We will endeavour to do both.

The state of New York contains one-seventh of the entire population of the Union. One seventh of 2,600,177 dollars, the whole amount of the "civil, diplomatic, and *miscellaneous* expenses" of the general government for the year (1826) is 371,453. This dividend includes more than one million of miscellaneous expenditure, such as "light houses," "stock in canal companies," and "payment of claims for buildings destroyed in the war," but no matter, we will take the amount in gross. Now the whole expenditure of the civil list of the state of New York, is about 350,000 dollars. The two sums make 721,453 dollars. Here you have 1,700,000 inhabitants receiving justice at their own doors, internal protection, legislation in the utmost convenient form possible; and *all* the more general advantages of government, for the sum of less than half a dollar a head annually. If you divide the military and naval expenses of the United States by seven, you have the entire pecuniary charge that they defray, not only for the current expenses, but for the material provisions they are making for future defence.★ The states are at no other material expenses than those attached to the civil list, unless it be for the purpose of domestic *improvements,* and even a great portion of the latter, is thus defrayed, in the salaries of the *employés.*

Of incidental expenses the American pays less, considering his means, than the inhabitant of any other nation. Their city corporations, with the exception of one or two, are cheap, and little or no money is expended in mere show. There are no church establishments, and the religious contributions are therefore voluntary. Still the clergy are supported. There are various manners of doing this, as you may suppose, in a country so diversified in condition. In many of the old congregations, there are endowments which have grown in value with the growth of the country, and which now serve to relieve the people of a large portion of the expense. A farm bought for that purpose, and a house erected when land and materials were cheap, become valuable and useful in time. There is a common practice of erecting a church by contributions, and then renting the pews, for the support of the clergymen. No general rule is, however, applicable to this particular branch of expense; but as no one taxes himself beyond his own pleasure, and as churches are, for the circumstances, exceedingly numerous, it is fair to presume that the population do not find the expense of supporting the clergy burthensome. Trifling additional taxes are also laid in the counties and towns to defray local expenses, and, among others, for the maintenance of the common schools. These taxes also vary according to circumstances, the county which is building a court house and gaol, or which is engaged in any other public work, paying more at the moment than the county which has already discharged that duty. The *whole* tax paid on a farm valued at 5000 dollars in one of the older counties of New York, was five dollars. This included every charge for that year, though the assessment is subject to variations, being sometimes more, and sometimes less. As the United States, in point of fact, imposes no taxes in time of peace, this charge

---

★ It should be remembered that all the expences of the general government (in time of peace) are paid by the importation duties.

was all the owner of this farm had to pay (as such) for the entire protection of government. It is true he contributed something in the way of duties on imported goods, but that is a contribution that depended entirely on his personal expenditure. The impositions of the general government are, as you already know, commonly much lighter than those laid in other commercial nations.

In order to make a correct estimate, however, of the comparative rate of the taxes paid by the American, it is necessary to consider the value of what he receives. He is required to pay for improvements in the country, which produce a direct influence on the increasing value of his property. The income and the price of his farm keep equal pace with the growth of the settlement in which he lives. He enjoys the means of giving a creditable education to his children, within a reasonable distance of his own dwelling, and all for the sum included in the state tax, if the cost of school-books, paper, &c. be excepted. He is certainly compelled to devote more or less of his time to working the highways,★ but then he takes care that the route by his own door shall be kept in as good order as that by the door of any body else.

As a whole, the public impositions in America, including taxes, duties, labour, militia service, clergy, and every thing else, are exceedingly light. But it is absolutely impossible to give any particular example which shall not be liable to so much exception as to destroy it as a rule. So much of the contribution is returned in the way of improvements which effect the value of the property taxed, that, had I all the statements in my head, I do not know that I could give you a clear idea of their relative amount. All those local impositions which exist in other countries, as octrois, &c. &c. are utterly unknown here.

I have heard it imputed to America as a fault, that her system leads to the loss of time and money in excessive litigation. It is said that there are more suits at law here than among any similar number of people in the known world. Although I cannot pretend to say that the fact is so, I should be surprised to learn that it was otherwise.

The whole territory of the United States covers 2,000,000 of square

---

★ This imposition is laid according to the property of the individual. A commutation in money at a very reduced rate is allowed, but it is impossible to give its amount, since it is an assessment that diminishes with the improvement of the country.

miles. It is true that the title to more than half of this immense surface still exists in the government, where a vast deal of it will probably continue for ages. But, in order to bring our calculations within the bounds of exactitude, let us again look at New York. This state has 46,000 square miles of territory, which is owned among, we will say (1828), 1,750,000 people. Now, to every foot of this land there is a title somewhere. Very little, indeed, is the property of the state. Here, then, is a plain and direct reason why the 1,750,000 inhabitants should have more questions about land titles than the same number any where else, simply because they are the owners of more of the article in dispute. Land is also greatly subdivided in all the older parts of America, and of course each subdivision has its separate title. Then the rapid transfer of property which is incidental to the condition of a country in progress of settlement, multiplies conveyances, and each new conveyance opens the way to litigation. The revolution, with its changes, also gave birth to disputes which time is just beginning to settle, as indeed it is beginning to settle all other controversies that grow exclusively out of the transfers of real estates.

The United States are, again, a more commercial nation, compared with their population, than any other in the world. Among such a people legal disputes must, of necessity, arise. Justice is comparatively cheap, and easy of access. Men have confidence in her decrees; and the fear of power, influence, and corruption is unknown. In such circumstances wrong headed persons, who are ever apt to fancy themselves in the right, make their appeals to the tribunals boldly. I do not believe that the system of the United States encourages litigation, except as it brings all men before the court on terms not of nominal, but of a true equality. Still I can believe that the great number of low practitioners of the law who are scattered up and down the country, do induce men to enter rashly into legal contests. In the older and more regulated states, litigation is far less frequent, *cæteris paribus,* than in those that are more new. The same is true of the proportion of taxes, as compared to the value of property. I am of opinion that, were it not for the great number of country lawyers in America, it would be found that litigation is less resorted to than in many other countries, notwithstanding the unavoidable causes of contention which exist in a new country. The number of the lawyers is undeniably an evil; but, besides being an evil which is likely to correct itself, and which is already beginning to correct itself, it is one that is not without its advantages. They serve to keep alive an active knowledge of their rights among the people, and although much abused as pettifoggers, they make, in common, exceedingly useful and intelligent local legislators.

There is a great fashion of decrying men of moderate acquirements in all things, as if life were not more a matter of experience than of theories. It is much easier to assume than to prove, that a set of profound thinkers would legislate better for a community than a set of active and half-educated men, who are familiar with the practices of the world. All the common passions of man are as well, and perhaps better known to the latter than to the former, and after legislation has provided against the dangers that are coincident to their existence, one must seek the rest of its duties in the world and not in books. But what says experience? It would be difficult to find any one country on earth in which the laws are better adapted to promote the true interests of the community, than in the most, I am not sure I could not say the least, favoured of the states of this republic. And yet legislation is the business of practical men altogether. At all events, they have contrived to obtain quiet and security at a cheaper rate than other people, and that, too, in many cases under all the unpropitious circumstances of great dispersion and the first stages of society.

It is a rule which applies to all salaries in this country, that little or no allowances are made for the support of mere dignity. The dignity of government is supposed to rest in the people themselves; and among their other provisions for its support, they have taken care to retain most of the money. The president receives a larger sum certainly than is necessary for his mere subsistence; but then the president is liable to a vast number of expenses that other functionaries escape; and, in his case, it is thought politic to bid a little higher than common, in order to command talent. It is not too much to say, that the president of the United States, if a prudent man, can save quite as much money out of his salary, each year, as a first rate lawyer in practice would gain; and I confess I see but one reason why he has the smallest right to ask any more. He has generally reached a time of life when he retires, that forbids further exertion; and perhaps it is wisest to attach a degree of consideration to this high office, which shall preclude men from descending subsequently to inferior duties. The latter point, however, is one that will certainly admit of dispute, and I do not think the former as strong as it first appears. Necessity will teach men the value of prudence and exertion in early life; nor is this the country that ought to wish to see its chief magistrate setting an example of useless, but attractive splendour. There are no vices so contagious as the corruptions which flow from the excessive use of money, for the desire to possess it is a passion that all men feel, since it is the medium by which all the ordinary good of life is obtained. The accountableness of the public agents, and the simplicity of men of station, are matters of so vast importance in a republic, that the one should never be neglected, and as little occasion as possible should be given to make any serious innovations on the other.

We have just had a proof that the government of the United States knows how to give with grace and liberality on a proper occasion. When La Fayette first came to America, he did not proceed on his distant and hazardous expedition empty handed. The new states were then so poor, and they had been kept, by the operation of colonial policy, so completely dependent on the mother country for supplies, that the contributions of an individual were not without moment to them. The arms and money of the young Frenchman were scarcely less acceptable than his sword and his heart. They had amply returned his love; but it still remained to discharge a debt whose obligations were scarcely less sacred.

During the last session, a bill was introduced, appropriating two hundred thousand dollars in money, and a township of land, to extinguish this debt. It was not pretended that the money borrowed, or rather given (for the devotion of La Fayette to the cause he had espoused knew none of the forms of bargaining) had not been already returned. But the Americans know that their venerable friend has long been a heavy sufferer by the revolution in his own country, and they also know that he took little account of the pecuniary interests of this life. The bill was not passed in enthusiasm, and with the hurry of dramatic effect, but it went through the forms of legislation with calmness and dignity. It was even resisted by one or two sturdy republicans, who paid a tribute to the manliness of the nation, by openly contending that, as the infirm and poorer agents of the revolution were still unrequited, they could not vote to bestow money on another, for services that were performed in common. But a vast majority of the two houses were of opinion that injustice to part, was no apology for injustice to the whole, and the case before them was one of too disinterested and too brilliant service to admit of a parallel.

The claims of La Fayette on America cannot, surely, be likened to the claims of even Washington. The immortal patriot of this country owed his allegiance, his services, and his life, to the land of his birth; and his exceeding merit is in the faith and ability with which he discharged the duties. But nature had imposed no such obligation on La Fayette. We may admire and extol the filial piety of the child in its degree; but without it, altogether, the offspring would become a reproach and a subject of scorn before mankind. The stranger who yields his aid under the influence of a general philanthropy, is alone entitled to deep and unqualified gratitude, since the universal obligations of society create indissoluble connections between the members of families and the citizens of the same communities.

But there was still a loftier claim in the case of La Fayette to the homage of a nation. His devotion to the cause of America was a devotion to the interests of humanity. The service he performed was chivalrous in its conception, bold in its moral attributes, and fearless in its execution. He dedicated youth, person, and fortune to the principles of liberty; and it was fitting that an example should be given to the world, that he who had suffered in such a cause was not to go unrequited. In this view of the case, it was just as incumbent on the Frenchman to receive, as it was the duty of the American to bestow. At a time when the servants of despotism and abject submission are receiving such ample gifts for their devotion, it is encouraging to see one splendid instance, at least, of virtue, and disinterestedness, and patient suffering, receiving a portion of the worldly rewards that should be the exclusive property of men devoted to the good of mankind.

Religion succeeds well, Cooper argues, without the aid of government. Over two hundred years of American history have proven that. The competition between various sects, furthermore, leads not to conflict but to unity and a virtuous society.

TO THE ABBATE GIROMACHI,
&c. &c.
Washington, ———

You inquire concerning the state of religion in the United States. I presume you ask the question in reference to its outward and visible signs, since it is not to be supposed that a layman, like myself, is sufficiently versed in its mysteries to go deeper than that which is apparent.

You know there is no establishment. Congress is prohibited by the constitution from creating one, and most (I believe all) of the state constitutions have the same provision. In point of fact, there is none whatever. The clergy, and all that pertains, therefore, to religion, are supported by voluntary contributions, or by endowments that have been made by devises, gifts, and other private means.

The first point to be considered, is the number and the nature of the sects. If the Presbyterians and Congregationalists, between whom there exists mere shades of difference in discipline and opinion; shall be considered as forming one sect, they are certainly the most numerous. It is computed that they possess near three thousand congregations. The Baptists are known to have more than two thousand. Perhaps the Methodists rank next in numbers. The Protestant Episcopal church is greatly on the increase.

I find, by the Ecclesiastical Register, that it contains ten bishops, and three hundred and ninety-four clergymen.* Most of the latter are settled, and many have two or three congregations under their charge. There are a good many Friends (Quakers) in Pennsylvania, New Jersey, and New York. The two former states were originally settled by religionists of this persuasion. The Roman Catholics are the most numerous in Maryland and Louisiana. The first was a Roman Catholic colony, and the latter has, as you know, been both French and Spanish. The Floridas must also contain some Catholics. Many of the Irish who come to this country, and who are settled in the more northern states, are also Catholics; but, including all, I should not think they rank higher, in point of numbers, than the sixth or seventh sect, after allowing for all the subdivisions among the Protestants themselves. There are some Lutherans and Moravians, and a great variety of less numerous or local sects.

---

* It may be interesting to those of a similar faith in England, to understand the constitution of this church in the United States. Where there are Episcopalians enough, the diocese is confined to a single state. But, as there are ten bishops, and twenty-four states, it is plain that several of the states are contained in one diocese. There are, in point of fact, however, eleven dioceses, that of Delaware being vacant. The highest spiritual authority known is, of course, a bishop. Priests and deacons being all the orders named in the Bible, are the only other orders known or used in America. The highest authority is exercised by the general convention. The general convention is composed of two bodies, a house of bishops, and a house of lay delegates. Each diocese has a convention for the regulation of its own affairs. The general convention consists of the bishops, who form the house of bishops, and of laymen, who are sent as delegates from the state of convention. The object of this body is to promote harmony and uniformity of doctrine in the whole church. The state conventions contain the clergy of the diocese, and a lay delegation from each church. In both conventions, the clergy (or bishops, as the case may be) and the laymen vote separately, a majority of each being necessary to an ordinance. Clergymen are presented by their congregations, and bishops are elected by the conventions of the diocese, and are approved of by the house of bishops. There is no salary yet given to any bishop, though provisions to a reasonable amount are making for that object. At present they are all rectors of churches. The oldest bishop for the time being, is called the presiding bishop, though he enjoys no exclusive authority. There have been, in all, twenty-one bishops of this church in the United States, and they hold their ordination from the archbishops of Canterbury and York, and from the non-juring bishops of the Episcopal church of Scotland, jointly.

The law recognizes these authorities to a certain extent, as it does the authorities of all other churches. The Catholics have their archbishops and bishops, the Methodists their bishops, and the Presbyterians, Baptists, &c. &c. their own particular forms of government.

The most important point that is proved by the condition of this country, is the fact that religion can, and does, exist as well without as with the aid of government. The experiment has been tried here, for two centuries, and it is completely successful. So far from competition (if I may use so irreverent a term on so grave a subject) weakening, it increases its influence, by keeping zeal alive. While the Episcopalian clergyman sees the Presbyterian priest existing in his neighbourhood, and enjoying all the advantages that he himself enjoys, he is clearly obliged to do one of two things; either to abandon the race, or to contend with watchfulness and care. Now this is exactly what is done here. The clergy are as chary as women of their characters, for they are certain of being proved, not by tests of their own establishing, but by those established by their competitors.

You may be inclined to ask if such a rivalry does not lead to strife and ill blood? Just the contrary. Each party knows that he is to gain, or to lose influence, precisely as he manifests the practice of the doctrines he teaches: and that, I apprehend, so far as Christianity is concerned, is charity and forbearance. At all events, with now and then an insulated and rare exception, great apparent good will and cordiality exists among the clergy of the different sects; and, I fancy, it is precisely for the reason that there is nothing to be gained, and a good deal to be lost, by a different line of conduct. This is considering the question solely on its temporal side, but you know I commenced with professing ignorance of spiritualities.

Freedom of thought on matters of religion, is so completely a consequence of intellectual advancement, that it is impossible to prevent men who think much from doing one of two things; they either choose their own course, in secret, or they become indifferent to the subject altogether. I have always been of opinion that sects carry their articles of faith too far, since it is next to impossible to get two intellectual men to view any long series of metaphysical propositions in precisely the same light; and it would be better to leave them to the dictates of their own consciences, and to the lights of their own intelligence in lesser matters, after they are once fairly of a mind on the more material truths of their creed. This desirable object is obtained in the United States, to a certain degree, though not entirely, by allowing every man to choose his church without attracting comment or censure. Charity is a consequence of such a state of things, at least that charity which manifests itself outwardly. The true object of religion is, to teach men the path to heaven, and that is an affair more affecting the individual than any body else. The moment society ceases to take the absolute direction of the matter into its own hands, individuals interest themselves rather than lose the object; and, unless they do interest themselves, under any system, I believe we are taught to think that establishments will do them no great good.

Still society has a wordly interest in the existence of religion—granted. But if it can obtain its object without an establishment, of what use is the latter? It is true, one does not see as many churches in a given number of square miles in America, as in a given number of square miles in France or England: nor are there as many people to use them. In order to institute a fair comparison, all things must be considered. In the first place, I am of opinion that the Americans have more places of worship than twelve millions of people in any other country of the globe; and if the peculiar condition of the new states be considered, I believe they have, in point of moral truth, twice as many. I am quite willing to admit that the cheapness of construction, the freedom of opinion, and necessity itself, may all contribute to produce such a result, but I cannot see how this negative proof is to demonstrate that religion suffers from the want of an establishment. Let us examine the progress of the sects in a parish.

Ten miles square of wilderness is laid out in a township. Settlers come into it from all quarters, and of all denominations. The state has reserved a few hundred acres of land, perhaps, for the support of religion. The first thing commonly done, is to erect a shop for a blacksmith, and there is generally an inn near it, both being, of course, established in some convenient place. The school house, (or three or four of them,) soon follows, and then people begin to think of a church. During the time that force for so important an object has been collecting, itinerant teachers, missionaries, &c., sent from the older parts of the country, have been in the habit of collecting the people in the school houses, barns, or some other building, in order to keep alive the remembrance of holy things. I think it may be taken as a rule that few settlements, in the more flourishing parts of the country, exist fifteen years without reaching the church building age. Some do it much sooner, and others, certainly, require more time to mature their efforts. But the church (the building) must have a faith, as well as its builders? Not necessarily. Churches are frequently built and kept in abeyance for a maturity of opinions, though nineteen times in twenty the very disposition to erect a church pre-supposes an understanding as to the denomination it is to serve. In coming to this understanding, the minority are, of course, obliged to yield, which is precisely what they would have to do if there were an establishment. But an establishment would keep men from error. Let us see how the truth lies on this point. How do the establishments of Scotland, England, Denmark, France, and Turkey, for instance, agree? It is quite plain, I think, that establishments have nothing to do with truth; and is it not equally plain, by the example of this country, that they are not necessary to the existence of religion? But America was settled by religionists, and the spirit they infused in the country is not yet extinct! Admitted. Is there any more likelihood, had the ancestors of the Americans been atheists, that the present generation would create an establishment, than that it would receive religion in sects? Did the apostles come into favour under an establishment? Or would not a country be more likely to receive religion in forms to suit tastes and opinions, than in any one form that could not suit all faculties, or appease all judgments? Here then, I think, we have some reason to believe that establishments neither introduce nor keep religion in a country. But let us go back to our settlement.

The church is built, and as the Presbyterians have given the most money, and are far the most numerous, the priest who is called is of their persuasion. Those who are firm in their own particular faith, cherish it in secret; and when the proper time comes, they join a congregation of their own people. They could do no more if the church was built under an establishment. Those who are not very rigid in their faith, most probably drop quietly into the communion of the church they find so convenient. An establishment would compel them to do precisely the same thing. In the course of a few years more, however, the people begin to separate, or rather to follow their own opinions; and then every thing settles down as quietly as men choose their wives, or make any other important selection that they have reason to think is particularly interesting to their individual happiness. But does not all this intermingling and indistinctness produce disorder and confusion? Just the contrary. While society is in its infancy it produces harmony, by inducing mutual support: and it weakens prejudice, and is fatal to superstition, by bringing the former in subjection to all it wants to destroy it—familiarity: and by rendering the other obnoxious to the ridicule and exposed to the reason of competitors. It is a known fact, that a century ago, the American religionists were among the most bigotted of their respective sects; and it is just as true now, that they have immensely improved, and that they are daily growing still more reasonable, as familiarity with each other teaches them how very little better any one man is than the rest of his fellow creatures.

But it will become necessary, in time, to make some use of the land which has been reserved for the support of the gospel. How is this to be done in such a manner as not to give offence to the minority? You will recollect that this fund has been created in the most insensible manner, and not by the aid of any imposition than is felt by the citizen. It is not so much a measure of general policy, as one that is intended to aid, to a reasonable extent, the wishes of the majority. Were there Jews or Mahommedans enough in the land, to make such a measure necessary, I take it for granted, they would get their share. It is the great merit of this government that it does not aim so much to satisfy theories as to produce wholesome practical results. It is the great fault of its enemies, that instead of looking at it as a government should be viewed, in its worldly and positive aspects, they are for ever endeavouring to find some inconsistency in theory which shall appease a sense of secret uneasiness, that is beginning to get a little too prevalent for their complacency, that it is a more enviable state of society than they wish to believe.

As respects the matter in question, the people of New York (for it is altogether an affair of the individual states,) have seen they must do nothing, under the most favourable circumstances for doing a great deal for the support of religion, or they must incur the risk of invading some perfectly dormant principle of a bald theory. They give land, which is of no value at the time, leaving the people to dispose of it when it does become of value. We will suppose this reservation now to be worth a division. The inhabitants of the town are then required to make their election. Every congregation, which is in truth a congregation, gets its share, and there the business is disposed of. The infidel, or the man of indifference, or perhaps a solitary Catholic, gets nothing, it is true, for he does not want it. You will at once see that this sort of provision is of use only to those who go through the hardship of settling a town, since their successors may have different religious persuasions; but it is meant for the encouragement and consolation of those who do undergo the privations incident to such a service. The best possible proof of the wisdom of the measure is, that it does good, without doing the least harm to any body. I can readily understand that they who have been long accustomed to quarrel, and to see others quarrel about the temporalities of churches, will find a thousand difficulties in disposing of such a grant as this I have named; but facts are daily proving here that it can be done, when men are once accustomed to meet on such occasions in a spirit of amity, without any difficulty at all.

I remember to have held a conversation with an innkeeper who resided within a few yards of an edifice that was then in the course of erection as a place of public worship. I asked him the denomination of the people to whom it belonged. His answer was, "The Presbyterians." "And you, you are a Presbyterian, no doubt?" "No, I was baptized in the Episcopal church, and I must say, I like it best after all." "Ah, then you have nothing to do with the cost of building this house?" "I have paid my share." "But how is it that you pay for the support of a church to which you do not belong?" "I do as I please, and I please to help my neighbours, who will help me in some other way, if not in this; besides, they are christians as well as myself: and I mean to have a pew, and go and hear their parson till I can hear one of my own church." "But you may be converted?" "Well," he said, smiling, "then I shall be a Presbyterian, and my wife and myself will be of the same mind; we are not afraid of looking the truth in the face in America, let it come out of what pulpit it may."

In fact, the utmost harmony and good-will prevails among the different sects. Controversy is but little known, though I have been present at a dispute of a very remarkable character. The parties were a Baptist and an Universalist. They met in a field at an appointed hour, and the ceremonial of the rencontre was arranged with as much precision as if they had met for a less pacific interview. They were to be placed so many feet asunder, in order that their voices should be audible. They were to speak alternately, and by the watch, so many minutes at a time; and each was to confine himself, according to an established protocol, to a certain set of opinions, during particular hours. The audience stood around as silent listeners.

It was a remarkable, and not an uninteresting scene. As you may suppose, the learning brought into the combat was none of the deepest, but the zeal and native shrewdness were great, and the discretion was admirable. I left the mooted point in as much doubt as I found it, though a great deal of absurdity was disposed of in the controversy, in a rough but sensible manner. This exhibition was, of course, as much of a novelty to the people of the country as it was to me.

I witnessed other scenes that were alike impressive and beautiful. The Methodists have, at stated periods, what are called camp meetings. They assemble in thousands in some wood, and hold their religious festivals, in a manner that is as striking by its peculiar simplicity, as it is touching by the interest and evident enjoyment they experience.

It is a fashion to ridicule and condemn these meetings, on the plea that they lead to excesses and encourage superstition. As to the former, the abuse is enormously exaggerated; though, beyond a doubt, there are individuals who attend them that would seek any other crowd to shield their vices; and as to the latter, the facts shew, that while new and awakened zeal, in ignorant persons, frequently breaks out in extravagance and folly, that they pass away with the exciting cause, and leave behind them tender consciences and a chastened practice. What are the weaknesses of these men to those that are exhibited in countries where faith is fettered by the law? Or, if you maintain an establishment, and let men follow their private opinions, in what does America differ from other countries, except in things that are entirely dependent on the peculiar temporal condition of the republic, and which could not be avoided, if the citizens were all in full communion with the church of Rome itself?

It is a mistake to believe that the liberality on religious subjects, which certainly exists to so eminent a degree in this country, is the effect of the want of an establishment. On the contrary, the fact that there is no establishment is owing to the liberal institutions, and to the sentiments of the people. You will remember, that the same political right to create establishments is to be found in the state governments, here, as is to be found any where else. *All* power that can belong to governments, and which has not been ceded to the United States, is the property of the states themselves, in their corporate capacities. It is true that most of them have decreed, in their constitutions, that no religious tests shall be known; but it is necessary to remember who have framed these imperative and paramount ordinances. The powers, too, that decreed these limitations can change them. But let us examine into the actual state of the law on this interesting subject.

The provision contained in the constitution of the United States is altogether prohibitory. It goes to say, that the government of the confederacy shall pass no law to create a religious establishment, or to prohibit the free exercise of religion. It is contained in an amendment, and is embodied in a paragraph which exposes rather a declaration of the limits of congressional power, than any concession of power itself. The object of this amendment was unquestionably to afford a clearer evidence of the public mind, and to set at rest for ever any questions which, by constructions of any previously-conceded rights, might by possibility arise on matters of such importance. Still the declaration that congress shall not have power to do this or that thing, only leaves the individual states more unequivocally in possession of the right to do it, since they possess all the rights of government except those conceded to the Union.

New England was settled by the Puritans. Whatever might have been the other good qualities of these zealots, religious liberality was not one of their virtues. It argues a somewhat superficial knowledge of the subject to contend that the Americans owe all their mental advancement, and freedom from prejudices, to the circumstance that they came into the country as reformers. It would be more true to say, that they came as dissentients; but though dissent may, it does not necessarily, infer liberality. The fact is, that no country ever possessed a more odious and bigoted set of laws, on the subject of conscience, than those first enacted by the Puritans. Independently of the little favour that was extended to witchcraft, it was made death for a Quaker to enter several of their colonies! This spirit, which they brought with them from England, was part of that noble and much-vaunted mental gift that the Americans received from the mother country. Fortunately, they had wisdom enough left to establish schools and colleges; and although it is quite probable that many worthy sectarians, who aided in this labour, thought they were merely fortifying their exclusive doctrines, the result has shewn that they then took the very measure that was likely to introduce liberality and promote christian charity in their land.

The Quakers themselves, though less sanguinary, for they did not deal in death at all, were not much more disposed to the intercourse than their eastern brethren. The Catholics in Maryland enacted the laws that Catholics are fond of adopting, and, in short, genuine, religious liberality was only to be found in those colonies where the subject was thought to be of so little interest as not to invite bigotry. Out of this state of things the present rational, just, charitable, novel, and, so far as man can judge, religious condition of society, has grown.

The unavoidable collision of sects has no doubt contributed to the result. It was not in nature to embitter life by personal and useless conflicts, and collected force did not exist in situations to produce combined oppositions. The Puritans had it all their own way in New England, until time had been given for reason to gather force: and, in the other colonies, adventitious circumstances aided to smother discussions. Liberality in politics, in some degree, drew religious freedom in its train; and when the separation from England occurred, the public mind was prepared to admit of great equality of rights in all things. Slavery was certainly retained, but it was retained much more from necessity than from any other cause.

Still the advancement of thought in America was rather gradual than sudden. Many of the original provisions of the states, on the subject of religion, imply a timid and undecided policy. In New Jersey *no Protestant can be denied any civil right on account of religion.* This is clearly a defensive enactment. In Pennsylvania, Mississippi, and Tenessee, a belief in God, and a future state of rewards and punishments, is necessary to enable a person to hold office. In North Carolina no person who *denies the truth* of the *Protestant religion,* or the divine authority of the Old and New Testament was capable of holding office. Many of these provisions have been changed, though some of them still remain. There is scarcely a year passes in which some law, that has been a dead letter, is not repealed in some one of the states, in order to bring the theory of the government more in unison with the practice. I believe I have quoted, above, all the states in which any thing approaching to religious tests has existed, within the last ten years. Massachusetts has certainly altered its constitution since that period, and a law disfranchising the Jews has just been repealed in the state of Maryland, which you know was originally a Catholic colony.

In New Hampshire the constitution *authorizes* the legislature to make provision for the support of *Protestant* ministers; and in Massachusetts the same duty is *enjoined.* The practice is simply this. An assessment is laid on all the inhabitants according to their estates. It is, like all other assessments in this country, exceedingly light, as its amount is regulated by the people themselves, through their immediate representatives. If a Baptist, for instance, resides in a parish where there is no baptist church, he is at liberty to prove that he has paid the assessment to a baptist church any where else; but should he not be disposed to take this trouble, the money is paid to the town collector, who gives it to the church nearest his place of residence, I believe. A similar practice prevailed not long since in Connecticut, but, as I have already said, gradual changes are making, and it is a little difficult to get at the precise conditions of the laws of so many different communities, that are fearlessly adapting their institutions to the spirit of the age.

In Maryland, Virginia, North Carolina, and Tenessee, ministers of the gospel are not eligible to the state legislatures. In South Carolina, Kentucky, and Mississippi, they can be neither governors nor legislators. In Missouri they can fill no other civil office, but that of justices of the peace. In New York, Delaware, and Louisiana, they can hold no civil offices at all. The constitution of the United States, and of all the other states, I believe, are silent on the matter, and, of course, clergymen can serve in any situation to which they may happen to be called. In all cases, I understand, the construction put on these regulations is applicable only to men in the actual exercise of clerical functions. The opinions of the whole nation are directly opposed to the union of civil and religious duties in the same person.

I have already told you, and I wish to repeat it, as an important fact that is always to be remembered, that, considering their scattered condition and circumstances, the people of this country manifest great zeal and interest in behalf of religions I honestly think more than any other nation I know, and I believe it is simply because they are obliged to depend solely on themselves for its comforts and security. Perhaps the activity of the nation has its influence on this as on other things. Remember, I do not say that we see spires and holy places as often here as in Europe: if we did, America would contain twenty times as many places of worship as the largest empire we have, being, Russia excepted, twenty times as large; and the state of New York alone, with 1,750,000 souls, (1828) would possess two-thirds as many churches as England with her twelve or fourteen millions of people.

English writers have not been ashamed to dwell on the comparative scarcity of churches in this country, compared with those in their own, as if the circumstance afforded any argument of a want of religion in the people. They might just as well quote the fact, that there were not as many tombstones to prove the same thing; or the American might make the circumstance that his country possesses more trees than England a matter of moral exultation.

You would be astonished to witness the perfect liberality between the sects which has grown up under this state of things. In the first place, there is nothing temporal to quarrel about, and the clergy are driven to their Bibles for their influence and power. I have asked several members of congress how many Catholics there were in that body, and nobody knew. I once asked an individual, in the interior of New York (and in a thriving and beautiful village), to what denomination a certain person we had just left belonged. "He is an Episcopalian," was the answer. This was disputed by a third person present. Proof was then adduced to show which was right. All parties agreed that the individual in question was a strictly religious man. One insisted that he had seen him commune the preceding Sunday in the Episcopal church. "What of that?" returned the other; "I have seen his wife commune among the Presbyterians; and every body knows that she and all her family are Episcopalians." But every body did not know any such thing, for the other disputant maintained exactly the converse of the proposition. An umpire was chosen in the street. This worthy citizen "really did not know, but he thought that both man and wife were very pious people! Stop," he continued, as he was coolly walking away, "you are right, John, Mr. —— is a Presbyterian, for I paid him the pew money last fall myself; and he would not have collected for the Episcopalians." But even *this* was disputed, and so, determined to settle the point, I went and asked the individual himself. He was a Presbyterian. "But you sometimes commune with the Episcopalians?" "Often." "And your wife?" "Is an Episcopalian." "And your children?" "We endeavour to make them christians, without saying much of sects; when they are old enough, they will choose for themselves." "But which church do they go to?" "Sometimes to one, and sometimes to the other." "But they are baptized?" "Certainly." "And by which clergyman?" "By the Episcopalian; because my church does not deny the validity of his ordination, though my wife's church disputes a little the validity of the ordination of the Presbyterian." "And your wife, what does she think about it herself?" "I believe she is of opinion that there is a good deal more said about it than is necessary." And there the matter rested. Now this may, according to some people's opinion, be dangerous intercourse, but, on the whole, I am inclined to think Christianity is the gainer.

Religion is kept as distinct as possible from the state. It is known that Mr. Adams, the president just elected, is an Unitarian; a persuasion that is repugnant to most Christian sects, and yet you see that he is in the chair. People at a distance would infer indifference to the subject of religion from such an excess of liberality; but the fact is, the most zealous religionist in this country knows that the salvation of Mr. Adams' soul is a matter of more moment to himself than to any body else, and that if he be in error, it is misfortune enough, without condemning him to a worldly persecution. Besides, they have sagacity enough to know that there is no more infallible way to give strength to any party, that cannot be positively crushed, than by giving it importance and energy by resistance.

The sheriff of the city of New York, an officer elected by the people, was, a few years ago, a Jew! Now all the Jews in New York united, would not probably make three hundred voters! Some kind hearted people got up a society to convert the Jews there, a short time since, and a notice soon appeared in a paper inviting the Jews to meet to concert means of converting the Christians.

Notwithstanding all this, the country is as much, or more, a Protestant and Christian country than any other nation on earth. I merely state a simple fact, on which you are at liberty to reason at pleasure. The sects are about as numerous as they are in the mother country, and all that one hears concerning Thumpers and Dunkers, and other enthusiasts, is grossly caricatured. They exist, when they do exist at all, as insulated and meagre exceptions; and it is odd enough, that perhaps half of these fantastical sects have been got up by emigrants from disciplined Europe, instead of being the natural offspring of the liberal institutions of the country itself. There is no doubt that many people come from our side of the ocean with strange notions of liberty and equality, and that they either quarrel with the Americans for not being as big fools as themselves, or set to work, in order to raise up creeds and political doctrines that they fondly hope will elevate man far above any thing heretofore known. In the mean time, the natives go on in their common sense and practical way, and say as little as possible about liberty, equality, or bigotry, and contrive to be the freest and the happiest, as they will shortly be, in my poor opinion, the wealthiest and most powerful nation of the globe, let other people like the prediction as they may.

I shall close this letter with giving you an account of one sect, that is as remarkable for its faith as for its practices. I mean the Shaking Quakers. I have been at three of the establishments of these people, viz. Hancock (in Massachusetts), and Lebanon and Niskayuna (in New York). I believe there is still another establishment, in one of the south-western states. The whole number of the sectarians is, however, far from great, nor is it likely to increase, since their doctrine denies the legitimacy of matrimony, or any of its results. There may be a thousand or fifteen hundred of them altogether.

The temporalities of the Shakers are held in common. They are not an incorporated company, but confidence is reposed in certain trustees, who are selected as managers and guardians of all their real estates, goods and chattels. They are an orderly, industrious sect, and models of decency, cleanliness, and of morality too, so far as the human eye can penetrate. I have never seen, in any country, villages so neat, and so perfectly beautiful, as to order and arrangement, without, however, being picturesque or ornamented, as those of the Shakers. At Hancock, the gate posts of the fences are made of white marble, hewn into shape and proportions. They are manufacturers of various things, and they drive a considerable trade with the cities of New York, Albany, and Boston. They are renowned retailers of garden seeds, brushes, farming utensils, &c. &c.

Though men and women, who, while living in the world, were man and wife, are often to be found as members of these communities, the sexes live apart from each other. They have separate dormitories, separate tables, and even separate doors by which to enter the temple.

But it is to the singular mode of worship of these deluded fanatics that I wish to direct your attention. You know, already, that no small portion of their worship consists in what they term the "labour of dancing." Their founder has contrived to lay his finger on one or two verses of the Old Testament, in which allusion is made to the custom of the Jews in dancing before the ark: and, I believe, they also place particular stress on the declaration of Solomon, when he says, "there is a time for all things," among which, dancing is enumerated. It is scarcely necessary to say, that none but the most ignorant, and, perhaps, the weakest minded men, can join such a sect from motives of conscience. I saw several negroes among them.

I went to attend their worship at Niskayuna. It was natural to suppose that their dancing was a sort of imitation of that of the dervishes, in which enthusiasm is the commencement, and exhaustion the close. On the contrary, it was quite a matter of grave preparation. The congregation (the Shakers) entered the meeting by different doors at the same time, the elders of the two sexes leading the advance, and one following the other in what is called single file. The men arranged themselves on one side of the room, and the women on the other. Their attire was rigidly simple and fastidiously neat. It was made nearly in the fashion of the highly respectable sect of Friends, though less rich in material. When silence was obtained, after the movement of the *entrée,* the whole group were formed in regular lines, and commenced singing certain spiritual songs of their own composition (I believe) to lively tunes, and with a most villainous nasal cadency. These songs were accompanied by a constant swinging of the bodies; and, from this commencement, I expected the access of the infatuated worship would grow by a regular increase of excitement. On the contrary, the songs were ended tranquilly, and others were sung, and always with the same quiet termination. At length, one of the elders gravely said, "Let us labour," just as you hear priests say from their desks, "Let us pray." The men then proceeded with gravity to take off their coats, and to suspend them from pegs; after which they arranged themselves in rows on one side of the room, the women occupying the other in the same order. Those who did not join the sets, lined the walls, and performed the duties of musicians with their voices. At the commencement of the song, the dancers moved forward, in a body, about three feet each, turned, shuffled, and kept repeating the same evolutions during the whole time of this remarkable service. It is scarcely possible to conceive any thing more ludicrous, and yet more lamentable. I felt disposed to laugh, and yet I could scarcely restrain my tears. I think, after the surprise of the ludicrous had subsided, that the sight of so much miserable infatuation left a deep and melancholy regret on the mind.

They appear to have an idea that a certain amount of this labour is requisite to salvation, for I learned that many of the elders had reached perfection, and that they had long since ceased to strive to reach heaven by pirouetting.

Now the laws of the different states where the small fragments of this sect exist, are far too wise and too humane to give their deluded followers any trouble. They are inoffensive and industrious citizens, and, in one or two instances, the courts have interpreted the laws as humanely in their favour as circumstances would reasonably allow. It is plain that the true bond of their union is the effect which concerted action and strict domestic government produces on the comforts of the grossly ignorant; but as the class of the very ignorant is quite limited in this country, and is daily getting to be comparatively still less numerous, there is no fear that this, or any other religious sect that is founded altogether on fanaticism and folly, will ever arrive at the smallest importance.

Vol. II, Letter 16

Cooper analyzes the geography of the southern states and their relationship to the "peculiar institution" of slavery. He admits the irony of the freest country also being one of the few in Christendom to permit slavery. Emancipation, however, comes down to property rights, an area over which the government(s) have no control. "There is not now, nor has there ever been since the separation of the colonies from the mother country, any power to emancipate the slaves, except that which belongs to their masters." Before Europeans criticize American slavery, though, Cooper writes they should look to their own history and see that they bear the guilt of creating the institution in the Americas.

TO SIR EDWARD WALLER, BART.
&c. &c.
New York, ——

It is an age since I wrote to any of the club. But though my pen has been necessarily quiet, the intervening time has not been unemployed. In the interval I have run over an immense surface in the southern and western states. It would be idle to attempt to describe all I have seen, and there would be the constant danger of leading you astray by exceptions, should I descend into detail. Still, as there is a great deal that is distinctive, I shall endeavour to convey to you some general ideas on the subject.

The first, and by far the most important feature, which distinguishes these states from their northern sisters, is slavery. Climate and productions induce some other immaterial differences. The laws, usages, institutions, and political opinions, with such exceptions as unavoidably grow out of states of society marked by such distinctions as the use or the absence of domestic slaves, are essentially the same.

There is a broad, upland region, extending through the interior of Virginia, the two Carolinas, and Georgia, where slaves are used, more as they were formerly used in New York and in the eastern states, than as they are now used in the other sections of the states named. That is to say, the farmer is the master of three or four labourers, and works in the field at their sides, instead of being a planter, who keeps a driver, and what are called gangs. Tenessee, and Kentucky also, with some exceptions, employ the negroes in a similar manner; while on the Mississippi, the Gulf of Mexico, and along the coast of the Atlantic, as far north as the Chesapeake, slavery exists much in the same forms as it is found in the English West India islands.

The country, on the whole coast of the United States, until one gets far northward and eastward, is low and champaign. It is healthy, or not, according to the degrees of latitude, and to local situation. The uplands are invariably salubrious. There is no region on earth more beautiful, or more fertile, than large parts of Virginia, Kentucky, and Tenessee. There is also much barren, or otherwise little valuable land, in the former state, as there is in the neighbouring states of North and South Carolina.

South Carolina and Louisiana are the only two states which, at the census of 1820, contained more blacks than whites. The former had 231,812 white inhabitants, and 258,497 blacks; leaving a balance of 26,685 in favour of the latter. Of the blacks, 251,783 were slaves, being 19,971 more slaves than whites. Louisiana had, at the same time, 73,383 whites, and 79,540 blacks; of the latter, 69,064 were slaves, being rather fewer slaves than whites. All people having black blood are enumerated as blacks. Georgia is the next considerable community which has so large a proportion of blacks. It had, in 1820, 189,566 whites, and 151,439 blacks. Virginia had 603,008 whites, and 462,042 blacks; and North Carolina 419,200 whites, and 219,629 blacks, or nearly two whites to one black. In Kentucky there were 434,644 whites to 129,491 blacks; and in Tenessee, which is much disposed to the habits of a free state, there were 339,727 whites to 82,826 blacks, a proportion of the latter not greater than what formerly existed in New York and New Jersey. Most of the blacks, in all these states, are slaves.

In 1790 there were 757,208 blacks in the United States; in 1800, 1,001,729; 1810, 1,377,810; in 1820, 1,764,836. By making premises of these facts, and taking the past rate of increase as a rule for the future, it would be found that there are now (1828) about 2,000,000 of blacks in the United States. In 1820 there were 233,400 *free* blacks in the United States. As the free blacks do not increase at the same rate as the slaves, this number cannot have accumulated in a full proportion, by natural causes. But emancipation has been busy since. New York, alone, has liberated more than 10,000 slaves since 1820. We will therefore assume that natural increase and emancipation have kept the free blacks up to the level of the increase of the whole number. This would leave us something like 1,750,000 for the whole amount of slaves in the country, at the present moment (1828). This result is probably not far from the truth. You will see, however, that my premises are a little faulty, because the increase of blacks between the years 1800 and 1810 was a good deal greater, in comparison with whole numbers, than between 1810 and 1820. This fact is owing to the abolition of the slave trade, which occurred between the two censuses of 1800 and of 1810, and which being known by a prospective law, induced extraordinary importations. Thus the increase between 1800 and 1810 was 376,581, whereas between 1810 and 1820 it was only 387,026, although there was so much larger a stock to increase from. Still, I think the amount of slaves cannot be much short of the number I have named. The white population, in the whole country, is now about 10,000,000. Of this number, however, at least 6,000,000, and probably a great many more, are in the free states. If we put the entire white population of the slave-holding states at 3,500,000, we shall probably give them quite as many as they possess. This would be making two whites to one slave in those states, and it is probably as near the truth as one can get at this distance of time from the census. But it has already been seen, that in many of these states the proportion of blacks is much larger than in others; South Carolina actually possessing more slaves than whites; and Tenessee having four whites to one black. There are, again, districts in these very states, in which the proportion of the whites to the blacks, and of the blacks to the whites, is even still greater.

In addition to these facts, it may be well to state that the whole white population of the country is known to have increased faster than the coloured, though the black population of the southern, or slave-holding states is thought to have increased a little faster than that of the whites.

In considering the question of slavery, as now existing in the United States, the subject naturally divides itself into the past, the present, and the future. It has been often said, that a people, claiming to be the freest of the earth, ought to have brought their practice more in conformity with their professions, and to have abolished slavery at the time they declared their independence. There are many unanswerable reasons against this allegation; or reasons that will be deemed unanswerable, by that portion of mankind who regard life as it actually exists, in its practical aspects and influences. There is not now, nor has there ever been since the separation of the colonies from the mother country, any power to emancipate the slaves, except that which belongs to their masters. This reason might satisfy most practical men of the impossibility of instantly achieving so desirable an object. That sort of humanity which regards the evils of a distant and alien people, and which, at the same time, turns a cold eye on the sufferings of those at hand, is, to say the least, as useless as it is suspicious. There is scarcely a nation in Europe, if, indeed, there be one, that has not a proportion of its population, that is quite equal to the proportion the slaves of America bear to the whites, which is not quite as low in moral debasement, the name of liberty alone excepted, and which, as a whole, endures much more of physical suffering than the negroes of America.

The condition of the American slave varies, of course, with circumstances. In some few portions of the country, he is ill dealt by. In most districts his labour is sufficiently light, his clothing is adapted to the climate, and his food is, I believe, every where abundant. The strongest evidence, after all, which can be given, that the amount of animal suffering among the American slaves is not great, (there are exceptions, of course), is the fact that they are a light hearted and a laughing race. I am very ready to grant that ignorance, and absence of care, are apt to produce hilarity, and that some of the most degraded and least intellectual people of the earth, are among the gayest; but I believe that it is a rule in nature, that where there is much animal suffering there is an animal exhibition of its existence.

There is still a higher, and a very numerous class of American slaves, who are far better instructed, better clothed, and better fed, and who are altogether a superior race to the lowest class of the European peasants. I mean the domestic servants, and those who labour as mechanics and artisans.

While on this branch of the subject, I shall take occasion to say, that

yearly meliorations in the condition of the slaves (and of the blacks generally), are taking place in some one part of the country or other. Several
unjust and exceedingly oppressive laws, that were the fruits of colonial policy, have been repealed, or greatly qualified, and public opinion is making a
steady advance to the general improvement, and, I think, to the final liberation of the race. Although these changes are not as rapid as they might be,
even with a due regard to policy, and far less rapid than most good men
could wish, it is a course that is more likely to be attended with less positive injury to the race of beings that true philanthropy would so gladly
serve, than one as headlong and as ill-advised as mere declaimers and pretenders would dictate.

I think no candid man will deny the difficulty of making two or three
millions of people, under any circumstances, strip themselves, generally of
half their possessions, and, in many instances, of all. There are few nations in
Europe, at this hour, in which the poorer classes would not be relieved from
serious pressure, would they, who have the means, tax themselves to discharge the debts which are the causes of so much of the heavy impositions
of their respective governments. Now, this would be a measure that would
do good to millions, great and almost inconceivable good, and harm to
none but to them that paid; whereas, a sudden, or any very violent emancipation of the slaves of America, would ruin those who did it, and scarcely
do less than ruin half, or even more, of those in whose behalf the charitable act would be performed. Let me be understood. I do not mean to say
that much more than is done might not be done, prudently, and with safety;
nor do I mean to say that most of those who find themselves in possession
of a species of property, that they have been educated to think a natural and
just acquisition, think much of the matter at all; but what I would wish to
express is, that they who do think calmly and sincerely on the subject, see
and feel all these difficulties, and that they weaken efforts that would otherwise produce an effect more visible than the sentiment which I think is
silently working its way throughout the whole of this nation.

In considering the question of American slavery, in reference to the past,
it is plain that Europe has been an equal participator in all that there is of
shame, or sin, in the transaction. There can be no charge more rapid and
unjust, than for an European to reproach the American with the existence
of slavery in his country. That the American is in the enjoyment of greater

power to do natural justice than the European, is just as true, as that, in most things, he does it. That slavery is an evil of which the great majority of the Americans themselves, who have no present agency in its existence, would gladly be rid of, is manifest, since they have abolished it in so many states already; but that it is an evil not to be shaken off by sounding declarations, and fine sentiments, any man, who looks calmly into the subject, must see. But so far as a comparison between Europe and America is concerned, let us, for an instant, examine the exceedingly negative merit of the former. Is it not a fact that the policy of all America was for more than a century controlled by Europe, and was not this scourge introduced under that policy? Has that policy, in Europe, been yet abandoned? Let us take the two most prominent nations boldly to task at once; does England or France, for instance, at this moment, own a foot of land on earth, where black slaves can be profitable, and where they do not use them?* It is absurd for France, or for England, to say we have no slaves in our respective kingdoms, properly so called, when every body knows that the one is at this moment filled with white beggars, and the other with paupers who are supported by the public purse, and both for the simple reason that they are overflowing with population. It is true, that two centuries ago, when they had more room, they did not import negroes from Guinea; but it is, also, just as true, that they sent their ships to convey them to colonies which are situated in climates where they might repay them for their trouble. It is as puerile as it is unjust, therefore, for these two countries, (most others might be included) to pretend to any exclusive exemption from the sin or the shame of slavery.

The merit of Christendom on the subject of the wrongs of Africa, is, at the best, but equivocal. Yet, such as it is, the meed is better due to the United States than to any other nation. They were the first to abolish the trade in human flesh, though the nation, of all others, that might most have reaped that short-sighted, but alluring profit, which tempted men to the original wrong. Had not the congress of the United States abolished this trade, there is no doubt millions of acres might have sooner been brought into lucrative cultivation, and the present generation at least would have been millions the richer. The whole body of the whites might have become a set of task-masters to gather wealth from the labour of the blacks. No doubt true

---

* It is well known that an Indian would be next to nothing in the Canadas, &c.

policy dictated the course they have taken, and they have but a very negative merit in pursuing it: still it should always be remembered, that what has
been done, was done by those who might have profited in security by a different course, and by those, too, who had been educated in the shackles of
a deeply rooted prejudice on the subject.

In reproaching the Americans with incongruity between their practices
and their professions, two or three points are very necessary to be remembered. In the first place, it is not true, as respects near 7,000,000 of the ten
that comprise their population; for *they* have given freedom and (essentially)
equal rights to those blacks who remain among them. The very condensa-
tion of the interests of slavery adds, however, to the difficulty of the subject,
since it makes the loss fall on a comparatively reduced number. The northern men had to do one of two things; to separate their fortunes from a portion of their countrymen, to whom they were bound by the ties of
fellowship, blood, common interests, and common descent, or submit to be
parties to an union in which some of the other parties were slave holders.
They were, in fact, slave holders themselves, at the time of the compact, so
that it would have been absurd to be very fastidious about the matter; and
there would have been but little wisdom in rejecting so much positive
good, in order to assert an abstract principle, that could be attended with
no single practical benefit. The southern states would have held their slaves,
had the northern refused to have joined them to make one nation; and, so
far as humanity is concerned, the negroes would not have been so well off,
since they now feel the influence of northern policy, while war and blood-
shed, and all the evils of a dangerous rivalry that would have arisen between
men whom nature had made friends and brothers are avoided. In short, this
is a reproach against the northern man, that is more likely to be made by
those who view the Union, and the continued harmony which pervades
these vast regions, with unquiet jealousy, than by any reasoning and practical philanthropist.

As to the southern man himself, he is placed, like so many nations of
other quarters of the globe, in an unfortunate predicament, that time and
society, and all the multiplied interests of life render so difficult to change.
The profession of the southern man is unquestionably that of equal rights;
and it is undeniable that he holds the black in slavery; but this does not
involve quite so great an absurdity as one would at first imagine. The slave

holders of the present day (viewed as a body) are just as innocent of the creation of slavery, as their fellow-citizens of New York or Connecticut; and the citizens of New York or Connecticut are just as innocent of the creation, of slavery as the citizens of London or Paris. But the citizens of the two former states have a merit in the matter that the citizens of neither of the towns named can claim, since they have stripped themselves of property to give freedom to their blacks, while those who were parties to the original wrong have contributed nothing to the measure they so much urge. But is it not possible to assert a principle under acknowledged limitations? The black man in the southern states of this Union is not considered a citizen at all. It would not be safe to consider him a citizen, in a country of equal political rights, since he is far too ignorant, and must for a generation at least, remain too ignorant to exercise, with sufficient discretion, the privileges of a citizen in a free government. It would, if any thing, be more prudent for the Virginian and Carolinian to admit boys of twelve years of age to vote, and to legislate, than to admit their blacks, in their present moral condition, without having any reference to the danger of a personal dissension. Equal rights do not, in any part of America, imply a broad, general, and unequivocal equality. It is the glory of the institutions of this country, that they have never run into practical excesses, in order to satisfy craving theories. By equal rights, the citizen of Connecticut, (and, I believe, no man doubts his rational and unlimited freedom,) understands that all who have reached a certain standard of qualification, shall be equal in power, and that all others shall be equal in protection. He does not give political power to the pauper, nor to females, nor to minors, nor to idiots, nor yet even to his priests. All he aims at is justice; and in order to do justice, he gives political rights to all those who, he thinks, can use them without abuse. He would be culpable only, if any class existed in his community, who might, with a little care, freely enjoy these rights, did he neglect to resort to that care. He therefore excludes only those who, on great, general, and lasting principles, are disqualified from exercising political power. The situation of the Carolinian is different, but his principle is quite the same: he excludes more; for, unhappily, when he arrived at the knowledge and the practice of a liberal policy himself, he found a numerous class of human beings existing within his borders, who were not competent to its exercise. He had but a choice between a seeming inconsistency, or the entire abandonment of what he thought a great good. He chose to make all equal, who can bear equality; and in that he has done exactly what his northern countryman has done, and no more. Should he unnecessarily neglect, however, to qualify these exceptions to enjoy a better state of being, he then becomes inconsistent.

I think these considerations must lead us to the conclusion, that most of the merits of this question lie in the fact of how much has been done and is now doing, towards effecting a change in what is admitted to be a prodigious evil. I feel confident that no discreet father, or husband, or brother, could ask a Carolinian, who was living in a state of highly polished society, and who enjoyed all the advantages of great moral improvement, to admit, at once, a body of men who had been nurtured in the habits of slavery, with all their ignorance and animal qualities, and who are numerically superior, to a participation of equal political rights. Such a measure would induce an absolute abandonment of their country and property on the part of the whites, or it would involve a degradation, and abuses that are horrible to reflect on. Individuals may and have parted with their means of personal indulgence to give liberty to their slaves; but it is too much to expect it from communities: nor would discreet individuals do it, if it were to be a general act, since a disorganization of society would be an inevitable consequence.

The true question, and that in which the friends of humanity should feel the deepest interest, is that connected with the steps that are taken to lead to the general emancipation, which must sooner or later arrive.

At the period of the declaration of the independence of the United States, slavery existed in all the British colonies. The blacks were not numerous in the northern provinces, for, there, the white was the better labourer. Still there were slaves in every one of the thirteen original states of this Union. The proportion of slaves in some of the middle states was nearly equal to what it now is in some of the southern. Massachusetts (which in 1790 had 5,463 blacks), put such a construction on its own bill of rights as abolished slavery. This was, I believe, the first measure of the sort that was ever taken on the American continent. The example has been successively followed, at different periods, by all the northern and middle states, until slavery is either abolished in fact, or by laws that have a prospective operation, in nine out of the fourteen states that adopted the present constitution in 1789. You may form some idea of the difficulty of getting rid of such an evil as slavery, by observing the caution with which these comparatively little incumbered states have approached the subject. Perhaps twenty years are necessary to effect the object humanely, even after the policy of a community is perfectly decided.

Numberless influences have, at the same time, been at work, however, to extend the limits in which slavery might exist. Alabama and Mississippi formed parts of Georgia; Kentucky and Tenessee were within the ancient limits of Virginia; and Louisiana, Missouri, and the Floridas were acquired by purchase. The people of Virginia and Georgia, in ceding their territory, were not disposed to cede the right of emigration, with the privilege of carrying their wealth with them, and slavery, in consequence, became extended over the four states named. Slaves were found in the two others, and in the Floridas. In this manner the eleven present slave-holding states came into existence. In the mean while, the states of Ohio, Indiana, and Illinois, were organized off what was once called the north-western territory. These, added to the nine states that had abolished the policy of slavery, and by the subsequent acquisition of Maine, brought their whole number up to thirteen.

I think that the influence of free opinions, if I may so express it, is steadily on the increase. It is not the smallest evil of slavery, that it begets in the master an indifference to its existence, and that it gives birth and durability to cruel and lasting prejudices. That these prejudices must be rooted out of the majority of the citizens of the southern states themselves, ere slavery shall cease to exist, is indisputable, since no power but their own can extinguish it. But my friend assures me, that within his recollection, an immense change has taken place in this particular. Twenty years ago, even in New York, a general and deep prejudice existed against this unfortunate class of human beings. It is rapidly disappearing. It is true, that the sort of commingling of the races, which a certain class of philanthropists are much fonder of proclaiming than they would be of practising, does not occur, nor is it likely very soon to occur in this country. Still there is every disposition to do the blacks justice, though there is none whatever to mingle the blood. I have heard of instances in which human beings of peculiar colour and form were esteemed in Europe as curiosities; but I fancy, if they abounded in any country, there would be found the same natural desire, in that portion of its inhabitants who believed themselves to possess the physical advantage to retain it, as is now found here. It is odd enough, that Europe, which, for so many centuries, has been making patents of nobility obstacles to matrimony, should decry so loudly against a people who hesitate a little at intermingling colours.

But there will still be a greater objection against this mingling of the races, for a long time to come. With few exceptions, the blacks of America belong to an ill-educated and inferior class. When free, they are left, like other men, to look after their own interests; and most of those, who have character and talent enough to rise above the condition of menials, push their fortunes in countries where they are not daily and hourly offended by the degradation of their caste. I think this circumstance must long keep them in a station which will prevent intermarriages. You will admit too, that matrimony is very much an affair of taste; and, although there well may be, and there are, portions of the world where white colour is not greatly admired, such is not the case here. The deep reluctance to see one's posterity exhibiting a hue different from one's own, is to be overcome, ere any extensive intercourse can occur between the blacks and the whites.

The probable future fate of the blacks of America, is a subject of deep and painful interest. I confess, however, I am not one of those who see any great danger to the whites in their increasing numbers. While they remain ignorant, their efforts must always be feeble and divided, and, as they become enlightened, they must see the utter impossibility of any continued success in a rising against a force numerically and morally so superior. Although the distances in America seem very great on the map, the inhabitants have contrived the means of bringing themselves wonderfully near to each other. The whites in the whole country increase faster than the blacks; and I think it will be found, that as emancipations multiply, the disproportion in numbers will be still greater, and always in favour of the former. It would not only be the duty of the northern men, but it would be a duty readily performed, to fly, in case of need, to the assistance of their southern neighbours. It is not easy to suppose circumstances in which the white population of the southern states, already (as a whole,) two to one against the slaves, armed, intelligent, organized, and possessing the immense moral superiority of their domestic relations, should not be sufficient of themselves to protect their persons and property against a rising. The only circumstances in which the danger could be very imminent or extensive, would be in the event of a foreign war; and then their common country would be a party, and the aid of states that will shortly number of themselves twenty or thirty millions, could be commanded in their defence.

But the danger of slavery, so far as it is connected with numbers, has its own cure. No man will keep a negro after he ceases to be profitable, any more than he will keep an extra supply of other animal force. If Carolina can bear 500,000 slaves, Carolina will probably accumulate that number; but after she has reached the point where policy says she must stop, instead of resorting to laws to retain her negroes, she will have recourse to laws to get rid of them. This to an European, and particularly to an Englishman, who knows that excessive population is the greatest burthen of his own country, may seem difficult; but in order to form a correct opinion of a question purely American, it is necessary to consider the actual state of things on this side of the Atlantic.

The already vast, and constantly increasing coasting trade of the United States, offers an easy, natural, and perfectly practicable drain, to the black population of the South. The blacks furnish, already, thousands of sailors, and useful sailors too, and they constitute a very important material for the supply of seamen, in considering the future commercial and nautical power of this confederation. The demand for domestics at the north, too, will, for many years, continue beyond the probability of a white supply. You will remember that experience has shewn that the free blacks have very little natural increase, and both these growing demands must therefore meet with most of their supplies from the slave-holding states. Then, again, the proximity of the West Indies, of Mexico, and of the South American States, in which a commingled population already exists, offer facilities for emigration, that Europe does not present. The slave population of the United States may reach 4 or 5,000,000, but (after a very short time) at a diminishing rate of increase,* and then I think it will be found that new means will be taken to get rid of them.

---

* At present the slave-holder has a motive for increasing his slaves, since he can sell them in the new states, but this demand will, of course, cease as the new states get full. Louisiana has recently passed a law, prohibiting the importation of slaves, a fact which the writer thinks proves the truth of his theory. The reader will always recollect that slaves cannot be *imported* into the United States, but that they can be *transported* from one state to another, unless prohibitions are made by the states themselves. This was part of the original compact, without which the southern states would not have consented to the present constitution.

In forming these conjectures, I have not regarded the narrowing of the limits of slavery by the constant advancement of opinion. It is true, that the surface on which slavery, in fact, exists, has, on the whole, been rather enlarged than otherwise since the existence of the confederation; but we should not lose sight of the circumstances under which this extension of the slave region has been effected.

It has spread with the diffusion of population, over districts that were originally the property of the slave-holders; and in no respect, except in mere territorial division, has there been any virtual enlargement of its political limits, unless one can thus call the enlargement of the borders of society. It is true, that when Missouri was admitted to the Union, an effort was made by the friends of the blacks (I use the term technically) to abolish slavery in that state. Had they succeeded, it would have been an inroad on the ancient limits; but their defeat ought not to be deemed an extension of the surface occupied by slaves, since slaves were there before. It was a sort of attempt to turn the flank of slavery, or to get into its rear; whereas I think it manifest that the great victory over habits and prejudices, which true policy will be sure to gain in time, is to be gained by pressing steadily on, in an open, manly, but cautious and conciliating manner, in its front. Ardent and steady a friend of universal liberty as you know me to be, I am, by no means sure, that, had I been a member of that congress, I would have given so violent an alarm to the slaveholders of the south as to have contributed to attempt to carry that law.

It is only necessary to witness the immense superiority that free labour possesses over slave labour, and to examine the different conditions of society in a state without slaves, and in one with, to see that a close contact must be destructive to the principles of slavery. The friends of emancipation have now a noble front, extending from the Atlantic to the Mississippi. I even think that accident has contributed to throw those communities most in advance, which are the least likely to retard the progress of emancipation. The honest and affluent, but quiet population of Pennsylvania, for instance, is much less suited to give the alarm to their neighbours of Maryland, than would be done by the more restless, everbusy people of New England, while their example is left to produce its undiminished effect. If I have been correctly informed, public opinion and sounder views of policy are making great progress in the latter state. The inhabitants begin to see that they would be richer and more powerful without their slaves than with them. This is the true entering wedge of argument, and juster views of moral truth will be sure to follow convictions of interest, as they have followed, and are still following, emancipation farther north.

The first and surest sign of a disposition to give freedom to the slaves, is the accumulation of the free blacks, since they are not only a positive proof that emancipation exists, but they argue an indifference to slavery in the whole community. In Maryland there were 145,429 blacks in 1810, and 147,128 in 1820. During the same time, the whites increased from 235,117 to 260,222. Emigration retarded the increase of the two races, no doubt; and yet, you see, contrary to the law of increase in most of the slave-holding states, the whites grew faster than the blacks. Now, of this number of 147,128 blacks, 39,730 were free. This is a very large proportion, and I hail it as a most auspicious omen. In point of fact, there were 4,109 fewer slaves in Maryland in 1820, than in 1810; while the whites had increased 25,105. Indeed, I heard very many enlightened and respectable men in Maryland regret that slavery existed among them at all; and the opinion is getting to be quite common, that free labour is the most profitable. Even in Virginia, the whites have increased 51,474, during the same ten years, while the blacks have increased only 38,954. It is true, the emigration renders these results a little doubtful; but the fact that there were, in 1820, 36,889 free blacks in Virginia, proves something. It is also of importance, that there exist, in so many of the slave-holding states, large bodies of their respective communities, who have very little interest in the perpetuation of the evil, except as their own personal welfare is connected with that of society. Although the latter influence is one of moment, it is also one that may influence a man both ways, since he may be as likely to believe that the interests of society call for some relief against the evil, as to think he ought to support it.

I have endeavoured to lay this important subject before you in a practical form. It has been done rapidly, and, I am quite certain, very imperfectly. It is proper to understand there is so much of intimate detail necessary to view the state of American slavery with discretion, that it is highly probable I may have fallen into error, but I still think you will find the views I have taken of it not without some plausibility. I shall sum them up, together with the leading facts, in as few words as possible.

I think liberal sentiments towards the blacks are rapidly gaining ground in most of the southern states.* Positive, political freedom is granted, or is in the course of being granted to them, in thirteen of the twenty-four communities of the confederation. Emancipation, geographically speaking, has now reached a formidable point of resistance (on account of the numbers of the slaves), but it is steadily advancing through the powerful agency of public opinion. When it has passed this point, its subsequent march will, I think, be easier and more rapid. Tenessee and Kentucky, the states that flank Virginia, have by no means so deep an interest in the maintenance of slavery, as the states further south; and I think it is not chimerical to hope that, by the aid of prospective laws, many are now living who may see slavery limited to the shores of the Atlantic, and to the Gulph of Mexico, with perhaps a belt for a little distance on each side of the Mississippi. In the mean time the advance of opinion is steady and great. Unless the christian world recedes, its final success is inevitable. I will not incur the charge of empiricism by pretending to predict the precise period.

I do not think that slavery, under any circumstances, can entail very serious danger on the dominion of the whites in this country, for at least a century or two. Districts might be ravaged beyond a doubt, but the prodigious superiority of the whites, in every thing that constitutes force, is the pledge of their power.

I am of opinion that the number of the slaves will be limited, as a matter of course, by necessity. There is a point beyond which they would be a burden. Nor is that point so distant as we commonly imagine. Perhaps it has been already attained in some of the older states.

I think that the free black population (except in the way of emancipation) does not increase, or, at least, not materially; and that the proportions between the whites and the blacks is steadily growing in favour of the former; that in future it will even grow faster; that emigration, the navy, commerce, and unsettled habits, will tend to repress the increase of the blacks, and to consume their numbers; and that the time of the intermingling of the races to any great extent is still remote.

Though there is much in these views to excite the regrets of a man of pure philanthropy, it appears to me that the cause of emancipation is far

---

* The writer does not mean that every man becomes in some degree sensible of the evil, but that a vast number do, and of men too, who are likely to have an effect on legislation.

from being as bad as it is generally supposed to be in Europe. Impatience is a characteristic of zeal. But impatience, though creditable to the feelings of the European, sometimes leads him, on this subject, into assertions that might provoke comparisons which would not be so honourable to his own society, perhaps, as he is apt to fancy. Impatience, however, on the part of the American, may even do worse; it may retard the very consummation he wishes. Mildness, candour, and conciliation are his weapons; and I think they will be irresistible. Although an ardent wisher for the happy moment of general emancipation, I always turn with disgust from those cold and heartless paragraphs which occasionally appear in the northern journals of this country, and which, under a superficial pretension to humanity, trifle with the safety and happiness of two of their fellow citizens in order to give an affected aid to the undoubtedly righteous cause of one black man. If this species of irritating language did good, if it did no harm by hardening men in their opinions, it would be disagreeable; but under the actual state of things it is far worse than useless. The general tone of the press, however, is sufficiently amicable, and all those who understand the difference between argumentation and judgment, have reason to hope it may long continue so.

But physical suffering, especially in a country like this, is not the prominent grievance of slavery. It is the deep moral degradation, which no man has a right to entail on another, that forms the essence of its shame. God has planted in all our spirits secret but lasting aspirations after a state of existence, higher than that which we enjoy, and no one has a right to say that such are the limits beyond which your reason, and, consequently, your mental being, shall not pass. That men, equally degraded, exist under systems that do not openly avow the principle of domestic slavery, is no excuse for the perpetuation of such a scourge, though circumstances and necessity may urge a great deal in extenuation of its present existence.

Vol. II, Letter 20

Cooper summarizes his arguments and predicts the future of the United States. The advancements of the Americans, he argues, stem from three advantages. First and most important, the American character is of the highest quality. Second, Americans use intelligently the room and resources of the frontier. Finally, republican institutions and the accompanying civil and religious freedom allow Americans to develop their natural and Godly gifts.

TO THE COUNT JULES DE BéTHIZY.

&c. &c.

Washington, ——

My pen grows weary, for I have seen so much, and written so little to the purpose, that I feel disposed to throw it away altogether. After making the tour of the coast of New England, and seeing all its large towns, I have returned here to prepare for my departure. I cannot quit the country, however, without giving you a summary of the information I have gained, or without indulging a little in speculations to which that information must naturally give rise.

The first reflection that is excited in the mind of an intelligent foreigner, after visiting these states, is an inquiry into the causes that have effected so much with means so limited, and in a time so short. A century ago the whole of the 1,000,000 of square miles that are now more or less occupied by these people, did not contain a million of souls. So late as the year 1776, the population was materially under 3,000,000, nor at the time did they actually cover more than 200,000 square miles, if indeed they covered as much. But since the peace of 1783, activity, enterprise, intelligence, and skill, appear to have been contending with each other, and they have certainly produced a result that the world has never before witnessed. I have heard Europeans say, that when they have heard that the Americans, of whom they had been accustomed to think as dwellers in remote and dark forests, possessed a million of tons of shipping, they believed their neutral character had made their flag a cloak for the enterprise and wealth of other nations. No doubt their commerce was somewhat unnaturally forced, and many frauds did exist, but the motives for deception have ceased these dozen years, and still America has a million and a half of tonnage. Perhaps no one demonstration of the energy of this population has excited in Europe the surprise that has been created by the boldness and dexterity with which they have constructed canals, that put to shame all similar works everywhere else. We understand the nature and the expense of this description of public works, and we know how to make a proper estimate of the enterprise necessary to effect them. But although the system of canals, which has broke so suddenly into existence in the United States, within the last ten years, argues an advanced and advancing state of society, it manifests no new principle of energy. It may be a higher exhibition of the quality, since the stage of improvement demands a superior manifestation of skill; but, believe me, the spirit which has produced it has not been dormant an hour since the British colonies have achieved their independence.

Although circumstances have lessened the interest which Europe has felt in America, it may be well questioned, whether the United States do not, at this hour, enjoy a higher consideration, on our side of the Atlantic, than the political doctrines, formerly in fashion, would have given to a people so dispersed, so few in numbers, and so remote. Their vast and growing commerce, of itself, makes them an object of the greatest attention, and the sure conviction that the child of that commerce, a marine, is likely soon to play its part in the great game of nations, gives additional interest to this republic. Still our anticipations are vague, founded on data but imperfectly understood, and, at all times, fettered by the prejudices and distinctive opinions of our own hemisphere.

In the first place, the influence of emigration on the growth of the United States has been usually overrated by Europeans. I have had occasion to say, already, that for thirty years it did not add many more than five thousand souls, annually, to the population. The fact is sufficiently known by the returns of the custom-houses, where all masters of vessels are obliged to report the number of their passengers. It is true, that thousands, who leave the mother country for the British provinces, find their way into the republic by land; but, perhaps, an equal number of natives have removed into the Canadas, the upper province of which is nearly, or quite half, peopled by emigrants from the states, or their descendants.

The first, the most important and the least understood, cause of the exceeding advance of the American states, is to be found in the character of their population. The general diffusion of a respectable degree of intelligence, would, of itself, produce an effect that it might be difficult to estimate precisely, but which may be always traced in its strongest point of view, in the respective conditions of the savage and of the civilized man. In addition to this general and mighty cause, the actual necessities of society supply an incentive to ingenuity and talent, that are wanted elsewhere. Were the American an indolent and contented being, nurtured in dulness, and kept in ignorance of the incentives which prompt men to exertion, this very state of necessity might serve to depress him still lower in the scale of being. But there is nothing more surprising in the country than the universal knowledge which exists of the condition of Europe. Their wants, therefore, feed their desires, and, together, they give birth to all the thousand auxiliaries of exceeding ingenuity. A proof of this fact is to be found in the manner in which the first canal of any importance was constructed. As it speaks volumes on the subject, I shall relate it.

Five-and-twenty years ago engineers from Europe began to make their appearance in America. They brought with them the rules of science, and a competent knowledge of the estimates of force, and the adaptation of principles to results; but they brought them all calculated to meet the contingencies of the European man. Experience showed that they neither knew how to allow for the difficulties of a novel situation, nor for the excess of intellect they were enabled to use. Their estimates were always wild, uncertain, and fatal, in a country that was still experimenting. But five-and-twenty years ago was too soon for canals in America. It was wise to wait for a political symptom in a country where a natural impulse will always indicate the hour for action. Though five-and-twenty, or twenty, or even fifteen years, were too soon, still ten were not. Ten years ago demonstrations had been made which enabled keen observers to detect that the time for extraordinary exertion had come. The great western canal of New York was conceived and planned. But instead of seeking for European engineers, a few of the common surveyors of the country were called to the aid of those who were entrusted with the duty of making the estimates; and men of practical knowledge, who understood the people with whom they had to deal, and who had tutored their faculties in the thousand collisions of active life, were brought to the task as counsellors. The result is worthy of grave attention. The work, in its fruits and in its positive extent, exceeded any thing of a similar nature ever attempted in Christendom. The authority to whom responsibility was due, was more exacting than any of our hemisphere. Economy was inculcated to a degree little known in other nations; and, in short, greater accuracy than usual was required under circumstances apparently the least favourable to attain it. Now, this canal was made (with such means) at a materially less cost, in infinitely less time, and with a boldness in the estimates, and an accuracy in the results, that were next to marvellous. There was not a man of any reputation for science employed in the work. But the utmost practical knowledge of men and of things was manifested in the whole of the affair. The beginning of each year brought its estimate of the expense, and of the profits, and the close its returns in wonderful conformity. The labour is completed, and the benefit exceeds the hopes of the most sanguine.

In this sketch of the circumstances under which the New York canal has been made, we may trace the cause of the prodigious advance of this nation. Some such work as this was necessary to demonstrate to the world, that the qualities which are so exclusively the fruits of liberty and of a diffused intelligence, have an existence elsewhere than in the desire of good. Without it, it might have been said, "The advance of America is deceptive; she is doing no more than our own population could do under circumstances that admitted of so much display; but she will find the difference between felling trees, and burning forests, and giving the finish which denotes the material progress of society." The mouths of such critics are now silenced. The American can point to his ploughs, to his ships, to his canals, to his bridges, and, in short, to every thing that is useful in his particular state of society, and demand, where a better or a cheaper has been produced, under any thing like circumstances of equality.

It is vain to deny the causes or the effects of the American system, dear Béthizy, nor should a man as philanthropist as yourself wish to deny them, since they rest on principles that favour the happiness and prosperity of the human race. We should not cavil about names, nor minor distinctions, in governments, if the great and moving principles are such as contemplate the improvement of the species in the mass, and not in exclusive and selfish exceptions.

The second great cause of the advancement of the United States is the abundance which is the consequence of room and of intelligence united, and which admits of so rapid an increase of its positive physical force. It is known that the population has doubled in about twenty-three years, though it is supposed that this rate of increase is gradually diminishing. It is probable that in the next fifty-five years there will be two more duplications of the amount. Of this number, supposing that slavery continues in its present form, and under its present influences (two things that cannot be rationally supposed), seven millions will be slaves, and forty-three millions free men. But slavery, though on the increase, as a whole, is known not to be on the increase in a ratio equal to that of the whites.

The third cause of the great progress of this country, and it is one intimately blended with all the other moral causes, is the perfect freedom of its civil and religious institutions, which gives the utmost possible play to the energies, and the strongest possible inducements to the laudable ambition of man.

There is unquestionably a powerful action and reaction between all these influences, which produce a vast combined result. A rapid review of what has been done in the way of general improvement, in the nation, may serve to give some idea of their effects.

I shall not write here of the condition of the army, and navy, and militia, since enough has been already said to furnish a sufficiently accurate knowledge of those branches of the subject.

The finances of the United States, you know to be prosperous. The public debt at the close of the last war (1813), amounted to about 120,000,000. On the first of October 1827, it was 68,913,541 dollars. But as seven millions of this debt was created for the purchase of the bank stock so often named, the true debt should not be estimated at more than 61,913,541 dollars.* This debt pays an interest of 6, 5, 4½, and 3 per cent. On 13,296,247 dollars an interest of 3 per cent. is paid; on 28,831,128, an interest of 6 per cent. is paid; on 15,993,972, an interest of 4½ per cent. is paid; on 5,792,000, an interest of 5 per cent. is paid. These sums make the amount named. The gradual diminution of the debt is taking place as fast as the terms of the loans will admit, and on those portions which pay the highest rate of interest. The last *may* be redeemed in 1835, and probably *will* be redeemed, at the present rate of diminution, before the end of the next dozen years, unless some new causes for loans should occur. In addition to these facts, it must be remembered that a stock which pays but three per cent. is never worth par. Thus, if the 13,296,247 of the 3 per cents. can be bought for 80 dollars, in the 100, this portion of the debt is also reduced in point of fact to 10,596,968 dollars. So that, all things considered, the whole actual debt of the United States cannot be considered as being more (on the 1st of July 1828) than 52,714,098 dollars, or something less than 12,000,000 of pounds sterling.

In a country so united in interests, but so separated by distance, a system of extended and easy internal communication is of vital importance. Without it, neither commerce, nor political harmony, nor intelligence, could exist to the degree that is necessary to the objects of the confederation. It has therefore been effected at some cost, but in a manner that is already returning its reward in pecuniary profit, as well as in the other great essentials named. The subject naturally divides itself into three branches, viz. that of information, that of internal trade, and that of personal communication.

For the first, the general post-office, with its numberless dependencies, has been established. The diffusion of intelligence is justly considered by the American statesmen to be no less important to the preservation of their institutions, than to the general advancement of the character and power of the nation. There are in the country about 7000 post-offices (1828), and a nearly incalculable distance of post route. The chief of this department says, that there is not now scarcely an inhabited district of any size in all these vast regions, to which the ramifications of these routes do not extend. The

---

* On the first of January 1828, it was estimated to be 67,413,377 dollars; or, deducting the seven millions for bank stock, at 60,413,377. The writer has since seen it announced, that 5,000,000 of principal will be paid on the 1st of July, 1828, so that the debt of the United States, on that day, will be about 55,413,377 dollars, if the cost of the bank stock shall be deducted.

same admirable economy exists in the management of this department, as in all the others of the government. Although it is quite plain that comparatively little correspondence can exist to defray the expenses of routes so extended, yet the department not only pays for itself, but it is beginning to yield a small revenue to the country. One would think that, under such circumstances, the cost of letters and journals was greater here than elsewhere. You shall judge for yourself. A letter for less than thirty miles pays six cents; for less than eighty and over thirty, ten cents; for less than one hundred and fifty miles, and over eighty, twelve and a half cents; for all distances over four hundred miles, twenty-five cents. A cent is one hundredth part of a dollar, or about an English half-penny, thus a letter will be transferred fifteen hundred miles, for a shilling sterling dollar. Double letters pay double, until they attain a certain weight, when they begin to pay by the ounce. Printed sheets, journals, or any thing else, pay one cent, for less than one hundred miles, per sheet, and one cent and a half for all distances over. The editors of public journals receive all their printed sheets gratis. The mail is carried in coaches a great proportion of the distance, in sulkies in other portions, and on horseback the rest.

The personal communication is effected by means of stage coaches and steam-boats. The vast rivers, and the prodigious facilities that are offered by means of the bays, enable passengers to travel with astonishing ease, rapidity and cheapness. The traveller may leave Boston by land. A ride of forty-five miles brings him to Providence; here he embarks for New York, 200 miles further, by the way of the sound of Long Island; the Naritan carries him to Brunswick; a few miles more of land carriage takes him to the Delaware; the river and bay of that name bring him to Newcastle; three hours by land, and he is on the waters of the Chesapeake; from the bay he may ascend half a dozen rivers, or proceed along the coast. At Norfolk, he enters a canal, and by means of sounds, bays, and a trifling land carriage, it is quite possible to reach the southern limits of Georgia. Most of this route is travelled in the manner I have described, and the rest of it is daily becoming more so.

The internal commerce of America exists with the least possible incumbrance. It is conducted chiefly by water, and an immense deal of it is done coast-wise, by means of the rivers, that are so many arteries penetrating the country in every direction. A license costs a few dollars, (two I believe,) and when a vessel is provided with such a document, there is no impediment to its passage into any of the public waters of the country. The whole confederation is unqualifiedly one nation in respect to commerce.

The government of the United States is also making certain military roads that are intended to intersect the country in those directions in which water does not flow. In addition to these improvements, states and chartered companies are effecting a vast deal more in the same way, that I have neither the room nor the knowledge necessary to communicate. As the debt is discharged, and larger sums come into the disposal of congress, it is to be presumed that they will increase the expenditures, by advancing the improvement of the country in all things that properly belong to their power.

In manufactures, the Americans have made immense progress since their separation from the mother country. The great Lord Chatham declared it should be the policy of England to prevent her colonies from manufacturing even a hobnail; and this plan of monopolizing wealth was tolerably successful, so long as the Americans were dependent on England, and even for many years afterwards. But, although the importations of this country, for home consumption, are greater now than they ever have been, its own manufactures have increased fifty fold.

The question of protecting manufactures by legislative enactments, is the one which involves more political warmth, at the present time, than any other question of mere policy. Indeed it may be said to be the only one. The disputants are chiefly men that are immediately interested in the result, though it is certain, that a few leading politicians adopt the opposite sides from policy or on principle. The only real point in dispute is, whether America has reached the period when it has become her interest to encourage her manufactures, at some little expense to her commerce, or rather at some little expense and loss to those who are engaged in particular branches of commerce, since it is obvious that nothing can have a greater tendency to increase the trade between different sections of a country like this, than increasing its objects. A vast deal is said, pro and con, on this subject. One party contends that it will destroy the shipping, and prove fatal to the revenue. If this reasoning be true, then the time is inevitable when the shipping and revenue of the United States must disappear, for nothing is more certain than that the time will come, when a vast proportion of their population finds that no great community can exist in prosperity, without a division of employment. But it is plain that these partisans utter absurdities, since it is a matter of perfect indifference to the citizen to whom or by what process he pays the dollar of duty that he is now obliged to pay for his coat. If the collector of some port does not receive it, some other collector can and will. But this dollar will be paid on an increased price, since the American manufacturer cannot bring his goods into the market so cheap as the foreign manufacturer, or he would not ask for protection. This may be true at the moment, and I am of opinion, that, (with the exception of articles that are deemed important to defence, and perhaps to certain articles that require some little time to give them the perfection necessary to competition,) no laws will be passed immediately on the subject. The question of manufactures is, however, clearly one of interest. Of their usefulness, and of their being one of the most active agents of wealth, as well as of the comfort of society, there can be no doubt. It is therefore like many other questions in America, purely one of time. Although it may not accord with her policy this year, to encourage them, or for her citizens to embark in them, the result is inevitable. A nation that lives so fast as this, does not compute time by ordinary calculations. Fifty years ago they manufactured next to nothing. They now manufacture almost every article of familiar use, and very many of them much better than the articles that are imported. They even begin to export. The coarse cotton goods of this country are already sent to South America, and I am told that they are preferred to the British. Importations of coarse cottons from India have entirely ceased; and indeed I was assured that their own coarse cottons were greatly preferred in their own markets to any other.

The American manufacturer has to contend with one difficulty that is unknown to the manufacturers of other countries. The unobstructed commerce of the United States admits of importations from all quarters, and of course the consumer is accustomed to gratify his taste with the best articles. A French duke might be content to use a French knife or a French lock; but an American merchant would reject both: he knows that the English are better. On the other hand, an English duchess (unless she could smuggle a little) might be content with an English silk; but an American lady would openly dress herself in silk manufactured at Lyons. The same is true of hundreds of other articles. The American manufacturer is therefore compelled of starting into existence full grown, or nearly so, in order to command success. I think this peculiarity will have, and has had, the effect of retarding the appearance of articles manufactured in the country, though it will make their final success as sure as their appearance will be sudden.

It is impossible to speak with certainty on the details of a question so complicated. A thousand articles are manufactured already, and may be considered as established. Twenty years ago, the Americans imported all their good hats; fifteen years ago they imported most of their coarse cottons; and ten years ago they imported most, if not all of their fine glass and ornamental hardware, such as fire-grates, &c. Many of these importations have ceased, and I am told that, considering the increase of the consumers, they are diminishing daily.

Though the particular matter that is now in dispute may be one of deep interest to certain merchants and manufacturers, it is clearly not the main question. Manufacturing is a pursuit so natural, and one so evidently necessary to all extended communities, that its adoption is inevitable at some day or other. The policy of the Americans wisely leaves them, in all cases except those of extraordinary necessity, (which become exceptions of course,) to the operation of natural influences. Policy will, nineteen times in twenty, indicate its own wants. If it be admitted that a people who possess the raw material in abundance, who enjoy the fruits of the earth to an excess that renders their cultivation little profitable, must have recourse to their ingenuity, and to their industry, to find new employments and different sources of wealth, then the Americans must become manufacturers. When the hour shall arrive, it will be vain to utter speculative reasons, for the wants of the nation will work out their own cure. If restrictive laws shall be necessary to effect it, the people will allow of a lesser evil to get rid of a greater. When the manufacturers of America are once fairly established, so that practice has given them skill, and capital has accumulated a little, there will be no fear of foreign competition. The exceeding ingenuity and wonderful aptitude of the people will give them the same superiority in the fabrication of a button or of a yard of cloth, as they now possess in the construction of a ship, or as they have manifested that they possess in the construction of a canal. A sufficient motive is all that is necessary to induce exertion. They have taken the infallible measure to ensure success, in bringing the greatest possible number of competitors into action, by diffusing intelligence so widely, and to so creditable an extent. I think that most questions of manufacturing will be settled practically in the next five-and-twenty years.

The vast extent of the United States affords all the means of wealth and comfort that climate, mines, and other natural facilities can supply. They are known to possess lead, copper, gold, iron, salt, and coal. The lead mines of Missouri are very extensive, and, with little or no skill, are already productive. The gold of Carolina is probably quite as abundant as is desirable. Copper is found in many places, but it is not yet much wrought. Iron is abundant, much worked, and some of it is more esteemed than any imported. Salt is found in quantities sufficient to supply the whole country, and even to furnish the article for exportation. It is not dug for yet, as the springs are found so saturated with the mineral as to render the process of boiling and evaporation more profitable. Coal exists in various parts of the country. It is procured, however, chiefly in Virginia, Pennsylvania, and Rhode Island. It is of various kinds, and of different degrees of excellence. That most in use is of the class *anthracite.* Of this species there are several gradations of quality. That of Pennsylvania is said to be the best. Mountains of coal exist in that state, and the people of the growing manufacturing town of Pittsburgh cut it out of the hills with as much facility as they would bring away an equal weight of dirt. Canals and railways are made to several of the coal mines, or rather coal *mountains,* and domestic coal is getting into very general use. The coal of eastern Pennsylvania is most fortunately placed. It lies within sixty or seventy miles of Philadelphia, to which place it is already conveyed by water. Philadelphia has a large capital, is now a great manufacturing town, and will probably be one of the largest in the world in the course of half a century. From Philadelphia, coal, or any thing else, can be carried by water to any part of the country which has a water communication with the ocean.

The cultivation of the vine has commenced. Wine is already made; though, as time is absolutely necessary to produce excellence in the quality of the grape, and as capital is still easily convertible to so many lucrative uses, it is possible that half a century may elapse before the United States export their liquors. That they will sooner or later do so is, I think, beyond a doubt. The silk worm is also beginning to attract attention, and plantations of the olive are coming daily more into fashion. In short, there is no means of comfort, indulgence, or wealth, that the Americans, in some one part of their country, cannot command; and it would be as weak, as it will unquestionably be false, to suppose that a people so sagacious and so active will neglect them beyond the moment when circumstances shall render their adoption profitable or convenient.

The construction of canals, on a practical scale, the mining for coal, the exportation of cotton goods, and numberless other improvements, which argue an advancing state of society, have all sprung into existence within the last dozen years.* It is a knowledge of these facts, with a clear and sagacious understanding of their immense results, coupled with exciting moral causes, that render the American sanguine, aspiring, and confident in his anticipations. He sees that his nation lives centuries in an age, and he feels no disposition to consider himself a child, because other people, in their dotage, choose to remember the hour of his birth.

How pitiful do the paltry criticisms on an inn, or the idle, and, half the time, vulgar comments on the vulgarity of a *parvenu* become, when objects and facts like these are pressing themselves on the mind! I have heard it said, that there are European authors who do not like to contract acquaintances with American gentlemen, because they feel a consciousness of having turned the United States into ridicule! I can tell these unfortunate subjects of a precipitate opinion, that they may lay aside their scruples. No American of any character, or knowledge of his own country, can feel any thing but commiseration for the man who has attempted to throw ridicule on a nation like this. The contest is too unequal to admit of any doubt as to the result, and the wiser way will be for these Quixotes in literature to say and think as little as possible about their American tilting match, in order that the world may not liken their lances to that used by the hero of La Mancha, and their helmets to barbers' basins.

---

* Forty years ago no cotton was raised in the United States.

PART II

A Letter to His Countrymen

Advertisement

This letter has been hastily written, with the hope of procuring its insertion in one of the daily prints. Its length having exceeded the writer's expectations, he has presented it to a son of his old and much esteemed publisher, the late CHARLES WILEY, who has given it its present form, for purposes connected with his own convenience.

To the Public

The private citizen who comes before the world with matter relating to himself, is bound to show a better reason for the measure than the voluntary impulses of self-love. In my own case, it might, perhaps, appear a sufficient excuse for the step now taken, that I am acting chiefly on the defensive; that the editors of several of the public journals have greatly exceeded their legitimate functions, by animadverting on my motives and private affairs; and that assertions, opinions, and acts, have been openly attributed to me, that I have never uttered, entertained, or done. When an individual is thus dragged into notice, the right of self-vindication would seem to depend on a principle of natural justice; and yet, if I know the springs of my own conduct, I am less influenced by any personal considerations in what I am now doing, than by a wish to check a practice that has already existed too long among us; which appears to me to be on the increase; and which, while it is degrading to the character, if persisted in, may become dangerous to the institutions of this country.

The practice of quoting the opinions of foreign nations, by way of helping to make up its own estimate of the degree of merit that belongs to its public men, is, I believe, a custom peculiar to America. That our colonial origin, and provincial habits, should have given rise to such a usage, is sufficiently natural; that journals which have a poverty of original matter, should have recourse to that which can be obtained not only gratuitously, but by an extraordinary convention, without loss of reputation, and without even the necessity of a translation, need be no mystery; but the readiness with which the practice can be accounted for, will not,

I think, prove its justification, if it can be shown that it is destructive of those sentiments of self-respect, and of that manliness and independence of thought, that are necessary to render a people great, or a nation respectable. Questions have now arisen between a portion of the press and myself, which give me more authority to speak in the matter than might belong to one whose name had not been so freely used, and it is my intention, while I endeavor to do myself justice, to make an effort to arrest the custom to which there is allusion; and which, should it continue to prevail, must render every American more or less subject to the views of those who are hostile to the prosperity, the character, and the power of his native land.

I am fully aware that every man must prepare himself to meet the narrowest constructions on his motives, when he assumes an office like this I have here undertaken; but I shall not complain, provided the opinion of the public receive a healthful impulse; while, at the same time, I shall not neglect the proper means to support my argument, by showing, as far as circumstances will permit, that I come to the discussion with clean hands. These constructions might have been obviated by having recourse to an anonymous publication, or by engaging some friendly pen to speak for me; but I have preferred the simpler, and, as I think, more manly course, of appearing in my own behalf. The nature of the proof I propose to offer, will compel me to mention myself oftener than I could wish, were not evidence of this nature less liable to be questioned, than that which comes from sources more indirect. I shall not shrink from my intention, therefore, on this account, while there is a hope that good may come of it. In vindicating myself, it will be necessary to reply to many attacks, without always quoting the papers in which they have appeared, which would swell this letter to an unreasonable size, and that, too, on a part of the subject that I could wish to treat as briefly as possible; but the reader is assured, that nothing of a direct personal nature will be said, that has not its warranty in some obvious allusion, insinuation, or open charge, in some one of the many journals of this country. In three instances, (those of the New-York American, the New-York Courier & Enquirer, and the New-York Commercial Advertiser,) it is my intention to answer the statements separately; distinctly marking the points at issue between each journal and myself, as is due to all the parties concerned.

I shall now proceed to execute the purpose of this letter, as briefly as the circumstances will allow, again begging the reader to remember that every statement which relates especially to myself, is either in reply to some unequivocal allegation to the contrary that is to be found in the public prints, or has a direct reference to the practice which it is so desirable to destroy.

First, then, I will show, that I come to this discussion with clean hands. At no period of my life have I had any connection with any review, notice or *critique* of any sort, that has appeared for or against me as a writer. With a single, and a very immaterial exception, I do not know to this hour, who are the authors of any favorable notice, biography, or other commentary, that has appeared on myself, or on any thing I have published; and in the case of the exception, I was made acquainted with the name of the writer, after the notice was written. As respects Europe, so far from having used any undue means to procure reviews, criticisms, or puffs, I am ignorant of the names of the writers of every thing of this sort that has appeared which has been in my favor; have probably not even read a dozen of these notices, with the exception of such as were to be found in the daily prints, since I have been absent; have refused numerous applications from the editors of periodicals, to send them critiques and copies of the books I had written; and, whenever it could be done, without obvious impropriety, have uniformly declined making the acquaintance of those who were known to be connected with what are called critical publications. In several instances, the very reviews which have made direct applications to me for favorable notices, have turned against me when it was understood that the request would not be complied with.★ In short, I affirm, that every report or asseveration that any review has been written in Europe, or any where else, by my connivance, or even with my knowledge, to produce an impression on the public mind at home, or with any other view, is founded in error or in malice. For a short time, I was a voluntary contributor of a periodical, that was edited by an old messmate, (Col. Gardner, the present Deputy

---

★ I am just informed by a friend, that he was lately applied to, by the editor of a literary journal in this city, to write a favorable notice of "The Headsman;" that he declined; and that an unfavorable one soon after appeared in the same publication!

Postmaster-General,) and I think he will remember the fact, that, when he declared his intention to obtain a favorable notice of "The Pioneers," I objected to it, on the ground of its being painful to me to see *critiques* of this kind in a publication with which I was connected, and that my objection prevailed.

I have been repeatedly and coarsely accused of writing for money, and exaggerated accounts of my receipts have been paraded before the public with views that it is not easy to mistake. That I have taken the just compensation of my labors, like other men, is true; nor do I see that he who passes a year in the preparation of a work, is not just as much entitled to the fruits of his industry, as he who throws off his crude opinions to-day, with the strong probability that on the morrow circumstances will compel him to admit that he was mistaken. Of this accusation, it is not my intention to say much, for I feel it is conceding a sacred private right to say any thing; but as it has been frequently pressed into notice by my enemies, I will add, that I never asked nor received a dollar for any thing I have written, except for the tales and the letters on America; that I have always refused to sacrifice a principle to gain, though often urgently entreated to respect the prejudices of foreign nations, with this very view; and that all the reports of the sums I have been soliciting and obtaining in France, Germany, and other countries, are either wholly untrue, or extravagant and absurd exaggerations.

I have been accused of undue meddling with the affairs of other nations. On this head it will be necessary to answer more at length, as the accusation takes two forms; one which charges me with entering impertinently into a controversy with the French government, and the other resting on the political tendency of some of the tales.

As respects the first, I shall say but little here, for I hope to be able to give the history of that controversy in a form less perishable than this letter.

In 1828, after a residence of two years in Europe, and when there had been sufficient opportunity to observe the disfavor with which the American character is viewed by nearly all classes of Europeans, I published a work on this country, whose object was to repel some of the hostile opinions of the other hemisphere, and to turn the tables on those who, at that time, most derided and calumniated us. This work was necessarily statistical in some of its features. In 1831, or about a year after the late revolution in France, there appeared at Paris, in a publication called *La Revue Britannique,* (the British Review, and this in France, be it remembered!) an article on the United States, which affected to prove that the cost of government in this country was greater than it was in France, or indeed in nearly every other country; and that a republic, in the nature of things, must be a more expensive form of government than a monarchy. This article, as has been stated, appeared in a review with a foreign title, at a moment when the French government professed great liberality, and just after the King of the French (taking the papers for authority) had spoken of the government of the United States as "the model government." There was no visible reason for believing that the French ministry had any connection with the review, and, although the fact might be and was suspected, the public had a perfect right, under all the laws of courtesy and usage, to assume exactly the contrary. In short, this dissertation of the Revue Britannique appeared, like any other similar dissertation, to be purely editorial, and it was clearly within the usual privileges of an author, whose positions it denied, as it denied those advanced in the work of mine just mentioned, to justify what he had already said. In addition to this peculiar privilege, I had that, in common with every citizen of the country whose facts were audaciously mutilated and perverted, of setting the world right in the affair, if I saw proper. Such a course was not forbidden by either the laws of France, any apparent connection between the review and the government, or the "reserve usually imposed on foreigners." I could cite fifty cases in which the natives of countries attacked have practised this right, from Baretti down to a countryman of our own, who has just exercised it in England. I did not exercise it. The article was pointed out to me; I was told that it was injuring the cause of free institutions; that it was depriving America of nearly the only merit Europe had hitherto conceded to her; and that I might do well to answer it. After a time, Gen. Lafayette called my attention to the same subject, and, without at all adverting to any personal interest he had in its investigation, pressed me to reply. I respectfully but firmly declined. I had seen so much of the ignorance of Europe in relation to ourselves; understood so thoroughly the design and bad faith on which it was bottomed, and so well knew the hopelessness of correcting the evil, (for it is a great evil, so far as the feelings, character and interests of every American are concerned,) that I felt no disposition to undertake the task. In addition to these general motives, I had the particular one of private interest. The vindication of the country already published, had occasioned a heavy pecuniary loss; it had even lost me the favor of a large party at home. I had many demands on my limited means, and was unable to make further sacrifices of this nature, to any abstract notions of patriotism or of truth. It was some months after the appearance of the review, that I was told the principal object of the article in question. It was to injure Gen. Lafayette. He had been stating, for forty years, that the American government was the cheapest known, and should the misstatements and sophistry of the Revue Britannique go uncontradicted, he would stand convicted before the French people of gross ignorance or of wilful fraud—or, to quote the language that was subsequently used by the Moniteur, of an "illusion or a lie." This fact presented the affair in an entirely new aspect. I determined to furnish the answer that was requested. Whatever may be the opinion of my countrymen on this point, it appeared to me that a man who stood in the relation which Gen. Lafayette occupied in respect to every American, ought not to be left to say that, when pressed upon hardest by his enemies, he had applied to a citizen of the country he had so faithfully served, and that, under the circumstances I have named, he had been denied what is due to even a criminal—the benefit of the truth. The "American" has lately insinuated that I am a "professed patriot." As I have never solicited nor received the usual rewards of professions of this nature, to me it seems that my conduct might have been referred to a simple and creditable sentiment of gratitude. Had I not been placed on the defensive, (so placed, I make no doubt, by designing men, who have felt my course to be a reproach to their own,) the world would never have been troubled with these details. The letter which I wrote on the matter in dispute, was given to Gen. Lafayette to secure my own self-approbation, and not to be made a merit of before the American people, of whom I never have, and do not now, ask more than a very negative justice. It was translated through the instrumentality of Gen. Lafayette, and, in this manner, it came before the French nation. I say it with regret, but I say it with a deep conviction of its truth, that I believe this to be the only country in the world in which a citizen would be placed on trial, for having refuted gross and unquestionable misstatements of the fair action of its own system, without any reference to the peculiar character that was given to this controversy, by the appeal and situation of Gen. Lafayette.

My letter, and one of Gen. Bernard which accompanied it, produced replies, containing fresh misstatements, mingled with great scurrility on the character, habits, and pursuits of the people of the United States. It was now a duty that I owed to myself, to the truth, and to all concerned, to answer. I did so in a short series of letters that was published in the "National." Throughout the whole discussion, care was had, on my part, to abstain from touching on the cost of government in France, though the comparison would have been perfectly justifiable, when the manner in which it was provoked is brought into the account. A few of my adversaries' contradictions were ridiculed, but with a slight exception of this sort, all I said had a strict reference to ourselves.

The dates of this controversy have some connection with that which is to follow. My first letter bears date Nov. 25th, 1831, and the last May 3d, 1832. The controversy on my part, however, would have ended in the commencement of March, but for a circumstance it may be well to name. After the appearance of my original letter, M. François Delassert, the vice-president of the Chamber of Deputies, published a letter from Mr. Leavitt Harris, of New-Jersey, who took grounds the very reverse of my own, who denied most of my facts, and who wrote virtually on the side of the Revue Britannique. To this letter I replied on the 3d of May as stated; that I did not prolong the discussion unnecessarily will, I think, be admitted, when the reader remembers, that Mr. Harris is the gentleman who has since been appointed to fill the office of chargè d'affaires at the court of France.

Having briefly stated an outline of the facts, in reference to the controversy on the cost of government, I proceed to the political tendency of the book that appeared about the same time, and to the circumstances accompanying its publication, so far as they have any connection with France.

The work in question is called the Bravo. Its outline was imagined during a short residence at Venice, several months previously to the occurrence of the late French revolution. I had had abundant occasion to observe that the great political contest of the age was not, as is usually pretended, between the two antagonist principles of monarchy and democracy, but in reality between those who, under the shallow pretence of limiting power to the *élite* of society, were contending for exclusive advantages at the expense of the mass of their fellow-creatures. The monarchical principle, except as it is fraudulently maintained as a cover to the designs of the aristocrats, its greatest enemies, is virtually extinct in christendom; having been supplanted by the combinations of those who affect to uphold it with a view to their own protection. Nicholas may still send a prince to the mines, but even Nicholas keeps not only his crown but his head, at the pleasure of the body of his aristocracy. This result is inevitable in an age when the nobles, no longer shut up in their holds and occupied in warring against each other, meet amicably together, and bring the weight of their united intelligence and common interests to bear upon the authority of the despot. The exceptions to such consequences arise only from brilliant and long continued military successes, great ignorance in the nobles themselves, or when the democratical principle has attained the ascendancy. With these views of what was enacting around me in Europe, and with the painful conviction that many of my own countrymen were influenced by the fallacy that nations could be governed by an irresponsible minority, without involving a train of nearly intolerable abuses, I determined to attempt a series of tales, in which American opinion should be brought to bear on European facts. With this design the Bravo was written, Venice being its scene, and her polity its subject.

I had it in view to exhibit the action of a narrow and exclusive system, by a simple and natural exposure of its influence on the familiar interests of life. The object was not to be attained by an essay, or a commentary, but by one of those popular pictures which find their way into every library; and which, whilst they have attractions for the feeblest intellects, are not often rejected by the strongest. The nature of the work limited the writer as to time and place, both of which, with their proper accessories, were to be so far respected as to preserve a verisimilitude to received facts, in order that the illusion of the tale should not be destroyed. The moral was to be inferred from the events, and it was to be enforced by the common sympathies of our nature. With these means, and under these limitations, then, the object was to lay bare the wrongs that are endured by the weak, when power is the exclusive property of the strong; the tendency of all exclusion to heartlessness; the irresponsible and ruthless movement of an aristocracy; the manner in which the selfish and wicked profit by its facilities, and in which even the good become the passive instruments of its soulless power. In short, I had undertaken to give the reader some idea of the action of a government, which, to use the language of the book itself, had neither "the high personal responsibility that sometimes tempers despotism by the qualities of the chief, nor the human impulses of a popular rule."

In effecting such an object, and with the materials named, the government of Venice, strictly speaking, became the hero of the tale. Still it was necessary to have human agents. The required number were imagined, care being had to respect the customs and peculiarities of the age, and of the particular locality of the subject. Little need be said of the mere machinery of such a plan, as the offence, if offence there be, must exist in the main design. One of those ruthless state maxims which have been exposed by Comte Daru, in his history of Venice, furnished the leading idea of the minor plot, or the narrative. According to this maxim, the state was directed to use any fit subject, by playing on his natural affections, and by causing him to act as a spy, assassin, or other desperate agent of the government, under a promise of extending favors to some near relative who might happen to be within the grasp of the law. As the main object of the work was to show the manner in which institutions that are professedly created to prevent violence and wrongs, become themselves, when perverted from their legitimate destination, the fearful instruments of injustice, a better illustration could not have been wished, than was furnished by the application of this rule. A pious son assumes the character of a Bravo, in the hope of obtaining the liberation of a father who had been falsely accused; and whilst the former is blasting his own character and hopes, under the delusion, and the latter is permitted to waste away his life in prison, forgotten, or only remembered as a means of working on the sensibilities of his child, the state itself, through agents whose feelings have become blunted by practice, is seen, forgetful of its solemn duties, intent alone on perpetuating its schemes of self-protection. This idea was enlarged upon in different ways. An honest fisherman is represented as struggling for the release of a grandson, who had been impressed for the galleys, while the dissolute descendant of one of the inquisitors, works his evil under favor of his rank. A noble, who claims an inheritance; an heiress; watermen; females of low condition, and servants, are shown as contributing in various ways to the policy of the soulless state. On every side there exist corruption and a ruthless action.

That some of the faces of this picture were peculiar to the Venitian polity, and to an age different from our own, is true; this much was necessary to the illusion of the tale; but it was believed that there remained enough of that which is eternal, to supply the moral.

Such was the Bravo, in intention at least. I confess I see nothing in its design of which an American need be ashamed. I had not been cooped up in a ward of New York, regarding things only on one side, and working myself into a fever on the subject of the imminent danger that impended over this great republic, by the machinations of a few "working-men," dreaming of Agrarian laws, and meditating on the neglected excellencies of my own character and acquirements on the one hand, and on the unmerited promotion of some neighbor, who spelt constitution with a *k* on the other: but it had been my employment for years to visit nations, and to endeavor to glean some general inferences from the comparisons that naturally suggested themselves. I knew that there existed at home a large party of *doctrinaires,* composed of men of very fair intentions, but of very limited means of observation, who fancied excellencies under other systems, much as the ultra-liberals of Europe, fancy perfection under our own; and, while I knew what I was doing was no more than one nail driven into an edifice that required a million, I thought it might be well enough to show the world that there was a writer among ourselves of some vogue in Europe, who believed that the American system was founded on just and durable principles. The book was thoroughly American, in all that belonged to it. The most grateful compliment I have ever received, was paid to me, unwittingly enough I believe, by a hostile English review, in reference to this very work. It said, in substance, that while Byron had seen in Venice, her palaces, her renown, and "England's glory" (!) the author of the Bravo had seen only her populace and her prisons. I take it this is just the difference that would be found, in such a case, between a right-thinking and a wrong-thinking man. Whether Lord Byron merited such a reproof, or not, I do not pretend to know—but I was grateful for the compliment.

I believe no sane man will deny the right of an American to produce such a work as the Bravo, considered purely in reference to its plan. But some, who will admit this, may be disposed to say that a book of such a nature should not have been published in France, at that particular moment. The distinction taken by these thin-skinned moralists (most of whom are liberal enough to all who write in honor of exclusion★) rests on a subterfuge. Had the Bravo been written and published among the mountains of Otsego, it would have been translated and republished at Paris, without any agency of mine. All that I had written, previously to arriving in Europe, was re-printed in this way; and the activity of the press is much too great at present, to leave any doubt on this head. I wrote in my own language, and had I caused an English edition to be printed at Paris, it would have been a sealed book to the French. There is no doubt that the tendency of the Bravo is directly opposed to the *intentions* of the French government party, and it has so been treated by writers of that country, both for and against; but it is by no means so clear that it is opposed to their *professions*. A stranger is bound to respect the laws and institutions of the country in which he may happen to be, but I do not know that he is obliged to dive into the secret and fraudulent intentions of its rulers. Let this be as it may, I stand acquitted of blame on any and all of these subtleties, for I did not cause the Bravo to be published in France at all. Even the sheets for the translation were obtained from another country, (I believe the work was actually translated in England,) and the re-prints in English which did appear, were surreptitious editions that an author without a copy-right could not prevent. I did not know of their existence until they had been before the world several weeks.

Such is the history of the intention and of the publication of the Bravo, so far as either is connected with the matter at issue. I do not know that its author had any great reason to be dissatisfied with its reception. The great mass of readers viewed it simply as a picturesque sketch of scenes and incidents, and in this respect it seems to have had sufficient interest to become tolerably popular. The publisher of the translation told me, shortly after it appeared, that it fared better than most of the works from the same pen.

★ Compare the language of these admirers of exclusive privileges, as respects me, and as respects Mr. G. Morris. The latter was an accredited agent of the United States, and was recalled at the complaint of the French government of that day, because he was believed to favor aristocracy! The London "Times," of Sept. 13, 1833, in speaking of the representatives of the United States, in Europe says—"They are very generally imbued with aristocratical sentiments, if possible more marked than those of the representatives of the European monarchies with whom they associate." Is this the character an American agent ought to earn abroad?

There were a few, however, who were accustomed to separate principles from facts. Some of these closer readers detected the intention of the book, and they were not slow in pointing it out. Figaro, without exception the wittiest journal in France, and one that was especially devoted to attacks on the *juste milieu,* contrary to its usual course, gave an especial article to the book, laying considerable stress on its political tendency. Praise from Figaro, on such a topic, almost inevitably drew censure from the other party, and from this time it became a fashion with a set to undervalue the work. I have a double purpose in dwelling on the reception of this book, and I hope the reader will overlook the weakness of an author, if I say a little more. There were several pictures from its scenes, at the French and English exhibitions of 1833; an opera has been written from it for the Académie de Musique,* at Paris; another for the Italian opera, at the same place; and when in London, Mr. Kenny told me he was writing an English opera on the same subject, for Drury Lane. I believe there have also been several melo-dramas in different languages. The critical notices of the work as I am told, for my own knowledge on this head is very limited, have been rather favorable, than otherwise. One of them, in particular, was so flattering, that I shall introduce it nearly entire, hoping its brevity will be its excuse.

"These volumes, we think, will add to his (Mr. Cooper's) *fame;* for though there is some careless writing, some repetitions, the effect of too much haste, and—for a novel—somewhat too much, perhaps, of political disquisition, there are touches of a master throughout. Of the females introduced, the gaoler's daughter is our heroine." [This, by the way, is a discovery, she being expressly called the heroine in the book!] "Her character is beautifully conceived and sustained; and the answer she gives to the venerable Carmelite, when he asks if she would not be afraid to plead before the Doge in behalf of her lover, is in the spirit, and worthy of the high-souled and conscientious *Jeanie Deans.* The fine old fisherman, Antonio, and the Bravo himself, are both strongly drawn. Venice is absolutely presented to the eye in the minute and picturesque descriptions of its canals, palaces, and squares; while its sports are admirably illustrated by the gorgeous ceremonial of the nuptials of the Adriatick, and the subsequent spirit-stirring race

---

* I do not know that this opera was accepted; I think it probable it was for obvious reasons refused; I was told, however, that the one for the Italian Opera had been received.

of the gondolas. But we are descanting on what all have read, or will read, and therefore forbear."

I had the more satisfaction in this short notice, because it bears on its face evidence of good faith, and because it appeared as editorial in the New-York American★ of December 3, 1831; a journal whose principal editor has justly obtained a respectable reputation for taste in literature.

As so much has been said of the Bravo, this would seem to be a proper place to introduce what I have to add, in reply to the three journals specifically named, as the subject is intimately connected with the history of that work. The American shall first occupy our attention. In answering this journal, I wish it to be understood that I decline all direct controversy with its correspondent who styles himself "Cassio." The tone of that person precludes him from the right to expect any reply, as a controversialist; and as a critic, I think the reader will agree with me, in believing that he is scarcely entitled to occupy our attention beyond the point which is necessary to prove my case.

The true matter at issue, between the American and myself is, whether a certain notice of the Bravo, which appeared in that paper, was, what it professed to be, of American manufacture, or of foreign; and, if the former, how far I had affirmed that it was not. I will now give a short history of the transaction.

It was, I believe, near the close of June, 1832, that Mr. Morse, the well known artist, (whose name is used with his own consent,) directed my attention to a *critique* on the Bravo, in the columns of the New-York American. Mr. Morse had read this pretended criticism, and while he could not forbear laughing at its exaggeration, he appeared to be provoked that a respectable journal at home, should admit so senseless a tirade against an absent countryman; and one too, who had just been seriously engaged in defending the common character of our common country, and this under circumstances of gravity that were known to him, although they might not have been so well understood by others. I must say, that I think the indignation expressed by this gentleman was creditable to him, both as a man and as an American. The warmth of my friend, induced me to examine the

---

★ The same paper, for June 24, 1833, has the following—"Of his novels, written in Europe, we do not now recollect one that does not, and should not impair his American fame." Of course, the "American fame" mentioned here, ought not to be confounded with the "fame" of the American.

article more closely than probably would have been done, had it fallen under my eye in the ordinary way. I gave it as my opinion, that this article was certainly written at Paris, (on its face it appeared, like any other communication, to have been written at home,) and that it most probably was a translation from the French, or had been written in English by some one who thought in the former language. Some of the reasons for this opinion shall be given. They are divided into those which depended on the disposition of the government party in France towards me, and on the internal evidence that existed in the article itself.

As respects the disposition of the government party towards myself, I had abundant proof. Figaro, the journal which had so warmly extolled the Bravo, was soon after bought up by the government; it of course changed its tone, and among others I was openly assailed in it, by name. An individual, filling a high official station, and who I have always believed spoke from authority, assured me that the part I had taken in the Finance Controversy would not be soon, to use his own words, "forgotten nor forgiven." During this controversy, the Revue Britannique more than once manifested a desire to frighten me from the field, by displaying its critical power, sometimes flattering and sometimes squibbing, according to the tactics of the moment. That very publication had previously furnished unequivocal evidence of the sort of faith that controls its decisions, by a long article on myself, which professed to be a translation from an English periodical. In this pretended translation, whole sentences were omitted or interpolated, evidently to suit the political views of its editor. In addition to this, I was familiar with the audacity and indifference to truth, with which these matters are usually conducted in that quarter of the world.

The internal evidence on which I believed the *critique* in the American to be virtually French, was not triffing. That it came from France, was to me beyond dispute; it was unquestionably written in bad faith; it abounded in faults of idiom and of grammar; most of the little reasoning it pretended to, was peculiarly French; it had an involved and obscure style, like that which characterizes insincere writing, and it violated, in an essential point, a received usage of English composition.

That it came from France, was evident enough to me at a glance. The critique contains a fling at these words in the title-page of the book, viz: "The Bravo, a Venitian story." Now, the words, "a Venitian story," form no part of the true title of the work. They are an unauthorized interpolation of the European booksellers, and are not to be found in the American, or the only authentic edition. Besides this fact, which was almost the first thing that caught my attention, the edition of M. Baudry, Paris, is quoted by name. This edition is spurious, and abounds with blunders, having been, in part, printed from uncorrected sheets, obtained from another country. With this proof, I could not hesitate to believe that the article was produced at Paris, as the alternative was to suppose that a writer at home had taken the bold measure of hunting up a spurious and foreign edition of an American book, in order to attack it through peculiarities that did not exist in the original. It has since been conceded that the communication was actually written at Paris, although its writer is said to be an American.

Under the circumstances of the case, when the fact was sufficiently established, that a critique on an American book, which appeared in an American journal, and as an American production, came in truth from a country where the writer of the work was openly assailed for party purposes, it created a strong presumption of foul play. But for this fact, I should have probably thrown the paper aside, consigning it to forgetfulness, along with a hundred more similar tirades that some of my countrymen have had the kindness to send to me, during my absence from home; or, at least, some who *pretend* to be my countrymen, although evidence is fast accumulating to show that a good many of them are foreigners, who have taken this, among other steps, to show their gratitude for the unusual liberality that is extended to them in this country. As the fact was at least curious, could it be proved, that the system of manufacturing ideas by which to judge our literature, was to be carried on by a foreign people, in this open manner, (that it had been done indirectly for a long time, I was fully aware,) I thought the matter merited an examination.

The style of the critique struck me, as having the involution of another language, and the vagueness of insincere writing. Let its first two sentences speak for themselves.—"We believe that, in conformity with all usage, it is the business of a critic to disclose to the world the merits or defects of authors; and, *of consequence,* his duty consists, ostensibly at least, in imparting information. Perhaps we shall forfeit all claim to the appellation (?) by commencing on a different plan, but even at *that* (anglice *this*) risk, we can adopt no other method of discussing the Bravo, than by first inquiring "what it's all about? &c. &c. &c."—I believe I may safely say, that the whole article is written in the same lively, perspicuous and logical manner, and with very much the same grammatical purity.

It abounds with faults of idiom and of grammar. The sentences just quoted, furnish proofs of what I say. To what does "appellation" properly refer? "That risk" should clearly have been "this risk," to be idiomatick, and the words contained between inverted commas, are a downright gallicism, or they are downright nonsense. "What it's all about?" as a mere quotation, is nonsense. Words might as well be quoted from a dictionary. The marks of quotation, therefore, must be intended to give the expression in a colloquial form; this is undeniably proved by their use in connection with the note of interrogation; and "what it's all about?" *as a speech,* means "what *it is* all about?" and this is very much as a Frenchman would be apt to ask the question. Any school-boy will see that it ought to have been written "what *is't* all about?" to be English. I have not cited these faults because they are the most obvious, but simply because the sentence was already before the reader, and because it was the first that offered. On this head it would be easy to write pages. "*No whit* superior," for instance, is some such English as if one should say "no bit taller." But I will quote one other sentence. "We cannot call *them*" (he is speaking of a man and a woman) hero *nor* heroine, for they have no claim to the *distinction.* These two worthies, who have nothing on earth to recommend *themselves,*" &c. &c. The fault of idiom, that of saying "*recommend themselves*" for "recommend them," struck me as an awkward translation of "*se recommander.*" It is unnecessary to point out the confusion in the grammar.

The violation of a usage of our language is this. In English, under a fiction of a plurality of writers, it is permitted to say *we,* when the writer alludes to himself; but it becomes obviously absurd, when it is expressly stated that there is but *one* writer. The *critique* is signed "Cassio;" and yet his communication is written in the first person plural. *We,* as applied to Cassio, and the Cassio of Shakspeare too, is a palpable absurdity. Now there prevails among the French critics, a custom of annexing to their communications an initial, or even the name of the critic, and it struck me, on seeing the obvious fault just alluded to, that the translator, finding the usual name at the foot of his original, and knowing it would not do to publish it, had fancied he showed his knowledge of English, by supplying its

place with that of one of Shakspeare's characters. These peculiarities might
certainly have passed as slovenly composition under other circumstances,
although a *critic* who is so vulnerable makes but an indifferent figure at
fault-finding; but under those which I have named, they became additional
evidence of the fact that was suspected.

The reasoning of the *critique* is French. It has a flavor of the academic
strut, very strangely mistyfied, it is true, by the manner in which it is presented. Thus, the writer thinks, or affects to think, that the leading idea of
the work is taken from a drama called Abællino; and, on this point he thus
expresses himself: "In our humble belief, no merit and no praise can belong
to a work, which in its principal design, is borrowed from the labors of
another's pen." There is a saying of an author of approved wisdom, which
might have taught the correspondent of the American a little moderation
on this head. Solomon tells us, "that the thing that hath been, is that which
shall be, and that which is done, is that which shall be done; and there is no
new thing under the sun." There is about as much resemblance in motive,
in character, in incident, and in all other points that form the true distinctions in cases of this sort, between Abællino and Jacopo, as there is between
the Lord Mortimer of an old-fashioned novel, and Tom Jones; but this is not
the point at issue. It has been admitted, that so much of the leading idea of
the tale, as is connected with Jacopo, or the Bravo, is taken from the history
of Monsieur Daru, and on this score there is no pretension to originality.
Was I to think, however, after the examples of Milton, Shakspeare, Byron,
Scott, and nearly every great name of the language, that a romance confessedly taken from a drama, or a drama from a romance, was in consequence to be hopelessly damned! There really appeared to me a temerity of
assertion in this charge, that could not belong to any one familiar with the
annals of English literature. I set it down as the opinion of a Frenchman,
who knew just enough of English to find fault with Shakspeare, and to
murder the language. I had no intention of commenting on the merits of
Cassio as a critic, but as the editor of the American has claimed him for a
favorite correspondent, I will give another touch of his quality, chiefly for
the purpose of making use of the circumstance in proving the bad faith
with which the article is written, although the occasion will be incidentally
improved, in order to show the editor of the American what a figure his
dwarf makes upon stilts.

It has been said that, in carrying out the principal design of the Bravo, a fisherman is introduced, soliciting the council for the release of his grandson from the galleys. The object was to exhibit the self-styled republic setting at nought another of the holiest of human affections. In the case of the Bravo, it trifled with the piety of the child; in that of Antonio, it was defeating parental care; and all at the expense of the many, for the particular advantages of the few. This grandson, a boy of tender years, is mentioned merely from the necessity of the case. The critic thinks, however, that he has detected an unpardonable sin, in the casual manner in which the lad is finally brought into the reader's presence. We will let him speak for himself. "There is a law with regard to romance," he says unhappily, without referring to the page of these critical pandects, "which forbids the introduction of the name, qualities and character of any person, who is not eventually introduced propria persona; and we learn the utility of the law by seeing it broken. The old fisherman, Antonio, has a grandson confined to the galleys" (he was pressed *for* the galleys) "and he makes it the business of his life★ to procure his liberation. To this end, he pleads with a member of the Council of Three," &c., &c., (the details are omitted as unnecessary,) "yet at the conclusion of all this, we find the following solitary reference to the subject:—'next to this characteristic equipage of the dead, walked a lad, whose brown cheek, half naked body, and dark roving eye, announced the grandson of the fisherman. Venice knew when to yield gracefully, and the boy was liberated, unconditionally, from the galleys; in pity, as it was whispered, for the untimely fate of the parent.' A line or two more informs (us) that he lived and died as other people do. It may be said, in reply to the commencement of this paragraph, that as the boy is actually introduced the rule is not infringed: *In letter* it is not, we admit, but it is in spirit. After half a book has been taken up to prepare an appearance, *such* an appearance is virtually none at all, either to satisfy an established rule, or the reader's expectations. We need not refer to *rules* to prove this an unpardonable fault."

All this parade about a rule, (whose very existence is a little equivocal)

★ It may be well to note the general exaggeration of the language. The grandfather was seventy, the grandson a boy, and the action of the tale, so far as the first was concerned, occupies about thirty hours!

savors of the academy, and is essentially French. If this rule were authority, the story of the Ephesian matron, for instance, would make but a scurvy figure in a tale, since the dear poor man, whose sainted qualities would fill the widow's heart for more than half a book, could only be presented to the reader as a ghost; a violation of probabilities that would quite unsettle the philosophy of *"ces quarantes qui ont l'esprit comme quatre."*

It is as easy to teach certain capacities rules, as it is to teach a parrot to speak; but there seems to be the same difficulty in causing the first to know when to apply what they have learned, as there is in causing the bird to think. If there had been a preparation for an "appearance," there certainly should have been an "appearance;" but as the only "appearance" contemplated, was that of strong human affections, ruthlessly violated, the ingenuity of our critic is quite thrown away.

I beg the reader will hear my account of the matter. Antonio demands the restoration of his child, who had been pressed to serve the state, while the children of the senators were permitted to go free. His suffering and his virtues raise the popular sympathy, and he is murdered in cold blood to get rid of him. The mistake of the multitude imputes the crime to Jacopo, whom the council allows to be executed, in order to conceal its own agency in the fisherman's death. The boy is introduced, at his grandfather's obsequies, for the old man is buried with public honors, with a view to show the manner in which the state continued to deceive, and not to satisfy any critical canon; the object of all being to demonstrate the fearful tendency of an irresponsible, soulless, arbitrary, political power. The whole of the reasoning of Cassio struck me as having the academic pretension of French criticism, in the hands of a bungler. As the editor of the American appears to take pride in the cleverness of his correspondent, however, I feel a particular desire to show him the beauty of the bantling to which he has so good-naturedly stood godfather. Let us imagine a suitable subject. The name of Solomon having been introduced already, in conjunction with that of his correspondent, luckily suggests the very one that is wanted. We will imagine a poet bent on working up the celebrated judgment of the king of Israel, into a tale of the usual size. He delineates the loves of the two mothers, their common delight in the birth of menchildren, and the yearnings of maternal affection over these precious gifts. Jerusalem, with its temple, its historical associations, and its usages, are successfully portrayed.* Then comes the appeal to the wise man of the earth for justice. The text is enriched with aphorisms from the lips of Solomon, with admirable touches of nature from the true mother, and with finely managed strokes of art from her who would deceive. The judgment follows, the whole concluding amid the wonder, the tears, and the admiration of the reader. It will be easy to fancy the writer of such a work in good humor with himself. Chance brings it, however, in the way of a certain person who is troubled with that most pernicious gift of providence, a whittling intellect. "Sir," suggests this exquisitely tempered mind, "your work has an unpardonable fault. 'There is a law of romance which forbids the introduction of the name, qualities, and character of any person, who is not eventually introduced propria persona.'You work upon our feelings, in relation to these babies, through two entire volumes, and conclude without making us sufficiently acquainted with either of them. I denounce the work. It is hopelessly damned." "You will remember, that the object was to portray maternal love; I had no occasion to do more than to represent the existence of one child, and the death of the other." "Sir, the rule." "Is not the wisdom of Solomon to your liking?" "The rule—the rule—the venerable, the sacred rule!" "You forget that, at least, one of the babies was dead." "You had the other. I do not know that even the dead might not have been brought to life, rather than violate so absolute a rule. At all events, you did nothing with the quick." "It was not possible to make a baby walk, talk, and act like a hero." "The rule, sir, the rule—you might have carried forward the time eighteen or twenty years, permitting the child to grow into these capabilities. Sir, you are little better than an ass, having overlooked an imperative rule." "To the devil with you and your rule; so long as the reader laughs when I laugh, weeps when I weep, and feels the force of the moral I would inculcate, I care not a straw for either." "Very well, sir; we shall see. I am about to denounce your book, for a violation of this very rule." "Denounce and welcome; you will only prove your own folly, and the world will laugh at you for your

---

* Or, to use the language of the New-York American, "Jerusalem, (pro hac vice) is absolutely presented to the eye in the minute and picturesque descriptions of its canals, palaces and squares; while its sports are admirably illustrated by the gorgeous ceremony of the nuptials of the"—king of the Jews with queen Sheba, for the want of a better.

pains." "Sir, you reckon without your host. I am by no means the man you take me for, but a favorite correspondent of the New-York American, whose editor is publicly pledged to cause all I write to be printed!"

As this affair of the "rule" is, I believe, the only serious attempt at ratiocination in the whole of "Cassio's" article, all the rest of it being modest assertions, whose value depends very much on the value of Cassio himself, I have been tempted into this little digression, out of respect to the subject. The reader should not complain, for he is certainly better off than before, having now two judgments of Solomon's, instead of one.

It remains to be shown, that the article was written in bad faith. This fact is, in my opinion, sufficiently apparent in its general tone. The editor of the American, who is a gentleman and an educated man, or I certainly should not take this pains to convince him of his error, must, I think, admit it himself, when he comes seriously to examine the communication. His correspondent pretty plainly intimates, for instance, that if the author of the Bravo wishes to escape the contempt of his fellow-creatures, he must write no more such books. When I compared this with the operas, the pictures, the dramas, and the other notices of the book, that of the American in particular, was I so wrong in thinking that such exaggerated censure could not be honestly given? There is also a supererogatory sensibility to the honor of America, on the part of the critic, that was exceedingly to be distrusted. The honor of America, which had nothing at all to do with the matter, is ostentatiously pressed into notice; and as for Cassio, he tells us in so many words, that if, as he has no doubt will be the case, the papers come out in favor of the book, he, for one, is prepared to blush for his country.* This asseveration of Cassio, by the way, is rather a pleasant commentary on the opinion of the American quoted.

But there is a circumstance which can leave no doubt on any reasonable mind, that the critique was written in bad faith. Its second paragraph contains these words:—"We have read the book as leisurely as novels require to be read, and yet, when the task is accomplished, *we have forgotten the plot, we have forgotten the hero and heroine, we have even forgotten in what small portion of the work we were interested.* We can recal, it is true, some 'tracery' of a preface,

---

* Let him speak for himself. "And we shall blush the deeper, if, as we expect, half the newspapers in the land come out with unqualified praise of 'the Bravo.'"

which appears to be 'any thing but to the purpose'—an occasional redundancy of moon-light—the *name* of Bravo—a few Italian interjections and masks—a few alarms—a few races and a few fainting fits, interspersed with formidable essays on political economy, &c. &c." It will be seen that there is no slip of the pen. The word *forgotten* is three times deliberately and pretendingly used, so that there can be no defence of inadvertency. Apart from some little distrust on the subject of so much ultra forgetfulness, I confess that this solemn and ponderous asseveration, a good deal astonished me. He who had so effectually forgotten the plot, the hero and heroine, and even the small part that interested him in a novel, was, virtually, so much in the situation of him who never knew any thing about them, that it was not easy to see what more a critic had to say. Now the reader, should he think the result worth his time, on examining the whole communication, will find that all he says of *those parts of the book, of which he admits he does retain some recollection,* is contained in the paragraph just quoted; and that he goes on to show, to the end of his article, that *he has* NOT *forgotten the plot, the hero and heroine,* and the small parts of the book in which he was interested; for he does little else than slash away at them all, right and left, during two closely printed columns of the New-York American! As if this were not sufficient, our acute observer goes on to furnish as minute a detail of self-refutation as, probably, ever figured in the annals of bastard criticism. On looking over the quotation from his article, where he undertakes to reason, it will be seen he says, that the *cursory* manner in which the grandson of the fisherman is presented to the reader, after so many previous allusions, is an unpardonable fault, in virtue of his "rule." Here, then, we have a critic, formally declaring that the plot of a novel is so worthless that he has forgotten it, and then, a few lines further on, damning it on account of the *cursory manner* in which one of its characters is introduced!

Language is mockery, or here is indubitable evidence that the correspondent of the American, either did not know, or did not care, what he said. I saw, in these facts, all the proof any man could desire, that the article was written in bad faith, and instead of believing that the Editor of the American would presume so boldly on the dulness of his readers, as to authorize the publication of this stuff, I thought at the time I first saw the *critique,* and said as much to the two gentlemen who were present, that it must have been admitted to the columns of his journal during his absence from town.

From internal evidence of this nature, and from much more of a similar character that might be adduced, particularly on the score of grammar and idiom, I gave it as my opinion to Mr. Morse, and the other gentleman present at the reading of the article, that this *critique* came from France, and that it was either a translation, or had been written by one who was not very conversant with the English language, and probably for the reasons I have named. This was but an opinion, nor could it, in the nature of things, convey any other impression to those who heard me. The second gentleman present, (I do not feel authorized to name him, for he is absent from the country,) took away the paper, declaring an intention to discover the truth, if possible. He thought, with Mr. Morse and myself, that if the agents of the French government had really carried their audacity so far, it was a fact worth knowing.

A few days after the occurrence of the interview, I left France, taking no steps whatever to inquire into this affair. At Aix-la-Chapelle, in Germany, about a month after my departure from Paris, I received an ordinary letter of friendship from Mr. Morse. It told me, among other things, that Mr.——, the gentleman already alluded to, had been as good as his word; that he had taken up the inquiry after the writer of the critique, with zeal; that he had ascertained the communication was certainly written at Paris, and that he had been promised the name of the writer. If he succeeded in getting the latter, it was to be sent to me. At Berne, other letters were received, that were silent on the subject. At Vevay, about two months after I had quitted France, I got a letter, which mentioned that Mr.—— had been completely successful, and the name of the writer (a Frenchman) was given. It will be seen that there was no precipitation in this inquiry. The parties through whom the intelligence was communicated to me, were both men of sense and of high respectability, and the intelligence was given as a naked fact, without any sort of reservation. I did what I presume any other person would have done in a similar situation; I believed what I was so distinctly and unreservedly told, and I set the whole affair down as one, among a great many more transactions of the same character, that had come to my knowledge within the last ten years.

When I returned to Paris, both Mr. Morse and the friend who had communicated the critic's name, had gone to America. The latter I have not since seen. Occasionally, when the good faith of the French government party was under discussion, I mentioned the fact, (giving my authorities,) as a proof how low they descended in their hostility; and once, in a burlesque publication that was intended to rebut their calumnies on this country, I playfully alluded to their critical zeal. Here the matter rested, so far as I was concerned, for several months. At the end of that time, I received another letter from Mr. Morse, in which the subject was again alluded to. He told me it was asserted in New-York, that the article in question was written *in this city,* by "an obscure clerk in a counting house;" he dwelt upon the malignancy of a party at home, who had constituted themselves my enemies;* and, Mr.—— being absent from America, he suggested the expediency of collecting proof on the spot, and of sending it home to refute this story. At the moment when this letter reached me, an article of the Commercial Advertiser had just attracted my serious attention. The article in the Commercial appeared to me (for reasons that shall be given in their place) to require some notice, while the story of the "obscure clerk" at New-York, did not. In answering the letter of Mr. Morse, however, I gave him full permission to make such use of all those parts of my letter that referred to either of the two journals, as he, on the spot, might deem expedient. As respects the article of the American, I told him, in brief, that I did not believe the report that it was written at New-York by the person in question, for there was abundant internal evidence that it came from France, a fact in which I could not easily be mistaken. I gave him to understand that I had "taken no particular pains" to investigate the affair since my return, but I had been informed, that the substance of the critique had been published in the Journal des Débats. In point of fact, I was told nearly this much by three different Americans; one saying he knew that certain parts existed in that journal; a second, that other parts were to be found in it; and a third giving the fact very much as I communicated it to Mr. Morse. I believed all this information, for there was no reason to doubt it, and in the haste of rapid and familiar writing, I at first stated as much without reservation in my letter, but on perusing what I had written, I took care to insert the words "as I understand," in order to show that I went on the information of others. The letter is not in my possession, but I am strongly impressed it will be found that these words "as I understand" were interlined for want

---

* The names of several of these individuals had been sent to me by another friend; they were persons utterly unknown to me.

of space, a circumstance that will give them more point, as it will show that they were written under a sense of responsibility. I very well remember to have taken great care not to say any thing as coming from myself, of which I was not morally certain. The letter has been printed, and speaks for itself. [See note A., end of pamphlet.] When a fact is first given, as imparted from others, all that is subsequently said about it, is necessarily qualified by that circumstance. After acquainting Mr. Morse with the character of the person whose name had been furnished by Mr.——, and making a few general remarks suggested by the subject, I turned to the communication in the Commercial, which it is only necessary to read my letter to see I treated as much the most important affair of the two.

It is now said, that all the information I have received on the subject of the origin of the critique, as well as my own conjectures, is erroneous; the article in question being written by an American, who was at Paris. I have little to do with this fact. Mr. Morse has handsomely admitted that he made the communications which have been stated as coming from him, and I do not doubt, did circumstances permit it, the other gentlemen alluded to, would do the same thing. They are all absent from America. The reasons for my *opinions* have been freely given, and I feel certain that no man, who understands French and who reflects on all the circumstances, will consider them light. The Editor of the American has a just claim to have the truth known, and I have taken some pains to state it, I hope clearly, though I honestly think he has put himself in a worse situation by avowing that "Cassio" was written by a known and esteemed correspondent, than he would have been left by my conjecture. Besides all this, I do not think that the fact that an American wrote the article, by any means clears it from the suspicions I have mentioned. Its bad faith is not changed by this circumstance, and as for Cassio himself, a witness who has forgotten so much that he remembers, and who remembers so much that he has forgotten, does not exactly stand before the public in the most favorable point of view.

In the warmth of the moment, the Editor of the American has permitted expressions to escape him that I think he will regret, when he looks more coolly at the affair. He says, in reference to me—"This gentleman and his flourishing backer (Mr. Morse) ascribe unhesitatingly the critique to the fears! and resentments! of the French government, roused by the popularity of Mr. Cooper's democratic writings; and the prefacing friend (Mr. Morse) gives us," &c. &c. Now, the manner in which I am coupled with Mr. Morse, in the commencement of this paragraph, and the manner in which Mr. Morse is made to speak for himself in its close, would give the reader just reason to think I had said what is here imputed to me. All I say is, that "the Bravo is certainly no very flattering picture for the upstart aristocrats of the new *regime,* and that nothing is more natural than their desire to undervalue the book." I leave the reader to compare these words with the language just quoted from the American. I was answering a letter, and many of my remarks had a direct reference to what had been previously said by my correspondent, and it is possible there may be some obscurity in its phrases. My own impression was, that the critique was more owing to the Finance Controversy than to any other cause, though I had abundant evidence that the substance of the Bravo itself was disagreeable to some of the new aristocracy. All that is said in the American of my "flouting" my Americanisms in the faces of foreigners, whose hospitality I had been enjoying, is unmerited; and all that is said, by contrast, of the deportment of the person who claims the honour of having written Cassio, will appear absurd to those who were in Paris during our common residence in that city. The circumstance that I believed the article to be written for political purposes, by no means justifies the language of the American in another point of view. Writers are employed, by political parties, generally, to assail their enemies, and to defend their friends; and it does not follow as a consequence of my impression, that I thought there was a meeting of the cabinet in order to decide that the communication should be sent to this country. I looked upon the whole affair much as I look upon one of the attacks of the American itself, against any one individual of the present government party at home, or as a thing to be done as a matter of course. I now quit the American, for the second of the journals named.

The Courier and Enquirer of June 15, 1833, has the following article on myself:

> *Mr. James Fenimore Cooper.*—We perceive by a letter from this distinguished gentleman, published in some of our newspapers, that his efforts to correct the misrepresentations of the *Doctrinaires* in Paris, on the subject of American taxation, has given great dissatisfaction in that quarter. It would seem, according to his statement, that in order to

revenge themselves for having been proved to be in the wrong, they have attacked him at a point where every author is most sensitive as well as vulnerable in his writings. Severe criticisms have subsequently appeared in the *Journal des Debats,* and other organs of that party, (1) *which Mr. Cooper ascribes to a feeling of political hostility, originating in the part he has taken in vindication of his country, whose Public Press he thinks ought to sustain him at this crisis, although it will be recollected he lately took occasion to set it at defiance, and express his contempt for its opinions.* (2) *He appears, however, to be most touched by a keen and severe criticism on the* Bravo which made its appearance some year or two since, in the columns of the New-York American, and which, (3) *if we are not mistaken, was antecedent to the circumstances supposed to have produced the hostility of the* Doctrinaires. (4) *He is mortified that any of his countrymen should* "appear" *to have turned against him, and states several facts which in his opinion go to prove that the criticism in the American was not written* "by an obscure clerk in a counting house," *as he terms him, but by a Frenchman in Paris, and is a mere translation of an article published in the Journal des Debats,* "a little altered to adapt it to the American reader."

We leave this question to be settled between Mr. Cooper and the writer who furnished the article for the American, (5) *and proceed to offer a few remarks on the insinuation thrown out by the former regarding the indisposition of his countrymen to sustain his literary reputation against the hostility of the* Doctrinaires, *which he has provoked by attempting their defence.* When a citizen of the United States goes to reside in a foreign country he places himself under the protection of its government and laws, to both of which he owes respect and obedience so long as he chooses to stay. If he don't like them, he should not make public his disgust; and if he wishes for the satisfaction of railing, he had better go home, and indulge his inclination there. In short, he has no business to meddle in politics.

(6) *But it is quite a different case, when the character of his country is assailed; its manners ridiculed, its morals and religion questioned, and its institutions exhibited in a contemptuous contrast with those of any other nation. He is then, we think, bound by every motive of patriotism, every duty of a citizen, to vindicate his country to the utmost extent of his power with his pen, as a soldier does with his sword. In this latter predicament was Mr.*

Cooper placed; his country was represented as taxed with burdens heavier than those borne by France and he was, we think, not only right in refuting the calumny, but he would have been emphatically wanting in duty to his country had he neglected the task. We think his country ought to be, and have no doubt she is, grateful for his good offices.

In our opinion he does great injustice to the people of the United States, in supposing them indifferent to, or inclined to detract from his reputation as a writer; or *that they, or any portion of them,* * *have, as he asserts, joined in a conspiracy with his enemies in France.* He is still one of the most popular writers of our country, which has done its part liberally in contributing to his fortune as well as his fame. If some of his later works have failed in supporting the reputation of the former ones, this is a misfortune which often befals men of the greatest genius. They cannot forever be quaffing at the fount of inspiration, nor does it always exhilirate alike. Neither does the public always judge alike. Its taste is perpetually altering, and mankind at length become tired of an old author, as voluptuaries do of an old mistress, whom they forsake for a new one, perhaps in reality not half so attractive. (7) *But why should Mr. Cooper suppose that an unfavorable criticism on a work, which did not peculiarly address itself to the feelings of his countrymen, is evidence of their indifference or hostility? If critics are in general so corrupt, as he insinuates, why should he appeal to his country and to the world against a criticism?* To our mind it would be much more dignified to treat all comments coming from such impure sources, with at least the affectation of indifference, and whatever he may feel, keep his feelings to himself. He has acquired a brilliant, and probably a lasting reputation; he can spare a leaf, without spoiling the wreath entwined round his brow.

(8) *He should remember, that when an American writer goes abroad to reap laurels, on a wider field, and a richer soil, though he may possess many advantages over such as remain in the obscurity of home, yet these are counterbalanced, by weights in the other scale. If he can only establish a reputation in any part of Europe, there will be little question of his talents here; they will be taken in a great degree on trust, as merchants receive their goods, on the faith of the*

---

* Query. How can an indifferent commentator know this?

invoice. But on the other hand, it will be necessary to lose his identity as a citizen of this obnoxious republic; to pay due deference to the claims of the well born, and yield prompt obedience to the long established rights of European superiority; to flatter their prejudices with indirect adroitness, and to avoid giving offence by retorting sarcasms, or refuting calumnies on his country; its institutions and character. In short, he must endeavour to speak, and if he writes to write, in such a decorous manner, that the most expert critic shall not be able to detect a single sentiment of affection or preference for the land of his birth. He may then possibly be pardoned the misfortune of having been born on this side of the Atlantic, and be hailed as a giant, for having attained the size of a man among a nation of pigmies!

But after all it is impossible to please every body, unless a man has the good fortune to have no opinions of his own. You cannot serve two masters; and it is the height of presumption to expect to retain possession, even if we should conquer, two worlds at a time. In the present war of interests and opinions, when those in high places abroad, perceive in the example and influence of the GREAT REPUB-LIC, the sources of imminent danger to their long established author-ity, it is to be expected that misrepresentations of every kind will be resorted to, for the purpose of weakening the force of that example. We hold it the duty of every American to do his best to refute and retort such manifestations of hostility, for, to use the strong words of an American writer, "we never yet saw an instance of a man or a nation, that gained aught but contempt by submission, or that did not thus invite a repetition of insult and injury." By pursuing a manly course of resistance to the injustice of foreign writers, an American must necessarily lose his popularity among that class of critics which in some measure directs, or at least indicates the taste of the aristoc-racy of Europe. (9) *Hence it is that writers must either suppress all expres-sions of partiality to their country and its government, or they will, like Mr. Cooper, become the object of frequent hostility. He must make his choice, and when made, submit with dignity to the sacrifice, with the assurance that a time will come, when in all probability the number of his American readers will far exceed those of France and England combined.* This is a sufficient remuneration, and with this we think he ought to be satisfied.

Assuredly Mr. Cooper has nothing to complain of, in regard to the return made by his countrymen, and indeed by the world at large, for the amusement he has afforded them in his writings. Let him compare his situation with that of Homer, Milton, Dryden, Otway, Fielding, Le Sage, Cervantes—the inimitable Cervantes!— the immortal labours of whose whole lives were insufficient to keep the wolf from the door. Let him remember the fate of these illustrious writers, and thank God for all his mercies.

I notice this article, although it appears as editorial, under the impression that it is not what it seems. It abounds in errors and misconstructions, some of which are of a nature almost to raise the suspicion that the finger of Cassio was concerned in producing them. It was especially sent to me (in duplicate) at Paris, along with the statement of the American and its correspondent Cassio, and I presume I am at least right in considering it as coming from the enemy. I have caused parts of this article to be *italicised* and numbered, for the convenience of reference. Let us commence with No. 1. Here is a great error. I have never meant to say that the Press of this country ought to sustain me at this crisis, [what crisis?] nor do I know that I have ever set it at defiance, or expressed any especial contempt for its opinions. My letter is there to answer for the first assertion. I do not think it contains a word to justify it. As for the second, I ask when and where I have set the press of this country at defiance? The press of this country is, like the men who control it, composed of good, bad, and indifferent, and any general character would be liable to great qualification.

No. 2. I certainly do not think I *seem* (the allusion is to my published letter) to be most touched by a keen and severe criticism on the Bravo. The criticism on the Bravo, as a criticism, never excited any feeling in me, nor did I ever express any in reference to it, beyond that which no intelligent man will need an interpreter to understand. Its importance was derived from its supposed origin. In the parts of my letter to Mr. Morse that are published some feeling, I admit, is betrayed in reference to the article in the Commercial, which excited a strong indignation, for I believed it to be the offspring of a piece of pitiful jesuitism and double-dealing. I believe so still. A simple, arithmetical process will prove that it was this article, and not the puerile attack of the American's correspondent, that I deemed the most

important. My remarks on the critique in the American, besides being necessary as an answer to the letter of Mr. Morse, and being much less strong
than those on the Commercial, fill just forty-eight printed lines of a newspaper, while those on the Commercial fill one hundred and sixty-five.
There is, I think, a misprint in my letter, where it is said that Mr. Morse had
alluded previously to the attack in the Commercial. He had certainly made
no such allusion, and all I say on this part of the subject is said at my own
suggestion. This assertion of the Courier and Enquirer appears to me to be
made to press the critique of Cassio into an importance I never gave it.

No. 3. This is another mistake. The *critique* of the American appeared
June 7th, 1832, and my letter to Gen. Lafayette bears date November 25,
1831; leaving an interval of six months between them. There was even time
to have sent an article from Paris after my *last* letter, (that to Mr. Harris,
published May 3, 1832,) and to get it inserted in the American of June 7th.

No. 4. I am unconscious of having expressed any such mortification, nor
can I find the word "appear," as here used, in any part of my letter. So far
from calling the writer of the *critique* "an obscure clerk in a counting-
house," I expressly tell Mr. Morse that I *do not believe* the story to that effect,
which he had sent me. This assertion is calculated to create an impression
that I estimate the intellectual value of a man according to his social position. On this point I can only say, that any such opinion is opposed to the
practice of a whole life.

No. 5. I cannot find any thing in my letter to justify this. I have complained that the Press did not support me in the Finance Controversy, in
which I thought the honor of the country concerned, but I cannot recall
any complaint of a want of support merely as a writer.

No. 6. I lay claim to no such patriotism, nor do I at all think it was the
"duty" of an American to refute the allegations of M. Saulnier, apart from
what he owed to General Lafayette. He might do it, or he might not, as he
saw proper. If such a duty had in truth existed, of all the men in America,
I was perhaps the one on whom it was the least imperative. I had already
made a heavy sacrifice to support the character of this country abroad, and
the effort had been so indifferently requited at home, that I should have
thought myself fairly exempt from any further service of the sort.

No. 7. All this, and indeed most that goes before it in the same paragraph, certainly is not justified by any thing I had said. It ascribes a meaning

to me, I think, quite without authority. I am not complaining of criticism, but of the Press lending itself to the views of our enemies. This is so obvious on the face of my letter, that I confess this portion of the article of the Courier and Enquirer, struck me as being expressly designed to give undue importance to the critique of the American.

No. 8. I never went abroad "to reap laurels on a wider field," nor did my presence in Europe in the slightest degree extend any little reputation I may possess as a writer, or add a dollar to my means. What I wrote was just as much before the European public before I quitted home, as it is now, and instead of making friends abroad to puff and sustain me, I made enemies, as will presently be shown, by refusing to submit to the practices of those who call themselves critics. All that Courier says on this head, therefore, is uttered under an erroneous impression, and is in no degree warranted by the facts.

No. 9. There is a singular misconception of the circumstances in this paragraph. My choice *was* made; it was in favor of my own country, her character and her institutions; and my complaint was not that foreigners abused me, but that *those in whose favor this choice had been made, helped to circulate their abuse.*

I could say a great deal more concerning this article of the Courier and Enquirer, but I presume enough has been shown to make it appear that it has not been written with sufficient attention to the facts of the case. I shall advert to only two more of its statements. My country is said to have advanced my fortune and my fame. The last is a word of pregnant signification, and is not to be used lightly. We have seen already the embarrassment into which the American has got, by flinging about this term too liberally. But putting the degree out of the question, the truth of this remark of the journal must depend on a principle that is general. If I owe reputation to my country, I owe gratitude; and if I owe both, other Americans are in the same predicament. Under what a load of obligation to their country, for instance, such men as Washington, Franklin, and Jay, *particularly the latter,* must have lived and died, if this novel doctrine of the Courier and Enquirer should happen to be true!

But I have more interest in settling the point of fortune. It is bad enough to have obligations of this sort thrown into one's face when they are true, but it becomes a little hard to be borne when there is no foundation whatever for the pretension. I cannot suppose that the journal means to be understood that I am indebted to those who may have bought any books I have written. So far from this being true, some of the latter are still indebted to me, and this too without much hope of payment. I presume a literary man does not intend to degrade literature, and yet it would be just as true to tell the grocer at his nearest corner, that the fortune he is making by his industry and judgment, is due to the liberality of the public, as it is to tell a writer that he is indebted to the public for the money that is paid him by his publisher. The public buys to please itself, and not to confer favors on authors; and, could the experiment be tried, I will answer for it, that were any popular book of a native writer to be pirated and sold at half price, it would be found that the rogue disposed of two copies to the honest dealer's one.* I am led to think that the writer of this article was under a mistake that I am afraid is sufficiently general, and which I hope now to be able to remove.

Since my return home, applications have been made to me to know the amount of the salary and of the emoluments of the consulate of Lyons, of which I was certainly the incumbent for a year or two. I have also understood, from a member of Congress, that there was an impression I had a salary from the government; and, in a pretended sketch of my life, that appeared lately in one of the papers, and in which, I think, thirteen alleged facts had just three truths, I am said to have filled the office of chargé d'affaires at Paris, a situation that would have given me $4,500 outfit, and as much of yearly salary. No part of all this is true. Mr. Clay (I wish it to be understood that this letter is written without the slightest view to party, for I shall never voluntarily lower myself from the condition of a freeman to become the mere political partizan of any man) very kindly acceded to my request of making me a consul, with a view that, while travelling, I might not have the air of expatriating myself. Lyons was chosen simply because

---

* It is an amusing commentary on this opinion of the journal, that a great many instances have come to my knowledge of Americans who have not read any thing I have written, for the avowed reason that nothing good could come from a countryman. A few days after my return, I met an old friend in the street. He appeared glad to see me— so glad, that I thought his reception one of the warmest it had been my good fortune to meet with! After a little conversation, I discovered that his joy proceeded from an impression that I had been dead some six or seven years. Here was immortality at once, in lieu of all this fame. Unhappily, there are many reasons why this country can give "fame" to no one; and among them is the degrading practice of leaning on others for so many of its opinions.

there was nothing to do. This office cost me just one hundred dollars in outfit, and returned to me just nothing. After a little time I resigned the nominal situation, under the conviction that gross abuses exist in a great deal that relates to our foreign appointments, abuses that I still hope to expose, and because I felt it was incumbent on me to set an example of the principles I professed.

This consulate was of no other use to me than that I have named. It gave neither money, social rank, nor personal consideration, and I claim no merit for the moderation of my views. As to the office of chargé d'affaires, I do not see how the mistake could well have arisen. It is a situation I certainly could not have taken for many reasons; for which I never in any manner applied; nor in any way desired. It is possible that the writer of the article in question, in the ardor of his patriotism, has supposed that the interest I manifested in the Finance Controversy may have been quickened by a fat salary. This opinion was not unnatural, for the secretary of state had made an appeal to all the governors to produce their statements to show, in defence of the action of free institutions, that our side of the question was right. With these views of the case, he has probably fallen into an error from some confusion in the facts. The office of chargé d'affaires was conferred on a gentleman who certainly had a part in the Finance Controversy; but, his opinions being directly opposed to those of General Lafayette and myself, he happened to take the opposite side of the question. As between me and my country, the account current of both profit and honor exhibits a blank sheet. I have never laid any claim to having conferred either, and I do not feel disposed to admit that I have received either. This is a subject on which I could gladly have been silent, but as it has been pressed into notice, it is due to myself to state the truth. The private feelings and interests of an individual can be of no great moment to the public, and I shall say no more, unless it be to add, that there is a facetiousness in the opinion of the journal on the subject of the "honor" I have received from my countrymen, that touches on mockery.

I come now to the article of the Commercial Advertiser. [See note B., end of pamphlet.] It consists of an extract from the Revue Encyclopédique on the Heidenmauer; of some joint comments of the editor of the journal, and of a correspondent, touching the impropriety of foreigners meddling with the politics of France; and an assertion, that France would not have abused us had certain of our countrymen not meddled with her private affairs. The allusions were obviously intended for me. Apart from a good deal of puerility in believing it any justification for vituperating a whole people, that one or two of its citizens had misbehaved, this article is written jesuitically as to manner, illogically as to its reasoning, and erroneously as to its facts. The history of the manner in which I entered into the discussion on the cost on governments has been given; and the reader is left to judge for himself how far I obtruded my opinions on a foreign people. If it be meant that I meddled privately with foreign politics it is a mistake, and all reports to the contrary are untrue. Whenever there was a question of bringing the example of America to bear upon the rest of the world, it was my wish that it should be done with truth, and as I strongly condemned the course taken by too many of our countrymen abroad; who defend our own system as the one best adapted to our immediate situation, when appealed to on this head, and on proper occasions, it was my habit to defend it on principle. I had early learned the use that was made by any concessions on this topic, and I determined that if any man quoted me against the action of free governments, he should quote me wrongfully. Even this has been done, so eager are the aristocrats to snatch anything like a concession from an American, but against such a fraud no human foresight can guard.

The letter to Mr. Morse was written chiefly to draw the attention of the public to particular facts. I believed then, and I believe still, that the article of the Commercial had its rise in the apprehensions of an agent of the United States, who felt that if I was right in the affair of the Finance Discussion, he had been very wrong; and who was desirous of forestalling public opinion, with a view to weaken the effect of any statement of the facts I might hereafter make. Added to this, was a wish on my part to check the degrading practice of quoting from the foreign journals to which there has so often been allusion. I had little interest in the result, for the letter to Mr. Morse, a great part of which has not been published, acquainted that gentleman with a resolution, that had long been made, of abandoning the pursuits of a writer, (a resolution that he well knew had not been lightly formed;) and that I only waited to comply with existing engagements to bring the tales to an end. This has been done, the last book of the series having been published. I did not go through the form of taking leave of the reader, for I had never known any other public than my own country, and I fully believe the editor of the American when he says, that I have been losing its favor since I went abroad. Under such circumstances, a leave-taking would have been mockery, and I only allude to the facts now, as a witness releases his rights in a contested claim, or to purge myself from the imputation of having an interest in the result. I wish what I am about to say not to be lost, but that it may serve those who come after me. I do not think this is a country in which any man can yet hope to be sustained as a writer, should he decide to take part frankly with the institutions and character of his country; the feelings of those who control public sentiment on subjects of this nature, are opposed to his success;* but should any young aspirant for literary reputation believe otherwise, I am willing to make an effort to afford him fair play. This opinion will probably surprise many of my readers, for there is a superabundance of patriotic profession; but let any discerning man look closely at the facts, and I believe he will come to my way of thinking.

The editor of the Commercial appears to have had some misgivings himself, as to the propriety of the course he was taking. He says that the review (la Revue Encyclopédique) was sent to him along with a letter from a correspondent; and when a foreign publication is thus introduced, the public has a right to believe that the "correspondent" is a correspondent abroad; and this the more especially when the allusion is made in a journal that is constantly flourishing its foreign correspondents before its readers.

I am now told that the article was concocted in this city, between the editor and a young man who was never out of his native country, to whom I was a perfect stranger, and who could know nothing of my private course abroad, except from the dangerous and uncertain evidence of vulgar rumour. I neither know nor care whether this report be true or false. I have been openly assailed; my discretion has been impugned; my conduct misrepresented, and the right to defend myself will not be denied. However direct may have been the agency of the diplomatic functionary alluded to, I have no doubt that his representations are at the bottom of the whole affair. As to this young man, if he prove not a man of straw, he will not be the first who has believed that he played the organ when he was only blowing the bellows. I repeat, then, it is my opinion that the said diplomatic agent is at the bottom of the whole affair. I thought I could detect even his

---

* The instinct of the selfish, sufficiently denotes the course that is dictated by expediency.

style in the language of the Commercial's correspondent; but if I was mistaken in this particular, then there are two persons who make such a parade of prepositions as "to, at and for," instead of one. At a future day, when better prepared, I shall speak more openly on this point. The editor of the Commercial himself appears to have distrusted the propriety of what he was doing, for he places its justification on his "knowledge of the fact that Mr. Cooper prefers the censure, to the praise, of the newspaper press. Of this peculiarity of his taste he has taken care to inform us in the preface to the Heidenmauer, in which he says in so many words—'Each hour, as life advances, am I made to see how capricious and *vulgar* is the immortality conferred by a newspaper.' " Now this sentence is made the apology of the editor of the Commercial for admitting into his columns an attack against the interests and character of an absent countryman; under cover of an article that was written by he knew not whom; which article contained a direct contradiction of itself to prove its worthlessness; which appeared in a periodical of little reputation, and which derived all its influence here, from a degrading practice which this editor did not hesitate to aid in upholding, in order to gratify his resentments. I now propose to furnish proof of the consistency and sincerity of the editor of the Commercial Advertiser.

First as to the application of the sentence from the preface of the Heidenmauer. I was giving an account of a journey which took me to the scene of the tale. The route led across the country which had just been traversed by the Prince of Orange in his celebrated march upon Brussels; a march which had so nearly effected a counterrevolution in Belgium. The journals were teeming with denunciations of the Dutch for their excesses, and the Prince of Orange was unhesitatingly consigned to lasting infamy, for the cruelties, conflagrations, and other outrages that he had permitted or ordered. These facts were subjects of public notoriety. On passing over the scene of this pretended violence, a few days after it was stated to have occurred, I looked in vain for the evidences of its truth. The remark, which the editor of the Commercial deems a justification of his course, was elicited by these facts. The word vulgar is used in its broad and true signification, and, in the sentence in which it was used, it meant commonplace or liable to popular error; but in the Commercial it is put in italics, as if its editor attached some such meaning to it, as would be bandied between two cobblers' wives that were disputing about the gentility of their respective *coteries.* This is a simple statement of the facts. I beg the reader to give a moment to their application.

In the New-York Commercial Advertiser, of June 17, 1833, among a good deal more to the same effect, I find these words: "The precipitate manner in which many conductors of papers condemn men and measures, upon slight evidence, is one of the prevailing *evils* or rather *sins* of this country. The conductors of public papers occupy a very responsible situation in society; many of them are men of talents; but party spirit has so far perverted the proper use of the press, that it has been seriously questioned by sensible men, whether, on the whole, the press serves most to enlighten public opinion with truth, or to pervert it with error." The letter of which this extract is a part, is signed N. Webster; a gentleman of great experience, who was once, I believe, editor of what is now the Commercial Advertiser, himself, and who probably understood very well what he was saying. This letter was doubtless, on the principle which justified the attack on me, introduced into the Commercial in order to furnish a justification of an attack against Dr. Webster's dictionary, or a reproof for his holding sound American opinions when he was in Europe; as, I am happy to say, is understood to have been the case:—no such thing: it is introduced by a merited eulogium on the venerable lexicographer, to whose especial benefit a whole column of the Commercial is devoted! It would offend the reader's common sense to say any more.

There seems to be an opinion prevalent among some of the editors of this country, that they who conduct the public press, are invested with peculiar privileges. The press is either a powerful instrument of good, or a terrible engine of evil. They who control it, do not possess a single right that is not equally the property of every one of their fellow-citizens; while, in place of these imaginary immunities, they exercise the self-assumed office under a moral responsibility that should cause every man of principle to hesitate before he undertakes duties so grave. A grosser abuse of accidental circumstances cannot be imagined, than that of a man of envious and malignant temperament, pouring out the workings of an evil spirit, under favour of these extraordinary means of publicity, carrying pain into the bosoms of families, making his crude opinions the arbiters of reputation, and pulling down, without the talent to build up again. The misconception on the subject of these imaginary privileges, has arisen from the fact that abitrary governments, aware of the influence of the journals, having curtailed even the power to do good, and free governments having restored to them this unquestionable right, some, who identify their own selfishness too closely with principles which ought to be sacred, have fancied that the emancipation from a wrong has brought with it a charter for licentiousness.

All that is believed to be necessary, has now been said in reply to the three journals particularly named, and I shall beg the reader to have patience, while I furnish some evidence of the quality of the mental aliment that is daily served out to the American public, by the practice of copying the opinions of foreigners. I shall be obliged to speak continually of myself, for the reasons already given; but, I trust, the apparent egotism will be pardoned, when it is remembered that in no other way could I command the same materials, or furnish evidence so little liable to error. The object is to let my countrymen into some of the secrets of the critical fraternity, at the same time that I show the danger of doing injustice by circulating calumnies of unknown origin, and lay bare the united ignorance and impudence of those abroad who affect to speak of us, as the greater experience of the old world would appear to entitle the sages of the east to treat the tyros of the west. In order to effect such a purpose, I shall cull, from a large mass of information that I possess, a set of facts, that may change the evidence in a way to meet most of the varieties of the abuse to which, from the practice named, we render ourselves liable.

It was in the autumn of 1830, that I first saw, *in an American journal,* a short article on myself, extracted from an English publication, which was particularly intended to wound my feelings and those of my family, and which was calculated to give the world a very erroneous opinion of, at least, one trait in my private character.

I had become the object of particular resentment to a certain portion of the English, from the circumstance of having written a statement of the causes of the hostility and prejudices which so generally exist in their country against our own. This resentment was greatly increased by the fact that the book I had written was translated into different languages, and circulated throughout Europe. Hitherto they had told their own story; but an American had now joined issue with them, and, for a novelty, had obtained a hearing at the bar of Europe. I was vituperated in England—a country whose reputation for this species of warfare is pretty well established—as a matter of course; for this I was prepared, having well weighed the matter beforehand; but here I had the pain of seeing an American journal stooping to become the instrument of English ribaldry against an absent countryman, who neither merited this particular act of injustice, nor any personal attack from the press of his own people. It may be well to examine the authority of this injurious tale, in order that the compliance of our own journalist may stand out in proper relief.

I regret that a long search has not enabled me to find the paragraph in question. It had been quoted into the ———— from an English journal, which had found it in a posthumous publication of the late Mr. William Hazlett, a writer whose reputation may teach caution to those who are addicted to indiscriminate deference for foreigners. But although it is not in my power to quote its words, I retain a very distinct recollection of its substance. It says that while Sir Walter Scott came to the reading rooms of the Messrs. Gagliniani, sitting down modestly in the outer room, I was in the habit of running about the streets of Paris (!!) and, furthermore, that in society I was in the practice of getting into corners and making faces, as if I would invite the company to admire the American Walter Scott. Puerile as all this may appear, in substance, Mr. William Hazlett did not hesitate to write it, his successors to print it, and the American journal in question to utter it to this country. It is evident on its face, that the writer himself had no very distinct idea of the nature of my sins, so far as they were connected with the shop of the Messrs. Gagliniani and the streets. Mr. Cooper running about the streets of Paris, and Sir Walter Scott taking his seat in the outer room at Gagliniani's, present no very striking images of criminality.

It is sufficiently plain that Mr. Hazlett, who was an utter stranger to me, had been charged with stories to my prejudice; and, probably feeling well disposed as an Englishman to resent the hardihood of an American who had presumed to tell the world a few naked truths on the points at issue between the countries, he gave vent to his animosity without making a particular draft on his logic. I could not desire a better proof of what I now wish to impress on my countrymen, than is to be found in this very paragraph. Here is a European writer of some eminence, permitting prejudice to escape him in a form to betray itself, and this too without the smallest qualification of common sense. What had my running about the streets of Paris to do with Sir Walter Scott's sitting down in the outer room at

Gagliniani's, or vice versa? I think I can explain this matter to the reader. The Messrs. Gagliniani had reprinted in the original, from sheets obtained in England, all my tales up to the time of my arrival at Paris. It was then necessary that I should take the charge of my own works, to secure my right at home; and I had an interview with one of the Messrs. Gagliniani on the subject. I was twice at their establishment. The first time, when nothing was determined or indeed proposed, I sat down too in the outer room, being fatigued; and when I was rested, I went away, without in the least suspecting I had done any thing particularly condescending. The second visit was made a short time afterwards, accompanied by a European friend. The interview took place in a garden, and I was treated with so much superciliousness, that my stay was short. The gentleman with me expressed strong indignation at the manners of Mr. Gagliniani, and observed that, in my place, he would have nothing more to do with him. This advice was exactly in conformity with my own feelings, and I have never entered the building of the Messrs. Gagliniani from that hour to this. A respectable bookseller assured me a few months after this occurrence, that he had heard Mr. Gagliniani threaten to injure the sale of my books, and to do me all the harm he could, a threat, I believe he was very capable of executing, so far as his means would allow. This man has probably repeated some of his tales to Mr. Hazlett, who, yielding to a prejudice, has so far forgotten himself as to record them in the puerile manner in which they appear; and an American journal does not hesitate to circulate what has thus been written by a foreigner! I will furnish one proof of the weight that ought to be attached to these loose opinions of the Messrs. Gagliniani. When Mr. Horatio Greenough and Mr. Morse came up from Italy to Paris, in 1831, they went to the Gagliniani's in order to obtain my address. On asking for me, as friends, they were led to believe that I was an habitué of the rooms, and an intimate there! As to my making faces in society, and standing in the corner—heaven save the mark! I never saw Mr. Hazlett but once; and never exchanged a syllable with him in my life. At one of the public evenings of Gen. Lafayette, I observed that the latter had been conversing with a stranger, who had the air of a student, and, as I thought, of an American. Believing it might be some one that I should be glad to know, I approached our illustrious host and asked if the conjecture was right. He told me that I was mistaken; that the stranger was Mr. Hazlett, offering to introduce me if I wished to make his acquaintance. I declined the introduction in conformity with the rule already named, and from which I have never voluntarily departed. There was not so much reason, moreover, agreeably to the usages of society, why I should have sought an introduction to Mr. Hazlett, as that Mr. Hazlett should have made the first advances to me. But, I did not care to make his acquaintance, and there the matter might very well have ended. It appears he did not think so; for he wrote me down as a coxcomb, possibly in consequence of my showing no *empressment* to make his acquaintance. The reader is not to suppose that Mr. Hazlett knew of Gen. Lafayette's offer, for he did not; but even if he had, it was no excuse for calumniating a man with whom he never exchanged a syllable. As to his assertion that I took pride in being called "The American Walter Scott," it will be seen it was quite gratuitous, and, if permitted to speak for myself on this point, I shall merely say that it gave me just as much gratification as any nick-name can give a gentleman. There exists in all large towns, like London and Paris, a set of very equivocal gentlemen and ladies, who aim at bringing themselves into notice without much respect for propriety. These people, who ordinarily want both breeding and intellect, and not unfrequently character, seek out every object of notoriety, less with a view to flatter him than to enhance their own importance. They are not easily repulsed by the quiet negatives of good breeding, but often urge their requests to importunity. If denied, they almost invariably take their revenge by endeavoring to undervalue the very *illustration,* as the French have it, that they had previously perhaps exaggerated. I was awkwardly placed as respects this troublesome class of patrons. A father and a husband, and one who did not choose altogether to overlook character in his associations, I have reason to think, that a great many enemies were made in this way, and that a great number of idle reports, that have reached me, had their rise in the vindictive resentments of troublesome, adventurers of this sort. I remember a ludicrous case of their modesty which shall be given. It was our misfortune to make a slight acquaintance with a family of this description in one of the Italian towns. The acquaintance, on our part, was managed with so much circumspection that it was confined to the exchange of a few cards, and when we sent the usual signs of leave-taking, previously to quitting the place, we congratulated ourselves that the thing was happily ended. It seems we reckoned without our host, for, at a moment when the trunks were packed, the lodgings discharged, and we were actually on the point of departing, we got a visit, I might almost say of reproach, for thinking of quitting the place without attending a rout that the family *intended* to give the following week, and to which we had not even received an invitation. The scene was ludicrously provoking. The modest proposal was made, and this by people who were now, for the first time, within my doors, that a large family should change all its arrangements, and postpone its departure, on a journey that was to transplant it from the centre of Italy to the centre of Germany, in order to attend "our party!" These people left us with the air of those who had received a serious injury, and, like Mr. Hazlett, may have ascribed my obstinacy to the fact that I was the American Walter Scott. A story founded on such an opinion would circulate widely in this country, to any man's disadvantage; and, although in the case of a writer of mere fiction the consequences are of importance to no one but himself, there might easily occur instances in which the reputations of grave defenders of our dearest rights would be undermined by the facility of which I complain.

I forbear to state a great many shameless deceptions that have actually been practised, at my individual expense, on the American Public. A brief recapitulation of two or three instances must suffice.

The New-York American published in 1827 the translation of a review of The Prairie, with a view, as was stated in the journal, to show the reader the light in which the author was held by foreigners. This critical notice (if the declaration of the man himself is to be believed) was written by an American who had changed his religion, renounced his country, and who shortly afterwards absconded from Paris with a reputation that no one can envy.

In 1828 I saw a statement, in a New-York journal, of an opinion that Sir Walter Scott had expressed concerning the stand I had taken on national questions, and which opinion was intended to lower me in the estimation of my countrymen. This statement very evidently came from the enemy. It referred to a time when I had never seen Sir Walter Scott; when we did meet, literally the first words he uttered was to express his respect for the very course which this statement intended to deride.

In 1829 an account of the manner in which I employed my time at Rome was published, although I did not visit that city till five months afterwards.

During a negotiation with a Paris bookseller,★ I was rudely assailed in a French journal, for the purpose, as was afterwards admitted, of lessening the value of the publications in my own eyes. Such expedients are constantly resorted to in France.

At Florence, in 1829, a person obtruded himself on me in a manner opposed to all the forms of society, impudently announcing himself to be a French critic who had done a great deal to extend the circulation of my works. I need scarcely say that an acquaintance, ushered in with such an introduction, was declined. Just before leaving Europe, I accidentally learned that this person wrote against me in every journal in which he could obtain admission for his articles. I believe the *critique* lately translated by the editor of the American, from the Journal des Débats, and which he compares with the communication of Cassio, in order to show that the latter was not borrowed, to have been written by this man. It is true I never saw the article in question before it appeared in the American; but it is

---

★ A French critic has lately intimated that I have been reaping large emoluments from his countrymen. I have never attempted to sell a copy-right any where but at home. It is true that one contract, written in England and sent to France for my signature, did express the contrary; but I remonstrated against the expression, and never permitted it to be used again. In England, the sheets of what I had written were sold, for the purchaser to do what he pleased with them. The same thing was done for Sir Walter Scott in America, and is constantly practised by other English authors. In France, I sold the sheets for translations, more with a wish to control the time of publication, by acting in concert with the publisher, than with a view to profit. The trifling amount received went to the uses of another. The sheets of three or four books were also sold in Germany, by the same person, and for his benefit. He died before the money for one book was received, and it remains unpaid to this hour. It will be remembered that there were, in all cases, translations previously to these arrangements.

As respects France, a calculation, made on known data, has shown that I paid to the French Government in taxes, during different residences in that country, considerably more money than was obtained from the sales of the sheets of fourteen books. France and Germany excepted, I never had even any indirect connexion with the translations.

The New-York Mirror has, more than once, adverted to the amount of my receipts, with a motive it is not easy to mistake. On what principle the editor of a journal can conceive himself authorized to meddle with the private affairs of a citizen, I do not know; but the statements of the journal in question on this subject, as they relate to myself, are not founded in truth. It remains for the public to decide whether it will tolerate or not this meddling with private interests, by every one who can get the command of a little ink and a few types. The usurpation of such a right is not only English imitation, but imitation of its lowest and least commendable school.

written in the temper, and has the initial letters of my modest visiter. I believe much the greater part of the hostile French *critiques* on myself, to have been written, in a spirit of revenge, by this man.

To such impositions is he liable who blindly copies from the journals of Europe. I could make this part of the case much stronger, but graver matter awaits our consideration.

The habit of fostering this deference to foreign opinion is dangerous to the very institutions under which we live. This is the point at which I have aimed from the commencement; for, while I feel that every defender of the action of our own system is entitled to fair-play, I have never had the weakness to believe that any personal interests of my own are a matter of sufficient importance to others, to require a publication like the present.

The practice of deferring to foreign opinion is dangerous to the institutions of the country.

In order to render the case that I wish to present clear, it will be necessary to take a short review of the institutions themselves.

The government of the United States is a peculiar confederation of many different bodies politic, for specified objects embracing certain of the higher functions of sovereignty, and to which we have given the appropriate name of a Union. The action of this government is obtained by a system of representation which, while it is compound and complicated in its elements, possesses, in fact, the redeeming and essential quality of simplicity, by providing that none but common interests shall be subject to its control. And, yet, while we actually possess, under the provisions of the Constitution, the essential requisite of an *ensemble* in the legal operation and spirit of the institutions, nothing is easier than to create an antagonist action, by overstepping the limits of the compact. A single glance at the instrument itself will explain my meaning.

A Union, from its very nature, must be a representative form of government; but the mere circumstance that a government is representative by no means establishes its character, which depends on the fact of whom the parties are that are represented. Under our system, each State is the arbiter of its own constituency, subject to the single condition that its form of polity shall be that of a Republic. A republic is a government in which the executive power is not hereditary, or in which the laws are administered in the name of a Commonwealth instead of that of a Prince. Venice, Poland, Frankfort,

Unterwalden, Berne and Connecticut, are or were all republics. New-York, in virtue of its reserved rights, has decided that its constituency shall be represented on the principle of universal suffrage. Virginia has a freehold qualification. Either of these States has a right to modify its representation as it shall think best for its own interests. In point of fact, it is true the states of this Union are nearly all democracies, but they have attained this near approach to harmony by their own acts; for, under the limitations of the Federal Constitution, it is quite within the legal competency of the several bodies corporate which compose the Union, to make that Union a representation of democracies, or of aristocracies, or of a mixture of both, by altering the characters of the respective constituencies. Did the government of the United States possess more minute powers, therefore, and were the States to exercise the privilege just mentioned, making their representations a mixture of aristocracies and democracies, disunion or revolution would inevitably follow. Although there are instances in which monarchies and aristocracies coalesce in confederations for defined objects, as in Germany, and in which aristocracies and democracies unite for the same purposes, there is no instance in history in which these antagonist principles have long existed, in the full exercise of equal powers, in the form of a consolidated community. The struggle between them has always produced revolution in fact, whatever may have been done in form. By studying, then, the danger of a union of great antagonist principles in a consolidated form of government, we are admonished to respect the conditions on which the possibility of their co-existence is admitted into our own system. Although Virginia, and certain other States, may possibly be termed representative democracies, when considered solely in reference to their white population, they are in truth, even now, mild aristocracies, when considered in reference to their whole population. Immaterial as the difference is in most cases between the polity of Virginia and that of New-York, there are some points of disagreement that sufficiently show how easy it is, by transcending the conditions of the Union, to awaken a spirit of hostility, and to endanger the existence of the compact that now binds them together. To these points of difference in principle may be added, as temporary causes of disunion, those interests which arise from difference of climate and productions.

Every government has two great classes of obstacles to contend with:—the propensities of human nature, and the difficulties that arise from its

particular manner of controling its own affairs. As the first is an evil that we
share in common with all men, it may be dismissed without comment; but
in the case of the second, it will be useful to allude here to one or two of
these particular causes of embarrassment as they exist under our own system.

The first great difficulty with which this government has to contend, is,
for reasons that are obvious, the accurate discrimination between the powers that are granted to the Union and those that are reserved by the states.
The contests which may arise on these vital questions can give birth to the
only true whigs and tories of America. The object of this Union was not
simply government—this was possessed in the several states—but it was to
extend a uniform system over so large a space, as to reap the greatest benefit from its action.

It has been said by others that the advantages of the Union, while they
are admitted to be of the last importance, are of a purely negative character. This, I apprehend, is little more than clothing a truism in pretending
language. The object of society in general is to enjoy the advantages of association and protection; to say, therefore, that we should be worse off without the Union, is but another method of saying that we are better off with
it. In Europe, when the enemies of this system (and they are the friends of
all others) are driven from position to position in the arguments that frequently occur between them and Americans, concerning the merits and
probable duration of our polity, they uniformly raise the objection, "that
your government is only a compromise." Every government is a compromise, or something worse. Every community that is not founded on such a
principle must sacrifice some of its interests to others; and, in our own case,
so far from believing that the mutual concessions that have been made in
the compact of the Union are opposed to the true spirit of government, I
shall contend that they are proofs that its real objects and just limitations
were properly understood. Disputes have certainly occurred, originating in
a diversity of employments; but we have not yet reached the period when
all the ordinary interests of civilized society are properly balanced. When
that period shall arrive, and it cannot be distant, I think it will be found that
this diversity of employments is an additional ligament to the Union. But,
while no great weight is to be given to a mere diversity of employments,
every attention is due to those feelings that enter into the daily habits and
prejudices of men. In this country, facts greatly outrun opinion. This is one

of the reasons that we see men looking behind them to Europe for precedents, instead of being willing to conduct their own affairs on their own
principles. Had congress the right to control those minute interests of society that touch the rooted practices of different sections of the Union, as
they are now controlled by the state legislatures, the revenue of the Union
would not be worth a year's purchase; for nothing but force would compel
the Virginian and the Vermontese to submit to the same detail of social
organization. In such a case we should quickly see the vicious influence of
the adverse principles of democracy and aristocracy. Still, the constitution
of the United States contemplates the co-existence of these antagonist
forces in our system, through the several states, and it fully admits of their
representation, for it leaves to each community the power to decide on the
character of its constituency. It follows as a corollary from the proposition,
that either the framers of the constitution were guilty of the gross neglect
of admitting into the government of the Union the seeds of its own
destruction, or that they devised means to obviate the natural conflict
between principles so irreconcileably hostile. They did the latter, by limiting the powers of the new government to the control of those interests that
take the same general aspects under every form of civilized society, let the
authority emanate from what sources it may. This provision, then, is our
only safeguard, and while it is respected there is little serious ground to
apprehend the downfall of the system; but as soon as innovation shall make
any serious inroads on these sacred limits, the bond which unites us will be
severed. From all this is to be inferred the immense importance of keeping
the action of the general government most rigidly within its defined
sphere, to the utter exclusion of all construction but that which is clearly
and distinctly to be inferred by honest deductions of powers that are conceded in terms.

To the danger which awaits any departure from a severe interpretation
of the constitution, as it is to be apprehended from the possibility, and
indeed it might be added the actual existence of different elements in the
federal constituency, may be added that which arises from the facility of
action through the organized forms of the state governments. The latter,
however, when considered as distinct from the difference in these elements
themselves, is a danger that arises solely from the inherent vices and weaknesses of man. They may or they may not lead to evil, as circumstances shall

direct; but the existence of antagonist principles, or of conflicting elements, in the construction of any government, *must lead to dissension,* unless some unusual preventive is devised. As has been seen, in our own case, the expedient is a limitation of powers.

The second embarrassment dependant on its own details, with which the federal government has to contend, is the possibility of an occasional want of concurrence in views and action between the different branches of the constituted authorities. This evil is peculiar to our own form of polity. It does not exist in England, and is almost the only solid advantage which that country, in a political point of view, possesses over our own.

As I am aware there will be a disposition to cavil at many of these positions, I may be permitted a word in the way of explanation. It has been said that in no other form of government is there the same danger from temporary collisions between the different branches of power, as in our own. To this would probably be objected the examples of England, at certain periods of her history, of France, since the restoration, and of divers of what are called the constitutional states of Germany; such as Bavaria, Saxony, Wurtemberg, the Hessen and Nassau. As respects the latter, while they are included in the reasons about to be given in relation to the two others, the instances they afford are entitled to no respect, for they are all under the control of an external and a superior force. Austria, Prussia and Russia would interfere to coerce the people,★ and the knowledge of this fact only has probably prevented revolution in them all.

England, so far from being an exception to the ground just taken, affords the strongest proof of its justice. The revolution of 1668 was owing to a struggle between the powers of the state. Previously to that period the prerogative was in the ascendant, and since that period it has been constantly on the wane, until it is completely annihilated as to all practical political authority. The laws are still administered in the name of the king it is true, his signature is necessary to certain acts, and he is yet called the head of the church and state; but aristocracy has cast its web about him with so much ingenuity, that the premier conducts his hand, the chancellor wields his conscience, and parliament feeds him, until he is reduced to the condition of a

---

★ France also might now be added to the list of those states that would directly, or indirectly, lend its influence to effect the same object.

well dressed lay-figure. There undeniably was a contest between parliament and the prerogative during the four reigns that preceded the last, and the result goes to prove the very position I have taken. This contest has wrought the effects of revolution, perverting the government from a monarchy to an oligarchy. The entire authority of the state, even to that of dictating his ministers to the king, is virtually in the hands of parliament. Open, palpable revolution has been carefully avoided, simply because the tendency of such convulsions is to elevate the low and to depress the great, and it was the wish of the aristocracy to effect its purpose by indirect means, and by the fictions of legality. The ascendancy of the thousand families who control the British empire has been obtained under the cry of liberty.

As the situation of France has not admitted of as much legal fraud as that of England, her example, since the restoration, is still more plainly in favor of the truth of our position. The contest between the crown and the chambers led Louis XVIII to alter the charter; and a few years later, when opinion had gathered force, and legislation began to assume most of its ordinary attributes, his successor lost his crown, in making a similar attempt.

Thus far, in quoting the examples of the European states, it has been the intention to show merely the inevitable tendency of struggles between the executive and the legislature, considered in connexion with leading principles, and under the supposition that the constituency and the representation are of the same mind. In the cases of what are called in Europe representative governments, the eventual★ danger has been somewhat lessened, and the temporary inconvenience removed, by a very simple expedient. The crown has power to prorogue or dissolve the legislature. The reasons, therefore, why the embarrassment that arises from temporary collisions between the executive and the legislature is greater in America than in England or France, are to be found in the fact that the chambers can be dissolved, and the fact that should the new elections be adverse to those who wield the power of the crown, the chambers, in their turn, compel a

---

★ In England the danger has been averted by virtually reducing all the powers of the government to one body. The constituency of England is, as to political effect, the property of the representation. In cases where the landlord does not control, the open vote gives the richest man nearly the certainty of being elected. The exceptions do not affect the rule.

change of ministers. The alternative, as was the case in France in 1830, is rev-olution. It is unnecessary to say that the executive of this country has no power to dissolve congress or congress any power to dissolve a ministry. The inevitable consequences of the continuance of such collisions, viz. revolu-tion, or changes equal in effect to revolution, is obviated only by the fre-quency of the elections.

We will return to our own polity.

It will be admitted that the government of the United States is one of powers delegated for limited and defined purposes. Its authority is to be found only in the constitution. Precedent, as it is derived from our own practice, is valuable merely as it has been established on sound principles, and as it is derived from the practices of others, is to be received with a cau-tious examination into its fitness for our peculiar condition.

The highest authority known to the constitution, in its spirit, is the con-stituency. It sits in judgment over all, and approves or condemns at pleasure. All the branches of the deputed government, executive, legislative and judi-cial, are equally amenable to its decisions. It has retained the power of even changing the characters of its several servants; of placing the authority of the president in the hands of a committee of congress, or in any other depository it shall select; of dispensing with the judiciary altogether, or of modifying its duties at pleasure; of re-modelling the legislature and of issu-ing to it new commissions, as it shall see fit. The only restraint it has laid on its own acts, is a provision pointing out the form in which its will is to be expressed, and a solitary condition touching that delicate point of the rights of the several states, which secures to each an equal representation in the senate. When the constituency and the people are identical, this becomes political liberty.

The highest attributes of the constituency are delegated to the legisla-ture, whose powers are as carefully and as distinctly defined, as the nature of things would well permit. The judiciary and executive are, in a great degree, subordinate to the will of the latter, on which there is no restraint but the provisions of the compact, and from which, when legitimately exer-cised, there is no appeal but to the constituency. Its members act with no other responsibility than that which they owe to their own body, and to the judgments that may be passed upon their measures by those who issued their commissions. Unlike the executive and the judiciary, they are liable to no impeachment.★ When the irresponsible nature of such a power, divided as it is among many, is taken in connexion with its extent, it is very obvious that far more danger is to be apprehended from the legislature, through innovations on the principles of the constitution under the forms of law, than from either of the two other branches of the government. They all exercise delegated powers, it is true, and powers that can be perverted from their legitimate uses; but congress is the least restrained, while it possesses the highest authority. It follows of necessity that it is the branch of this government most likely to abuse its trust.

Obvious as are these facts, what has just been said is not the popular manner of viewing the subject. The English aristocracy has so long been innovating on the prerogative of the crown, under the cry of liberty, and the *theory* of the English constitution has so artfully favored such a mystification, that we have caught the feeling of another country, and are apt to consider those to whom we have confided the greatest authority under the least responsibility, the exclusive guardians of our liberties! Such an opinion can only be entertained by a sacrifice of both fact and reason. The constituency is its own protector, or our pretension to real liberty would be idle. The executive is a creature of our own forming, and for our own good, and it is manifestly a weakness to confound him or his authority, with a prince and his prerogative, the latter being based on the divine right.

In a monarchy power is supposed to be the prerogative of the crown, and what is called liberty is no more than concessions obtained from the sovereign in behalf of the subject. Under really free institutions, government itself is no more than a concession of powers for the benefit of protection and association. It is very possible that these mutual concessions should produce an exactly similar set of subordinate ordinances or laws, and yet one government shall enjoy real freedom, and the other possess no more than its shadow. The essence of liberty is in the ultimate power to control, as residing in the body of the nation. Its form is exhibited through the responsibility of the public agents.

★ This is an instance in which imitation has led us astray from the commencement. What sufficient reason can be given why the representative, in a system like ours, should not be tried and punished for an abuse of trust, as well as a judge, or the president? In countries in which the representative is either an advocate or a master, there is good cause for his impunity, but in ours, where he is only a servant, there is none.

The inference that I could wish to draw from this brief statement is the absolute necessity of construing the Constitution of the United States on its own principles; of rigidly respecting the spirit as well as the letter of its provisions; and of never attempting to avert any evil which may arise under the practice of the government, in any other manner than that which is pointed out by the instrument itself. On no other terms can this Union be perpetuated, and on these terms, there is reason to believe that our prospect of national happiness and power exceeds that of any other people on the globe.

I now propose to mention two or three cases in which the habit of admitting foreign examples into the administration of our own system, has violated the essential principles of the great national compact. I shall commence with the executive, although it might not be difficult to show that the habit of reasoning of American interests on English principles, has led, in some particulars, to the original error of modeling the institutions themselves into forms but indifferently suited to our actual condition. As my space is limited, I shall endeavor to be brief.

The appointing power of the president is contained in Art. II. Sec. 2, of the Constitution, and is expressed in these words:—"And he shall nominate, and by and with the advice and consent of the senate, shall appoint ambassadors, other public ministers and consuls, &c. &c." So far as these particular officers are concerned, there is no other constitutional mode of appointing them, unless under the provision of clause 3d, same section, which goes on to say, that "the president shall have power to fill *all vacancies* that may happen during the recess of the senate, by granting commissions which shall expire at the end of their next session." This provision was evidently made to prevent the necessity of calling the Senate together uselessly, and, at the same time, to prevent the public service from suffering.

Two practices have prevailed in the government as to the manner of deciding what offices shall be created. In the one case, it is commanded by law that there shall be certain offices, and it becomes the duty of the president and senate to name the persons who are to fill them. In the other, it is left to the discretion of those who hold the appointing power to settle the question, congress retaining the check of refusing the money by which they are to be paid. In the latter case it is understood that the appointment is legal, although a salary should be refused, provided the nominee will serve for nothing. As respects foreign ministers, their number, rank and destination, have never been determined in any other manner than by the simple exercise of the appointing power.

Mr. W. C. Rives, of Virginia, was regularly and legally appointed a minister to the court of France, in 1829. In 1832, he returned home, and resigned. Soon after, Mr. Leavitt Harris was appointed, *by the President and Senate,* a chargé d'affaires to fill the vacant mission. In the absence of any law to the contrary, this was the only method of determining what the rank of that mission should be. Some months later, and during the recess of the senate, Mr. Harris either resigned or was removed, and Mr. Livingston was appointed an *Envoy Extraordinary and Minister Plenipotentiary* in his place. Whence did the president derive his power for making this appointment? I see no other source than an inference that might be drawn from the appropriations; but can congress, even by a direct law, give a power to the president to name a citizen to an original office during the recess of the senate? It had been determined that the mission to France should be that of a chargé d'affaires, precisely in the same manner that it had been determined that a great many other missions should be lowered in rank; and the president, it appears to me, had just as much legal warranty for removing the chargé d'affaires to Colombia, during the recess of the senate, and for appointing a minister in his place, as he had to name Mr. Livingston to fill the vacancy occasioned by the resignation or removal of Mr. Harris. When a lieutenant of the navy dies, the president surely has no power to appoint a captain to succeed him, even though the appropriations might meet the difference in the respective amounts of pay. The practice is liable to great abuse. Mr. Erving was nominated as minister to Constantinople, but was rejected by the senate, on the ground that the rank of the mission should be limited to that of a chargé d'affaires. Mr. David Porter was eventually appointed in the latter capacity. Now, if the doctrine prevail that the president has a right to name a minister to succeed a chargé during the recess of the senate, what was there to prevent him from pursuing his original intention, by removing Mr. Porter and putting Mr. Erving in his place with the rank of minister?*

---

* It is scarcely necessary to say, that nothing offensive is intended to the gentleman appointed, for whose talents I have the greatest respect; nor is any particular blame attached to the present executive, for the looseness of the practice of the government had crept into a precedent.

Take a much stronger case.

Consuls can only be appointed *by the President with the consent of the Senate,* unless to fill vacancies in the recess of the latter, and then the appointment can only be made by the president. The language of the Constitution on this point will not admit of misconception. In 1833, Mr. Barnet, then consul at Paris, died. Mr. Niles had been left chargé des affaires of the legation a short time previously. The difference between a chargé d'affaires and a person left chargé des affaires of a legation is very material, or, rather, under our system, *it ought to be* very material. A chargé d'affaires is the lowest officer in the ranks of diplomacy that is ever charged with a mission. He can execute the same political powers as an ambassador or the highest; but a secretary left chargé des affaires is no more than one who remains to keep open the communications between the two countries, and receives his appointment from the minister. It may be questioned whether one can be legally appointed at all under our compact. Mr. Rives himself was no other than an agent of the American states commissioned to execute certain defined functions. When he left the mission with Mr. Niles, the latter became, in one sense, his deputy. The commission which the latter held as secretary of legation, gave him no legal claim to the trust, which Mr. Rives might, had he seen fit, have confided to another. On the death of Mr. Barnet, Mr. Niles, in virtue of powers contained in the regular instructions, (as I understand,) appointed a consul to succeed him. Here, then, we have an office, which the constitution expressly says shall be filled only by the president and senate, except in the case of a single contingency, and in the event of that contingency by the president alone, filled by a substitute's substitute!

I understand that the commanders of the Mediterranean squadrons are instructed to appoint consuls, and that they have often done so. In one instance, there is good reason to think that the functions of a consul were for a long time executed by a woman, who had no other commission than her dying husband's request.

The foreign agents of the government are in the habit of naming attachés to the different legations, and the consuls frequently commission what are called vice-consuls.

An attaché is either an officer or he is not. If an officer, he is appointed directly in the face of the constitution; if not, his appointment is an imposition on foreign countries, who believe him to be one, and treat him accordingly. Great injustice is done to the example of our institutions, by the practice of naming attachés. Many intelligent men and sound Americans have unquestionably obtained the appointments; but, in too many instances, vain and ignorant young persons seek the distinction, get into a society that turns their heads, and begin to deride the republican institutions which they are thought to represent. To such a pass did this abuse extend, that serious thoughts were entertained by some of our countrymen, who were in Europe a year or two since, to address a memorial to congress on the subject. Even the president, as the law stands, has no power to appoint a vice-consul, and yet there are some scores of these functionaries in existence! No civil officer of this government can be appointed legally, except in one of two manners, viz. either by the president and senate, as pointed out in the constitution, or by the president himself, the head of a department, or a court of law, in virtue of an act of congress. I found that the consular instructions *supposed* a power in the consul to appoint his agents, who, in many cases, perform all his duties. I did as others had done before me, and named an agent; but seeing the error, as has been said in an earlier part of this letter, the office was resigned. I mention the circumstance merely to show that what is here advanced is advanced on principle, and with no view to criminate any particular man, or any set of men.

All these abuses, and a great many more of a similar character that might be named, arise from the habit of seeking authorities for our practice among other nations, instead of taking those which form the compact between the states. The king of England, or those who wield the prerogative in his name, are the fountains of honor, and they make such appointments as they please, and in any mode or form they shall see fit, and any objection raised to the course taken by our government is usually met by some precedent derived from the usages of England. He who points to the constitution is answered by a saying of Mr. Burke, or a decision of my Lord Mansfield! These cases have been mentioned because they have occurred openly, and even party spirit has so far acquiesced in the authority of European precedent, that it has never assailed those who have been the agents of permitting their existence.

Let us see if congress itself is exempt from the sinister influence of foreign example.

The late events connected with the removal of the deposits are known to every one. The president directs the secretary of the treasury to remove the public moneys from the Bank of the United States, and on receiving a refusal, he removes the incumbent, and fills the place with an officer disposed to comply. This officer, agreeably to a provision of the law which gave him authority to perform the act, makes a report of his reasons to congress. The senate of the United States, after a long debate on the subject matter of the report, passes a separate resolution declaring, in substance, that the interference of the president in this affair was unconstitutional. To this vote the president asks leave to enter a solemn protest, principally on the ground that it is, in effect, a judgment pronounced without the forms of law.

With the legality of the course pursued by the president, or with the justness of the exceptions he has taken to the vote of the senate, so far as they relate to its judicial effect, the objects of this letter have no connection. But as every citizen who expresses his opinions with due moderation, and with a suitable deference to the sentiments of others, has a right to lay his objections to the acts of any or every department of the government before the public, I shall attempt to show, that, by the letter of the constitution, by a fair construction of its spirit, and from all just reasoning through inferences to be drawn from the good and evil of the step it has taken, the senate of the United States had no authority whatever to pass any separate resolution at all on the subject, whether in favor of, or against the conduct of the executive; and that all the authority which can or has been quoted to the contrary, is derived from a state of things so essentially different from our own, as to be valueless, or worse than none. The reader will at once perceive that if this position can be made good, it will be in perfect conformity with the general drift of this letter.

In analysing the authority of congress, we are to look nowhere but to the constitution. Burke and De Lolme and Hallam were all able writers; Pitt, Fox, any many others, have been eloquent speakers, but neither of them had any concern with the compact that binds these states together. It is purely a bargain of our own making, and it should be a bargain of our own construing. So far as precedent is connected with mere parliamentary usage, in reference to forms only, and to principles as they relate to forms, the authority of the statesmen named may be entitled, with many exceptions, to their weight; but when there is question of the great principles of our government, or of its peculiar action, authorities from such a source are to be received like advice from an enemy. The liberty of which they speak is not our liberty. It means no more than power wrested from the repository which has held it for ages by the accidents and usages of monarchy and feodality, and is meant to descend no lower than a particular caste. The liberty with which we are concerned is regularly based on the foundations of the people, and is intended for their benefit.

The senate of the United States has passed a separate resolution pronouncing the conduct of the president to be unconstitutional in reference to a certain exercise of authority. On the mere merits of this step the public mind is divided, although very few indeed question its right to take a separate resolution, except as it is prejudging a case on which its members may be called to decide as triers under an impeachment. So rooted is the feeling that the legislature is the guardian of our liberties, that most men do not see that, under a system like our own, every particle of power it exercises is abstracted from the constituent! The concessions that have been made to congress may all have been made in the interest of order and good government; but, so far as a blind jealousy is in any manner to be justified, it is no more than common sense to take care that it shall be felt on our own side of the question. Let us now look for the authority under which the senate has acted.

The *manner* in which the constitution has delegated power to congress is of some moment in such an investigation. That instrument commences with saying, that all legislative authority shall reside in the *two* houses of congress. It then speaks of the organization and of the elements of the respective bodies, and of the forms of elections. An entire section is next devoted to the *separate* powers of each house. If any *direct* authority for the vote of the senate is contained in the constitution, it is naturally to be looked for in this section.★ The only clause that contains anything, which the most fertile imagination has attempted to torture into authority to take a vote of censure on the acts of the president, is the second. By the second clause "each house may determine the rules of its proceedings, &c." But to determine the *manner* of performing functions so obviously does not infer a right to create them, that this opinion is entitled to no respect.

In those sections which treat of the organization of the respective

★ See Note D, end of pamphlet.

houses, there are clauses giving to each body the power to choose its own officers, with an exception in the case of the senate, and which give to the house of representatives the sole power of impeachment, and to the senate the right to sit in judgment. The constitution, in speaking of the manner of electing the president, refers the choice to the house of representatives in a certain contingency, and it gives to the senate the power to count the votes that come from the electoral colleges. These several clauses embrace all the powers directly granted to each house to act separately, that is contained in the instrument from which all the power they have to act at all is derived. It is a just inference from the minute specification of the powers which are expressly granted, many of which are of a kind that were indispensably requisite for the action of the respective houses, and might safely have been left to construction, if it had been intended to leave any *principle* whatever to construction, that no other authority was in any case to be exercised by either house of congress *separately*. Even the power to keep a separate record of its own proceedings is granted to each house in terms, a right that might fairly enough be supposed to be incidental to that of proceeding at all. It must be conceded, then, that the constitution has granted no *direct* authority to the senate to pass a simple vote of censure on the acts of the president, or on those of the meanest citizen of the land. Unless it can be found in a just and fair construction, therefore, of some power that has been *directly* granted, we shall be driven to our old enemy imitation, and imitation of a system so opposed to our own as to render it doubly hazardous.

Construction is a fruitful source of power. The constitution has provided, however, an important check against its abuse, by declaring that all powers which are not delegated to the United States, nor prohibited to the states, "are reserved to the states respectively, *or to the people.*" By the people is meant, as a matter of course, the constituency. Common prudence would seem to say, that construction, under a compact like our own, should be jealously limited to clear inferences from the powers that are granted in terms. In this view of the case, the act of the senate can be sustained by no sufficient authority, since there is no authority expressly granted to that body to act separately that can, in any manner, be tortured into such an inference. This difficulty has been foreseen, and they who sustain the conduct of the senate, depend on precedent and general principles, or maintain that its act was merely preparatory to ordinary legislation.

There can be no doubt that congress (not the senate alone) had a right to act on the report of the secretary of the treasury in relation to the removal of the deposites. It had full power to order them to be restored to the Bank of the United States. This could be done, it is to be presumed, under the spirit of the charter, by a simple resolution or order. But the constitution commands that "every order, resolution or vote," which requires the concurrence of the two houses, that of adjournment alone excepted, shall be sent to the president for his approval, as in the case of a bill, and in the event of his disapproving, that it shall be carried by a two-thirds vote in each house, before it take effect. No one can believe that the president would approve of a resolution to restore the deposites, or of a vote of censure on himself. It is matter of notoriety, that the house of representatives is of the same way of thinking. An attempt at legislation, therefore, would have failed. This is probably the reason that there has been no attempt at legislation.* The vote of the senate is a simple, unqualified vote of censure, as to its effect, and in its form it is the mere expression of an opinion of that body. To say that it has any connexion with ordinary legislation is to insult the meanest intellect. We are consequently driven to general principles, or to precedent for the authority we are seeking.

Precedent derived from our own practices may be adduced in extenuation of even an erroneous procedure, beyond a question; but, unless the procedure itself can be justified on principles that arise from our own state of things, so far as the argument of this letter is concerned, the more the practice has prevailed, the greater is the evil which it is its object to expose.

It is claimed as a parliamentary usage, from time immemorial, for legislative bodies to express their opinions on public measures in this mode. The justification of the senate is rested on this circumstance more than on any other, and certainly it is the best attempt at justification that has been made. Let us examine its validity.

The practices of the colonial legislatures must be identified with those of parliament, for the struggle, or the pretence of a struggle, between the prerogative of the crown and the franchises of the people was common to

---

* Notice of an attempt at legislation on this subject has just been given by the very senator who introduced the vote of censure, a circumstance that of itself shows he did not keep legislation in view in the original step.

all, inducing the same modes of attack and defence. The practices of the state legislatures, if opposed to the principles of their respective governments, or not warranted by direct concessions from the people, are liable to the same objection as the act of the senate, and only go to prove the extent of the evil, like precedents derived from congress.

Were the argument to rest here, I should be prepared to say for one, that the senate, having no sufficient power delegated by the constitution, overstepped its authority in passing any resolution on the subject at all, as unconnected with legislation, and in the absence of the forms of impeachment, let precedent decide as it might. I do not believe that congress itself, far less one of its bodies separately, can find authority in the constitution for passing a resolution of this nature, with no other view than a mere expression of its opinion; and I cannot but think, that the constitution of the United States ought to prevail against precedent, let it come from what source it may. But it is my intention to give the argument all the benefit it can receive from the practices of parliament, reserving the right to make use of principles to defeat their effect, for such an illustration is the precise point to which I most desire to bring the reader.

It will be conceded that some legitimate good must be the object of every general construction of power in a state, or the measure becomes an act of tyranny as well as of usurpation.

The two houses of parliament do pass resolutions, both separate and concurrent, censuring the conduct of those who are termed "his majesty's ministers," but who are, in truth, the ministers of parliament. They censure those who are responsible to themselves, who are appointed at their pleasure, and who retire before their frown. An honorable member of the senate has lately said that he was not *his* senator, in allusion to the executive, and it was well said. He might have gone farther, and have added, nor am I *my own* senator. He is *our* senator, and the president is *our* president, and we commissioned both to discharge certain important public trusts, under very positive limitations of authority.

There is a *motive* for the censure of parliament. It is a test of parties, and the precursor of a change. Either parliament or ministers must yield. There is, in fact, no popular constituency in the question. The peers represent themselves, and the commons represent the money of the rich, that of the peers included. So closely was the price of a seat in the lower house calculated, before the late reform, that it was generally estimated it cost £1000 a year, taking into the account the chances of a dissolution. A vote of censure on the king cannot be passed, for parliament still respects the fictions of the constitution, and it would be useless; but votes of censure on the ministers are common: they are the usual method of ascertaining the strength of parties, and the ordinary mode of producing a change of measures, or, at least, of men.

What has all this in common with the principles or the ordinances of the American constitution? The censures of congress cannot drive a president from his chair, or even a secretary from his cabinet. They both virtually hold their places by the same tenure as that of congress itself. They are equally the servants of the people, who have reserved to themselves the right to judge of their conduct. But while the vote of the senate can do no good, it may and has done much harm. It has brought into action the second great embarrassment peculiar to the details of this form of government, that of creating dissension between its different branches, by which the interests not of "his majesty," but of the people, suffer. The supplies of this very year have been so long delayed, in consequence of the determination of the opposition to embarrass the executive, according to the English mode, that individuals have been compelled to pay heavy penalties for the benefit of the imitation. Government cannot be sued,* and contractors must await its justice. It is not agreeable, however, to pay three per cent. a month for money that would be forthcoming if Burke and Chatham, and the Parliamentary History of England, were less in the hands of some of our legislators, and the constitution more.

The cry of withholding the supplies has reached the press, and, in some cases, the people. If these supplies are not just in themselves, if they are extravagant in amount, or prodigal in expenditure, they should never have been granted at all; but for a legislator to manifest that he is opposed to granting them merely with a view to embarrass an administration, is a direct insult on

---

* This is another instance of error, arising from imitation at the commencement. In countries in which the rights of the subject are no more than concessions from power, we can understand why a government should not be sued; but under our polity, reason and justice would both say that every facility should be given to the weak to enforce their claims against the strong.

the intelligence of the constituency. It is not withholding *its* supplies, but it is withholding *our* supplies. Parliament, by adopting a system of withholding the supplies, has annihilated the prerogative, except as it is wielded for its own purposes. The president will still be president, though congress refuse to vote a dollar, and the faith of this nation will be violated if his salary be not punctually paid. If he commit grave faults pending the legal term of service, impeachment and punishment are the remedies, and every four years the people sit in judgment on the merits of his acts. This measure of withholding the supplies is peculiarly English; it is the means by which parliament has destroyed whatever of balance the government ever had, and is the simplest, the most obvious, and the most dangerous of all the modes of legislative usurpation. It is time to begin to consider our legislators in their true character; not as sentinels to watch the executive merely, but as those of the public servants the most likely to exceed their delegated authority.

I am quite prepared for the feeling to which these remarks will be likely to give birth. It is one of the prominent evils of this system of imitation, that the minds of the constituency themselves get to be poisoned. A false direction is given to the public watchfulness. Already we have the president, an officer created for our special benefit, compared to the king of England. It may be useful here to institute a short comparison between the authorities of these two functionaries. The king, it is true, now merely *represents* the prerogative, the latter being wielded at the will of parliament, but we will consider him as he exists in theory, and as other kings yet exist in fact.

The right of the king to his crown is derived from descent, and is inalienable. He can declare war and make peace. He is the head of the church, the fountain of honor, and can do no wrong. Here is certainly no resemblance to a president. Both command the armies, but on very different conditions. The president is merely a generalissimo, Congress being an aulic council to direct him as it shall please, and he must do very much as it shall direct; being, in his military capacity, virtually as much under the law as the lowest corporal in the ranks. Parliamentary usurpation may have reduced the king of England as low, it is true, compelling him as civil king to bind himself as military king; but it is not so in France, and other countries where the prerogatives are still exercised by the sovereigns. The king of France can raise as many men by enlistment as he shall see fit, provided he can find means to pay them. The army is his army. In such a state of things, there may be a good reason for withholding the supplies. As keepers of the public moneys, the trusts and duties of both king and president are the same. It is no more than to name competent agents, and so far from being a benefit, in both cases, it is an onerous charge; such a charge as men in commercial life ordinarily ask two and a half per cent. on the amounts received and paid for assuming, and this, too, with the additional advantage of mingling them, for the time being, with their private resources. The king can do no wrong; the president is responsible for his acts, both by the ordinary law and under an impeachment. It follows that there is no great analogy between a president and a king.

To return to the act of the senate. We have already considered it in relation to its authority, and we will now look for its real character. It is not legislative beyond a doubt. It is neither more nor less than a solemn expression of an opinion by that honorable body, in its collected capacity. As, in the absence of direct authority, it is required to justify the act on principles applicable to our especial condition, we must look to all its probable results in estimating its propriety.

An expression of an opinion that has so clear a tendency to embarrass the action of a government especially created for the sole benefit of the constituency, should have some high countervailing advantage. It cannot have been uttered to the world for the information of the senators themselves, or in order that they may know their own minds. It was not expected, at least not plausibly expected, that it would cause the president to retrace his steps; to reappoint Mr. Duane and to restore the deposites. If such was the intention, the failure might have been foreseen. From this quarter it has produced a protest, and feelings between the president and senate of which much evil and no good to the public service are to be the consequences. But, I shall be informed, it is telling the nation what the senate thinks of the conduct of its executive. This is very true, and in reply, as was very reasonably to be anticipated, the president, in his turn, has told the nation what he thinks of the conduct of the senate. It remains for the nation now to say what it thinks of the conduct of both. If the senate has passed this resolution for the benefit of the nation, (and all its formal acts have a false direction that have not this tendency,) it remains to be seen in what manner. We have not been told a fact, but the senate's *opinion* of a fact. The fact was as well known to us all, as to the senate itself. Why has the senate given us its opinion in this matter? In order to extract ours in reply? At the proper time our opinion would have been made known, without this interference of the senate. But, it will be said, the senate is a learned and an intellectual body, and its opinion will have weight with the constituency, and influence the public mind. There has been a great deal said, and said cleverly too, on the subject of the right of the constituent to instruct his representative, but this doctrine savors strongly of a right in the representative to instruct his constituent! The senate was never commissioned to act in this manner on the public will, and the practice is liable to the grossest abuses. If the president can be censured, candidates for the presidency can be censured too. Means will never be wanting, and the two houses of congress will degenerate into mere electioneering caucuses.

But is not this a free country, freer than England;—is not congress our representation, and shall not congress do that which parliament does daily? God forbid that congress should ever have power to do that which parliament does daily; and, on the other hand, God forbid that the president should not do daily that which the king of England (of his own will) cannot do at all! Parliament has seized upon the executive powers, and rendered the king a cypher; it wields the prerogative in his name; it has pulled down and set up dynasties; it is both law and constitution; it has established a religion and is about to destroy one; it has rendered the judges dependent on its pleasure; and, quite lately, it has even changed its own elements! Parliament is absolute. Who is there bold enough in this nation to say that he wishes congress to possess the powers of parliament? Congress is composed of what the lawyers call "attorneys in fact," and when we see it overstepping in the least its delegated functions, our feelings should be like those of one who has authorized another to sell, in his name, a single acre of his land, and who learns that his agent has so interpreted his authority, that he is about to dispose of the whole estate.

If the president could do no more than the king of England can do in fact, (putting fictions out of the question,) we should be incurring the evils of periodical elections, and paying $25,000 a year to one of our own citizens to live in the White House and do nothing.

If the vote of the senate is not authorized by any direct power delegated by the constituency in the great national compact; if it cannot be justified by fair deductions from any power that is so delegated; and if a just consideration of the uses and origin of similar authority, as it is exercised in other countries, shows that its exercise here, on the same principles, is opposed to the spirit of our own institutions, where are we to look for the vindication of the step of that body? It can be found only in precedents derived from our own practice, and precedents of evil derived from our own practice and founded on the usages of the English parliament, only make the case it is my wish to present so much the stronger.

The evil is not limited to the vote of the senate. The house of representatives, as anxious to support as the senate is to condemn the course of the executive, has sent a committee to investigate the affairs of the bank, and, the directors of the institution refusing to acquiesce in the measure, a resolution is introduced to arrest the whole body for contempt. Whence is the power derived by which congress itself can take such a step? Why parliament does it! But it has been seen that parliament does a great deal that it would be considered tyranny and usurpation for congress to attempt. The constitution gives no power to congress to arrest any one for contempt. Each house is master of its own hall, and there its police power ends. But the constitution gives congress power to pass all laws necessary to carry the defined powers into effect, and this measure is required to extort information that is important to the public good. The constitution *has* given this authority to congress, and it will be time enough for any branch of the government to use it, when congress, by law, has vested it with the necessary authority.

It would be more respectable, and far safer, were we to make an effort to conduct our own affairs on our own principles. If this Union shall ever be destroyed by any error or faults of an internal origin, it will not be by executive, but by legislative usurpation. The former is easily enough restrained, while the latter, cloaked under the appearance of legality and representation, is but too apt to carry the public sentiment with it. England has changed its form of government, from that of a monarchy to that of an exceedingly oppressive aristocracy, precisely in this manner.

The habit of listening to another people, and of imbibing their prejudices and peculiar ways of thinking, does not limit its injury to the representation of the country. The constituency itself becomes tainted by the communion, and ceases to judge of its own interests on its own principles. This is the penalty we pay for being the younger and the less important nation. The question that has just been considered furnishes proof of what is said.

The contest between the executive and the senate has very naturally aroused the friends of the respective parties, and strange political heresies are rife among us. My limits will admit of but one or two brief examples.

In his protest, the president lays down the doctrine that the keeping of the public moneys must be confided to those whose tenure of office is left to his official discretion, and whose manner of discharging their trusts must of necessity be submitted to his supervision and approval. Now against this plain, constitutional position, there is raised a cry from one extremity of the Union to the other, which, to say the least, is not of the most prudent and reflecting character. It is highly probable that some precedent may be found in the speeches of Lord Chatham or Mr. Burke, in which the danger of executive usurpation in some way connected with the public money is pointed out, and which, *if admitted as authority,* will make Gen. Jackson appear in but very indifferent colors in the eyes of his fellow citizens. But Gen. Jackson, although he can do what the king of England cannot do, is not the king of England after all. He is our fellow citizen, named to a high trust for definite period, and with a defined authority. Common sense and common honesty would tell us, therefore, the expediency of looking into the conditions of the bargain under which he has accepted service, before we open the vials of our wrath upon his head. What says the constitution which we have compelled him to swear he will defend? It says, in so many words, that he shall have the power of appointing all the officers of the government (with the consent and advice of the senate) with the exception of those whose appointment is provided for by the constitution itself, and of certain *inferior officers,* whose appointment congress can, by law, place in the gift of either the president alone, of the heads of departments, or of the courts of law. It will be well for us to remember that "power," as it is used in the American constitution, is but, another word for *duty.* As the constitution is silent on the subject of the appointment of a treasurer of the United States, and the office is certainly a very important office, and not an inferior one, it follows as a matter of course that the keeping of the money cannot be placed beyond the supervision and authority of the executive. Congress can say that the money shall be kept where or in whatever manner it shall please; it can put the trust in the hands of commissioners, and as many as it shall see fit to order; but it cannot say who those commissioners shall be, for the simple reason that the constitution is silent as to the existence of any such power in congress, and has spoken as plainly as words can speak, to say that another shall possess it. English reasoning has so far prevailed, however, that we have been plainly told congress can raise a committee of its own body to keep the money, or it can put it in the custody of the vice-president and of the judges, who are independent of the president, and thus rescue us from tyranny. As for the judges, they have already spoken their minds on this subject, and have told congress, in the matter of the pensions, that they shall assume no duties that the constitution has not authorized. The vice-president may certainly be named as a commissioner for keeping the public money, by the president and senate, holding the appointment at the pleasure of the former, but it is far beyond the power of congress to give him a character *as vice-president,* that is not bestowed already by the constitution.* It would be just as lawful for the executive to pretend to give new powers to congress itself. The powers or duties of the several branches of government can only be varied by the highest legislation of the land—that of the constituency, convened in the representation prescribed by the national compact. Congress having no power to hold the money itself, can grant none to a committee of its own body. It is exclusively a legislative corps, (as congress,) and it can exercise even that authority only, subject to the limitations mentioned in the constitution.

Many who read this letter will feel disposed to exclaim against a state of things which places so much power in the hands of one man. I see far less apprehension of executive than of legislative usurpation in this country. Still, I am willing to admit that the president has too much authority for our form of government. This is precisely one of the points in which imitation led the framers of the constitution astray. It would be better, for instance, if congress had power to appoint a treasurer, as is practised in most of the state governments. But should congress attempt to remedy the evil by simple parliamentary action, it will, as I humbly object, be carrying imitation to a still more dangerous extreme. Before we are Burked out of our constitutional existence, let us at least make an attempt to try some of the expedients of our own system.

---

* The writer is here answering an argument used by one of his personal friends at a public meeting, and which has been sent to him in one of the newspapers of the day.

I have reserved the gravest instances of dependance on foreign opinion to the last.

Combinations exist to coerce the citizen.* The laborer is menaced; he is discharged if he will not vote in conformity with the will of his employer. This is striking at the root of the social compact—at the rights of the constituency itself. It is an accursed principle imported from that land which, while I fully admit its greatness and its importance even to ourselves in many particulars, moral as well as physical, has probably sent us quite as much evil as good.

The pretence that the employer has a right to coerce the vote of the employed, is neither more nor less than maintaining the doctrine of the *representation* of property in its worst, because in its most oppressive and fraudulent, form. We have solemnly decreed that property *shall not be represented;* even those states that still exact a money *qualification* in the voters, limit the demand to that of a *qualification* only; we have protected the elector by the ballot, and various other legal safeguards, and yet, so pernicious is the influence of that country from which we so largely imbibe our opinions, that the heresy is openly maintained by perhaps a majority of those who are most in the habit of looking abroad for rules of thought.

The power to use another's vote is thoroughly English. Parliament itself is no other than a collection of the rich (or of their nominees) who command the electors themselves to give them authority. The system is a pure mistification, and the day when it really gets root in this country may be looked upon as the commencement of a rule that is to subvert the institutions, and to place us where England is placed to-day, in the hands of the selfish, the mercenary and the purchased, without any other relief from their usurpations than such as is to be obtained from the throes of the oppressed. We may get reform as England has got reform, by tumults, and conflagrations, and threats of revolution; but we shall no longer obtain redress by the quiet, safe, and humane expedient of the ballot boxes.

Another baneful effect of this foreign domination is the fact, that our best and least rewarded servants are rendered subject to an influence that is hostile to our rights, our national character, and our nearest interests. All

---

* There will probably be a disposition to deny the fact. The writer only asserts what he has heard openly defended, and that which, it is in evidence, has been practised.

who can recall the events of the last war, must remember with what a niggardly spirit applause was meted out to those who shed their blood in the nation's defence, by the *doctrinaires* created by this habit of deferring to strangers. One legislature solemnly voted that our soldiers and seamen were no better than so many mercenaries, fighting against God and his truth! This was not merely party spirit; party spirit exists in England and in France to an extent quite equaling any thing of the same nature that ever existed here, but the English and the French never refuse to honor their defenders. In this country, without pensions, orders, titles, or even military rank, we strip patriotism to the skin, leaving it little more than opinion for its reward, and, by the propensity of which there is complaint, we rob it, in part, of even this insufficient recompense.

What can be more grievous than the case of a citizen who ventures upon the high seas, under the protection of his country's flag, and who is violently dragged, with insults and not unfrequently with robbery, into the service of another people, where he is made to risk both life and morals, to uphold a state of things that, rightly considered, is perhaps more antagonist to the system under which he was born than any other that can be named? Such was impressment. We all know its practice; and yet, to such an extent did mental dependance carry subserviency among us, that, I am not sure I might not say, a majority of our theorists as stoutly maintained the right of England to enter our ships, exacting from us the proofs of citizenship, and of exercising a power so insulting and so injurious, as if they were contending for the privileges of their liege lord. I know not what Mr. Burke might have said on this subject, but I happen to know the opinion of that upright, practical and gallant old seaman, Lord Collingwood, and it was simply that, were the case reversed, England herself would not submit to such a practice for an hour. If England wishes the services of her seamen, the simplest rules of justice prescribe that she should find means to keep them at home, and that she is not to enforce her own municipal regulations by invading the sovereignty of foreign nations. What renders the practice still more insulting, is the fact that, at the very time she practised this wrong on others, she drew into her own marines, both military and commercial, all the foreigners she could entice, in addition to those who were compelled to serve her.

Do not deceive yourselves with the belief that these things are not seen and understood by others. There exists in this country an unaccountable delusion on the subject of the manner in which the American name and character are viewed in foreign countries. Diplomatic courtesy, the exaggerated expressions of European intercourse, and the deceptions of the designing, appear to have aided vanity in throwing a film before the eyes of too many of us, on this point. He who could wish the estimation of his countrymen to be lower than it actually is, must have a zest for humility that will one day procure canonization. Heaven knows how willingly I would tell you the contrary, if, in honesty, I could; but, in order to tell you the truth, I am compelled to say that I believe there is not another nation of christendom whose people enjoy less positive favor than our own. We are not so generally hated as the English, it is true; but I am far from being sure that the alternative is any better. I feel certain that one of the chief causes of this state of feeling, springs from the fact that we are so often untrue to ourselves. The impression that our infidelity makes on foreigners is painfully humiliating. I will close this disagreeable portion of my letter with one instance, taken from a hundred within my own experience, to show the truth of what is here said.

In 1828 accident threw me into the society of the present chancellor of England, then Mr. Brougham, and I was honored with an introduction. The interview took place in passing rapidly from one room to another. The usual terms of courtesy occupied us until we reached the place to which we were going, an interval of perhaps a minute, when this distinguished man turned short upon me, and abruptly inquired—"What is the reason that so many of your countrymen desert the distinctive opinions of their country on coming to Europe?" My answer was that "I hoped the fact was not so." *"My experience would say it is."* "To what class of men do you allude?" "To your foreign ministers in particular." "Something will depend on the character of the man; will you name one?" He did, adding, however, that he meant the remark as general, I could only say that I supposed these gentlemen were willing to carry prudence to an excess, and that they aimed at making themselves agreeable. "I understand you—you think they affected what they did not feel, for the sake of quiet." But he looked as if he knew better, and I much fear that I looked as if I knew better too. It is some consolation to know that Mr. Brougham did not live in the intimacy of the Franklins, and Jays and Jeffersons of our diplomacy.

One of the most melancholy consequences of this habit of deferring to other nations, and to other systems, is the fact that it causes us to undervalue the high blessings we so peculiarly enjoy; to render us ungrateful towards God, and to make us unjust to our fellow men, by throwing obstacles in their progress towards liberty.

There is an impatience of existing practical evils that causes many of the best-disposed men of this nation to overlook the real merits of the great question that is now agitating christendom. No one will deny that we have our own particular causes of complaint, and that a very great proportion of them are the offspring of democracy. Were it not for this we should be perfect. All the evil that is dependent on polity, and which is peculiarly our own, has this origin. It can have no other, for there is no monarch, nor aristocracy (practically and politically considered) to produce a different. But let him who has known both England and America intimately compare the disadvantages of the systems, and, if an honest and a sensible man, he will tell you to be content with your lot. Artful, intriguing demagogues get uppermost among us too often, beyond a doubt; but where do they not? The difference between a demagogue and a courtier is not worth disputing about. We have the certainly of knowing that when such men do arrive at power, they are reduced to something very near the *minimum* of harm; whereas, in other countries, the abuse is pretty sure to be at the expense of a very great majority.

The liberals of Europe (the term *whig* is going fast out of fashion in England, where it means no more than a modified aristocrat, or a liberal of the last century,) complain that Americans do them as much harm with their tongues, as the institutions of the country do good by their example.

The disposition to respect the sayings and opinions of England, leads us to credit, with a dangerous facility, the audacious charges that the agents of her hostile institutions bring against our own. We appear, in the eyes of others, like a people who do not more than half believe in the evidence of our own facts, and who are not sincere in our own professions. This is one of the reasons that Europe fancies we are living under a violent and rude democracy, which compels the wise and good to submit to its dictation, under the penalty of losing life and property. It is a common impression in Europe that this country is rent by civil wars and violence.

In the finance controversy the truth was entirely on our side, as subsequent investigation has triumphantly established. The French government, or, to speak more properly; its writers announced their intention to send to this country for documents to prove us in the wrong, and it is understood at Paris that they have abandoned the design, under a conviction that the facts are against them. And yet, what portion of our *doctrinaires* espoused our cause, which was in effect the cause of freedom? At Paris, I believe much the larger portion of our countrymen were against us. Mr. Rives,★ the minister, was openly cited by the French premier, in the chamber of deputies, as being of that opinion; the secretary of legation, I have it in proof, was also against us; and it has been seen that Mr. Harris, the gentleman who was afterwards named to be chargé d'affaires, actually wrote a letter against us, which the *juste millieu* caused to be printed in an extra number of the Revue Britannique. These gentlemen had a perfect right to their convictions, certainly, but if their course was in any manner influenced by a wish to propitiate the French government, the public will judge between me and them. If they had political effect in view, the high and honorable condition of our relations with France, just at this moment, must be exceedingly flattering to their diplomatic sagacity.

The Prefect of the Loiret, our principal antagonist, frequently referred to certain honorable Americans, *(plusieurs honorables Americains)* who, he asserts, were too liberal to confound their duty to the truth with their duty to their country, and who were much too wise to believe that national honor and national expenditure were the same thing. These writers, agreeably to his account of the matter, carried their liberality so far as to furnish him with various documents to enable him to prove that we were very wrong. M. Saulnier had the indiscretion to publish one of these documents, and I believe it was proved, to the satisfaction of every man who took the trouble to read the controversy, that this precious evidence was extracted from a very worthless statistical table that is to be found in the travels of Captain Basil Hall!

So far as I have been able to ascertain the fact, the opinion at home, among the *doctrinaires*, was also very generally against us in the finance

---

★ It is due to this gentleman to say, that he affirms M. Perier quoted him wrongfully; but he was quoted, and his opinion was triumphantly cited against us in all the ministerial journals, and, to the best of my knowledge, the statement is uncontradicted to this hour.

question, much the greater part of these persons having jumped to their conclusions without even knowing the real points that were mooted. There must be something very unsound in the state of public opinion, when so many of what are called the *elite* of a country, go off at half-cock against the effects of its own institutions.

I turn from interests like these to myself again with humility and regret. But the purpose of this letter would not be accomplished were I to bring it too abruptly to a close. Still I cannot force myself to the completion of its original design. I did intend, my countrymen, to expose to you the exultation and interested satisfaction with which other nations view this dependance on themselves; the derision mingled with art, with which they play upon the weakness, and the deep design of destroying your growing power and prosperity that lies at the bottom of all. This is a duty that will probably fall to some pen better qualified for its performance. But I cannot take my leave of you, without so far trespassing on your good nature as to venture a kind word at parting.

I came before you, as a writer, when the habit of looking to others for mental aliment most disqualified the public to receive a native author with favor. It has been said lately that I owe the little success I met with at home, to foreign approbation. This assertion is unjust to you. Accident first made me a writer, and the same accident gave a direction to the subject of my pen. Ashamed to have fallen into the track of imitation, I endeavored to repair the wrong done to my own views, by producing a work that should be purely American, and of which love of country should be the theme. This work most of you received with a generous welcome that might have satisfied any one that the heart of this great community is sound. It was only at a later day, when I was willing more obviously to substitute American *principles* for American *things,* that I was first made to feel how far opinion, according to my poor judgment, still lags in the rear of facts. The American who wishes to illustrate and enforce the peculiar principles of his own country, by the agency of polite literature, will, for a long time to come, I fear, find that *his* constituency, as to all purposes of distinctive thought, is still too much under the influence of foreign theories, to receive him with favor. It is under this conviction that I lay aside the pen. I am told that this step will be attributed to the language of the journals, and some of my friends are disposed to flatter me with the belief that the journals misrepresent the public sentiment. On this head, I can only say that, like others similarly situated, I must submit to any false inferences of this nature to which accident shall give birth. I am quite unconscious of giving any undue weight to the crudities of the daily press, and as to the press of this country in particular, a good portion of the hostility it has manifested to myself, is so plainly stamped with its origin, that it never gave me any other uneasiness, than that which belongs to the certainty that it must be backed by a strong public opinion, or men of this description would never have presumed to utter what they have. The information on which I act is derived from sources entitled to more respect than the declamations of the press.

I confess I have come to this decision with reluctance, for I had hoped to be useful in my generation, and to have yet done something which might have identified my name with those who are to come after me. But it has been ordered differently. I have never been very sanguine as to the immortality of what I have written, a very short period having always sufficed for my ambition; but I am not ashamed to avow, that I have felt a severe mortification that I am to break down on the question of distinctive American thought. Were it a matter of more than feeling, I trust I should be among the last to desert my post. But the democracy of this country is in every sense strong enough to protect itself. Here, the democrat is the conservative, and, thank God, he has something worth preserving. I believe he knows it, and that he will prove true to himself. I confess I have no great fears of our modern aristocracy, which is wanting in more of chivalry than the *accolade*.

Had I not been dragged before you rudely, through the persevering hostility of one or two of the journals, this duty to myself would have been silently performed. With the exception of the extract of the letter published by Mr. Morse, this is the only instance, during the many years that we have stood to each other in the relations of author and reader, in which I have ever had occasion to trouble you, either directly or indirectly, with any thing personal to myself, and I trust to your kindness to excuse the step I have now taken. What has here been said, has been said frankly, and I hope with a suitable simplicity. So far as you have been indulgent to me, and no one feels its extent more than myself, I thank you with deep sincerity; so far as I stand opposed to that class among you which forms the public of a writer, on points that, however much in error, I honestly believe to be of vital importance to the well being and dignity of the human race, I can only lament that we are separated by so wide a barrier as to render further communion, under our old relations, mutually unsatisfactory.

J. FENIMORE-COOPER

POSTSCRIPT

This letter was already written and sent to press, as mentioned in the introductory notice, when the condition of trade caused the bookseller to hesitate about publishing. The writer was also averse to appear before the public at a moment so gloomy, with matter that was necessarily of a personal nature. With this double motive, the pamphlet has been kept back till now.

Hasty writing and hasty printing (for the work was pushed while it was actually proceeding) have occasioned a few inadvertences of style, most of which will be attributed by the reader to their true causes. There are, however, one or two of these mistakes that call for correction. "Grateful for the compliment," should be "gratified by the compliment"—page 15, line 22.

By insinuating that the foreigners who have attacked the writer in this country, were guilty of ingratitude to the latter, there is no intention of identifying the interests of the two; the idea has been imperfectly expressed. It was meant to say that the writer has been thus assailed by these men, *because he has presumed to defend the interests of his native land against those of their own.*

The delay in publishing induced the writer to destroy more than half of what he had originally written, in order to illustrate his position by events of more notorious and recent occurrence, such as those connected with the removal of the deposites.

Since the letter has been printed, the writer has received a communication from General Lafayette, on the subject of the finance controversy. In alluding to Mr. Rives, there was a delicacy of saying more than was already public, but it is due to that gentleman now to say, that General Lafayette, in his name, has informed the French people that Mr. Rives did not say what M. Perier attributed to him. The writer was privy to the fact that Mr. Rives authorized General Lafayette, after some delay, to say this much in the chambers, and that it was not done on account of the illness and subsequent death of M. Perier. But the point on which Mr. Rives and the writer are at issue, is that the former owed it to the country not to permit any foreign minister to quote him against the action of its system, without promptly and effectually causing it to be contradicted. General Lafayette was merely authorized to do that which the writer thinks Mr. Rives should have taken care was done with great promptitude. In consequence of the delay or indecision of Mr. Rives, this country presented the singular spectable of its secretary of state (Mr. Livingston) calling upon all the governors for facts to disprove the statements of the Revue Britannique, *in the interests of free institutions,* while the American minister at Paris was openly quoted by the French premier, in the chamber of deputies, as giving an opinion directly on the other side of the question!

The tone of many Americans in Europe was often the subject of discussion between General Lafayette and the writer. The latter knew that some of his countrymen were among the most bitter deriders of the venerable patriot when in reverses, and that most of these men crowded about him in the hour of his triumph, in a way even to exclude his true friends. While this country has manifested, at home, its attachment to the venerable patriot, it has not always respected his feelings, or observed that delicacy which was due to his eminent and disinterested services. The manner in which he has been spoken of in the memoirs of some of his revolutionary contemporaries might have been spared, for, while it could do no good, it has furnished his enemies with materials of attack. There are two sides to every question. The opinion of Mr. Gouverneur Morris is known, and it may be well now to hear what can be said in answer. The following is an extract from General Lafayette's last letter to the writer. It is scarcely necessary to say that the allusion is to Mr. Morris:—

"I have read the memoirs of a distinguished statesman, to whose memory I am bound by the seal of an early friendship, and an affectionate gratitude for the great services he rendered in the most dangerous times to my wife and children; yet I cannot deny that his communications with the royal family, representing me as an ultrademocrat and republican, even for the meridian of the United States, were among the numerous causes which encouraged them in their opposition to my advice and to the side of public opinion. For my part, I have, in the course of my long life, ever experienced that distance, instead of relaxing, does enliven and brace my sentiments of American pride."

It is time that this country took more care that its public agents abroad do not at least *misrepresent* public opinion at home. Neutrality is a duty, but it is not neutrality to compromise a principle when there is a just occasion to speak; nor is it neutrality for an agent of this country to be "*howling against reform*," as the conduct of one was described to the writer by a distinguished English liberal—not a *whig*. This country owes it to itself to strip the tinsel from the coats of its foreign agents, and to send them abroad in the attire they use at home. Even the half-civilized Turk has too much dignity and self-respect to change his turban for a hat, when he goes to the Tuileries or St. James', and why should we forever bend to the habits of other people? We lose instead of gaining respect by the course, and in losing respect we lose influence. A *tailor* at Paris once showed the writer, with a sneer, a coat he had been making for an American agent, with a star as large as the evening planet on each breast, wrought in gold thread! After all, it was but a pitiful imitation of the Toison d'Or and St. Esprit. Simplicity is as much the characteristic of a gentleman as magnificence—in the name of Heaven let us have one or the other!

It was the original intention of the writer to expose the manner in which the British aristocratic journals, however much opposed to each other on certain points, rally to support their distinctive privileges and national interests. The Quarterly and Edinburgh usually mix like oil and vinegar, but the latter was selected to assail the writer, because it was believed it passed as a more liberal work in this country. In England a *tory* means an oligarchist; a *whig* is merely an aristocrat; a *liberal* is one who wishes rational freedom, founded on the base of the people, and a *radical* is one who is for overturning every thing and beginning *de novo*. The Edinburgh Review is strictly whig, and it has been contending for taking away the close boroughs from my Lords A. B. and C., in order to make a new distribution of power among the few—not the few in *its* sense, for this would be oligarchical; but the *few* in our sense, which is aristocratical. The writer had selected four or five cases of the exceeding ignorance of the Edinburgh, in order to show with what instruction it discussed American subjects, but his limits have forced the matter out. There is one case, however, to which he could wish to say a word. Mr. Rush, in his late work on England, observes that men of different parties meet sociably in society, appearing for the moment to forget their political antipathies. In reviewing this book the critic asks, with a sneer, and in reference to this remark of Mr. Rush, if Mr.

Cooper remembers his answer when he was told that Pitt and Fox never met in private life. The writer does not remember his answer, nor does he remember ever to have been before told the circumstance in question. As he is told it now, however, he will make an answer, viz. "That the fact contradicts the statement of Mr. Rush, and that the reviewer does not appear to have had sufficient sagacity to see it."

On re-examining the constitution, the writer perceives that the power of each house to keep a separate journal is given rather in the character of an injunction than in that of a concession. Of course he has used the fact improperly as an illustration of his argument, which it does not sustain, while, at the same time, it does not oppose it.

The writer has succeeded in finding the paragraph from the pen of Mr. Hazlett, which is alluded to in page 52. It is given below:—

"There are two things I admire in Sir Walter, his capacity and his simplicity; which indeed I am apt to think are much the same. The more ideas a man has of other things, the less he is taken up with the idea of himself. Every one gives the same account of the author of Waverly in this respect. When he was in Paris, and went to Galignani's, he sat down in an outer room to look at some book he wanted to see: none of the clerks had the least suspicion who it was. When it was found out, the place was in a commotion. Cooper, the American, was in Paris at the same time: his looks and manners seemed to announce a much greater man. He strutted through the streets with a very consequential air; and in company held up his head, screwed up his features, and placed himself on a sort of pedestal to be observed and admired, as if he never relaxed in the assumption nor wished it to be forgotten by others, that he was the American Walter Scott."

NOTES

A.

Since my arrival from Switzerland, I have taken no particular pains to investigate the affair of the critique on the Bravo, that appeared in the New-York American, though one or two circumstances have occurred to corroborate what I never doubted, that it was a translation of one of the attacks of the Juste Milieu, a little altered to adapt it to the American reader, for, as you may remember, it professes to come from an American. The Journal des

Debats, the oracle of the party of the Doctrinaires, published, some time before, the original, allowing for the translation and the necessary alterations, as *I understand*. This fact alone would put the question of its origin at rest, were there not sufficient internal evidence to prove it, without referring to the stupid blunder of quoting the Paris edition of the work! I take the report you mention, of this critique having been written by "an obscure clerk in a counting-house," to be a subterfuge. [The following are the words of Mr. Morse:—"I gave you the name of the writer (of the critique) in Paris, on the authority of———; since I have been at home, it has been declared to me that the review was written *here* by an obscure clerk in a counting-house, and ——— was cited to me as having assured my informant of the fact." It will be seen that this attributing of the article to *an obscure person* did not come from either Mr. Morse or myself, neither of whom believed the story, but actually from the other side. ———, the person alluded to by Mr. Morse, is a personal and political friend of the editor of the American, and if Cassio dislikes this description of his employments, he must reserve his spleen for those who originated it.] It might have been forwarded to the American through such a channel, or it might have been translated by such a pen, for the work is done in so bungling a manner, that, as you will recollect, I detected its French origin before twenty lines were read. I am not disposed to deny the obscurity of the translator. When work of this description is done, it is usually committed to understrappers. Depend on it, however, that it was translated at Paris, clerk or no clerk. The Bravo is certainly no very flattering picture for the upstart aristocrats of the new regimes, and nothing is more natural than their desire to undervalue the book; but the facility betrayed by our own journals, in an affair of this nature, in a source of deep mortification to every American of right feeling. I ought to have said, there is a gentleman now at Paris, who (I am told) says he was present when one of the editors of the American wrote the article. You may take this statement as the companion to the report of the agency of the "obscure clerk;" both stories cannot be true, since they contradict each other. I have no doubt that Mr.——— discovered the truth, and that ——— is the true author of the article, with, perhaps, the exception of the alterations which exist in the translation. This ——— is a common hack writer—was then in the employment of the Journal des Debats, and would have written an eulogium on the Bravo, or any thing else, the next day, for a hundred francs. It is unnecessary to say any thing to you touching the venality of the French and English reviews. As a general rule, nothing appears in either without favor or malice.

You have not alluded to the attack on me, contained in the Commercial Advertiser of Feb. 1st last. I consider this article much more worthy of attention than the pitiful affair of the translation of Mr. ———'s criticism on the Bravo. I think, were the truth known, that, with the exception of the article on the Heidenmauer, translated from the Revue Encyclopedique, and which has looseness enough to contain its own refutation, this is purely of American origin. "We clearly perceive," says the reviewer, "that Cooper has long ceased to dwell in America. It awakens no more recollections in his soul." Here is the 'ercles vein with a vengeance! Now, just twenty-three lines lower down, in the column of the Commercial, this grinder of ideas adds—"Cooper does not speak of a site, &c. without stopping to say, 'Oh, this is much better in America,' &c. &c. It is easy to see that *he must think of his own country to excite himself, and to arrive at the end of his book.*" All this stuff is well enough for the ordinary French reader, who is not usually a very great stickler for facts, or consistency. But why is it translated for the Commercial? I think I can tell you.

The Commercial shows that the review is sent by a "correspondent." It even gives some of the opinions, and, luckily, some of the language too, of this correspondent. Here is what he says of me: "He has *constituted himself the literary antagonist* of the monarchy, aristocracy and feudality of all Europe, and particularly of England, *to, at, and for* which last country he especially writes." I have italicised the eleven feet. "To, at, and for!" I know but one potentate capable of parading these prepositions. Had he been as skillful in enumerating the cost of government, in the finance discussion, these innocent little parts of speech would never have been dragged forth so unmercifully. Let us look at him again. Lower down he says, "He is an American (not a French) Voltaire, at Paris, (not Fernay)." Here is pith for you! By these few words we learn that Voltaire was a Frenchman, and that I am a Yankee that once lived at Fernay, and the other at Paris. We had at Cooperstown, some thirty or forty years ago, a political writer who put his parentheses into one another, like spare pill-boxes, but he wanted altogether the lucid arrangement of the correspondent of the Commercial!

The jesuitism of this digested attack in the Commercial is worthy of notice. First I am shown up by the Theban of the French review; then comes an article *against* Mrs. Trollope to prove the impartiality of the periodical quoted,—afterwards the editor says, in his own person, though I strongly suspect he uses even the language of his "correspondent"—"We regret the existence of unfriendly feelings to us among the French. France—our early friend—has always been popular in America, *through and with* all her faults, &c." Again—"We believe now, that even the French government-party in France would have no inclination to attack us, if Americans abroad had pursued *the same reserve in politics which we enforce upon Europeans here.*" All this is meant for me, and it all comes from the fact that I gave my testimony in favor of General Lafayette, when it suited the French government to affirm, in the face of Europe, that all our old friend had been saying for forty years, concerning the effect of our institutions, was false; and that, in fact, we paid more taxes than the French.

I do not believe that the editor of the Commercial, who passed ten years of his life in calling the French any thing but gentlemen, wrote the words "France has always been popular in America, &c." Rely on it, they are calculated; and come from his "correspondent." The *"through and with"* savor of the "to, at, and for;" nothing but a rear-guard to the main body. "The unfriendly feeling of the French," means of the French government-party, for the French, as a nation, are in a comfortable state of indifference as respects America and all it contains. The government hatred has been excited by the dread of a republic, which would, of course, be death to itself.—"The same reserve in politics we enforce from Europeans!" A residence in America about as long as mine has been in France, entitles the stranger to become a citizen. It is notorious that foreigners are constantly employed about the American press; as reporters in congress, and in a variety of ways that act on public opinion. When I left New-York a paper was published in the city that was openly called the Albion, and whose color was decidedly English. Now, we will suppose that the Globe, or any other government paper with us, should pretend to prove that England had a debt of thrice its real amount, and that the Englishman pays three times the taxes he does, will any man affirm that this Albion would hesitate about showing the truth, let the motive for the misrepresentation be what it might; or that public opinion in America would inflict a punishment for its so doing? Suppose an American had served England as Lafayette has served us, and that the motive was to crush this American, and you have a case completely parallel to my interference with the finance discussion. But to render the remark of the Commercial still more flagrant, one of the proprietors and editors of that very paper is, or was quite lately, an Englishman! I have seen some very extraordinary and some impudent transactions in my time, but I can recall none more flagrant than this of putting an American on his trial, at the bar of public opinion, and that, too, in his own country, for having told the truth in defence of General Lafayette, at a great pecuniary loss to himself, and without the smallest possibility of personal advantage. Every hour convinces me, more and more, that we are a nation in name only, let Mr. Webster and Mr. Calhoun say what they please about it.

As respects the finance discussion, it is my intention, however, to publish its details, not for any interest I have in it personally, but from a wish to set the history of the part played by the agents of our government in foreign countries generally before the public. Nothing but publicity is needed to extort the corrective. The subject grows in my hands, and may make a small volume. If I help to produce a change in the tone of the agent abroad, I shall not have lived entirely for nothing. Europe will gain in rights, and we shall gain in character. Heaven knows how much it is wanted, even for the simplest purposes of true policy. We have a fair specimen of the effect of the nose-of-wax system, by the recent course of the French government. Here is a solemn treaty, duly ratified, to pay a certain sum on a certain day. Our bill is protested, under the pretence that there has been no appropriation. Now, the chambers have been in session near nine months since the ratifications were exchanged, and not a word has been said by the ministry on the subject. Would England, or Austria, or Russia, or Prussia, or even poor little Sardinia, be treated so cavalierly?

We flatter and play the courtier, and act on the all-things-to-all-men principle, when we should assume the frank attitude of the republicanism we profess, ask only what is right, and take nothing less. I may finish the little work over which we used to laugh so much a year since, but it has lain ten months untouched.

The editor of the Commercial has a naive avowal "that he might have hesitated to admit this attack, but for the knowledge that Mr. Cooper prefers the censure to the praise of the daily press." If I have this humor, it must be one of those tastes which are formed by habit. Were I to answer the editor, it would be in the words of the French saying—"Il y a de la Rochefaucauld et de la Rochefaucauld."

How much longer America means to tolerate this slavish dependance on foreign opinion, without which editors would not dream of extracting remarks on ourselves from hostile journals, you are in a situation to know better than I. All the familiar thoughts and illustrations of English literature are in direct and dangerous opposition to our own system, and yet we are unwilling to support a writer in the promulgation of those that are in harmony with our profession, and which I think are abstractly true. The English in particular see and profit by this weakness. It is manifestly their interest to do our thinking if possible, that they may do other things for us that are more lucrative; and they are not scrupulous about the means employed to effect this object. They systematically attack and undervalue every man they believe independent of their influence, and extol those to the skies who will do their work. When all is done, they deride us for our folly, despise their instruments heartily, and respect those most who most respect themselves. John Bull, "through and with" all his faults, is at least manly, and has a great contempt for a "dough face."

This letter was written to the very person who had sent me the name of the writer of Cassio, who knew that I had taken no steps to inquire into the affair previously to going to Switzerland, and who is now told that I had taken none since my return. A good deal of the letter is not published.

B.

Extract from the Commercial Advertiser.

REVUE ENCYCLOPEDIQUE.—We have received the October number of the *Revue Encyclopedique.* On a hasty glance at its contents, we discover two articles, which it may be interesting to our readers to notice.

The first is a brief notice of Cooper's *Heidenmauer,* in which the French Reviewer treats this last work of "our distinguished countrymen," with no small degree of severity, as will be seen:—

"*We clearly perceive,* (says the Reviewer,) *that Cooper has long ceased to dwell in America. It awakens no more recollections in his soul. It calls up no more poetical images—no more simple and original creations—no more descriptions so picturesque, so fresh, so attractive.* He has become a quiet citizen, who no more quits the land. He has forgotten that other world, which he has made us so much love, the Sea—the sea with its infinite variety in infinite uniformity—the sea, with the sailor's faith and boldness—the sea, with all the poetry of sublime nature united to the genius of man.—It is as melancholy a thing as death, to see this powerful inspiration depart—or rather exhaust itself upon itself. Walter Scott is no more, and Cooper also is no more, for we have known him only by his genius, and his genius is dead."

After a brief account of the work, in which the writer acknowledges that there is an occasional brilliancy, he concludes thus:—

"I do not wish to analyze this romance, which every one has read. All must have been impatient of the often fatiguing prolixity of the descriptions, and of the singular prejudices of Cooper, which make him, on each page, while recounting the events of the sixteenth century, establish a parallel between the manners, belief, and political institutions of America and of Europe. *Cooper does not speak of a site—he does not bring one of his heroes on the scene or describe the spirit of the epoch, without stopping to say—'Oh! this is much better in America—you see nothing like this there.'—It is easy to see that he is not interested in his subject, and that he must think of his own country to excite himself, and to arrive at the end of his book.*"

"I know not, indeed, why there is not in these men of genius a secret and benevolent voice, to bid them to cease, and tell them that they have done enough for glory, and that they must not sully beautiful and ravishing remembrances by the weakness of an exhausted talent, which has given all it could give to the world."

"I wish I had not read any of the romances of Scott, after the Fair Maid of Perth, nor any of Cooper's since his Puritan of America."

"I hope, as to Cooper, that this may be the last work I shall read, and especially I wish it may be the last which I shall have to review."

By the *Puritan of America,* we presume, is meant the *Wept of the Wisht-on-Wish,* and we rejoice to believe that the most ridiculous of names has not travelled abroad.

A correspondent, whose letter accompanies the review, thinks the Frenchman has not hit upon the true cause of Cooper's incessant references to politics in his late works. "He has constituted himself," says our friend, "the literary antagonist of the monarchy, aristocracy and feudality of all Europe, and particularly of England, *to, at, and for which last country* he especially writes. He is an American (not a French) Voltaire, at Paris, (not Fernay,) and is undermining thrones and principalities, and changing the destinies of Europe. After all, perhaps the interests of mankind would not materially suffer, and his readers would be better pleased, if he would leave off the high-heeled buskin and become the mere good-tempered novelist once more." This vain of censure is rather severe, and we should have declined its insertion, were it not for the knowledge of the fact that Mr. Cooper prefers the censure, to the praise, of the newspaper press. Of this peculiarity of his taste he has taken care to inform us in the preface to the *Heidenmauer*, in which he says in so many words:—"Each hour, as life advances, am I made to see how capricious and *vulgar* is the immortality conferred by a newspaper!"

The second article of this review, to which we alluded, is on "The United States of America." *It is an amiable and sensible article, vindicating us from the tory calumnies of England, and dispassionately commenting on our present political difficulties.*

After some severe remarks on the English travellers in America, the writer says—"It is melancholy—it is humiliating to observe that this vile use of calumny, and of paltry spite towards America, which characterizes the sentiments of a certain party in England, has been imported among us; and that France, whose glory it is that she contributed to free America from the English yoke, has turned round and joined her old enemies to condemn the social grossness of the Americans. But is it not to the mother country that they owe, in a great measure, these coarseness of manners?

"All the sins which they can accumulate against that detested word— *Republic*—are lavished en masse, without rhyme or reason, on North America; and all the vices and defects with which they reproach her are ascribed, without exception, to the equality, which reigns there and to the absence of an hereditary sovereign.

"This blind and unreasonable argument, we can conceive of and even respect in the mouth of an English tory, for with him loyalty and royalism form a species of religion. The superannuated sentiment of personal attachment to a royal race, which formerly prevailed universally in Europe, exists still in England, while it is extinct with us. If we have royalists, it is from reason and reflection that they are so: if they maintain royalty, it is from the idea of its necessity or its utility. The right divine is an empty word to them—a farce at best, good only for the peasants of La Vendee.—The belief in the right divine naturally carries an English tory to condemn the name and existence of a republic, wherever he finds them, whether in history or in existence. But for our royalists from utility to launch the same anathemas, and affect the same disgust, is intolerable—it is acting fanaticism without the excuse of faith.

"This war of the tory critics, and of our '*juste milieu*' against America is carried on, not so much by a regular attack on the political institutions of the republic, as by satire on the manners of the people. As it is no longer possible to deny that the Americans are well and cheaply governed, they undertake to prove that at least they are not a *fashionable* people—a proposition which is not difficult to demonstrate. But, granting that the want of elegance is a crime in a young nation, can they seriously blame the Americans for it? Would America have shunned this defect, by remaining tory, or by continuing to be governed by English viceroys for the last fifty years? If the States of North America had maintained the monarchy, would their manners have been softened? Would they have been less provincial, or less coarse? or rather, would not an English novelist a-la-mode, like Mrs. Trollope, have found much richer materials for caricature in the burlesque affections of the petty courts of their English viceroys."

"We are Americans enough to deny the very defect, which our friendly advocate would palliate, and verily believe that our countrymen are not comparatively deficient in elegance, if our English critics, who hold up to us the models of refinement—if Captain Hall and Mistress Trollope are, in their individual persons, 'the great sublime they draw.' But we sincerely regret the existence of unfriendly feelings to us among the French. France—our early friend—has been always popular in America, *through and with* all her faults, and we believed our feelings were reciprocated. Even the royalists, from conviction and feeling, have spoken well of us, and we remember, at this moment, an eulogium upon America, pronounced in the Chamber of Deputies by Hyde de Neuville, the amiable minister, once resident among us—himself an ultra-royalist. *And we believe now, that even the government-party in France would have no inclination to attack us, if Americans abroad had pursued the same reserve in politics which we enforce upon Europeans here.*"

C.

Extract from the New-York Commercial Advertiser of April 11, 1834.

"During the whole contest (the election) it was both *melancholy* and *amusing* to see *the immense number of foreigners* who were driving up every moment to the marine court to get out certificates of naturalization. *Almost every five minutes an omnibus came up filled with them.* Nine-tenths of them were of the lowest class, and many not long enough in the country to wear out the clothes they brought on their backs. They went to the court *foreigners in every sense of the word,* altogether ignorant of the institutions of the country, and of almost every thing else; *but the moment they enter*—hoc presto, they are instantly changed, and in five minutes they come out intelligent American citizens, burning with love of country and patriotism, *and are sent off to the polls to support the Constitution and break men's heads.*"

Now this is the editor who coolly tells his readers that France would not have vituperated this country, had certain Americans at Paris observed "the same reserve in politics, which we *enforce* upon foreigners here!"

D.

Extracts from the Constitution.
ARTICLE 1.—Section 5.

1. Each house shall be the judge of the elections, returns and qualifications of its own members; and a majority of each shall constitute a quorum to do business; but a smaller number may adjourn from day to day, and may be authorized to compel the attendance of absent members, in such manner and under such penalties as each house may provide.

2. Each house may determine the rules of its proceedings, punish its members for disorderly behaviour, and, with the concurrence of two thirds, expel a member.

3. Each house shall keep a journal of its proceedings, and from time to time publish the same, excepting such parts as in their (its) judgment require secrecy; and the yeas and nays of the members of either house, on any question, shall, at the desire of one fifth present, be entered on the journal.

4. This clause relates to adjournments, and is entirely prohibitory.

The foregoing clauses contain all the powers to act separately that are conceded to each house, and which are common to both. The clauses that follow contain all the powers for each house to act separately that are not common to both.

ARTICLE 1.—*Section 2.*

5. The house of representatives shall choose their speaker and other officers, and shall have the sole power of impeachment.

Section 3.

5. The senate shall choose their other officers, (the vice-president being its speaker or president) and also a president pro tempore, in the absence of the vice president, or when he shall exercise the office of President of the United States.

6. The senate shall have the sole power to try all impeachments, &c.— (The rest of the clause prescribes the forms of such trials.)

The senate has the power to approve of nominations and treaties, the president commissioning and ratifying. It has the exclusive right to count the votes of the electors, and to declare the result. The house of representatives has power, in the event of their being no election by the colleges, to choose a president in a prescribed manner.

In addition to these cases of separate power, the members of the two houses have a few personal privileges which do not, however, at all bear upon the point at issue. The house of representatives has also the right to originate all bills for raising revenue.

The following are the powers of the two houses acting conjointly.

ARTICLE 1.—*Section 8.*

The congress shall have power—

1. To lay and collect taxes, duties, imposts, and excises; to pay the debts and provide for the common defence and general welfare of the United States; but all duties, imposts, and excises, shall be uniform throughout the United States—

2. To borrow money on the credit of the United States—

3. To regulate commerce with foreign nations, and among the several states, and with the Indian tribes—

4. To establish a uniform rule of naturalization, and uniform laws on the subject of bankruptcies throughout the United States—

5. To coin money, regulate the value thereof, and of foreign coin, and fix the standard of weights and measures—

6. To provide for the punishment of counterfeiting the securities and current coin of the United States—

7. To establish post offices and post roads—

8. To promote the progress of science and useful arts, by securing, for limited times, to authors and inventors, the exclusive right to their respective writings and discoveries—

9. To constitute tribunals inferior to the supreme court: To define and punish piracies and felonies committed on the high seas, and offences against the law of nations—

10. To declare war, grant letters of marque and reprisal, and make rules concerning captures on land and water—

11. To raise and support armies; but no appropriation of money to that use shall be for a longer term than two years—

12. To provide and maintain a navy—

13. To make rules for the government and regulation of the land and naval forces—

14. To provide for calling forth the militia to execute the laws of the union, suppress insurrections, and repel invasions.

15. To provide for organizing, arming, and disciplining the militia, and for governing such part of them as may be employed in the service of the United States, reserving to the states respectively, the appointment of the officers, and the authority of training the militia according to the discipline prescribed by congress—

16. To exercise exclusive legislation in all cases whatsoever, over such district (not exceeding ten miles square) as may, by cession of particular states, and the acceptance of congress, become the seat of government of the United States, and to exercise like authority over all places purchased, by the consent of the legislature of the state in which the same shall be, for the erection of forts, magazines, arsenals, dock-yards, and other needful buildings—and,

17. To make all laws which shall be necessary and proper for carrying into execution the foregoing powers, and all other powers vested by this constitution in the government of the United States, or in any department or officer thereof.

In addition to these powers congress, by obvious implication, can give authority to the several states to keep troops and raise revenue; it can determine the time of choosing the electors of president; it can put the appointments of certain inferior officers of the government in the president alone, in the heads of departments, or in the courts of law; it can declare the punishment of treason, under definite limitations; it can propose amendments to the constitution; it can dispose of and make all needful rules and regulations concerning the territory or other property belonging to the United States; it can admit new states into the Union; it can make appropriations of all moneys to be expended for the public service; it can make regulations for the choosing of its own bodies, with certain restrictions; it can name the day of its own assembling; it can give permission to the public agents to accept of titles, presents, offices, &c. from foreign governments; it has power to name the officer who shall act as president in a certain contingency, and it has power to name the places where the courts for the trials for certain crimes shall be held.

PART III

The American Democrat,
or Hints on the Social and
Civic Relations of the
United States of America

INTRODUCTION

This little work has been written, in consequence of its author's having had many occasions to observe the manner in which principles that are of the last importance to the happiness of the community, are getting to be confounded in the popular mind. Notions that are impracticable, and which if persevered in, cannot fail to produce disorganization, if not revolution, are widely prevalent, and while many seem disposed to complain, few show a disposition to correct them. In those instances in which efforts are made to resist or to advance the innovations of the times, the writers take the extremes of the disputed points, the one side looking as far behind it, over ground that can never be retrod, as the other looks ahead, in the idle hope of substituting a fancied perfection for the ills of life. It is the intention of this book to make a commencement towards a more just discrimination between truth and prejudice. With what success the task has been accomplished, the honest reader will judge for himself.

The Americans are obnoxious to the charge of tolerating gross personalities, a state of things that encourages bodies of men in their errors while it oppresses individuals, and which never produced good of any sort, at the very time they are nationally irritable on the subject of common failings. This is reversing the case as it exists in most civilized countries, where personalities excite disgust, and society is deemed fair game. This weakness in the American character might easily be accounted for, but, the object being rather to amend than to explain, the body of the work is referred to for examples.

Power always has most to apprehend from its own illusions. Monarchs have incurred more hazards from the follies of their own that have grown up under the adulation of parasites, than from the machinations of their enemies; and, in a democracy, the delusion that would elsewhere be poured into the ears of the prince, is poured into those of the people. It is hoped that this work, while free from the spirit of partizanship, will be thought to be exempt from this imputation.

The writer believes himself to be as good a democrat as there is in America. But his democracy is not of the impracticable school. He prefers a democracy to any other system, on account of its comparative advantages, and not on account of its perfection. He knows it has evils; great and increasing evils, and evils peculiar to itself; but he believes that monarchy and aristocracy have more. It will be very apparent to all who read this book, that he is not a believer in the scheme of raising men very far above their natural propensities.

A long absence from home, has, in a certain degree, put the writer in the situation of a foreigner in his own country; a situation probably much better for noting peculiarities, than that of one who never left it. Two things have struck him painfully on his return; a disposition in the majority to carry out the opinions of the system to extremes, and a disposition in the minority to abandon all to the current of the day, with the hope that this current will lead, in the end, to radical changes. Fifteen years since, all complaints against the institutions were virtually silenced, whereas now it is rare to hear them praised, except by the mass, or by those who wish to profit by the favors of the mass.

In the midst of these conflicting opinions, the voice of simple, honest, and what, in a country like this, ought to be fearless, truth, is nearly smothered; the one party effecting its ends by fulsome, false and meretricious eulogiums, in which it does not itself believe, and the other giving utterance to its discontent in useless and unmanly complaints. It has been the aim of the writer to avoid both these errors also.

No attempt has been made to write very profound treatises on any of the subjects of this little book. The limits and objects of the work forbade it; the intention being rather to present to the reader those opinions that are suited to the actual condition of the country, than to dwell on principles more general. A work of the size of this might be written on the subject of "Instruction" alone, but it has been the intention to present reasons and facts to the reader, that are peculiarly American, rather than to exhaust the subjects.

Had a suitable compound offered, the title of this book would have been something like "Anti-Cant," for such a term expresses the intention of the writer, better, perhaps, than the one he has actually chosen. The work is written more in the spirit of censure than of praise, for its aim is correction; and virtues bring their own reward, while errors are dangerous.

CONTENTS

On Government

Man is known to exist in no part of the world, without certain rules for the regulation of his intercourse with those around him. It is a first necessity of his weakness, that laws, founded on the immutable principles of natural justice, should be framed, in order to protect the feeble against the violence of the strong; the honest from the schemes of the dishonest; the temperate and industrious, from the waste and indolence of the dissolute and idle. These laws, though varying with circumstances, possess a common character, being formed on that consciousness of right, which God has bestowed in order that men may judge between good and evil.

Governments have many names, which names, in all cases, are dependent on some one of the leading features of the institutions. It is usual, however, to divide governments into despotisms, limited monarchies, and republicks; but these terms are too vague to answer the objects of definitions, since many aristocracies have existed under the designation of monarchies, and many monarchies have been styled republicks.

A despotism is a government of absolute power, in which the entire authority is the possession of the prince. The term "despot," as applied to a sovereign, however, is not properly one of reproach. It merely signifies a ruler who is irresponsible for his acts, and who governs without any legal restraint on his will. The word "tyrant" had originally the same meaning, though, in a measure, both have become so far corrupted as to convey an idea of abuses.

A limited monarchy is a government in which the will of the sovereign is restrained by certain provisions of the state, that cannot lawfully be violated. In its true signification, the word monarch means any prince at the head of a state. Monarchs are known by different titles; such as emperors, kings, princes, grand dukes, dukes, &c. &c.; but it is not now common to apply the term to any below the rank of kings. The title of sovereign is of more general use, though properly meaning the same thing as that of monarch.

A republick is a government in which the pervading acknowledged principle is the right of the community as opposed to the right of a sovereign. In other words, the term implies the sovereignty of the people, in lieu of that of a monarch. Thus nations which have possessed kings, dukes, and princes at their heads, have been termed republicks, because they have reserved the right to elect the monarchs; as was formerly the case in Poland, Venice, Genoa, and in many other of the Italian states, in particular. Even Napoleon continued to style France a republick, after he had assumed the imperial diadem, because his elevation to the throne was sanctioned by the votes of the French nation. The term, in his case, however, was evidently misapplied, for the crown was made hereditary in his family, while the polity of a republick supposes a new election on the death of the last ruler, if not oftener. In the case of Napoleon, the people elected a dynasty, rather than a prince.

In a republick the chief of the state is always elective. Perhaps this fact is the most accurate technical distinction between a monarchy and this form of government, though the pervading principle of the first is the right of the sovereign, and of the last the right of the community. The term republick, (*respublica) means the public things, or the common weal. Hence the term commonwealth, the word wealth, in its political sense, meaning prosperity in general, and not riches in particular.

If these theoretical distinctions were rigidly respected, it would be easy to infer the real character of a government from its name; but nothing can be less alike than governments ordinarily are, in their action, and in their professions. Thus despotism can scarcely be said to exist in truth, in any part of christendom; monarchs being compelled to govern according to established laws, which laws are formed on principles reasonably just, while they are restrained in the exercise of their will by an opinion that has been created by the advanced intelligence of the age.

---

* *Res,* a thing; *publica,* public—"public things."

Some kings are monarchs only in name, the power having essentially passed into the hands of a few of their nominal subjects; and, on the other hand, some princes, who, by the constitutional principles of the system, are deemed to be but a part of the state, effectually control it, by means of bribes, rewards, and political combinations, submitting to little more restraint than the nominal despots. Just at this time, Prussia is an instance of the first of these truths, England of the second, and France of the last.

Prussia, though a despotism in theory, is governed as mildly, and, apart from political justice, as equitably and legally, as any other country. The will of the sovereign is never made to interfere, arbitrarily, with the administration of law, and the law itself proceeds from the principles that properly influence all legislation, though it can only receive its authority from the will of the king. That country furnishes a proof of the progress of opinion, as well as of its power to check abuses. It was only the great grandfather of the present sovereign who caused tall men to marry tall women at his command, in order to gratify a silly desire to possess a regiment of the tallest troops in the world. The influence of opinion on governments has been greatly aided by the wars and revolutions of the last, and of the present century, in which privileges have been diminished, and the rights, as well as, what is perhaps of more importance, the knowledge of their rights among the people, have been greatly augmented.

England, which is called a monarchy, is in fact a complicated but efficient aristocracy. Scarcely one of the powers that is attributed to the king by the constitution, and which were in truth exercised by his predecessors, is possessed by the present monarch in fact. By the constitution, the king of England is supposed to form a balance between the nobles and the people, whereas, in truth, his utmost influence is limited to holding a balance between parties, and this only in cases of a nearly equal force between contending factions. The extent of the authority of the king of England, at the present day, amounts to little more than the influence which he is permitted to use in minor cases, the aristocracy having devised expedients to control him on all occasions that are deemed of moment. As the mode in which this change has been effected, illustrates the manner in which governments are made to take one character, while they profess to belong to another, a brief exposition will aid the reader in understanding the subject.

The king of England can do no wrong, but the ministers are responsible to parliament. As the country has no written constitution, and laws enacted by the king, lords and commons, have the force of constitutional provisions, a system has been established, by taking advantage of the necessities of different sovereigns, by which no executive act is legal, that is not sanctioned by at least one responsible minister. It follows, the monarch can do nothing to which his parliament is seriously opposed, since no minister will incur the risk of its displeasure. It is true that the nominal assent of the king is necessary to the enactment of a law, but the ministers being responsible for the consequences if it is withheld, and the parliament alone being the judge of these consequences, as well as of the criminals, while it has an active jealousy of its own power, no instance of the exercise of this authority has occurred for more than a century. The right to withhold supplies has been the most efficient agent of the parliament, in subduing the authority of the crown.

By the theory of the British constitution, the king can declare war. Formerly this prerogative was exercised by different warlike sovereigns for personal motives. Now, the right exists only in name, for no minister would consent to give the declaration the legal forms, with the certainty of being impeached, and punished, unless acting in accordance with the wishes of parliament.

Although parliament exercises this authority in all cases of importance, the ministers are permitted to perform most minor acts of authority unquestioned, so long as they have a party in the legislature to sustain them. This party, however, is necessary to their remaining in the ministry, and it follows that the majority of parliament controls the very appointment of ministers, the only important political function that the king can now, even in theory, exercise without the intervention of a responsible minister. Were he, however, to appoint a minister in opposition to the wishes of parliament, that body would refuse the required laws. The first requisite, therefore, on the formation of a new ministry, is to enquire who can "meet parliament," as it is termed; or, in other words, what ministers will be agreeable to a majority of the legislature.

Thus, while the king of England says who shall be his ministers, the parliament says who they shall not be; and, in this instance, supported as it is by a control of all legislation, the negative power is found to be stronger than the affirmative. In reality, the ministers of Great-Britain are appointed by the parliament of the country, and not by the king, and this is virtually neutralizing, if not directly annihilating, all the available authority of the latter.

In theory, the government of France and that of Great-Britain have the same general character. In practice, however, owing to the greater political advancement of the last of these two countries, France, to-day, is not far from the point where England stood a century since. Then the king of England ruled through his parliament, whereas now the parliament rules through the king. On the other hand, with much of the machinery of a free state, the king of the French governs himself. A dread of the people's getting the ascendancy, causes the aristocracy to lend itself to the power of the crown, which not only dictates the law, but, in many cases, proves to be stronger than the law itself. Of the three countries, perhaps legality is more respected in Prussia and Austria, both despotisms in theory, than in France, which has the profession of a limited monarchy. This difference is owing to the security of the two first governments, and to the insecurity of the last.

These facts show the necessity of distinguishing between names and things in governments, as well as in other matters. The institutions of no country are rigidly respected in practice, owing to the cupidity and passions of men; and vigilance in the protection of principles is even more necessary in a democracy than in a monarchy, as their violation is more certain to affect the interests of the people under such a form of government than under any other. A violation of the principles of a democracy is at the loss of the people, while, in a monarchy, it is usually their gain.

ON REPUBLICKS

Republics have been as liable to frauds, and to departures from their professions, as any other polities, though no government can properly be termed a republick at all, in which the predominant authority of a single hereditary ruler is acknowledged. In all republicks there must be more or less of direct representation, however much its influence is lessened by the duration and by the magnitude of the trusts.

Poland was formerly termed a republick, because the kingly office was elective, and on account of the power of the Diet. At that time any member of this body could defeat a law by exclaiming in Latin, *Veto,* (I forbid it,) from which usage the word *veto* has been adopted as a substantive, in most of the languages of christendom, to express the same power in the different executive rulers; which it is now common to term the "veto-power."

The exercise of this right was found so inconvenient in practice, that, at length, in cases of gravity, the nobles of the Diet would draw their swords, and menace the dissenting member with death, unless he withdrew his "veto." As a negative authority often has the efficiency of that which is affirmative, it is scarcely possible to conceive of a system in which the will of a majority was less consulted than in this.

The republick of Venice was an hereditary aristocracy, as, in a great measure, was that of ancient Rome. The term, in its true signification, perhaps, infers a free government, for it means a representation of the general interests of the state, but, as in practice, this representation became confined purely to the interests of the state, and the state itself was under the control of a few who did not fail to turn their authority to their private advantage, the system has oftener resulted in abuses than even that of monarchies. The profession of a free government, in which the facts do not frankly concur, usually tends to gross wrongs, in order to conceal and protect the frauds. In Venice, such was the jealousy and tyranny of the state, that a secret council existed, with an authority that was almost despotick, while it was inquisitorial, and which was removed from the usual responsibility of opinion, by an expedient that was devised to protect its members from the ordinary liabilities of common censure. This council consisted of three nobles, who held their office for a limited period, and were appointed by drawing lots, each person concealing the fact of the lot's having fallen on himself, until he met his associates at an appointed place. It is an extraordinary fact, that the same expedient was devised to conceal the murderers, in the well known case of Morgan, who fell a victim to the exaggeration and weakness of some of the members of the Masonic Fraternity.

By examining the different republicks of ancient and modern times, it would be found that most of them had little more than the profession of liberty, though all substituted in them the right of the community for that of a monarch, as a primary principle. This feature, then, must be taken as the distinction between this form of government and that of kingdoms, or of the sovereignties in which one rules, or is supposed to rule.

Republicks may be aristocratical, or democratical; and they may so nearly approach both, as to render it matter of doubt to which class they properly belong; for the political combinations of communities, in a practical sense, are so numerous as almost to defeat accurate general definitions.

On the Republick of the United States of America

The government of the United States, differs from all others that have preceded it, though some imitations have been attempted in the southern parts of this continent. Its novelty, no less than its complicated nature, arising from its double system, has given birth to many errors in relation to its principles and its action, even among its own citizens, as well as among strangers.

The polity of the United States is that of a confederated republick, but the power of the federal government acting in most instances on the body of the community, without the intervention of the several states, it has been better styled a Union. This word, which is original as applied to a political system, was first given to this form of confederation, and is intended to express the greater intimacy of the relations of the parties, than those of all previous examples. It exists in the constitution, however, only as it is used in setting forth the motives for substituting that instrument for the old articles of confederation: the constitution being silent as to the particular polity of the country, except as it recognizes the general term of a republick.

The word constitution, of itself, properly implies a more identified form of government, than that which is usually understood to exist under a confederation; the first inferring a social compact, fundamental and predominant, the last a league between independent sovereignties. These distinctions have a certain weight, though they are rather arbitrary than logical, since men may create any degree of allegiance, or of liability they may deem expedient, under any form, or modes of government. To deny this is to deny to bodies of human beings the right of self-government, a gift of nature. Though possessing a common end, governments are, in reality, subject to no laws but those of their own establishing.

The government of the United States was formed by the several states of the Union, as they existed at the period when the constitution was adopted, and one of its leading principles is, that all power which is not granted to the federal authority, remain in the states themselves, or what is virtually the same thing, in the people of the states. This principle follows as a necessary consequence from the nature of the grants to the federal government, but it has been clearly expressed in a clause of the instrument, that was introduced by way of amendment, in 1801. This feature distinguishes this federal government from all the federal governments that have gone before it, as it was the general and ancient rule that liberty existed as a concession from authority; whereas, here, we find authority existing as a concession from the ruled. Something like the same principle exists in the governments of the several states, and it once existed in the ancient democracies, though, in no other known system perhaps, as clearly and as unequivocally as in this, since it is a general maxim that governments should have all power, however much they may restrain themselves in its exercise.

In the conflict of parties, the question by whom the federal government was formed, has been agitated with more seriousness than the point at issue merited, since, the fact admitted that the power which framed it did not exceed its authority, it is much more essential to know what was done, than to ascertain who did it. The notion that the *people* of the United States, in the popular signification of the word, framed the government, is contrary to fact, and leads to a wrong interpretation of many of the distinctive features of the system. The constitution of the United States was formed by a convention composed of delegates elected by the different states, in modes prescribed by their several laws and usages. These delegates voted by states, and not as individuals, and the instrument was referred back to conventions in the respective states for approval, or ratification. It is a governing principle of political maxims, that the power to ratify, is the power that possesses the authority in the last resort. Thus, treaties between independent sovereignties, are never valid until ratified by the high treaty-making powers of the respective countries. As the several states of this Union first acted through delegates of their own appointing, and then ratified their acts, in conventions also chosen by constituencies of their own selection, it is not easy to establish any thing more plainly than the fact, that the constitution of the United States was framed by the states then in existence, as communities, and not by the body of the people of the Union, or by the body of the people of the states, as has been sometimes contended.

In favor of the latter opinion, it is maintained that the several states were an identified nation previously to the formation of the government, and the preamble of the constitution itself, has been quoted to prove that the compact was formed by the *people,* as distinct from the states. This preamble commences by saying that "We the people of the United States," for reasons that are then set forth, have framed the instrument that follows; but in respecting a form of phraseology, it, of necessity, neither establishes a fact, nor sets up a principle, and when we come to examine the collateral circumstances, we are irresistably led to regard it merely as a naked and vague profession.

That the several states were virtually parts of one entire nation previously to the formation of any separate general government, proves nothing in the premises, as the very circumstance that a polity distinct from that of Great Britain was established by our ancestors, who were members of the great community that was then united in one entire nation, sufficiently shows that these parts can separate, and act independently of each other. Such a circumstance might be, and probably it was, a strong motive for forming a more identified government, but it cannot properly be quoted as authority for, or against any of its provisions. The latter are a mere question of fact, and as such their construction must depend on their intention as explained in language.

The term "people," like most other substantives, has its general and its specific significations. In its general signification, the people of a country, means the population of a country; as the population of a country includes the women and children, nothing can be clearer than that the "people," in this signification, did not form the American constitution. The specific significations of this word are numerous, as rich, poor, wise, silly, good and bad people. In a political sense, the people means those who are vested with political rights, and, in this particular instance, the people vested with political rights, were the constituencies of the several states, under their various laws, modifications and constitutions, which is but another name for the governments of the states themselves. "We the *people,*" as used in the preamble of the constitution, means merely, "We the *constituencies* of the several states."

It follows, that the constitution of the United States was formed by the states, and not by the people of the entire country, as contended; the term used in the preamble being used in contra-distinction to the old divine right of sovereigns, and as a mode of expressing the general republican character of the government. The states, by a prescribed majority, can also amend the constitution, altering any of its provisions, with the exception of that which guaranties the equal representation of the states in the senate. It might be shown, that states possessing a minority of all the people of the Union can alter the constitution, a fact, in itself, which proves that the government of the United States, though a republick, is not necessarily a popular government, in the broadest meaning of the word. The constitution leaves the real character of the institutions of the country, with the exception that it prohibits monarchies, to be settled by the several states themselves.

On the other hand, too much importance is attached to what is called the reserved sovereignties of the several states. A community can hardly be termed sovereign at all, which has parted with all the great powers of sovereignty, such as the control of foreign relations, the authority to make war and peace, to regulate commerce, to coin money, keep fleets and armies, with all the other powers that have been ceded by the states to the federal government. But, admitting that the rights reserved are sovereign in their ordinary nature, they are scarcely so in the conditions under which they are enjoyed, since, by an amendment of the constitution, a state may be deprived of most of them, without its own consent. A community so situated can scarcely be deemed sovereign, or even independent.

The habit of drawing particular inferences from general theories, in matters as purely practical as those of government, is at all times dangerous, and the safest mode of construing the constitution of the United States, is by looking only at the instrument itself, without adverting to other systems, except as they may serve to give the proper signification of the terms of that instrument, as these terms were understood at the time it was framed.

Many popular errors exist on the subject of the influence of the federal constitution on the rights and liberties of the citizen. The rights and liberties of the citizen, in a great degree, depend on the political institutions of the several states, and not on those of the Union. Many of these errors have arisen from mistaking the meaning of the language of the constitution. Thus, when the constitution says that no laws shall be passed abridging the rights of the citizen in any particular thing, it refers to the power which, under that particular constitution, has the authority to pass a law at all. This power, under the government of the United States, is Congress, and no other.

An example will better show the distinction. In art. 6th of the amendments to the constitution, we find the following clause: "In all criminal prosecutions, the accused shall enjoy the right of a speedy and *public* trial, by an impartial *jury,*" &c. &c. &c. It is not the meaning of this provision of the constitution, that, under the laws of the several states, the citizen shall be entitled to a *public* trial by a *jury,* but that these privileges shall be assured to those who are accused of crimes against the laws of the United States. It is true, that similar privileges, as they are deemed essential to the liberties of their citizens, are assured to them by the constitutions of the several states, but this has been done by voluntary acts of their own, every state having full power, so far as the constitution of the United States has any control over it, to cause its accused to be tried in secret, or without the intervention of juries, as the people of that particular state may see fit.

There is nothing in the constitution of the United States, to prevent all the states, or any particular state, from possessing an established religion, from putting the press under the control of censors, from laying restrictions and penalties on the rights of speech, or from imposing most of the political and civil restraints on the citizen, that are imposed under any other form of government.

The guarantees for the liberties of the citizen, given by the constitution of the United States, are very limited, except as against the action of the government of the Union alone. Congress may not pass any law establishing a religion, or abridging the freedom of speech, or of the press, but the provisions of the constitution relating to these subjects, have no reference to the rights of the states. This distinction is very essential to a correct understanding of the institutions of the country, as many are misled on the subject. Some of the states, for example, are rigid in enforcing respect for the sabbath, and a popular notion has prevailed that their laws are unconstitutional, since the federal compact guaranties liberty of conscience. This guarantee, like most of the others of the same nature, is only against the acts of Congress, and not against the acts of the states themselves. A state may pass any law it please to restrain the abuses of the sabbath, provided it do not infringe on the provisions of its own constitution, or invade a right conceded to the United States. It cannot stop the mail for instance, or the passage of troops in the service of the federal government, but it may stop all who are not thus constitutionally protected by the superior power of the Union.

This reading of the constitution is in conformity with all the rules of construction, but that it is right, can be shown from the language of the instrument itself. In article 1st, section 9th, clause 3d, we find this provision—"No bill of attainder, or *ex post facto* law, shall be passed." In article 1st, section 10th, clause 1st, which section is composed entirely of restraints on the power of the states, we find this provision—"No *state* shall pass any bill of attainder, *ex post facto* law, &c. &c." Had the provision of clause 3d, sect. 9th, been intended to limit the powers of the states, clause

1st, sect. 10th, would clearly have been unnecessary. The latter provision therefore, is one of the few instances, in which the power of the states themselves, is positively restrained by the constitution of the United States.

Although the several states have conceded to the United States most of the higher attributes of sovereignty, they have reserved to themselves nearly all of the functions that render governments free, or otherwise. In declaring war, regulating commerce, keeping armies and navies, coining money, which are all high acts of sovereignty, despotisms and democracies are alike; all forms of governments equally controlling these interests, and usually in the same manner.

The characters of institutions depend on the repositories of power, in the last resort. In despotisms the monarch is this repository; in aristocracies, the few; in democracies, the many. By the constitution of the United States, its government is composed of different representations, which are chosen, more or less directly, by the constituencies of the several states. As there is no common rule for the construction of these constituencies, their narrowness, or width, must depend on the fundamental laws of the states, themselves. It follows that the federal government has no fixed character, so far as the nature of its constituency is concerned, but one that may constantly vary, and which has materially varied since the commencement of the government, though, as yet, its changes have always been in the direction of popular rights.

The only distinctive restriction imposed by the constitution of the United States on the character of the state governments, is that contained in article 4th, section 4th, clause 1st, which guaranties to each state a republican form of government. No monarchy, therefore, can exist in this country, as existed formerly, and now exists, in the confederation of Germany. But a republican form of government is not necessarily a free government. Aristocracies are oftener republicks than any thing else, and they have been among the most oppressive governments the world has ever known.

No state can grant any title of nobility; but titles of nobility are oftener the consequence than the cause of narrow governments. Neither Venice, Poland, Genoa, Berne, (a canton of Switzerland,) nor most of the other narrow aristocracies of Europe, had any titular nobles, though some of these countries were afflicted by governments of great oppression. Any state of this Union, by altering its own constitution, may place the power of its own government, and, by consequence, its representation in the government of the United States, in any dozen families, making it perpetual and hereditary. The only guarantee against such an act is to be found in the discretion of the people of the several states, none of whom would probably part with power for such a purpose, and the check which the other states might hold over any one of their body, by amending the constitution. As this instrument now exists, however, there can be no reasonable doubts of the power of any one, or of all the states, so to alter their polities.

By considering these facts, we learn the true nature of the government, which may be said to have both a theoretical character, and one in fact. In theory, this character is vague, and, with the immaterial exception of the exclusion of a monarchy and the maintenance of the representative form, one altogether dependent on the policy of the states, by which it may be made a representative aristocracy, a representative democracy, or a union of the two. The government, in fact, is a near approach to that of a representative democracy, though it is not without a slight infusion from a few mild aristocracies. So long as slavery exists in the country, or, it were better to say, so long as the African race exists, some portion of this aristocratic infusion will probably remain.

Stress is laid on the foregoing distinctions, because the government of the Union is a compact between separate communities, and popular misconceptions on the nature of the institutions, in a nation so much controlled by popular opinion, not only lead to injustice, but may lead to dissension. It is the duty of every citizen to acquire just notions of the terms of the bargain before he pretends to a right to enforce them.

On Distinctive American Principles

Distinctive American principles as properly refer to the institutions of the states as to those of the Union. A correct notion of the first cannot be formed without keeping the latter constantly in view.

The leading distinctive principle of this country, is connected with the fact that all political power is strictly a trust, granted by the constituent to the representative. These representatives possess different duties, and as the greatest check that is imposed on them, while in the exercise of their offices, exists in the manner in which the functions are balanced by each other, it is of the last importance that neither class trespass on the trusts that are not especially committed to its keeping.

The machinery of the state being the same in appearance, in this country and in that from which we are derived, inconsiderate commentators are apt to confound their principles. In England, the institutions have been the result of those circumstances to which time has accidentally given birth. The power of the king was derived from violence, the monarch, before the act of succession, in the reign of Queen Anne, claiming the throne in virtue of the conquest by William, in 1060. In America, the institutions are the result of deliberate consultation, mutual concessions, and design. In England, the people may have gained by diminishing the power of the king, who first obtained it by force; but, in America, to assail the rightful authority of the executive, is attacking a system framed by the constituencies of the states, who are virtually the people, for their own benefit. No assault can be made on any branch of this government, while in the exercise of its constitutional duties, without assaulting the right of the body of the nation, which is the foundation of the whole polity.

In countries, in which executive power is hereditary, and clothed with high prerogatives, it may be struggling for liberty to strive to diminish its influence; but, in this republick, in which the executive is elective, has no absolute authority in framing the laws, serves for a short period, is responsible, and has been created by the people, through the states, for their own purposes, it is assailing the rights of that people, to attempt in any manner to impede its legal and just action.

It is a general law in politics, that the power most to be distrusted, is that which, possessing the greatest force, is the least responsible. Under the constitutional monarchies of Europe, (as they exist in theory, at least,) the king, besides uniting in his single person all the authority of the executive, which includes a power to make war, create peers, and unconditionally to name to all employments, has an equal influence in enacting laws, his veto being absolute; but, in America, the executive, besides being elective, is stripped of most of these high sources of influence, and is obliged to keep constantly in view the justice and legality of his acts, both on account of his direct responsibilities, and on account of the force of public opinion.

In this country, there is far more to apprehend from congress, than from the executive, as is seen in the following reasons:—Congress is composed of many, while the executive is one, bodies of men notoriously acting with less personal responsibilities than individuals; congress has power to enact laws, which it becomes the duty of the executive to see enforced, and the really legislative authority of a country is always its greatest authority; from the decisions and constructions of the executive, the citizen can always appeal to the courts for protection, but no appeal can lie from the acts of congress, except on the ground of unconstitutionality; the executive has direct personal responsibilities under the laws of the land, for any abuses of his authority, but the member of congress, unless guilty of open corruption, is almost beyond personal liabilities.

It follows that the legislature of this country, by the intention of the constitution, wields the highest authority under the least responsibility, and that it is the power most to be distrusted. Still, all who possess trusts, are to be diligently watched, for there is no protection against abuses without responsibility, nor any real responsibility, without vigilance.

Political partisans, who are too apt to mistake the impulses of their own hostilities and friendships for truths, have laid down many false principles on the subject of the duties of the executive. When a law is passed, it goes to the executive for execution, through the executive agents, and, at need, to the courts for interpretation. It would seem that there is no discretion vested in the executive concerning the constitutionality of a law. If he distrust the constitutionality of any law, he can set forth his objections by resorting to the veto; but it is clearly the intention of the system that the whole legislative power, in the last resort, shall abide in congress, while it is necessary to the regular action of the government, that none of its agents, but those who are especially appointed for that purpose, shall pretend to interpret the constitution, in practice. The citizen is differently situated. If he conceive himself oppressed by an unconstitutional law, it is his inalienable privilege to raise the question before the courts, where a final interpretation can be had. By this interpretation the executive and all his agents are equally bound to abide. This obligation arises from the necessity of things, as well as from the nature of the institutions. There must be somewhere a power to decide on the constitutionality of laws, and this power is vested in the supreme court of the United States, on final appeal.

When called on to approve a law, even though its principle should have been already pronounced on by the courts, the executive is independent.

He is now a legislator, and can disregard all other constructions of the constitution, but those dictated by his own sense of right. In this character, to the extent of his veto-power, he is superior to the courts, which have cognizance of no more than each case as it is presented for their consideration. The president may approve of a law that the court has decided to be unconstitutional in principle, or he may veto a law that the court has decided to be constitutional in principle. The legislator himself, is compelled to submit to the interpretation of the court, however different his own views of the law may have been in passing it, but as soon as he comes to act again as a legislator, he becomes invested with all his own high duties and rights. The court cannot make the constitution, in any case; it only interprets the law. One court may decide differently from another, and instances often occur in which the same judges see reason to change their own decisions, and it would be, to the last degree, inexpedient, to give the court an authority beyond the necessity of the circumstances.

Although the court can render a law null, its power does not extend beyond the law already passed. Congress may re-enact it, as often as it please, and the court will still exercise its reason in rejecting it. This is the balance of the constitution, which invites inquiry, the constituencies of the states holding a legal authority to render that constitutional which the courts have declared to be unconstitutional, or vice versa, by amendments to the instrument itself; the supremacy of the court being merely temporary, conditional, and growing out of expediency and necessity.

It has been said that it is a vital principle of this government, that each of its branches should confine itself to the particular duties assigned it by the constitution, and in no manner exceed them. Many grave abuses have already arisen from loosing sight of this truth, and there is danger that the whole system will be perverted from its intention, if not destroyed, unless they are seasonably corrected. Of these, the most prevalent, the one most injurious to the public service, that which has been introduced the most on foreign and the least on American principles, is the practice of using the time and influence of the legislatures, for the purpose of acting on the public mind, with a view to affect the elections. The usage has already gained so much footing, as seriously to impede the course of legislation.

This is one of the cases, in which it is necessary to discriminate between the distinctive principles of our own government, and those of the government of the country from which we are derived. In England, by the mode in which the power of the executive has been curtailed, it is necessary that the ministerial contests should be conducted in the legislative bodies, but, in this country, such a course cannot be imitated, without the legislators' assuming an authority that does not belong to them, and without dispossessing the people, in some measure, of their rights. He who will examine the constitution for the powers of congress, will find no authority to pass resolutions on, or to waste the time, which is the property of the public, in discussing the matters, on which, after all, congress has no power to decide. This is the test of legislative authority. Congress cannot properly even discuss a subject, that congress cannot legally control, unless it be to ascertain its own powers. In cases that do not admit of question, this is one of the grossest abuses of the institutions, and ought to be classed with the usurpations of other systems.

There is a feeling connected with this subject, that it behoves every upright citizen cautiously to watch. He may be opposed to the executive, for instance, as a party-man, and yet have an immediate representative in congress, of his own particular way of thinking; and it is a weakness of humanity, under such circumstances, for one to connect himself most directly with his own immediate candidate, and to look on his political opponent with distrust. The jealousy created by this feeling, induces unreflecting men to imagine that curbing their particular representatives, in matters of this nature, is curtailing their own rights, and disposes them to defend what is inherently wrong, on personal motives.

Political systems ought to be, and usually are, framed on certain great and governing principles. These principles cannot be perverted, or lost sight of, without perverting, or rendering nugatory the system itself; and, under a popular government, in an age like this, far more is to be apprehended from indirect attacks on the institutions, than from those which are direct. It is usual to excuse these departures from the right on the plea of human propensities, but human institutions are framed expressly to curb such propensities, and no truth is more salutary than that which is contained in the homely saying, that "law makers should not be law breakers."

It is the duty of the citizen to judge of all political acts on the great principles of the government, and not according to his own political partialities, or prejudices. His own particular representative is no more a representative of the people, than the representative of any other man, and one branch of the government is no more representative than another. All are to keep within their respective spheres, and it may be laid down as a governing maxim of the institutions, *that the representative who exceeds his trusts, trespasses on the rights of the people.*

All comparisons between the powers of the British parliament and those of congress are more than useless, since they are bodies differently constituted, while one is absolute, and the other is merely a special trustee for limited and defined objects.

In estimating the powers of congress, there is a rule that may be safely confided in, and which has been already hinted at. The powers of congress are express and limited. That body therefore, can have no right *to pass resolutions* other than those which affect their own police, or, in a moral sense, even to make speeches, except on subjects on which *they have a right to pass laws.* The instant they exceed these limits, they exceed the bounds of their delegated authority. By applying this simple test to their proceedings, any citizen may, in ordinary cases, ascertain how far the representatives of the nation abuse their trusts.

Liberty is not a matter of words, but a positive and important condition of society. Its great safeguards, after placing its foundations on a popular base, is in the checks and balances imposed on the public servants, and all its real friends ought to know that the most insidious attacks, are made on it by those who are the largest trustees of authority, in their efforts to increase their power.

The government of the United States has three branches. The executive, the legislative and the judicial. These several branches are independent of each other, though the first is intended to act as a check on the second, no law or resolution being legal that is not first submitted to the president for his approval. This check, however, does not render the first an integral part of the legislature, as laws and resolutions may be passed without his approval, by votes of two thirds.

In most constitutional monarchies, the legislatures, being originally secondary powers, were intended as checks on the action of the crown, which was possessed of the greatest, and, by consequence, of the most dangerous authority; whereas, the case is reversed in America, the executive using his veto as a check on congress. Such is the intention of the constitution, though the tactics of party, and the bitterness of opposition, have endeavored to interpret the instrument differently, by appealing to the ancient prejudices derived from England.

On the Powers of the Executive

The president "sees the laws faithfully executed." In order to render this power efficient, he appoints to office and removes all officers, but the judges, and those whom they are authorized by congress to appoint, who form an independent portion of the government. As this has been a disputed authority, it may be well to explain it more distinctly.

The president *nominates* to the senate, and with its "advice and consent," *appoints* all the officers of the government, with the exception of those whose appointment congress has authority to vest, by law, in the heads of departments, or in the courts of justice. The functionaries appointed by the courts of law are not removable, either directly, or indirectly, by the president, that branch of the government being independent, and not *executing,* but merely *interpreting* the laws. Although the president cannot remove the officers who are appointed by the heads of departments, he can remove those heads of departments themselves, thereby securing a prompt and proper execution of their duties. In this manner all the executive agents are subject to the supervisory power of the president, as, there can be no just doubt, was the intention of the constitution.

The right of the president to remove from office has been disputed, but on insufficient grounds. Unless the constitution shall be so interpreted as to give him this power, all officers must hold their places until removed by death, or impeachment, as it is clear no other branch of the state, separately, or in connection with a second, possesses this authority. A brief examination of the instrument will demonstrate this truth, the reader bearing in mind that there is now question, only, of those officers who are appointed by the executive, and not of those who are appointed by the courts of law, or the heads of departments.

The language of the constitution is as follows:—"He (the president) shall have power, by and with the advice and consent of the senate, to make treaties, provided two thirds of the senators concur; and he shall *nominate,* and, by and with the advice and consent of the senate, *appoint* ambassadors," &c. &c. and all the other officers of the government, with the exceptions already named. From this phraseology it has been contended that, as the senate has a voice in appointing, it ought to have a voice in removing from office, the constitution leaving the latter authority entirely to construction.

In addition to the paragraph just quoted, we find that "he (the president) shall *commission* all officers of the United States." All the direct provisions of the constitution on this subject, are contained in these two parts of sections.

The pretension in behalf of the senate's voice in removals, is made under an erroneous notion of its power in appointments. The senate in no manner *appoints* to office. This is proved by the language of the constitution, which reads, by taking away the parenthetical part of the sentence, "*he* (the president) shall appoint," &c. &c. In no other way, can grammar be made of the sentence. The president, therefore, and not the senate appoints to office, and by construction, the president decides on the removal. The consent of the senate, in the cases of treaties and offices, is a bestowal of authority on the president, alone, by which consent he receives a complete power to act in the premises, as he shall judge expedient. Thus a treaty is not ratified, because the senate approves of it, nor a citizen appointed to office because the senate consents to his appointment; the authority granted in both cases being given to the president, and not to the instrument in the case of a treaty, or to the individual in the case of an appointment. The president may refuse to ratify a treaty, which is the consummation of such a compact, or to commission an officer, which is his authority to act, after having received the consent of the senate, in both cases. The power of the senate is merely a negative power in appointments and in treaties, its dissent defeating the intention of the president, but its assent in no manner obliging him to adhere to his first resolution. Or, it would be better still to say, the senate has power to complete the authority of the president.

In some countries a parent negatives the marriage of the child. This is a similar case in principle, for when the father consents, he does not marry, but permits his child to perform the affirmative act.

The powers of the president are three-fold, in the cases of appointments. He "nominates," he "appoints" and he "commissions." To nominate is to propose, or name; to appoint, is to determine in the mind, or, in this case to settle on consultation; and to commission, is to empower. The last act, is the one by which the nominee receives his authority, and it would seem to be a just construction that the authority which appoints and empowers should have the right to withdraw its commission.

They who object to this reasoning, say that the power to "commission" is merely a ministerial power. No part of the constitution can be thus limited in its signification. *All* the powers of the executive named in the instrument, are strictly executive powers, and are to be construed solely on the great principles that regulate all executive authority. This is in conformity with the letter and spirit of the constitution, which has instituted this high office, not as a ministerial, but as an executive office.

The distinction between an executive and a ministerial function is great and manifest. The last is positive, and limited by the provisions of the law to be executed; the first has a wide discretion, and is always to be interpreted on as liberal and broad principles, as the nature of the case will allow; it being the intention that high political considerations should have their due weight on the acts of such an agent. But a quotation from the constitution, itself, will show our meaning. The section which contains the power of the president to commission, is in these words: "He (the president,) shall, from time to time, give to congress information of the state of the Union, and recommend to their consideration such measures as *he shall judge necessary and expedient;* he may, on extraordinary occasions, convene both houses, or either of them, and, in case of disagreement between them, with respect to the time of adjournment, he may adjourn them to such time *as he may think proper;* he shall receive ambassadors and other public ministers; he shall take care that the laws be faithfully executed; and *he shall commission* (empower, in an executive sense) *all the officers of the United States.* "

Each and all of these high functions are executive, and are to be discharged on the great principles of executive power. Thus the president is not *obliged* to "receive ambassadors and other public ministers," as they shall present themselves, like a mere minister of state, when the act is contrary to the interests and character of the nation; but he is the depository of that discretionary authority, to receive, or to reject them, which by the usages of nations and in the necessity of things, must somewhere abide in all governments. Under the confederation this power resided in congress; under the constitution it is in the president. Were this function merely a ministerial function, the president would have no power to decline receiving a foreign agent, and the country would be destitute of a necessity means to protect the interests and dignity of the state.

On the same principle, the right to commission (or empower) as an executive right, in the absence of any specific fundamental law to the contrary, infers the right to withdraw that commission; or in other words, to remove from office.

All the different powers of the president confirm this construction. He is commanded "to take care that the laws be faithfully executed," a duty than can be discharged in no other manner, than by displacing unworthy agents, and entrusting the authority to worthier; he nominates, or originates the appointment; with the consent of the senate, he settles the matter in his own mind, or appoints; and according to the true and technical signification of the word, he commissions, or empowers; unless it be intended that all offices shall be held during good behaviour, he removes.

That the constitution did not intend that officers should be irremovable, is to be inferred from the fact that duties are assigned the president, that can be discharged in no other manner than by displacing delinquents; from the general usages of governments; and from the fact that certain officers are named, in the way of exceptions, as those who are to hold their trusts during good behaviour.

An example will show the necessity of this power's existing in the president. A collector is commanded to perform certain acts, which he neglects to do, to the great injury of the country. The executive is ordered by the constitution to take care that this, as well as the other laws, be faithfully executed. He admonishes the delinquent, who pertinaciously adheres to his illegal course. In what manner is the president to enforce the law? Impeachment is not in his power, in the first place; and in the next place, it does not enforce the law, but punishes the offender. He may, in some cases, order the law officers of the government to prosecute for penalties, perhaps, but the law officers may also refuse to do their duties, and thus the whole intention of the institutions would be set at naught.

Errors have arisen, on these subjects, by misconceiving the meaning of the terms. "Nominate," "appoint" and "commission," are to be construed in their broadest significations, in an instrument as dignified and comprehensive as a constitution, and with strict reference to the general character of the functions with which they are connected, functions that are purely executive and in no manner ministerial. This is the only statesmanlike view of the question, though the practice of permitting common-law lawyers to expound the great national compact, has had the effect to narrow and degrade the instrument, favoring the views of political factions, and not unfrequently disturbing the country without a commensurate object.

The practice of the government has always been in conformity with this reasoning, though, it is believed that no commentator has ever given a sufficiently broad signification to the power to commission. If this power be strictly executive, as it is just to deem it, it must be taken like the power to receive ambassadors, or as a duty vested with high executive discretion. The president has consequently the same authority to withold, or to withdraw a commission, in the one case, as in the other, to receive or to decline receiving a foreign minister.

It follows that all the affirmative power in making treaties, in appointing to office, and in removing, is in the president alone, the advice and consent of the senate not authorising the several acts, but merely completing the right of the executive to perform these high functions himself.

The president of the United States, besides his civil duties, is the military commander in chief of the army and navy of the United States, at all times, and of the militia of the several states whenever the latter is called into the field.

He is the representative of the constituencies of the states, under a peculiar modification, and for the purposes set forth in the constitution. He has no prerogative, which implies an inalienable and exclusive right or privilege, for his functions take the character of duties, and the states can legally, and under prescribed forms, not only modify those duties, but they can altogether destroy the office, at will.

As a rule, there is far more danger that the president of the United States will render the office less efficient than was intended, than that he will exercise an authority dangerous to the liberties of the country. Some of his powers perhaps, are too imitative, and are unnecessary; that of dismissing military officers, for instance. But it is a greater evil to attempt reducing them, except in conformity with the provisions of the constitution, than to endure them. Even these questionable points of power, have been seldom abused, and, as a whole, the history of the country shows ten instances of presidents' evading responsibility, to one of their abusing power. A recent case is that of the executive's assenting to an indirect law recognizing the independence of Texas, a measure that is purely diplomatick and international, and which, of course, ought to be regulated by treaty, and in no other manner. A step of this gravity, if referred to the proper authority, would have required the sanction of a two thirds vote in the senate, and consequently a deliberation and prudence that might do better justice, and possibly avoid a war.

On Equality

Equality, in a social sense, may be divided into that of condition, and that of rights. Equality of condition is incompatible with civilization, and is found only to exist in those communities that are but slightly removed from the savage state. In practice, it can only mean a common misery.

Equality of rights is a peculiar feature of democracies. These rights are properly divided into civil and political, though even these definitions are not to be taken as absolute, or as literally exact.

Under the monarchies of the old world, there exist privileged classes, possessed of exclusive rights. For a long period the nobles were exempted from taxes, and many other charges, advantages that are still enjoyed by them, in certain countries. In England, even, the nobles are entitled to hereditary advantages that are denied to those who are of inferior birth. All these distinctions are done away with in principle, in countries where there exists a professed equality of rights, though there is probably no community that does not make some distinctions between the political privileges of men. If this be true, there is strictly no equality of political rights, any where, although there may be, and is, a nearer approach to an equality of civil rights.

By political rights we understand, the suffrage, eligibility to office, and a condition of things that admits of no distinction between men, unless on principles that are common to all. Thus, though a man is not qualified to vote until he has reached the age of twenty-one, the regulation does not effect political equality, since all are equally subjected to the rule, and all become electors on attaining the same age.

With an equality of civil rights, all men are equal before the law; all classes of the community being liable equally to taxation, military service, jury duties, and to the other impositions attendant on civilization, and no one being exempted from its control, except on general rules, which are dependent on the good of all, instead of the exemption's belonging to the immunities of individuals, estates, or families. An equality of civil rights may be briefly defined to be an absence of privileges.

The distinction between the equality of civil and of political rights is material, one implying mere equality before the administration of the law, the other, equality in the power to frame it.

An equality of civil rights is never absolute, but we are to understand by the term, such an equality only, as is compatible with general justice and the relations between the different members of families. Thus, women nowhere possess precisely the same rights as men, or men the same rights as women. The wife, usually, can neither sue nor be sued, while the husband, except in particular cases, is made liable to all legal claims on account of the wife. Minors are deprived of many of their civil rights, or, it would be better to say, do not attain them, until they reach a period of life that has been arbitrarily fixed, and which varies in different countries, according to their several policies.

Neither is equality of political rights ever absolute. In those countries where the suffrage is said to be universal, exceptions exist, that arise from the necessity of things, or from that controlling policy which can never be safely lost sight of in the management of human affairs. The interests of women being thought to be so identified with those of their male relatives as to become, in a great degree, inseparable, females are, almost generally, excluded from the possession of political rights. There can be no doubt that society is greatly the gainer, by thus excluding one half its members, and the half that is best adapted to give a tone to its domestic happiness, from the strife of parties, and the fierce struggles of political controversies. Men are also excluded from political rights previously to having attained the age prescribed by law. Paupers, those who have no fixed abodes, and aliens in law, though their lives may have been principally passed in the country, are also excluded from the enjoyment of political rights, every where. Thus birth-right is almost universally made a source of advantage. These exceptions, however, do not very materially affect the principle of political equality, since the rules are general, and have been made solely with a reference to the good of society, or to render the laws less liable to abuses in practice.

It follows, that equality, whether considered in connection with our civil or political rights, must not be taken as a general and absolute condition of society, but as such an equality as depends on principles that are equitable, and which are suited to the actual wants of men.

ON AMERICAN EQUALITY

The equality of the United States is no more absolute, than that of any other country. There may be less inequality in this nation than in most others, but inequality exists, and, in some respects, with stronger features than it is usual to meet with in the rest of christendom

The rights of property being an indispensable condition of civilization, and its quiet possession every where guarantied, equality of condition is rendered impossible. One man must labor, while another may live luxuriously on his means; one has leisure and opportunity to cultivate his tastes, to increase his information, and to refine his habits, while another is compelled to toil, that he may live. One is reduced to serve, while another commands, and, of course, there can be no equality in their social conditions.

The justice and relative advantage of these differencies, as well as their several duties, will be elsewhere considered.

By the inequality of civil and political rights that exists in certain parts of the Union, and the great equality that exists in others, we see the necessity of referring the true character of the institutions to those of the states, without a just understanding of which, it is impossible to obtain any general and accurate ideas of the real polity of the country.

The same general exceptions to civil and political equality, that are found in other free countries, exist in this, though under laws peculiar to ourselves. Women and minors are excluded from the suffrage, and from maintaining suits at law, under the usual provisions, here as well as elsewhere. None but natives of the country can fill many of the higher offices, and paupers, felons and all those who have not fixed residences, are also excluded from the suffrage. In a few of the states property is made the test of political rights, and, in nearly half of them, a large portion of the inhabitants, who are of a different race from the original European occupants of the soil, are entirely excluded from all political, and from many of the civil rights, that are enjoyed by those who are deemed citizens. A slave can neither choose, nor be chosen to office, nor, in most of the states, can even a free man, unless a white man. A slave can neither sue nor be sued; he can not hold property, real or personal, nor can he, in many of the states be a witness in any suit, civil or criminal.

It follows from these facts, that absolute equality of condition, of political rights, or of civil rights, does not exist in the United States, though they all exist in a much greater degree in some states than in others, and in some of the states, perhaps, to as great a degree as is practicable. In what are usually called the free states of America, or those in which domestic slavery is abolished, there is to be found as much equality in every respect as comports with safety, civilization and the rights of property. This is also true, as respects the white population, in those states in which domestic slavery does exist; though the number of the bond is in a large proportion to that of the free.

As the tendency of the institutions of America is to the right, we learn in these truths, the power of facts, every question of politics being strictly a question of practice. They who fancy it possible to frame the institutions of a country, on the pure principles of abstract justice, as these principles exist in theories, know little of human nature, or of the restraints that are necessary to society. Abuses assail us in a thousand forms, and it is hopeless to aspire to any condition of humanity, approaching perfection. The very necessity of a government at all, arises from the impossibility of controlling the passions by any other means than that of force.

The celebrated proposition contained in the declaration of independence is not to be understood literally. All men are not "created equal," in a physical, or even in a moral sense, unless we limit the signification to one of political rights. This much is true, since human institutions are a human invention, with which nature has had no connection. Men are not born equals, physically, since one has a good constitution, another a bad; one is handsome, another ugly; one white, another black. Neither are men born equals morally, one possessing genius, or a natural aptitude, while his brother is an idiot. As regards all human institutions men are born equal, no sophistry being able to prove that nature intended one should inherit power and wealth, another slavery and want. Still artificial inequalities are the inevitable consequences of artificial ordinances, and in founding a new governing principle for the social compact, the American legislators instituted new modes of difference.

The very existence of government at all, infers inequality. The citizen who is preferred to office becomes the superior of those who are not, so long as he is the repository of power, and the child inherits the wealth of the parent as a controlling law of society. All that the great American proposition, therefore, can mean, is to set up new and juster notions of natural rights than those which existed previously, by asserting, in substance, that God has not instituted political inequalities, as was pretended by the advocates of the Jus Divinum, and that men possessed a full and natural authority to form such social institutions as best suited their necessities.

There are numerous instances in which the social inequality of America may do violence to our notions of abstract justice, but the compromise of interests under which all civilized society must exist, renders this unavoidable. Great principles seldom escape working injustice in particular things, and this so much the more, in establishing the relations of a community, for in them many great, and frequently conflicting principles enter, to maintain the more essential features of which sacrifices of parts become necessary. If we would have civilization and the exertion indispensable to its success, we must have property; if we have property, we must have its rights; if we have the rights of property, we must take those consequences of the rights of property which are inseparable from the rights themselves.

The equality of rights in America, therefore, after allowing for the striking exception of domestic slavery, is only a greater extension of the principle than common, while there is no such thing as an equality of condition. All that can be said of the first, is that it has been carried as far as a prudent discretion will at all allow, and of the last, that the inequality is the simple result of civilization, unaided by any of those factitious plans that have been elsewhere devised in order to augment the power of the strong, and to enfeeble the weak.

Equality is no where laid down as a governing principle of the institutions of the United States, neither the word, nor any inference that can be fairly deduced from its meaning, occurring in the constitution. As respects the states, themselves, the professions of an equality of rights are more clear, and slavery excepted, the intention in all their governments is to maintain it, as far as practicable, though equality of condition is no where mentioned, all political economists knowing that it is unattainable, if, indeed, it be desirable. Desirable in practice, it can hardly be, since the result would be to force all down to the level of the lowest.

All that a good government aims at, therefore, is to add no unnecessary and artificial aid to the force of its own unavoidable consequences, and to abstain from fortifying and accumulating social inequality as a means of increasing political inequalities.

On Liberty

Liberty, like equality, is a word more used than understood. Perfect and absolute liberty is as incompatible with the existence of society, as equality of condition. It is impracticable in a state of nature even, since, without the protection of the law, the strong would oppress and enslave the weak. We are then to understand by liberty, merely such a state of the social compact as permits the members of a community to lay no more restraints on themselves, than are required by their real necessities, and obvious interests. To this definition may be added, that it is a requisite of liberty, that the body of a nation should retain the power to modify its institutions, as circumstances shall require.

The natural disposition of all men being to enjoy a perfect freedom of action, it is a common error to suppose that the nation which possesses the mildest laws, or laws that impose the least personal restraints, is the freest. This opinion is untenable, since the power that concedes this freedom of action, can recall it. Unless it is lodged in the body of the community itself, there is, therefore, no pledge for the continuance of such a liberty. A familiar, supposititious case will render this truth more obvious.

A slave holder in Virginia is the master of two slaves: to one he grants his liberty, with the means to go to a town in a free state. The other accompanies his old associate clandestinely. In this town, they engage their services voluntarily, to a common master, who assigns to them equal shares in the same labor, paying them the same wages. In time, the master learns their situation, but, being an indulgent man, he allows the slave to retain his present situation. In all material things, these brothers are equal; they labor together, receive the same wages, and eat of the same food. Yet one is bond, and the other free, since it is in the power of the master, or of his heir, or of his assignee, at any time, to reclaim the services of the one who was not legally manumitted, and reduce him again to the condition of slavery. One of these brothers is the master of his own acts, while the other, though temporarily enjoying the same privileges, holds them subject to the will of a superior.

This is an all important distinction in the consideration of political liberty, since the circumstances of no two countries are precisely the same, and all municipal regulations ought to have direct reference to the actual condition of a community. It follows, that no country can properly be deemed free, unless the body of the nation possess, in the last resort, the legal power to frame its laws according to its wants. This power must also abide in the nation, or it becomes merely an historical fact, for he that was once free is not necessarily free always, any more than he that was once happy, is to consider himself happy in perpetuity.

This definition of liberty is new to the world, for a government founded on such principles is a novelty. Hitherto, a nation has been deemed free, whose people were possessed of a certain amount of franchises, without any reference to the general repository of power. Such a nation may not be absolutely enslaved, but it can scarcely be considered in possession of an affirmative political liberty, since it is not the master of its own fortunes.

Having settled what is the foundation of liberty, it remains to be seen by what process a people can exercise this authority over themselves. The usual course is to refer all matters of choice to the decision of majorities. The common axiom of democracies, however, which says that "the majority must rule," is to be received with many limitations. Were the majority of a country to rule without restraint, it is probable as much injustice and oppression would follow, as are found under the dominion of one. It belongs to the nature of men to arrange themselves in parties, to lose sight of truth and justice in partizanship and prejudice, to mistake their own impulses for that which is proper, and to do wrong because they are indisposed to seek the right. Were it wise to trust power, unreservedly, to majorities, all fundamental and controlling laws would be unnecessary, since they might, as occasion required, emanate from the will of numbers. Constitutions would be useless.

The majority rules in prescribed cases, and in no other. It elects to office, it enacts ordinary laws, subject however to the restrictions of the constitution, and it decides most of the questions that arise in the primitive meetings of the people; questions that do not usually effect any of the principal interests of life.

The majority does not rule in settling fundamental laws, under the constitution; or when it does rule in such cases, it is with particular checks produced by time and new combinations; it does not pass judgment in trials at law, or under impeachment, and it is impotent in many matters touching vested rigths. In the state of New York, the majority is impotent, in granting corporations, and in appropriating money for local purposes.

Though majorities often decide wrong, it is believed that they are less liable to do so than minorities. There can be no question that the educated and affluent classes of a country, are more capable of coming to wise and intelligent decisions in affairs of state, than the mass of a population. Their wealth and leisure afford them opportunities for observation and comparison, while their general information and greater knowledge of character, enable them to judge more accurately of men and measures. That these opportunities are not properly used, is owing to the unceasing desire of men to turn their advantages to their own particular benefit, and to their passions. All history proves, when power is the sole possession of a few, that it is perverted to their sole advantage, the public suffering in order that their rulers may prosper. The same nature which imposes the necessity of governments at all, seems to point out the expediency of confiding its control, in the last resort, to the body of the nation, as the only lasting protection against gross abuses.

We do not adopt the popular polity because it is perfect, but because it is less imperfect than any other. As man, by his nature, is liable to err, it is vain to expect an infalliable whole that is composed of fallible parts. The government that emanates from a single will, supposing that will to be pure, enlightened, impartial, just and consistent, would be the best in the world, were it attainable for men. Such is the government of the universe, the result of which is perfect harmony. As no man is without spot in his justice, as no man has infinite wisdom, or infinite mercy, we are driven to take refuge in the opposite extreme, or in a government of many.

It is common for the advocates of monarchy and aristocracy to deride the opinions of the mass, as no more than the impulses of ignorance and prejudices. While experience unhappily shows that this charge has too much truth, it also shows that the educated and few form no exemption to the common rule of humanity. The most intelligent men of every country in which there is liberty of thought and action, yielding to their interests or their passions, are always found taking the opposite extremes of contested questions, thus triumphantly refuting an arrogant proposition, that of the exclusive fitness of the few to govern, by an unanswerable fact. The minority of a country is never known to agree, except in its efforts to reduce and oppress the majority. Were this not so, parties would be unknown in all countries but democracies, whereas the factions of aristocracies have been among the fiercest, and least governable of any recorded in history.

Although real political liberty can have but one character, that of a popular base, the world contains many modifications of governments that are, more or less, worthy to be termed free. In most of these states, however, the liberties of the mass, are of the negative character of franchises, which franchises are not power of themselves, but merely an exemption from the abuses of power. Perhaps no state exists, in which the people, either by usage, or by direct concessions from the source of authority, do not possess some of these franchises; for, if there is no such thing, in practice, as perfect and absolute liberty, neither is there any such thing, in practice, as total and unmitigated slavery. In the one case, nature has rendered man incapable of enjoying freedom without restraint, and in the other, incapable of submitting, entirely without resistance, to oppression. The harshest desposts are compelled to acknowledge the immutable principles of eternal justice, affecting necessity and the love of right, for their most ruthless deeds.

England is a country in which the franchises of the subject are more than usually numerous. Among the most conspicuous of these are the right of trial by jury, and that of the *Habeas Corpus*. Of the former it is unnecessary to speak, but as the latter is a phrase that may be unintelligible to many, it may be well to explain it.

The literal signification of *Habeas Corpus*★ is, "thou may'st have the body." In arbitrary governments, it is much the usage to oppress men, under the pretence of justice, by causing them to be arrested on false, or trivial charges, and of subjecting them to long and vexatious imprisonments, by protracting, or altogether evading the day of trial. The issue of a writ of *Habeas Corpus,* is an order to bring the accused before an impartial and independent judge, who examines into the charge, and who orders the prisoner to be set at liberty, unless there be sufficient legal ground for his detention.

★ *"Habeas,"* second person singular, present tense, subjunctive mood, of the verb *"Habere,"* to have; *"Corpus,"* a noun, signifying "body."

This provision of the English law has been wisely retained in our system, for without some such regulation, it would be almost as easy to detain a citizen unjustly, under a popular government, as to detain the subject of a monarchy; the difference in favor of the first, consisting only in the greater responsibility of its functionaries.

By comparing the privileges of the *Habeas Corpus,* where it exists alone, and as a franchise, with those of the citizen who enjoys it merely as a provision of his own, against the abuses of ordinances that he had a voice in framing, we learn the essential difference between real liberty and franchises. The Englishman can appeal to a tribunal, against the abuse of an existing law, but if the law be not with him, he has no power to evade it, however unjust, or oppressive. The American has the same appeal against the abuse of a law, with the additional power to vote for its repeal, should the law itself be vicious. The one profits by a franchise to liberate his person only, submitting to his imprisonment however, if legality has been respected; while the other, in addition to this privilege, has a voice in getting rid of the obnoxious law, itself, and in preventing a recurrence of the wrong.

Some countries have the profession of possessing a government of the people, because an ancient dynasty has been set aside in a revolution, and a new one seated on the throne, either directly by the people, or by a combination that has been made to assume the character of a popular decision. Admitting that a people actually had an agency in framing such a system, and in naming their ruler, they cannot claim to be free, since they have parted with the power they did actually possess. No proposition can be clearer than that he who has given away a thing is no longer its master.

Of this nature is the present government of France. In that country the ancient dynasty has been set aside by a combination of leaders, through the agency of a few active spirits among the mass, and a prince put upon the throne, who is virtually invested with all the authority of his predecessor. Still, as the right of the last sovereign is clearly derived from a revolution, which has been made to assume the appearance of popular will, his government is termed a government of the people. This is a fallacy that can deceive no one of the smallest reflection. Such a system may be the best that France can now receive, but it is a mystification to call it by any other than its proper name. It is not a government of consultation, but one of pure force as respects a vast majority of Frenchmen.

A good deal of the same objection lies against the government of Great Britain, which, though freer in practice than that of France, is not based on a really free system. It may be said that both these governments are as free as comports with discretion, as indeed may be said of Turkey, since men get to be disqualified for the possession of any advantage in time; but such an admission is only an avowal of unfitness, and not a proof of enjoyment.

It is usual to maintain, that in democracies the tyranny of majorities is a greater evil than the oppression of minorities in narrow systems. Although this evil is exaggerated, since the laws being equal in their action it is not easy to oppress the few without oppressing all, it undeniably is the weak side of a popular government. To guard against this, we have framed constitutions, which point out the cases in which the majority shall decide, limiting their power, and bringing that they do possess within the circle of certain general and just principles. It will be elsewhere shown that it is a great mistake for the American citizen to take sides with the public, in doubtful cases affecting the rights of individuals, as this is the precise form in which oppression is the most likely to exhibit itself in a popular government.

Although it is true, that no genuine liberty can exist without being based on popular authority in the last resort, it is equally true that it can not exist when thus based, without many restraints on the power of the mass. These restraints are necessarily various and numerous. A familiar example will show their action. The majority of the people of a state might be in debt to its minority. Were the power of the former unrestrained, circumstances might arise in which they would declare depreciated bank notes a legal tender, and thus clear themselves of their liabilities, at the expense of their creditors. To prevent this, the constitution orders that nothing shall be made a legal tender but the precious metals, thus limiting the power of majorities in a way that the government is not limited in absolute monarchies, in which paper is often made to possess the value of gold and silver.

Liberty therefore may be defined to be a controlling authority that resides in the body of a nation, but so restrained as only to be exercised on certain general principles that shall do as little violence to natural justice, as is compatible with the peace and security of society.

On the Advantages of a Monarchy

The monarchical form of government has the advantages of energy for external purposes, as well as of simplicity in execution. It is prompt and efficient in attack. Its legislation is ready, emanating from a single will, and it has the means of respecting treaties with more fidelity than other systems.

As laws are framed on general principles, they sometimes work evil in particular cases, and in a government of the will, the remedy is applied with more facility than in a government of law.

In a monarchy, men are ruled without their own agency, and as their time is not required for the supervision or choice of the public agents, or the enactment of laws, their attention may be exclusively given to their personal interests. Could this advantage be enjoyed without the abuses of such a state of things, it would alone suffice to render this form of government preferable to all others, since contact with the affairs of state is one of the most corrupting of the influences to which men are exposed.

As a monarchy recedes from absolutism, and takes the character of constitutionality, it looses these advantages to a certain extent, assuming more of those of legality.

On the Advantages of an Aristocracy

The aristocratical form of government, though in an unmitigated form one of the worst known, has many advantages when tempered by franchises. This latter is the real polity of Great Britain, though it is under the pretence of a monarchy. No government, however, can properly be called a monarchy, in which the monarch does not form a distinct and independent portion of the state. The king of England, by the theory of the constitution, is supposed to hold a balance between the lords and the commons, whereas he, in truth, may be said merely to hold a casting vote between the several factions of the aristocracy, when the forces of these factions neutralize each other.

Aristocracies have a facility in combining measures for their interests that is not enjoyed by democracies. The power being in the hands of a few, these few can act with a despatch and energy, which, though unequaled by those of a monarchy, commonly have the material advantage of better agents. In an aristocracy, influence among the aristocrats themselves depending chiefly on the manly qualities, history shows us that the public agents are usually more chosen for their services than in a monarchy, where the favor of the prince is the chief requisite for success; it may therefore be assumed that the higher qualities of those who fill the public trusts, in an aristocracy, more than neutralize the greater concentration of a monarchy, and render it the most efficient form of government, for the purposes of conquest and foreign policy, that is known. Aristocracy has an absorbing quality, if such a term may be used, by which the active and daring of conquered territories, are induced to join the conquerors, in order to share in the advantages of the system. Thus we find that almost all the countries that have made extensive conquests over civilized people, and who have long retained them, have been aristocracies. We get examples of the facilities of aristocracies to extend their influence, as well as to retain it, in Rome, England, Venice, Florence and many other states.

An aristocracy is a combination of many powerful men, for the purpose of maintaining and advancing their own particular interests. It is consequently a concentration of all the most effective parts of a community for a given end; hence its energy, efficiency and success. Of all the forms of government, it is the one best adapted to support the system of metropolitan sway, since the most dangerous of the dependants can be bribed and neutralized, by admitting them to a participation of power. By this means it is rendered less offensive to human pride than the administration of one. The present relations between England and Ireland, are a striking instance of what is meant.

An aristocracy, unless unusually narrow, is peculiarly the government of the enterprising and the ambitious. High honors are attainable, and jealousy of rewards is confined to individuals, seldom effecting the state. The tendency of the system, therefore, is to render the aristocrats bold, independent and manly, and to cause them to be distinguished from the mass. In an age as advanced as ours, the leisure of the higher classes of an aristocracy, enable them to cultivate their minds and to improve their tastes. Hence aristocracies are particularly favorable to knowledge and the arts, as both grow under patronage.

It is necessary to distinguish, however, between a political and a merely social aristocracy. These remarks apply chiefly to the former, which alone has any connexion with government. The term aristocracy, in fact, applies properly to no other, though vulgar use has perverted its signification to all nobles, and even to the gentry of democracies.

Advantages of a Democracy

The principal advantage of a democracy, is a general elevation in the character of the people. If few are raised to a very great height, few are depressed very low. As a consequence, the average of society is much more respectable than under any other form of government. The vulgar charge that the tendency of democracies is to levelling, meaning to drag all down to the level of the lowest, is singularly untrue, its real tendency being to elevate the depressed to a condition not unworthy of their manhood. In the absence of privileged orders, entails and distinctions, devised permanently to separate men into social castes, it is true none are great but those who become so by their acts, but, confining the remark to the upper classes of society, it would be much more true to say that democracy refuses to lend itself to unnatural and arbitrary distinctions, than to accuse it of a tendency to level those who have a just claim to be elevated. A denial of a favor, is not an invasion of a right.

Democracies are exempt from the military charges, both pecuniary and personal, that become necessary in governments in which the majority are subjects, since no force is required to repress those who, under other systems, are dangerous to the state, by their greater physical power.

As the success of democracies is mainly dependant on the intelligence of the people, the means of preserving the government are precisely those which most conduce to the happiness and social progress of man. Hence we find the state endeavoring to raise its citizens in the scale of being, the certain means of laying the broadest foundation of national prosperity. If the arts are advanced in aristocracies, through the taste of patrons, in democracies, though of slower growth, they will prosper as a consequence of general information; or as a superstructure reared on a wider and more solid foundation.

Democracies being, as nearly as possible, founded in natural justice, little violence is done to the sense of right by the institutions, and men have less occasion than usual, to resort to fallacies and false principles in cultivating the faculties. As a consequence, common sense is more encouraged, and the community is apt to entertain juster notions of all moral truths, than under systems that are necessarily sophisticated. Society is thus a gainer in the greatest element of happiness, or in the right perception of the different relations between men and things.

Democracies being established for the common interests, and the publick agents being held in constant check by the people, their general tendency is to serve the whole community, and not small portions of it, as is the case in narrow governments. It is as rational to suppose that a hungry man will first help his neighbor to bread, when master of his own acts, as to suppose that any but those who feel themselves to be truly public servants, will first bethink themselves of the publick, when in situations of publick trust. In a government of one, that one and his parasites will be the first and best served; in a government of a few, the few; and in a government of many, the many. Thus the general tendency of democratical institutions is to equalize advantages, and to spread its blessings over the entire surface of society.

Democracies, other things being equal, are the cheapest form of government, since little money is lavished in representation, and they who have to pay the taxes, have also, directly or indirectly, a voice in imposing them.

Democracies are less liable to popular tumults than any other polities, because the people, having legal means in their power to redress wrongs, have little inducement to employ any other. The man who can right himself by a vote, will seldom resort to a musket. Grievances, moreover, are less frequent, the most corrupt representatives of a democratick constituency generally standing in awe of its censure.

As men in bodies usually defer to the right, unless acting under erroneous impressions, or excited by sudden resentments, democracies pay more respect to abstract justice, in the management of their foreign concerns, than either aristocracies or monarchies, an appeal always lying against abuses, or violations of principle, to a popular sentiment, that, in the end, seldom fails to decide in favor of truth.

In democracies, with a due allowance for the workings of personal selfishness, it is usually a motive with those in places of trust, to consult the interests of the mass, there being little doubt, that in this system, the entire community has more regard paid to its wants and wishes, than in either of the two others.

ON THE DISADVANTAGES OF A MONARCHY

A monarchy is liable to those abuses which follow favoritism, the servants of the prince avenging themselves for their homage to one, by oppressing the many.

A monarchy is the most expensive of all forms of government, the regal state requiring a costly parade, and he who depends on his own power to rule, must strengthen that power by bribing the active and enterprising whom he cannot intimidate. Thus the favorites of an absolute prince, in connection with the charges of himself and family, frequently cost the state as much as its necessary expenditures.

It is the policy of a monarchy to repress thought, a knowledge of human rights being always dangerous to absolute, or exclusive power. Thus the people of monarchies are divided into the extremes of society, the intermediate and happiest classes being usually small, and inclined to favor their superiors from apprehension of the brutal ignorance of those below them.

Monarchies are subjected to the wars and to the policies of family alliances, the feelings and passions of the prince exercising a malign influence on the affairs of the state.

In monarchies the people are required to maintain a military force sufficient to support the throne, the system always exacting that the subject should pay the troops that are kept on foot to hold him in subjection.

Truth is trammelled in a monarchy, the system dreading collision with a power so dangerous to all factitious and one-sided theories.

Monarchies, especially those in which the crown possesses a real and predominant power, discourage sincerity and frankness of character, substituting appearances for virtue, and flattery and deception for wholesome facts.

Women often exercise an improper influence, and this from an impure motive, in monarchies, history tracing even wars to the passions of an offended mistress.

The public money is diverted from legitimate objects, to those which support the personal views, passions, caprices, or enmities of the prince.

Monarchies are subject to all those abuses, which depend on an irresponsible administration of power, and an absence of publicity; abuses that oppress the majority for the benefit of a few, and which induce subserviency of character, frauds, flatteries and other similar vices.

If, in this age, monarchies exhibit these results of the system in milder forms, than in other centuries, it is owing to the increasing influence of the people, who may control systems, though in a less degree, indirectly as well as directly.

On the Disadvantages of an Aristocracy

Aristocracy has, in common with monarchy, the evils of an expenditure that depends on representation, the state maintaining little less pomp under aristocrats, than under princes.

It is compelled to maintain itself against the physical superiority of numbers also, by military charges that involve heavy personal services, and large expenditures of money.

Being a government of the few, it is in the main, as a necessity of human selfishness, administered in the interests of the few.

The ruled are depressed in consequence of the elevation of their rulers. Information is kept within circumscribed limits, lest the mass should come to a knowledge of their force, for horses would not submit to be put in harness and made to toil for hard taskmasters, did they know as much as men.

Aristocracies partaking of the irresponsible nature of corporations, are soulless, possessing neither the personal feelings that often temper even despotism, nor submitting to the human impulses of popular bodies. This is one of the worst features of an aristocracy, a system that has shown itself more ruthless than any other, though tempered by civilization, for aristocracy and barbarism cannot exist in common.

As there are many masters in an aristocracy, the exactions are proportionably heavy, and this the more so, as they who impose the burthens generally find the means to evade their payment: the apophthegm that "it is better to have one tyrant than many," applying peculiarly to aristocracies, and not to democracies, which cannot permanently tyrannize at all, without tyrannizing over those who rule.

Aristocracies have a natural tendency to wars and aggrandizement, which bring with them the inevitable penalties of taxes, injustice, demoralization and blood-shed. This charge has been brought against republicks generally, but a distinction should be made between a republick with an aristocratical base, and a republick with a democratical base, their characters being as dissimilar as those of any two forms of government known. Aristocracies, feeling less of the better impulses of man, are beyond their influence, while their means of combining are so great, that they oftener listen to their interests than to those sentiments of natural justice that in a greater or less degree always control masses.

Aristocracies usually favor those vices that spring from the love of money, which there is divine authority for believing to be "the root of all evil." In modern aristocracies, the controlling principle is property, an influence the most corrupting to which men submit, and which, when its ordinary temptations are found united to those of political patronage and power, is much too strong for human virtue. Direct bribery, therefore, has been found to be the bane of aristocracies, the influence of individuals supplying the place of merit, services and public virtue. In Rome this system was conducted so openly, that every man of note had his "clients," a term which then signified one who depended on the favor of another for the advancement of his interests, and even for the maintenance of his rights.

Aristocracies wound the sense of natural justice, and consequently unsettle principles, by placing men, altogether unworthy of trust, in high hereditary situations, a circumstance that not only offends morals, but sometimes, though possibly less often than is commonly imagined, inflicts serious injuries on a state.

On this point however, too much importance must not be attached to theories, for in the practices of states a regard is necessarily paid to certain indispensable principles, and the comparative merits of systems are to be established from their general tendencies, rather than from the accidental exceptions that may occasionally arise: the quality in the *personnel* of administrations depending quite as much on the general civilization of a nation, as on any other cause.

On the Disadvantages of a Democracy

Democracies are liable to popular impulses, which, necessarily arising from imperfect information, often work injustice from good motives. Tumults of the people are less apt to occur in democracies than under any other form of government, for, possessing the legal means of redressing themselves, there is less necessity to resort to force, but, public opinion, constituting, virtually, the power of the state, measures are more apt to be influenced by sudden mutations of sentiment, than under systems where the rulers have better opportunities and more leisure for examination. There is more feeling and less design in the movements of masses than in those of small bodies, except as design emanates from demagogues and political managers.

The efforts of the masses that are struggling to obtain their rights, in monarchies and aristocracies, however, are not to be imputed to democracy; in such cases, the people use their natural weapon, force, merely because they are denied any participation in the legal authority.

When democracies are small, these impulses frequently do great injury to the public service, but in large states they are seldom of sufficient extent to produce results before there is time to feel the influence of reason. It is, therefore, one of the errors of politicians to imagine democracies more practicable in small than in large communities, an error that has probably arisen from the fact that, the ignorance of masses having hitherto put men at the mercy of the combinations of the affluent and intelligent, democracies have been permitted to exist only in countries insignificant by their wealth and numbers.

Large democracies, on the other hand, while less exposed to the principal evil of this form of government, than smaller, are unable to scrutinize and understand character with the severity and intelligence that are of so much importance in all representative governments, and consequently the people are peculiarly exposed to become the dupes of demagogues and political schemers, most of the crimes of democracies arising from the faults and designs of men of this character, rather than from the propensities of the people, who, having little temptation to do wrong, are seldom guilty of crimes except through ignorance.

Democracies are necessarily controlled by publick opinion, and failing of the means of obtaining power more honestly, the fraudulent and ambitious find a motive to mislead, and even to corrupt the common sentiment, to attain their ends. This is the greatest and most pervading danger of all large democracies, since it is sapping the foundations of society, by undermining its virtue. We see the effects of this baneful influence, in the openness and audacity with which men avow improper motives and improper acts, trusting to find support in a popular feeling, for while vicious influences are perhaps more admitted in other countries, than in America, in none are they so openly avowed.

It may also be urged against democracies, that, nothing being more corrupting than the management of human affairs, which are constantly demanding sacrifices of permanent principles to interests that are as constantly fluctuating, their people are exposed to assaults on their morals from this quarter, that the masses of other nations escape. It is probable, however, that this evil, while it ought properly to be enumerated as one of the disadvantages of the system, is more than counterbalanced by the main results, even on the score of morals.

The constant appeals to public opinion in a democracy, though excellent as a corrective of public vices, induce private hypocrisy, causing men to conceal their own convictions when opposed to those of the mass, the latter being seldom wholly right, or wholly wrong. A want of national manliness is a vice to be guarded against, for the man who would dare to resist a monarch, shrinks from opposing an entire community. That the latter is quite often wrong, however, is abundantly proved by the fact, that its own judgments fluctuate, as it reasons and thinks differently this year, or this month even, from what it reasoned and thought the last.

The tendency of democracies is, in all things, to mediocrity, since the tastes, knowledge and principles of the majority form the tribunal of appeal. This circumstance, while it certainly serves to elevate the average qualities of a nation, renders the introduction of a high standard difficult. Thus do we find in literature, the arts, architecture and in all acquired knowledge, a tendency in America to gravitate towards the common center in this, as in other things; lending a value and estimation to mediocrity that are not elsewhere given. It is fair to expect, however, that a foundation so broad, may in time sustain a superstructure of commensurate proportions, and that the influence of masses will in this, as in the other interests, have a generally beneficial effect. Still it should not be forgotten that, with the exception of those works, of which, as they appeal to human sympathies or the practices of men, an intelligent public is the best judge, the mass of no community is qualified to decide the most correctly on any thing, which, in its nature, is above its reach.

It is a besetting vice of democracies to substitute publick opinion for law. This is the usual form in which masses of men exhibit their tyranny.

When the majority of the entire community commits this fault it is a sore grievance, but when local bodies, influenced by local interests, pretend to style themselves the publick, they are assuming powers that properly belong to the whole body of the people, and to them only under constitutional limitations. No tyranny of one, nor any tyranny of the few, is worse than this. All attempts in the publick, therefore, to do that which the publick has no right to do, should be frowned upon as the precise form in which tyranny is the most apt to be displayed in a democracy.

Democracies, depending so much on popular opinion are more liable to be influenced to their injury, through the management of foreign and hostile nations, than other governments. It is generally known that, in Europe, secret means are resorted to, to influence sentiment in this way, and we have witnessed in this country open appeals to the people, against the acts of their servants, in matters of foreign relations, made by foreign, not to say, hostile agents. Perhaps no stronger case can be cited of this weakness on the part of democracies, than is shown in this fact, for here we find men sufficiently audacious to build the hope of so far abusing opinion, as to persuade a people to act directly against their own dignity and interests.

The misleading of publick opinion in one way or another, is the parent of the principal disadvantages of a democracy, for in most instances it is first corrupting a community in order that it may be otherwise injured. Were it not for the counteracting influence of reason, which, in the end, seldom, perhaps never fails to assert its power, this defect would of itself, be sufficient to induce all discreet men to decide against this form of government. The greater the danger, the greater the necessity that all well-intentioned and right-minded citizens should be on their guard against its influence.

It would be hazardous, however, to impute all the peculiar faults of American character, to the institutions, the country existing under so many unusual influences. If the latter were overlooked, one might be induced to think frankness and sincerity of character were less encouraged by popular institutions than was formerly supposed, close observers affirming that these qualities are less frequent here, than in most other countries. When the general ease of society is remembered, there is unquestionably more deception of opinion practised than one would naturally expect, but this failing is properly to be imputed to causes that have no necessary connection with democratical institutions, though men defer to publick opinion, right or wrong, quite as submissively as they defer to princes. Although truths are not smothered altogether in democracies, they are often temporarily abandoned under this malign influence, unless there is a powerful motive to sustain them at the moment. While we see in our own democracy this manifest disposition to defer to the wrong, in matters that are not properly subject to the common sentiment, in deference to the popular will of the hour, there is a singular boldness in the use of personalities, as if men avenged themselves for the restraints of the one case by a licentiousness that is without hazard.

The base feelings of detraction and envy have more room for exhibition, and perhaps a stronger incentive in a democracy, than in other forms of government, in which the people get accustomed to personal deference by the artificial distinctions of the institutions. This is the reason that men become impatient of all superiority in a democracy, and manifest a wish to prefer those who affect a deference to the publick, rather than those who are worthy.

ON PREJUDICE

Prejudice is the cause of most of the mistakes of bodies of men. It influences our conduct and warps our judgment, in politics, religion, habits, tastes and opinions. We confide in one statesman and oppose another, as often from unfounded antipathies, as from reason; religion is tainted with uncharitableness and hostilities, without examination; usages are contemned; tastes ridiculed, and we decide wrong, from the practice of submitting to a preconceived and an unfounded prejudice, the most active and the most pernicious of all the hostile agents of the human mind.

The migratory propensities of the American people, and the manner in which the country has been settled by immigrants from all parts of the christian world, have an effect in diminishing prejudices of a particular kind, though, in other respects, few nations are more bigotted or provincial in their notions. Innovations on the usages connected with the arts of life are made here with less difficulty than common, reason, interest and enterprise proving too strong for prejudice; but in morals, habits and tastes, few nations have less liberality to boast of, than this.

America owes most of its social prejudices to the exaggerated religious opinions of the different sects which were so instrumental in establishing the colonies. The quakers, or friends, proscribed the delightful and elevated accomplishment of music, as, indeed, did the puritans, with the exception of psalmody. The latter confined marriage ceremonies to the magistrates, lest religion should be brought into disrepute! Most of those innocent recreations which help the charities, and serve to meliorate manners, were also forbidden, until an unnatural and monastic austerity, with a caustic habit of censoriousness, got to be considered as the only outward signs of that religious hope, which is so peculiarly adapted to render us joyous and benevolent.

False and extravagant notions on the subject of manners, never fail to injure a sound morality, by mistaking the shadow for the substance. Positive vice is known by all, for happily, conscience and revelation have made us acquainted with the laws of virtue, but it is as indiscreet unnecessarily to enlarge the circle of sins, as it is to expose ourselves to temptations that experience has shown we are unable to resist.

The most obvious American prejudices, connected with morality, are the notions that prevail on the subject of mispending time. That time may be mispent is undeniable, and few are they who ought not to reproach themselves with this neglect, but the human mind needs relaxation and amusement, as well as the human body. These are to be sought in the different expedients of classes, each finding the most satisfaction in those indulgences that conform the nearest to their respective tastes. It is the proper duty of the legislator to endeavor to elevate these tastes, and not to prevent their indulgence. Those nations in which the cord of moral discipline, according to the dogmas of fanatics, has been drawn the tightest, usually exhibit the gravest scenes of depravity, on the part of those who break loose from restraints so ill judged and unnatural. On the other hand, the lower classes of society, in nations where amusements are tolerated, are commonly remarkable for possessing some of the tates that denote cultivation and refinement. Thus do we find in catholic countries, that the men who in protestant nations, would pass their leisure in the coarsest indulgences, frequent operas and theatrical representations, classes of amusements which, well conducted, may be made powerful auxiliaries of virtue, and which generally have a tendency to improve the tastes. It is to be remarked that these exhibitions themselves are usually less gross, and more intellectual in catholic, than in protestant countries, a result of this improvement in manners.

The condition of this country is peculiar, and requires greater exertions than common, in extricating the mind from prejudices. The intimate connexion between popular opinion and positive law is one reason, since under a union so close there is danger that the latter may be colored by motives that have no sufficient foundation in justice. It is vain to boast of liberty, if the ordinances of society are to receive the impression of sectarianism, or of a provincial and narrow morality.

Another motive peculiar to the country, for freeing the mind from prejudice, is the mixed character of the population. Natives of different sections of the United States, and of various parts of Europe are brought in close contact, and without a disposition to bear with each other's habits, association becomes unpleasant, and enmities are engendered. The main result is to liberalize the mind, beyond a question, yet we see neighborhoods, in which oppressive intolerance is manifested by the greater number, for the time being, to the habits of the less. This is a sore grievance, more especially, when, as is quite frequently the case, the minority happen to be in possession of usages that mark the highest stage of civilization. It ought never to be forgotten, therefore, that every citizen is entitled to indulge without comment, or persecution, in all his customs and practices that are lawful and moral. Neither is morality to be regulated by the prejudices of sects, or social classes, but it is to be left strictly to the control of the laws, divine and human. To assume the contrary is to make prejudice, and prejudice of a local origin too, more imperious than the institutions. The justice, not to say necessity of these liberal concessions, is rendered more apparent when we remember that the parties meet as emigrants on what may be termed neutral territory, for it would be the height of presumption for the native of New York, for instance, to insist on his own peculiar customs, customs that other portions of the country perhaps repudiate, within the territory of New England, in opposition not only to the wishes of many of their brother emigrants, but to those of the natives themselves.

ON STATION

Station may be divided into that which is political, or publick, and that which is social, or private. In monarchies and aristocracies the two are found united, since the higher classes, as a matter of course, monopolize all the offices of consideration; but, in democracies, there is not, nor is it proper that there should be, any intimate connexion between them.

Political, or publick station, is that which is derived from office, and, in a democracy, must embrace men of very different degrees of leisure, refinement, habits and knowledge. This is characteristick of the institutions, which, under a popular government, confer on political station more power than rank, since the latter is expressly avoided in this system.

Social station is that which one possesses in the ordinary associations, and is dependent on birth, education, personal qualities, property, tastes, habits, and, in some instances, on caprice, or fashion. Although the latter undeniably is sometimes admitted to control social station, it generally depends, however, on the other considerations named.

Social station, in the main, is a consequence of property. So long as there is civilization there must be the rights of property, and so long as there are the rights of property, their obvious consequences must follow. All that democracies legitimately attempt is to prevent the advantages which accompany social station from accumulating rights that do not properly belong to the condition, which is effected by pronouncing that it shall have no factitious political aids.

They who have reasoned ignorantly, or who have aimed at effecting their personal ends by flattering the popular feeling, have boldly affirmed that "one man is as good as another;" a maxim that is true in neither nature, revealed morals, nor political theory.

That one man is not as good as another in natural qualities, is proved on the testimony of our senses. One man is stronger than another; he is handsomer, taller, swifter, wiser, or braver, than all his fellows. In short, the physical and moral qualities are unequally distributed, and, as a necessary consequence, in none of them, can one man be justly said to be as good as another. Perhaps no two human beings can be found so precisely equal in every thing, that one shall not be pronounced the superior of the other; which, of course, establishes the fact that there is no natural equality.

The advocates of exclusive political privileges reason on this circumstance by assuming, that as nature has made differences between men, those institutions which create political orders, are no more than carrying out the great designs of providence. The error of their argument is in supposing it a confirmation of the designs of nature to attempt to supplant her, for, while the latter has rendered men unequal, it is not from male to male, according to the order of primogeniture, as is usually established by human ordinances. In order not to interfere with the inequality of nature, her laws must be left to their own operations, which is just what is done in democracies, after a proper attention has been paid to the peace of society, by protecting the weak against the strong.

That one man is not deemed as good as another in the grand moral system of providence, is revealed to us in Holy Writ, by the scheme of future rewards and punishments, as well as by the whole history of those whom God has favored in this world, for their piety, or punished for their rebellion. As compared with perfect holiness, all men are frail; but, as compared with each other, we are throughout the whole of sacred history made to see, that, in a moral sense, one man is not as good as another. The evil doer is punished, while they who are distinguished for their qualities and acts, are intended to be preferred.

The absolute moral and physical equality that are inferred by the maxim, that "one man is as good as another," would at once do away with the elections, since a lottery would be both simpler, easier and cheaper than the present mode of selecting representatives. Men, in such a case, would draw lots for office, as they are now drawn for juries. Choice supposes a preference, and preference inequality of merit, or of fitness.

We are then to discard all visionary theories on this head, and look at things as they are. All that the most popular institutions attempt, is to prohibit that one *race* of men shall be made better than another by law, from father to son, which would be defeating the intentions of providence, creating a superiority that exists in neither physical nor moral nature, and substituting a political scheme for the will of God and the force of things.

As a principle, one man is as good as another in rights. Such is the extent of the most liberal institutions of this country, and this provision is not general. The slave is not as good as his owner, even in rights. But in those states where slavery does not exist, all men have essentially the same rights, an equality, which, so far from establishing that "one man is as good as another," in a social sense, is the very means of producing the inequality of condition that actually exists. By possessing the same rights to exercise their respective faculties, the active and frugal become more wealthy than the idle and dissolute; the wise and gifted more trusted than the silly and ignorant; the polished and refined more respected and sought, than the rude and vulgar.

In most countries, birth is a principal source of social distinction, society being divided into castes, the noble having an hereditary claim to be the superior of the plebeian. This is an unwise and an arbitrary distinction that has led to most of the social diseases of the old world, and from which America is happily exempt. But great care must be had in construing the principles which have led to this great change, for America is the first important country of modern times, in which such positive distinctions have been destroyed.

Still some legal differences, and more social advantages, are produced by birth, even in America. The child inherits the property, and a portion of the consideration of the parent. Without the first of these privileges, men would not exert themselves to acquire more property than would suffice for their own personal necessities, parental affection being one of the most powerful incentives to industry. Without such an inducement, then, it would follow that civilization would become stationary, or, it would recede; the incentives of individuality and of the affections, being absolutely necessary to impel men to endure the labor and privations that alone can advance it.

The hereditary consideration of the child, so long as it is kept within due bounds, by being confined to a natural sentiment, is also productive of good, since no more active inducement to great and glorious deeds can offer, than the deeply seated interest that man takes in his posterity. All that reason and justice require is effected, by setting bounds to such advantages, in denying hereditary claims to trusts and power; but evil would be the day, and ominous the symptom, when a people shall deny that any portion of the consideration of the ancestor is due to the descendant.

It is as vain to think of altogether setting aside sentiment and the affections, in regulating human affairs, as to imagine it possible to raise a nature, known to be erring and weak, to the level of perfection.

The Deity, in that terrible warning delivered from the mount, where he declares that he "will visit the sins of the fathers upon the children, unto the third and fourth generation," does no more than utter one of those sublime moral truths, which, in conformity with his divine providence, pervade nature. It is merely an announcement of a principle that cannot safely be separated from justice, and one that is closely connected with all the purest motives and highest aspirations of man.

There would be a manifest injustice in visiting the offence of the criminal on his nearest of kin, by making the innocent man participate in the disgrace of a guilty relative, as is notoriously done most, by those most disposed to rail at reflected renown, and not to allow of the same participation in the glory. Both depend upon a sentiment deeper than human laws, and have been established for purposes so evidently useful as to require no explanation. All that is demanded of us, is to have a care that this sentiment do not degenerate to a prejudice, and that, in the one case, we do not visit the innocent too severely, or, in the other, exalt the unworthy beyond the bounds of prudence.

It is a natural consequence of the rights of property and of the sentiment named, that birth should produce some advantages, in a social sense, even in the most democratical of the American communities. The son imbibes a portion of the intelligence, refinement and habits of the father, and he shares in his associations. These must be enumerated as the legitimate advantages of birth, and without invading the private arrangements of families and individuals, and establishing a perfect community of education, they are unavoidable. Men of the same habits, the same degree of cultivation and refinement, the same opinions, naturally associate together, in every class of life. The day laborer will not mingle with the slave; the skilful mechanic feels his superiority over the mere laborer, claims higher wages and has a pride in his craft; the man in trade justly fancies that his habits elevate him above the mechanic, so far as social position is concerned, and the man of refinement, with his education, tastes and sentiments, is superior to all. Idle declamation on these points, does not impair the force of things, and life is a series of facts. These inequalities of condition, of manners, of mental cultivation must exist, unless it be intended to reduce all to a common level of ignorance and vulgarity, which would be virtually to return to a condition of barbarism.

The result of these undeniable facts, is the inequalities of social station, in America, as elsewhere, though it is an inequality that exists without any more arbitrary distinctions than are indispensably connected with the maintenance of civilization. In a social sense, there are orders here, as in all other countries, but the classes run into each other more easily, the lines of separation are less strongly drawn, and their shadows are more intimately blended.

This social inequality of America is an unavoidable result of the institutions, though nowhere proclaimed in them, the different constitutions maintaining a profound silence on the subject, they who framed them probably knowing that it is as much a consequence of civilized society, as breathing is a vital function of animal life.

ON THE DUTIES OF STATION

The duties of station are divided into those of political or public station, and those of social, or private station. They are not necessarily connected, and shall be considered separately.

ON THE DUTIES OF PUBLICK OR POLITICAL STATION

By the duties of publick station, we understand those of the private citizen, as well as those of the citizen who fills a publick trust. The first lie at the root of the social compact, and are entitled to be first enumerated.

On the manner in which the publick duties of the private citizen are discharged, in a really free government, depend the results of the institutions. If the citizen is careless of his duties, regardless of his rights, and indifferent to the common weal, it is not difficult to foresee the triumph of abuses, peculation and frauds. It is as unreasonable to suppose that the private servant who is not overlooked, will be faithful to his master, as to suppose that the publick servant who is not watched, will be true to his trusts. In both cases a steady, reasoning, but vigilant superintendance is necessary to the good of all concerned; to the agent by removing the temptation to err, and to the principal by securing an active attention to his interests.

The American citizens are possessed of the highest political privileges that can fall to the lot of the body of any community; that of self-government. On the discreet use of this great power, depends the true character of the institutions. It is, consequently, an imperious duty of every elector to take care and employ none but the honest and intelligent, in situations of high trust.

Every position in life has its peculiar dangers, men erring more from an inability to resist temptation, than from any morbid inward impulses to do wrong without an inducement. The peculiar danger of a democracy, arises from the arts of demagogues. It is a safe rule, the safest of all, to confide only in those men for publick trusts, in whom the citizen can best confide in private life. There is no quality that more entirely pervades the moral system than probity. We often err on certain points, each man having a besetting sin, but honesty colors a whole character. He who in private is honest, frank, above hypocrisy and double-dealing, will carry those qualities with him into publick, and may be confided in; while he who is the reverse, is, inherently, a knave.

The elector who gives his vote for one whom he is persuaded on good grounds is dishonest in his motives, abuses the most sacred of his public duties. It is true, that party violence, personal malice and love of gossip, frequently cause upright men to be distrusted, and that great care is necessary to guard against slander, the commonest of human crimes, and a besetting vice of a democracy; but the connection between the constituent and the representative is usually so close, that the former, by resorting to proper means, can commonly learn the truth. Let it be repeated, then, that the elector who gives his vote, on any grounds, party or personal, to an unworthy candidate, violates a sacred publick duty, and is unfit to be a freeman.

Obedience to the laws, and a sacred regard to the rights of others, are imperative publick duties of the citizen. As he is a "law-maker," he should not be a "law-breaker," for he ought to be conscious that every departure from the established ordinances of society is an infraction of his rights. His power can only be maintained by the supremacy of the laws, as in monarchies, the authority of the king is asserted by obedience to his orders. The citizen in lending a cheerful assistance to the ministers of the law, on all occasions, is merely helping to maintain his own power. This feature in particular, distinguishes the citizen from the subject. The one rules, the other is ruled; one has a voice in framing the ordinances, and can be heard in his efforts to repeal them; the other has no choice but submission.

In Democracies there is a besetting disposition to make publick opinion stronger than the law. This is the particular form in which tyranny exhibits itself in a popular government; for wherever there is power, there will be found a disposition to abuse it. Whoever opposes the interests, or wishes of the publick, however right in principle, or justifiable by circumstances, finds little sympathy; for, in a democracy, resisting the wishes of the many, is resisting the sovereign, in his caprices. Every good citizen is bound to separate this influence of his private feelings from his publick duties, and to take heed that, while pretending to be struggling for liberty, because contending for the advantage of the greatest number, he is not helping despotism. The most insinuating and dangerous form in which oppression can overshadow a community is that of popular sway. All the safeguards of liberty, in a democracy, have this in view, as, in monarchies, they are erected against the power of the crown.

The old political saying, that "the people are their own worst enemies," while false as a governing maxim, contains some truth. It is false to say that a people left to govern themselves, would oppress themselves, as monarchs and aristocrats, throughout all time, are known to oppress the ruled, but it is true to say, that the peculiar sins of a democracy must be sought for in the democratical character of the institutions. To pretend otherwise, would be to insist on perfection; for, in a state of society in which there is neither prince nor aristocrats, there must be faultlessness, or errors of a democratic origin, and of a democratic origin only. It is, therefore, a publick duty of the citizen to guard against all excesses of popular power, whether inflicted by mere opinion, or under the forms of law. In all his publick acts, he should watch himself, as under a government of another sort he would watch his rulers; or as vigilantly as he watches the servants of the community at home; for, though possessing the power in the last resort, it is not so absolutely an irresponsible power as it first seems, coming from God, and to be wielded on those convictions of right which God has implanted in our breasts, that we may know good from evil.

On the Private Duties of Station

The private duties of the citizen, as connected with social station, are founded chiefly on the relations between man and man, though others may be referred to a higher source, being derived directly from the relations between the creature and his creator.

A regard for the duties of private station, are indispensable to order, and to the intercourse between different members of society. So important have they always been deemed, that the inspired writers, from the Saviour through the greatest of his apostles down, have deemed them worthy of being placed in conspicious characters, in their code of morals.

The first direct mandates of God, as delivered on Mount Sinai, were to impress the Jews with a sense of their duties to their Heavenly Father; the next to impress them with the first of their social duties, that of honor and obedience to their parents.

The fifth commandment, then, may be said to contain the first of our social duties. It is strictly one of station, for it enforces the obligation of the child to its parents. Nor is this all; the entire extent of the family relations are included in principle, since it cannot be supposed that those who precede our immediate parents, are excluded from the general deference that we owe to the greater experience, the love, and the care of our predecessors.

It is apparent throughout the code of christian morals, that a perfect reciprocity between the duties of social station is nowhere inferred. "Nevertheless," says St. Paul, "let every one of you in particular, so love his wife, even as himself; and the wife *see* that she *reverence* her husband." There is an obligation of deference imposed on the wife, that is not imposed on the husband. "Servants be obedient to them that are your masters according to the flesh, with fear and trembling, in singleness of heart, as unto Christ." By these, and many similar mandates, we perceive that the private duties of station are constantly recognized, and commanded, by the apostles, as well as by the Saviour.

The old abuses of power, with the attendant reaction, have unsettled the publick mind, in many essential particulars, on this important point. Interested men have lent their aid to mislead the credulous and vain, until a confusion in the relations between the different members of society has arisen, that must, more or less, lead to confusion in society itself.

After the direct family relations, come the private duties that are generally connected with station, as between master and servant.

Whoever employs, with the right to command, is a master; and, whoever serves, with an obligation to obey, a servant. These are the broad signification of the two words, and, in this sense they are now used.

It is an imperative obligation on those who command, to be kind in language, however firm, and to use a due consideration in issuing their orders. The greater the duty of those, whose part it is to obey, to comply with all just and reasonable requisitions, or, in other words, to conform to the terms of their service, the greater is the duty of the master to see that he does not exact more than propriety will warrant. On the other hand, they who serve owe a respectful and decorous obedience, showing by their manner as well by their acts, they understand that without order and deference, the different social relations can never be suitably filled. So far from republican institutions making any difference in this respect, in favor of him who serves, they increase the moral duty to be respectful and assiduous, since service in such a case, is not the result of political causes, but a matter of convention, or bargain.

The relations between the master and the domestic servant, are peculiar, and are capable of being made of a very endearing and useful nature. The house servant, whether man or woman, fills a more honorable, because a much more confidential station, than the lower mechanic, or farm laborer. The domestics are intrusted with the care of the children of those they serve, have necessarily charge of much valuable property, and are, in a manner, intrusted with the secrets of the domestic economy. The upper servants of a considerable and well bred family, or of those who are accustomed to the station they fill, and have not been too suddenly elevated by the chances of life, are often persons of a good education, accustomed to accounts, and, in a measure, familiarized to the usages of polite life, since they see them daily practised before their eyes. Such persons invariably gain some of the refinement and tone of mind that marks the peculiar condition of their employers.

The rule of most civilized nations, is for the master to treat the servant as an humble friend. In the more polished countries of Europe, the confidential domestic holds a high place in the household, and, after a long service, is commonly considered as an inferior member of the family.

It is a misfortune of America to admit so many of the dogmas of the country from which she is derived, while living in a state of society so very different. An attempt to treat and consider a domestic, as domestics are treated and considered in England, is unwise, and, in fact, impracticable. The English servant fares worse, in many particulars, than the servant of almost every other nation. France would be a better and a safer model, in this particular, the masters of France being usually much milder and more considerate than those of England, while the servants are altogether superior. The French servant is not as cleanly and thorough in his work, as the English servant, a difference in the habits of the country forbidding it; but he is generally more attached, better informed, more agreeable as a companion, quite as serviceable, the exception mentioned apart, and more faithful, honest and prudent. This is true of both sexes; the female domestics of France, while less tidy in household work than those of England or America, being altogether superior to both, in moral qualities, tastes, general usefulness and knowledge.

A beautiful instance of the effect of the duties of social station is before the eyes of the writer, even while he pens this paragraph; that of an aged woman, who passed her youth in the service of one family, ministering to the wants of three generations, and is now receiving the gratitude which long and patient toil has earned. On the one side is affection, delicacy, and attention to the wants of age; on the other a love little short of that of a mother's, softened by the respect that has always marked the life of one in whom a sense of the duties of social station has never been weakened. Nothing still makes this venerable servant more happy, than to be employed for those whom she has seen ushered into life, whom she first fondled on the knee, while these, again, mindful of her years and increasing infirmities, feel it a source of pleasure to anticipate her little wants, and to increase her comforts. The conditions of master and servant are those of co-relatives, and when they are properly understood they form additional ties to the charities and happiness of life. It is an unhappy effect of the unformed habits of society in this country, and of domestic slavery, that we are so much wanting in this beautiful feature in domestic economy.

The social duties of a gentleman are of a high order. The class to which he belongs is the natural repository of the manners, tastes, tone, and, to a certain extent, of the principles of a country. They who imagine this portion of the community useless, drones who consume without producing, have not studied society, or they have listened to the suggestions of personal envy, instead of consulting history and facts. If the laborer is indispensable to civilization, so is also the gentleman. While the one produces, the other directs his skill to those arts which raise the polished man above the barbarian. The last brings his knowledge and habits to bear upon industry, and, taking the least favorable view of his claims, the indulgence of his very luxuries encourages the skill that contributes to the comforts of the lowest.

Were society to be satisfied with a mere supply of the natural wants, there would be no civilization. The savage condition attains this much. All beyond it, notwithstanding, is so much progress made in the direction of the gentleman, and has been made either at the suggestions, or by the encouragement of those whose means have enabled, and whose tastes have induced them to buy. Knowledge is as necessary to the progress of a people as physical force, for, with our knowledge, the beasts of burthen who now toil for man, would soon compel man to toil for them. If the head is necessary to direct the body, so is the head of society, (the head in a social, if not in a political sense,) necessary to direct the body of society.

Any one may learn the usefulness of a body of enlightened men in a neighborhood, by tracing their influence on its civilization. Where many such are found, the arts are more advanced, and men learn to see that there are tastes more desirable than those of the mere animal. In such a neighborhood they acquire habits which contribute to their happiness by advancing their intellect, they learn the value of refinement in their intercourse, and obtain juster notions of the nature and of the real extent of their rights. He who would honor learning, and taste, and sentiment, and refinement of every sort, ought to respect its possessors, and, in all things but those which affect rights, defer to their superior advantages. This is the extent of the deference that is due from him who is not a gentleman, to him who is; but this much is due.

On the other hand, the social duties of an American gentleman, in particular, require of him a tone of feeling and a line of conduct that are of the last importance to the country. One of the first of his obligations is to be a guardian of the liberties of his fellow citizens. It is peculiarly graceful in the American, whom the accidents of life have raised above the mass of the nation, to show himself conscious of his duties in this respect, by asserting at all times the true principles of government, avoiding, equally, the cant of demagogueism with the impracticable theories of visionaries, and the narrow and selfish dogmas of those who would limit power by castes. They who do not see and feel the importance of possessing a class of such men in a community, to give it tone, a high and far sighted policy, and lofty views in general, can know little of history, and have not reflected on the inevitable consequences of admitted causes.

The danger to the institutions of denying to men of education their proper place in society, is derived from the certainty that no political system can long continue in which this violence is done to the natural rights of a class so powerful. It is as unjust to require that men of refinement and training should defer in their habits and associations to the notions of those who are their inferiors in these particulars, as it is to insist that political power should be the accompaniment of birth. All, who are in the least cultivated, know how irksome and oppressive is the close communion with ignorance and vulgarity, and the attempt to push into the ordinary associations, the principles of equality that do and ought to govern states in their political characters, is, virtually, an effort to subvert a just general maxim, by attaching to it impracticable consequences.

Whenever the enlightened, wealthy, and spirited of an affluent and great country, seriously conspire to subvert democratical institutions, their leisure, money, intelligence and means of combining, will be found too powerful for the ill-directed and conflicting efforts of the mass. It is therefore, all important, to enlist a portion of this class, at least, in the cause of freedom, since its power at all times renders it a dangerous enemy.

Liberality is peculiarly the quality of a gentleman. He is liberal in his attainments, opinions, practices and concessions. He asks for himself, no more than he is willing to concede to others. He feels that his superiority is in his attainments, practices and principles, which if they are not always moral, are above meannesses, and he has usually no pride in the mere vulgar consequence of wealth. Should he happen to be well born, (for birth is by no means indispensable to the character,) his satisfaction is in being allied to men of the same qualities as himself, and not to a senseless pride in an accident. The vulgar-minded mistake motives that they cannot feel; but he, at least, is capable of distinguishing between things that are false, and the things which make him what he is.

An eminent writer of our own time, has said in substance, that a nation is happy, in which the people, possessing the power to select their rulers, select the noble. This was the opinion of a European, who had been accustomed to see the liberal qualities in the exclusive possession of a caste, and who was not accustomed to see the people sufficiently advanced to mingle in affairs of state. Power cannot be extended to a *caste*, without *caste's* reaping its principal benefit; but happy, indeed, is the nation, in which, power being the common property, there is sufficient discrimination and justice to admit the intelligent and refined to a just participation of its influence.

AN ARISTOCRAT AND A DEMOCRAT

We live in an age, when the words aristocrat and democrat are much used, without regard to the real significations. An aristocrat is one of a few, who possess the political power of a country; a democrat, one of the many. The words are also properly applied to those who entertain notions favorable to aristocratical, or democratical forms of government. Such persons are not, necessarily, either aristocrats, or democrats in fact, but merely so in opinion. Thus a member of a democratical government may have an aristocratical bias, and *vice versa*.

To call a man who has the habits and opinions of a gentleman, an aristocrat, from that fact alone, is an abuse of terms, and betrays ignorance of the true principles of government, as well as of the world. It must be an equivocal freedom, under which every one is not the master of his own innocent acts and associations, and he is a sneaking democrat, indeed, who will submit to be dictated to, in those habits over which neither law nor morality assumes a right of control.

Some men fancy that a democrat can only be one who seeks the level, social, mental and moral, of the majority, a rule that would at once exclude all men of refinement, education and taste from the class. These persons are enemies of democracy, as they at once render it impracticable. They are usually great sticklers for their own associations and habits, too, though unable to comprehend any of a nature that are superior. They are, in truth, aristocrats in principle, though assuming a contrary pretension; the ground work of all their feelings and arguments being self. Such is not the intention of liberty, whose aim is to leave every man to be the master of his own acts; denying hereditary honors, it is true, as unjust and unnecessary, but not denying the inevitable consequences of civilization.

The law of God is the only rule of conduct, in this, as in other matters. Each man should do as he would be done by. Were the question put to the greatest advocate of indiscriminate association, whether he would submit to have his company and habits dictated to him, he would be one of the first to resist the tyranny; for they, who are the most rigid in maintaining their own claims, in such matters, are usually the loudest in decrying those whom they fancy to be better off than themselves. Indeed, it may be taken as a rule in social intercourse, that he who is the most apt to question the pretensions of others, is the most conscious of the doubtful position he himself occupies; thus establishing the very claims he affects to deny, by letting his jealousy of it be seen. Manners, education and refinement, are positive things, and they bring with them innocent tastes which are productive of high enjoyments; and it is as unjust to deny their possessors their indulgence, as it would be to insist on the less fortunate's passing the time they would rather devote to athletic amusements, in listening to operas for which they have no relish, sung in a language they do not understand.

All that democracy means, is as equal a participation in rights as is practicable; and to pretend that social equality is a condition of popular institutions, is to assume that the latter are destructive of civilization, for, as nothing is more self-evident than the impossibility of raising all men to the highest standard of tastes and refinement, the alternative would be to reduce the entire community to the lowest. The whole embarrasment on this point exists in the difficulty of making men comprehend qualities they do not themselves possess. We can all perceive the difference between ourselves and our inferiors, but when it comes to a question of the difference between us and our superiors, we fail to appreciate merits of which we have no proper conceptions. In face of this obvious difficulty, there is the safe and just governing rule, already mentioned, or that of permitting every one to be the undisturbed judge of his own habits and associations, so long as they are innocent, and do not impair the rights of others to be equally judges for themselves. It follows, that social intercourse must regulate itself, independently of institutions, with the exception that the latter, while they withold no natural, bestow no factitious advantages beyond those which are inseparable from the rights of property, and general civilization.

In a democracy, men are just as free to aim at the highest attainable places in society, as to obtain the largest fortunes; and it would be clearly unworthy of all noble sentiment to say, that the grovelling competition for money shall alone be free, while that which enlists all the liberal acquirements and elevated sentiments of the race, is denied the democrat. Such an avowal would be at once, a declaration of the inferiority of the system, since nothing but ignorance and vulgarity could be its fruits.

The democratic gentleman must differ in many essential particulars, from the aristocratical gentleman, though in their ordinary habits and tastes they are virtually indentical. Their principles vary; and, to a slight degree, their deportment accordingly. The democrat, recognizing the right of all to participate in power, will be more liberal in his general sentiments, a quality of superiority in itself; but, in conceding this much to his fellow man, he will proudly maintain his own independence of vulgar domination, as indispensable to his personal habits. The same principles and manliness that would induce him to depose a royal despot, would induce him to resist a vulgar tyrant.

There is no more capital, though more common error, than to suppose him an aristocrat who maintains his independence of habits; for democracy asserts the control of the majority, only, in matters of law, and not in matters of custom. The very object of the institution is the utmost practicable personal liberty, and to affirm the contrary, would be sacrificing the end to the means.

An aristocrat, therefore, is merely one who fortifies his exclusive privileges by positive institutions, and a democrat, one who is willing to admit of a free competition, in all things. To say, however, that the last supposes this competition will lead to nothing, is an assumption that means are employed without any reference to an end. He is the purest democrat who best maintains his rights, and no rights can be dearer to a man of cultivation, than exemptions from unseasonable invasions on his time, by the coarse-minded and ignorant.

On Demagogues

A demagogue, in the strict signification of the word, is "a leader of the rabble." It is a Greek compound, that conveys this meaning. In these later times, however, the signification has been extended to suit the circumstances of the age. Thus, before the art of printing became known, or cheap publications were placed within the reach of the majority, the mass of all nations might properly enough be termed a rabble, when assembled in bodies. In nations in which attention is paid to education, this reproach is gradually becoming unjust, though a body of Americans, even, collected under what is popularly termed an "excitement," losing sight of that reason and respect for their own deliberately framed ordinances, which alone distinguish them from the masses of other people, is neither more nor less than a rabble. Men properly derive their designations from their acts, and not from their professions.

The peculiar office of a demagogue is to advance his own interests, by affecting a deep devotion to the interests of the people. Sometimes the object is to indulge malignancy, unprincipled and selfish men submitting but to two governing motives, that of doing good to themselves, and that of doing harm to others. The true theatre of a demagogue is a democracy, for the body of the community possessing the power, the master he pretends to serve is best able to reward his efforts. As it is all important to distinguish between those who labor in behalf of the people on the general account, and those who labor in behalf of the people on their own account, some of the rules by which each may be known shall be pointed out.

The motive of the demagogue may usually be detected in his conduct. The man who is constantly telling the people that they are unerring in judgment, and that they have all power, is a demagogue. Bodies of men being composed of individuals, can no more be raised above the commission of error, than individuals themselves, and, in many situations, they are more likely to err, from self-excitement and the division of responsibility. The power of the people is limited by the fundamental laws, or the constitution, the rights and opinions of the minority, in all but those cases in which a decision becomes indispensable, being just as sacred as the rights and opinions of the majority; else would a democracy be, indeed, what its enemies term it, the worst species of tyranny. In this instance, the people are flattered, in order to be led; as in kingdoms, the prince is blinded to his own defects, in order to extract favor from him.

The demagogue always puts the people before the constitution and the laws, in face of the obvious truth that the people have placed the constitution and the laws before themselves.

The local demagogue does not distinguish between the whole people and a part of the people, and is apt to betray his want of principles by contending for fancied, or assumed rights, in favor of a county, or a town, though the act is obviously opposed to the will of the nation. This is a test that the most often betrays the demagogue, for while loudest in proclaiming his devotion to the majority, he is, in truth, opposing the will of the entire people, in order to effect his purposes with a part.

The demagogue is usually sly, a detractor of others, a professor of humility and disinterestedness, a great stickler for equality as respects all above him, a man who acts in corners, and avoids open and manly expositions of his course, calls blackguards gentlemen, and gentlemen folks, appeals to passions and prejudices rather than to reason, and is in all respects, a man of intrigue and deception, of sly cunning and management, instead of manifesting the frank, fearless qualities of the democracy he so prodigally professes.

The man who maintains the rights of the people on pure grounds, may be distinguished from the demagogue by the reverse of all these qualities. He does not flatter the people, even while he defends them, for he knows that flattery is a corrupting and dangerous poison. Having nothing to conceal, he is frank and fearless, as are all men with the consciousness of right motives. He oftener chides than commends, for power needs reproof and can dispense with praise.

He who would be a courtier under a king, is almost certain to be a demagogue in a democracy. The elements are the same, though, brought into action under different circumstances, ordinary observers are apt to fancy them the extremes of opposite moral castes. Travellers have often remarked, that, Americans, who have made themselves conspicuous abroad for their adulation of rank and power, have become zealous advocates of popular supremacy, on returning home. Several men of this stamp are, at this moment, in conspicuous political stations in the country, having succeeded by the commonest arts of courtiers.

There is a large class of political men in this country, who, while they scarcely merit the opprobium of being termed demagogues, are not properly exempt from the imputation of falling into some of their most dangerous vices. These are they, whose habits, and tastes, and better opinions, indeed, are all at variance with vulgar errors and vulgar practices, but, who imagine it a necessary evil in a democracy to defer to prejudices, and ignorance, and even to popular jealousies and popular injustice, that a safe direction may be given to the publick mind. Such men deceive themselves, in the first place, as to their own motives, which are rather their private advancement than the publick good, and, admitting the motives to be pure, they err greatly both in their mode of construing the system under which they live, and in the general principles of correcting evil and of producing good. As the greatest enemy of truth is falsehood, so is the most potent master of falsehood, truth. These qualities are correlatives; that which is not true, being false; and that which is not false, being true. It follows, as a pervading rule of morals, that the advancement of one is the surest means of defeating the other. All good men desire the truth, and, on all publick occasions on which it is necessary to act at all, the truth would be the most certain, efficient, and durable agency in defeating falsehoods, whether of prejudices, reports, or principles. The perception of truth is an attribute of reason, and the ground-work of all institutions that claim to be founded in justice, is this high quality. Temporary convenience, and selfish considerations, beyond a doubt, are both favored by sometimes closing the eyes to the severity of truth, but in nothing is the sublime admonition of God in his commandments, where he tells us that he "will visit the sins of the fathers unto the third and fourth generations of their children," more impressively verified, than in the inevitable punishments that await every sacrifice of truth.

Most of the political men of the day belong to this class of doubtful moralists, who, mistaking a healthful rule, which admonishes us that even truth ought not to be too offensively urged, in their desire to be moderate, lend themselves to the side of error. The ingenuity of sophisms, and the audacity of falsehoods receive great support from this mistaken alliance, since a firm union of all the intelligent of a country, in the cause of plain and obvious truths, would exterminate their correlative errors, the publick opinion which is now enlisted in the support of the latter, following to the right side, as a matter of course, in the train of combined knowledge. This is the mode in which opinions rooted in the wrong have been gradually eradicated, by the process of time, but which would yield faster, were it not for the latitude and delusion that selfishness imposes on men of this class, who flatter themselves with soothing a sore that they are actually irritating. The consequence of this mistaken forbearance, is to substitute a new set of errors, for those which it has already taken ages to get rid of.

On the subject of government and society, it is a misfortune that this country is filled with those who take the opposite extremes, the one side clinging to prejudices that were founded in the abuses of the feudal times, and the other to the exaggerations of impracticable theories. That the struggle is not fiercer, is probably owing to the overwhelming numbers of the latter class, but, as things are, truth is a sufferer.

The American *doctrinaire* is the converse of the American demagogue, and, in his way, is scarcely less injurious to the publick. He is as much a visionary on one side, as the extreme theoretical democrat is a visionary on the other. The first deals in poetry, the last in cant. The first affirms a disin-terestedness and purity in education and manners, when exposed to the corruption of power, that all experience refutes; and the last an infallibility in majorities that God himself has denied. These opposing classes produce the effect of all counter-acting forces, resistance, and they provoke each other's excesses.

In the *doctrinaire,* or theorist of the old school, we see men clinging to opinions that are purely the issue of arbitrary facts, ages after the facts themselves have ceased to exist, confounding cause with effect; and, in the demagogue, or his tool, the impracticable democrat, one who permits envy, jealousy, opposition, selfishness, and the unconsciousness of his own inferiority and demerits, so far to blind his faculties, as to obscure the sense of justice, to exclude the sight of positive things, and to cause him to deny the legitimate consequences of the very laws of which he professes to be proud. This is the dupe who affirms that, "one man is as good as another."

These extremes lead to the usual inconsistencies and follies. Thus do we see men, who sigh for titles and factitious and false distinctions, so little conscious of truth, as to shrink from asserting the real distinctions of their social station, or those they actually and undeniably possess; as if nature ever intended a man for an aristocrat, who has not the manhood to maintain his just rights; and those, again, who cant of equality and general privileges, while they stubbornly refuse to permit others to enjoy in peace a single fancied indulgence or taste, unless taken in their company, although nature, education and habits have all unfitted them to participate, and their presence would be sure to defeat what they could not, in the nature of things, enjoy.

The considerate, and modest, and just-minded man, of whatever social class, will view all this differently. In asserting his own rights, he respects those of others; in indulging his own tastes, he is willing to admit there may be superior; in pursuing his own course, in his own manner, he knows his neighbor has an equal right to do the same; and, most of all, is he impressed with the great moral truths, that flatterers are inherently miscreants, that fallacies never fail to bring their punishments, and that the empire of God is reason.

On Representation

Representation is the vital principle of all free governments, with the exception of those which rule over unusually small territories. A pure democracy infers institutions under which the people, in primary assemblies, enact their own laws; a system of which the good is questionable under any circumstances, and which is evidently impracticable in large communities. The governments of the several states of this Union, with some slight modifications, are representative democracies, and as the federal government receives its distinctive character from the states, themselves, the latter is necessarily a confederated representative democracy. Representation, therefore, lies at the root of the entire American system.

Conflicting opinions exist on the subject of the relations between the representative and his constituent, impracticable notions and contradictory errors being equally maintained. These notions may be divided into those of two schools, equally ultra, one taking its rise in the sophisms and mystifications of English politics, the other arising from the disposition of men to obtain their objects, by flattering popular power. The subject is grave, and all important to a country like this.

With the exception of a few popular boroughs, and a county or two, England has no free representation. In most of the counties, even, the control of the elections is in the hands of the great land-holders; in far the larger number of the boroughs, the power of the landlords is so great, that they name the successful candidate, as openly as the minister himself names to official employments. In the case of contested elections, even, the struggle is really between the power of two or more great families, and not between bodies of the electors, seats for boroughs being bought and sold like any other commodity. Under such circumstances, it is quite apparent that instructions from a constituency, that is itself instructed whom to return, would be a useless mockery. We are not to look at England, therefore, for principles on this subject, the fundamental systems of the two countries being so dissimilar; one giving power to property, the other to numbers.

There is no doubt it is the intention of the American system, that the will of the constitutional majorities, to a certain extent, should be properly regarded by the representative; and that when the latter, who has been elected with the express understanding that he is to support a particular measure, or a particular set of principles, sees reason to change his opinion, he would act most in conformity with the spirit of the institutions, by resigning his trust. All human contracts are made subject to certain predominant moral obligations, which are supposed to emanate from Divine Truth. Thus, a representative, conscientiously entertaining convictions in its favour, may give a pledge to support a particular measure, as a condition of his election, there being no sufficient reason to doubt that the doctrine of specific pledges is sound, the people having a free option to exact them, and the candidate as free an option to withhold them, as each may see fit. These pledges, however, must be in conformity with the spirit and letter of the constitution, and not opposed to good morals; the first being a governing condition of the social compact, and the last a controlling principle of human actions. But, while this much is admitted in favor of the power of the constituency, great care must be had not to extend it too far.

In the first place, no constituency has a right to violate the honest convictions of a representative. These are a matter of conscience, and, if the subject be of sufficient magnitude to involve conscientious scruples, the power of the representative is full and absolute. This freedom of conscience is an implied obligation of the compact between the parties; therefore, in a case of importance, that admits of moral doubts, and one in which the will of the constituency is unequivocally expressed, it becomes the representative to return the trust, and this, too, in season, circumstances allowing, to permit the other party to be represented in the matter, agreeably to its own opinions. As there are so many governing circumstances of great delicacy, in all such cases, it is evident they must be rare, and that the rule exists as an exception, rather than as one of familiar practice.

Great care must be always taken to see that the wishes of the constituency are actually consulted, before the American representative is bound, morally even, to respect their will; for there is no pretence that the obligation to regard the wishes of his constituents is more than implied, under any circumstances; the social compact, in a legal sense, leaving him the entire master of his own just convictions. The instant a citizen is elected he becomes the representative of the minority as well as of the majority, and to create any of the implied responsibility that has been named, the opinion of the first, so far as their numbers go, is just as much entitled to respect, as the opinion of the last. The power to decide, in cases of elections, is given to the majority only from necessity, and as the safest practicable general rule that can be used, but, it is by no means the intention of the institutions to disfranchise all those who prefer another to the successful candidate. The choice depends on a hundred considerations that are quite independent of measures, men judging differently from each other, in matters of character. Any other rule than this might be made the means of putting the government in the hands of the minority, as the following case will show.

A, is elected to congress, by a vote of one thousand and one, against a vote of nine hundred and ninety-nine. He has, consequently, two thousand constitutents, supposing all to have voted. The majority meet to instruct their representative, and the instructions are carried by a vote of five hundred and one to five hundred. If these instructions are to be received as binding, the government, so far as the particular measure is concerned, may be in the hands of five hundred and one electors, as opposed to fourteen hundred and ninety-nine. This case may be modified, by all the changes incidental to numbers.

To assume that majorities of caucuses, or of *ex parte* collections of electors, have a right to instruct, is to pretend that the government is a government of party, and not a government of the people. This notion cannot honestly be maintained for an instant. Recommendations emanating from such a source may be entitled to a respectful consideration, but not more so than a counter-recommendation from an opposing party. In all such cases, the intention of the representative system is to constitute the representative a judge between the conflicting opinions, as judges at law are intended to settle questions of law, both being sworn to act on the recognized principles that control society.

In the cases that plainly invade the constitution, the constituents having no power themselves, can dictate none to their representative. Both parties are bound equally to respect that instrument, and neither can evade the obligation, by any direct, or indirect means. This rule covers much of the disputed ground, for they who read the constitution with an honest desire to understand it, can have little difficulty in comprehending most of its important provisions, and no one can claim a right to impose sophistry and selfishness on another, as reason and justice.

As doubtful cases may certainly arise under the constitution, the right of the constituency to influence the representative in instances of that sort, may plausibly be supposed to be greater than in those of constructions plainly proceeding from the excitement and schemes of partisans. Still the power of the constituency to interfere, *after an election,* beyond the right to urge their own sentiments, as opinions entitled to particular respect from their particular representative, is very questionable. The constitution contains the paramount laws of society. These laws are unchangeable, except as they are altered agreeably to prescribed forms, and until thus altered, no evasion of them is admissible. In the necessity of things, every public functionary must be permitted to interpret this instrument for himself, subject to the liabilities and responsibilities, official and otherwise, of his station. In this respect, the legislator, by the nature of his trust, having full power to enact and to repeal, knows no other control than his conscience. The expressed compact between the representative and the constituent, gives to the first an absolute discretionary power, subject to this great rule, and, by the implied, no instructions can ever weaken this high obligation, since it is clearly a governing condition of the bargain between them.

A judge is representative, in a government like this, in a general sense, since he acts for and through the people. Now, it will not be pretended that the people can instruct the courts how to interpret the constitution, although they can alter it, nor should it be contended that the constituency can instruct a representative how to interpret the constitution, when it involves a matter of conscience. The remedy, in the one case, is to alter the constitution; and in the other, to send a new representative, with pledges given previously to the election, to interpret the constitution according to the conceptions of the right, entertained by the constituency. Of course such a pledge ought not to be given, unless given conscientiously.

The constitution specifically guaranties the right of the citizens to assemble and *petition* congress, a provision that would be a mockery, did that instrument suppose a right to *instruct*.

It has been said that the representative, has the same relations to the minority, as to the majority of his constituents, when elected. In a broader and equally binding sense, he has the same relations to the entire country, as to his own immediate constituents, else would legislation be reduced to a mere contest of local interests, without a regard to justice or to general principles. If this be true, and it must be true, or all the fundamental governing rules of the social compact become of no account, the constituents of a particular representative can have no right even to request, much less to instruct him to support their local interests at the expence of others, and least of all can they have a right to violate the constitution, in order to do so. In this particular, the question has been involved in the same sophisms, and, to a degree, is to be settled by the same principles, as those which appertain to the relations between the accused and his legal counsel. Some latitudinarians in morals have contended that the legal adviser of an accused has a right to do in his defence, whatever the accused himself would do; that he is an attorney, with full powers to execute all that the other's feelings, interests and passions might dictate. This is monstrous and untenable doctrine, being destructive of all moral responsibility, to say nothing of the laws. The counsel, has a *right* to do no more than his client has a *right* to do, nor can the constituent, in any case, have a right to instruct his representative to do that which he has no right, in a moral or legal sense, to do himself, even admitting the general doctrine of instruction to be sound.

Although the principle that the representative chosen by a few, becomes the representative of all, is sound as a general principle, it is not an unqualified rule any where, and still less so in the federal government. The constitution requires that the representative should reside in the state from which he is sent, expressly to identify him with its particular interests, and in order to prevent that concentration which exists in other countries. Half the French deputies are from Paris, and a large portion of the English members of parliament are virtually from the capital. Their systems are peculiarly systems of concentration, but ours is as peculiarly a system of diffusion. It may be questioned, therefore, how far the American representative ought to sacrifice the good of his particular state, in order to achieve the general good. Cases may certainly occur, in which the sacrifice ought to be made, but the union of these states is founded on an express compromise, and it is not its intention to reach a benefit, however considerable, by extorting undue sacrifices from particular members of the confederacy. All cases to the contrary should be clear, and the necessary relations between the good and evil, beyond cavil.

In identified governments, the principle that a few shall be sacrificed to the general good, must always, in a greater or less degree, prevail; but it is not the intention of the American compact that any one state should ruin itself, or even do itself any great and irreparable injury, that the rest of the Union should become more prosperous. In this sense, then, the member of congress represents his immediate constituents, or perhaps it would be better to say his immediate state, and although he has no right to further its interests at the expense of the interests of other states, he is not called on to sacrifice them for the benefit of the sisters of the Union. This is one of the cases in which the doctrines of English representation do not apply to the American system. The difference arises from the circumstance that, in the one case, government is a compact between persons; in the other, a compact between states.

In a government like that of the United States, the executive is as much representative as the legislature. Will it therefore be pretended that the president is also bound to respect the instructions of the people? Is he to appoint those whom the people will, remove those whom the people denounce, pardon those whom the people order, and approve of such bills as the people dictate? Is he to command the army and navy, see that the laws are executed, and conduct the negotiations of the country according to the opinions and intimations of a majority of his constituents, or according to his own conceptions of duty, and the light of his own knowledge and experience? If the representative is bound to obey the will of his constituents, all this must the president do, or prove false to the institutions. As the commander in chief, his own soldiers would have a right to instruct him in the mode of performing his military functions, as, indeed, they would have a right to tell congress, when and against whom to declare war!

If the representative of the executive functions is thus bound to respect instructions, a majority of the people might virtually repeal an unpopular law, by instructing the president not to see it enforced, and thus destroy the rights of third parties. Such a doctrine would throw society into confusion, leave nothing stable, and set up a dangerous and irresponsible power, that would be stronger than the institutions themselves.

A principle reason for sending representatives to congress, is the impossibility of masses of men meeting to legislate with due knowledge and deliberation, and it can scarcely be contended that the results which cannot be obtained by any expedient of law, method and arrangement, are to be expected from extra-legal, voluntary and immethodical means. We ought not, consequently, to give an authority to those opinions of the people informally expressed, that the constitution would seem to show cannot be rendered available, when formally expressed.

The term representative implies full power to act, or, at least, full power to act under the limitations that environ the trust. A delegate is less gifted with authority, and is understood to act under instructions. These are ancient distinctions, and, existing as they did at the time the constitution was framed, they are entitled to respect, as explaining its intention. A representative is a *substitute;* a delegate an *ambassador.* It is, moreover, an admission of imbecility to suppose that the institutions infer a right to instruct, when no such right is expressed. All the machinery of the state is opposed to it, while in other countries, as in Switzerland, where the delegate acts under instructions, the machinery of the state is framed to meet such an end.

Upon the whole, when we take into consideration the received signification of terms, as they were understood when the constitution was framed; the legal effect of legislative acts, which are binding, though the entire constituency instruct to the contrary; the omission in the constitution to point out any legal means of instructing, and the practical difficulties in obtaining instructions that shall be above the reproach of being *ez parte* and insufficient; the permanent obligations of the constitution; the doubt and indecision instructions would introduce into a government, that was expressly framed to obviate these weaknesses; the dangers that constantly arise from the activity of the designing, and the supineness of the well-meaning; the want of unity, and of fixed principles, it might give to a legislation that controls peace and war, and the foreign relations; as well as the exposure to foreign influence directly exercised over irresponsible men; and the general character of deliberation and examination which is secured to congress, which may be called on to act on information known only to itself; we are led to conclude that the doctrine of instruction is unconstitutional, whether as applied to the senate, or to the house of representatives, and that so far from being a doctrine that is adapted to secure the domination of real majorities, it is rather an invention of intriguing politicians to effect their own wishes, in opposition to those of the nation. Exceptions may occur, but governing principles are to be settled on general rules, and by general effects.

It being established that the representative is placed beyond the control of instructions, as beyond doubt is, at least, his legal position, the importance of making careful selections, becomes apparent. There is no safer rule in selecting a representative, than that already named; or that of choosing the man for public confidence, who may be relied on, in private. Most of all is the time-server and demagogue to be avoided, for such a man is certain to use power as an instrument of his private good. It is a mistake to suppose, on correct principles, that the representative is the obliged party. The man who faithfully does his duty in congress, is a servant to whom a difficult task is assigned, with a very insufficient compensation; and such a man should always be selected with care, and rewarded with a frank gratitude.

It is a painful admission, extorted by truth, that in human institutions, the intention is never long respected. Representation may not be in practice, what it was intended for, in theory, but, still, it might be drawn much nearer to what it ought to be, than it actually is. If party be not necessary to this government as a good, it is, perhaps, unavoidable as an evil. But no elector should ever submit himself so implicitly to party as to support a man whose private acts prove him to be unfit for a public trust. The basis of the representative system is character, and without character, no man should be confided in. In discriminating between candidates, however, it should be remembered that there are "wolves in sheep's clothing," in character, as well as in other things. Personal vanity induces ordinary men to confide most in those who most flatter their frailties, but, it is a tolerably safe rule that he who is not afraid to speak the truth, is not afraid to act the truth; and truths, moral, political and social, are peculiarly the aim of this government.

ON CANDOR

Candor is a proof of both a just frame of mind, and of a good tone of breeding. It is a quality that belongs, equally to the honest man and to the gentleman: to the first, as doing to others as we would ourselves be done by; to the last, as indispensable to the liberality of the character.

By candor we are not to understand trifling and uncalled for expositions of truth; but a sentiment that proves a conviction of the necessity of speaking truth, when speaking at all; a contempt for all designing evasions of our real opinions; and a deep conviction that he who deceives by necessary implication, deceives wilfully.

In all the general concerns, the publick has a right to be treated with candor. Without this manly and truly republican quality, republican because no power exists in the country to intimidate any from its exhibition, the institutions are converted into a stupendous fraud.

Foreigners reproach the Americans with a want of directness and candor, in conducting their ordinary intercourse. It is said that they dissemble thoughts that might properly be expressed, in the presence of the parties interested, to express them openly and in a way to insinuate more than is asserted, behind their backs. It is to be feared that this is a vice of humanity, but, still, one people may be more under its influence than another. It would be a singular and a false effect of freedom, to destroy a nation's character for candor; but we are not to be deceived by names, it being quite possible that a tyranny of opinion should produce such results, even in a democracy.

America is under many powerful influences, that have little connection with the institutions. The want of large towns, the scattered population, and the absence of much marked inequality of condition, necessarily lend a provincial character to the population, a character that every where favors the natural propensity of man to bring all his fellows within the control of his own strictures. The religionists who first settled the country, too, have aided in bringing individual opinion in subjection to publick opinion, and, as the latter is always controlled by combinations and design, consequently more or less to error. There is no doubt that these combined causes have had the effect to make a large portion of the population less direct, frank, candid and simple in the expression of their honest sentiments, and even in the relation of facts, than the laws of God, and the social duties require. It is to this feeling that the habit has arisen of making cautious and evasive answers, such as "I guess," "I conclude," "I some think," "I shouldn't wonder, if such a man had said so and so," when the speaker is the whole time confident of the fact. This practice has the reproach of insincerity and equivocation, is discreditable, makes intercourse treacherous and unsafe, and is beneath the frankness of freemen. In all these respects, a majority of the American people might take a useful lesson from the habits of England, a country which though remarkable for servility to superiors, can boast of more frankness in ordinary life, than our own.

Candor has the high merit of preventing misconceptions, simplifies intercourse, prevents more misunderstandings than equivocation, elevates character, inculcates the habit of sincerity, and has a general tendency to the manly and virtuous qualities.

ON LANGUAGE

Language being the medium of thought, its use enters into our most familiar practices. A just, clear and simple expression of our ideas is a necessary accomplishment for all who aspire to be classed with gentlemen and ladies. It renders all more respectable, besides making intercourse more intelligible, safer and more agreeable.

The common faults of American language are an ambition of effect, a want of simplicity, and a turgid abuse of terms. To these may be added ambiguity of expression. Many perversions of significations also exist, and a formality of speech, which, while it renders conversation ungraceful, and destroys its playfulness, seriously weakens the power of the language, by applying to ordinary ideas, words that are suited only to themes of gravity and dignity.

While it is true that the great body of the American people use their language more correctly than the mass of any other considerable nation, it is equally true that a smaller proportion than common attain to elegance in this accomplishment, especially in speech. Contrary to the general law in such matters, the women of the country have a less agreeable utterance than the men, a defect that great care should be taken to remedy, as the nursery is the birth-place of so many of our habits.

The limits of this work will not permit an enumeration of the popular abuses of significations, but a few shall be mentioned, in order that the student may possess a general clue to the faults. "Creek," a word that signifies an *inlet* of the sea, or of a lake, is misapplied to running streams, and frequently to the *outlets* of lakes. A "square," is called a "park;" "lakes," are often called "ponds;" and "arms of the sea," are sometimes termed "rivers."

In pronunciation, the faults are still more numerous, partaking decidedly of provincialisms. The letter *u,* sounded like double *o,* or *oo,* or like *i,* as in vir*too,* for*tin,* for*tinate*; and *ew,* pronounced also like *oo,* are common errors. This is an exceedingly vicious pronunciation, rendering the language mean and vulgar. "New," pronounced as "*noo,*" is an example, and "few," as "*foo;*" the true sounds are "*nu*" and "*fu,*" the *u* retaining its proper soft sound, and not that of "*oo.*"

The attempt to reduce the pronunciation of the English language to a common rule, produces much confusion, and taking the usages of polite life as the standard, many uncouth innovations. All know the pronunciation of p l o u g h; but it will scarcely do to take this sound as the only power of the same combination of final letters, for we should be compelled to call t h o u g h, thou; t h r o u g h, throu; and t o u g h, tou.

False accentuation is a common American fault. Ensign (insin,) is called en*syne,* and engine (injin,) en*gyne.* Indeed, it is a common fault of narrow associations, to suppose that words are to be pronounced as they are spelled.

Many words are in a state of mutation, the pronunciation being unsettled even in the best society, a result that must often arise where language is as variable and undetermined as the English. To this class belong "clerk," "cucumber" and "gold," which are often pronounced as spelt, though it were better and more in conformity with polite usage to say "clark," "*cow*-cumber," (not cow*cum*ber,) and "goold." For *loote*nant (lieutenant) there is not sufficient authority, the true pronunciation being "*leute*nant." By making a familiar compound of this word, we see the uselessness of attempting to reduce the language to any other laws than those of the usages of polite life, for they who affect to say *loote*nant, do not say "*loote*nant-co-lo-nel," but "*loote*nant-kurnel."

The polite pronunciation of "either" and "neither," is "i-ther" and "ni-ther," and not "eether" and "neether." This is a case in which the better usage of the language has respected derivations, for *"ei,"* in German are pronounced as in "height" and "sleight," *"ie"* making the sound of *"ee."* We see the arbitrary usages of the English, however, by comparing these legitimate sounds with those of the words "lieutenant colonel," which are derived from the French, in which language the latter word is called *"co-lo-nel."*

Some changes of the language are to be regretted, as they lead to false inferences, and society is always a loser by mistaking names for things. Life is a fact, and it is seldom any good arises from a misapprehension of the real circumstances under which we exist. The word "gentleman" has a positive and limited signification. It means one elevated above the mass of society by his birth, manners, attainments, character and social condition. As no civilized society can exist without these social differences, nothing is gained by denying the use of the term. If blackguards were to be *called* "gentlemen," and "gentlemen," "blackguards," the difference between them would be as obvious as it is to-day.

The word "gentleman," is derived from the French gentilhomme, which originally signified one of noble birth. This was at a time when the characteristics of the condition were never found beyond a caste. As society advanced, ordinary men attained the qualifications of nobility, without that of birth, and the meaning of the word was extended. It is now possible to be a gentleman without birth, though, even in America, where such distinctions are purely conditional, they who have birth, except in extraordinary instances, are classed with gentlemen. To call a laborer, one who has neither education, manners, accomplishments, tastes, associations, nor any one of the ordinary requisites, a gentleman, is just as absurd as to call one who is thus qualified, a fellow. The word must have some especial signification, or it would be synonymous with man. One may have gentleman-like feelings, principles and appearance, without possessing the liberal attainments that distinguish the gentleman. Least of all does money alone make a gentleman, though, as it becomes a means of obtaining the other requisites, it is usual to give it a place in the claims of the class. Men may be, and often are, very rich, without having the smallest title to be deemed gentlemen. A man may be a distinguished gentleman, and not possess as much money as his own footman.

This word, however, is sometimes used instead of the old terms, "sirs," "my masters," &c. &c., as in addressing bodies of men. Thus we say "gentlemen," in addressing a publick meeting, in complaisance, and as, by possibility, some gentlemen may be present. This is a license that may be tolerated, though he who should insist that all present were, as individuals, gentlemen, would hardly escape ridicule.

What has just been said of the word gentleman, is equally true with that of lady. The standard of these two classes, rises as society becomes more civilized and refined; the man who might pass for a gentleman in one nation, or community, not being able to maintain the same position in another.

The inefficiency of the effort to subvert things by names, is shown in the fact that, in all civilized communities, there is a class of men, who silently and quietly recognize each other, as gentlemen; who associate together freely and without reserve, and who admit each other's claims without scruple or distrust. This class may be limited by prejudice and arbitrary enactments, as in Europe, or it may have no other rules than those of taste, sentiment and the silent laws of usage, as in America.

The same observations may be made in relation to the words master and servant. He who employs laborers, with the right to command, is a master, and he who lets himself to work, with an obligation to obey, a servant. Thus there are house, or domestic servants, farm servants, shop servants, and various other servants; the term master being in all these cases the correlative.

In consequence of the domestic servants of America having once been negro-slaves, a prejudice has arisen among the laboring classes of the whites, who not only dislike the term servant, but have also rejected that of master. So far has this prejudice gone, that in lieu of the latter, they have resorted to the use of the word *boss,* which has precisely the same meaning in Dutch! How far a subterfuge of this nature is worthy of a manly and common sense people, will admit of question.

A similar objection may be made to the use of the word "help," which is not only an innovation on a just and established term, but which does not properly convey the meaning intended. They who aid their masters in the toil may be deemed "helps," but they who perform all the labor do not assist, or help to do the thing, but they do it themselves. A man does not usually hire his cook to *help* him cook his dinner, but to cook it herself. Nothing is therefore gained, while something is lost in simplicity and clearness by the substitution of new and imperfect terms, for the long established words of the language. In all cases in which the people of America have retained the *things* of their ancestors, they should not be ashamed to keep the *names.*

The love of turgid expressions is gaining ground, and ought to be corrected. One of the most certain evidences of a man of high breeding, is his simplicity of speech; a simplicity that is equally removed from vulgarity and exaggeration. He calls a spade, a "spade." His enunciation, while clear, deliberate and dignified, is totally without strut, showing his familiarity with the world, and, in some degree, reflecting the qualities of his mind, which is polished without being addicted to sentimentalism, or any other bloated feeling. He never calls his wife, "his lady," but "his wife," and he is not afraid of lessening the dignity of the human race, by styling the most elevated and refined of his fellow creatures, "men and women." He does not say, in speaking of a dance, that "the attire of the ladies was exceedingly elegant and peculiarly becoming at the late assembly," but that "the women were well dressed at the last ball;" nor is he apt to remark, "that the Rev. Mr. G— gave us an elegant and searching discourse the past sabbath," but, that "the parson preached a good sermon last sunday."

The utterance of a gentleman ought to be deliberate and clear, without being measured. All idea of effort should be banished, though nothing lost for want of distinctness. His emphasis ought to be almost imperceptible; never halting, or abrupt; and least of all, so placed as to give an idea of his own sense of cleverness; but regulated by those slight intonations that give point to wit, and force to reason. His language should rise with the subject, and, as he must be an educated and accomplished man, he cannot but know that the highest quality of eloquence, and all sublimity, is in the thought, rather than in the words, though there must be an adaptation of the one to the other.

This is still more true of women than of men, since the former are the natural agents in maintaining the refinement of a people.

All cannot reach the highest standard in such matters, for it depends on early habit, and particularly on early associations. The children of gentlemen are as readily distinguished from other children by these peculiarities, as by the greater delicacy of their minds, and higher tact in breeding. But we are not to abandon all improvement, because perfection is reached but by few. Simplicity should be the first aim, after one is removed from vulgarity, and let the finer shades of accomplishment be acquired as they can be attained. In no case, however, can one who aims at turgid language, exaggerated sentiment, or pedantic utterance, lay claim to be either a man or a woman of the world.

On the Press

It would seem that providence, for some of its own great ends, has denied to man any particular blessing, which his own waywardness is not destined to lessen, if not entirely to neutralize. In nothing connected with human happiness, is this grave truth more apparent than in the history of the press.

In despotisms, where the weakness of the bodies of nations, is derived from an ignorance of their force, and from the want of means to act in concert, the press is the lever by which the thrones of tyrants and prejudices are the most easily overturned, and, under such circumstances, men often contend for privileges in its behalf, that become dangerous to the peace of society, when civil and political rights are obtained.

In a popular government, so far from according an entire immunity from penalties to the press, its abuses are those which society is required, by its very safety, to visit with its heaviest punishments. In a democracy, misleading the publick mind, as regards facts, characters, or principles, is corrupting all that is dear to society at its source, opinion being the fountain whence justice, honors; and the laws, equally flow.

It is a misfortune that necessity has induced men to accord greater license to this formidable engine, in order to obtain liberty, than can be borne with less important objects in view; for the press, like fire, is an excellent servant, but a terrible master.

It may be taken as rules, that without the liberty of the press, there can be no popular liberty in a nation, and with its licentiousness, neither publick honesty, justice, nor a proper regard for character. Of the two, perhaps, that people is the happiest which is deprived altogether of a free press, since private honesty, and a healthful tone of the publick mind are not incompatible with narrow institutions though neither can well exist under the constant corrupting action of a licentious press.

The governing principle connected with this interest, would seem to depend on a general law, which, under abuses, converts the most beneficial moral agents to be the greatest enemies of the race. The press is equally capable of being made the instrument of elevating man to the highest point of which his faculties admit, or of depressing him to the lowest.

In struggling for liberty and emancipation from errors and prejudices, men have not always paused to reflect on the influence of the agents they have employed, when those agents, from contending with a powerful enemy, shall have become conquerors, and have begun to look about them for the fruits of victory. The press, so efficient as the opponent of tyrants, may become despotic itself; it may substitute new errors for those it has eradicated, and, like an individual spoiled by success, may generally abuse its advantages.

Many false notions have been introduced into society, in the desire to vindicate the rights of so powerful an agent. Of these, one of the worst is the admission of a claim in the press to interfere, in any manner, with private character. The good of such an interference, is at the best but doubtful, and the oppression, in those cases in which injustice is done, is of the most intolerable and irreparable kind.

It would be a proper and a just, though an insufficient atonement, in cases of established libel, to vest a power in the courts to compel the libeller to publish, for a series of weeks, or months, or even years, his own condemnation in his own columns, that the antidote might accompany the poison; though it is to be feared, that the possession of popular rights is still too recent, to permit the majority of men to entertain correct notions concerning an instrument that, they rightly fancy, has been so serviceable in the conflict they have just escaped.

It ought never to be forgotten, that the press, contending for natural but forbidden rights, is no more like the press when these rights are obtained, than the man struggling with adversity, and chastened by misfortune, is like the man flushed with success and corrupted by prosperity.

The history of the press is every where the same. In its infancy it is timid, distrustful, and dependant on truth for success. As it acquires confidence with force, it propagates just opinions with energy; scattering errors and repelling falsehood, until it prevails; when abuses rush in, confounding principles, truths, and all else that is estimable, until it becomes a serious matter of doubt, whether a community derives most good or evil, from the institution.

On the Liberty of the Press

What is called the liberty of the press, is very generally misconceived. In despotic, or narrow governments, persons, styled censors, are appointed to examine the columns of journals, *before the latter are issued,* with power to suppress all offensive or injurious articles. This, of course, is putting the press under the control of government, and the press is not a free press, since it cannot publish what its editors please. By the liberty of the press, we are to understand, only, an exemption from this restraint, or a condition of things which enables the citizen to publish what he please, as he can utter what he may please with his tongue.

All men, in a civilized country, however, are responsible for what they say, or publish. If a man speak slander against another, he is liable to the individual injuried, in damages. If a man publish a libel, he incurs the same liability. Some persons suppose that the press possesses privileges, in this respect, that are not accorded to individuals; but the reverse is the fact, as a man may utter with impunity, that which he cannot publish with impunity. The distinction arises from the greater circulation, and the greater power to injure, of a published libel, than of a spoken slander. The editor of a journal, therefore, does not possess the same immunities as an editor, that he possesses as a private citizen. Without such a distinction the community would possess a set of men in its bosom, who would enjoy a power to tyrannize over it, with impunity, through its means of publicity.

The liberty of the press, in principle, resembles the liberty to bear arms. In the one case, the constitution guaranties a right to publish; in the other, a right to keep a musket; but he who injures his neighbor with his publications may be punished, as he who injures his neighbor with his musket may be punished.

The constitution of the United States does not guaranty even the right to publish, except as against the laws of congress, as has been previously stated; the real liberty of the press depending altogether on the provisions of the several state governments, in common with most of the other liberties and rights of the citizen.

ON THE AMERICAN PRESS

The newspaper press of this country is distinguished from that of Europe in several essential particulars. While there are more prints, they are generally of a lower character. It follows that in all in which they are useful, their utility is more diffused through society, and in all in which they are hurtful, the injury they inflict is more wide-spread and corrupting.

The great number of newspapers in America, is a cause of there being so little capital, and consequently so little intelligence, employed in their management. It is also a reason of the inexactitude of much of the news they circulate. It requires a larger investment of capital than is usual in this country, to obtain correct information; while, on the other hand, the great competition renders editors reckless and impatient to fill their columns. To these circumstances may be added the greater influence of vague and unfounded rumours in a vast and thinly settled country, than on a compact population, covering a small surface.

Discreet and observing men have questioned, whether, after excluding the notices of deaths and marriages, one half of the circumstances that are related in the newspapers of America, as facts, are true in their essential features; and, in cases connected with party politics, it may be questioned if even so large a proportion can be set down as accurate.

This is a terrible picture to contemplate, for when the number of prints is remembered, and the avidity with which they are read is brought into the account, we are made to perceive that the entire nation, in a moral sense, breathes an atmosphere of falsehoods. There is little use, however, in concealing the truth; on the contrary, the dread in which publick men and writers commonly stand of the power of the press to injure them, has permitted the evil to extend so far, that it is scarcely exceeding the bounds of a just alarm, to say that the country cannot much longer exist in safety, under the malign influence that now overshadows it. Any one, who has lived long enough to note changes of the sort, must have perceived how fast men of probity and virtue are loosing their influence in the country, to be superseded by those who scarcely deem an affectation of the higher qualities necessary to their success. This fearful change must, in a great measure, be ascribed to the corruption of the publick press, which, as a whole, owes its existence to the schemes of interested political adventurers.

Those who are little acquainted with the world are apt to imagine that a fact, or an argument, that is stated publickly in print, is entitled to more credit and respect than the same fact or argument presented orally, or in conversation. So far from this being true, however, in regard to the press of this country, it would be safer to infer the very reverse. Men who are accustomed daily to throw off their mistatements, become reckless of the consequences, and he who would hesitate about committing himself by an allegation made face to face, and as it were on his personal responsibility, would indite a paragraph, behind the impersonality of his editorial character, to be uttered to the world in the irresponsible columns of a journal. It is seldom, in cases which admit of doubt, that men are required to speak on the moment; but, with the compositor in waiting, the time pressing, and the moral certainty that a rival establishment will circulate the questionable statement if he decline, the editor too often throws himself into the breach. The contradiction of to-day, will make a paragraph, as well as the lie of yesterday, though he who sees the last and not the first, unless able to appreciate the character of his authority, carries away an untruth.

Instead of considering the editor of a newspaper, as an abstraction, with no motive in view but that of maintaining principles and disseminating facts, it is necessary to remember that he is a man, with all the interests and passions of one who has chosen this means to advance his fortunes, and of course, with all the accompanying temptations to abuse his opportunities, and this too, usually, with the additional drawback of being a partisan in politics, religion, or literature. If the possession of power, in ordinary cases, is a constant inducement to turn it to an unjust profit, it is peculiarly so in the extraordinary case of the control of a public press.

Editors praise their personal friends, and abuse their enemies in print, as private individuals praise their friends, and abuse their enemies with their tongues. Their position increases the number of each, and the consequence is, that the readers obtain inflated views of the first, and unjust notions of the last.

If newspapers are useful in overthrowing tyrants, it is only to establish a tyranny of their own. The press tyrannizes over publick men, letters, the arts, the stage, and even over private life. Under the pretence of protecting publick morals, it is corrupting them to the core, and under the semblance of maintaining liberty, it is gradually establishing a despotism as ruthless, as grasping, and one that is quite as vulgar as that of any christian state known. With loud professions of freedom of opinion, there is no tolerance; with a parade of patriotism, no sacrifice of interests; and with fulsome panegyrics on propriety, too frequently, no decency.

There is but one way of extricating the mind from the baneful influence of the press of this country, and that is by making a rigid analysis of its nature and motives. By remembering that all statements that involve disputed points are *ex parte*; that there is no impersonality, except in professions; that all the ordinary passions and interests act upon its statements with less than the ordinary responsibilities; and that there is the constant temptation to abuse, which ever accompanies power, one may come, at last, to a just appreciation of its merits, and in a degree, learn to neutralize its malignant influence. But this is a freedom of mind that few attain, for few have the means of arriving at these truths!

The admixture of truth and falsehood in the intelligence circulated by the press, is one of the chief causes of its evils. A journal that gave utterance to nothing but untruths, would loose its influence with its character, but there are none so ignorant as not to see the necessity of occasionally issuing truths. It is only in cases in which the editor has a direct interest to the contrary, in which he has not the leisure or the means of ascertaining facts, or in which he is himself misled by the passions, cupidity and interests of others, that untruths find a place in his columns. Still these instances may, perhaps, include a majority of the cases.

In a country like this, it is indispensable to mental independence, that every man should have a clear perception of the quality of the political news, and of the political opinions circulated by the press, for, he who confides implicitly to its statements is yielding himself blindly to either the designed and exaggerated praises of friends, or to the calculated abuse of opponents.

As no man is either as good, or as bad, as vulgar report makes him, we can, at once, see the value that ought to be given to such statements.

All representations that dwell wholly on merits, or on faults, are to be distrusted, since none are perfect, and it may, perhaps, be added, none utterly without some redeeming qualities.

Whenever the papers unite to commend, without qualification, it is safe to believe in either venality, or a disposition to defer to a preconceived notion of excellence, most men choosing to float with the current, rather than to resist it, when no active motive urges a contrary course, feeding falsehood, because it flatters a predilection; and whenever censure is general and sweeping, one may be almost certain it is exaggerated and false.

Puffs, political, literary, personal and national, can commonly be detected by their *ex parte* statements, as may be their counterpart, detraction. Dishonesty of intention is easily discovered by the man of the world, in both, by the tone; and he who blindly receives either eulogium or censure, because they stand audaciously in print, demonstrates that his judgment is still in its infancy.

Authors review themselves, or friends are employed to do it for them; political adventurers have their dependants, who build their fortunes on those of their patrons; artists, players, and even religionists, are not above having recourse to such expedients to advance their interests and reputations. The world would be surprised to learn the tyranny that the press has exercised, in our own times, over some of the greatest of modern names, few men possessing the manliness and moral courage that are necessary to resist its oppression.

The people that has overturned the throne of a monarch, and set up a government of opinion in its stead, and which blindly yields its interests to the designs of those who would rule through the instrumentality of newspapers, has only exchanged one form of despotism for another.

It is often made a matter of boasting, that the United States contain so many publick journals. It were wiser to make it a cause of mourning, since the quality, in this instance, diminishes in an inverse ratio to the quantity.

Another reason may be found for the deleterious influence of the American press, in the peculiar physical condition of the country. In all communities, the better opinion, whether as relates to moral or scientific truths, tastes, manners and facts, is necessarily in the keeping of a few; the great majority of mankind being precluded by their opportunities from reaching so high in the mental scale. The proportion between the intelligent and whole numbers, after making a proper allowance on account of the differences in civilization, is probably as great in this country, as in any other; possibly it is greater among the males; but the great extent of the territory prevents its concentration, and consequently, weakens its influence. Under such circumstances, the press has less to contend with than in other countries, where designing and ignorant men would stand rebuked before the collected opinion of those who, by their characters and information, are usually too powerful to be misled by vulgarity, sophistry and falsehood. Another reason is to be found in the popular character of the government, bodies of men requiring to be addressed in modes suited to the average qualities of masses.

In America, while the contest was for great principles, the press aided in elevating the common character, in improving the common mind, and in maintaining the common interests; but, since the contest has ceased, and the struggle has become one purely of selfishness and personal interests, it is employed, as a whole, in fast undermining its own work, and in preparing the nation for some terrible reverses, if not in calling down upon it, a just judgment of God.

As the press of this country now exists, it would seem to be expressly devised by the great agent of mischief, to depress and destroy all that is good, and to elevate and advance all that is evil in the nation. The little truth that is urged, is usually urged coarsely, weakened and rendered vicious, by personalities; while those who live by falsehoods, fallacies, enmities, partialities and the schemes of the designing, find the press the very instrument that the devils would invent to effect their designs.

A witty but unprincipled statesman of our own times, has said that "speech was bestowed on man to conceal his thoughts;" judging from its present condition, he might have added, "and the press to pervert truth."

ON PROPERTY

As property is the base of all civilization, its existence and security are indispensable to social improvement. Were it possible to have a community of property, it would soon be found that no one would toil, but that men would be disposed to be satisfied with barely enough for the supply of their physical wants, since none would exert themselves to obtain advantages solely for the use of others. The failure of all attempts to form communities, even on a small scale, with a common interest, goes to prove this. Where there is a rigid equality of condition, as well as of rights, that condition must necessarily be one of a low scale of mediocrity, since it is impossible to elevate those who do not possess the requisite qualities any higher. Thus we see that the societies, or religious sects, in which a community of property prevails, are content with merely supplying the wants of life, knowing little or nothing of its elegancies, refinements, or mental pleasures. These communities, moreover, possess an outlet for their idle and dissolute, by resorting to expulsion, a remedy that society itself cannot apply.

The principle of individuality, or to use a less winning term, of selfishness, lies at the root of all voluntary human exertion. We toil for food, for clothes, for houses, lands, and for property, in general. This is done, because we know that the fruits of our labor will belong to ourselves, or to those who are most dear to us. It follows, that all which society enjoys beyond the mere supply of its first necessities, is dependant on the rights of property.

It is not known that man exists anywhere without establishing rules for the protection of property. Even insects, reptiles, beasts and birds, have their several possessions, in their nests, dens and supplies. So completely is animal exertion, in general, whether in man or beast, dependant on the enjoyment of this right, under limitations which mark their several conditions, that we may infer that the rights of property, to a certain extent, are founded in nature. The food obtained by his toil, cannot be taken from the mouth of man, or beast, without doing violence to one of the first of our natural rights. We apply the term of robber, or despoiler, to the reptile or bird, that preys on the aliment of another animal, as well as to the human thief. So long as natural justice is admitted to exist, the party assailed, in such cases, has a right to defend his own.

The rights of property become artificial and extended, as society becomes civilized. In the savage state the land is without owners, property consisting in the hut, the food, and the arms used in war and in the chase. In pastoral, or semi-barbarous states, use gives claims, not to individuals, but to tribes, and flocks are pastured on grounds that belong to one entire community, but to that one only. Private property is composed of cattle, sheep, tents, horses, camels, with the common claims to share in the common fields.

Civilization has established various, and in some cases, arbitrary and unjust distinctions, as pertaining to the rights of property. These are abuses, the tendency of man being to convert into curses things that Providence designed to prove benefits. Still, most of the ordinances of civilized society, that are connected with this interest, are founded in reason, and ought to be rigidly maintained.

The first great principle connected with the rights of property, is its inviolability in all cases in which the laws leave it in possession of the proprietor. Every child should be taught to respect the sanctity of his neighbour's house, garden, fields and all that is his. On those parts of another's possessions, where it is permitted to go, he should go with care not to abuse the privilege, and from those parts which he is forbidden to use, he should religiously abstain. The child that is properly impressed in infancy, with the rights of property, is in little danger of committing theft in after life, or, in any other manner of invading that which is the just possession of another.

The doctrine that any one "may do what he please with his own," however, is false. One may do with his own, whatever the laws and institutions of his country allow, and no more. One may even respect the letter, and yet violate the spirit of those laws and institutions, committing a moral, if not a legal offence, in so doing. Thus, he, who would bring his money to bear upon the elections of a country like this, abuses his situation, unless his efforts are confined to fair and manly discussions before the body of the people.

In nations where the mass have no political rights, means have been found to accumulate power by the aid of wealth. The pretence has been that none but the rich have a stake in society. Every man who has wants, feelings, affections and character, has a stake in society. Of the two, perhaps, the necessities of men are a greater corrective of political abuses, than their surplus means. Both may lead to evil, beyond a doubt, but, as laws which are framed by all, must be tolerably impartial and general in their operation, less danger arises from the rule of the former, than from the rule of the latter. When property rules, it rules alone; but when the poor are admitted to have a voice in government, the rich are never excluded. Such is the nature of man, that all exclusive power is uniformly directed to exclusive purposes. Property always carries with it a portion of indirect political influence, and it is unwise, and even dangerous, to strengthen this influence by adding to it constitutional privileges; the result always being to make the strong stronger, and the weak weaker.

On the other hand, all who love equal justice, and, indeed, the safety of free institutions, should understand that property has its rights, and the necessity of rigidly respecting them. It is the right of the possessor of property to be placed on an equal footing with all his fellow citizens, in every respect. If he is not to be exalted on account of his wealth, neither is he to be denounced. In this country, it is the intention of the institutions, that money should neither increase nor lessen political influence.

There are habits that belong to every condition of life. The man of hereditary wealth, is usually a man of leisure, and he little understands the true spirit of democracy, who supposes that such a man is not to enjoy the tastes and inclinations, which are the fruits of leisure and cultivation, without let or hindrance. Democracy leaves every man the master of his acts and time, his tastes and habits, so long as he discharges his duty to the publick, and respects the laws. He who declaims against another for holding himself aloof from general association, arrogates to himself a power of censure that he does not rightly possess, and betrays his own consciousness of inferiority. Men of really high social station never make this complaint, for they are above jealousy; and they who do, only discover a feeling that is every way removed from the manliness and spirit of true independence.

One may certainly be purse-proud, and of all the sources of human pride, mere wealth is the basest and most vulgar minded. Real gentlemen are almost invariably above this low feeling, and they who attribute habits, that have their rise in sentiment, tastes, knowledge and refinement, to such a cause, usually make the mistake of letting their own ignorance of the existence of motives so elevated, be known. In a word, if the man of property has no more personal legal immunities, than the man who has none, neither has he fewer. He is privileged to use his own means, under the general regulations of society, in the pursuit of his own happiness, and they who would interfere with him, so far from appreciating liberty, are ignorant of its vital principles.

If left to itself, unsupported by factitious political aid, but sufficiently protected against the designs and rapacity of the dishonest, property is an instrument of working most of the good that society enjoys. It elevates a national character, by affording the means of cultivating knowledge and the tastes; it introduces all above barbarism into society; and it encourages and sustains laudable and useful efforts in individuals. Like every other great good, its abuses are in proportion to its benefits.

The possessor of property is not, half the time, as much the object of envy as the needy imagine, for its corrupting influence endangers eternal peace. Great estates are generally of more benefit to the community than to their owners. They bring with them anxiety, cares, demands, and, usually, exaggerated notions, on the part of the publick, of the duties of the rich. So far from being objects of envy, their possessors are oftener the subjects of commiseration; he who has enough for his rational wants, agreeably to his habits and education, always proving the happier man.

The possessions of new families are commonly exaggerated in the publick mind, while those of long established families are as commonly diminished.

A people that deems the possession of riches its highest source of distinction, admits one of the most degrading of all influences to preside over its opinions. At no time, should money be ever ranked as more than a means, and he who lives as if the acquisition of property were the sole end of his existence, betrays the dominion of the most sordid, base, and grovelling motive, that life offers.

Property is desirable as the ground work of moral independence, as a means of improving the faculties, and of doing good to others, and as the agent in all that distinguishes the civilized man from the savage.

Property has been made the test of political rights, in two distinct forms. It has been *represented,* and it has been established as a *qualification.* The *representation* of property is effected in two modes; first, by giving the proprietor more votes than one, according to the number and situation of his freeholds; and, secondly, by raising the test of qualification so high, as to exclude all but the affluent from the franchise. The first was the English system, previously to the recent changes; the last, is the actual system of France.

A government founded on the representation of property, however direct or indirect, is radically vicious, since it is a union of two of the most corrupting influences to which man is subject. It is the proper business of government to resist the corruptions of money, and not to depend on them.

To a qualification of property, if placed so low as to embrace the great majority of the people, there is no very serious objection, though better tests might, perhaps, be devised. Residence, character, information, and fixed relations with society, ought to be added to this qualification; and it might be better, even, could they be made entirely to supersede it. In local governments, or those of towns and villages, which do little more than control property, a low property qualification is the true test of the franchise, though even in these cases, it might be well to add information and character.

ON UNIVERAL SUFFRAGE

There is no more a literal universal suffrage, than a literal equality. All these terms must be received in a limited sense, their meaning amounting merely to a comparison with other and older conditions of society. One half of every population is excluded from the suffrage on account of sex, and more than half of the remainder on account of age. From the class that these two great rules do not affect, another, but a small portion, is excluded for their extreme poverty, their crimes, a want of residence or as vagabonds, or for some other cause. The most popularly governed of the American states admit these doctrines.

The policy of adopting a suffrage as wide as that which is commonly called universal, has been much and plausibly contested. Better political tests, perhaps, might be applied than those which now exist, and there can be little doubt that the present system is carried too far in its application and under the particular circumstances of the country, if not too far as a general principle.

The governments of towns and villages, for instance, are almost entirely directed to the regulation of property, and to the control of local interests. In such governments universal suffrage is clearly misplaced, for several grave and obvious reasons, a few of which shall be mentioned.

Towns and villages having no legislative control over the greater interests, such as the general protection of life, the person, the character, and property, there is neither the same necessity for, nor the same justice in, letting in all classes to participate in power. The laws which control the great and predominant interests, or those which give a complexion to society, emanate from the states, which may well enough possess a wide political base. But towns and villages regulating property chiefly, there is a peculiar propriety in excluding those from the suffrage who have no immediate local interests in them. An undue proportion of the dissolute, unsettled, vicious and disorganizing, collect in towns, and that balance of society, which, under other circumstances, might neutralize their influence, is destroyed, leaving, as a consequence, the power to control their governments, under a suffrage that is universal, in the hands of the worst part of community; for, though these persons may not be in sufficient force absolutely to elevate men of their own class to office, they hold a balance between conflicting parties, uniformly act together, and commonly in favor of those who are most disposed to sacrifice principle to expediency. A system must be radically wrong, when the keeper of a tavern, or of a grocery, through his facilities in humoring one of the worst of our vices, can command more votes than a man of the highest attainments, or of the highest character.

The great immigration of foreigners into the country, and the practice of remaining, or of assembling, in the large towns, renders universal suffrage doubly oppressive to the citizens of the latter. The natives of other countries bring with them the prejudices of another and an antagonist state of society; or what is still worse, their reaction; and it is a painful and humiliating fact, that several of the principal places of this country, are, virtually, under the control of men of this class, who have few convictions of liberty, beyond those which arise from a love of licentiousness, who are totally ignorant of its governing principles, and who, in their hearts and language, are hostile to the very people whose hospitality they enjoy. Many of these men cannot even speak the language of the land, and perhaps a majority of them cannot read the great social compact, by which society is held together. Whatever may be said, on general principles, of the necessity of giving to a government the broadest possible base, few will contend that circumstances like these, ought not to qualify the regulation in practice.

Local and limited governments, like those of towns and villages, are best managed in the hands of men who have permanent and fixed interests within their boundaries, and there is little propriety in admitting the more floating part of the population to a participation of an authority that scarcely controls a single right which affects transient persons.

Universal suffrage, in the more extended sense, cannot be received as a naked proposition, without reference to facts. Some nations are totally unqualified to exercise this trust, intelligently and safely, while in others, it may be the best and most sure foundation of society. As a general rule it would be highly dangerous, though the communities that can safely bear it are to be envied and esteemed.

Systems are to be appreciated by their general effects, and not by particular exceptions. Principles also become modified in practice, by facts, and universal suffrage presents very different results in one state of society, from that which it presents in another. So long as the laboring classes of a country can receive high wages, the love of independence that is natural to man, will induce them to give their votes according to their own interests, pleasure, judgment, passions or caprices; for these are equally governing motives of human actions; but when the pressure of society shall become so great as to compel the man of small means to depend on the man of large for his comforts, or even for his bread, as is the natural tendency of all civilized society, the power of money will probably be felt adversely under a suffrage that includes all, or as nearly so, as is practicable. It may then become necessary to liberty, itself, to limit the suffrage.

The representative will necessarily have a direct moral relation to his constituency. In a community that contains many men of character and intelligence, the representation will be of a higher order, than in a community that contains few. We are not to judge of the general effects of the American system, therefore, by the present condition of its representation, though those who have the best means of observation, are of opinion that it will even now sustain a favorable comparison with that of any other country.

There are periods in the histories of all countries, in which entire nations may be said to be on their good behavior. These are the times of struggles and changes, when attention is drawn to the acts of publick men, and principles have unusual influence. Such was the case at the commencement of the American revolution; at one period of the French; and is, in a degree, the present state of the British parliament. At such periods, the same representative acts under impulses very different from those which commonly influence him, and care must be had, in comparing systems, to take into the account all the facts that would be likely to affect them.

Universal suffrage is capricious and uncertain in its minor consequences, often producing results directly contrary to those which were expected.

The transitory nature of the American population renders universal suffrage less advantageous and more injurious, than it would prove to be in a less vacillating condition of society. Thus it is, we see new men, and even strangers, filling offices in places that they entered a year previously, to quit the year that will succeed. The effect of this passing connection with a community is bad, on many accounts, but it becomes seriously so, when the floating and unstable members of society have sufficient interest to unsettle its concerns with their own fluctuating interests.

ON THE PUBLICK

There is a disposition, under popular governments, to mistake the nature and authority of the publick. Publick opinion, as a matter of course, can only refer to that portion of the community that has cognizance of the particular circumstances it affects, but in all matters of law, of rights, and of principles, as they are connected with the general relations of society, the publick means the entire constituency, and that, too, only as it is authorized to act, by the fundamental laws, or the constitution. Thus the citizen who asserts his legal rights in opposition to the wishes of a neighborhood, is not opposing the publick, but maintaining its intentions, while the particular neighborhood is arrogating to itself a power that is confided to the whole body of the state.

Tyranny can only come from the publick, in a democracy, since individuals are powerless, possessing no more rights than it pleases the community to leave in their hands. The pretence that an individual oppresses the publick, is, to the last degree, absurd, since he can do no more than exercise his rights, as they are established by law; which law is enacted, administered and interpreted by the agents of the publick.

As every man forms a portion of the publick, if honest and influenced by right principles, the citizen will be cautious how he takes sides against particular members of the community, for he is both deciding in his own case, a circumstance under which few make impartial judges, and combining with the strong to oppress the weak.

In this country, in which political authority is the possession of the body that wields opinion, influences that elsewhere counteract each other, there is a strong and dangerous disposition to defer to the publick, in opposition to truth and justice. This is a penalty that is paid for liberty, and it depends on the very natural principle of flattering power. In a monarchy, adulation is paid to the prince; in a democracy to the people, or the publick. Neither hears the truth, as often as is wholesome, and both suffer for the want of the corrective. The man who resists the tyranny of a monarch, is often sustained by the voices of those around him; but he who opposes the innovations of the publick in a democracy, not only finds himself struggling with power, but with his own neighbors. It follows that the oppression of the publick is of the worst description, and all real lovers of liberty, should take especial heed not to be accessaries to wrongs so hard to be borne. As between the publick and individuals, therefore, the true bias of a democrat, so far as there is any doubt of the real merits of the controversy, is to take sides with the latter. This is opposed to the popular notion, which is to fancy the man who maintains his rights against the popular will, an aristocrat, but it is none the less true; the popular will, in cases that affect popular pleasure, being quite as likely to be wrong, as an individual will, in cases that affect an individual interest.

It ought to be impressed on every man's mind, in letters of brass, *"That, in a democracy, the publick has no power that is not expressly conceded by the institutions, and that this power, moreover, is only to be used under the forms prescribed by the constitution. All beyond this, is oppression, when it takes the character of acts, and not unfrequently when it is confined to opinion."* Society has less need of the corrective of publick opinion, under such a system, than under a narrow government, for possessing all the power, the body of the community, by framing the positive ordinances, is not compelled to check abuses by resisting, or over-awing the laws. Great care should be had, therefore, to ascertain facts, before the citizen of a free country suffers himself to inflict the punishment of publick opinion, since it is aiding oppression in its worst form, when in error, and this too, without a sufficient object.

Another form of oppression practised by the publick, is arrogating to itself a right to inquire into, and to decide on the private acts of individuals, beyond the cognizance of the laws.

Men who have designs on the favor of the publick invite invasions on their privacy, a course that has rendered the community less scrupulous and delicate than it ought to be. All assumptions of a power to decide on conduct, that is unaccompanied by an authority to investigate facts, is adding the danger of committing rank injustice, to usurpation. The practice may make hypocrites, but it can never mend morals.

The publick, every where, is proverbially soulless. All feel when its rights, assumed or real, are invaded, but none feel its responsibilities. In republicks, the publick is, also, accused of ingratitude to its servants. This is true, few citizens of a democracy retaining the popular favor, without making a sacrifice of those principles, which conflict with popular caprices. The people, being sovereign, require the same flattery, the same humouring of their wishes, and the same sacrifices of truths, as a prince.

It is not more true, however, that the people in a democracy, are ungrateful, than that monarchs are ungrateful. The failing is common to all power, which, as a rule, is invariably as forgetful of services as it is exacting. The difference in the rewards of the servants of a prince, and the rewards of the servants of a democracy, is to be found in the greater vigilance of the first, who commonly sees the necessity of paying well. No dignities or honors conferred on a subject, moreover, can raise him to a level with his master, while a people reluctantly yield distinctions that elevate one of their own number above themselves.

In America, it is indispensable that every well wisher of true liberty should understand that acts of tyranny can only proceed from the publick. The publick, then, is to be watched, in this country, as, in other countries kings and aristocrats are to be watched.

The end of liberty is the happiness of man, and its means, that of leaving the greatest possible personal freedom of action, that comports with the general good. To supplant the exactions of the laws, therefore, by those of an unauthorized publick, is to establish restraints without the formalities and precision of legal requirements. It is putting the prejudices, provincialisms, ignorance and passions of a neighborhood in the place of statutes; or, it is establishing a power equally without general principles, and without responsibility.

Although the political liberty of this country is greater than that of nearly every other civilized nation, its personal liberty is said to be less. In other words, men are thought to be more under the control of extra-legal authority, and to defer more to those around them, in pursuing even their lawful and innocent occupations, than in almost every other country. That there is much truth in this opinion, all observant travellers agree, and it is a reproach to the moral civilization of the country that it should be so. It is not difficult to trace the causes of such a state of things, but the evil is none the less because it is satisfactorily explained. One principal reason, beyond a question, is the mistake that men are apt to make concerning the rights and powers of the publick in a popular government.

The pretence that the publick has a right to extend its jurisdiction beyond the reach of the laws, and without regard to the principles and restraints of the fundamental compact that binds society together, is, indeed, to verify the common accusation of the enemies of democracy, who affirm that, by substituting this form of government for that of a despotism, people are only replacing one tyrant by many. This saying is singularly false as respects the political action of our institutions, but society must advance farther, the country must collect more towns, a denser population, and possess a higher degree of general civilization, before it can be as confidently pronounced that it is untrue as respects the purely social.

The disgraceful desire to govern by means of mobs, which has lately become so prevalent, has arisen from misconceiving the rights of the publick. Men know that the publick, or the community, rules, and becoming impatient of any evil that presses on them, or which they fancy presses on them, they overstep all the forms of law, overlook deliberation and consultation, and set up their own local interests, and not unfrequently their passions, in the place of positive enactments and the institutions. It is scarcely predicting more than the truth will warrant, to say, that if this substitution of the caprices, motives and animosities of a portion of the publick, for the solemn ordinances of the entire legal publick, should continue, even those well affected to a popular government, will be obliged to combine with those who wish its downfall, in order to protect their persons and property, against the designs of the malevolent; for no civilized society can long exist, with an active power in its bosom that is stronger than the law.

On Deportment

Much of the pleasure of social communication depends on the laws of deportment. Deportment may be divided into that, which, by marking refinement and polish, is termed breeding; and that, which, though less distinguished for finesse and finish, denoting a sense of civility and respect, is usually termed manners. The first can only be expected in men and women of the world, or those who are properly styled gentlemen and ladies; while an absence of the last is a proof of vulgarity and coarseness, that every citizen of a free state should be desirous of avoiding. Breeding is always pleasant, though often arbitrary in its rules; but manners are indispensable to civilization. It is just as unreasonable to expect high breeding in any but those who are trained to it, from youth upward, as it would be to expect learning without education; but a tone of manners, that shall mark equally self-respect and a proper regard for others, is as easily acquired as reading and writing.

The gentleman should aim at a standard of deportment that is refined by sentiment and taste, without the sickliness of overstrained feelings; and those beneath him in condition, at a manly humanity, that shall not pretend to distinctions the party does not comprehend, while it carefully respects all the commoner observances of civilized intercourse.

A refined simplicity is the characteristic of all high bred deportment, in every country, and a considerate humanity should be the aim of all beneath it.

ON AMERICAN DEPORTMENT

The American people are superior in deportment, in several particulars, to the people of Europe, and inferior in others. The gentlemen have less finesse, but more frankness of manner, while the other classes have less vulgarity and servility, relieved by an agreeable attention to each other's rights, and to the laws of humanity in general. On the whole, the national deportment is good, without being polished, supplying the deficiency in this last essential, by great kindness and civility. In that part of deportment which affects the rights of all, such as the admission of general and common laws of civility, the absence of social selfishness, and a strict regard to the wants and feebleness of woman, all other nations might be benefitted by imitating this.

The defects in American deportment are, notwithstanding, numerous and palpable. Among the first, may be ranked insubordination in children, and a general want of respect for age. The former vice may be ascribed to the business habits of the country, which leave so little time for parental instruction, and perhaps, in some degree, to the arts of political agents, who, with their own advantage in view, among the other expedients of their cunning, have resorted to the artifice of separating children from their natural advisers, by calling meetings of the young, to decide on the fortunes and policy of the country. Every advertisement calling assemblies of the young, to deliberate on national concerns, ought to be deemed on insult to the good sense, the modesty, and the filial piety of the class to which it is addressed.

The Americans are reproached, also, with the want of a proper deference for social station; the lower classes manifesting their indifference by an unnecessary insolence. As a rule, this charge is unmerited, civility being an inherent quality of the American character; still, there are some who mistake a vulgar audacity for independence. Men and women of this disposition, require to be told that, in thus betraying their propensities, they are giving the strongest possible proofs that they are not what their idle vanity would give reason to suppose they fancy themselves, the equals of those whom they insult by their coarseness.

More of this class err from ignorance, want of reflection, or a loose habit of regulating their conduct in their intercourse with others, than from design. The following anecdote will give an instance of what is meant, and, as the circumstance related is true, the reader will perceive the ludicrous impression that is left, by these gross improprieties of behaviour. A gentleman, who shall be called Winfield, perceiving a girl of eight or ten years of age, endeavoring to find an entrance to his house, enquired her errand. "I have some hats for *Winfield's girls,*" was the answer. Although shocked at this rudeness, Mr. Winfield told the child, that by going to a certain door, she would find a servant to receive her. "Oh!" replied the girl, "I have already seen the *Irish lady,* in the kitchen." This Irish *lady,* was the cook, a very good woman in her way, but one who had no pretensions to be so termed!

Such a confusion in the ideas of this child, is a certain proof of a want of training, for the young ladies who were treated so disrespectfully, were not the less ladies, nor did the cook become more than a cook, for the vulgarity. Facts are not to be changed by words, and all they obtain, who fancy their language and deportment can alter the relations of society, is an exposure of their own ignorance.

The entire complexion, and in many respects, the well being of society, depends on the deportment of its different members, to each other. It behoves the master to be kind to the servant, the servant to be respectful and obedient to his master; the young and inexperienced to defer to the aged and experienced; the ignorant to attend to the admonitions of the wise, and the unpolished to respect the tastes and habits of the refined.

In other countries, where positive ordinances create social distinctions in furtherance of these ends, it is believed they cannot be obtained in any other manner; but it is to be hoped that America is destined to prove, that common sense and the convictions of propriety and fitness, are as powerful agents as force. The servility and arrogance of a highly artificial social scale are not to be desired, but, having positive social facts, also, which cannot be dispensed with, it is vain to resist them. Civility and respect, are the sure accompaniments of a high civilization, and the admission of obvious facts is an indispensable requisite of common sense, as their denial is evidence of infatuation and folly.

There is a moral obligation in every man to conduct himself with civility to all around him. Neither are his particular notions of what is proper, to be taken as an excuse for his rudeness and insults. Refinement and the finesse of breeding are not expected from the majority, but none are so ignorant, in this country, as not to distinguish between what is proper and what is improper in deportment.

Some men imagine they have a right to ridicule what are termed "airs," in others. If it could be clearly established what are "airs," and what not, a corrective of this sort might not be misapplied. But the term is conventional, one man experiencing disgust at what enters into the daily habits of another. It is exceedingly hazardous, therefore, for any but those who are familiar with the best usages of the world, to pronounce any thing "airs," because it is new to them, since what has this appearance to such persons may be no more than a proof of cultivation and of a good tone of manners.

On the other hand, many who have been thrown accidentally and for short periods, into the society of the more refined classes, adopt their usages without feeling or understanding their reasons and advantages, caricaturing delicacy and sentiment, and laying stress on habits, which, though possibly convenient in themselves, are not deemed at all essential by men and women of the world. These affectations of breeding are laughed at, as the "silver-forkisms" of pretenders. To the man of the world it is unnecessary to point out the want of taste in placing such undue stress on these immaterial things, but it may not be unnecessary to the novice in the usages of the better circles, to warn him that his ignorance will be more easily seen by his exaggerations, than by his deficiencies of manner. The Due de Richlieu is said to have detected an impostor by his *not* taking olives with his fingers.

But these are points of little interest with the mass, while civility and decency lie at the root of civilization. There is no doubt that, in general, America has retrograded in manners within the last thirty years. Boys, and even men, wear their hats in the houses of all classes, and before persons of all ages and conditions. This is not independence, but vulgarity, for nothing sooner distinguishes a gentleman from a blackguard, than the habitual attention of the former to the minor civilities established by custom. It has been truly said, that the man who is well dressed respects himself more, and behaves himself better, than the man that is ill dressed; but it is still more true that the man who commences with a strict observance of the commoner civilities, will be the most apt to admit of the influence of refinement on his whole character.

On Publick Opinion

Publick opinion is the lever by which all things are moved, in a democracy. It has even become so powerful in monarchies, as, virtually, to destroy despotism in all really civilized countries, holding in check the will and passions of princes.

Publick opinion, however, like all things human, can work evil in proportion to its power to do good. On the same principle that the rebound is proportioned to the blow in physics, there can be no moral agent capable of benefitting man that has not an equal power to do him harm. Publick opinion rightly directed is the highest source of national virtue, as publick opinion, which has taken a wrong direction, is the surest means of serving the devil.

In a democracy, as a matter of course, every effort is made to seize upon and create publick opinion, which is, substantially, securing power. One of the commonest arts practised, in connection with this means of effecting objects, is to simulate the existence of a general feeling in favor, or against, any particular man, or measure; so great being the deference paid to publick opinion, in a country like this, that men actually yield their own sentiments to that which they believe to be the sentiment of the majority.

In politics, however, and, indeed, in all other matters that are of sufficient magnitude to attract general attention, there are adverse sentiments, which, were it not for the absurdity of the phrase, might almost be termed two publick opinions. This is the result of party feeling, which induces men to adopt in gross, the prejudices, notions and judgments of the particular faction to which they belong, often without examination, and generally without candor. When two men of equal intelligence, of the same means of ascertaining facts, and of the same general fairness of disposition, hold the opposite extremes of opinion on the character of a particular individual, or of a particular measure, we see the extent to which a bias may be carried, and the little value that those who wish only to support the truth ought to attach even to publick opinion, in matters that will admit of doubt.

As no reparation can ever be made, in this world, to the individual who has been wronged by publick opinion, all good men are cautious how they listen to accusations that are unsupported by testimony, vulgar report being more likely to be wrong than to be right.

In matters that admit of investigation and proof, publick opinion in the end, when passion, prejudice and malice have had their day, is very apt to come to a just decision, but this is often too late to repair the wrong done to the sufferer. In matters that, by their nature, cannot be clearly established, artifice, the industry of the designing, and studied misrepresentations, permanently take the place of facts, history itself being, as a whole, but an equivocal relation of all the minor events, and a profound mystification as to motives.

Publick opinion will be acted on in this country, by its enemies, as the easiest and most effectual mode of effecting their purposes, bodies of men never being sufficiently clear-sighted to detect remote consequences. It is said to be a common practice in Europe, for the governments to incite commotions, when they wish to alarm the country on the subject of any particular opinion, as the surest and promptest method of checking its advance. The excesses of the French revolution are now attributed to the schemes of agents of this sort; the opponents of liberty finding it impossible to stem the torrent, having recourse to the opposite policy of pushing it into revolting extremes.

Excitement is a word that, as regards the publick in a country like this, ought to be expunged from its dictionary. In full possession of the power, there is every motive for deliberation and enquiry on the part of the people, and every inducement to abstain from undue agitation. "Excitement," may favor the views of selfish individuals, but it can never advance the interests of truth. All good citizens should turn a deaf ear to every proposal to aid in producing an "excitement," as it is calling into existence a uniform enemy of reason, and the most certain agent of defeating the intention of the institutions, which are based on investigation and common sense.

Whenever the government of the United States shall break up, it will probably be in consequence of a false direction having been given to publick opinion. This is the weak point of our defences, and the part to which the enemies of the system will direct all their attacks. Opinion can be so perverted as to cause the false to seem the true; the enemy, a friend, and the friend, an enemy; the best interests of the nation to appear insignificant, and trifles of moment; in a word, the right the wrong, and the wrong the right.

In a country where opinion has sway, to seize upon it, is to seize upon power. As it is a rule of humanity that the upright and well intentioned are comparatively passive, while the designing, dishonest and selfish are the most untiring in their efforts, the danger of publick opinion's getting a false direction, is four-fold, since few men think for themselves. Perhaps there is not, in all America, apart from general principles, a sentiment that is essentially just, and which is recognized as publick opinion; a sufficient proof of which is to be found in the fact that publick opinion is constantly vibrating around truth, which alone is unchangeable.

Publick opinion has got a wrong, if not a dangerous direction, already, in this country, on several essential points. It has a fearfully wrong direction on the subject of the press, which it sustains in its tyranny and invasions on private rights, violating all sanctity of feeling, rendering men indifferent to character, and, indeed, rendering character itself of little avail, besides setting up an irresponsible and unprincipled power that is stronger than the government itself. One of its consequences is a laxity of opinion on the subject of wrongs committed by the press, that amounts to a denial of justice. Another, and a still graver result, is to give an unrestrained supremacy to an engine that is quite as able, and perhaps more likely, to corrupt and destroy society than to reform it. This fearful state of things, which is better adapted than any other, to restrain good, and to prefer bold and bad men, has been brought about by the action of the press, itself, on publick opinion, and is an example of the manner in which this tremendous agent can be perverted to evil, in a popular government. It follows, that publick opinion should be watched and protected from receiving a wrong bias, as we would protect and overlook the first impressions of a child.

Publick opinion in America is exposed to another danger, growing out of the recent colonial origin of the country. There is no question that the people of this country defer in an unusual manner to foreign opinions, more particularly to those of the nation from which they are derived. The proof of this is ample, but one may constantly see quotations from English journals, in support of the pretensions of politicians, writers, artists, and all others, who are liable to the decisions of their fellow citizens for the estimation in which they are held. An opinion is seldom given in Europe, of any thing American, unless from impure motives. The country attracts too little attention in the other hemisphere, to be included in the ordinary comments of the civilized world. There are, and may be, an occasional exception, but this is the rule. As many of the interests of this country are opposed to the interests of European nations, efforts are constantly made to influence opinion here, in favor of interests there. The doctrine of free trade, as it is called, has this origin, having been got up by English writers, to prevent other states from resorting to the same expedients to foster industry, that have so well succeeded in Great Britain. The factitious condition of all things in that great empire, renders any derangement hazardous, and while America trifles with her welfare, like a vigorous youth who is careless of his health through reliance on his constitution, England watches over every material concern, with the experience, vigilance and distrust of age. Hence it is that every means is resorted to, to extol men who have become the dupes of English sophistry, and to depreciate those who resist her schemes.

We have lately seen, on the part of France, an open and a direct attempt to interfere between the people and the government, in an affair touching the character and highest interests of the country, and although the appeal injured the cause of those who urged it, by exposing their sophistry and bad faith, it proves the reliance that foreign powers have on their ability to influence publick opinion, here, even in matters touching our own dearest interests!

Another familiar and recent instance of the efforts of foreigners to influence American opinion, may be cited in connection with the late quarrel with France. It is known that the English government mediated to prevent a war. This mediation was accepted on the part of the American government, with the express reservation that France must comply with the terms of the treaty. In other words, we merely conditioned to delay acting, until the effort should be made to induce France to comply with all we asked. France saw reasons to change her policy, and to comply with our terms, before the acceptance of the English mediation was known, and yet strong efforts have been made to persuade the American people that the accommodation was produced through English mediation, and that England was

pledged to see this accommodation effected, in the character of an arbitra-
tor. The first is untrue as to fact, and the last is opposed to all the principles
of arbitration, as nothing was placed at the decision of the English government. The case is a recent proof of the vigilance that is necessary to keep
publick opinion independent of foreign domination.

Opinion is the moving power of this country, and it would be extreme
weakness to suppose that other nations, which are ever ready to lavish their
treasure and to shed their blood, in order to effect their purposes, would
neglect means so sure, easy and noiseless, as that of acting on the common
mind. The danger of evil from this source will increase with the growing
power of the country, or, as her policy will be likely to influence foreign
interests, in a ratio proportioned to her strength and wealth.

No nation can properly boast of its independence while its opinion is
under the control of foreigners, and least of all, a nation with institutions
dependant on the popular will.

On Civilization

Civilization means a condition of society that is the opposite of the savage,
or barbarous state. In other languages this term is more strictly applied to
the arts of life, than in the English, in which we are more apt to associate
with it the moral condition of a country.

England stands at the head of modern civilization, as a whole, although
many countries surpass her in particular parts. The higher tastes of England
are not as refined and cultivated, perhaps, as those of Italy and France, but
the base of society is infinitely more advanced.

America occupies a middle place in the scale, wanting most of the
higher tastes, and excelling in that species of civilization which marks ease
and improvement in the middling and lower classes. There is one feature
connected with the civilization of this country that is peculiar; for while the
people have long been accustomed to the habits of England, they have not
been possessed of those arts by which the different objects of the comforts
they have enjoyed are produced. For a long time articles as humble as hats,
shovels and hoes, were not fabricated in the country, though the time never
has been when the Anglo-Americans were unaccustomed to their use.

Although there is a difference between the civilization of the towns, and that of the country, in America, it is less marked than in Europe. The disparity between the refinement, mental cultivation and the elegances of life, is much less apparent than usual, as between an American capital and an American village, though the localities, of course, make some distinctions. As a whole, civilization, while it is less perfect in this country than in the European nations, is more equally diffused throughout the entire community. Still it better becomes the American people to strive to advance their condition than to manifest a weak, unmanly and provincial sensibility to the faults that are occasionally commented on, nations, like individuals, merely betraying a consciousness of their own demerits, by meeting admonition with insult and anger.

The Americans are deficient on many points of civilization, solely for the want of physical force in given places, the practice of covering large surfaces unavoidably retarding the improvements of the nation. This is rather the subject of regret, than a matter of reproach. They are almost ignorant of the art of music, one of the most elevating, innocent and refining of human tastes, whose influence on the habits and morals of a people is of the most beneficial tendency. This taste and knowledge are not only wanting to the people, but an appreciation of their importance. They are also wanting in most of the high tastes, and consequently in the high enjoyments, that accompany a knowledge of all the fine arts in general, and in much that depends on learning, research, and familiarity with the world.

The Americans excel in humanity, in the ordinary comforts, though inferior to the English in this respect, in general civility, in the means of motion while confined to great routes, in shipping and most of the facilities of trade, in common instruction and an aptitude to ordinary pursuits, and in an absence of the sophisms that beset older and more artificial systems. It is, however, to be regretted, that as the nation recedes from the struggle that created the present system, the truths that came uppermost in the collision, are gradually yielding to a new set of sophisms, more peculiar to the present order of things.

There is a familiar and too much despised branch of civilization, of which the population of this country is singularly and unhappily ignorant; that of cookery. The art of eating and drinking, is one of those on which more depends, perhaps, than on any other, since health, activity of mind, constitutional enjoyments, even learning, refinement, and, to a certain degree, morals, are all, more or less, connected with our diet. The Americans are the grossest feeders of any civilized nation known. As a nation, their food is heavy, coarse, ill prepared and indigestible, while it is taken in the least artificial forms that cookery will allow. The predominance of grease in the American kitchen, coupled with the habits of hasty eating and of constant expectoration, are the causes of the diseases of the stomach so common in America. The science of the table extends far beyond the indulgence of our appetites, as the school of manners includes health and morals, as well as that which is agreeable. Vegetable diet is almost converted into an injury in America, from an ignorance of the best modes of preparation, while even animal food is much abused, and loses half its nutriment.

The same is true as respects liquors. The heating and exciting wines, the brandies, and the coarser drinks of the laboring classes, all conspire to injure the physical and the moral man, while they defeat their own ends.

These are points of civilization on which this country has yet much to learn, for while the tables of the polished and cultivated partake of the abundance of the country, and wealth has even found means to introduce some knowledge of the kitchen, there is not perhaps on the face of the globe, the same number of people among whom the good things of the earth are so much abused, or ignorantly wasted, as among the people of the United States. National character is, in some measure, affected by a knowledge of the art of preparing food, there being as good reason to suppose that man is as much affected by diet as any other animal, and it is certain that the connection between our moral and physical qualities is so intimate as to cause them to react on each other.

On the Right of Petition

The right of petition is guarantied to the American citizen by an amendment to the constitution, made in 1801. By this clause, *congress* is prohibited from passing any law to prevent the *people* from *peaceably assembling,* in order to petition the government for a redress of grievances. This prohibition, like those on the subjects of the liberty of the press, liberty of speech and liberty of conscience, was perfectly supererogatory, the states having conceded to congress no authority to pass any law to the contrary. It is understood that all these provisions were introduced through the influence of Mr.

Jefferson, who was desirous that the constitution should exhibit on its face, what might be termed its profession of political faith, since foreigners did not comprehend the negative restrictions on the power of the federal government, that grow out of the fact of its being purely a government of deputed and defined authority.

The right of petition is by no means an important political right in this country, where the constituents hold so strong a check on their representatives, and where no important laws can long exist without their approbation. In countries in which the people cannot assemble to cause publick opinion to act on their rulers, and in which the great majority are disfranchised, or never possessed a vote, the right of petition is an all important right. Men confound the characters of the institutions of different nations, when they ascribe the same importance to it here.

Although the people have a right to petition, congress is not bound to waste its time in listening to and in discussing the matter of petitions, on the merits of which that body has already decided. A discretionary power rests in congress to receive, or to reject a petition, at pleasure, the right going no farther than the assembling and petitioning; else would it be in the power of a small proportion of the people to occupy all the time of the national legislature on vexatious and useless questions.

A state has no right to petition congress at all. The legislature of a state has its limited powers as well as congress, and, did the constitution of a particular state include this among the other powers of its legislature, the governing principle of the federal constitution is opposed to it. The right of petition as claimed by a state can do no legitimate good, and may lead to much evil, as a brief examination will show. The federal government acts directly on the people, through agents of its own; for whenever it accepts the agency of a state, the agents of that state are in effect the agents of the general government. Now, the representation in one body of congress, is not a state representation, but it is a representation founded on numbers. As a state, if possessing authority to petition, one state ought to have the weight of another, whereas, in congress, one state has much more influence than another, as the following example will show. The senators of fourteen states may vote for the passage, or the repeal of a law, under the influence of petitions from their several state legislatures, and yet the veto of the representatives of the remaining twelve states shall defeat the measure in the other house. It follows that the states, purely as states, are not so strictly constituents of congress as to claim a *right* to petition. The danger of the practice is derived from the tendency of creating local feelings, through the agency of the local governments, and of thus endangering the peace of the Union.

It would be difficult to show that a state has more right to petition congress, than congress has to petition a state. This interference of the different parts of a complicated and nicely balanced machine, might derange its entire movement.

ON COMMERCE

Commerce, in a general sense, is trade, but it is also usual to apply the word particularly to the traffick between nations. Navigation is not commerce, but a means of conducting commerce.

Commerce is merely an incident of civilized society, though there is always a strong disposition in commercial communities to treat it as a principal. The interests of commerce, in a general sense, depend on certain great principles, which ought always to be respected; but, as these interests, by their nature, are also liable to be influenced by the constant vicissitudes arising out of the fluctuations of trade, there is a strong disposition in those connected with commerce, to sacrifice all governing rules, to protect the interests of the day. This disposition is common to man, but it is more active in merchants, on account of the magnitude and precarious nature of the risks they run. The agriculturist who loses a crop, suffers an injury, more or less serious, that another year will repair; but the merchant who loses his adventures, is usually ruined.

It follows, that a community governed by men in trade, or which is materially influenced by men in trade, is governed without any fixed principles, every thing being made to yield to the passing interests of the hour, those interests being too engrossing to admit of neglect, or postponement.

It is a mistake to suppose commerce favorable to liberty. Its tendency is to a monied aristocracy, and this, in effect, has always been the polity of every community of merchants. Commerce is an enemy of despotic power in the hands of a prince, of church influence, and of hereditary aristocracies, from which facts it has obtained its reputation of sustaining freedom; but, as a class, merchants will always be opposed to the control of majorities.

The true office of commerce is to facilitate exchanges of articles between men, to the amount that their wants and interests require; but as every transfer of property leaves a profit with the merchant, he has a disposition to increase his gains, by pushing his transactions beyond the just limits of trade. This disposition is best checked by the penalties of bankruptcies, but, in a country like this, in which no such penalty exists, the consequence is to produce an unbroken succession of commercial reverses, that affect the value of all the property in the nation, almost periodically.

Commerce is entitled to a complete and efficient protection in all its legal rights, but the moment it presumes to control a country, or to substitute its fluctuating expedients for the high principles of natural justice that ought to lie at the root of every political system, it should be frowned on, and rebuked.

The merchant who is the immediate agent in paying the duties on goods, has no more claims than another, as the money eventually comes from the pocket of the consumer, and the factor is amply paid for his services in his profits.

All legislation affecting the currency, commerce and banking, in a country like this, ought to be limited, as far as circumstances will allow, to general and simple provisions, the nature of the institutions forbidding the interference that is elsewhere practised with advantage. A familiar example will show our meaning. In all commercial communities there is a commercial mart, or a capital, where exchanges are effected, cargoes disposed of in gross, and where all the great interests of trade concentrate, as the blood flows to and from the heart. In identified governments, like that of England, for instance, legislation may respect this natural tendency to concentration in commerce, and enact laws for its especial benefit and protection. Thus an English law may have an especial relation to the interests of London, as the mart that regulates the entire currency of the kingdom. But, on the other hand, in a government like that of America, there is a principle of diffusion, which requires that the legislation should be general in its application. New York and New Orleans, for instance, regulate the currency and exchanges of the whole country; but congress cannot pass a law to aid these legitimate efforts of trade, since any legislation that should favor New York at the expense of Philadelphia, in appearances even, would be opposed to the controlling principle of the compact. It follows, that the interference of the government with all such questions, in this country, should be unfrequent and cautious, since it possesses a power to injure, with very little power to benefit.

The real merchant is a man of a high pursuit, and has need of great general knowledge, much firmness of character, and of far-sighted views, to succeed in his objects. He is a principal agent in extending knowledge and civilization, and is entitled to a distinguished place in the scale of human employments. But the mere factor, who is the channel of communication between the producer and the consumer, in what is called a regular trade, has no more claims to this character, than the clerk who copies a treaty has a claim to be considered a negotiator.

ON THE CIRCULATION MEDIUM

Necessity has induced men to establish a certain standard of value, by means of the precious metals, to represent property. As it is desirable that this standard of value should fluctuate as little as possible, laws have been passed rendering it illegal to receive more than a fixed rate of interest for money. There can be no question that these laws would be singularly useful, did not dealers find means to evade them, for a variation in the value of the representative of property, renders all contracts liable to the hazards of a fluctuation, in addition to that of the article purchased. It is to be feared, however, that nothing short of making usury criminal, will ever effect this object; if, indeed, such a remedy be practicable.

As the world does not contain a sufficiency of the precious metals to represent any considerable amount of its debts, it has been found necessary to resort to a system of credits, for the purposes of commerce, that is based on gold and silver. This system is so simple, that any one can understand it. The precious metals have a currency throughout christendom, while the credit of an individual, or of a banking institution, is limited. All that is required of the two latter, therefore, is, that its paper should be redeemed in specie, as specie shall be wanted.

In a country like America, a purely specie currency is utterly impracticable. Although money is not actually wanted for a tithe of the debts that are due, at any one moment, so much more is wanted than can be obtained in the precious metals, that a recourse to the credit system is unavoidable, as a single feature of the true condition of the country will show.

America, in the states and territories, contains about twelve hundred thousand square miles. This immense country is in the course of settlement, and the transfers of real estate, are a hundred-fold what they are in Europe, on the same extent of surface. A piece of land is frequently sold several times in the course of a single year, whereas centuries often elapse in older countries, without the sale of a given property. Every transfer of title causes an indebtedness, and consequently a necessity for a circulating medium to represent it. The earth does not probably contain a sufficiency of the precious metals, at their present value, to represent all the debts of this one country.

On the other hand, nothing is easier than to abuse a system of credits. The unrestrained issue of papermoney, with its attendant contractions, keeps the value of property unsettled, creates pressures and bankruptcies, and otherwise produces the instability that so peculiarly marks the condition of American trade.

Specie should be the basis of all currency. There should also be enough of the precious metals floating in the community, to meet its minor daily wants, the proper office of credit being to represent money in large sums, and not to represent money in small sums. For all the purposes of payments from the pocket, nothing is so convenient, or so safe, as gold and silver, as all who have tried it well know. Indeed, so palpable is the fact, that in Europe, men of wealth almost invariably use gold for this purpose, even in those countries in which it is slightly above the standard of value in price, and it may be questioned if any paper ought to be issued of a value less than fifty or a hundred dollars. In short, the precious metals are intended to circulate among those who have not the leisure nor knowledge to ascertain the credit of paper, while the credit system is to facilitate the operations of trade, and to supply the deficiency in gold and silver in the payment of larger sums. Any effort to make paper do more than legitimately belongs to its office, is an attempt to supplant the interests of society by serving the interests of money dealers.

ON SLAVERY

Domestic slavery is an institution as old as human annals, and probably will continue, in its spirit, through different modifications, as long as man shall remain under the different degrees of civilization that mark his actual existence. Slavery is no more sinful, by the christian code, than it is sinful to wear a whole coat, while another is in tatters, to eat a better meal than a neighbor, or otherwise to enjoy ease and plenty, while our fellow creatures are suffering and in want. According to the doctrines of Christ, we are "to do as we would be done by," but this law is not to be applied to slavery more than to any other interest of life. It is quite possible to be an excellent christian and a slave holder, and the relations of master and slave, may be a means of exhibiting some of the mildest graces of the character, as may those of king and subject, or principal and dependant, in any of the other modifications of human institutions.

In one sense, slavery may actually benefit a man, there being little doubt that the African is, in nearly all respects, better off in servitude in this country, than when living in a state of barbarism at home.

But, while slavery, in the abstract, can no more be considered a sin, than most human ordinances, it leads to sin in its consequences, in a way peculiarly its own, and may be set down as an impolitic and vicious institution. It encourages those faults of character that depend on an uncontrolled will, on the one side, and an abject submission, on the other. It usually limits the moral existence of the slave, too, as there is a necessity of keeping him ignorant, in order that he may be held in subjection.

Slavery is of two kinds; one in which the slave is a chattel, and can be disposed of as such, and one in which he is attached to the soil, like a fixture, and can only be sold with the land. The former is the condition of the American slave; the latter the condition of the European serf. All Europe, formerly, had serfs, or slaves, of the latter class, though their existence is now confined to a few countries in the north and east of that quarter of the world. Still, the consequences of the old system are, more or less, to be traced, in most European countries, and, though differing in degree, their people may as fairly be termed slaves in principle, as those of our own southern states.

ON AMERICAN SLAVERY

American slavery is of the most unqualified kind, considering the slave as a chattel, that is transferable at will, and in full property. The slave, however, is protected in his person to a certain extent, the power of the master to chastise and punish, amounting to no more than the parental power.

American slavery is distinguished from that of most other parts of the world, by the circumstance that the slave is a variety of the human species, and is marked by physical peculiarities so different from his master, as to render future amalgamation improbable. In ancient Rome, in modern Europe generally, and, in most other countries, the slave not being thus distinguished, on obtaining his freedom, was soon lost in the mass around him; but nature has made a stamp on the American slave that is likely to prevent this consummation, and which menaces much future ill to the country. The time must come when American slavery shall cease, and when that day shall arrive, (unless early and effectual means are devised to obviate it,) two races will exist in the same region, whose feelings will be embittered by inextinguishable hatred, and who carry on their faces, the respective stamps of their factions. The struggle that will follow, will necessarily be a war of extermination. The evil day may be delayed, but can scarcely be averted.

American slavery is mild, in its general features, and physical suffering cannot properly be enumerated among its evils. Neither is it just to lay too heavy stress on the personal restraints of the system, as it is a question whether men feel very keenly, if at all, privations of the amount of which they know nothing. In these respects, the slavery of this country is but one modification of the restraints that are imposed on the majority, even, throughout most of Europe. It is an evil, certainly, but in a comparative sense, not as great an evil as it is usually imagined. There is scarcely a nation of Europe that does not possess institutions that inflict as gross personal privations and wrongs, as the slavery of America. Thus the subject is compelled to bear arms in a quarrel in which he has no real concern, and to incur the risks of demoralization and death in camps and fleets, without any crime or agency of his own. From all this, the slave is exempt, as well as from the more ordinary cares of life.

Slavery in America, is an institution purely of the states, and over which the United States has no absolute control. The pretence, however, that congress has no right to entertain the subject, is unsound, and cannot be maintained. Observing the prescribed forms, slavery can be legally abolished, by amending the constitution, and congress has power, by a vote of two thirds of both houses, to propose amendments to that instrument. Now, whatever congress has power to do, it has power to discuss; by the same rule, that it is a moral innovation on the rights of the states to discuss matters in congress, on which congress has no authority to legislate. A constitutional right, and expediency, however, are very different things. Congress has full power to declare war against all the nations of the earth, but it would be madness to declare war against even one of them, without sufficient cause. It would be equal madness for congress, in the present state of the country, to attempt to propose an amendment of the constitution, to abolish slavery altogether, as it would infallibly fail, thereby raising an irritating question without an object.

On Slavery in the Distric of Columbia

Congress having all power to legislate for the District of Columbia, there can be no reasonable doubt of its power to legislate on slavery, as well as any other interest, under the limits of the constitution. A plausible question might even be raised whether the ordinary restrictions of the constitution apply at all to the legislation of the District, and whether the powers of congress over this particular portion of the country, are not as absolute as the powers of parliament in Great Britain.

Still the legislation for the District, in principle, depends on that general rule which ought to guide all just legislators. To pretend that a member of congress from Vermont, or a member of congress from Louisiana, is to respect the opinions of his own immediate constituents, in legislating especially for the District of Columbia, is like pretending that the emperor of Austria, who is equally sovereign of both countries, should consult the interests of the people of the kingdom of Bohemia, in establishing laws for the kingdom of Hungary. The relation between the constituent of the member and the District, is altogether anomalous, and, on no just principle, can be made to extend to this absolute control.

All legislation that is especially intended for the District, should keep the interests of the District alone in view, subject to the great reasons for which this territory was formed, and to the general principles of morality. So far as any influence beyond that of the District is concerned, on the question of slavery, this legislation should be more in the interest of the slave-holding states, than in the interests of the non-slave-holding states, as with the latter it is purely a negative question, whereas, with the former, it has a positive affirmative connection with their immediate interests, in more senses than one. Thus the slave-holder has a claim to be able to visit the seat of government, attended by his body servants, and this, too, without incurring any unpleasant risks of their loss merely to satisfy the abstract notions of right of the citizens of the non-slave-holding states. This claim may not be so great as to over-shadow those of the inhabitants of the District itself, should they demand a law for the emancipation of their slaves, but is quite great enough to over-shadow the negative interests of the resident of a non-slave-holding state.

In the management of this interest, in general, it ought to be remembered, that to the citizen of the non-slave-holding state, slavery offers little more than a question of abstract principles, while to the citizen of the slave-hold-ing state it offers a question of the highest practical importance, and one that, mis-managed, might entirely subvert the order of his social organization.

On Party

It is commonly said that political parties are necessary to liberty. This is one of the mistaken opinions that have been inherited from those who, living under governments in which there is no true political liberty, have fancied that the struggles which are inseparable from their condition, must be com-mon to the conditions of all others.

England, the country from which this people is derived, and, until the establishment of our own form of government, the freest nation of Chris-tendom, enjoys no other liberty than that which has been obtained by the struggles of parties. Still retaining in the bosom of the state, a power in the-ory, which, if carried out in practice, would effectually overshadow all the other powers of the state, it may truly be necessary to hold such a force in check, by the combinations of political parties. But the condition of Amer-ica, in no respect, resembles this. Here, the base of the government is the constituencies, and its balance is in the divided action of their representa-tives, checked as the latter are by frequent elections. As these constituencies are popular, the result is a free, or a popular government.

Under such a system, in which the fundamental laws are settled by a written compact, it is not easy to see what good can be done by parties, while it is easy to see that they may effect much harm. It is the object of this article, to point out a few of the more prominent evils that originate from such a source.

Party is known to encourage prejudice, and to lead men astray in the judgment of character. Thus it is we see one half the nation extolling those that the other half condemns, and condemning those that the other half extols. Both cannot be right, and as passions, interests and prejudices are all enlisted on such occasions, it would be nearer the truth to say that both are wrong.

Party is an instrument of error, by pledging men to support its policy, instead of supporting the policy of the state. Thus we see party measures almost always in extremes, the resistance of opponents inducing the leaders to ask for more than is necessary.

Party leads to vicious, corrupt and unprofitable legislation, for the sole purpose of defeating party. Thus have we seen those territorial divisions and regulations which ought to be permanent, as well as other useful laws, altered, for no other end than to influence an election.

Party, has been a means of entirely destroying that local independence, which elsewhere has given rise to a representation that acts solely for the nation, and which, under other systems is called the country party, every legislator being virtually pledged to support one of two opinions; or, if a shade of opinion between them, a shade that is equally fettered, though the truth be with neither.

The discipline and organization of party, are expedients to defeat the intention of the institutions, by putting managers in the place of the people; it being of little avail that a majority elect, when the nomination rests in the hands of a few.

Party is the cause of so many corrupt and incompetent men's being preferred to power, as the elector, who, in his own person, is disposed to resist a bad nomination, yields to the influence and a dread of factions.

Party pledges the representative to the support of the executive, right or wrong, when the institutions intend that he shall be pledged only to justice, expediency and the right, under the restrictions of the constitution.

When party rules, the people do not rule, but merely such a portion of the people as can manage to get the control of party. The only method by which the people can completely control the country, is by electing representatives known to prize and understand the institutions; and, who, so far from being pledged to support an administration, are pledged to support nothing but the right, and whose characters are guarantees that this pledge will be respected.

The effect of party is always to supplant established power. In a monarchy it checks the king; in a democracy it controls the people.

Party, by feeding the passions and exciting personal interests, overshadows truth, justice, patriotism, and every other publick virtue, completely reversing the order of a democracy, by putting unworthy motives in the place of reason.

It is a very different thing to be a democrat, and to be a member of what is called a democratic party; for the first insists on his independence and an entire freedom of opinion, while the last is incompatible with either.

The great body of the nation has no real interest in party. Every local election should be absolutely independent of great party divisions, and until this be done, the intentions of the American institutions will never be carried out, in their excellence.

Party misleads the public mind as to the rights and duties of the citizen. An instance has recently occurred, in which a native born citizen of the United States of America, the descendant of generations of Americans, has become the object of systematic and combined persecution, because he published a constitutional opinion that conflicted with the interests and passions of party, although having no connection with party himself; very many of his bitterest assailants being foreigners, who have felt themselves authorized to pursue this extraordinary course, as the agents of party!

No freeman, who really loves liberty, and who has a just perception of its dignity, character, action and objects, will ever become a mere party man. He may have his preferences as to measures and men, may act in concert with those who think with himself, on occasions that require concert, but it will be his earnest endeavour to hold himself a free agent, and most of all to keep his mind untrammelled by the prejudices, frauds, and tyranny of factions.

ON INDIVIDUALITY

Individuality is the aim of political liberty. By leaving to the citizen as much freedom of action and of being, as comports with order and the rights of others, the institutions render him truly a freeman. He is left to pursue his means of happiness in his own manner.

It is a curious circumstance, that, in endeavouring to secure the popular rights, an effect has been produced in this country totally opposed to this main object. Men have been so long accustomed to see oppression exercised in the name of one, or in the name of a few, that they have got to consider the sway of numbers as the only criterion of freedom. Numbers, however, may oppress as well as one or a few, and when such oppression occurs, it is usually of the worst character.

The habit of seeing the publick rule, is gradually accustoming the American mind to an interference with private rights that is slowly undermining the individuality of the national character. There is getting to be so much publick right, that private right is overshadowed and lost. A danger exists that the ends of liberty will be forgotten altogether in the means.

All greatness of character is dependant on individuality. The man who has no other existence than that which he partakes in common with all around him, will never have any other than an existence of mediocrity. In time, such a state of things would annihilate invention and paralyze genius. A nation would become a nation of common place labourers.

The pursuit of happiness is inseparable from the claims of individuality. To compel all to follow this object in the same manner, is to oppress all above the average tastes and information. It can only be done at the expense of that which is the aim of liberty.

An entire distinct individuality, in the social state, is neither possible nor desirable. Our happiness is so connected with the social and family ties as to prevent it; but, if it be possible to render ourselves miserable by aspiring to an independence that nature forbids, it is also possible to be made unhappy by a too obtrusive interference with our individuality.

Of all Christian countries, individuality, as connected with habits, is perhaps the most encouraged in England; and of all Christian countries this is the one, perhaps, in which there is the least individuality of the same nature. The latter fact would be extraordinary, could it not be referred to the religious discipline that so much influenced the colonists, and which in a measure supplied the place of law. In communities in which private acts became the subject of publick parochial investigation, it followed as a natural consequence, that men lived under the constant corrective of publick opinion, however narrow, provincial, or prejudiced. This feature of the American character, therefore, is to be ascribed, in part, to the fanaticism of our ancestors, and, in part, to the natural tendency in democracies to mistake and augment the authority of the publick.

"They Say"

"They say," is the monarch of this country, in a social sense. No one asks *"who* says it," so long as it is believed that *"they* say it." Designing men endeavor to persuade the publick, that already "they say," what these designing men wish to be said, and the publick is only too much disposed blindly to join in the cry of "they say."

This is another consequence of the habit of deferring to the control of the publick, over matters in which the publick has no right to interfere.

Every well meaning man, before he yields his faculties and intelligence to this sort of dictation, should first ask himself "who" is "they," and on what authority "they say" utters its mandates.

Rumour

The people of the United States are unusually liable to be imposed on by false rumours. In addition to the causes that exist elsewhere, such as calculated and interested falsehoods, natural frailty, political machinations, and national antipathies, may be enumerated many that are peculiar to themselves.

The great number of, and the imperfect organization of the newspaper establishments, as has already been shown, is a principal reason; necessity, in some degree, compelling a manufacture of "news," when none exists in reality.

The great extent of the country, the comparative intelligence of the inhabitants, an intelligence that is often sufficient to incite inquiry, but insufficient for discrimination, the habit of forming opinions, which is connected with the institutions, the great ease of the population, which affords time for gossip, and the vast extent of the surface over which the higher intelligence, that can alone rebuke groundless and improbable rumours, is diffused, are so many reasons for the origin and increase of false reports.

Falsehood and truth are known to be inseparable, every where, but as rumour gains by distance, they are necessarily more mixed together in this country, than in regions where the comparative smallness of surface renders contradiction easier.

The frequency and all controlling character of the elections keep rumours of a certain sort in constant circulation, bringing in corruption and design in support of other motives.

The ability to discriminate between that which is true and that which is false, is one of the last attainments of the human mind. It is the result, commonly, of a long and extensive intercourse with mankind, But one may pass an entire life, in a half-settled and half-civilized portion of the world, and not gain as much acquaintance with general things, as is obtained by boys who dwell in regions more populous. The average proportion between numbers and surface in America, is about twelve to the square mile, whereas, it approaches three hundred, in the older countries of Europe! On this single fact depends much more, in a variety of ways, than is commonly believed.

On Religion

As reason and revelation both tell us that this state of being is but a preparation for another of a still higher and more spiritual order, all the interests of life are of comparatively little importance, when put in the balance against the future. It is in this grand fact that we are to seek for the explanations of whatever may strike us as unjust, partial, or unkind in the dispensations of Providence, as these dispensations affect our temporal condition. If there is no pure and abstract liberty, no equality of condition, no equal participation in the things of the world that we are accustomed to fancy good, on remembering the speck of time passed in the present state, the possibility that what to us may seem a curse, may in truth be a blessing, the certainty that prosperity is more corrupting than adversity, we shall find the solution of all our difficulties.

In a religious point of view, it may be permitted to endeavor to improve our temporal condition, by the use of lawful and just means, but it is never proper to repine. Christ, in the parable of the vine dressers, has taught as a sublime lesson of justice, by showing that to the things which are not our own, we can have no just claim. To this obvious truth, may be added the uncertainty of the future, and the ignorance in which we exist of what is good, or what is evil, as respects our own wants.

There is but one true mode of viewing life, either in a religious, or in a philosophical sense, and that is to remember it is a state of probation in which the trials exceed the enjoyments, and that, while it is lawful to endeavor to increase the latter, more especially if of an intellectual and elevated kind, both form but insignificant interests in the great march of time.

Whatever may be the apparent inequalities here, and even they are less real than they appear to be, it is certain that we bring nothing with us into the world, and that we take nothing out of it. Every thing around us serves to teach the lesson that, though inequality of condition here is as probably intended for some great end as it is unavoidable, we come from a state of being in which we know of no such law, to go to one that we have divine revelation for believing will render the trifling disparities and the greatest advantages of this life, matters of insignificance, except as they have had an influence on our deportment, characters and faith. It would be just as discreet for a man who is suffering with hunger to murmur at having been created with such a want, while others are feeding, as to repine that another enjoys advantages he cannot possess. In this country, the aim has been to reduce all the factitious inequalities of station, condition, wealth and knowledge, to a state as natural as comports with civilization, and beyond this it exceeds the power of man to go, without returning to the condition of the savage. Let him, then, on whom the world bears hard, seek his consolation in that source which is never drained, and where more contentment is to be found that shadows a throne, or smiles on riches and power. If it be a positive thing to be a gentleman, or a lady, and as much a folly to deny it as to deny that a horse is an animal, it is equally positive that we carry in us a principle of existence that teaches us, however good and pleasant may seem the outward blessings of the world, that there are still blessings of infinitely greater magnitude, that have the additional merit of being imperishable.

The limits and objects of this work neither require, nor admit of very profound dissertations, but a few words on the peculiarities of religion and of religious feeling in America, may not be misplaced.

The causes which led to the establishment of the principal American colonies, have left a deep impression on the character of the nation. In some respects this impression has been for good, in others for evil. Our business is with the latter.

Fanaticism was the fault of the age, at the time our ancestors took possession of the country, and its exaggerations have entailed on their descendants many opinions that are, at the best, of a very equivocal usefulness. These opinions are to be detected by the contracted notions of those who entertain them, and by a general want of that charity and humility, which are the most certain attendants of the real influence of the meek and benef-icent spirit of Christ.

In America the taint of sectarianism lies broad upon the land. Not con-tent with acknowledging the supremacy of the Deity, and with erecting temples in his honor, where all can bow down with reverence, the pride and vanity of human reason enter into and pollute our worship, and the houses that should be of God and for God, alone, where he is to be hon-ored with submissive faith, are too often merely schools of metaphysical and useless distinctions. The nation is sectarian, rather than Christian.

Religion's first lesson is humility; its fruit, charity. In the great and sub-lime ends of Providence, little things are lost, and least of all is he imbued with a right spirit who believes that insignificant observances, subtleties of doctrine, and minor distinctions, enter into the great essentials of the Chris-tian character. The wisest thing for him who is disposed to cavil at the immaterial habits of his neighbor, to split straws on doctrine, to fancy tri-fles of importance, and to place the man before principles, would be to dis-trust himself. The spirit of peace is not with him.

The institutions of the country, by wisely breaking down all artificial and unnecessary distinctions, while they have preserved the ordinances nec-essary to civilized society, have removed the factitious barriers from one particular vice, which, while it belongs to the nature of man, may be termed a besetting sin of this country. We shall conclude this article, therefore, by simply quoting the stern mandate of the tenth commandment: "Thou shalt not covet thy neighbor's house; thou shalt not covet thy neighbor's wife; nor his man-servant, nor his maid-servant, nor his ox, nor his ass, nor any thing that is thy neighbor's."

CONCLUSION

The inferences to be drawn from the foregoing reasons and facts, admitting both to be just, may be briefly summed up as follows.

No expedients can equalize the temporal lots of men; for without civ-ilization and government, the strong would oppress the weak, and, with them, an inducement to exertion must be left, by bestowing rewards on talents, industry and success. All that the best institutions, then, can achieve, is to remove useless obstacles, and to permit merit to be the artisan of its own fortune, without always degrading demerit to the place it ought naturally to fill.

Every human excellence is merely comparative, there being no good without alloy. It is idle therefore to expect a system that shall exhibit faultlessness, or perfection.

The terms liberty, equality, right and justice, used in a political sense, are merely terms of convention, and of comparative excellence, there being no such thing, in practice, as either of these qualities being carried out purely, according to the abstract notions of theories.

The affairs of life embrace a multitude of interests, and he who reasons on any one of them, without consulting the rest, is a visionary unsuited to control the business of the world.

There is a prevalent disposition in the designing to forget the means in the end, and on the part of the mass to overlook the result in the more immediate agencies. The first is the consequence of cupidity; the last of short-sightedness, and frequently of the passions. Both these faults need be vigilantly watched in a democracy, as the first unsettles principles while it favors artifice, and the last is substituting the transient motives of a day, for the deliberate policy and collected wisdom of ages.

Men are the constant dupes of names, while their happiness and well-being mainly depend on things. The highest proof a community can give of its fitness for self government, is its readiness in distinguishing between the two; for frauds, oppression, flattery and vice, are the offspring of the mistakes.

It is a governing principle of nature, that the agency which can produce most good, when perverted from its proper aim, is most productive of evil. It behoves the well-intentioned, therefore, vigilantly to watch the tendency of even their most highly prized institutions, since that which was established in the interests of the right, may so easily become the agent of the wrong.

The disposition of all power is to abuses, nor does it at all mend the matter that its possessors are a majority. Unrestrained political authority, though it be confided to masses, cannot be trusted without positive limitations, men in bodies being but an aggregation of the passions, weaknesses and interests of men as individuals.

It is as idle to expect what is termed gratitude, in a democracy, as from any other repository of power. Bodies of men, though submitting to human impulses generally, and often sympathetic as well as violent, are seldom generous. In matters that touch the common feeling, they are avaricious of praise, and they usually visit any want of success in a publick man, as a personal wrong. Thus it is that we see a dozen victories forgotten in a single defeat, an irritable vanity in the place of a masculine pride, and a sensitiveness to opinion, instead of a just appreciation of acts.

Under every system it is more especially the office of the prudent and candid to guard against the evils peculiar to that particular system, than to declaim against the abuses of others. Thus, in a democracy, instead of decrying monarchs and aristocrats, who are impotent, it is wiser to look into the sore spots of the only form of government that can do any practical injury, and to apply the necessary remedies, than to be glorifying ourselves at the expense of charity, common sense, and not unfrequently of truth.

Life is made up of positive things, the existence of which it is not only folly, but which it is often unsafe to deny. Nothing is gained by setting up impracticable theories, but alienating opinion from the facts under which we live, all the actual distinctions that are inseparable from the possession of property, learning, breeding, refinement, tastes and principles, existing as well in one form of government, as in another; the only difference between ourselves and other nations, in this particular, lying in the fact that there are no other artificial distinctions than those that are inseparable from the recognised principles and indispensable laws of civilization.

There is less real inequality in the condition of men than outward circumstances would give reason to believe. If refinement brings additional happiness, it also adds point to misery. Fortunately, the high consolations of religion, in which lies the only lasting and true relief from the cares and seeming injustice of the world, are equally attainable, or, if there be a disadvantage connected with this engrossing interest, it is against those whose lots are vulgarly supposed to be the most desirable.

NOTE ON THE EDITORS

BRADLEY J. BIRZER

Dr. Bradley J. Birzer is assistant professor of history at Hillsdale College in Michigan. His specialties include the American frontier, Jacksonian American, and the Civil War. He is also a senior fellow with the Center for the American Idea in Houston.

JOHN WILLSON

Dr. John Willson is Salvatori Professor of History and Traditional Values at Hillsdale College. A recepient of numerous awards for excellence in teaching, Dr. Willson specializes in the history of the eighteenth- and early nineteenth-century American republic.

CHRISTOPHER B. BRIGGS

Conservative Leadership Series editor Christopher B. Briggs holds degrees from Bowdoin College and The Catholic University of America. Assistant editor of *Humanitas,* a journal of the humanities published in Washington, D. C., he writes and edits from northern Virginia.

INDEX